The State of Open Data
Histories and Horizons

The State of Open Data

Histories and Horizons

African Minds
Cape Town

International Development Research Centre
Ottawa • Amman • Montevideo • Nairobi • New Delhi

Open Data for Development (OD4D) Network

HOW TO CITE THIS VOLUME

Davies, T., Walker, S., Rubinstein, M., & Perini, F. (Eds.). (2019). *The State of Open Data: Histories and Horizons*. Cape Town and Ottawa: African Minds and International Development Research Centre.

First published in 2019 by African Minds and the International Development Research Centre (IDRC).

African Minds
4 Eccleston Place
Somerset West, 7130
Cape Town, South Africa
www.africanminds.org.za

A co-publication with
International Development Research Centre
PO Box 8500, Ottawa, ON, K1G 3H9, Canada
www.idrc.ca / info@idrc.ca

© Contributors 2019. Licensed under the Creative Commons Attribution 4.0 International licence (http://creativecommons.org/licenses/by/4.0/).

The research presented in this publication was carried out with the aid of the Open Data for Development (OD4D) Network and a grant from the International Development Research Centre, Ottawa, Canada. The views expressed herein do not necessarily represent those of IDRC or its Board of Governors.

ISBNs:
Print edition 978-1-928331-95-7
eBook edition (IDRC): 978-1-55250-612-7
ePub edition: 978-1-928331-96-4

Orders:
African Minds
4 Eccleston Place, Somerset West, 7130, Cape Town, South Africa
info@africanminds.org.za
www.africanminds.org.za

For orders outside Africa:
African Books Collective
PO Box 721, Oxford OX1 9EN, UK
orders@africanbookscollective.com

Contents

Acknowledgements		viii
About the editors		x
Foreword by Beth Simone Noveck		xi
Introduction		1

SECTION 1: OPEN DATA SECTORS AND COMMUNITIES

Introduction		12
Chapter 1.	Accountability and anti-corruption *Jorge Florez and Johannes Tonn*	17
Chapter 2.	Agriculture *Ruthie Musker, Ben Schaap, Martin Parr, and André Laperriere*	35
Chapter 3.	Corporate ownership *Jack Lord*	51
Chapter 4.	Crime and justice *Sandra Elena*	65
Chapter 5.	Development assistance and humanitarian action *Catherine Weaver, Josh Powell, and Heather Leson*	77
Chapter 6.	Education *Javiera Atenas and Leo Havemann*	91
Chapter 7.	Environment *Selwyn Willoughby*	103
Chapter 8.	Extractives *Anders Pedersen*	119
Chapter 9.	Geospatial *Renée Sieber*	137
Chapter 10.	Government finances *Cécile Le Guen*	151
Chapter 11.	Health *Mark Irura*	166
Chapter 12.	Land ownership *Tim Davies and Sumandro Chattapadhyay*	181
Chapter 13.	National statistics *Shaida Badiee, Caleb Rudow, and Eric Swanson*	196
Chapter 14.	Telecommunications *Stephen Song*	207
Chapter 15.	Transport *Pieter Colpaert and Julián Andrés Rojas Meléndez*	215
Chapter 16.	Urban development *Jean-Noé Landry*	225

SECTION 2: ISSUES IN OPEN DATA

Introduction — 238

Chapter 17. Algorithms and artificial intelligence — 243
Tim Davies

Chapter 18. Data infrastructure — 260
Leigh Dodds and Peter Wells

Chapter 19. Data literacy — 274
Mariel Garcia Montes and Dirk Slater

Chapter 20. Gender equity — 287
Ana Brandusescu and Nnenna Nwakanma

Chapter 21. Indigenous data sovereignty — 300
Stephanie Carroll Rainie, Tahu Kukutai, Maggie Walter, Oscar Luis Figueroa-Rodríguez, Jennifer Walker, and Per Axelsson

Chapter 22. Measurement — 320
Danny Lämmerhirt and Ana Brandusescu

Chapter 23. Privacy — 339
Teresa Scassa

SECTION 3: OPEN DATA STAKEHOLDERS

Introduction — 352

Chapter 24. Civil society — 355
Christopher Wilson

Chapter 25. Donors and investors — 367
Fernando Perini and Michael Jarvis

Chapter 26. Governments — 381
Barbara-Chiara Ubaldi

Chapter 27. Journalists and the media — 395
Alex Howard and Eva Constantaras

Chapter 28. Multilateral organisations — 406
Craig Hammer

Chapter 29. Private sector — 418
Joel Gurin, Carla Bonina, and Stefaan Verhulst

Chapter 30. Researchers — 430
François van Schalkwyk

SECTION 4: OPEN DATA AROUND THE WORLD

Introduction		446
Chapter 31.	Eastern Europe and Central Asia	450
	Lejla Sadiku and Yaera Chung	
Chapter 32.	European Union	465
	Rufus Pollock and Danny Lämmerhirt	
Chapter 33.	Latin America and the Caribbean	485
	Silvana Fumega and Maurice McNaughton	
Chapter 34.	Middle East and North Africa	503
	Nagla Rizk, Nancy Salem, and Stefanie Felsberger	
Chapter 35.	North America, Australia, and New Zealand	517
	David Eaves, Ben McGuire, and Audrey Carson	
Chapter 36.	South, East, and Southeast Asia	535
	Michael Canares	
Chapter 37.	Sub-Saharan Africa	549
	Leonida Mutuku and Teg-wende Idriss (Tinto)	

Conclusion and recommendations   565

Acknowledgements

The editors would like to thank the International Development Research Centre (IDRC) for its support of the State of Open Data project from inception to conclusion, without which this publication would not have been possible.

We wish to also acknowledge the ongoing efforts of the Open Data for Development (OD4D) network to help create open data ecosystems around the world in order to spur social change, increase government transparency, support the Sustainable Development Goals (SDGs), and for its ongoing commitment to promoting and understanding the impact of open data, resulting in the publication of this volume. OD4D has received support from IDRC, the World Bank, the United Kingdom's Department for International Development (DFID), the William and Flora Hewlett Foundation, and Global Affairs Canada.

The State of Open Data project is the result of a collaboration, drawing on input from over 200 individuals. Authors have benefitted from independent reviews by members of the Editorial Board and invited reviewers, as well as the input of many more contributors during the early online "Environment Scan" stage of the project. We have endeavoured to credit all non-anonymous contributions, but know there will have been input and suggestions offered at workshops or in conversations that are not recorded below. If you were a contributor to the State of Open Data project in any way, we thank you.

The State of Open Data project owes its greatest debt to all of the authors who have come together to contribute chapters to this volume, bringing to the project an unprecedented level of expertise and knowledge, as well as a diversity of invaluable experience. We have included more specific information on every author in each chapter.

We would like to recognise and thank all the members of The State of Open Data's dedicated Editorial Board, our extremely knowledgeable team of peer reviewers, and all those who have provided additional assistance to the authors through their contribution to the environmental scans or to the development of the chapters in this volume.

Editorial Board

Ania Calderon, Craig Hammer, Fiona Smith, Joel Gurin, Katelyn Rogers, Lejla Sadiku, Maurice McNaughton, Muchiri Nyaggah, Nancy Salem, Nnenna Nwakanma, Shaida Badiee, Stefaan Verhulst, and Teg-wende Idriss (Tinto).

Peer reviewers

Abed Khooli, Ali Rebaie, Amanda Smith, Amy Guy, Anca Matioc, Ania Calderon, Caleb Rudow, Claire Schouten, Claudia Schwegmann, David McNair, Eric Swanson, Francesca De Chiara, Giuseppe Sollazzo, Hatem Ben Yacoub, Jacqueline Klopp, Jean-Noé Landry, Jenna Slotin, Joshua Powell, Julian Tait, Keitha Booth, Krishna Sapkota, Krzysztof Izdebski, Leigh Dodds, Maya Forstater, Mollie Hanley, Omenogo Mejabi, Oscar Montiel, Paul Walsh, Paulina Bustos Arellano, Pyrou Chung, Raed M. Sharif, Rafael García Aceves, Riyadh Al-Balushi, Rob Kitchin, Rosario Pavese, Satyarupa Shekhar, Tom Orrell, Willow Brugh, and Yan Naung Oak.

Environment scan and chapter contributors

Carlos Iglesias, Enrique Zapata, Arjan El Fassed, Stefanie Felsberger, Alan Hudson, Kshitiz Khanal, Michal Kubáň, Carla Bonina, Devangana Khokhar, James McKinney, Khairil Yusof, Pierre Chrzanowski, Adrián Pino, Ana Brandusescu, Andrea Borruso, Anne-Marie Heemskerk, Bart Hanssens, Ben Parker, Christian Medina-Ramirez, Eduard Martin-Borregon, Elise Dufief, Eva Constantaras, Francois van Schalkwyk, Joshua Tauberer, Lindsay Read, Manuel Acevedo, Marina Godoy Crotto, Martin Noblecourt, Martín Szyszlican, Matteo Brunati, Paige Kirby, Rachel Rank, Rupert Simons, Aaron Wytze, Adam Kariv, Alannah Hilt, Alla Morrison, Andi Pawelke, Andrea Ayres Deets, Andrew Nicklin, Andrew Therriault, Andrew Young, Anna Alberts, Anna Fleming, Anna Powell-Smith, Anton Ruehling, Antonio Jesús Sánchez Padial, Arturo Muente-Kunigami, Audrey Ariss, Bierta Thaci, Carole Excell, Chang Liu, Chipo Msengezi, Chris Taggart, Daniel Carranza, Darko Brkan, David Moore, David Rae, David Sasaki, David Selassie Opoku, David Wasylciw, Denice Ross, Dhanaraj Thakur, Dheeraj Ravindranath, Diego Cuesy, Duncan Edwards, Edafe Onerhime, Edward Saperia, Eliza Niewiadomska, Fabrizio Scrollini, Felipe Amaya Salazar, Feng Gao, Gabe Sawhney, Gabriel Mercado, Gabriela Rodriguez, Gaurav Godhwani, Georges Labreche, German Stalker, Gerry Tychon, Gwen Phillips, Hari Subhash, Hossein Maleknejad, Jason Lally, Jason M. Hare, Jay Daley, Jeff Geipel, Joel Nativdad, Jonathan van Geuns, Jorge Florez, Jorge Umaña, Jose M. Alonso, Joshua Powell, Juan Ortiz Freuler, Juan Pablo Marin Diaz, Kate Vang, Katie Clancy, Krystina Shveda, Krzysztof Madejski, Kyle Copas, Laura Meggiolaro, Lisa Walmsley, Liz Dodds, Liz McGrath, Maciej Możejewski, Madeleine Ngeunga, Maggie Walter, Manuel Acevedo, Marnie Webb, Martin Bader, Martin Noblecourt, Matthew McNaughton, Michael Schnuerle, Mike Davies, Mikhail Parfentiev, Miles Litvinoff, Momi Peralta Ramos, Mor Rubinstein, Nadiia Babynsky Virna, Nancy Salem, Natalia Mazotte, Nikesh Balami, Nikhil VJ, Nino Macharashvili, Noémie Girard, Nora Lester Murad, Owen Boswarva, Pablo Cruz Casas, Paloma Baytelman, Paola Mosso, Paul Bradshaw, Paul Hindriks, Paul Stone, Paulina Bustos, Pedro Manrique, Philip Horgan, Pınar Dağ, Rachel Murray, Ruba Ishak, Scott McQuarrie, Selene Yang, Sidi Zakari Ibrahim, Stefaan Verhulst, Steven Adler, Sym Roe, Tara Susman-Peña, Thomas Lassourd, Tina Appiah, Tyler Kleykamp, Valentina Delgado, Virginia Brussa, Walter Palmetshofer, Will Skora, Yacine Khelladi, Yanina Bellini Saibene, Yohanna Loucheur, and Zukiswa Kota.

The editors also wish to thank and acknowledge Jean-Noé Landry and the team at OpenNorth for their invaluable support of the project's administrative processes.

Special thanks are due to the entire African Minds production team: Simon Chislett, Leith Davis, and Tessa Botha, as well as African Minds Director, François van Schalkwyk, for his partnership in the publishing process. Finally, the project also owes a great debt to Nola Haddadian, the Publisher at IDRC, for her tireless support and patience throughout the publishing and editorial review process without which the project would not have been realised.

About the editors

Tim Davies is an activist, researcher, and social entrepreneur, who has been working on themes related to open data since 2009. He was Research Lead for the first two years of the IDRC/World Wide Web Foundation's "Exploring the Emerging Impacts of Open Data in Developing Countries" research network and coordinated the first two editions of the global Open Data Barometer. He co-founded Open Data Services Co-op in 2015 to support ongoing development of open data infrastructures, including the Open Contracting Data Standard (OCDS) and data standards for corporate transparency. He was series editor for the Open Data Charter Open-Up Guides on anti-corruption and agriculture. A social researcher by training, Tim has been a fellow of the Berkman Centre for Internet and Society and has studied at the Oxford Internet Institute and University of Southampton Web Science Centre. He blogs at http://www.timdavies.org.uk and tweets at https://www.twitter.com/timdavies.

Stephen B. Walker is the former Director General responsible for leading open government and open data for the Government of Canada, where he developed and implemented national policies, programmes, and infrastructure to advance open data. At the international level, Steve was directly involved in the development of the G8 Open Data Charter as well as the Open Data Charter. He also chaired the Open Government Partnership's Working Group on Open Data. More recently, Steve has worked with the Open Data for Development (OD4D) network and managed the International Open Data Conference. Steve also runs his own consulting company, True North Consulting, specialising in advancing open data and transparency policies and practices. Steve tweets infrequently at https://www.twitter.com/sbwalker61.

Mor Rubinstein is an open data practitioner with more than ten years of experience. She was a Community Coordinator and the Lead Researcher for Open Knowledge International's Global Open Data Index. She is currently the Labs Manager for 360Giving, a UK initiative for opening up philanthropic grants data for better grant-making. She is also the co-founder and coordinator of the Open Heroines community, a global community for women in open data, open government, and civic tech. She holds a Master of Science in Social Science of the Internet from the Oxford Internet Institute. You can follow her on Twitter at https://www.twitter.com/morchickit.

Fernando Perini is a Senior Programme Specialist at Canada's International Development Research Centre (IDRC), where he coordinates the Open Data for Development (OD4D) programme. OD4D is a global partnership that supports southern leadership and locally led data ecosystems around the world as a way to spur positive social change and sustainable development. You can follow Fernando on Twitter at https://www.twitter.com/fperini.

Foreword

It was a long day in early December 2008. Thirteen hours alone on a Sunday in a windowless room of the presidential transition HQ on 6th Street in DC. The transition team that had started as a dozen people the previous summer had ballooned after the election to almost 700 people who were now responsible for planning the first hundred days of the Obama administration. It was a microcosm of the government, designing initiatives to launch the new presidency with a socially impactful and politically practical bang.

Coming on the heels of the Bush Administration and plummeting rates of trust in government, it was imperative that we govern differently, not behind closed doors, but in the open. Although the iPhone had only just been invented and social media platforms, Facebook and Twitter, were still comparatively new, it was clear that the internet, especially new data science tools and methods, might make it possible to strive for more evidence-based policy-making and better solutions to public problems.

At that juncture, I was chairing the Technology, Innovation and Government Reform (TIGR) working group, a small band of people passionate about the potential for using new technology to modernise and improve the workings of government. Our policy initiatives were designed to cut across the usual topics of economy, education, foreign policy, and health to promote a different way of working. We wanted to be "one bullet point of every five" and help each of the subject-matter teams to use technology, data, and innovation to accelerate the implementation of their goals.

We had a motley array of cross-cutting suggestions to put forward to the President-elect. They included new websites, such as USASpending.gov that would lay bare the money we were spending on the bailout after the financial crisis, and new hires, including the creation of a new Chief Technology Officer position, an expanded Chief Information Officer role, and a technology "SWAT" team that would go into each agency and assess the state of its infrastructure, as well as a new open government policy. As is now well known, that policy had three inextricably intertwined prongs: transparency, participation, and collaboration.

Inspired by the way the publication of weather data had spawned a billion-dollar forecasting industry or the sharing of government-collected genomic data had birthed the biotech revolution, we were convinced that opening up the information that government collects would accelerate solutions to public problems if designed to go beyond mere transparency to create incentives for a wide range of actors across government, academia, and industry to use information for public good.

Just as open source software development – creating code with a larger group of people often outside the confines of one organisation to accelerate the process of both writing and testing software – opening up government data could make it possible for those outside of government to scrutinise and use government information more productively than government acting on its own.

Now ten years into the open data revolution, it is almost hard to remember how radical an idea open data – or transparency plus participation and collaboration – was at the time.

First, it upended 50 years of thinking about the right-to-know strategies embodied in Freedom of Information (FOI) legislation. Open data complicated our reliance on FOI as the bedrock of transparency policy by shifting the underlying theoretical understanding of the relationship between the state and the public from the adversarial to the collaborative.

FOI is an inherently confrontational tactic focused on prying secrets out of government. Open data is not. It depends upon the institution that collects the data wanting to publish it in order to attract knowledgeable and passionate members of the public who want to use it. Because governments in an open data regime must proactively publish their data with the intent that people will use it, the normative essence of open data is participation rather than litigation. The role of the public has always been to scrutinise and criticise. The idea that the public and government can work together to augment the manpower and skills in under-resourced public institutions continues to demand a major shift of mindset.

Second, many transparency and good government activists were actively hostile toward the new policy because it did not focus squarely on publishing information only about the workings of government such as budget data that is designed to produce greater government accountability. By catalysing public engagement to promote both the scrutiny of data by the public and collaboration with the public in building new analytical tools and websites, open data galvanised collaboration between institutions and the public to create value of *different* kinds, especially to advance solutions to hard problems.

Opening up the corpus of patent data – one of our earliest projects – while laudable, struck many as a distraction from the all-important goal of enhancing government accountability. The fact that such data could unlock our understanding of the innovation economy was not yet well understood. Similarly, the idea that open data could be a key asset in developing tools to help passengers know which flights were likely to be delayed, help patients choose between hospitals, or help parents make more informed decisions about colleges, ran contrary to what open government meant for many people.

It took many years of experience with open data to temper the discontent and persuade the naysayers. Creating apps for the Health Datapalozza by using newly published datasets from Health and Human Services began to change minds. Witnessing first-hand the reforms to the criminal justice system in the United States made possible by opening up police data was a sign that the movement was maturing. Thousands of lives saved by CPR-trained bystanders responding to texts specifying the locations of people experiencing cardiac arrest, generated by a real-time open data feed of emergency 911 calls, drove home the point that open data is a vital new tool for advancing social justice. The countless examples from around the world sprinkled throughout this volume, and the over 70 countries making commitments to publishing open data as part of their participation in the Open Government Partnership, have created widespread awareness of the power of open data as a new tool in the toolkit for public problem solving.

The explosion of newly available data coupled with mounting evidence (as this book so thoroughly demonstrates) that data catalyses productive, problem-solving partnerships between government and the governed suggests that the use of open data as a tool of governing will continue to grow. If the trend continues, open data will lead to new empirically informed ways to hold government and others accountable, spurring consumer choice and expanding the range of approaches to tackling human rights and development challenges.

Yet a week does not go by when I do not still have to debate with those in government about the value of opening data. Open data in many places is still under threat from the move toward more closed governments and closed societies. Even in more enlightened regimes, however, many still argue that it is better to sell than give away the data that was paid for by, and belongs to, taxpayers. I still plead with those who doubt whether people will use the open data we invest in publishing in machine-readable formats rather than PDFs.

These doubts stem, in part, from the lack of data-analytical skills among public servants. We know more in 2019 than we did a decade ago about how to use data for good. But even when governments know to open and publish their data, they still often lack the ability to use the data themselves. This may slowly change as agencies like Digital Canada, the Argentinian government lab (LabGobAr), and the multi-university Coleridge Initiative in the US, train people in government in how to use data to solve problems.

To be sure, there have been times when the potential for open data has been over-hyped, especially when naively assuming that data publication, in and of itself, will solve problems, neglecting the importance of investing in the original idea that participation and collaboration are vital for getting multi-disciplinary teams of people inside and outside of government scrutinising, visualising, and using the data to create value.

But, fundamentally, the challenge for open data – and open government more broadly – is the shift in mindset it demands to embrace the original values and learn the practices of transparency, participation, and collaboration.

Open government shifts the focus of transparency from monitoring government after the fact to mechanisms that encourage the public to participate actively in improving societal outcomes. Open data fosters more active citizenship and more collaborative democratic institutions that draw directly on the collective expertise of the population to solve public problems. Ultimately, open data gives us a vision for a new kind of government to strive for – not bigger or smaller – but one that ensures collaboration makes our public institutions more effective and legitimate and our democracy stronger. By taking stock of the current state of open data, this book acts as a key resource and charts a course for future action to keep open data on track as a transformative tool of more open, collaborative, innovative, and participatory governance.

Beth Simone Noveck
Professor, New York University and Director, The Governance Lab
New York City, 2019

Introduction

A decade ago, open data was more or less just an idea, emerging as a rough point of consensus for action among pro-democracy practitioners, internet entrepreneurs, open source advocates, civic technology developers, and open knowledge campaigners. Calls for "open data now" offered a powerful critique of the way in which governments and other institutions were hoarding valuable data paid for by taxpayers – data that if made accessible, could be reused in a myriad of different ways to bring social and economic benefits and democratic change.

Ten years on, open data is much more than just an idea. First, it was a movement, and then a label applied to vast quantities of data from genomics and geospatial data to land registers, contracting, and parliamentary voting. Today, it's a term found on government portals, in global policy documents, and in job descriptions. Thousands of businesses around the world owe their existence or their growth to the release of open government data, and hundreds of civil society organisations have embraced open data as a key element of their social change toolkit.

For a while, it may have been possible to identify a cohesive open data movement united by shared interests, working simply to gain access to more data and establishing the principle that government data should be open. However, as the movement has evolved, stakeholders have turned their focus to linking data use to specific needs and to questions of how to quantify the return on investment in advancing open data. Within this fast growing and organic open data movement, an ever-increasing number of networks and communities of practice have become more diverse, fluid, and cross-sectoral.

So what is the open data movement today? What has it achieved over the last decade? Answering these questions is at the core of this publication. It is a collective effort to explore what we can learn from the past, to identify how to build on the investments made to date, and to look at how open data policy and practice have started to address challenges such as mainstreaming and sectorisation.

Exploring these questions is not just important for historical purposes. It can yield important insights on how best to move forward. This publication is also an invitation to identify the issues that may sustain this broad coalition into the future. We believe that a deep reflection about the movement, even a reflection on whatever cracks have appeared or on the gaps between promise and reality, provides a vital opportunity to discuss where realignment and rethinking are needed.

This collection of essays is the product of an 18-month journey that has brought together almost 70 authors, supported by over 200 other contributors, to produce 37 short chapters on the current state of open data from a range of different perspectives, offering the most comprehensive attempt to explore the breadth and depth of the open data field to date.

Histories and horizons

Ten years may seem like a short period of time, but, when technology is involved, it constitutes a generational age. Institutional memories are curiously short, and in the cultural context of open data where amateurs are often welcome and professional barriers to entry are low, it is easy for work to proceed with little awareness of the past. This last decade has seen many succeeding phases of activity, so we have encouraged our authors to take a comparatively long view (when set against other contemporary writing on open data) to document the past in order to lay stronger foundations for future research and action.

We have also sought to understand open data as a global movement. Although some accounts have a tendency to focus on the North American or European roots of open data, tracing histories back to the launch of data.gov under Barack Obama's presidency, open data practice has been shaped by interventions from across the globe. To gain a vantage point on open data as a global movement, this collection draws upon the editors' engagement with the Open Data for Development (OD4D) network[1] which has been closely engaged in regional networks in the Global South and involved in a range of global initiatives, including the Open Data Barometer (ODB), the Open Data Charter, the Open Government Partnership (OGP) Open Data Working Group, the Impact Map, and the Open Data Leaders Network.

Since 2015, OD4D has also been the permanent co-host of the International Open Data Conference (IODC), and the editors of this volume have been involved in preparing conference reports, including shared roadmaps for action, for the third, fourth, and fifth IODC meetings. We have seen how, over its five editions, IODC has shifted from a focus on open data, in and of itself, toward discussions that are thematic, sectoral, regional, and issue oriented, fostering critical debates on open data. The conference tracks and sessions at IODC have ultimately provided many of the chapter titles in this book, reflecting the many subcommunities of the open data field that have emerged. The debates at IODC over the last nine years also provide a useful proxy for debates across the wider field of open data, so a survey of the IODC conferences offers us one route to explore, in broad strokes, a history of how the focus of the open data movement has evolved.

The evolution of a movement

The first IODC was hosted by the United States Department of Commerce and took place in November 2010 in Washington, DC.[2] At the same time, in London, a civil-society led conference, the Open Government Data Camp, was taking place.[3] These parallel events captured the growing excitement about open data from both governments and civil society and marked the end of a year in which open data had moved from idea to initiative and from inception to the earliest stages of institutionalisation. Over time, the boundaries between government and civil society networks have become more fluid with both positive and negative effects. The focus of these early events was on showcasing the platforms that had been built and discussing the potential for open data across sectors. However, even at this early stage, questions were being asked about how the impact of open data might be tracked, and whether bold claims being made on the transformative potential of open data could actually be realised.

By the time of the second IODC, hosted by the World Bank in July 2012,[4] the question of how to measure emerging impact was firmly on the agenda. At this point, open data was being discussed in the context of international development and the movement had broadened to include a number of open data leaders from developing countries. Yet, while many of the projects profiled were still platform-focused, it was becoming clear that simply releasing data was not enough and that the quality of data available was far from perfect. Early discussions turned to whether the potential returns of open data had been overstated and how to deal with the growing gap between rhetoric and reality. That early sense of an impact gap still pervades many of the chapters in this collection with several authors exploring the various reasons that could explain less than promised progress on transformative use. However, we note that the perception of an impact gap is rarely reflected by a similar level of difficulty in sourcing case studies of open data use, raising questions about the perception and the reality of progress on open data, as well as the influence of early conceptual models for open data impact on current critical practice.

By the time of the third IODC in Ottawa in May 2015, the focus had moved to an examination of how open data ideas and practices were developing in different sectors and regions.[5] The conference captured a period of dramatic regional and sectoral growth of open data activity with increasingly diverse representation from across the globe. There was growing recognition that opening data alone was not enough to create impact. Instead, as many of the chapters in this collection explore, to secure outcomes from open data, clear goals need to be established and a series of strategic interventions identified. Policy design, intermediaries, and capacity building were all on the agenda. As more stories of open data in use to solve specific problems were shared, there was a growing recognition that impacts secured in one context or sector may not automatically translate to another. And with this recognition came an understanding that, rather than a single open data movement, there may be many overlapping, interwoven movements, drawing on particular elements of open data to address many different agendas.

The third IODC also made explicit the potential links between open data and sustainable development, highlighting that open data was no longer the only data game in town. Instead, in the context of international development, open data now had to find its place alongside renewed efforts to build the capacity of long-established statistical agencies, as well as newer initiatives seeking to tap into the potential of big data from proprietary private sector providers.

The fourth IODC, held in Madrid in October 2016, was framed in terms of "Global Goals, Local Impact", reflecting increased consolidation of global advocacy and a continued focus on shared global principles, which was evolving in parallel with the growth of subnational and thematic initiatives.[6] Although the open data agenda had matured and become well-established as part of global policy-making, discussions explored concerns that it risked becoming a niche issue, destined to be the focus of only a small group of the "usual suspects". Issues of privacy, gender equity, diversity, inclusion, and Indigenous data rights, all competed for space on the agenda, along with a new space for more critical discussion of how open data impact might be realised and the potential for more nuanced approaches to open data practice.

These critical threads continued into the fifth IODC that was held in Buenos Aires in September 2018.[7] New on the agenda were discussions related to artificial intelligence (AI), and the conference saw a stronger focus on data standards and open data infrastructure. Although these later issues have long been discussed by a small but dedicated element of the open data community, there was increased recognition that they are not just technical issues. They also involve questions of data governance with political choices embedded in the use of data standards and structures, having substantial consequences for who can use and benefit from data.

In 2018, for the first time, the IODC agenda also featured a session on "Open Data Under Threat", capturing a sense that continued progress was by no means assured. Against the backdrop of a deepening crisis of diminishing government support for openness around the world and much more public debate around the positive and negative potential of technology, concerns voiced over open data were no longer solely about a perceived impact gap. They also involved a deeper questioning of when and where openness can be safely practised and whether open data should be a priority for donors, advocates, and activists in the future.

A look at the 2018 IODC agenda also illustrates sectoral and regional sessions going deeper into the specific concerns of their fields and localities. In this, we find a reflection of the increasing diffusion of open data ideas, representing both a marker of success but also a potential risk to any future coherence of open data activity. In putting together this collection, while drawing on the OD4D network and IODC as a starting point, we have been conscious of the need to move beyond to capture wider activity on open data and to explore how an early open data movement has now become many overlapping movements. By working with a diverse community of authors, encouraging them to draw on both published literature and their own domain-based networks, as well as on wider online outreach to the community, we have looked to capture insights into the open data world from far beyond the core IODC community.

Taking stock

Culture and temperament inevitably shape any qualitative review of progress. As with any invested community, a substantial number of people and organisations engaged with open data have a tendency toward critique. For many, the idea that data should be open was ultimately born out of a critical opposition to the way governments were handling data and an ambitious imagining of an alternative future in which access and capacity to gain benefit from data is more evenly distributed. Coupled with the differences in pace between rapid technological change and comparatively glacial governmental reform, this critical approach combined with well-meaning ambition can lead to the progress of the last decade being underplayed. Challenges on the horizon ahead can too often serve to mask the steps that have been taken in order for those challenges to become visible.

In looking across the chapters that follow, we are struck by the extent to which open data ideas have become established across the globe. For instance, in Chapter 28 (Multilateral organisations),

Hammer describes how, from 2010 onward, global development banks have integrated open data into their own methodologies, helping to popularise open data initiatives in developing and developed countries. In Chapter 29 (Private sector), Gurin, Bonina, and Verhulst illustrate the private sector's widespread use of open data with examples from Asia, Africa, Latin America, Europe, and America. And since the Sustainable Developments Goals were adopted in 2015, robust, comparable, and open data has been emphasised as a critical tool to both inform and monitor development efforts. Across the entire section on Open Data Sectors and Communities, examples of open data being used to drive socioeconomic benefits or to shape policy debates are too numerous to mention here.

The adoption of open data as a central tool used in a number of major global policy initiatives of the last decade is particularly notable. The OGP, the International Transparency Initiative, the Extractives Industry Transparency Initiative (see Chapter 8: Extractives), and the Global Legal Entity Identifier Foundation which was created to respond to the last financial crisis (see Chapter 3: Corporate ownership), have all embraced open data within their work. Within the OGP in particular, commitments related to open data have been some of the most popular and successful.[8] As Chapter 17: Algorithms and artifical intelligence explores, even as public attention shifts from open data toward a new wave of excitement about AI, open data ideas appear firmly established as a foundation for governmental AI policy.

So why is the current period for open data one of re-evaluation, rather than of celebrating progress? Put simply, the adoption of open data as part of the global development toolbox has opened it (rightly) to substantial scrutiny. How quickly are efforts to open up data leading to change? What is the return on investment from open data-related reforms? What are the factors that shape whether or not open data leads to impact? And finally, how does work on open data interact or integrate with other core issues of sustainable development, such as gender equity, Indigenous rights, and good governance? Questions such as these have received increasingly detailed attention over the last few years. Although hardly any of these questions have simple answers, by looking at both progress and challenges, this volume seeks to bring together evidence, examples, and analysis that can support efforts to address them more clearly than before.

Looking to the future: An impending identity crisis

For all the steps forward described above, as we look to the horizons of open data, we are confident in stating that policy excitement about open data has peaked. Ten years in, we are past the peak of a hype cycle and past the point where promise has to give way to evidence of practical impact. As a result, many open data communities are fast approaching their difficult teenage years with a deepening identity crisis.

Over the last decade, debates around the role of data in society have moved to centre stage, but arguments for openness now have to share the spotlight with newer excitement over the economic potential of big data, machine learning, and growing fears about the negative impacts of data stemming from data-driven manipulation of politics or the corporate invasion of personal privacy. Although early narratives around open data may have been able to present increased access to data as an unalloyed public good, contemporary advocacy must confront a much more complex landscape in which power, politics, and the question of who gains or loses from unfolding regimes of data access cannot be ignored.

This presents a number of key challenges with which the following chapters attempt to grapple. As open data has spread globally, the way in which open data ideas have manifested across different sectors, communities, countries, and stakeholder groups has increasingly varied. Regional distinctions of emphasis have developed, with, for example, some downplaying the importance of open licences (see Chapter 37: Sub-Saharan Africa) and others talking of innovation rather than of openness in order to avoid political resistance (see Chapter 34: Middle East and North Africa). As sectoral efforts deepen, it is domain or subject matter experts, rather than data specialists, who drive activity forward, so that the challenges of creating cross-sectoral linkages and building shared data infrastructure become even greater. Increased emphasis on inclusion places a substantial demand on problem-centred initiatives, which, in light of low levels of data literacy, must choose whether to focus on data for expert communities or to actively pursue the promise of open data as a tool of wider popular empowerment. When the focus shifts from calling for access to data to creating data infrastructure and putting data to work, the divergent goals of those who formed an initial open data movement come clearly into view and managing the tensions that emerge can be complex.

It was in mid-2017, as these tensions were becoming more apparent, amid a sense that overall momentum for open data may be faltering, that the State of Open Data project was conceived. Our objective:

> *To critically review the current state of the open data movement, assessing its progress and effectiveness in addressing challenges related to social and economic development and democratisation around the world.*

Based on such a broad stock-taking of open data activity, we may not be able to fully resolve questions about the future of open data, but we can provide an account that helps practitioners, policy-makers, and community advocates to step back from their own position to gain a view of the wider landscape. By doing this, we hope to offer a rich and timely perspective and the groundwork for constructive debates that will shape the next decade of open data.

A collaborative review: The approach

The open data field already benefits from a number of semi-regular quantitative studies of the progress of open data, such as the ODB[9] and Open Data Index,[10] both also supported by OD4D. To complement these, the approach to the State of Open Data project was designed, from the outset, to be more qualitative and narrative in style, involving a five-stage process.

1. **Selection.** Working with the OD4D network, potential chapters were identified based on open data communities, regions, stakeholder groups, and cross-cutting issues. Authors were then invited to lead on creating these chapters. The introduction to each section of this book provides details on the selection of chapter topics.

2. **Engagement.** Authors were asked to create an initial "environment scan": a community brainstorming of issues, evidence, key actors, and events related to their topic. Scans were posted online for public comment and additions to gather more examples, case studies, articles, and input from beyond the authors' own networks.

3. **Writing and review.** Responding to a common set of questions and prompts, authors then completed full chapter drafts, drawing on the input received from the environmental scans. These draft chapters were sent for peer review by independent reviewers and by members of our editorial board. Reviews were sent to authors who completed chapter revisions based on the input received.

4. **Public drafts and discussion.** Public drafts for the majority of the chapters were posted online ahead of the IODC in Buenos Aires in September 2018, where emerging themes were discussed. Panel discussions on themes from the work were also held at the OGP Summit in Tbilisi, Georgia, followed by additional opportunities for revision.

5. **Synthesis and recommendations.** Based on a collective review of all chapters, the editors have worked to draw out key findings and recommendations, which are summarised in section introductions and the book's conclusion, including recommendations for research, funding, policy-making, and practitioner communities.

The authors and contributors to this project have been drawn from a wide range of backgrounds. Some have been active in the open data field for many years, while others are relative newcomers. Some are advocates and activists, while others are observers or academics. Some are open data generalists, while others specialise in a particular field. Many draw upon a range of different roles and positions.

When considering all of the authors, contributors to the environment scans, independent reviewers, and the editorial board, input has been received from over 220 individuals from around the world. Representing the diversity of the open data community with regard to gender, diversity, and global inclusivity has been the key principle underlying our approach to this volume. The goal was to achieve a 50–50 gender split in terms of authorship, although we fell short of this with a 58–42 split in favour of men.

Definitions and scope: Open government data

Our focus in this volume is primarily, but not exclusively, on open government data. That is, data which traditionally originates from governments, is created or used during the business of governing, or is created or published at the request of governments. We have intentionally adopted a broad definition here, cognisant that, over recent years, the traditional monopoly of national-level governments both in data collection and in being a primary site of governance has been eroded. For example, satellite imagery data from

> private companies or crowdsourced data from citizen scientists can all fall within the broad landscape of open data either traditionally collected by governments or used for governing. Similarly, data that results from academic research networks, but which informs public decision-making and action, forms a component of some chapters within this volume. However, reflecting the way that communities of practice around open data are generally organised, we have mostly stayed away from looking at open data in terms of open science or evaluating the extent to which different scientific disciplines and communities are approaching data sharing, access, and openness. This is well addressed in other work.[11]
>
> When it comes to defining open data, we draw upon the widely used definition of open data as data that is accessible, machine-readable, and free of licensing restrictions on reuse. However, we apply the definition heuristically rather than legalistically. This recognises, for example, that in some countries and contexts, the lack of a fully "open licence" is less of a barrier to reuse in practice than in others, or that, at times, data may not be provided in machine-readable formats at source but has been easily converted for reuse by intermediaries. Rather than rule out such cases from exploration on a technicality, they are included in the scope of this study with their limitations noted where relevant.

Targeting the core stakeholders

One of the notable features of open data is the way in which it has been adopted and shaped by so many different stakeholders. Unlike "big data", for example, which appears to be primarily a corporate concept marketed to governments and civil society, networks around "open data" have always been much more diverse, fluid, and cross-sectoral. More than anything, this breadth and fluidity lies at the root of the impending identity crisis of the open data movement. For a long time, it may have been possible to manage the tension between different interests via a short-term focus on simply gaining access to more data. However, when stakeholders turn their focus to data use and the need to quantify the return on their investment of time and resources, a broader open data coalition is much harder to sustain. Determining what the open data movement can (and should) yield moving forward, how to maximise every investment made, and how to take on the challenges of mainstreaming and sectoralisation simultaneously, is at the core of the movement's identity crisis. The cracks that may appear need not lead to crisis. Rather, they should serve to highlight in relief where realignment and rethinking are needed for the future.

In editing this collection, we have sought to work with all of the authors to address the needs of four main groups: researchers, funders, policy-makers, and practitioners.

For researchers, each chapter draws upon available academic and grey literature, providing detailed citations and suggesting further reading. The hope is that researchers will use these chapters as a primer on open data within particular contexts to identify critical research gaps in need of further attention. In particular, the inclusion of further reading is designed to assist the use of these chapters in a teaching context.

For funders, we have sought to highlight key organisations and stakeholders in each sector and region and to point out instructive examples of what is being done with open data, noting, where appropriate, gaps in the available resources needed to develop new ideas or to scale what works in more locations for larger impact. A dedicated chapter on donors and investors (see Chapter 25) also considers the need for greater coordination of funding, and, as with most chapters, points to current areas of underinvestment, particularly around the infrastructure needed for sustainability and high-quality data delivery, as well as capacity building, to create a widespread culture of data use.

For policy-makers, we have encouraged authors to address both progress and challenges in the implementation of open data. In many cases, you will find more on the persistent challenges, reflecting not so much a lack of progress but rather the shared critical and progressive mindset of our authors who seek ambitious social change through the application of open data. We have sought, however, to keep chapters focused on a relatively small number of issues, prioritising those that most deserve policy attention at present.

For practitioners interested in detail on open data projects, whether focused on data publication or use, we have sought to provide them with both critical reflection and inspiration. The hope is that by reviewing chapters related to a specific sector from multiple perspectives, practitioners will discover new ways of framing old problems and practical ideas about how to move forward in using open data as a tool of entrepreneurial development or social progress.

Crucially though, we do not know how many of the readers of these essays will, in the future, associate themselves with the label of "open data practitioner" or "researcher", or whether they will simply perceive their role as someone who engages with open data as one tool among many. This is perhaps core to the identity crisis the movement may be currently experiencing and to the corresponding adjustments that open data communities will need to make in the second decade of open data. Is there still a need for a sustained movement that identifies the technical and licensing regime around open data as its core objective? What ethical and normative approaches need to be integrated into any future engagement with open data? Is it a good thing for the debate to move on from openness to adopt other narratives related to "good data",[12] "data justice",[13] or "data rights"[14]? We will return to these questions after our review of the state of open data offered in the following chapters, when we will be better placed to discuss what stands to be gained or lost in the years ahead.

Endnotes

1. https://www.od4d.net/
2. https://web.archive.org/web/20101128112407/https://www.data.gov/conference/
3. https://web.archive.org/web/20101218004117/http://opengovernmentdata.org/camp2010/
4. https://web.archive.org/web/20120821060331/http://www.data.gov/communities/conference
5. https://web.archive.org/web/20150716100733/http://opendatacon.org/
6. https://web.archive.org/web/20161104210854/http://opendatacon.org/
7. https://web.archive.org/web/20190127062831/https://www.opendatacon.org/

8   Khan, S. & Foti, J. (2015). Aligning supply and demand for better governance: Open data in the Open Government Partnership. *Open Government Partnership*, 1 January. https://www.opengovpartnership.org/resources/aligning-supply-and-demand-better-governance-open-data-open-government-partnership

9   https://opendatabarometer.org/

10 https://index.okfn.org/

11 Digital Science. (2018). *The state of open data report 2018*. London: Digital Science and FigShare. https://digitalscience.figshare.com/articles/The_State_of_Open_Data_Report_2018/7195058

12 Daly, A., Mann, M., & Devitt, S.K. (2019). *Good data*. Amsterdam: Institute of Network Cultures.

13 Taylor, L. (2017). What is data justice? The case for connecting digital rights and freedoms globally. *Big Data & Society, 4(2)*. https://doi.org/10.1177/2053951717736335

14 Tisne, M. (2018). It's time for a bill of data rights. *MIT Technology Review*, 14 December. https://www.technologyreview.com/s/612588/its-time-for-a-bill-of-data-rights/

Section 1

Open Data Sectors and Communities

CONTENTS

Introduction		12
Chapter 1.	Accountability and anti-corruption	17
Chapter 2.	Agriculture	35
Chapter 3.	Corporate ownership	51
Chapter 4.	Crime and justice	65
Chapter 5.	Development assistance and humanitarian action	77
Chapter 6.	Education	91
Chapter 7.	Environment	103
Chapter 8.	Extractives	119
Chapter 9.	Geospatial	137
Chapter 10.	Government finances	151
Chapter 11.	Health	166
Chapter 12.	Land ownership	181
Chapter 13.	National statistics	196
Chapter 14.	Telecommunications	207
Chapter 15.	Transport	215
Chapter 16.	Urban development	225

The chapters in this section explore sixteen different sectors and communities where open data has been applied.

The earliest advocates turned to open data because they faced particular problems. They were not seeking data in general, but rather specific datasets to help them solve those problems. In the years that have followed, a broad movement on open data has secured access to data on thousands of different topics. How useful this data has been in solving problems or meeting social challenges is dependent on both the data and on the particular problems and challenges that were targeted. Open data is not a one-size-fits-all solution, but instead plays out in different ways in different settings. As the chapters in this section will illustrate, to understand the state of open data, we need to look at open data in context, exploring the particular sectors where it has evolved and the communities that have developed around it.

Open data sectors ...

There are very few sectors where open data might not have a role. However, to provide a broad overview of open data developments, the focus chapters in this section were selected based on an analysis of the agenda and discussions at recent editions of the International Open Data Conference (see Introduction), as well as themes identified in the 2015 Sustainable Development Goals (SDGs)[1] and the categories of high-value data identified in the G8 Open Data Charter[2] and global measurement tools (see Chapter 22). We have sought to select sectors at varying stages of progress, ranging from government finances (Chapter 10) where budget and subsidy datasets have had a pivotal role in shaping early work on open data through to telecommunications (Chapter 14), a sector largely overlooked to date as an area of focus for open data initiatives. Our coverage is by no means comprehensive, and, inevitably, there are different choices that could have been made on the scope of each sector. Water and air quality, for example, could arguably have been addressed as sectors in their own right, although, in this volume, they find their place as sub-themes within the essay on the environment (Chapter 7).

The key advantage of a sectoral approach in a review of open data is that it requires us to take a step back and to understand open data in context. Understanding and intervening in the struggles around land ownership data (Chapter 12), for example, requires an appreciation of the different systems related to land ownership and a recognition of the role that records and data play in securing land rights. Progress on opening up corporate ownership data (Chapter 3) can also be better understood in the context of the global financial crisis and the search for policy responses at that point in time when "shovel-ready" open data approaches were available to draw on. Sectoral engagement with open data is far from inevitable but instead relies on the right combination of advocacy, infrastructure, and backing at key opportunity points. These opportunities can evolve quickly from external events, as in the 2008 financial crisis, or from the alignment of different stakeholder interests over time, such as with agriculture (Chapter 2), where a case can be made for opening up new pre-competitive space and a sectoral shift from closed to open models of data production and use.

The histories and horizons of open data vary from sector to sector. We have worked with the authors of each chapter to identify key dates in the development of open data in their sectors.

These timelines are published as part of the online companion to this book. Taking this long view helps us to understand the way in which open data ideas enter into an existing landscape of data systems, political attitudes, stakeholder relationships, and programmes of action. In the crime and justice sector, for example (Chapter 4), the history of open data might have started with interactive crime mapping in 2005, but new technological approaches have to contend with long-established and localised legacy ICT systems and the conservative ethos of many judicial institutions. The crime and justice chapter also draws important attention to the way open data work unfolds between different branches of government, encouraging us to consider government stakeholders beyond just the executive branch.

A sectoral approach also allows us to look beyond the "usual suspects" who self-identify with open data to locate other important stakeholders who have, to date, been on the periphery of the open data discourse. In the health chapter, for example (Chapter 11), the creators of an open source health management information system (HMIS) emerge as central players whose actions, in tandem with national-level policy activity, can contribute to improvements in the availability of aggregated open health data. Chapters on education (Chapter 6) and geospatial data (Chapter 9) also identify key stakeholder groups (the open education working group and open geospatial community, respectively) who have had relatively weak links to wider open data communities in spite of their relevant expertise and knowledge. A sectoral approach also reveals common influences across sectors. Eleven of the sixteen chapters in this section, for example, mention either the Open Data Charter[3] or the Open Government Partnership[4] as an influence on open data advances, and nine chapters draw on evidence from the Open Data Barometer[5] to understand progress.

Finally, a sectoral lens can help us to assess open data maturity and explore how embedded open data has become across a sector. To comprehensively assess the state of open data in a particular sector might require looking at the proportion of data generated in that sector which is ultimately available as open data, or it might involve an audit of use cases, identifying how far open data approaches have been adopted in addressing key sectoral challenges. While the chapters that follow are indicative rather than exhaustive, they show very different states of open data adoption. For example, the chapter on development assistance and humanitarian action (Chapter 5) suggests that the idea of open by default has become reasonably embedded in the sector, allowing stakeholders to shift their focus to developing and embedding more mature data-use practices. However, the chapter authors also note the ongoing challenge of building a data, and open data, culture in the sector, particularly given complex relationships between international, national, and local stakeholders. In the extractives sector (Chapter 8), work on governance, looking at issues such as contracts, tax, and royalty payments, has progressively integrated open data over the last decade, resulting in increased data availability and use. Yet, at the same time, the wider sector has seen a vast growth in proprietary data collection by commercial firms using emerging technologies, meaning that while the absolute quantity of open data available may have grown, the relative proportion of open to closed data has likely declined. A similar issue appears to be at play in the transport sector (Chapter 15), where route-planning apps have been a poster-child of the open data movement, but where the authors report that only a fraction of the data used to drive these apps is actually provided as open data. Even when open data is available, it may only cover a limited portion of the transportation experience. If a small group of stakeholders have access to superior but restricted-access application programming interfaces, the ideal conditions for innovation in the development of solutions will not develop.

One factor evident throughout the chapters in this section (and indeed throughout this volume) is that while open data has a technical foundation, progress relies upon policy, people, and collaboration. Open data tends to enter the discourse of a sector through the actions of one or more small groups that are able to enrol a wider group around them to develop and explore the application of open data. These are the open data communities that this section also attempts to bring into focus.

... and communities

The original working title for this section of the book was "Open data communities" rather than "Open data sectors and communities". Yet, it became clear that for most chapters, there was an open question as to the extent to which a coherent and recognisable community could be said to exist around the chapter subject. For most, the idea of community invokes a group with some degree of shared values, attitudes, and goals, and whose members have some degree of interaction. Although there are many successful "thematic" open data communities, in some sectors there are many different groups, each with distinct agendas, and with varying levels of interconnection, whilst in other sectors the sense of a distinct open data community is much more nascent.

By looking at the extent of community networking within, and across, sectors, we bring into focus a number of the drivers for community cohesion, including levels of collaboration, learning, and progress on securing impact from open data. For example, in the broad accountability and anti-corruption field (Chapter 1), we find strong connections have been made between distinct communities of investigative journalists, open contracting and procurement specialists, and individuals acting under a "follow the money" banner. While often meeting separately, these groups also benefit from a high degree of fluidity and the exchange of ideas through events, multilateral meetings, and field-building publications. By contrast, although the crime and justice chapter (Chapter 4) identifies many individual projects looking at open data, there is little evidence of a sustained global or regional community pushing open data forward in this sector, and instead the landscape is made up of ad-hoc initiatives by governments or other stakeholders without the evidence of substantial community development. Using a community lens can highlight how differing sectoral cultures, and different levels of investment in community coordination, impact on the degree to which action has been mobilised to address open data.

A community lens also brings to the fore questions about the people involved in steering and shaping open data activity within particular domains, inviting an exploration of whether communities are diverse or whether they are globally representative. Ultimately, all of the chapters serve to illustrate that community building requires intentional effort and sustained investments of time, resources, and energy. For example, substantial efforts have gone into outreach and to providing travel support to enable participants from lower-income countries to participate in open data events, such as the International Open Data Conference,[6] the GODAN Summit focusing on agriculture,[7] Open Contracting global events,[8] or meetings of the

International Aid Transparency Initiative's Technical Advisory Group.[9] We should also note that global community building often requires bridging language barriers, and the flow of learning and conversation between different linguistic open data communities is worthy of further investigation.

Lastly, a community lens can be used to examine the position of an open data community within a wider sector as a whole. Are open data specialists simply talking to each other or are they reaching out to shape wider sectoral work? The picture is varied, although, in almost all cases, there are opportunities to improve the integration of open data practitioners into existing sectoral communities of practice and to leverage open data to broaden those communities. A level of cultural adaptation is generally required as open data communities interface with existing communities of practice. For example, the national statistics chapter (Chapter 13) calls for improved connections between open data and national statistics offices (NSOs), recognising the need to focus on building mutual respect and understanding between statistics professionals and open data communities. The urban development chapter (Chapter 16) also illustrates the challenges of inserting an open data community into the mainstream of the sector, where, although open data has become a central topic in community discussions of resilient cities, within the commercial-led smart-cities marketplace, open data is treated as a minor tool rather than a transformative agenda.

Future states

The chapters in this section identify hundreds of different organisations engaging with the open data agenda and many different projects opening data and putting it to use. However, they also reveal that increasing open data adoption and impact across a sector is by no means inevitable. The process of making data open and ensuring that datasets can serve a much wider range of use cases than those for which they were originally created has resulted in a myriad of issues around data quality and interoperability that are only now starting to be addressed. Many chapters also point to major bottlenecks caused by endemic capacity gaps around data analysis and use, as well as the limited deployment of strategic actions to connect data analysis with policy change. In many sectors, the full potential of open data is being missed, in part, due to a shortage of sustained specialist work on technical and policy challenges and difficulty in finding non-profit or for-profit models that can bring the extended focus needed to move beyond pilots into long-term projects and programmes.

What is clear, however, is that although, in 2009, open data was promoted as a general reform, today, it is primarily seen as an asset to be used in meeting specific goals (including the SDGs). This raises many new questions for the open data movement as a whole, including whether it can be said that there is even a single overarching open data movement or whether we have many divergent sectoral movements and communities. How can open data be used to go deeper into sectoral problem solving while still maintaining cross-cutting learning and connections between communities? The chapters that follow are intended to address these questions and more.

Endnotes

1. https://sustainabledevelopment.un.org
2. Cabinet Office. (2013). G8 Open Data Charter and Technical Annex. GOV.UK, 18 June. https://www.gov.uk/government/publications/open-data-charter/g8-open-data-charter-and-technical-annex
3. https://opendatacharter.net/
4. https://www.opengovpartnership.org
5. https://opendatabarometer.org/
6. http://opendatacon.org/
7. https://www.godan.info/pages/godan-summit-2016
8. http://www.opencontracting2017.org/
9. https://iatistandard.org/en/about/tag/

001.

Accountability and anti-corruption

Jorge Florez and Johannes Tonn

Key points

- An established international field working on anti-corruption and accountability has existed only marginally longer than the open data movement itself. Open data for anti-corruption holds great potential, but efforts often face the common challenge that data availability does not automatically translate into effective data use.

- Strategies employed by reformers to address corruption and anti-corruption include strengthening the capacity of different local stakeholders to work with open data and tailoring the implementation of technical solutions to the institutional and political dynamics of particular contexts.

- Research indicates that the relationship between transparency and accountability is not necessarily causal or linear. Anti-corruption practitioners continue to debate how to best address the challenges at the heart of corruption problems.

- Future efforts need to focus on strengthening the connections between open data and anti-corruption practitioners, and ensuring the sharing of evidence and lessons learned.

Introduction

The expectations that open data might serve as a strategic tool for reformers around the world to improve anti-corruption and accountability results has been a key driver behind the push by open data advocates for more and better open government data. The underlying theory appears straightforward: open data "can reinforce anti-corruption efforts by strengthening transparency, increasing trust in governments, and improving public sector integrity and accountability by reinforcing the rule of law through dynamic citizen participation, engagement, and multi-stakeholder collaboration".[1]

Excitement over the promise of open data has been shared by large and small organisations alike. The G7 and the G20 have recognised its value, and multilaterals, such as the World Bank and the Inter-American Development Bank, have invested heavily in programmes to support open data. Bilateral aid agencies, including the Department for International Development (DFID) in the United Kingdom (UK) and the United States Agency for International Development (USAID), and philanthropic foundations, such as members of the Transparency and Accountability Initiative,[2] have also supported open data work. Additionally, multi-stakeholder initiatives like the Open Government Partnership, the Open Contracting Partnership (OCP), and the International Aid Transparency Initiative (IATI), among others, have facilitated and promoted efforts by government agencies, civil society, and media organisations across the world.

Current evidence about the impact of this work is relatively scant. Some argue that open data efforts have proven successful in "improving government by tackling corruption and increasing transparency, and enhancing public services and resource allocation", and in "empowering citizens [...] by enabling more informed decision making and new forms of social mobilisation".[3] Yet, at the same time, others have pointed out that open data has not been widely used in corruption investigations.[4] Other research questions the linearity and simplicity of the assumption that data availability leads to results, arguing that "transparency, information or open data are not sufficient to generate accountability".[5] It is fair to conclude that challenges exist in measuring the impact of open data to improve accountability and anti-corruption results. This raises questions about whether, and how, the open data community can convince the general public that greater access to open data is key to achieving results.

One reason why the evidence is patchy is that the relevant literature lacks common definitions of accountability and anti-corruption.[6] Definitions are often overly broad, defining accountability as the combination of answerability, the obligation to inform and justify public decisions, and enforceability, the ability to sanction or remedy contravening behaviour.[7] Corruption, in turn, is often used as an umbrella term to group behaviours related to the abuse of entrusted power, ranging from bribery and embezzlement to clientelism.[8] Both accountability and anti-corruption are about preventing, detecting, and disrupting abuses of power. Open data is a very powerful tool to reduce information asymmetries that lead to a power imbalance; however, more open information is not enough to actually negate the institutional and political dynamics that allow those in power to abuse it and remain impune.

Open data activists often assume that the solutions needed to strengthen accountability and to reduce corruption are already known by specialists, and that open data will increase the effectiveness of those working to implement such solutions. However, international development work focused on anti-corruption and accountability has been around only marginally longer than work on open data,[9,10] and the communities working on these issues have not yet reached consensus on several issues. Debates related to anti-corruption and accountability revolve around: concerns over how to prioritise and address corruption challenges in different contexts;[11] exploration of how to design, monitor, and implement interventions;[12] questions related to understanding and tracking changes in the political and technical dynamics that shape institutional reform and behavioural change;[13] discussions regarding how to identify and assess impact;[14] and ways to ensure that interventions actually empower marginalised groups and provide them with the means to improve their lives.[15]

Reflection on the overlap between the open data and the anti-corruption and accountability agendas offers important opportunities to methodically test underlying assumptions about the impact that power abuses have in practice and the role opening information can play in addressing these abuses. However, up to this point, such work has often been done by "pioneers" with little collaboration across agendas and with little attention given to the movement from simple data availability to using it strategically to address systemic or sectoral problems and achieving real impact.

This chapter will highlight the challenges, gaps, and progress made on key issues at the intersection between open data, accountability, and anti-corruption.

Open data for accountability and anti-corruption

In the mid-2000s, reformers pushing for open data began to demand the publication of data by governments in reusable formats that could be accessed by the general public. This effort later evolved toward identifying and then closing gaps in the publication of datasets,[16] with an additional focus on the implementation of data standards and data interoperability. Advocates have been successful in framing the open data agenda, advocating for standards, and convincing civil society, governments, and, to a lesser extent, the private sector to engage.

Open data initiatives have tended to focus on the release of data summarising existing government processes, while paying little attention to uses and users of the data, often treating open data as an end in itself. This has created momentum for the publication of datasets, but has also led to some governments focusing solely on transparency around selected issues without paying attention to opening up the underlying processes behind that data which are used internally to support transactions and decision-making. Open data and open government advocates have labeled these types of efforts as "passing off the release of inconsequential government-held data as transparency"[17] or "open-washing".

The mostly implicit theory of change in many open data initiatives is that more information will (almost) automatically lead to its use by those working on anti-corruption and accountability and enable them to produce better outcomes and achieve impact. However, while information and technical improvements are great tools to better understand accountability and corruption challenges, they are not sufficient to address entrenched power structures that oppose governance reform and generate systemic changes.

In 2016, the Open Data Barometer found that a number of datasets relevant to anti-corruption work (e.g. budgets, company registries, spending, contracting, and land ownership) "still tend to be highly opaque, and often the least open", and that important differences persist within and across regions.[18] A review of key datasets in five G20 countries also indicates that these relevant datasets are often not yet published, that public officials lack the skills to leverage open data, and that initiatives to strengthen citizen engagement using open data rarely link to anti-corruption or sectoral areas.[19]

In 2017, the "Open up guide: Using open data to combat corruption"[20] identified 30 key datasets[21] for fighting corruption (see sample in Figure 1), as well as standards that can make these datasets interoperable. The guide was tested in Mexico,[22] which produced evidence on the

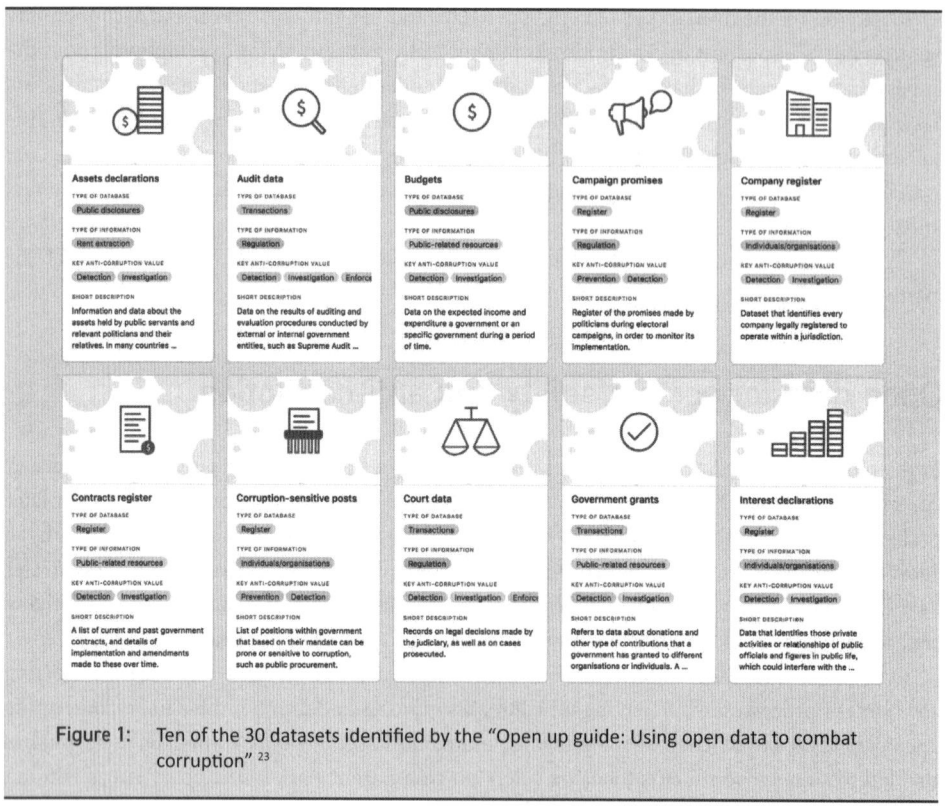

Figure 1: Ten of the 30 datasets identified by the "Open up guide: Using open data to combat corruption"[23]

value of the guide for enabling government officials to open key datasets. It also highlighted the need to define clear data governance frameworks and to promote dialogue between data users and producers in government and civil society.

Top down and bottom up access to data

Efforts to open up data that is directly relevant to local accountability and corruption challenges are becoming more frequent, but they remain siloed, with a low degree of interoperability among released datasets that are often used by only a limited number of stakeholders active in a specific issue area. Such efforts are often led by civil society and, to a lesser extent, by governments. Examples of government-led efforts include the publication of commercial agreements, business relations, payments, and gifts to health providers by the private sector in France[24] and Germany,[25] as well as budget and/or spending data by many governments at different levels, often with support from international actors such as the Global Initiative for Fiscal Transparency,[26] the World Bank,[27] and Open Budgets.[28] These government-led efforts have also spread to government performance data, such as the publication of data on the use of public resources for natural risk management and response by Italy[29] and Mexico.[30]

In other cases, civil society and media organisations have stepped in to close important gaps in the official publication of data related to accountability and anti-corruption. Most commonly,

> ### Testing the "Open up guide: Using open data to combat corruption" – Mexico[31]
>
> A joint effort by the government, Cívica Digital, Transparencia Mexicana, the Open Data Charter, and the Inter-American Development Bank tested the Open up Guide in Mexico by publishing a number of the key datasets it identifies.[32] This work provided insights into the challenges and opportunities of opening key datasets to fight corruption:
>
> - Access to a list of key datasets and guidelines for data publication facilitates collaboration with institutions; however, this collaboration can be improved by prioritising data publication based on locally relevant corruption challenges and user needs. The process also provides entry points for opening datasets beyond the executive branch.
>
> - Data publication needs to be complemented with capacity building for work on data and the provision of targeted support concerning gaps, legal challenges, and data use. The Mexico pilot enabled researchers to produce a process that can be used by governments elsewhere in their efforts to improve the publication of key datasets related to anti-corruption.
>
> - Agencies with the mandate to open government data and civil society organisations are both key to ensuring the actual implementation of commitments to open data and to improving the processes and practices that underlie data production and use. This collaboration can be improved by instituting and/or strengthening formal data governance frameworks.

these efforts focus on those areas where governments have not indicated a willingness to act (or even explicitly oppose the publication of datasets) by using a wide array of strategies to achieve the release of information which is then transformed into open data. Such efforts often seek to pressure governments by accessing and releasing information in ways that will create incentives for government officials to publish the same information as open data. Some of the strategies used to access data when official open data is lacking include:

1. Making public information requests[33] and publishing structured data from the results, such as the work by *La Nacion* newspaper on asset declarations.[34]

2. Obtaining data from candidates running for public office and from government officials on assets, tax compliance, and interests, as with the work done by the civil society coalition behind the "tres de tres" initiative in Mexico.[35]

3. Scraping documents and connecting different sources of data, such as with the publication of open data on political finance[36] in Peru by "Ojo público" and in Taiwan[37] by the Council Voting Guide.

4. Transforming complex data into open formats as has been done by "Ciudadano Inteligente"[38] in Chile with regard to party financing.

5. Turning information published by non-government actors (e.g. reports by private companies) into open data, as with the Data Extractors Programme by Publish What You Pay.[39]

6. Combing through public records and linking up data to enable the investigations of potentially corrupt transactions, such as the work by the Open Data Institute (ODI) in Kenya[40] and the Organised Crime and Corruption Reporting Project in Eastern Europe.[41]

7. Collating and systematising data from different sources and jurisdictions, such as the work by Open Ownership, merging public registers, government reports, and voluntary disclosure[42] to reveal beneficial ownership, or the work by Govtrack[43] with regard to the US Congress.

These efforts hold great potential, but have often faced challenges to translate data gathering into data use with tangible impact. Data often remains both siloed and dispersed, with information on the same topic being scattered across different agencies or levels of government, which provide the data in different ways and formats. Even where data can be collected and connected, concerns about its quality, completeness, usability, and sustainability are common. When working with data, questions of trust inevitably arise. Data users often doubt the reliability of the data and question whether the design and evaluation of public policies and decisions are actually based on that data. Finally, many potential data users face the emerging tendency of many governments to close civic space.[44]

Opening sensitive data in closed contexts

Most conversations around open data are based on experiences from those countries with some willingness to release open data on contentious issues, yet there are also efforts to open data for accountability and anti-corruption led by civil society mavericks in repressive countries with high levels of secrecy.

In Venezuela, the Transparency International chapter and the Instituto de Prensa y Sociedad de Venezuela have led an effort to compile, systematise, and publish open data[45] about regulations and decisions with regard to the use of public money. In Malaysia, the Sinar Project and the Web Foundation have produced and linked data about politically exposed persons[46] in an effort to shed light on how power is used and misused in the country. These admirable efforts challenge repressive and secretive governments and put issues of corruption and accountability up for public debate.

Over the last decade, progress and challenges in achieving accountability and anti-corruption results have led the community to gradually revise the theory and practice underlying their work on open data. Activists are now moving beyond models based on the supply and demand of data[47] to focus their work on more locally relevant problems, seeking to unpack the different elements needed to connect data production to use and impact. Some of the key ideas that may be coalescing into a revised theory of change include:

1. The need to make explicit the steps needed to go from data production through to taking actions that can activate institutional responses.[48]
2. A move from linear models to the use of cyclical and iterative approaches that enable a focus on specific governance challenges and the use of learning and adaptation.[49]
3. Integrating open data into the operation of existing anti-corruption institutions and mechanisms.[50]
4. Revising how to measure progress in the implementation of open data initiatives.[51]

The following sections will provide a deeper exploration of the different mechanisms connecting data availability and action with regard to existing anti-corruption systems and initiatives.

Moving from availability to use

Progress in the publication of data, even if uneven and patchy, has raised important questions about who will use that data, how they will use it, and what results can be achieved. There are no silver bullets when it comes to promoting the use of open data by local stakeholders to address corruption and accountability challenges. The approaches that have been used to bridge the gap between data production and use can be classified into three overlapping groups: those focused on data standardisation and technological tools, those focused on engaging users and particular problems, and those focused on changing government processes and practices.

First, those initiatives that have focused on standardisation and technological tools have paid great attention to the development of data standards and their implementation by governments. They aim to improve the quality and comparability of published data and enable the development of tools that can be adapted according to the needs of audiences in different contexts. These efforts have targeted a variety of areas from democratic processes to resource flows and, to a lesser extent, development results. Examples[52] include the IATI standard,[53] Fiscal Data Package,[54] the Popolo data specification,[55] the OpenCorporates schema,[56] and the Open Contracting Data Standard.[57]

The development and management of data standards related to accountability and anti-corruption have shown a similar trend to that of the broader open data space. Initially, standardisation was focused on finding ways to better present the information that was produced by governments, but later those leading the standards began to pay greater attention to data users' needs, moving beyond representing government processes into using data to reshape those processes. Important challenges still remain in terms of the technical features and tools needed to make the implementation of data standards more useful and in relation to ensuring that stakeholders have the capacity to use the standards to address locally relevant challenges. Increased collaboration between standard developers, implementers, and data users at the global and national level is needed to develop technical solutions in a way that is sensitive to local capacities to produce the data and to put it to use within complex political systems.

Even though there are a number of stakeholders working to implement data standards, promote interoperability, and develop tools to facilitate data use, the actual use of open data has not increased proportionally. New projects that pay greater attention to supporting users trying to use data presented according to data standards are now emerging with strategies to promote data use[58] and to explore the use of open data to fight corruption in particular countries.

Second, those initiatives that have paid greater attention to engaging users and achieving particular outcomes have shown important results. A clear example is the work of journalists at the national and international levels involved in collaborative networks such as the International Consortium of Investigative journalists (ICIJ). Recent scandals, such as those exposed by the Panama[59] and Paradise[60] Papers, have not only uncovered corruption, but have led to the consequential launch of prosecutions and the resignation of public officers and even presidents.[61] After publishing such stories, data has been made available in open formats that can enable the work or analysis by others. While these examples could be used to question the value of open government data on politically salient issues when compared to data obtained through leaks, the disparity in outcomes may indicate more about the differences in the way this data is being produced, treated, and used.

Leaked data often includes full versions of documents that are then used to stimulate collaboration among networks of journalists, both online and offline. These networks review the data thoroughly to organise it, clean it, and make sense of it. The same networks then use the data to find leads that are further corroborated and developed through other sources, including open government data, documents, and on-the-ground research. This intense work is not focused on merely making the information available; it is aimed at making the information useful to further identify and expose illegal activities carried out by those in power.

Lastly, there are a number of initiatives that have focused on fostering and supporting changes in government processes and administrative practices. Some of this work relies heavily on data to explore the value of new technologies like machine learning, blockchain,[62] and algorithms;[63] however, using these tools to analyse open government data has not yet reached a widespread level of popularity.[64] Interest in these still emerging technologies leads inevitably to a range of challenges with regard to potential violation of privacy, the possibility of reproducing and increasing existing biases, and the threat of using automation to hide questionable decisions and practices.[65]

Other important work to promote change in government practices through the use of open data is led by multi-stakeholder initiatives on procurement, international aid, extractives, and public infrastructure. Even though these initiatives are at different levels in their uptake and maturity, all of them seek to alter long-established government processes. While some initiatives use formal multi-stakeholder forums for the production, verification, and use of open data, others promote the integration of open data into government processes beyond the simple publication of data. These initiatives have led to important, if not yet widespread, results,[66] ranging from identifying money flows in the extractives sector[67] and the misuse of public resources[68] to achieving savings and better service delivery through improvements in the planning and implementation of government processes (see the box opposite).

> ## Open contracting: From open data to improved results
>
> From saving millions in public resources[69] to fueling citizen mobilisation demanding accountability[70] and improving the implementation of service delivery programmes,[71] open contracting is one of the most successful uses of open data to improve anti-corruption and accountability results. Three features place the work of the OCP and its local partners[72] at the forefront of work on open data:
>
> - Open contracting principles and the data standard to regularise the opening of procurement information were developed in collaboration with government reformers, lawyers, private sector companies, and the media.
>
> - Sectoral efforts have gone beyond the development of a standard to focus on work with local reformers to address concrete challenges related to increasing value for money, strengthening public integrity, boosting market opportunities, enhancing internal efficiency, and improving the quality of goods and services.
>
> - Reformers have used agile and adaptive ways for promoting the implementation of procurement reforms, user engagement, and the actual use of data, learning on the go and adjusting strategies as needed.
>
> Opening information on government contracts is increasing the capacity of activists and journalists to understand and challenge existing structures and protocols that allow the siphoning of public resources and unfair contracting practices.
>
> An example of this work in action is the joint effort by the municipal government of Bogotá and Colombia's procurement agency, Colombia Compra Eficiente (CCE), to use open data to identify inefficiencies and corrupt practices in the delivery of school meals in the city.[73] The use of this data by government and suppliers has led to reshaping the way the programme is tendered, opening opportunities for more suppliers to participate, and enabling the busting of a price-fixing scheme for fruit. This improved the accountability of the process and enhanced the quality and timeliness of the meals provided.

The wide variety of approaches by government and civil society to address anti-corruption and accountability challenges should not be read as an attempt to identify the single best strategy to achieve results. Instead, the open data community needs to distil, share, and debate the lessons emanating from both successes and failures, reflecting on what these lessons mean for developing and implementing further projects moving forward. Additionally, it is not only a matter of choosing between approaches focused around a particular technology, stakeholder group, or government reform. It will be necessary to identify and explore, in practice, how a combination of these approaches can help to address particular corruption and accountability challenges within specific contexts.

Moving from use to impact

As discussed above, more data does not necessarily lead to a proportional increase in either the use of data or anti-corruption and accountability results; however, increased access to standardised, machine-readable, and reusable data has enabled sharper investigations into instances of corruption and abuses of power, additional research to identify inefficiencies in the use of public resources, and greater awareness of systematic biases against particular groups. Nonetheless, current advances are generally insufficient to address the root causes that underpin corruption and accountability challenges: the ways in which power is distributed in a given society and the subversion of existing (democratic) institutions for private gain.

There are several emerging efforts to improve openness beyond the executive branch[74,75] and address corruption and accountability challenges[76] in other branches of government, including activities at the heart of the democratic process, such as monitoring elections and the undue influence of money in politics through campaign and party financing. Some initiatives, like those of organisations in the Openingparliament.org[77] network, have paid particular attention to the legislative branch.[78] These efforts to open and communicate information about legislators, how they perform their duties, and about legislation itself[79] have been at the centre of work to strengthen democracy, with consequent benefits for anti-corruption work. Yet, these emerging efforts often face important challenges in relation to the availability of data in machine-readable formats to support the accountability of members of parliament, as well as in relation to implementing lobbying reforms. While legislatures may be happy to see accessible data on aspects of government operations, they may be more resistant to opening up structured data on their own activities and interests.

A number of national governments have also been subject to interesting efforts to open up data about the judiciary[80] and oversight bodies, such as audit institutions. Their aim is to get a more complete picture of how cases are assigned to judges and how those cases progress until judgment is rendered. However, these efforts are not yet widespread and often face claims that they may hamper due process during trials.

Crucially, even when data is made available, initiatives tend to remain limited in their focus on particular branches of government or processes and generally have weak formal connections to the institutional systems in which they operate (e.g. the functioning of democratic institutions, the use of public resources, and the application of effective sanctions against those who engage in corrupt practices). This makes it challenging to follow cases of corruption from identification through to final resolution and sanctions, and, ultimately, hinders lasting impact and influence on future activities. Without ongoing scrutiny of democratic systems of power to enforce anti-corruption measures, individuals and institutions are able to continue to act with impunity, and the consolidation and replication of corrupt networks is facilitated.

The theory of change behind the idea of using open data for anti-corruption and accountability also highlights the potential value data can have in empowering citizens and enabling social mobilisation. Some organisations have used data to pursue an activist approach to crafting stories, uncovering wrongdoing, and identifying entry points that enable others to get involved. However, these approaches can put activists in peril, and, as of today, there are no established safety networks for this work, such as those that exist to protect human rights defenders or journalists. The absence of such safeguards, and the weaker links to established mechanisms for protection, may lead activists to take unnecessary risks and expose them to legal, reputational, or physical attacks.

Opening up the judiciary and advocating for greater accountability results

Due process and the effective management of evidence during trials is often seen by reformers as an excuse taken to the extreme by judicial bodies, preventing public disclosure of the most basic information on how cases are moved through the judicial system after a corruption scandal has been uncovered. However, some initiatives in this area have had an impact. One example of an open data initiative to obtain and use such information is the work done by the "Asociación Civil por la Igualdad y la Justicia" (ACIJ) in Argentina.

After years of litigation efforts to access information on corruption cases from the judiciary, and the burdensome work of turning hard copies into machine-readable data, ACIJ was able to create an observatory of cases.[81] This has enabled the public to demand greater accountability regarding the delivery of justice in corruption-related cases. Recently, this work has been further enabled by the opening of judicial information by the Argentine government.[82] Investigations into how corruption cases are allocated[83] have resulted in significant insights into how impunity is sustained, and there are now calls for reform to tackle more profound systemic issues in the judicial system.

Despite the emergence of various activist approaches, it is generally organisations that focus on governance, transparency, participation, and accountability that most frequently lead initiatives to address accountability and anti-corruption. These organisations play an important role, but still need to find effective ways to engage other key stakeholders, such as organisations working in particular sectors or territories, those working on rights protection, those active in social movements, or those working through other alternative mechanisms, such as strategic litigation. The minimal connections that often exist between open data initiatives and a broader range of stakeholders can deepen the challenges related to the usability, and actual use, of the data and hinder real impact in addressing problems that affect citizens.

The assumption that an improved capacity to identify instances of corruption leads to activating institutional oversight mechanisms is not necessarily wrong; however, assuming that those mechanisms will actually deliver results in the form of successful reforms, grievance redress, or sanctions without additional effort is, at the very least, an oversimplification. Open data can be a tool useful not only to identify instances of corruption, but also to engage, challenge, and reform the institutional designs and practices that enable corruption. Turning this potential into reality requires the use of approaches that consider the institutional and political environments in which data is produced and used. Adopting such approaches will enable sharper thinking about how the use of data can be more effective in practice, how to counter the forces that oppose openness (be they for private gain or from an aversion to change), and how to build stronger bridges between advocates for open data, activists working on sectoral and systemic challenges, and the democratic forces that can act on the findings and evidence obtained from the use of open data.

The open data community needs to explore and test innovative ways of using data that take all of these slowly acquired insights into consideration: to effectively challenge institutional mechanisms and practices that perpetuate impunity, inefficiencies, and the abuse of power; to reach out to unusual stakeholders by finding ways to integrate their needs and interests; to tap into existing social mobilisation processes; and to link the efforts of the different stakeholders engaging on reform with government branches and institutions.

Reflections and the road ahead

Over the past decade, reformers have used open data to create ripples and, in some cases, waves, in uncovering and prosecuting corruption. In a few cases, these efforts have resulted in the reform of systems where corruption had been the norm. Through their work, these reformers have generated insights that can help us to understand how to use open data more effectively to fight against corruption going forward. One of the key insights open data reformers have started to embrace is the value of adopting a problem-driven approach to the publication and use of data in order to address much more specific corruption and accountability challenges. These approaches also call for more collaborative models that are more grounded in the environmental context in which they are to be implemented, building on the needs and interests of local reformers and moving away from the replication of generalised practices toward the development of tailored "best-fit" solutions.

This shift in thinking on how to best use open data for accountability and anti-corruption does not represent a break with the ideals at the core of the open data movement, such as "open by default", but it does call for some refinement of our thinking around how to articulate advocacy goals, learning aims, and the desired impact. There is, and will continue to be, value in demanding that governments open up data on key issues related to accountability and anti-corruption; however, these demands should be based on a clear understanding of the users and usefulness of data, as well as the technical, political, and institutional environments in which it will be used.

To grapple with the implications of these insights, stakeholders would benefit from engaging with each other to develop non-linear approaches to better address particular corruption and accountability challenges. Learning about other perspectives and approaches will provide useful insights to improve how we devise and test methods, monitor progress and results, and spur dialogue on how and why specific approaches might yield better results. In particular, it is important to explicitly address the following questions:

1. How can the field facilitate and strengthen the work of local champions, including government, civil society, and the private sector, to generate and use data evidence to demand accountability and to lead in the fight against corruption?

2. What are the needs of different local stakeholders with regard to using open data? How can these insights help to tailor technical tools and methodological approaches to better support stakeholders in different sectors and contexts?

3. How can stakeholders build stronger and more effective connections among those working on open data, accountability, and anti-corruption, and those who work in sectors on specific issue areas?

4. What are the potential risks associated with using emerging technologies, such as machine learning, and artificial intelligence, in relation to accountability and anti-corruption? How can these tools and methods be combined with the social mobilisation and institutional mechanisms needed to generate and sustain change?

5. How can actors link the technical capacities needed to use open data with the political strategies needed to effectively change systems and ensure sustainable results?

Success in addressing these questions over the next decade will enable reformers to achieve significant accountability and anti-corruption results, but future work will require the community to develop holistic theories of change and the willingness to test them, implementing interventions in an iterative manner that enables reformers to ensure that open data is useful and used, while strengthening collaboration among stakeholders to achieve systemic reform and explicitly addressing entrenched power dynamics. In addition, the community must move beyond simple dichotomies that either highlight the production or the use of data toward models that start with identifying a specific problem to be solved, include the identification of the opportunities and challenges faced by local champions, and embrace learning and adaptation to develop solutions that are a better fit in specific environmental contexts.

Further reading

Carolan, L. (2017). *Mapping open data for accountability*. Transparency and Accountability Initiative and Open Data Charter. http://www.transparency-initiative.org/wp-content/uploads/2017/06/taiodc_draft_data4accountabilityframework.pdf

McGee, R., Edwards, D., Hudson, H., Anderson, C., & Feruglio, F. (2017). *Appropriating technology for accountability: Messages from making all voices count*. Brighton: Institute of Development Studies. https://opendocs.ids.ac.uk/opendocs/bitstream/handle/123456789/13452/RR_Synth_Online_final.pdf

OECD. (2017). *Compendium of good practices on the publication and reuse of open data for anti-corruption across G20 countries: Towards data-driven public sector integrity and civic auditing*. Paris: Organisation for Economic Co-operation and Development. http://www.oecd.org/corruption/g20-oecd-compendium-open-data-anti-corruption.htm

Santiso, C. (2018). Will Blockchain disrupt government corruption? *Stanford Social Innovation Review*, 5 March. https://ssir.org/articles/entry/will_blockchain_disrupt_government_corruption

Vrushi, J. & Hodess, R. (2017). *Connecting the dots: Building the case for open data to fight corruption*. Berlin: Transparency International and World Wide Web Foundation. http://webfoundation.org/docs/2017/04/2017_OpenDataConnectingDots_EN-6.pdf

About the authors

Jorge Florez leads Global Integrity's work on fiscal governance. He focuses on helping country-level partners to use data strategically to address accountability and corruption challenges. Follow Jorge at https://www.twitter.com/j_florezh and learn more about Global Integrity at https://www.globalintegrity.org.

Johannes Tonn leads Global Integrity's anti-corruption work and supports partners in designing and implementing problem-driven, data-informed, and learning-centred approaches to solving governance challenges. Follow Johannes at https://www.twitter.com/johntonn and learn more about Global Integrity at https://www.globalintegrity.org.

How to cite this chapter

Florez, J & Tonn, J. (2019). Open data, accountability, and anti-corruption. In T. Davies, S. Walker, M. Rubinstein, & F. Perini (Eds.), *The state of open data: Histories and horizons* (pp. 17–34). Cape Town and Ottawa: African Minds and International Development Research Centre. http://stateofopendata.od4d.net

This work is licensed under a Creative Commons Attribution 4.0 International (CC BY 4.0) licence. It was carried out with the aid of a grant from the International Development Research Centre, Ottawa, Canada.

Endnotes

1. OECD. (2017). *Compendium of good practices on the publication and reuse of open data for anti-corruption across G20 countries: Towards data-driven public sector integrity and civic auditing*. Paris: Organisation for Economic Co-operation and Development, p. 11. http://www.oecd.org/corruption/g20-oecd-compendium-open-data-anti-corruption.htm
2. http://www.transparency-initiative.org/who-we-are/
3. GovLab. (2016). Open data's impact: Open data is changing the world in four ways. http://odimpact.org/
4. Segato, L. (2015). *Revolution delayed: The impact of open data on the fight against corruption*. Torino: Research Centre on Security and Crime, p. 2. https://www.transparency.it/wp-content/uploads/2015/09/2015-TACOD-REPORT.pdf
5. McGee, R., Edwards, D., Hudson, H., Anderson, C., & Feruglio, F. (2017). *Appropriating technology for accountability: Messages from making all voices count*. Brighton: Institute of Development Studies, p. 11. https://opendocs.ids.ac.uk/opendocs/bitstream/handle/123456789/13452/RR_Synth_Online_final.pdf

6. Fox, J. (2018). The political construction of accountability keywords: Lessons from action-research. *TICTeC 2018*, Lisbon. https://tictec.mysociety.org/2018/presentation/political-construction-of-accountability-keywords
7. Stapenhurst, R. & O'Brien, M. (n.d). *Accountability in governance*. Washington, DC: World Bank. https://siteresources.worldbank.org/PUBLICSECTORANDGOVERNANCE/Resources/AccountabilityGovernance.pdf
8. Menocal, R.A. & Taxell, N. (2015). *Why corruption matters: Understanding causes, effects and how to address them*. London: Department for International Development. https://assets.publishing.service.gov.uk/government/uploads/system/uploads/attachment_data/file/406346/corruption-evidence-paper-why-corruption-matters.pdf
9. Carothers, T. & Brechenmacher. S. (2014). *Accountability, transparency, participation, and inclusion: A new development consensus?* Washington, DC: Carnegie Endowment for International Peace. https://carnegieendowment.org/files/new_development_consensus.pdf
10. Savedoff, W. (2016). *Anti-corruption strategies in foreign aid: From controls to results*. CDG Policy Paper. Washington, DC: Center for Global Development. https://www.cgdev.org/sites/default/files/CGD-policy-paper-Savedoff-anticorruption-agenda.pdf
11. Heywood, P. (2016). *Tackling corruption overseas – Written evidence*. London: Parliament of the United Kingdom. http://data.parliament.uk/writtenevidence/committeeevidence.svc/evidencedocument/international-development-committee/tackling-corruption-overseas/written/29840.html
12. Marquette, H. (2016). *Tackling corruption: Why we need to do things differently*. London: Parliament of the United Kingdom. http://data.parliament.uk/writtenevidence/committeeevidence.svc/evidencedocument/international-development-committee/tackling-corruption-overseas/written/30710.pdf
13. Menocal, R.A. & Taxell, N. (2015). *Why corruption matters: Understanding causes, effects and how to address them*. London: Department for International Development. https://assets.publishing.service.gov.uk/government/uploads/system/uploads/attachment_data/file/406346/corruption-evidence-paper-why-corruption-matters.pdf
14. Malito, D.V. (2014). *Measuring corruption indicators and indices*. EUI Working Paper. Robert Schuman Centre for Advanced Studies. San Domenico di Fiesole: European University Institute. http://cadmus.eui.eu/bitstream/handle/1814/29872/RSCAS_2014_13.pdf
15. McGee, R., Edwards, D., Hudson, H., Anderson, C., & Feruglio, F. (2017). *Appropriating technology for accountability: Messages from making all voices count*. Brighton: Institute of Development Studies. https://opendocs.ids.ac.uk/opendocs/bitstream/handle/123456789/13452/RR_Synth_Online_final.pdf
16. Web Foundation. (2017). *Open Data Barometer – Global report*. 4th edition. Washington, DC: World Wide Web Foundation. https://opendatabarometer.org/4thedition/report/
17. Khan, S. & Foti, J. (2015). *Aligning supply and demand for better governance: Open data in the Open Government Partnership*. Washington, DC: Open Government Partnership. https://www.opengovpartnership.org/resources/aligning-supply-and-demand-better-governance-open-data-open-government-partnership
18. Web Foundation. (2017). *Open Data Barometer – Global report*. 4th edition. Washington, DC: World Wide Web Foundation. https://opendatabarometer.org/4thedition/report/
19. Vrushi, J. & Hodess, R. (2017). *Connecting the dots: Building the case for open data to fight corruption*. Berlin: Transparency International and World Wide Web Foundation. http://webfoundation.org/docs/2017/04/2017_OpenDataConnectingDots_EN-6.pdf
20. Open Data Charter. (2018). Open up guide: Using open data to combat corruption. https://open-data-charter.gitbook.io/open-up-guide-using-open-data-to-combat-corruption/
21. https://airtable.com/shrHY9KFJ5bircwvx/tblOY2aw1hYUuJze9
22. Open Data Charter. (2017). Anti-corruption open up guide: Road-testing methodology. https://drive.google.com/file/d/0B44SovahLueTUTlxaUZBVldrWDQ/view
23. https://airtable.com/universe/exppzIHMSvEHE3ZCB/using-open-data-to-combat-corruption
24. http://www.transparence.sante.gouv.fr

25 Vrushi, J. & Hodess, R. (2017). *Connecting the dots: Building the case for open data to fight corruption*. Berlin: Transparency International and World Wide Web Foundation. http://webfoundation.org/docs/2017/04/2017_OpenDataConnectingDots_EN-6.pdf

26 http://www.fiscaltransparency.net/

27 http://boost.worldbank.org/

28 https://openbudgets.eu/

29 http://italiasicura.governo.it/site/home.html

30 http://www.transparenciapresupuestaria.gob.mx/es/PTP/fuerzamexico

31 Echeverria, A., D'Herrera, D., & Alanís, R. (2018). *Open up guide: Testing how to use open data to combat corruption in Mexico*. Washington, DC: Inter-American Development Bank. https://opendatacharter.net/open-up-guide-testing-how-to-use-open-data-to-combat-corruption-in-mexico/

32 https://datos.gob.mx/busca/group/guia-de-datos-abiertos-anticorrupcion

33 Fumega, S.V. (2016). Transformations in international civil society organisations working towards a greater access and use of governmental informational resources. PhD Thesis, University of Tasmania. https://eprints.utas.edu.au/23437/

34 http://interactivos.lanacion.com.ar/declaraciones-juradas/

35 https://www.3de3.mx/

36 Luna Amancio, N. (2018). Cinco desafíos para investigar el dinero, la política y el crimen desde los datos estructurados [Five challenges to investigate money, politics and crime using structured data]. *OjoPúblico*. https://fondosdepapel.ojo-publico.com/data/cinco-desafios-para-investigar-el-dinero-la-politica-y-el-crimen-desde-los-datos/

37 Pei-yi, C. (2018). How Taiwan uses open data to follow the money in politics. *G0v.News*, 28 March. https://g0v.news/how-taiwan-uses-open-data-to-follow-the-money-in-politics-779cb58a648d

38 https://partidospublicos.cl/

39 https://web.archive.org/web/20180726074721/http://www.publishwhatyoupay.org/our-work/using-the-data/

40 Young, A. & Verhulst, S. (2016). *Kenya's Open Duka: Open data for transactional transparency*. GovLab and Omidyar Network. http://odimpact.org/files/case-study-kenya.pdf

41 Radu, P. (2016). Follow the money: How open data and investigative journalism can beat corruption. *Global Investigative Journalism Network*, 25 March. https://gijn.org/2016/05/25/follow-the-money-how-open-data-and-investigative-journalism-can-beat-corruption/

42 https://openownership.org/what-we-do/

43 https://www.govtrack.us/

44 https://monitor.civicus.org/

45 https://vendata.org/site/

46 Canares, M., Yusof., K., & Meng, S. (2017). *Collaborating for open data. Building an open database on politically exposed persons in Malaysia: A case study*. Washington, DC: World Wide Web Foundation. http://webfoundation.org/docs/2017/08/RP-Collaboration-For-Open-Data-082017.pdf

47 Khan, S. & Foti, J. (2015). Aligning supply and demand for better governance: Open data in the Open Government Partnership. *Open Government Partnership*, 1 January. https://www.opengovpartnership.org/resources/aligning-supply-and-demand-better-governance-open-data-open-government-partnership

48 Carolan, L. (2017). *Mapping open data for accountability. Transparency and Accountability Initiative and the Open Data Charter*. http://www.transparency-initiative.org/wp-content/uploads/2017/06/taiodc_draft_data4accountabilityframework.pdf

49 Davies, T. & Perini, F. (2016). Researching the emerging impacts of open data: Revisiting the ODDC conceptual framework. *The Journal of Community Informatics*, *12(2)*. http://ci-journal.org/index.php/ciej/article/view/1281

50 Open Data Charter. (2018). Open up guide: Using open data to combat corruption. https://open-data-charter.gitbook.io/open-up-guide-using-open-data-to-combat-corruption/

51. Brandusescu, A. & Lämmerhirt, D. (2018). Open Data Charter measurement guide. *Open Data Charter*, 22 May. https://opendatacharter.net/4869-2/
52. For more examples, see https://airtable.com/shrHY9KFJ5bircwvx/tblOY2aw1hYUuJze9
53. International Aid Transparency Initiative Standard. http://iatistandard.org/
54. Kariv, A. (2018) Introducing version 1 of the Fiscal Data Package Specification. *Open Knowledge International Blog,* 28 May. https://blog.okfn.org/2018/05/28/introducing-version-1-of-the-fiscal-data-package-specification/
55. McKinney, J. (2013). Introducing Popolo, an Open Government Data Specification. *OpenNorth.* http://www.opennorth.ca/2013/02/21/update-on-opengovernment.html
56. https://opencorporates.com/info/about
57. https://www.open-contracting.org/data-standard/
58. IATI. (2017). *IATI data use strategy 2017-19.* https://drive.google.com/file/d/1Oh_tFfe5sahfkeUISRynR2U6dm4lPQSS/view?usp=embed_facebook
59. International Coalition of Investigative Journalists (ICIJ). (2016). The Panama Papers: Exposing the rogue offshore finance industry. https://www.icij.org/investigations/panama-papers/
60. ICIJ. (2018). Paradise Papers: Secrets of the global elite. https://www.icij.org/investigations/paradise-papers/
61. Fitzgibbon, W. & Díaz-Struck, E. (2016) Panama Papers have had historic global effects – and the impacts keep coming. *International Coalition of Investigative Journalists*, 1 December. https://www.icij.org/investigations/panama-papers/20161201-global-impact/
62. Santiso, C. (2018). Will Blockchain disrupt government corruption? *Stanford Social Innovation Review*, 5 March. https://ssir.org/articles/entry/will_blockchain_disrupt_government_corruption
63. World Economic Forum. (2018). Tech for integrity. https://widgets.weforum.org/tech4integrity/
64. See, for example, https://github.com/okfn-brasil/serenata-de-amor
65. Rieke, A., Bogen, M., & Robinson, D.G. (2018). *Public scrutiny of automated decisions: Early lessons and emerging methods.* Upturn and Omidyar Network. https://www.omidyar.com/sites/default/files/file_archive/Public%20Scrutiny%20of%20Automated%20Decisions.pdf
66. Brockmyer, B. & Fox, J.A. (2015). Assessing the evidence: The effectiveness and impact of public governance-oriented multi-stakeholder initiatives. *SSRN.* https://papers.ssrn.com/abstract=2693608
67. EITI. (2012). *Nigeria EITI: Making transparency count, uncovering billions. Case studies.* Oslo: Extractives Industry Transparency Initiative. https://eiti.org/sites/default/files/documents/Case%20Study%20-%20EITI%20in%20Nigeria.pdf
68. CoST Honduras. (2016). Why we make infrastructure transparent in Honduras. *Open Government Partnership* [Blog post], 6 December. https://www.opengovpartnership.org/stories/why-we-make-infrastructure-transparent-honduras
69. Brown, S. (2016). "Everyone sees everything": Overhauling Ukraine's corrupt contracting sector. *Open Contracting Stories*, 28 November. https://medium.com/open-contracting-stories/everyone-sees-everything-fa6df0d00335
70. Brown, S. & Neumann, G. (2017). Paraguay's Transparency Alchemists: How citizens are using open contracting to improve public spending. *Medium* [Open contracting stories], 2 October. https://medium.com/open-contracting-stories/paraguays-transparency-alchemists-623c8e3c538f
71. Brown, S. & Neumann, G. (2018). The deals behind the meals: How open contracting helped fix Colombia's biggest school meal program. *Medium* [Open contracting stories], 9 April. https://medium.com/open-contracting-stories/the-deals-behind-the-meals-c4592e9466a2
72. https://www.open-contracting.org/why-open-contracting/worldwide/#/
73. Ibid.
74. Naser, A., Ramírez-Alujas, Á., & Rosales, D. (Eds.). (2017). *Desde el Gobierno abierto al Estado abierto en América Latina y el Caribe* [From open government to the open state in Latin America and the Caribbean]. Santiago: Comisión Económica para América Latina y el Caribe. https://repositorio.cepal.org/bitstream/handle/11362/41353/1/S1601154_es.pdf

75 OECD. (2017). *Compendium of good practices on the publication and reuse of open data for anti-corruption across G20 countries: Towards data-driven public sector integrity and civic auditing.* Paris: Organisation for Economic Co-operation and Development. http://www.oecd.org/corruption/g20-oecd-compendium-open-data-anti-corruption.htm

76 Open Data Charter. (2016). *Open Data for anti-corruption: Investigation and Enforcement: Workshop Report,* 24 April. https://docs.google.com/document/d/1cnnjwfX1aDjNVjUhl-0gWGRwLVfU1T2gFeJDuDBiSwY/edit?usp=embed_facebook

77 See more at https://www.openingparliament.org/ and at https://www.transparencialegislativa.org/

78 See more at https://beta.openparldata.org/about/ and http://everypolitician.org/

79 https://www.regardscitoyens.org/la-fabrique-de-la-loi/

80 See, for example, the open data portal of the judiciary in Argentina at http://datos.jus.gob.ar/, the publication of data gathered by audit institutions in the city of New York at https://www.checkbooknyc.com/, and the state of Veracruz in Mexico at http://sistemas.orfis.gob.mx/simverp

81 See http://acij.org.ar/

82 A new version of the observatory is being built using data from the Supreme Court. https://www.cij.gov.ar/causas-de-corrupcion.html

83 For more information, see https://conocimientoabierto.github.io/visualizaciones/sorteosJudiciales/

002

Agriculture

Ruthie Musker, Ben Schaap, Martin Parr, and André Laperriere

Key points

- High level leadership, private sector engagement, and academic networks have put open data on the agenda across the agriculture sector.

- Issues of ethics, ownership, power, culture, and capacity all need to be addressed before the sector is "open by default".

- Mapping information flows through agriculture value chains can help policy-makers and practitioners to identify pre-competitive spaces for open data sharing and to understand the implications of opening data more broadly.

- Donors and governments have a key role to play in establishing the policy framework for openness and supporting the infrastructure needed for a sustainable open data commons for agricultural research and practice.

Introduction

Goal 2 of the Sustainable Development Goals (SDGs) commits United Nations member states to both achieve food and nutrition security and to promote sustainable agriculture. The world population is projected to exceed 9 billion people by 2050,[1] and the corresponding growing demand for food is exerting massive pressure on the use of water, land, and soil, which is further exacerbated by global warming. The majority of the world's food is still harvested by smallholder farmers,[2] many of whom are poor and food insecure themselves.[3]

Agriculture is a knowledge intensive industry. Government and private sector-supported research and agricultural extension work (e.g. farmer education) is central to improving crop yields, understanding and implementing sustainable practices, and getting food to market. However, it is only in the past two decades that the agricultural sector has valued data as a tool for generating, sharing, and exploiting knowledge to improve yields, reduce losses, and increase overall agricultural business outcomes.

Rapid internet and mobile phone penetration, especially in the developing world, the accessibility of satellite and remote sensing data, and new data collection and analytical approaches all play a role in the "datification" of agriculture. While data-related opportunities are increasing, challenges still exist in the policy, ethical, and data standards domains, and key datasets remain absent or inaccessible. This is especially true in terms of nutrition-related data, which is largely under-utilised in the field of agriculture. Despite some progress in raising consumers' awareness of the nutritional value of the food they consume, demand has not been significantly redirected to the production of more nutritious food, especially in the developing world.

Networks and leadership: A history of open data in agriculture

Work on open data in agriculture has emerged from a long history of knowledge management practice and international networking. Agricultural libraries in the United States (US) have been sharing bibliographical data since the 1940s. In the 1980s, the Food and Agriculture Organization (FAO) of the United Nations developed AGROVOC[4] initially as a printed thesaurus of terms and later established it as the first real data standard (vocabulary) for an open agriculture information ecosystem. FAO also created the first network to support agricultural information sharing in 2003, known as GLOBAL.RAIS (Global Alliance of the Regional Agricultural Information Systems).[5] In 2008, they launched the Coherence in Information for Agricultural Research for Development (CIARD) initiative,[6] a global movement dedicated to open agricultural knowledge, working to align the efforts of national, regional, and international institutions, and to improve information sharing and services.

The importance of considering not only data, but open data, came to the fore in 2012, when the US convened an international conference on Open Data for Agriculture, the result of a G8 commitment, with an emphasis on making "reliable agricultural and related information available to African farmers, researchers, and policymakers".[7] This led to the creation of Global Open Data for Agriculture and Nutrition (GODAN) as a convening network to bring together public, private, and non-profit stakeholders to find ways to open up and use data more effectively.

GODAN was conceived to focus on awareness raising and advocacy as reflected in its statement of purpose,[8] but, from the outset, it was found that change through advocacy results only when partners are brought together to debate the issues and obstacles to making open data for agriculture a reality, especially when they can draw on provocative policy-focused research and recommendations. An approach to "Convene, Equip, and Empower" now frames the overall GODAN theory of change.[9]

Other notable networks that advocate for open data in agriculture through high-level communications, research, and events include the Global Partnership for Sustainable Development Data, the Research Data Alliance, Global Forum for Agricultural Research, Presidents United to Solve Hunger, and AgriCord.[10]

A value chain perspective

When we consider the potential and use of open data in agriculture, there are numerous facets that reflect the breadth and diversity of the sector, especially when one also considers nutrition as a key element of the field. Whether it is food price data, geodata, plant genomes, country statistics, nutrition data, or data from a grassroot initiative to quantify food composition, published open data sets can be used by a wide variety of stakeholders to generate impact.[11] The actors involved are similarly diverse. Consider, for example, the single value chain for cheese production illustrated below.

Products	Inputs	Feed	Cows	Milk	Cheese
Actors	• Industry • Government • NGOs • University • Farmer	• Farmer • Industry • University	• Farmer • Industry • University • Government	• Farmer • Industry • University • Government	• Farmer • Industry • University • Government
Example data	• Amount of fertiliser applied • Soil quality • Pest risk	• Yield • Market price • Weather • Transport	• Milk produced • Animal health • Amount eaten • Living conditions • Methane emissions	• Market price • Nutritional information • Machinery used for processing • Food safety measures	• Market price • Nutrition • Food safety • Transport to market • Consumer data

Figure 1: Single value chain for cheese production
Source: Authors

Cheese is made of milk produced with the involvement of feed producers, dairy farmers, transporters, and processing factories. Each actor has an interest in understanding the provenance of their inputs and the markets they operate in. Some of the production chain involves data that can be made open. In other cases, data will be seen as a commercial asset. Regulators may be interested in product traceability, nutritional content, and labelling, and in providing this information to consumers. Producers are also interested in investment opportunities and risk reduction. In this simple value chain, there are various ancillary datasets that may be considered pre-competitive, yet still have some commercial value (weather data, transportation data, genetic data on livestock, etc.). These datasets can inform production, allowing producers to adjust the sourcing of inputs or to modify the production process to improve both the quality and the volume of their crops. Openness is clearly a tool to facilitate the flow of data across this value chain and to realise the maximum potential of data, yet openness requires policy choices, private sector engagement, and consumer awareness. It also requires that consideration be given to how different actors will be able to use the data that becomes available based on its level of interoperability. This chapter will attempt to unpack a number of these issues in more depth.

Open data issues in agriculture

Connecting stakeholders

Agriculture is a complex sector, and it can be difficult to define its boundaries. Agriculture and food systems integrate seamlessly into other systems, such as ecology, human health, and the built environment. Sustainable agriculture is considered a "wicked problem",[12] where too many elements are involved in order for the problem to ever be considered "solved". The data and metadata that are collected within agricultural systems are equally complex because they are generated by thousands of global stakeholders from multiple sectors, using an incredible range of types, formats, and ontologies. However, when we consider some of the primary forms and uses of agricultural data, such as research, production management, and statistical monitoring, we can start to map out some of the roles that different stakeholders play as illustrated in Figures 2 and 3.

Governments collect and share data in the form of national and international statistics (e.g. US National Agriculture Census[13] and FAOSTAT[14]), but often also support farmers and agricultural practices by publishing key datasets used for ICT-enabled farm extension and to empower consumers in food supply chains. Governments may also provide policy-relevant open data, including data related to national standards and frameworks used by service providers who help farmers or processors meet regulatory requirements.[15] Government also uses open data to

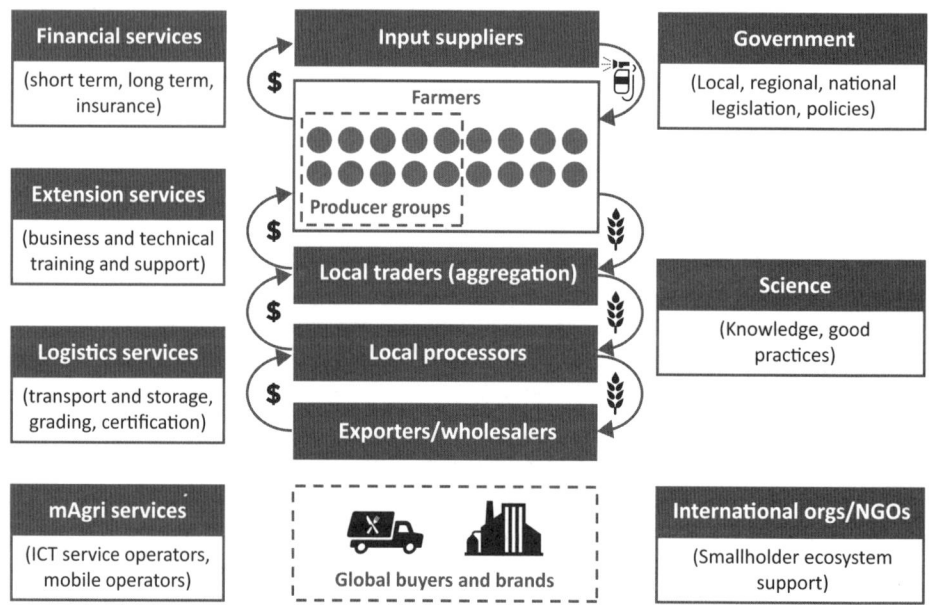

Figure 2: Different actors in the agriculture sector
Source: Jellema, A., Meijninger, W., & Addison, C. (2015). *Data and smallholder food and nutritional security*. CTA Working Paper 15/1. Wageningen, The Netherlands: Technical Centre for Agricultural and Rural Cooperation

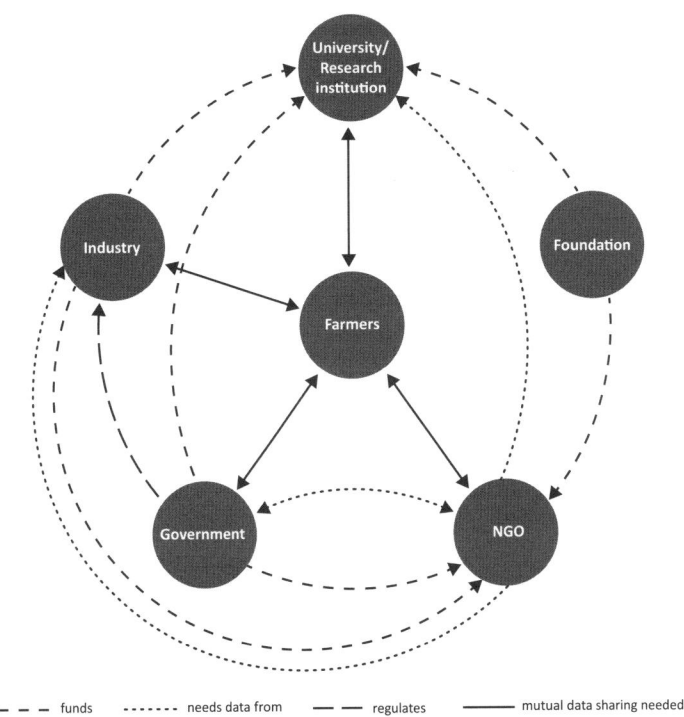

Figure 3: The relationships and data flows between various actors in the agriculture sector
Source: Authors and Technical Centre for Agricultural and Rural Cooperation (CTA)

promote transparency in their operations, with registers of land ownership a key example.[16] They are able to use their regulatory power to collect, or require the publication of, key data from private actors. Since 2012, a number of governments have developed and implemented open data policies to help embed open data practice in their own organisations or use their role as donors, funders, and commissioners to bring open data into the mainstream of agricultural development work.

Larger agricultural businesses are increasingly interested in open data, and companies are exploring opportunities to act as both data producers and consumers.[17] Some larger companies recognise that they are being held accountable by society and that greater transparency is a key foundation of their licence to operate.[18] In 2014, with the support of the Open Data Institute, Syngenta, a multi-billion dollar firm, placed open data at the core of its transparency strategy;[19] however, for many firms, operational "transparency" remains more opaque with information buried in corporate reports and the lack of structured background data. This presents challenges not only for public scrutiny, but also for investors seeking to target more sustainable investments.[20] Due to the nature and size of the value chains of larger corporate entities in the agri-food business that operate on a truly global level, they can have a significant impact on countries that lag behind in terms of reaching the SDGs.

Many **farmers** in developed countries are turning to data-based precision agriculture. Even in the developing world, farming involves increasing amounts of data collection and analysis. However, smallholder farmers often lack the technical capacity to manage or exploit the open data they create or that is provided by external producers. Instead, they often rely on intermediaries from the private sector or government. These intermediaries typically develop portals, apps, and tools that allow farmers to benefit from data on a range of topics, such as weather, infestations, or soil quality, that would otherwise be unavailable to them. Farmers' organisations have raised questions about the potential exploitation of data from farmers, with it being used against the interests of farmers unless it is well governed. In some countries, farmers have decided to take data management into their own hands by collectively developing portals and tools for themselves.

Academia and research have a long history of sharing data, and the cultural environment is shifting in a more open direction as open science is being embraced by more researchers,[21] donors,[22] and research networks.[23,24] The FAIR (Findable, Accessible, Interoperable, Reusable) data principles[25] have seen very rapid adoption in the scientific community, and open data has an important, albeit not exclusive, role within these principles. In partnership with international institutions, researchers have built a range of research infrastructure, including the European Open Science Cloud,[26] and networks for the discovery of data, such as the CIARD Ring.[27] The Interest Group on Agricultural Data (IGAD) at the Research Data Alliance (RDA)[28] connects a global community of researchers in the agricultural domain to exchange state-of-the-art research data on agriculture. However, access to research data remains fragmented. Although good permanent repositories exist,[29] it is not uncommon for data associated with a research project to be published, but then disappear when funding for the project tied to maintaining the data servers is no longer available.

Overall, although the supply of open data from all these different stakeholders is increasing, there remain large gaps, quality issues, and challenges in making data interoperable, as well as difficulties in establishing appropriate incentives for the stakeholders that are most relevant within the value chain.

Toward a global (open) data ecosystem for agriculture and food

Agricultural data includes social, environmental, physical, and financial factors. If viewed through the value chain, this includes inputs (fertilizer, pesticides, seeds), production (soil, weather, growth, land and water use), harvest (farmer income, yield, storage), and transport to market (food prices, road conditions, CO_2 emissions). This data is collected using several methods: in-situ sensors, household surveys/interviews and on-the-ground collection, and, increasingly, through technology, such as satellites and drones, and sensors on farm equipment.

With all this data, what would it take to secure the best access to data for improving agriculture and food security? This is the question addressed by Syngenta and GODAN partners in articulating their vision for a global data ecosystem for agriculture and food.[30] A global data ecosystem encompasses open standards and frameworks that enable decentralised data exchange. In an ideal open data ecosystem, all data, from geospatial to household surveys, could be layered together and used by any actor within the ecosystem. This is a socio-technical project: combining principles (such as the FAIR principles), technology, and stakeholder engagement.

Standards

Standards are explicit guidelines for the collection, management, and organisation of data. They can dramatically improve the interoperability of data between different stakeholders across agricultural value chains. Standards take many forms, including vocabularies, taxonomies, measurement protocols, data models, and equipment interfaces. The field of agriculture has long engaged in processes of standardisation for specific purposes, such as food safety, cross compliance of subsidies, machine engineering, and lab analysis, yet the existence of many sub-fields in agriculture has led to a proliferation of standards. These various standards have a surprisingly low degree of interoperability as they were developed to primarily serve the specific sub-fields; however, the need to use data from different sources for new applications (including big data and artificial intelligence applications) has made interoperability increasingly important. The starting point for greater interoperability is increased transparency on the development and use of current standards.

In order for standards to be more useful for research and for decision-making, they must be online, open, and machine-readable. GODAN Action (see box below) has completed a mapping of agri-food standards[31] and discovered that 16% of the standards are not online, only 56% are machine-readable, and only 21% are clearly available under open licences, thereby limiting their use for open data. The relative openness of standards is often related to the sub-field where they originated. For example, plant science standards are more likely to be open than soil-related standards, and supply chain standards are even less likely to be open.

GODAN and the Agricultural Information Management Standards (AIMS) initiative, hosted by FAO, have developed the VEST Registry[32] to make standards more open and useful by cataloguing ontologies in use in different agricultural sub-fields.[33] The RDA/IGAD,[34] started in 2013, works specifically on methods to make agricultural data more interoperable across crop-specific themes (such as rice and wheat) by developing joint standardised vocabularies, such as the Global Agricultural Concept Scheme.[35] Identifying and describing the standards in use provides a first step to increasing interoperability and rationalising standards; however, it is also important to increase widespread adoption of standards by embedding their use requirements in the development of guidelines and policies on open data.

GODAN Action

GODAN Action[36] is a three-year multi-sector project funded by the Department for International Development (DFID) in the UK and implemented by the Open Data Institute (ODI), GODAN, the Technical Centre for Agricultural and Rural Cooperation (CTA), Wageningen UR, and FAO, which aims to enable data users, practitioners, and intermediaries to work effectively with open data in the agriculture and nutrition sectors. GODAN Action works on three focal areas that will help overcome open data challenges: promoting standards and best practices, measuring open data impact, and building capacity with stakeholders. GODAN Action is applying these three focal areas to three specific data themes: weather data (2017), nutrition data (2018), and land use data (2019).

Policy

Over the past decade, open access and open data policies have become more prominent among governments and funders of agricultural programmes. The US and the United Kingdom (UK) made some of the first efforts toward the creation of open data policies. In 2013, US President Obama signed an executive order[37] toward making data open by default, which led to the US Department of Agriculture's (USDA) launch of the Food, Agriculture, and Rural virtual community[38] on data.gov. The UK created its open data policy in 2012[39] and has since opened thousands of agriculture-related datasets through the Department for Food and Rural Affairs,[40] and the European Union (EU) has undertaken similar work through the EU Open Data Portal.[41] These examples illustrate the potential for public policy development in support of the publication of agriculturally relevant data.

Several governments in Africa are in the process of developing open data policies specifically for agriculture. In 2017, Kenya held a Ministerial Conference on Open Data for Agriculture and Nutrition, which culminated in the Nairobi Declaration, a 16-article statement on open data policy in agriculture and nutrition.[42] The statement was signed by 15 African ministers, who have formed a network to develop policies for their respective countries. Francophone Africa is developing a similar network to support public policy development, the Conférence d'Afrique Francophone sur les Données Ouvertes (CAFDO).[43]

In 2016, a beta version of an International Open Data Charter Open Up Guide on Agriculture was published,[44] setting out a call for all governments to adopt a focus on agriculture within their wider open data policies and providing guidance on policy and practice specifically in the agricultural domain. The full version of the Open Up Guide[45] was subsequently launched in 2018 at the International Open Data Conference in Buenos Aires, Argentina.

Funders of agricultural research and development have developed open access policies, although these generally require only open journal publication of the research conclusions without necessarily requiring the underlying data to also be published as open data. Since 2012, the UK's DFID, the US Agency for International Development (USAID), and the Gates Foundation, among others, have established policies that require their funded researchers to share both research publications and research data under conditions that permit access and reuse.[46] However, a review of these policies in 2017 found they lacked clear open data definitions, suggesting a need to strengthen understanding of open data as a distinct concept alongside open access. There is also growing recognition that funded projects need support to understand and apply open data principles to their work, as well as access to technical data infrastructures to ease data publication and sharing. Several initiatives, such as the Gates Foundation funded Initiative for Open Ag Funding,[47] which ran from 2016 to 2018, have explored how to make programmatic data (financial and administrative data about funded programmes) open as well, building on the International Aid Transparency Initiative.[48]

A large gap also exists in the development of any coherent open data policy or practice among the private sector actors within the agricultural industry, although when put into place, such data policies would likely seek to balance open access with business interests, thereby limiting open data benefits and overall transparency.

Ethics

The widely cited case of John Deere tractors has become a key reference point in discussions related to data ethics. These "smart machines" not only plough the soil, but also capture vast amounts of data, which, under their "terms of service", are fed back to John Deere to analyse and exploit with no guarantee of benefits or data going back to the farmer.[49] Cases like this[50] have helped to spark an emphasis on data ethics in agriculture, exploring perceived power imbalances between farmers and big agribusiness and triggering initiatives, such as the EU Code of Conduct on Agricultural Data Sharing by Contractual Agreement,[51] endorsed by hundreds of equipment manufacturers.

Data privacy and security issues relate to the management and use of personally identifiable data, whether it is photographic, geospatial, financial, or demographic. There are many issues and ongoing discussions underway related to the degree of access that industry, government, and research institutions should have to data on the choices (e.g. agricultural practice, land use, product use) that an individual farmer makes. The norm is that data should not be made open when farm and farmer data privacy and security are at risk. There is general acceptance that sensitive data can be made available at times if aggregated, but not at the individual level. Data collectors must make every effort to prevent data breaches and inform farmers how data about them is used.[52] One such initiative that is now gaining traction in opening up data across agricultural companies, such as tractor companies and farm sourcing corporations, is the Open Ag Data Alliance[53] which has built an open source framework to allow farmers to access and control their own data.

Data ownership and legal rights issues are a difficult and complex component of the data ethics debate within the agriculture domain.[54] If data is to be increasingly made open by default, the sector would benefit from improved clarity around legal data ownership and governance frameworks. Legal issues that affect access to, and the use of, data at the international, national, and subnational level include copyright, database rights, technical protection measures, trade secrets, patents, plant breeders' rights, privacy, and even tangible property rights.[55] Within the sector, there is general agreement that farmers should steward their own data and that legal frameworks should be transparent, but the discussions are complex,[56] and many worry that more stringent mechanisms around farm data ownership could hurt innovation.[57]

Responsible data relates to employing data in ways that do not increase power imbalances. Careful examination of context can result in data being opened, shared with a chosen group, or kept closed.[58] Governments may publish data to improve accountability, as a policy instrument or as a service to citizens, especially if collection has been paid for by taxes. The Open Data Charter[59] encourages governments to make their data "open by default" for this reason, but accepts that there may be cases when data cannot be opened.

There is growing recognition in the field that to release data responsibly, the effects on vulnerable communities, especially women, Indigenous populations, and migrant workers must be considered.[60] The sensitive information at issue in this case is not always personally identifiable information, but rather knowledge that, if made open, may allow others to profit from it to the detriment of others. For example, if data released indicates that women are managing or using land without obtaining the legal rights to do so, external actors may undertake to gain control of the land at the expense of the women.[61] Trust between stakeholders around appropriate data responsibilities is important, but little guidance currently exists on best practices.

Preliminary work on issues of privacy, responsible data, and data ownership in agriculture has been carried out, and numerous farm organisations, manufacturers, and other entities have expressed interest in participating in further conversations around data ethics to build a new consensus, especially as it pertains to smallholder rights.[62] This work is still at an early stage.

Capacity

While smallholder farmers could benefit significantly from open data-driven knowledge on when and where to plant and harvest, and what current market prices are, at present it is highly resourced stakeholders who appear to be the primary beneficiaries of open data in agriculture. To ensure all stakeholders have the technical resources, knowledge, and capabilities to collect, publish, or reuse open data, efforts over the last few years have sought to overcome major capacity gaps among governments, data intermediaries, and farmers. For example, the GODAN Capacity Development Working Group and GODAN Action host webinars and provide a conversation space for those exploring how to use open data to create benefit for themselves or their organisations.[63]

Early learning from the field is showing that forming relationships among organisations and individuals, building trust, and ensuring a high diversity of stakeholders are all important in moving from awareness of open data to implementation of new business models and data use strategies. Researchers, governments, donors, NGOs, and farmers' organisations have all discussed trust as an essential component of capacity development and willingness to commit to open data in agriculture.[64]

Evidence shows, however, that digital skills, including access to technology, access to the internet, and even simple word processing and spreadsheet management skills are lacking in rural farming areas, especially in developing countries, and among women and vulnerable communities. To seek to address these issues, CTA has invested in IT capacity development efforts and e-Learning specifically for women and girls.[65] As mobile phones are increasingly available in developing countries, advocates expect that skills will increase, especially in rural agricultural areas. However, it is also anticipated that more capacity development efforts will be needed to ensure that all farmers can access, use, and share open data, including through the use of mobile platforms.

Looking ahead

As we have seen, agriculture is diverse, as is the potential for applying open data to support a range of activities in the sector, from providing remote sensing data for precision agriculture applications to bringing farming extension advice to smallholder farm owners. Although the stakeholders may look very different, overarching sector goals remain mostly unchanged: to grow nutritious food as efficiently as possible, balanced with the need to secure the basic livelihood of people everywhere, using successful business models. As outlined in this chapter, the burgeoning ecosystem for open agricultural data is only beginning to address a myriad of issues as evidenced by the series of discussions that took place at the GODAN Summit in 2016 (see Figure 4). In the light of a growing world population and ever-increasing pressures on resources, we need technological improvements and innovative approaches in many areas of agriculture and nutrition to meet this goal, and data will be central to that effort.

Figure 4: Drawnalism artwork by Alex Hughes captured at the GODAN Summit, September 2016

To date, the private sector has shown only minimal interest in publishing their data openly for reuse. A much greater emphasis on incentives and business models that encourage the release of open data at all levels of agricultural value chains is necessary. Both researchers and companies need to undergo a cultural shift from closed and proprietary to shared and open, recognising the value of open data in promoting innovation, cost-sharing, and improved value chain efficiencies. The extent to which the FAIR principles have caught on, at least in the rhetoric of the sector, is encouraging and highlights the value of communicating open data ideas as part of a broader normative agenda for advancing agriculture.

In 2018, the meaningful sharing of useful (both anonymised and identifiable) on-farm data was often curtailed by legitimate privacy concerns raised by farmers and their organisations, or by farm machinery and farm management systems that operate in a proprietary space. The open data community needs to increasingly involve stakeholders who are trusted by farmers, such as farm cooperatives, in order to promote innovation using on-farm data. Right now, for those wanting to innovate with data, obtaining large satellite datasets from governments or agents who have already adopted an open data policy is a lot easier than opening up on-farm data or nutrition data from surveys. Yet inclusive innovation also requires remote sensing to provide ground-truth data, highlighting the need for ongoing efforts to secure granular data about farms with the acceptance and support of farmers and their communities. As the agri-food industry increasingly needs a "licence to operate" from the public, they have begun to release more data on their sustainability performance. Early examples of this data publication and of the private sector's involvement in tracking SDG progress is promising in that regard. In addition, open data for agriculture has almost exclusively focused on food security, but, thus far, has neglected to consider textiles and forestry, which bear a large environmental cost and should be priority areas for future focus.

The seeds are sown for the growth of open data in agriculture, but, as yet, the evidence of lasting impact is limited. Creating the right ecosystem will need more than awareness raising. It will require all stakeholders to grapple with challenging ethical issues by turning debates and discussions into consensus, capacity development, guidance, and common approaches that can be deployed at scale.

Further reading

Allemang, D. & Teegarden, B. (2017). A global data ecosystem for agriculture and food (version 1; not peer reviewed). *F1000Research, 6(1844)*. https://doi.org/10.7490/f1000research.1114971.1

Carolan, L., Smith, F., Protonotarios, V., Schaap, B., Broad, E., Hardinges, J., & Gerry, W. (2015). How can we improve agriculture, food and nutrition with open data? *Open Data Institute* [Article], 27 May. https://theodi.org/article/improving-agriculture-and-nutrition-with-open-data/

De Beer, J. (2017). Ownership of open data: Governance options for agriculture and nutrition (version 1; not peer reviewed). *F1000Research*, *6(1002)*. https://doi.org/10.7490/f1000research.1114298.1

Ferris, L. & Rahman, Z. (2017). Responsible data in agriculture (version 1; not peer reviewed). *F1000Research*, *6(1306)*. https://doi.org/10.7490/f1000research.1114555.1

Smith, F., Fawcett, J., & Musker, R. (2017). Donor open data policy and practice: An analysis of five agriculture programmes (version 1; not peer reviewed). *F1000Research*, *6(1900)*. https://doi.org/10.7490/f1000research.1115013.1

Wilkinson, M.D., Dumontier, M., Aalbersberg, Ij.J., Appleton, G., Axton, M., Baak, A., Blomberg, N. et al. (2016). The FAIR Guiding Principles for scientific data management and stewardship. *Scientific Data*, 3(160018). https://www.nature.com/articles/sdata201618

About the authors

Ruthie Musker is Strategic Projects and Partnerships Lead for GODAN. Follow Ruthie at http://www.twitter.com/ruthiemusker and learn about GODAN at https://www.godan.info.

Ben Schaap is Research Lead at GODAN, where he works on research to support advocacy goals for open data through the mapping of impact case studies. You can follow Ben at https://twitter.com/benschp and learn more about GODAN at https://www.godan.info.

Martin Parr is currently Director of Data & Services, Digital Development, at the Centre for Agriculture and Biosciences International (CABI). He has been involved in open data and open knowledge projects in the agricultural sector for many years, and was involved in drafting the Global Open Data for Agriculture and Nutrition declaration. You can follow Martin at https://www.twitter.com/parr2_parr and learn more about CABI at https://www.cabi.org.

André Laperriere is Executive Director of the Secretariat for GODAN. Follow André at https://www.twitter.com/a_laperriere and learn more about GODAN at https://www.godan.info.

How to cite this chapter

Musker, R., Schaap, B., Parr, M., & Laperriere, A. (2019). Open data and agriculture. In T. Davies, S. Walker, M. Rubinstein, & F. Perini (Eds.), *The state of open data* (pp. 35–50). Cape Town and Ottawa: African Minds and International Development Research Centre. http://stateofopendata.od4d.net

This work is licensed under a Creative Commons Attribution 4.0 International (CC BY 4.0) licence. It was carried out with the aid of a grant from the International Development Research Centre, Ottawa, Canada.

Endnotes

1. Thomson Reuters. (2015). How will we fill 9 billion bowls by 2050? | #9billionbowls. http://reports.thomsonreuters.com/9billionbowls/
2. Graeub, B.E., Chappell, M.J., Wittman, H., Ledermann, S., Kerr, R.B., & Gemmill-Herren, B. (2016). The state of family farms in the world. *World Development*, *87*, 1–15. https://www.sciencedirect.com/science/article/pii/S0305750X15001217?via%3Dihub
3. Rapsomanikis, G. (2015). *The economic lives of smallholder farmers: An analysis based on household data from nine countries*. Rome: Food and Agriculture Organization of the United Nations. http://www.fao.org/3/a-i5251e.pdf
4. AIMS (Agricultural Information Management Standards). (2018). AGROVOC. http://aims.fao.org/vest-registry/vocabularies/agrovoc
5. GFAR. (2003). *GLOBal ALliance of the Regional Agricultural Information Systems (GLOBAL.RAIS): Project document*. Rome: Global Forum on Agricultural Research. http://www.fao.org/docs/eims/upload/216229/GLOBAL.RAIS_Project.pdf
6. https://ring.ciard.net/about-ring
7. http://www.godan.info/events/g8-conference-open-data-agriculture
8. http://godan.info/pages/statement-purpose
9. http://www.godan.info/pages/theory-change
10. http://www.data4sdgs.org/, https://www.rd-alliance.org/, http://www.gfar.net/, http://wp.auburn.edu/push/ and https://www.agricord.org/en, respectively.
11. Carolan, L., Smith, F., Protonotarios, V., Schaap, B., Broad, E., Hardinges, J., & Gerry, W. (2015). *How can we improve agriculture, food and nutrition with open data?* London: Open Data Institute and Global Open Data for Agriculture and Nutrition. https://theodi.org/article/improving-agriculture-and-nutrition-with-open-data/
12. Van Latesteijn, H.C. & Rabbinge, R. (2012). Wicked problems in sustainable agriculture and food security, the TransForum experience. *International Food and Agribusiness Management Review*, *15 (Special Issue B)*, 89–94. https://www.ifama.org/resources/Documents/v15ib/Latesteijn-Rabbinge.pdf
13. https://www.nass.usda.gov
14. http://www.fao.org/faostat/en/
15. For example, https://data.food.gov.uk/catalog
16. Smith, F. & Jellema, A. (2016). *Introducing the Agriculture Open Data Package. BETA version*. Wallingford: Global Open Data for Agriculture and Nutrition. http://www.godan.info/sites/default/files/GODAN_Agriculture_Open_Data_Package_BETA_1.pdf
17. Beardmore, D. (2017). The value of open data for the private sector. *Open Data Institute* [Article], 23 June. https://theodi.org/article/the-value-of-open-data-for-the-private-sector/
18. Menzies, T. (2015). What does "social license" mean for agriculture? *CropLife Canada*, 3 November. https://croplife.ca/what-does-social-license-mean-for-agriculture/
19. https://www.syngenta.com/site-services/transparency.aspx
20. Odier, P. (2017). Why lack of data is the biggest hazard in "green investing". *Financial Times*, 6 March. https://www.ft.com/content/be8e5db2-0249-11e7-aa5b-6bb07f5c8e12
21. Government of The Netherlands. (2016). *Amsterdam call for action on open science*. Amsterdam: Ministry of Education, Culture and Science. https://www.government.nl/documents/reports/2016/04/04/amsterdam-call-for-action-on-open-science
22. Smith, F., Fawcett, J., & Musker, R. (2017). Donor open data policy and practice: An analysis of five agriculture programmes (version 1; not peer reviewed). *F1000Research*, *6(1900)*. https://doi.org/10.7490/f1000research.1115013.1
23. See, for example, the GoFAIR Initiative, https://www.go-fair.org/go-fair-initiative

24. Zervas, P., Manouselis, N., Karampiperis, P., Hologne, O., Janssen, S., & Keizer, J. (2018). E-ROSA D3.7: Foresight roadmap paper. *Zenodo*, 17 October. https://zenodo.org/record/1479659#.XMaPFegzZPY
25. https://www.nature.com/articles/sdata201618#author-information
26. EC (European Commission). (2018). European Open Science Cloud (EOSC). https://ec.europa.eu/research/openscience/index.cfm?pg=open-science-cloud
27. http://ring.ciard.net/
28. https://www.rd-alliance.org/groups/agriculture-data-interest-group-igad.html
29. See, for example, the *Open Data Journal for Agricultural Research* at http://library.wur.nl/ojs/index.php/odjar/ and AgTrials at http://www.agtrials.org/
30. Allemang, D. & Teegarden, B. (2017). A global data ecosystem for agriculture and food (version 1; not peer reviewed). *F1000Research*, *6(1844)*. https://doi.org/10.7490/f1000research.1114971.1
31. Pesce, V., Tennison, J., Mey, L., Jonquet, C., Toulet, A., Aubin, S., & Zervas, P. (2018). A map of agri-food data standards (version 1; not peer reviewed). *F1000Research*, *7(177)*. https://doi.org/10.7490/f1000research.1115260.1
32. https://vest.agrisemantics.org/about/vest-agroportal
33. Jonquet, C., Toulet, A., Arnaud, E., Aubin, S., Dzalé Yeumo, E., Emonet, V., Graybeal, J., Laporte, M.A., Musen, M.A., Pesce, V., & Larmande, P. (2018). AgroPortal: A vocabulary and ontology repository for agronomy. *Computers and Electronics in Agriculture*, *144*, 126–143. https://doi.org/10.1016/j.compag.2017.10.012
34. https://www.rd-alliance.org/groups/agriculture-data-interest-group-igad.html
35. https://agrisemantics.org/GACS/
36. http://www.godan.info/godan-action
37. Obama, B. (2013). Executive Order: Making open and machine readable the new default for government information. *The White House*, 9 May. https://obamawhitehouse.archives.gov/the-press-office/2013/05/09/executive-order-making-open-and-machine-readable-new-default-government-
38. https://www.data.gov/food/
39. HM Government of the United Kingdom. (2012). *Open data: Unleashing the potential*. White Paper. London: HM Government UK. https://assets.publishing.service.gov.uk/government/uploads/system/uploads/attachment_data/file/78946/CM8353_acc.pdf
40. Defra (Department for Food and Rural Affairs, UK). (2017). About Defra's data programme. *Gov.UK/Defra Digital*. https://webarchive.nationalarchives.gov.uk/20180801164029oe_/https://defradigital.blog.gov.uk/about-defras-data-programme/
41. https://open-data.europa.eu/
42. GODAN (Global Open Data for Agriculture and Nutrition). (2017). Statement of the ministers: Building resilience on food security and nutrition through open data. *Ministerial Conference on Agriculture and Nutrition Data, 14–16 June 2017, Nairobi, Kenya*. http://assets.aims.fao.org.s3-eu-west-1.amazonaws.com/public/posts/attachments/Conference%20Statement%20-%20Open%20Data%20-%20GODAN%20-%20JUne%202017.pdf
43. Banzet, A. (2017). #CAFDO2017: The first Francophone African Conference on Open Data and Open Government. *Open Government Partnership*, 15 June. https://www.opengovpartnership.org/stories/cafdo2017-first-francophone-african-conference-on-open-data-and-open-government
44. Smith, F. & Jellema, A. (2016). *Introducing the Agriculture Open Data Package. BETA version*. Wallingford: Global Open Data for Agriculture and Nutrition. http://www.godan.info/sites/default/files/GODAN_Agriculture_Open_Data_Package_BETA_1.pdf
45. Jellema, A., Musker, R., Smith, F., Brandusescu, A., & Davies, O. (2018). Open up guide for agriculture. https://openupguideforag.info/
46. Smith, F., Fawcett, J., & Musker, R. (2017). Donor open data policy and practice: An analysis of five agriculture programmes (version 1; not peer reviewed). *F1000Research*, *6(1900)*. https://doi.org/10.7490/f1000research.1115013.1

47 InterAction. (2017). Initiative for Open Ag Funding. https://interaction.org/project/open-ag-funding/overview
48 https://iatistandard.org/en/
49 Baarbé, J. & De Beer, J. (2017). A data commons for food security. Open AIR Working Paper 7(17). *SSRN*, 1 August. https://dx.doi.org/10.2139/ssrn.3008736
50 EIP-AGRI (European Innovation Partnership for Agricultural Productivity and Sustainability). (2016). *Data revolution: Emerging new data-driven business models in the agri-food sector*. Seminar Report. https://ec.europa.eu/eip/agriculture/sites/agri-eip/files/eip-agri_seminar_data_revolution_final_report_2016_en.pdf
51 https://copa-cogeca.eu/img/user/files/EU%20CODE/EU_Code_2018_web_version.pdf
52 Ferris, L. & Rahman, Z. (2017). Responsible data in agriculture (version 1; not peer reviewed). *F1000Research*, *6(1306)*. https://doi.org/10.7490/f1000research.1114555.1
53 http://openag.io/
54 Davies, T. (2015). Data, openness, community ownership and the commons. *Tim's Blog*, 2 September. http://www.timdavies.org.uk/2015/09/02/openness-community-ownership-and-the-commons/
55 De Beer, J. (2017). Ownership of open data: Governance options for agriculture and nutrition (version 1; not peer reviewed). *F1000Research*, *6(1002)*. https://doi.org/10.7490/f1000research.1114298.1
56 Cosgrove, E. (2017). Congress wades into farm data "ownership" debate. *AgFunderNews*, 17 July. https://agfundernews.com/congress-wades-farm-data-ownership-debate.html/
57 Heath, R. (2017). Could farmer data "ownership" kill innovation? *Australian Farm Institute*, 13 June. http://www.farminstitute.org.au/ag-forum/could-farmer-data-ownership-kill-innovation
58 (ODI) Open Data Institute. (2015). The data spectrum. https://theodi.org/about-the-odi/the-data-spectrum/
59 Open Data Charter. (2015). Principles. https://opendatacharter.net/principles/
60 Maru, A., Berne, D., De Beer, J., Ballantyne, P., Pesce, V., Kalyesubula, S., Fourie, N., Addison, C., Collett, A., & Chaves, J. (2018). Digital and data-driven agriculture: Harnessing the power of data for smallholders (version 1; not peer reviewed). *F1000Research, 7(525)*. https://doi.org/10.7490/f1000research.1115402.1
61 Ferris, L. & Rahman, Z. (2017). Responsible data in agriculture (version 1; not peer reviewed). *F1000Research*, *6(1306)*. https://doi.org/10.7490/f1000research.1114555.1
62 Ibid.
63 http://www.godan.info/working-groups/capacity-development
64 Musker, R. & Schaap, B. (2018). Global Open Data in Agriculture and Nutrition (GODAN) Initiative Partner Network Analysis. *F1000Research*, *7(47)*. http://dx.doi.org/10.12688/f1000research.13044.1
65 CTA (Technical Centre for Agricultural and Rural Cooperation). (2018). Women need access to open data with potential application for agriculture. https://www.cta.int/en/article/women-need-access-to-open-data-with-potential-application-for-agriculture-sid0c13ea34e-27e6-40d5-895a-67d434b0f933

003

Corporate ownership

Jack Lord

Key points

- The availability of standardised and openly licensed corporate data "at source" from corporate registries is limited, but through intermediaries like OpenCorporates, significant open data can be accessed and reused.

- Big strides have been made over the last decade in laying the technical and policy foundations for more open data on corporate structures, ownership, and control, but although progress has been made on the balance between openness and privacy in corporate data, there are still issues to resolve.

- Evidence suggests open corporate data can be a key tool in improving risk management and holding the powerful to account, but progress may also bring increasing hostility to openness from some entities in the private sector.

- A concerted effort will be needed in the coming years to build on the foundations laid to date in order to deliver a global, robust, and reliable supply of open data on corporate identity and ownership.

Introduction

Basic corporate data is essential for understanding our world. The name of a company, its legal form, registration number, formation date, the identities of its directors, and the registry where this information is held are all fundamental to knowing who we are doing business with and who our employers are, as well as which entities should be taxed and in which jurisdiction. Access to that data over time allows us to assess the performance and structure of the economy as businesses form, merge, break apart, and fail. Another layer of analysis opens up if we move from simply identifying corporate entities to identifying their owners and those who ultimately control them, a concept referred to as beneficial ownership. The more jurisdictions that require corporate ownership data to be open, the easier it becomes to navigate through a myriad of shell companies, regardless of where they are located, to identify the actual owners.

Information provided as open corporate data is of interest to public, private, and civil society stakeholders, and has a universal geographical applicability. G20 leaders have discussed the need to use corporate data to improve financial stability and efficiency, to combat corruption, and to improve the exchange of tax information between jurisdictions.[1] These same goals are reflected in the Sustainable Development Goals (SDGs). SDGs 16 and 17 address the need to reduce illicit financial flows, ensure the return of stolen assets, reduce corruption, promote investment, and develop capacities for domestic tax collection, all of which are supported by improving the availability and use of corporate data.[2]

Progress, impacts, and challenges

Progress: Data availability and technical infrastructure

Despite the relevance of information on corporates, progress on releasing it as open data has been slow. In the fourth edition of the *Open Data Barometer*, corporate data, identified as company register data, had the third lowest score of all the datasets surveyed, and only 5% of all company register data was available as open data.[3] Nor has there been a significant shift over time to open these datasets. The first edition of the *Open Data Barometer* in 2013 found that only 3 of 74 company register datasets were available as open data; by the time of the fourth edition in 2017, only 6 of 109 datasets were open.[4] Corporate registers still lack a universal data standard that could be used to make opening these datasets easier in the future.

A more hopeful picture can be found from OpenCorporates, an aggregator that provides corporate data under an open licence. In 2018, OpenCorporates provided corporate data from 127 registries in 73 different countries; however, much of this comes from OpenCorporates' own scraping work rather than from the release of open datasets at source. For the platform to move toward more comprehensive global coverage, more jurisdictions will need to open their company register data and remove the paywalls that limit access.

Although datasets containing basic corporate information were found in all but one of the jurisdictions assessed by the 2017 *Open Data Barometer*, albeit at many different levels of openness and machine-readability, data related to corporate ownership often did not exist at all.[5] In the latest Financial Action Task Force (FATF) consolidated assessment, only 19 of 69 countries listed are compliant with transparency requirements for beneficial ownership, and these requirements mandate only that information on beneficial ownership is obtainable by competent authorities, not by the public.[6,7] Very little open data on corporate ownership exists at the present time. Open registers on beneficial ownership are available for Denmark (which also has a register of legal ownership), the UK, and the Ukraine, and a state contractors' register is available in Slovakia. Furthermore, while the policy advances discussed below are likely to create more ownership registers in the future, these will not necessarily be open, free-to-access, or machine-readable.

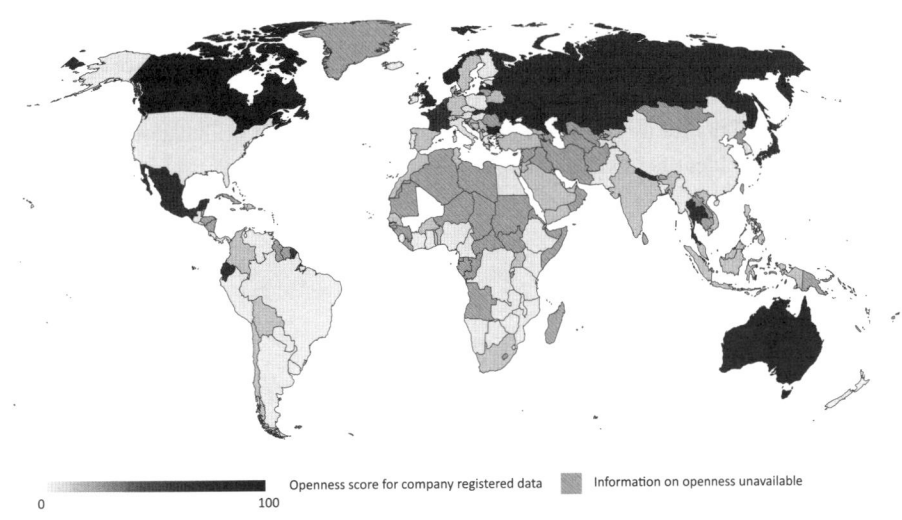

Figure 1: The *Open Data Barometer* (ODB) uses ten different variables to assess the presence and openness of company register datasets using an expert survey. The fourth edition of the ODB found just six company register datasets that met the full open definition.
Source: https://opendatabarometer.org/?_year=2017&indicator=ODB

However, important advances have been made. These advances might be described as "infrastructural", providing the technical components that support the dynamic and international nature of corporate information, as well as the legislative and civil society support that have made these technical advances possible.

The most fundamental requirement for open corporate data is the availability of identifiers that are unique, stable, and interoperable across jurisdictions and that are openly licensed. In this respect, a great deal of progress has been made. Two systems are operational. Thomson Reuters' PermID assigns identifiers and offers them, plus basic company and officer information, under an open license for over 3.4 million legal entities.[8] The Global Legal Entity Identifier Foundation (GLEIF) takes a different approach, requiring legal entities to sign up for an identifier through a local operating unit. The LEI data they provide also contains basic company information and will soon also contain "Level Two" data on an entity's accounting parent. Over 1.3 million LEIs have been issued to date; however, despite their universal applicability, identifier coverage is greater across the wealthiest countries with almost 25% of the LEIs issued coming from the UK and USA alone (see Figure 2).[9]

Another supporting development has been the emergence of lists and services to point publishers and data users toward the right sources of corporate identifiers. One example of this is org-id.guide, which has evolved from the organisation identifiers registry list maintained by the International Aid Transparency Initiative to help encourage the use of stable identifiers from existing registers for all types of legal entities across the world.[10] Launched at the 2016 International Open Data Conference and developed to meet a commitment of the IODC Roadmap,[11] it has been fostered by a collaboration of open data standards providers, but has not yet seen wide adoption. GLEIF also maintains a list of corporate registries with unique identifiers known as the Registration Authorities List that is used in LEIs.[12] One danger here is that we face a proliferation of competing open standards to the point that tooling for crosswalks between identifiers will need to be part of the future landscape of open corporate data. GLEIF's dataset linking LEIs to SWIFT's Business Identifier Codes is a welcome step in this direction.[13]

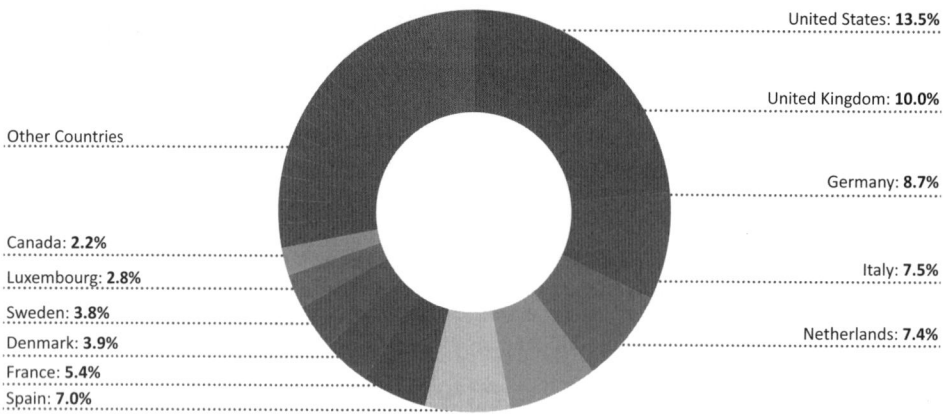

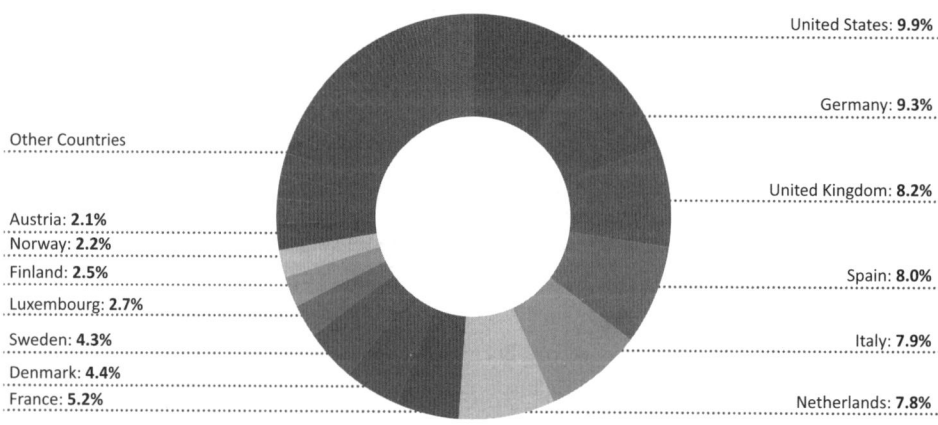

Figure 2: Over 1.3 million LEIs have been issued, although the global distribution of identifiers, and the extent to which they are attached to verified data, varies by country.
Source: https://www.gleif.org/en/lei-data/global-lei-index/lei-statistics

The final technical component of progress on open corporate data is the emergence of universal data platforms. These services offer an advantage over national platforms in that corporate activity often crosses borders, so identifying corporates often requires searching multiple corporate registers maintained on national platforms. Reconciliation of company names and disambiguation of company officers is a significant value-added service that such platforms can provide. OpenCorporates is the most well-established example, offering access to open corporate data via search and an API. More recently, OpenOwnership, funded by the UK's Department for International Development, has sponsored the development of the Beneficial Ownership Data Standard and brought together beneficial ownership information from several existing national registers on its own platform with plans to extend further and to allow self-submission by companies and individuals.[14]

An introduction to beneficial ownership

In the context of corporate ownership, "beneficial ownership" refers to the identification of the natural person or persons who benefit from, or control, legal entities, persons, or arrangements. Beneficial ownership can be achieved through such means as formal rights, like votes or dividend rights attached to shareholdings, or informal rights, like the ability to influence the direction of a company outside a formal ownership relationship. The identification of beneficial ownership involves looking through otherwise complex corporate ownership chains to find the "ultimate" beneficial owner regardless of how many shell companies or secrecy-based jurisdictions may stand in the way.

Beneficial ownership is also partly defined in the negative. While the "beneficiary" of an asset can be any legal person, natural person, or arrangement, a beneficial owner must be a natural person, because, regardless of how complex a corporate structure may be, control over it ultimately resolves to one or more natural persons. Beneficial ownership is also distinct from "legal ownership", which refers only to ownership of legal title. For example, one natural person may legally own a company, while another natural person is the beneficial owner through a trust or nominee structure. Legal title is not necessary for beneficial ownership, because control may be exercised through informal means.[15]

The concept of beneficial ownership has its origins in trust law, but, beginning in the 1970s, it has become part of the lexicon of international tax, anti-money laundering, and illicit financial flows. More recently, beneficial ownership has moved out of these specific fields into the broader policy debate on corruption and transparency.[16] Of particular importance is the emergence of the OpenOwnership project, which is focused on enabling the publication of open beneficial ownership data and creating its own global register of this data. The project has a steering group comprised of civil society groups, such as the Open Contracting Partnership and OpenCorporates, and has built links with organisations like the Open Government Partnership and the Extractives Industry Transparency Initiative that have existing commitments to beneficial ownership transparency.

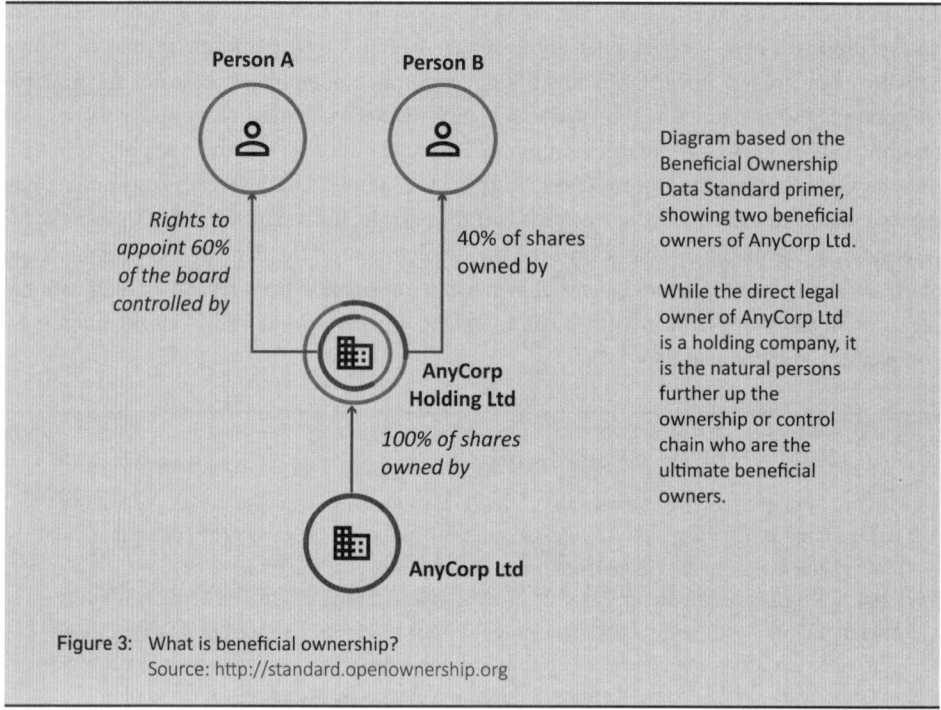

Figure 3: What is beneficial ownership?
Source: http://standard.openownership.org

Progress: Policy and legislation

The foundational work for progress on opening data corporate ownership has involved winning the policy and legislative argument that corporate ownership data should be made available. At a high-level, these arguments are summarised in two communiqués from the G8 and G20 in 2013 around the themes of anti-corruption and open societies,[17] which, in October of that year, led to the first public commitment to an open register of beneficial owners by the UK at an Open Government Partnership (OGP) conference in London.[18]

The motivation for opening up corporate data has three interlocking themes. First, the financial crisis ushered in a historical period of reform centred around the dangers of uncertain information and unknown actors in financial markets. This has been particularly important in the G20 driving forward the Global Legal Identifier Foundation, which is based on their linking of time-consuming and uncoordinated practises for identifying counterparties to the potential for exposure to liabilities and consequent financial instability.[19] Second, the use of anonymous corporate vehicles in corruption cases and other illicit financial flows was highlighted in the World Bank's influential 2011 *Puppet Masters* report.[20] Corporate anonymity has since been identified as a contributor to terrorist-financing, to corruption, to the expropriation of shareholders, and to impeding development goals.[21] Third, the technical requirements of tax-sharing and anti-money laundering requirements increased the demand for interchangeable data on natural persons and legal entities.[22] Together, these three themes have been critical drivers of the beneficial ownership agenda.

The concrete outcome of these policy initiatives has been national- and regional-level legislation to mandate open registers of business data and the systematic collection of beneficial ownership data (to which access may still be restricted). While early adopters were single European nations, new regional leaders like Indonesia are starting to emerge in the Global South.[23] In the European Union, the Anti-Money Laundering Directive (AMLD) obligates member states to create public central registers of beneficial ownership. In a major legislative advance in 2017, the AMLD was updated to include trusts and trust-like arrangements and to make that data accessible to those with a legitimate interest.[24]

Multilateral organisations have also drawn a wider range of entities into contact with the infrastructure for identifying and describing corporates and for publishing this information as open data. The Extractive Industry Transparency Initiative (EITI) 2016 Standard requires countries to publish roadmaps for beneficial ownership transparency in the extractives sector and a recommendation that beneficial ownership registers be public. As of March 2017, 21 countries had committed to a establishing a public register.[25] The Open Government Partnership also recommends robust registers of beneficial ownership as an intermediate commitment to open government, and recommends providing open access to machine-readable data from these registers as an advanced commitment.[26]

There is also a less visible layer of work related to corporate registers that is not yet yielding open datasets but still establishes concrete targets for advocacy work in this area. In many jurisdictions, such as Hong Kong, Singapore, Switzerland, Zambia, and others, governments have passed legislation to require closed beneficial ownership registers to comply with anti-money laundering standards.[27] Similarly, the implementation of the Markets in Financial Instruments Directive II (MiFID II) requires trusts wishing to trade in financial instruments to have an Legal Entity Identifier as of January 3, 2018,[28] so that prior to the implementation of the revised AMLD in the EU, we will get signals about which trusts in the region are economically active and another identifier that can be incorporated into central registers.

Case study: OpenCorporates

OpenCorporates was founded in 2010 and has received funding from the Alfred P. Sloan Foundation, ODINE, and EU Horizon 2020. OpenCorporates collects corporate data from public open data sources, official APIs, and data scrapings, and transforms it all into a standard form. Covering 127 registries, OpenCorporates offers a search engine, access to free and paid APIs, corporate data, company gazettes, and LEIs. The site also offers curated datasets on out-of-state corporations in the US. In 2017, OpenCorporates took the Quebec corporate registry to court after receiving a takedown notice for information originally accessed from that registry. The case indicates both how far the movement for open corporate data has come and the role that OpenCorporates has played and how much work is still left to be done.

Impacts: Markets for corporate data

Even at this relatively early stage, the opening up of corporate data has had significant impact. There is a significant market for data on corporate entities, and startups in this ecosystem have both built new business models based on available open data sources and challenged information providers. Significant businesses that have emerged in this space: OpenCorporates, providing standardised corporate and financial data; DueDil, offering credit checking and anti-money laundering checks; Arachnys, offering automated and manual tools for due diligence; and Calcbench, offering standardised accounts data for US companies.[29] Encouragingly, many of these businesses support the rhetoric around the expected impacts of open corporate data by serving to reduce the compliance costs for businesses, making decision-making about investment and risk more transparent, giving minority shareholders visibility on who controls legal entities, and allowing diagnostics for individual businesses and whole sectors of the economy through the use of detailed data. There is still an obvious absence of businesses from the Global South; however, the coverage of OpenCorporates and Arachnys, in particular, is also deliberately global and constrained only by data availability. This is an encouraging sign that businesses built on open corporate data can be supply-led rather than demand-led and that we will see a more diverse customer profile emerge as a result.

Impacts: Civil society users of open corporate data

Corporate data has been fertile ground for civil society with the origins of movement closely tied to transparency goals and now closely aligned with the Sustainable Development Goals. The NGO, Global Witness, has used corporate data to investigate corruption in Myanmar's jade industry (see box) and money-laundering associated with Panamanian companies and the Trump Ocean Club.[30] Investigations that combine leaked and official data simultaneously illustrate both the promise of joining up data and the difficulties of investigating ownership when so many legal entities are registered in jurisdictions that support secret registration for corporations. As another example, Transparency International, when investigating foreign ownership of properties in London, combined information from the International Consortium of Investigative Journalists' Offshore Leaks Database and official sources; however, despite combining sources, the report was unable to find information on 46% of the companies concerned.[31] When open data sources are available, the potential for civil society to investigate and exert pressure is clear. For example, court documents from a Brazilian case linked to the Odebrecht bribery scandal, enabled journalists in Scotland to both examine the role of Scottish Limited Partnerships (SLPs) as a possible money-laundering vehicle and highlight the lack of compliance with disclosure rules in the UK's open register.[32] The UK has since signalled reforms on SLPs.[33] Similarly, campaigners have also demonstrated the potential impact of tying data standards together. In Malaysia, the Sinar Project's Telus website, for example, will use the Open Contracting Data Standard, Popolo, and the Beneficial Ownership Data Standard to link legal entities and natural persons in public procurement disclosures as a way of finding corruption.[34]

> ### Case Study: Global Witness and the Jade Industry
>
> The Global Witness investigation of the jade industry in Myanmar involved unstructured source data that was turned into structured data by OpenCorporates. This process also meant that full access to the dataset was preserved even as director and shareholder details were being scrubbed from the original source.[35] Global Witness was then able to see links within the jade industry using official data and to disambiguate legal entities and natural persons with the support of on-the-ground interviews. Together, these techniques allowed for precise documentation on how important figures from government, the military, and the narcotics trade were heavily involved in the jade industry. As this example suggests, the investigative use of corporate data often requires anchoring in a particular external context. This might, as in Myanmar, provide information on the local significance of patterns of corporate ownership or, as with large-scale leaks like the Panama Papers, point investigators toward possible wrongdoing.

Challenges: Data quality

A significant challenge that is likely to become more acute over time is the quality assurance of data held in open registers, especially when legal entities self-submit and information is verified on a risk-assessment basis. In these situations, the information provided by honest actors is of variable quality, and the information provided by dishonest actors is often hard to disentangle. This problem is particularly acute when new compliance regimes are introduced and submitters' understanding of their statutory duties is limited. A report from Global Witness has found that the UK's person of significant control (PSC) register, which is unverified and has some unvalidated data fields, has serious data quality issues.[36] Verified data, or data submitted through a corporate service provider, is likely to be high quality, but imposes higher costs on corporates. The poor quality of open registries, and the high cost of verified alternatives, was used as an argument against open and verified corporate registries in a 2011 report by the Stolen Asset Recovery Initiative.[37] The same argument has resurfaced more recently in the context of registers of beneficial ownership.[38] Proponents of open corporate data will need to be wary of poor data creating negative feedback around corporate transparency. A possible solution is to adopt the LEI approach, where local operating units validate information for a small fee and accuracy remains high.[39] There will also need to be a push for verified data, using traceable processes by authorised persons to reduce the opportunity for plausible deniability when false information is entered into a register.[40] To guard against honest mistakes, registries may also be able to improve data quality through automated error detection, better guidance to submitters, and improved data validation.

Challenges: Data protection and useful data

Other than data quality, the other major challenge to improving open data on corporate identity and ownership may be the potential negative reaction from some corners to increases in transparency, primarily because arguments around privacy and data protection are currently unresolved. While the European court has ruled that there is no "right to be forgotten" for natural persons in company registers, legislation has not removed ambiguities around how long data can be stored for, who has the right to access it, and how far should it go to identify individuals.[41] While campaigners have made cogent arguments against privacy for beneficial owners, the argument is likely to re-emerge as ownership transparency is tied into legal reforms associated with corporations and to the fundamental rights of individuals. Given that extracting value from corporate ownership data involves making sometimes uncertain connections between datasets held in different jurisdictions, practitioners and civil society will need to balance the arguments for transparency with the need for coordination and harm prevention for individuals exempt from disclosure and for individuals who, while not exempt, may nonetheless be exposed to harm by the joining up of datasets.

One more challenge arising from success will be the need to encourage positive uses for ownership data, while discouraging detrimental or adversarial uses. There is a significant risk that some combination of poor data quality, complex or non-interoperable data, and a lack of capacity will lead to registers being created but not used. In this regard, it is useful to have sector-specific guidance (e.g. NRGI's work on extractives) or targets for success or failure (e.g. increasing revenue collection in the Global South).[42] While positive uses of ownership data will need to be cultivated, adversarial uses of registers are likely to increase unsupervised. Dishonest actors will become familiar with the rules and find it easier to skirt disclosure requirements, and as long as secrecy-based jurisdictions still exist, they will also have the option to simply close legal entities and open new ones not subject to scrutiny.[43] This could itself be seen as a sign of success, but it will be crucial to be able to measure such behavioural changes.

Conclusion

Much progress on open data related to corporate identity and ownership has been made. While it might appear that the amount of open corporate data is still relatively limited, much of the infrastructure required for success, such as policy, legislation, and technical architecture is now in place or being developed. Moreover, progress to date has involved a broad base of stakeholders from government, multilateral institutions, civil society, and the private sector. Great advances have been made in creating a shared understanding that we need to be able to unambiguously identify legal entities using universal identifiers, which has led to an emerging ecosystem of links to complex corporate data. A more recent development is that the policy argument in support of beneficial ownership seems to have been won. We have seen early examples of registers providing ownership data as open data, as well as the legislative basis for many more to come in the near future mostly as the result of a civil society movement committed to opening up asset ownership as part of economic transparency. However, the withdrawal of the US from the EITI on the basis that it is a "burden for business" demonstrates the fragility of the achievements to date and the difficulty of maintaining corporate disclosure as a desirable goal.[44] For open corporate data to fulfil its promise for the SDGs, any momentum that has been created in Europe and North America will need to be recreated across the Global South.

Further reading

FATF & Egmont Group. (2018). *Concealment of beneficial ownership*. Paris: Financial Action Task Force. https://www.fatf-gafi.org/media/fatf/documents/reports/FATF-Egmont-Concealment-beneficial-ownership.pdf

Gray, J. & Davies, T. (2015). Fighting phantom firms in the UK: From opening up datasets to reshaping data infrastructures? *SSRN*. https://papers.ssrn.com/sol3/papers.cfm?abstract_id=2610937

Knobel, A., Meinzer, M., & Harari, M. (2017). What should be included in corporate registries? A data checklist part 1: Beneficial ownership information, 2017. *SSRN*. https://ssrn.com/abstract=2953972

Prichard, W. (2018). *Linking beneficial ownership transparency to improved tax revenue collection in developing countries*. Summary Brief 15. Brighton, UK: International Centre for Tax and Development. http://opendocs.ids.ac.uk/opendocs/handle/123456789/13753

Westenberg, E. & Sayne, A. (2018). *Beneficial ownership screening: Practical measures to reduce corruption risks in extractives licensing*. Briefing May 2018. New York, NY: Natural Resource Governance Institute. https://resourcegovernance.org/sites/default/files/documents/beneficial-ownership-screening_0.pdf

About the author

Jack Lord is a Data and Policy Analyst at Open Data Services Co-operative. He is co-chair of the Beneficial Ownership Data Standard working group and is works with OpenOwnership to provide technical assistance to countries implementing beneficial ownership transparency. Follow Jack at https://www.twitter.com/jacklord and follow his work at https://www.opendatanotes.com.

How to cite this chapter

Lord, J. (2019). Corporate Ownership. In T. Davies, S. Walker, M. Rubinstein, & F. Perini (Eds.), *The state of open data: Histories and horizons* (pp. 51–64). Cape Town and Ottawa: African Minds and International Development Research Centre. http://stateofopendata.od4d.net.

This work is licensed under a Creative Commons Attribution 4.0 International (CC BY 4.0) licence. It was carried out with the aid of a grant from the International Development Research Centre, Ottawa, Canada.

Endnotes

1. G20. (2013). Communiqué: Meeting of finance ministers and central bank governors. http://www.g20.utoronto.ca/2013/2013-0720-finance.html
2. UN (United Nations). (2015). Transforming our world: The 2030 Agenda for Sustainable Development. https://sustainabledevelopment.un.org/post2015/transformingourworld
3. Web Foundation. (2017). *Open Data Barometer – Global report*. 4th edition. Washington, DC: World Wide Web Foundation. https://opendatabarometer.org/doc/4thEdition/ODB-4thEdition-GlobalReport.pdf
4. Davies, T. (2013). *Open Data Barometer: 2013 global report*. Washington, DC: World Wide Web Foundation. http://opendatabarometer.org/doc/1stEdition/Open-Data-Barometer-2013-Global-Report.pdf
5. Web Foundation. (2017). *Open Data Barometer – Global report*. 4th edition. Washington, DC: World Wide Web Foundation. https://opendatabarometer.org/doc/4thEdition/ODB-4thEdition-GlobalReport.pdf
6. FATF (Financial Action Task Force). (2018). FATF methodology for assessing compliance with the FATF recommendations and the effectiveness of AML/CFT systems. http://www.fatf-gafi.org/publications/mutualevaluations/documents/fatf-methodology.html
7. FATF (Financial Action Task Force). (2018). Consolidated assessment ratings. http://www.fatf-gafi.org/publications/mutualevaluations/documents/assessment-ratings.html
8. Thomson Reuters. (2018). Open PermID: Entity search. https://developers.thomsonreuters.com/open-permid/open-permid-entity-search-restful-api
9. GLEIF (Global Legal Entity Identifier Foundation). (2018). Global LEI Index: LEI statistics. https://www.gleif.org/en/lei-data/global-lei-index/lei-statistics
10. http://org-id.guide/
11. IDRC. (2015). *Enabling the data revolution: An international open data roadmap. Conference report*. Ottawa: International Development Research Centre. http://1a9vrva76sx19qtvg1ddvt6f.wpengine.netdna-cdn.com/wp-content/uploads/2015/09/IODC2015-Final-Report-web.pdf
12. GLEIF (Global Legal Entity Identifier Foundation). (n.d.). GLEIF registration authorities list. https://www.gleif.org/en/about-lei/gleif-registration-authorities-list
13. Wolf, S. (2018). GLEIF and SWIFT introduce the first open source BIC-to-LEI relationship file to allow for interoperability across multiple ID platforms. *GLEIF Blog*, 8 February. https://www.gleif.org/en/newsroom/blog/gleif-and-swift-introduce-the-first-open-source-bic-to-lei-relationship-file-to-allow-for-interoperability-across-multiple-id-platforms
14. OpenOwnership. (2018). About the project. https://openownership.org/about/
15. FATF & Egmont Group. (2018). *Concealment of beneficial ownership*. Paris: Financial Action Task Force. https://www.fatf-gafi.org/media/fatf/documents/reports/FATF-Egmont-Concealment-beneficial-ownership.pdf
16. Gray, J. & Davies, T. (2015). Fighting phantom firms in the UK: From opening up datasets to reshaping data infrastructures? *SSRN*. https://papers.ssrn.com/abstract=2610937
17. Lough Erne G8 Leaders' Communiqué, 18 June 2013. https://www.gov.uk/government/publications/2013-lough-erne-g8-leaders-communique; G20 Meeting of Finance Ministers and Central Bank Governors, Moscow, 20 July 2013. http://www.g20.utoronto.ca/2013/2013-0720-finance.html
18. The background to this commitment is described in Gray, J. & Davies, T. (2015). Fighting phantom firms in the UK: From opening up datasets to reshaping data infrastructures? *SSRN*. https://papers.ssrn.com/abstract=2610937
19. Couillault, B., Mizuguchi, J., & Reed, M. (2017). Collective action: Toward solving a vexing problem to build a global infrastructure for financial information. https://www.fsa.go.jp/common/conference/danwa/20170202.pdf
20. Halter, E.M., Harrison, R.M., Park, J.W., Sharman, J.C., & Van der Does de Willebois, E.J.M. (2011). *The puppet masters: How the corrupt use legal structures to hide stolen assets and what to do about it*. Washington, DC: World Bank. http://documents.worldbank.org/curated/en/784961468152973030/The-puppet-masters-how-the-corrupt-use-legal-structures-to-hide-stolen-assets-and-what-to-do-about-it

21 Global Witness. (2013). *Poverty, corruption and anonymous companies: How hidden company ownership fuels corruption and hinders the fight against poverty*. London: Global Witness. https://www.globalwitness.org/en/archive/anonymous-companies-global-witness-briefing/; O'Donovan, J., Wagner, H.F., & Zeume, S. (2016). The value of offshore secrets: Evidence from the Panama Papers. *SSRN*. https://papers.ssrn.com/abstract=2771095; Ohlbaum, D. (2013). *Terrorism, Inc.: How shell companies aid terrorism, crime, and corruption*. New York, NY: Open Society Foundations. https://www.opensocietyfoundations.org/sites/default/files/Terrorism%20INC%20Final%2010-24-13%20FINAL.pdf

22 FATF. (2017). *Guidance on transparency and beneficial ownership*. October 2014. Paris: Financial Action Task Force. http://www.fatf-gafi.org/publications/fatfrecommendations/documents/transparency-and-beneficial-ownership.html; OECD. (2017). *Standard for automatic exchange of financial account information in tax matters*. 2nd edition. Paris: Organisation of Economic Co-operation and Development Publishing. http://dx.doi.org/10.1787/9789264267992-en

23 SSEK Indonesian Legal Consultants – Suwana, A.S. & Erlan, B.B. (2018). Mandatory disclosure of beneficial owners in Indonesia. https://www.lexology.com/library/detail.aspx?g=57148873-1811-4daf-852f-d207dd474313

24 EUR-Lex. (2017). Proposal for a Directive of the European Parliament and of the Council amending Directive (EU) 2015/849 on the prevention of the use of the financial system for the purposes of money laundering or terrorist financing and amending Directive 2009/101/EC – Analysis of the final compromise text with a view to agreement ST 15849 2017 INIT - 2016/0208 (COD). http://eur-lex.europa.eu/legal-content/EN/TXT/?qid=1514903266840&uri=CONSIL:ST_15849_2017_INIT

25 EITI. (2015). *The EITI Standard 2016*. Oslo: Extractive Industries Transparency Initiative. https://eiti.org/sites/default/files/documents/the_eiti_standard_2016_-_english.pdf; EITI. (2017). The EITI Board Approved the Recommendations of the Implementation Committee Related to Beneficial Ownership. 36th Board meeting in Bogota, Colombia. 9 March 2017. https://eiti.org/BD/2017-31

26 Open Government Partnership. (n.d.). Beneficial ownership, illustrative commitments. https://www.opengovpartnership.org/theme/beneficial-owners

27 Baker McKenzie. (2017). Survey of beneficial ownership disclosure in Hong Kong, Singapore, Switzerland and the UK. 5 December. https://www.bakermckenzie.com/en/insight/publications/2017/12/survey-of-beneficial-ownership

28 ESMA (European Securities and Markets Authority). (2017). Legal Entity Identifier. Briefing Note 9, October 2017. https://www.esma.europa.eu/document/legal-entity-identifier-briefing-note

29 EUR-Lex. (2017). Proposal for a Directive of the European Parliament and of the Council amending Directive (EU) 2015/849 on the prevention of the use of the financial system for the purposes of money laundering or terrorist financing and amending Directive 2009/101/EC – Analysis of the final compromise text with a view to agreement ST 15849 2017 INIT – 2016/0208 (COD). http://eur-lex.europa.eu/legal-content/EN/TXT/?qid=1514903266840&uri=CONSIL:ST_15849_2017_INIT

30 Global Witness. (2015). Jade: A Global Witness investigation into Myanmar's "big state secret". https://www.globalwitness.org/jade-story/; Global Witness. (2017). Narco-a-Lago: Money laundering at the Trump Ocean Club, Panama. November 2017. https://www.globalwitness.org/en/campaigns/corruption-and-money-laundering/narco-a-lago-panama/

31 Transparency International. (2016). London property: A top destination for money launderers. http://www.transparency.org.uk/publications/london-property-tr-ti-uk/; ICIJ (International Consortium of Investigative Journalists). (2018). Offshore leaks database. https://offshoreleaks.icij.org/

32 Leask, D. (2018). Scots shell firms play key role in Latin America's bribery "mega scandal". *The Herald Scotland*, 3 February. http://www.heraldscotland.com/news/15917473.Scots_shell_firms_play_key_role_in_global_web_of_bribery/

33 Settle, M. (2018). Theresa May set to ban secretive Scottish shell companies to halt flow of dirty Russian money. *The Herald Scotland*, 22 March. http://www.heraldscotland.com/news/16103825.Banned__Scotland_s_secret_tax_havens_for_Putin_cronies/

34 Yusof, K. (2017). Telus (Transparency). 5 November. https://docs.google.com/presentation/d/1nVO30WSfdHXcvyDMUU80pmazoXCpcqH6nVFaJZARk6w; Sinar/Telus. (2017). Telus: Joined up data transparency project for PEPs, OCDS & beneficial ownership. *GitHub* [Post]. https://github.com/Sinar/telus

35 OpenCorporates. (2015). How open company data was used to uncover the powerful elite benefiting from Myanmar's multi-billion dollar jade industry. White Paper. *Medium* [Blog post], 27 October. https://medium.com/opencorporates/how-open-company-data-was-used-to-uncover-the-powerful-elite-benefiting-from-myanmar-s-multi-1ef35f88d6bd

36 Global Witness & Open Ownership. (2017). Learning the lessons from the UK's public beneficial ownership register. 23 October. https://www.globalwitness.org/en/campaigns/corruption-and-money-laundering/learning-lessons-uks-public-beneficial-ownership-register/

37 StAR (Stolen Asset Recovery Initiative). (2011). *Barriers to asset recovery*. Washington, DC: World Bank. https://star.worldbank.org/sites/star/files/Barriers%20to%20Asset%20Recovery.pdf

38 Comments by Pascal Saint-Amans, Director of the OECD's Centre for Tax Policy in 2016, in Rumney, E. (2016). Time not right for public registers of beneficial ownership, says OECD tax chief. *Public Finance International*, 15 June. http://www.publicfinanceinternational.org/news/2016/06/time-not-right-public-registers-beneficial-ownership-says-oecd-tax-chief; Forstater, M. (2017). *Beneficial openness? Weighing the costs and benefits of financial transparency*. CMI Working Paper 3. Bergen, Norway: Christian Michelson Institute. https://www.cmi.no/publications/6201-beneficial-openness

39 Less than 0.01% of LEI records failed an accuracy check in the GLEIF data quality report, see GLEIF (Global Legal Entity Identifier Foundation). (2018). Global LEI data quality report. https://www.gleif.org/en/lei-data/gleif-data-quality-management/about-the-data-quality-reports/download-data-quality-reports/download-global-lei-data-quality-report-february-2018

40 Sztykowski, Z. & Taggart, C. (2017). What we really mean when we talk about verification: Authentication and authorization (Part 2 of 4). *Open Ownership* [News post], 26 September. https://openownership.org/news/what-we-really-mean-when-we-talk-about-verification-authentication-and-authorization-part-2-of-4/

41 Judgment of the Court (Second Chamber) of 9 March 2017, *Camera di Commercio, Industria, Artigianato e Agricoltura di Lecce vs Salvatore Manni*, No. ECLI:EU:C:2017:197; Fowler, N. (2016). Beneficial ownership and disclosure of trusts: Challenging the privacy arguments. *Tax Justice Network* [Blog post], 7 December. http://www.taxjustice.net/2016/12/07 beneficial-ownership-disclosure-trusts-challenging-privacy-arguments/

42 Westenberg, E. & Sayne, A. (2018). *Beneficial ownership screening: Practical measures to reduce corruption risks in extractives licensing*. Briefing 15 May. New York, NY: Natural Resource Governance Institute. https://resourcegovernance.org/sites/default/files/documents/beneficial-ownership-screening_0.pdf; Prichard, W. (2018). *Linking beneficial ownership transparency to improved tax revenue collection in developing countries*. ICTD Summary Brief 15. Brighton, UK: International Centre for Tax and Development. http://opendocs.ids.ac.uk/opendocs/handle/123456789/13753

43 When Scottish Limited Partnerships were brought into the UK's beneficial ownership disclosure regime, the number of registrations fell from 5 215 in 2016 to 2 823 in 2017, see Bellingcat Investigation Team. (2018). Scottish Limited Partnerships: Scottish in name only. *Bellingcat*, 2 March. https://www.bellingcat.com/news/uk-and-europe/2018/03/02/scottish-limited-partnerships-scottish-name/

44 EITI Secretariat. (2017). EITI Chair statement on United States withdrawal from the EITI. *Extractive Industries Transparency Initiative* [News post], 2 November. https://eiti.org/news/eiti-chair-statement-on-united-states-withdrawal-from-eiti

004

Crime and justice

Sandra Elena

Key points

- Some of the earliest open data experiments revolved around crime data and were driven by public and journalistic interest in local crime data; however, the open data community related to crime and justice data remains one of the least developed.

- Open data work in the crime and justice domain faces particular challenges related to privacy, legacy systems, and interoperability, and often involves working with some of the most conservative institutions.

- Donors and international organisations have increasingly recognised the potential links between open data and the crime and justice sector, but there are many cultural and coordination barriers to be overcome.

- A strong and sustainable judicial open data ecosystem has the potential to create more transparent and accountable judicial institutions and to improve the quality and effectiveness of judicial public policy, leading to greater access to justice and safer environments for all.

Introduction

In May 2005, a month before the official Google Maps application programming interface (API) was launched, ChicagoCrime.org was launched, a pioneering experiment that took crime data from the Chicago Police Department and presented it on an interactive map. Not only did this inspire a plethora of diverse mapping mash-ups,[1] but it also sparked many other data-driven crime maps and acted as a key reference point for early open data arguments.[2] Yet despite this strong beginning, crime and justice probably remains one of the least developed sectors for open data. Outside of the publication of administrative data by police forces, usually at the local level to enable crime incident mapping, the release of open data from judiciaries or other entities within the justice system remains rare, and governments are generally more reluctant to open up crime and justice data to the public. According to the last edition of the Open Data Barometer, only 17% of surveyed governments had, by 2017, made any crime data available to the public as open data.[3]

There is, however, a growing awareness of "open justice" as a public good and the need to apply open data principles to enhance transparency, accountability, and citizen participation related to the activities of the government agencies dealing with crime and justice matters. Evidence of this movement toward "open justice" can be seen in the growing number of worldwide judicial commitments included by member countries of the Open Government Partnership (OGP) in their National Action Plans. In 2011, only two out of a total of 170 commitments delivered by member states related to the judiciary, while the last three years have seen an increase to 63 (16 in 2015, 25 in 2016, and 22 in 2017). Of the total of 100 justice-related commitments delivered within the OGP system since 2011, 24 are based on the use of open data (see box, Examples of OGP justice-related commitments based on the use of open data).

The importance of open crime and justice data derives from the need to reinforce transparency and accountability. Crime and justice institutions have historically been seen as rather aloof institutions, detached from social influence; however, these institutions take actions and make decisions that should really not be considered any differently from other public institutions with regard to the need to be transparent and subject to constant public scrutiny.[4]

Government is often divided into three branches: legislative, executive, and judicial. Open government data programmes have predominantly focused on the executive, which has responsibility for the delivery of government services and the implementation of legislation, leading to the release of crime data and crime mapping from police institutions or ministries. However, there has been much less focus on the availability of open data from the judicial branch of government.

This must be addressed as a core issue of democracy as the justice system should be a citizen-centred public service, where decisions are actually made by civil servants who are entrusted with the task of observing the law but are in no way above it.[5] Greater levels of open data from the judiciary can help the system become not only more transparent and accountable, but also more efficient. Open data should inform judicial public policy. While, at present, policies are often designed from the top down and can result in poor quality services, the use of open data to build sound judicial policies through data analysis and citizen engagement will provide more efficient judicial services. Jimenez-Gomez recently described the worldwide state of the art of "open justice" initiatives more broadly and identifies the use of open data as a core element that should be taken into account to enhance the accountability of the courts.[6]

There are many elements that go into open justice, often involving the innovative use of technology in the crime and justice space. This chapter is intended to be an examination of the evolution of open data specifically pertaining to crime and justice, and is not intended to include the additional analysis of policies related to civic participation or technology other than those related to open data.

> **Examples of OGP justice-related commitments based on the use of open data**
>
> **France (2015), National Action Plan 1, Commitment 12: Open Legal Resources[7]**
>
> This commitment received a starred rating after evaluation by the OGP's Independent Reporting Mechanism due to its potentially transformative impact. It includes further developing the provision of legal and legislative resources as reusable open data and deepening citizen participation in developing innovative services and open source tools to facilitate the understanding and preparation of legislative texts, as well as in the drafting (*avant-projet de loi*) of the Digital Bill.
>
> **Spain (2017), National Action Plan 3, Commitment 4.1: Open Justice in Spain[8]**
>
> This current commitment focuses on advancing open data as an instrument for achieving openness in Spain's judicial branch. It seeks to promote the citizen's right to access judicial information, including the initial steps required to transform the existing model of judicial statistics into a new system based on open data with improved characteristics regarding the quality of data, its collection, and management.

Lessons learned: Open crime and justice data

The most common sources of open data in this domain are the government agencies responsible for delivering services and implementing policies related to crime and justice. Hence, it makes sense that a vast majority of open data initiatives are national projects driven by institutions of the executive branch and the judiciary, with a few of them carried out by international organisations such as the European Union (EU) or the United Nations Office for Drugs and Crime (UNODC). While there is a not negligible amount of crime and justice data collected by private sector institutions, such as law firms, the potential contribution of these sources is yet to be realised.

Bargh, Choenni, and Meijer have accurately identified "three typical challenges" for the implementation of open data in the judicial field, highlighting privacy, legacy, and interoperability as significant challenges that should be taken into account in further development.[9]

Privacy relates to the required balance between the transparency of data and privacy for the real-life persons whose sensitive attributes, such as names, birth dates, crime types, or judgments, must be protected by removal or anonymisation.

Legacy refers to the very nature of legal data and the semantic evolution over time caused by continuous changes to rules and regulations. New crimes under the law need to be codified and old crimes can have their names changed or be redefined. Managing legacy data also becomes a challenge when government reform initiatives involve switching to new IT landscapes, requiring the migration of large amounts of accumulated data (data historically stored on paper) and then transferred to newer electronic systems. In order to make this data open and reusable, the importance of effective independent management of legacy systems cannot be underestimated.

Finally, the challenge of **interoperability** alludes to the necessity of ensuring that different sets of data, gathered by a large number of different agencies, be collected, stored, and then released using standardised criteria and processes, allowing the data to be integrated and combined with data from external sources. The justice system also needs to advance the use of unique identifiers that would make it easier to connect data across institutions and avoid redundancies in data collection between multiple partners across the judiciary who may be recording the same information.

The structure of the judiciary within federal governments deserves a special mention as the existence of national and sub-national levels (involving different judicial systems within one country) requires complicated inter-institutional coordination, making synchronisation and interoperability especially difficult to accomplish. Collaboration between different branches of government also presents challenges to reforms driven by the openness agenda as the transversal interaction required is perceived, in some cases, as a threat to the separation of powers (i.e. judicial independence).

Political and cultural barriers are still common hurdles for the implementation of the open data agenda in the public sector. Those barriers tend to be even higher in the case of institutions dealing with crime and justice (law enforcement agencies, the judiciary), which are traditionally some of the most conservative and independent institutions. As Roberto Gargarella notes, this is based on a conception of impartiality that holds dear the idea of isolated reflection by an individual (or a small elite of individuals) as a requisite for making correct or unbiased decisions.[10]

Another challenge is created when police and justice institutions lag behind in terms of technological capacity (i.e. hardware, software, skills, and expertise). Universities and scientific agencies could, and should, play a key role in building capacity for the use of data and emerging technologies in the police and justice sector.

Additionally, the involvement of civil society is still very limited in this field. Few civil society networks have projects looking specifically at open data in the crime and justice domain, with even fewer being large enough to be known internationally. However, there are some emerging examples of civil society organisations (CSOs) working independently or in collaboration with government agencies, including Measures for Justice in the United States (US), OpenGiustizia in Italy, La Nación Data in Argentina, and the Justice Data Lab[11] in the United Kingdom (UK).

Measures for Justice[12] is a civil society initiative launched in 2011 that has developed a data-driven set of performance measures aimed at assessing and comparing different aspects of the criminal justice system in state jurisdictions of the US. The analysis, using data extracted from administrative case management systems, covers three main categories: fiscal responsibility, fair process, and public safety.

OpenGiustizia[13] was a project focused on organisational innovation and optimisation for the Court and the Public Prosecutor of Napoli, developed by three Italian universities and financed by the EU's Social Fund between 2007 and 2013. Among the project's objectives was the creation of interoperability within the system's databases and the provision of tools for accountability and performance evaluation.

La Nación Data[14] is a data journalism initiative which has been underway since 2012 by one of the main newspapers of Argentina. It consists of a news portal and blog based on data collected from various sources. It makes an intensive use of open crime and justice data, delivering content on themes such as femicide, high-profile judicial cases, and the penitentiary system.

Justice Data Lab[15] is a service run by the Ministry of Justice of the UK and New Philanthropy Capital. Set up in 2013, it is aimed at organisations providing offender rehabilitation services. It uses administrative data on re-offenders to conduct on-demand impact evaluations, so that these organisations can assess the actual impact of their work through data-based evidence.

For most of these initiatives, data availability and interoperability remain a challenge. Measures for Justice, for example, covers just six US states at present. The next section will explore the different kinds of data that could or should be available on crime and justice, and the various actors involved in creating and using it.

Making crime and justice open data available

The primary focus of opening data within the crime and justice sector is on three main categories of information:

1. Case data: information on judgments and court rulings issued by crime and justice institutions (e.g. courts, tribunals, etc.).

2. Jurisdictional data: performance and activity data from crime and justice agencies, such as statistical data related to cases, reported crimes, arrests, citizen complaints, etc.

3. Structural data: information on the internal characteristics of crime and justice agencies, such as their organisation, their internal processes, how they allocate their budget, infrastructure, rules of procedure, staff and salaries, procurement, etc.

Data produced or collected by institutions within the crime and justice system is generally made available in three main ways:

1. As primary data (i.e. unprocessed, as it was collected at the source) in downloadable datasets or files (CSV, XML, DOC, XLS, PDF).

2. As aggregated statistical data (i.e. as processed, and anonymised if necessary, data) in the form of downloadable files or datasets.

3. In aggregate form, but as graphical presentations either in static visualisations of statistical data or through the use of user-facing data visualisation and analysis tools.

As the box below illustrates, while jurisdictional and structural data may originate with either the judicial or executive branches of government, case data tends to be solely within the province of the judiciary.

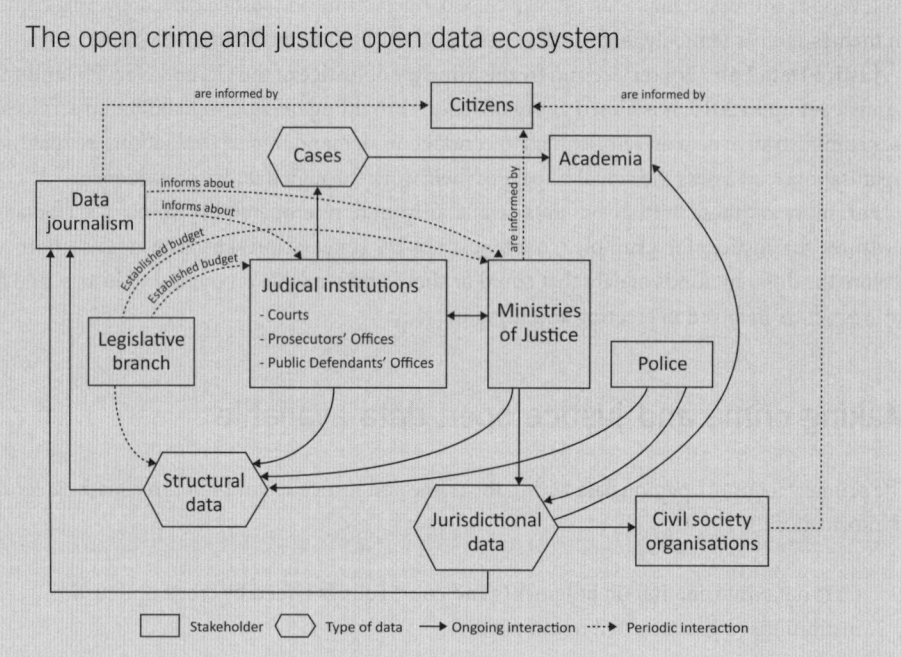

Using a data ecosystem mapping methodology,[16] this diagram represents the crime and justice open data ecosystem as described in this chapter. Unbroken lines represent constant interaction between the actors involved, while dotted arrows represent a direct but non-continuous bond. Information producers (e.g. the judiciary, ministries of justice, the police) are often also active consumers and users of the information produced. Stakeholders, such as academia, CSOs, and data journalists, act as intermediaries, using raw data and transforming it into user-friendly information products for a broader range of users (citizens).[17]

The way in which open crime and justice data are combined and delivered to users can vary substantially. Table 1 gives 18 examples of data projects, although, for the sake of this chapter, detailed analysis is restricted to four illustrative cases: Openjustice (US), Data.police.uk (UK), Datos.jus.gob.ar (Argentina), and ECourts (India).

Openjustice[18] is an open data project developed by the Office of the Attorney General of the Department of Justice of California (US) to establish a criminal justice data portal which was first launched in 2015. It currently delivers jurisdictional data from all enforcement agencies across the State of California, covering crime, deaths in custody, hate crimes, homicides, juvenile court and probation, citizen complaints, and the use of force. Structural data on the portal includes lists of law enforcement and criminal justice personnel, as well as county-level contextual data (educational attainment, income, poverty, and unemployment levels) for each county. The data is made available as downloadable datasets and through visualisation tools.

Data.police.uk[19] is an open data portal maintained by the Home Office of the United Kingdom that provides data about crime and policing in England, Wales, and Northern Ireland.

Open Data Sectors and Communities I Crime and Justice   71

Table 1: Open crime and justice data projects around the world

INITIATIVES	TYPE OF DATA			FORMATS		
	Cases	Jurisdictional data	Structural data	Primary data (dataset)	Aggregate data (dataset)	Aggregate data (graphic)
OpenJustice (US)		X	X	X	X	X
data.police.uk (UK)		X	X	X	X	X
datos.jus.gob.ar (Argentina)		X	X	X	X	X
ECourts (India)	X	X	X			X
Measures for Justice[20] (US)		X	X		X	X
Mapa del Delito CABA[21] (Argentina)		X		X	X	X
Datos Abiertos del Poder Judicial de Costa Rica[22]		X	X		X	X
Data Portal Singapore's Public Data[23]		X	X		X	X
Productivity Commission[24] (Australia)		X	X		X	X
Dados Abertos MPRS[25] (Brazil)		X	X		X	X
Judicial Department[26] (Russia)	X	X	X		X	
Statistics Canada Crime and Justice[27]		X	X		X	X
The Judiciary[28] (Liberia)	X	X			X	
data.unodc.org[29] (UNODC)		X	X		X	
ISS Crime Hub[30] (South Africa)		X	X			X
Otvorené Súdy[31] (Slovakia)	X	X	X			
Eur-lex[32] (EU)	X		X			
De Rechstpraak[33] (Netherlands)	X		X			

It was launched in 2013[34] and delivers jurisdictional data on reported crimes and all kinds of police activity, including drug seizures, the issuance of firearms certificates, breath tests, or the setting up of cordons under the Terrorism Act. It also contains structural data on the police workforce, procurement, salaries, etc. Both primary and aggregated statistical data is available, and the update frequency is either quarterly or annually depending on the subject matter.

Datos.jus.gob.ar[35] is the open data portal of the Ministry of Justice and Human Rights of Argentina, containing overall data on the country's justice sector. The portal was launched in 2016 and offers data on a range of jurisdictional activities, such as the delivery of pre-judicial mediation and the provision of access to justice, as well as information on criminal policy, the prison system, and structural data on institutions of the judicial branch and the Ministry of Justice. Primary and aggregate data are available as downloadable datasets as well as via visualisation tools. The update frequency of datasets depends on the subject matter, ranging from daily or monthly to annually.

ECourts[36] is a service provided by the Ministry of Law and Justice and the Supreme Court of India. Online since 2013, it contains real-time judicial data for all jurisdictions subject to the Indian judiciary. It aims to serve as a dynamic source of information on the judicial system. It is based upon a "National Judicial Data Grid", which works as a nationwide data warehouse for case data and aggregated data delivered through visualisations.

Additional examples of open crime and justice data initiatives are highlighted in Table 1, classified according to the categories mentioned previously.[37]

The potential impact on social and economic development

Open crime and justice data is expected to play a key role in measuring and delivering progress in terms of social and economic development. Although the UNODC has been working on crime and justice statistics for many years, the United Nations 2030 Agenda for Sustainable Development places a fundamental importance on open data at all levels to promote accountability and inclusive decisions, to support reductions in crime and violence, and to improve access to justice for all over the next 11 years. Although data will play a vital role in showcasing national progress toward over 169 global targets encompassed within the Sustainable Development Goals (SDGs), it will also allow decision-makers in all three branches of government to be able to rely on quality information for the design of public policies, based on evidence, to achieve those global targets. Key SDGs for crime and justice data include SDG 16, aimed at the reduction of violence, the reduction of organised crime, the development of effective, accountable, and transparent institutions, and ensuring access to justice and public information, and SDG 5, which focuses on gender equality and the total elimination of violence against women and girls.

With regard to SDG 5, two specific examples of effective initiatives should be noted: the provision of primary open data on sexual offences by the Colombian government through their Open Data Portal[38] and the specific section on gender issues of the Open Judicial Data Portal of the Ministry of Justice of Argentina, datos.jus.gob.ar,[39] where primary data is made available on femicides, human trafficking, and assistance granted to victims of violence.

The potential of open crime and justice data with regard to the SDGs will probably have a crucial impact in the future allocation of resources and funding for associated projects and initiatives. International organisations, such as The Hague Institute for Innovation of Law or the Latin American Open Data Initiative (ILDA), are already orienting their funding priorities in this direction as are other significant actors like the Open Data Institute, Transparency International, and the Open Society Foundations. Crime and justice open data is also increasingly on the agenda for key international organisations that are pushing for open government-oriented reforms in the public sector, including the International Development Research Centre, the OGP, and mySociety, among others.

Conclusions

An enabling environment is currently emerging for the spread of open data by and between crime and justice institutions. International organisations and governments have begun to consider crime and justice data as a raw material to use in implementing and evaluating public policies. At the same time, data journalists, academia, and CSOs are learning how to use open data to promote more transparent and accountable judicial institutions.

There are still, however, many barriers to the implementation of quality open data initiatives and specifically to the extended use of judicial open data. The main barriers are traditional cultural and political forces against openness within the judicial system, the lack of adequate financial and human resources invested in capacity building, and current inadequate or restrictive legal frameworks, including those that create a barrier to publishing data from judicial cases. Another hurdle to overcome is the difficult but necessary coordination of the various public institutions producing judicial data, as well as the lack of consistent standards around the production and publishing of judicial information and the relatively weak expertise of civil society and other actors in analysing the data.

Ultimately, two main actions are required in order to strengthen the judicial open data ecosystem. First, at the institutional level, governments should include the judicial sector within their access to information laws and open data policies and regulations. At the same time, justice institutions should commit to country-wide and transversal open data strategies. These strategies must take into account open judicial data intermediaries, such as academia and CSOs. It is recommended that one judicial institution in the country (e.g. the Ministry of Justice, the Supreme Court, or the Judicial Council) takes on the leadership role and coordinates the development and implementation of open data policies and plans. Additionally, judiciaries should set goals, targets, and indicators for justice delivery, and the resulting performance data should be available and evaluated through open data.

Second, concerning the use of open judicial data, each judicial system must establish a balance between publication and privacy protection. Privacy should not be used as an excuse for avoiding openness. Governments and international organisations should promote the use of open judicial data through different tools (curricula, hackathons, journalism, etc.) and public participation mechanisms should be put in place to assess and set priorities for the data release process. We also recommend setting up open judicial data portals to contain the totality of available data for each judicial system. Open judicial data should not only be provided in the format of open datasets, but also through visualisations and data stories in order to reach a wide variety of users. Advancing the interoperability of the data held in the systems of numerous institutions producing open judicial data is a must. Governments, working with leading international organisations, should promote the definition and adoption of specific standards for open judicial data. International organisations should also promote the creation of open judicial data networks and working groups, as well as the participation of open judicial data experts and leaders in relevant conferences and debates wherever they are taking place. With success in these endeavours, the next decade should see the ongoing development of a strong and sustainable judicial open data ecosystem that can enable more transparent and accountable judicial institutions while delivering more effective access to justice and safer environments for all.

Further reading

Elena, S. (2015). Open data for open justice: A case study of the judiciaries of Argentina, Brazil, Chile, Costa Rica, Mexico, Peru and Uruguay. Presented at *Open Data Research Symposium*, 27 May 2015, Ottawa, Canada. http://www.opendataresearch.org/dl/symposium2015/odrs2015-paper10.pdf

Elena, S. (2018) *Justicia Abierta: Aportes para una agenda en construcción* [Open Justice: Contributions for an agenda under construction]. Ediciones SAIJ. http://www.bibliotecadigital.gob.ar/items/show/1818

Huang, Y. (2017). Open data portal for Champaign racial and criminal justice: Towards greater transparency in policy making. Master's Thesis, Urban Planning, University of Illinois. http://hdl.handle.net/2142/98538

Jiménez-Gómez, C.E. (2017). Hacia el Estado abierto: Justicia Abierta en America Latina y el Caribe [Towards the Open State: Open Justice in Latin America and the Caribbean]. In A. Naser, Á. Ramírez-Alujas, & D. Rosales (Eds.), *Desde el gobierno abierto al Estado abierto en América Latina y el Caribe* [From open government to the open state in Latin America and the Caribbean]. CEPAL. https://repositorio.cepal.org/handle/11362/41353

Jiménez-Gómez, C.E. & Gascó-Hernández, M. (2016). Achieving open justice through citizen participation and transparency. *IGI Global.* https://www.igi-global.com/book/achieving-open-justice-through-citizen/148515

Marković, M. & Gostojić, S. (2018). Open judicial data: A comparative analysis. *Social Science Computer Review.* https://journals.sagepub.com/doi/10.1177/0894439318770744

About the author

Sandra Elena is an open data and open government expert based in Buenos Aires. She currently coordinates the Open Justice Program, Ministry of Justice and Human Rights, which is implementing the first open data initiative in Argentina's judiciary. You can follow Sandra at https://www.twitter.com/sandra_elena1 and learn more about her work at https://datos.jus.gob.ar.

How to cite this chapter

Elena, S. (2019). Open data, crime and justice. In T. Davies, S. Walker, M. Rubinstein, & F. Perini (Eds.), *The state of open data: Histories and horizons* (pp. 65–76). Cape Town and Ottawa: African Minds and International Development Research Centre. http://stateofopendata.od4d.net

This work is licensed under a Creative Commons Attribution 4.0 International (CC BY 4.0) licence. It was carried out with the aid of a grant from the International Development Research Centre, Ottawa, Canada.

Endnotes

1. Holovaty, A. (2018). In memory of Chicagocrime.Org. *Holovaty.Com*, 31 January. http://www.holovaty.com/writing/chicagocrime.org-tribute/
2. Huijboom, N. & Van den Broek, T. (2011). Open data: An international comparison of strategies. *European Journal of EPractice, 12(1)*, 4–16. http://unpan1.un.org/intradoc/groups/public/documents/UN-DPADM/UNPAN046727.pdf
3. Web Foundation. (2018). Open Data Barometer. 3rd edition. https://opendatabarometer.org/3rdedition/data/
4. Montero, G. (2017). Del gobierno abierto al Estado abierto: la mirada del Centro Latinoamericano de Administración para el Desarrollo [From open government to the open state: The view of the Latin American Center for Administration for Development]. In A. Naser, A. Ramirez, & D. Roslaes (Eds.), Desde el gobierno abierto al Estado abierto en América Latina y el Caribe [From open government to open state in Latin America and the Caribbean] (pp. 53–81). Santiago: Comisión Económica para América Latina y el Caribe [Economic Commission for Latin America and the Caribbean] (our translation). https://repositorio.cepal.org/handle/11362/41353
5. Mora, L.P.M. (2006). Jueces y Reforma Judicial en Costa Rica [Judges and judicial reform in Costa Rica]. *Revista de Ciencias Jurídicas, 109*, 15–32. https://revistas.ucr.ac.cr/index.php/juridicas/article/view/9717 (our translation)
6. Jiménez-Gómez, C.E. (2016). Open judiciary worldwide: Best practices and lessons learnt. In C.E. Jiménez-Gómez & M. Gascó-Hernández (Eds.), *Achieving open justice through citizen participation and transparency* (pp. 1–15). Hershey, PA: IGI Global. https://www.researchgate.net/publication/307598204_Open_Judiciary_Worldwide_Best_Practices_and_Lessons_Learnt
7. https://www.opengovpartnership.org/starred-commitments/open-legal-resources
8. https://www.opengovpartnership.org/documents/spain-action-plan-2017-2019
9. Bargh, M.S., Choenni, S., & Meijer, R.F. (2016). Integrating semi-open data in a criminal judicial setting. In C.E. Jiménez-Gómez & M. Gascó-Hernández (Eds.), *Achieving open justice through citizen participation and transparency* (pp. 137–156). Hershey, PA: IGI Global. https://www.igi-global.com/chapter/integrating-semi-open-data-in-a-criminal-judicial-setting/162839

10. Gargarella, R. (1996). *La justicia frente el gobierno* [Justice against the government](our translation). Barcelona: Ariel.
11. https://www.gov.uk/government/publications/justice-data-lab
12. https://measuresforjustice.org/
13. http://www.opengiustizia.it/
14. https://www.lanacion.com.ar/data
15. https://www.gov.uk/government/publications/justice-data-lab
16. http://www.opendataresearch.org/emergingimpacts/methods.html
17. Elena, S., Aquilino, N., & Riviére, A. (2014). Emerging impacts in open data in the judiciary branches in Argentina, Chile and Uruguay. Center for the Implementation of Public Policies Promoting Equity and Growth. http://www.opendataresearch.org/content/2014/658/emerging-impacts-open-data-judiciary-branches-argentina-chile-and-uruguay.html
18. https://openjustice.doj.ca.gov/
19. https://data.police.uk/
20. https://measuresforjustice.org/
21. https://mapa.seguridadciudad.gob.ar/
22. https://datosabiertospj.eastus.cloudapp.azure.com/
23. https://data.gov.sg/dataset?organization=ministry-of-home-affairs-singapore-prison-service
24. https://www.pc.gov.au/research/ongoing/report-on-government-services/2018/justice
25. http://dados.mprs.mp.br/dados_abertos/
26. http://www.cdep.ru/
27. https://www150.statcan.gc.ca/n1/en/subjects/crime_and_justice
28. http://judiciary.gov.lr/
29. https://data.unodc.org/
30. https://issafrica.org/crimehub
31. https://otvorenesudy.sk/
32. https://eur-lex.europa.eu/
33. https://www.rechtspraak.nl/
34. Smith, A.M. & Heath, T. (2014). Police.uk and Data.police.uk: Developing open crime and justice data for the UK. *JeDEM – EJournal of EDemocracy and Open Government, 6(1)*, 87–96. https://jedem.org/index.php/jedem/article/view/326/273
35. http://datos.jus.gob.ar/
36. http://ecourts.gov.in/ecourts_home/
37. Information available at Open Data Portals as of 13 March 2018.
38. https://www.datos.gov.co/Seguridad-y-Defensa/Delitos-Sexuales-2016/3j7m-zgyi/data
39. http://datos.jus.gob.ar/pages/datos-de-justicia-con-perspectiva-de-genero

005

Development assistance and humanitarian action

Catherine Weaver, Josh Powell, and Heather Leson

Key points

- From the mid-2000s, organisations and individuals working in the field of development assistance and humanitarian action have identified significant gaps in the data sharing needed to support effective coordination of funding and operational work. Early adopters of open data, from 2008 onwards, have worked to fill these gaps and have continued to pioneer open data projects.

- Availability and accessibility of open data have increased substantially, often outstripping the capacity of organisations to reliably use this data, and more work is needed to ensure that data sharing reflects the principles of data protection.

- Greater investment is needed in joining up data and establishing common languages and standards for aid-related data. Open data approaches have a key role in breaking down silos between aid, budget, and demographic data.

- Research must now move beyond qualitative case studies to rigorous testing of theories of change through quantitative longitudinal studies.

Introduction

Bureaucracies like to "hug" data[1] for many diverse reasons, and international development aid and humanitarian agencies are no exception. For decades, the complex aid regime has been plagued by information silos and technical, political, and cultural barriers to data sharing. This legacy presents a distinct challenge to effective global assistance in an era of unprecedented humanitarian crises and persistent poverty, especially in conflict-ridden states. Doing no harm and ensuring protection are key principles in development assistance and humanitarian action; therefore, ensuring data protection must also be a principle. Sharing data requires a delicate balance of effective coordination and protection of the most vulnerable. Organisations involved in aid and humanitarian action have limited funding allocated to upskilling staff and developing infrastructure. Gaps in technology and digital literacy are often barriers to building open data processes within the complex aid delivery structures.

According to the international transparency movement's theory of change, open data is the key to unlocking the potential of international aid. Opening data related to development assistance and humanitarian action will improve donor coordination, improve the efficiency of humanitarian action, facilitate a faster response regarding relief assistance and development spending, better inform resource planning and management, and empower stakeholders and communities to push for greater participation.[2,3,4,5,6,7,8,9] Open data, simply put, will make development aid and humanitarian action more accountable and effective. But how far have we come in realising this potential?

This chapter will provide a brief overview of the state of open data in the development and humanitarian space, focusing on data collected and published by development agencies, private philanthropic organisations, and humanitarian relief organisations. It will also supply a critical assessment of the progress and pitfalls in the global transparency movement. We find that there have been significant achievements in building consensus, standards, and technical platforms around open aid data. Yet, the supply of open data has not always matched the demand, nor has the open data revolution incited the expanded use of data in the area of international aid that may have been expected.

The key challenges lingering today involve the need to improve the quality and consistency of available data. This is difficult insofar as the data models, infrastructure, training, and business risk analysis/workflow for open data in aid and humanitarian action are often insufficiently funded. At the same time, we need to build broader awareness and expand the use of open data with the objective of building data literacy and improving (and proving) the impact of open data on decisions and outcomes. Likewise, we need to make open data accessible and useful to all stakeholders, while also addressing difficult issues, such as data privacy, protection, and responsible use. Finally, to sustain the momentum behind this data revolution, we need to garner greater evidence of impact to demonstrate the benefits of open data in the field of development and humanitarian assistance.

Background

In the context of development assistance, the open data agenda has grown out of larger debates on aid accountability and effectiveness. Since the Second and Third High Level Forums on Aid Effectiveness in Paris in 2005 and Accra in 2008, several definitions and standards on aid transparency and open data have emerged, as well as numerous efforts to construct monitoring and verification systems around compliance with international agreements and transparency guarantees. At the Fourth High Level Forum on Aid Effectiveness in Busan, South Korea, in November 2011, most major donor countries and agencies, including many from the Global South, committed to reporting their aid information according to a common standard that combined three complementary systems: the Organisation for Economic Co-operation and

Development (OECD) Development Assistance Committee (DAC) Creditor Reporting System (CRS++),[10] the OECD DAC Forward Spending Survey (FSS),[11] and the International Aid Transparency Initiative (IATI).[12]

The open data movement in international development has seen the development of a rich set of supranational initiatives,[13] national-level policies, and international non-governmental organisations (NGOs), and networks devoted specifically to the advocacy and production of transparent and open aid data. Today, the principals and goals of open data are embedded in the United Nations (UN) 2030 Sustainable Development Goals (SDGs). In 2014, the UN's Independent Expert Advisory Group (IEAG) published *A world that counts: Mobilising the data revolution for sustainable development*.[14] The report called for investments in new technologies and capacity building to improve the quantity and quality of data to address the inequalities in data access between countries and for donors to promote the use of data in decision-making, participation, and accountability.[15] Similar commitments were made in the 2015 African Data Consensus,[16] the 2016 G8 Open Data Charter,[17] the Grand Bargain for the Global Humanitarian Agenda,[18] and, more recently, the March 2018 UN Statistical Commission's 49th Session on "Better Data, Better Lives".[19] The open data movement as it pertains to international development and humanitarian aid has shared a similar trajectory in terms of the evolution of influential policies and activities.

The growth and support of open data as applied to humanitarian action is often tied to large-scale humanitarian crisis events. This work often starts with determining workflows and best practices for sharing data that will not do harm, and the first data that needs to be shared is most often geospatial data. The Global Facility for Disaster Reduction and Recovery (GFDRR), created in 2006,[20] has been instrumental in advocating and piloting open data for both resilience and disaster recovery, primarily through its OpenDRI initiative established in 2011.[21] The GFDRR has connected key humanitarian actors with technical communities. Open data, including OpenStreetMap (OSM),[22] has become more central for humanitarian action after its use during the response to the 2010 Haiti earthquake. By engaging volunteers, the global OSM community can quickly contribute essential geospatial data, such as location data on buildings and roads. Having the most up-to-date data can provide those involved in delivering humanitarian aid with the information needed to make strategic decisions. The UN Foundation sponsored *Disaster relief 2.0* report outlined the potential impact of this kind of information sharing. The GFDRR, the World Bank, the United Nations Office for the Coordination of Humanitarian Affairs (UN OCHA), and government agencies collaborated with the open data community during this response.[23]

Many other emergency response activities have included organised efforts of global open data advocates within the humanitarian network or within digital humanitarian networks like the Digital Humanitarian Network or CrisisMappers.[24] The Humanitarian OpenStreetMap Team (HOT),[25] founded in 2010, has worked to coordinate technology communities, mappers, and humanitarians to deliver geospatial data for both international aid and humanitarian action. Missing Maps, founded in 2014 by the American Red Cross, British Red Cross, Medicine Sans Frontiers/Doctors Without Borders UK (United Kingdom), and HOT, promotes the use of open map data for humanitarian action from disaster responses to health programming.[26] The UN OCHA's establishment of the Humanitarian Data Exchange in 2014 builds on years of effort by multiple humanitarian groups to open data.²⁷ UN Global Pulse, the United Nations International Children's Emergency Fund (UNICEF), the World Food Programme, the United Nations High Commissioner for Refugees (UNHCR), and other UN agencies all work with open data. In the humanitarian space, the CrisisMappers Conference and the State of the Map events²⁸ have convened businesses, technologists, researchers, open data enthusiasts, funders, and governments. Burgeoning support for open data has also been reinforced by the proliferation of work by civil society organisations (CSOs), NGOs, technologists, businesses, and researchers, much of which has been initiated as a result of global and regional events, including the annual International Open Data Conference,²⁹ Open Data Day,³⁰ and the Data for Development Festival.³¹

The International Aid Transparency Initiative (IATI)

IATI was launched in Accra, Ghana in 2008 at the Third High Level Forum on Aid Effectiveness. IATI is a multi-stakeholder, voluntary initiative created to better capture timely, detailed, comparable information on aid from traditional multilateral and bilateral donors, new and emerging donors (such as the BRICS countries, Brazil, Russia, India, China, and South Africa), NGOs, and foundations.

IATI offers a common standard for reporting and promoting the principles of open aid by making all data publicly accessible, machine-readable, and downloadable for replication and integration with other datasets. It also makes a variety of aid information available, including data on forward spending and subnational activity locations. IATI is supported by a governing board, a technical secretariat, and a Members Assembly, and currently has over 600 publishers. In 2009, Publish What You Fund (PWYF) was created to monitor donor compliance with IATI and other aid transparency commitments through an annual Aid Transparency Index (see Figure 1).

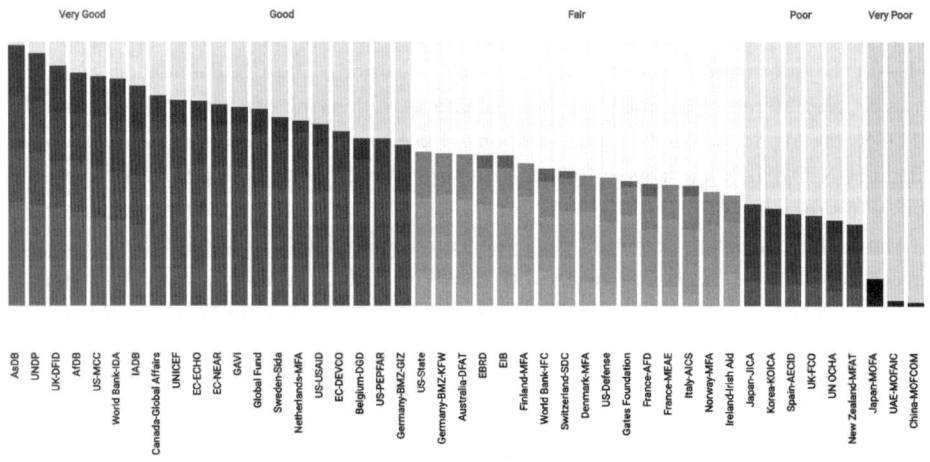

Figure 1:   Overview of the 2018 Aid Transparency Index
             Source: http://www.publishwhatyoufund.org/the-index/2018

In the development aid space, key leaders in the open data movement include the Members' Assembly of IATI, PWYF, Development Initiatives, the World Bank Open Aid Partnership and Mapping for Results team, Development Gateway, AidData, the International Development Research Centre, the Transparency and Accountability Initiative, Interaction, and the Open Data Research Network. These actors have been central to establishing the broad momentum for open aid and establishing the methodologies and platforms needed to provide open aid data within developing and emerging market economies (through country-owned aid information management systems, such as Development Gateway's Aid Management Platforms),[32] bilateral and multilateral aid donor dashboards,[33] and international datasets (including the IATI registry, Development Initiatives' Development Data Hub, and AidData's project-level aid datasets).[34]

Progress

As discussed above, one clear success in the open aid data movement is the emergence of a clear consensus on the need to open data and to establish robust policies to ensure the provision of standardised aid data by development and humanitarian organisations, national governments, and supranational institutions. There has been considerable progress in developing the infrastructure, in particular the systems and standards needed to collect, store, and publish open data, such as the IATI XML standard and the Humanitarian Data Exchange.[35] To reinforce the transparency movement, monitoring and rating systems have been established to oversee aid donor performance, including one aid-specific index, PWYF's Aid Transparency Index, and others with a broader focus on open data, such as Open Data Watch's Open Data Inventory, Open Knowledge Foundation's Government Open Data Index, and the World Wide Web Foundation's Open Data Barometer.

The Centre for Humanitarian Data and HDX

The UN OCHA's Humanitarian Data Exchange (HDX) is an open data platform for sharing data across organisations and crises. Early HDX iterations included support from technology communities at hackathons leading up to the official HDX launch in 2014. HDX has a series of features, including organisation pages, country pages, and crisis pages. HDX also includes tools for automated charting based on the Humanitarian Exchange Language (HXL), a data standard based on using hashtags in spreadsheets.

HDX provides step-by-step guidance for sharing data while adhering to strict practices of organisational and individual accountability. All datasets are reviewed to ensure they do not include personal identifiable data. As of March 2018, there are over 6 500 datasets and hundreds of participating organisations sharing a wide range of open data, including assessments, geospatial, population, and more.

There are HDX Labs in Dakar, Senegal and Nairobi, Kenya, and, building on its success to date, the UN OCHA launched the Centre for Humanitarian Data in The Hague, Netherlands, in late 2017 with a focus on four areas: data policy, data literacy, data services, and network engagement.

More recently, the open aid data movement has introduced innovations to improve access to data in forms useful to stakeholders and decision-makers. This has produced platforms that enable interactive use and easily downloadable data. Perhaps, more critically, the collection of data has taken on more inclusive approaches. From mapathons to hackathons, the entire data lifecycle has changed with new mobile and community engagement programmes. This improves the timeliness and usefulness of data and increases awareness and community buy-in. Simultaneously, there is growing attention to the need to "join up" open data across sectors (e.g. open aid data with open budget data) to increase its usefulness to key stakeholders.

Gaps

Despite the progress described above, there remain numerous challenges to realising the promise of open data in international development and humanitarian action. There are four main issues: persistent problems in providing consistent, standardised data across a proliferating number of sites; concerns about privacy and data protection; a lack of organisational investment in technology; and the lack of clear evidence of the cost benefits and impact of open aid data.

(In)Consistencies in the supply of open data

One challenge facing open aid data is widespread inconsistency in how multilateral organisations report their data.[36] While the IATI registry has been increasingly used by development agencies, reporting has been uneven across organisations and across key data points, especially disbursement and procurement data. Some multilateral organisations, such as the World Bank Group, provide more financial information on their websites, although not necessarily as open data. Other organisations, such as the OECD, United Nations Environment Programme (UNEP), International Organisation for Migration (IOM), and the International Monetary Fund (IMF), have been slow to release open financial data.

Likewise, there is often conflicting data across different open data systems. For example, in collecting and attempting to code data on aid projects in Nepal and Bangladesh, the Complex Emergencies and Political Stability in South Asia (CEPSA) team at the University of Texas collated all project documents, financial information, and geolocation data from Nepal's Aid Management Platform, Bangladesh's Ministry of Finance, IATI, AidData, OECD CRS++, and the websites of numerous donors, including the World Bank, Asian Development Bank, Japan, the United States (US), and the United Kingdom (UK). The CEPSA team found dramatically different totals on the number of projects and surprising gaps in the availability of activity-level data across the different sources, including project titles, funding amounts, and project data. The CEPSA team even found significant inconsistencies in the data coming from individual donor countries. For example, in attempting to assess patterns in US development assistance in Nepal and Bangladesh, there were discrepancies in the data provided by the US Congressional Greenbook, OECD CRS++, USAID Foreign Aid Tracker, and the US State Department Foreign Aid Dashboard.[37]

A root cause of these inconsistencies may be the lack of common data sharing protocols. One key exception is in the health sector, where there are data sharing protocols for pandemic and epidemic emergencies available via the World Health Organization (WHO). There are also informal informational working groups in the humanitarian sector, as well as country-level donor sector working groups and donor coordinated forums in the development sector. However, efforts to "join up" data on a global level are nascent, including initiatives such as the Joined-Up Data Standards (JUDS) Project (closed in 2017)[38,39] and the Global Partnership for Sustainable Development Data (GPSDD)[40] working group on SDG Data Interoperability. Nonetheless, the irony is that the open data movement may be moving too fast as many data sources have yet to converge upon a common standard (with common fields) for collecting and reporting data.

Data privacy, protection, and responsible use

Concerns about data privacy, protection, and responsible use are valid and persuasive reasons why some organisations have been reluctant to open and share data. Choosing which data to share, and for what purpose, is very complex for humanitarian organisations. Any discussion of data sharing needs to start with ensuring the protection of the most vulnerable communities. Coordination is key for delivering effective humanitarian responses guided by international humanitarian law and standards like Sphere.[41] Information managers need to collaborate to determine data sharing workflows that adhere to data protection guidance and responsible data use while still improving coordination. This is complicated by the lack of business analysis of workflows that would better support incorporating open data practices into processes, procedures, and tools. Similarly, there needs to be more effort to reconcile open data with domestic and international privacy laws and protections (e.g. the European Union's General Data Protection Regulation), and, therefore, a need for open data advocates to understand that humanitarians may not be able to share all data given the sensitive situations in which they work.

Addressing all of these issues requires a wholesale change in how development practitioners and humanitarians work, as well as the development and adoption of data protection and responsible use policies. The International Committee of the Red Cross (ICRC) has sought to develop such protocols in their *Professional standards for protection work*[42] and *Handbook on data protection*.[43] The United States Agency for International Development (USAID) has created guidance for its implementing partners under ADS Chapter 508[44] and has implemented a research programme on responsible data, although results are not yet public.[45] The *Responsible data handbook* also lays out principles for handling data privacy in development projects.[46]

Technology and data literacy

Sharing and opening data requires tools, knowledge, and established workflows. International humanitarian and development organisations have funding structures focused on either rapid response or programmatic delivery. There is rarely sufficient investment in upgrading technology infrastructure and business workflows to prepare for all the potential changes noted in the *Fourth industrial revolution*.[47] A data revolution needs a technology revolution first. Improved data opening and sharing is also related to upskilling organisations and individuals in these sectors. Data literacy is essential for improving advocacy and the use of open data everywhere and critically important in the area of development and humanitarian assistance. Investment in data literacy, operational changes, technology innovation, and back office workflows are rarely the priority given the pressing humanitarian needs.[48] This funding gap inhibits the critical changes required to properly implement tools and workflows to better support open data.

Data culture

While innovation in open data has been a top priority of many development agencies at the headquarters level, these innovations often fail to appeal to country office staff, limiting impact and implementation at local levels. For example, while publishing and using IATI has been a top priority of many agencies, country staff are often unaware of IATI and are occasionally resistant to its use, creating inconsistencies between data published locally and that published internationally. More broadly, research has shown that agency staff at the country level often rely more heavily on interpersonal relationships rather than openly accessible data.[49] These misalignments suggest a combination of factors:

- International open data publishers often do not understand the needs of local users, leading to a top-down push for data use that results in country office fatigue and resistance.

- Data published internationally often does not reflect local realities or it lacks the attributes (e.g. subnational locations and results data) needed to answer key questions on aid efficacy.

- Country-level agency staff are often sceptical of the value of data generally, as local conversations and negotiations are seen as more effective means for gathering information.

- Fostering data literacy requires a data culture of learning and sharing, meaning new approaches to leadership, sharing, and trust building with local stakeholders. Current systems and processes for knowledge exchange are often outdated.

- Theories of change around open data still need to grapple with the necessary cultural change for data producers and data consumers. Work to advance open data should recognise that trust in, and the use of, open data can vary greatly across countries and sectors where data may be highly politicised and contested, and where the practice of evidence-based decision-making is not yet ingrained in policy-making.

An increased focus on enhancing the partnership between headquarters and country offices with the aim of tackling local challenges and improving the effective dissemination and uptake of open aid data is necessary. Examples of this include UNICEF's partnership with Development Gateway, Development Initiatives' work with partner governments and country offices to localise IATI data to solve priority challenges,[50] and the Netherlands' and the Department for International Development's (DFID) engagement with suppliers and country offices to encourage disaggregated publication and use of IATI data.

Evidence

There are a number of new studies that attempt to provide evidence on the impact of open data (see box, Building the evidence base: Studies of open aid data use and impact). Each of these studies seeks to fill the gap on what we know about the extent to which key stakeholders are actually aware of open data, as well as their willingness and ability to access and use these systems. Ultimately, with the realisation that an "if we build it, they will come" approach is simply not enough, attention has shifted from developing to testing the open aid data theory of change.

> **Building the evidence base: Studies of open aid data use and impact**
>
> While evidence of the longer-term impact remains sparse, there are several recent studies that have attempted to directly measure the levels of awareness, use, and outputs related to open aid data.
>
> Studies by USAID (2015: *Aid transparency country pilot assessment*),[51] Development Gateway (2016: *Use of IATI in country systems*),[52] and Development Initiatives (2017: *Reaching the potential of IATI data*)[53] have studied the awareness and use of IATI data globally and within specific countries, such as Zambia, Ghana, and Bangladesh. Similar studies have examined awareness and use of in-country aid information management systems, including in Nepal (with a 2014 study by Freedom Forum),[54] in Sierra Leone (in a 2017 Oxfam study),[55] and in Timor Leste, Senegal, and Honduras (in a 2017 report from AidData).[56]
>
> Fewer studies have attempted to measure the actual impact of open aid data on other variables, such as accounting in development finances, donor coordination, citizen empowerment, and development outcomes (with the exception of PWYF's 2017 work in Benin and Tanzania,[57] papers by GovLab in 2017,[58] and Kotsadam et al. in 2018 in Nigeria[59]).

To date, evaluations related to open aid data have been largely qualitative and limited to non-generalisable case studies. In many instances, these case studies reveal little awareness of open aid data systems and engagement with that data. As a step prior to measuring impact, research must first better understand the conditions that enable or constrain data awareness and use. Such conditions often boil down to simple capacity issues with respect to accessing and analysing data, which often require higher bandwidth, sufficient server capacity, and the availability of computers and smartphones. Access and use also require sufficient expertise to navigate data that is supplied in foreign languages (especially English) or complex programs (ArcGIS, XML formats, and dense CSV files). To understand awareness and use, research must also address the complex political economy around data ecosystems. This includes developing a sensitivity to the cultures of data production and sharing, the politics behind resource allocation, the delegation of authority for open data systems, the role of the media and data journalists in serving as intermediaries, and the historical relationships between governments, donors, and civil society groups.[60]

Conclusions and recommendations

The past decade of the application of open data to development assistance and humanitarian action has provided critical lessons for moving forward. We offer four key recommendations to the international open data community on how to address the key challenges faced in making open data work in the delivery of development assistance and humanitarian action.

1. The release and use of open data faces organisational hurdles. This may include a lack of resources and infrastructure needed to ensure quality and timely data collection or a lack of a data culture that encourages data use. Data is only useful if it is seen by end users as central to information products, evidence, decisions, and knowledge sharing. Open data advocates need to ensure that the mechanisms designed to supply open data are informed by, and integrated into, organisational structures in ways that are consistent with local data cultures and existing capacities. A common language is needed to develop an understanding between data consumers and data producers. The key to success is understanding the culture and context, then building capacity and usage with early adopters. The talking points about "why open data matters" need to incorporate and acknowledge the barriers and aim for opportunities that show true impact.

2. More investment is needed to support joined-up data initiatives. The evidence we have to date suggests strongly that stakeholders want open data around aid and humanitarian assistance, but would find it more useful if such data was more effectively integrated across sectors, especially with respect to domestic budgets and essential demographic information. We need to break down silos and manage open data with a comprehensive, holistic approach.

3. Successfully addressing data privacy, protection, and responsible use will continue to be critical to the success of the open data movement. Setting minimum data standards is the starting point for data sharing. Improving education on the impact and value of data sharing while still adhering to data protection and responsible data use will require a constant balance. Open data and data sharing can occur if data-driven projects are built with privacy protection by design. Data controllers, data producers, and data consumers will need to plan and manage risks and benefits by incorporating proven practices into standard operating procedures.

4. The open data community, and the broader community of donors engaged in international development and humanitarian action, need to invest more in basic research on awareness, use, and impact. Investment in technology and business analysis will also aid the implementation of open data practices. To sustain momentum for open data, we need to rigorously test the theory of change and hypothesised effects on outcomes, such as aid accountability, effectiveness, donor coordination, improved budget management, and timely and inclusive decision-making in the allocation of scarce resources.[61] These studies need to go beyond static, qualitative case studies to include more longitudinal studies that are capable of capturing the larger societal costs and benefits and the long-term impacts of open data.

Further reading

Clare, A., Verhulst, S., & Young, A. (2016). *Open aid in Sweden.* Brooklyn, NY: GovLab. http://odimpact.org/files/case-study-sweden.pdf

Friends of Publish What You Fund. (2016). *How can data revolutionize development?: Putting data at the center of US global development – an assessment of US foreign aid transparency.* Washington, DC: Friends of Publish What You Fund. http://media.wix.com/ugd/9a0ffd_2ce18150803b48989905acabf9bb91d6.pdf

GovLab. (2016). The GovLab selected readings on data and humanitarian response. http://thegovlab.org/data-and-humanitarian-response/

Gutman, J. & Horton, C. (2015). *Accessibility and effectiveness of donor disclosure policies: When disclosure clouds transparency.* Washington, DC: Brookings Institution. https://www.brookings.edu/wp-content/uploads/2016/07/donor-disclosure-policies-gutman.pdf

About the authors

Catherine Weaver is an Associate Professor and Associate Dean of Students at the University of Texas at Austin (LBJ School of Public Affairs), and Co-Director of Innovations for Peace and Development (IPD). Learn more about IPD at https://www.ipdutexas.org. Follow Kate at https://www.twitter.com/kateweaverUT.

Josh Powell is the Deputy CEO at Development Gateway and has been involved with the International Aid Transparency Initiative (IATI) and open data since 2010. Follow Josh at https://www.twitter.com/joshuacpowell and learn more about Development Gateway at https://www.developmentgateway.org.

Heather Leson is Data Literacy Lead at the International Federation of Red Cross Red Crescent Societies (IFRC), is on the board of the OpenStreetMap Foundation, and is a member of the Humanitarian OpenStreetMap Team. Follow Heather at https://www.twitter.com/heatherleson and learn more about her work at https://www.ifrc.org.

How to cite this chapter

Weaver, C., Powell, J., & Leson, H. (2019). Open data and development assistance and humanitarian aid. In T. Davies, S. Walker, M. Rubinstein, & F. Perini (Eds.), *The state of open data: Histories and horizons* (pp. 77–90). Cape Town and Ottawa: African Minds and International Development Research Centre. http://stateofopendata.od4d.net

This work is licensed under a Creative Commons Attribution 4.0 International (CC BY 4.0) licence. It was carried out with the aid of a grant from the International Development Research Centre, Ottawa, Canada.

Endnotes

1. Khokar, T. (2017). Hugs and databases: In memory of Hans Rosling. *World Bank: The Data Blog*, 13 February. https://blogs.worldbank.org/opendata/hugs-and-databases-memory-hans-rosling
2. Florini, A. (Ed.). (2007). *The right to know: Transparency for an open world*. New York, NY: Columbia University Press.
3. Fox, J. (2007). The uncertain relationship between transparency and accountability. *Development in Practice, 17(4/5)*, 663–671. https://www.jstor.org/stable/25548267
4. Collin, M., Zubairi, A., Nielson, D., & Barder, O. (2009). *The costs and benefits of aid transparency*. Wells, UK: Aidinfo/Development Initiatives. http://bit.ly/2ShVCfu
5. PWYF. (2009). *Why aid transparency matters, and the global movement for aid transparency*. PWYF Briefing Paper 1. London: Publish What You Fund. http://www.publishwhatyoufund.org/wp-content/uploads/2017/01/Briefing-Paper-1-Why-Aid-Transparency-Matters.pdf
6. Mulley, S. (2010). *Donor aid: New frontiers in transparency and accountability*. London: Transparency and Accountability Initiative. http://www.transparency-initiative.org/archive/wp-content/uploads/2011/05/donor_aid_final1.pdf
7. Carothers, T. & Brechenmacher, S. (2014). *Accountability, transparency, participation, and inclusion: A new development consensus?* Washington, DC: Carnegie Endowment for International Peace. https://carnegieendowment.org/files/new_development_consensus.pdf
8. Herrling, S. (2015). The business proposition of open aid data: Why every US agency should default to transparency. *Publish What You Fund* [Blog post], 30 June. https://web.archive.org/web/20150914193510/http://www.publishwhatyoufund.org/updates/by-country/us/business-proposition-open-aid-data-why-every-u-s-agency-should-default-transparency/
9. Barder, O. (2016). Aid transparency: Are we nearly there? *Center For Global Development* [Blog post], 13 April. https://www.cgdev.org/blog/aid-transparency-are-we-nearly-there
10. https://stats.oecd.org/Index.aspx?DataSetCode=CRS1
11. https://stats.oecd.org/Index.aspx?DataSetCode=FSS
12. http://www.aidtransparency.net/
13. See, for example, the EU Aid Transparency Guarantee and the Global Partnership for Effective Development Cooperation.
14. IEAG. (2014). *A world that counts: Mobilising the data revolution for sustainable development*. Independent Expert Advisory Group Secretariat. http://www.undatarevolution.org/report/
15. Ibid., p. 6.
16. ECA. (2015). *Africa data consensus*. Addis Ababa: Economic Commission for Africa. https://www.uneca.org/sites/default/files/PageAttachments/final_adc_-_english.pdf
17. G8. (2013). Policy paper: G8 open data charter and technical annex. London: Government of the United Kingdom. https://www.gov.uk/government/publications/open-data-charter/g8-open-data-charter-and-technical-annex
18. Grand Bargain Signatories. (2016). *The Grand Bargain: A shared commitment to better serve people in need*. New York, NY: Agenda for Humanity. https://www.agendaforhumanity.org/initiatives/3861
19. https://unstats.un.org/unsd/statcom/49th-session/
20. https://www.gfdrr.org
21. https://opendri.org/
22. https://www.openstreetmap.org/
23. Harvard Humanitarian Initiative. (2011). *Disaster relief 2.0: The future of information sharing in humanitarian emergencies*. Washington, DC and Berkshire, UK: UN Foundation & Vodafone Foundation Technology Partnership. https://hhi.harvard.edu/sites/default/files/publications/disaster-relief-2.0.pdf

24 http://crisismappers.net/ and http://digitalhumanitarians.com/
25 https://www.hotosm.org/
26 http://www.missingmaps.org/about/ and https://wiki.openstreetmap.org/wiki/Missing_Maps_Project
27 https://data.humdata.org/faq
28 https://wiki.openstreetmap.org/wiki/State_Of_The_Map
29 https://www.opendatacon.org/
30 http://opendataday.org/
31 http://www.data4sdgs.org/news/data-development-festival
32 Mitchell, L. (2017). Systematically tracking the aid tracking systems. *Medium: Leigh Mitchell's Blog*, 27 July. https://medium.com/@leighmitchell/tracking-the-tracking-systems-ddd3d6578fef
33 See, for example, https://devtracker.dfid.gov.uk/, https://openaid.se/, http://openaid.um.dk/, https://explorer.usaid.gov/, https://open.unicef.org/, and https://open.undp.org/
34 See https://www.iatiregistry.org/, http://data.devinit.org/, and http://aiddata.org/datasets
35 http://iatistandard.org/203/schema/, https://digitalprinciples.org/, and https://data.humdata.org/
36 https://openstate.github.io/multitest/
37 GAO. (2016). *Foreign assistance: Actions needed to improve transparency and quality of data on Foreignassistance.gov*. Washington, DC: United States Government Accountability Office. https://www.gao.gov/products/D14383
38 http://juds.joinedupdata.org/
39 Steele, L. & Orrell, T. (2017). *The frontiers of data interoperability for sustainable development*. London: Development Initiatives & Publish What You Fund. http://www.publishwhatyoufund.org/wp-content/uploads/2017/11/JUDS_Report_Web_061117.pdf
40 http://www.data4sdgs.org/
41 http://www.sphereproject.org/
42 ICRC. (2013). *Professional standards for protection work*. 2013 edition. Geneva: International Committee of the Red Cross. https://reliefweb.int/sites/reliefweb.int/files/resources/Professional%20standards%20for%20protection%20work%20carried%20out%20by%20humanitarian%20and%20human%20rights%20actors%20in%20armed%20conflict%20and%20other%20situations%20of%20violence.pdf
43 Kuner, C. & Marelli, M. (Eds.). (2017). *Handbook on data protection in humanitarian action*. Geneva: International Committee of the Red Cross. https://shop.icrc.org/handbook-on-data-protection-in-humanitarian-action.html?___store=default
44 USAID. (2014). *USAID ADS chapter 508: Privacy program*. Washington, DC: United States Agency for International Development. https://www.usaid.gov/sites/default/files/documents/1868/508.pdf
45 USAID. (2018). *An introduction to USAID's work on responsible data*. USAID & FHI360. Washington, DC: United States Agency for International Development. http://devinfo.digitaldevelopment.org/resources/introduction-usaids-work-responsible-data
46 Responsible Data Forum. (2016). *The hand-book of the modern development specialist*. The Engine Room. https://the-engine-room.github.io/responsible-data-handbook/assets/pdf/responsible-data-handbook.pdf
47 Schwab, K. (2017). *The fourth industrial revolution*. New York, NY: Currency.
48 Obrecht, A. & Warner, A.T. (2016). *More than just luck: Innovation in humanitarian action*. An HIF/ALNAP Study. London: ALNAP & Open Data Institute. https://www.alnap.org/help-library/more-than-just-luck-innovation-in-humanitarian-action
49 Custer, S. & Sethi, T. (Eds.). (2017). *Avoiding data graveyards: Insights from data producers and consumers*. Washington, DC: AidData at the College of William and Mary. https://www.aiddata.org/publications/avoiding-data-graveyards-insights-from-data-producers-users-in-three-countries
50 https://www.developmentgateway.org/sites/default/files/2018-06/Learning%20from%20Using%20UNICEF%20IATI%20Data%20in%20Madagascar%20and%20Senegal%20AMPs_DetailReport.pdf

51. USAID. (2015). *Aid transparency country pilot assessment*. Washington, DC: United States Agency for International Development.
52. Cisse, H., Ferreyra, F., Irura, M., Musoni, F., Ngom, O., Powell, J., & Sanchez, V. (2016). *Use of IATI in country systems: Final report*. Washington, DC: Development Gateway. https://www.developmentgateway.org/sites/default/files/2017-02/IATI-UseinCountrySystems-FINAL.pdf
53. Ntawiha, W. & Zellmann, C. (2017). *Reaching the potential of IATI data*. Bristol, UK: Development Initiatives. http://devinit.org/wp-content/uploads/2017/03/reaching-the-potential-of-IATI-data.pdf
54. Sapkota, K. (2014). *Exploring the emerging impacts of open aid data and budget data in Nepal*. Kathmandu: Freedom Forum. http://www.opendataresearch.org/sites/default/files/publications/Open%20Aid%20and%20Budget%20Data%20in%20Nepal%20-%2015th%20Sept-print.pdf
55. Grabowski, A. (2017). *Transparency is more than dollars and cents: An examination of informational needs for aid spending in Sierra Leone and Liberia*. Oxford: Oxfam. http://hdl.handle.net/10546/620330
56. Custer, S. & Sethi, T. (Eds.). (2017). *Avoiding data graveyards: Insights from data producers and consumers*. Washington, DC: Aid Data at the College of William and Mary. https://www.aiddata.org/publications/avoiding-data-graveyards-insights-from-data-producers-users-in-three-countries
57. PWYF. (2017). *With publication comes responsibility: Using open data for accountability in Benin and Tanzania – A Discussion Paper*. London: Publish What You Fund. http://www.publishwhatyoufund.org/wp-content/uploads/2017/09/With-Publication-Brings-Responsibility-A-discussion-paper.pdf
58. Verhulst, S. & Young, A. (2016). *Open data impact: When demand and supply meet*. Brooklyn, NY: GovLab. http://odimpact.org/files/open-data-impact-key-findings.pdf
59. Kotsadam, A., Østby, G., Rustad, S.A., Tollefsen, A.F., & Urdal, H. (2018). Development aid and infant mortality. Micro-level evidence from Nigeria. *World Development, 105*, 59–69.
60. Custer, S. & Sethi, T. (Eds.). (2017). *Avoiding data graveyards: Insights from data producers and consumers*. Washington, DC: Aid Data at the College of William & Mary. https://www.aiddata.org/publications/avoiding-data-graveyards-insights-from-data-producers-users-in-three-countries
61. Carolan, L. (2017). *Mapping open data for accountability*. Washington, DC: Transparency and Accountability Initiative and the Open Data Charter. http://www.transparency-initiative.org/wp-content/uploads/2017/06/taiodc_draft_data4accountabilityframework.pdf

006

Education

Javiera Atenas and Leo Havemann

Key points

- Open data can help researchers and policy-makers understand the education landscape, provide information for parents and children about education facilities and their performance, and serve as a key element in the creation of open educational resources (OER).

- Attention must move beyond the simple availability of data on education to also question how the data is contextualised, presented, and used to ensure it does not result in the reinforcement of pre-existing biases and social divides.

- There has been relatively limited intersection to date between the open education and open data communities. There are opportunities for future strengthening of these links, increasing the use of open data as a key educational resource, and supporting more applied civic education.

Introduction

According to United Nations (UN) Sustainable Development Goal (SDG) 4,[1] states must "ensure inclusive and quality education for all and promote lifelong learning". In this chapter, we consider the ways in which open data can support the achievement of this goal. In the education sector, open data released by governments and educational institutions, as well as by national and international organisations, can support a wide range of interventions, including strategies to improve the quality of education, the design of effective education policies, the creation of educational resources, and the development of the key literacies needed to operate and participate in today's "datafied society".[2]

The education ecosystem is made up of a complex network of systems and practices developed to address a wide range of sociopolitical and economic issues. Despite the enormous efforts made by countries to guarantee equal access to quality education, there are still challenges to overcome for which open data can provide insight, perspective, and a wide range of tools to further our understanding of core educational problems and to support the development of solutions. It has also been argued that open data can be used as part of a series of quality indicators to help people to make better decisions related to educational opportunities and methodologies and to choose among education providers. More overtly, open data used in the development of open educational resources (OER) can be considered a key tool in promoting citizenship and democratic values and developing the transversal literacies that citizens require in order to participate in a datafied society. Figure 1 indicates three main ways in which open data and the broader education sector intersect. You can also think of this in terms of how open data use intersects with the three main education stakeholder groups: policy-makers, parents and learners, and educators.

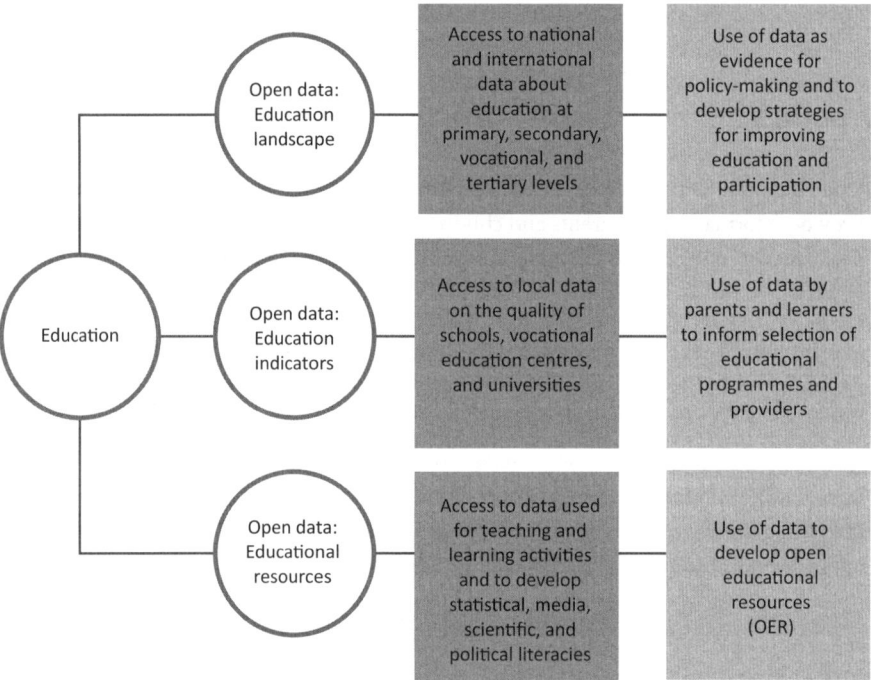

Figure 1: Open data in education
Source: Authors

In this chapter, we will explore both the opportunities and challenges that open data presents across the education sector, drawing upon examples from around the world, and wider critical arguments and studies related to open data.[3] We are aware that while open data can promote public participation and social innovation, it can also reinforce pre-existing biases by connecting performance with the poor and vulnerable in an unfair manner, helping to further marginalise those who cannot choose where to live or study. The evidence we have gathered suggests that although impact to date has been mixed, there are many opportunities to substantially strengthen existing networks and activities around open data and education in the future.

Open data and the education landscape

Understanding the current state of education and identifying ways to improve education, are vital tasks for policy-makers. Davies,[4] Niemi,[5] Burns, Köster,[6] and the 2017 EU Eurydice Report[7] argue that policy-makers need better access to evidence in order to address policy issues. Data that describes achievements, attainment, enrolment, or the distribution of learning are all important to determine whether educational systems are working or not. The United Nations Educational, Scientific and Cultural Organization (UNESCO)[8] has indicated the need to ground policy on reliable evidence to ensure that educational policies are effective, efficient, and implementable. They argue for the use of comparable indicators and for ensuring that data is available disaggregated by gender, administrative area, geographical location, sociocultural groupings, education level, and type of provider to enable a comparison between the different groups and to identify those who are educationally disadvantaged.

Motivans,[9] in exploring data availability to monitor the SDGs, also calls for educational data that is relevant, valid, reliable, timeless, punctual, clear, transparent, comparable, accessible, affordable, consistent, and with potential for disaggregation. There has been some progress on making this data available (and open), but major gaps remain. Notably, educational data from countries such as Kenya, South Africa, Ecuador, or Montenegro[10] is scarce and neither widely nor openly available, making it difficult to assess their progress in relation to SDG 4.

While some states have had standardised testing since the 1950s, it is only in the last 20 years that standard national assessments have become the norm in Europe, and the majority of the world's population still resides in countries without such testing.[11] International initiatives have stepped in to fill the gap. The best-known example of performance data provided at the international level is the Organisation for Economic Co-operation and Development's (OECD) Programme for International Student Assessment (PISA) test[12] initiated in 2000, providing data about learner performance in science, mathematics, and reading. The results of this standard test, linked to sociodemographic data, enable comparative analysis regarding differences in performance among diverse groups of learners, taking into account gender, social background, migrant learners, and ethnicity. In 2015, 72 countries participated in the PISA survey, generating data that is commonly used in evidence-based policy-making to help educational stakeholders to target specific problems guided by clear information. Individual (anonymous) student results from the study are published in downloadable structured data formats for common statistical software.

When open data is available as disaggregated data then a wide range of actors can get involved in its analysis. Academics are clearly major users of education-related data, but private consultancies and non-profit organisations have also taken advantage of available datasets. For example, in the United Kingdom (UK), the FTT Education Datalab[13] was established by a non-profit education services company to help policy-makers improve educational practice. International organisations, such as the OECD, UNESCO, and the World Bank, make use of data (combined with qualitative research) to contribute to the international collection of policies, presentations, policy tools, and frameworks intended to support evidence-based policy-making. Van Schalkwyk (2017) has also drawn attention to the way in which institutions providing performance data (in particular, higher education institutions in South Africa[14]) take advantage of cross-institution comparisons for benchmarking and how making more granular information available as open data has provided "a new fuel for transformation".[15]

However, when approaching educational data for research and policy purposes, there are at least two important considerations to keep in mind. First, the privacy of educators and learners must be protected when using or sharing data, particularly administrative and statistical data containing personally identifiable information. Surfacing and addressing patterns of educational disadvantage requires a careful balance because it is important that educational data can be disaggregated by gender, sociocultural background, educational level, and type of school. In the UK, controversy has emerged a number of times over the intrusiveness and level of data disclosure from the National Pupil Database.[16]

Second, it is important to consider the capacity to create and use data, not just its availability. In this area, one project to watch is the CapED initiative.[17] This project, active in 25 of the least developed countries (LDCs), aims to connect national education policies with data sources, and to support states in their use of this data in the development of their national action plans to achieve SDG 4. As each national CapED project works with UNESCO's Institute of Statistics to implement a data component, there may be opportunities to further emphasise open data approaches.

When microdata cannot be disclosed, the design of indicators that describe the data landscape is also of crucial importance. At the national level, one example that demonstrates this is the Data Chile education indicators site[18] that provides information from the National System of Performance Evaluation (SNED). SNED has been constructed using six indicators: school effectiveness, improvement, initiative, improvement of working conditions, equal opportunities, and the integration of teachers, parents, and guardians (see Figure 2). In an open data context, it is important to think about who gets involved in defining the indicators that will shape the sources of data that will be available in future.

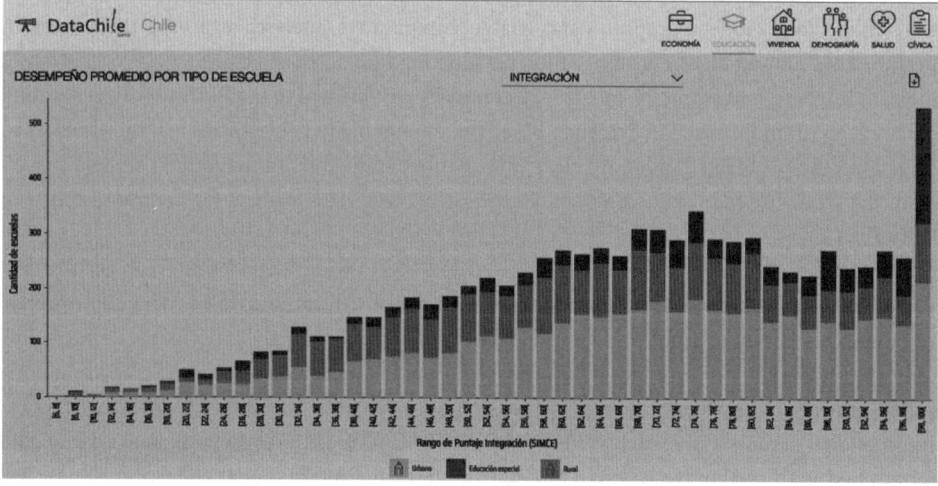

Figure 2:   National System of Performance Evaluation (SNED) data: Integration
Source: DataChile, https://es.datachile.io/geo/chile#education

In summary: demand is high for data across the education landscape, but supply varies. When open data is available, established policy-makers can be joined by new actors, including entrepreneurs and journalists, to debate and shape education performance and policy; however, even in the absence of globally comparable data or the use of that data by policy-makers, datasets on educational institutions can also drive change through parent and pupil behaviours.

Open data about educational institutions

In many countries, parents and/or pupils have some degree of choice over educational institutions. Statistics have long played a role in decisions related to the selection of learning products, programmes, and providers. With the availability of open data, a range of interactive platforms have emerged that use institutional or third-party assessment data to inform parents and learners, providing them with indicators and information they can use to make informed choices.[19,20] The data made available about educational institutions tends to focus on performance (e.g. university ratings) by using standardised metrics, but also may provide detailed information on programmes and prerequisites.

The last decade has seen the launch of numerous portals around the world that provide the means to compare the quality of education at different institutions using data provided by national and local authorities. Some examples include the Identicole portal in Peru, MIME from the Ministry of Education in Chile, JedeSchule run by non-profit organisations in Germany, the mobile app-based Conozca su escuela in Costa Rica run by Programa Estado De La Nación, and Scholen Keuze and Scholen op de Kaart in the Netherlands.[21]

A number of platforms go beyond using data to encourage "shopping around" in the selection of schools. For example, Mejora tu escuela in Mexico,[22] created by El Instituto Mexicano para la Competitividad (IMCO) with funding from the Omidyar Network, places an emphasis on gathering feedback from users of the platform and equipping them to advocate for improvements to their existing schools. In the UK, School Cuts,[23] created with the backing of major teachers' unions, places the emphasis on how funding cuts in education are impacting individual schools and was used as an advocacy tool in the last election. One of the unions funding the project claimed it helped to change "750 000 votes during the election and resulted in the government stumping up another £1.3 billion for schools in July".[24] However, the vast majority of platforms focus on maps and rankings. Figures 3 and 4 show two further examples from the UK. The first one, School Atlas, was developed by the Mayor of London and showcases the impact of income deprivation on children in London. The second example is a map of schools in London developed by a private firm, Locrating Ltd, which places the emphasis on school quality, cross-referencing data from Ofsted (the inspector of schools) and the Department of Education (UK). It showcases schools by area, displaying school quality as "inadequate", "requires improvement", "good", or "outstanding"; however, if we look at the data from a critical perspective, we can note the biases this information may portray by reinforcing preconceived notions of privilege and disadvantage.

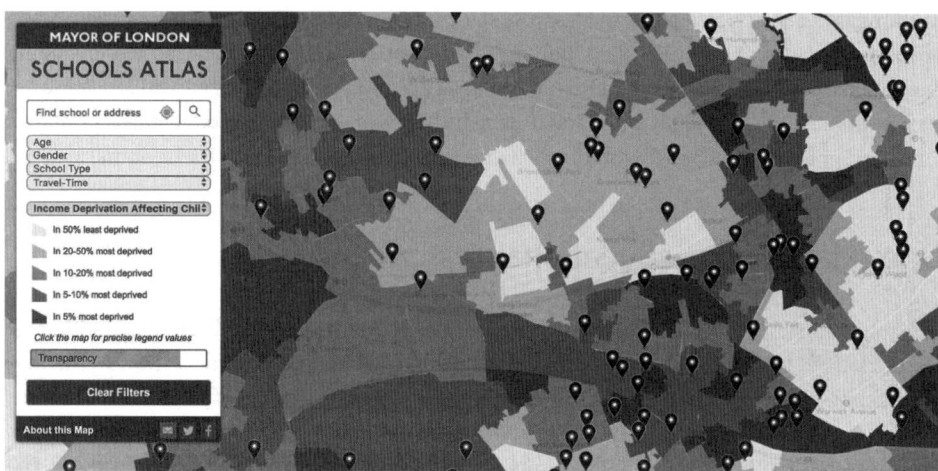

Figure 3:   Mayor of London – Schools Atlas
Source: https://maps.london.gov.uk/schools/

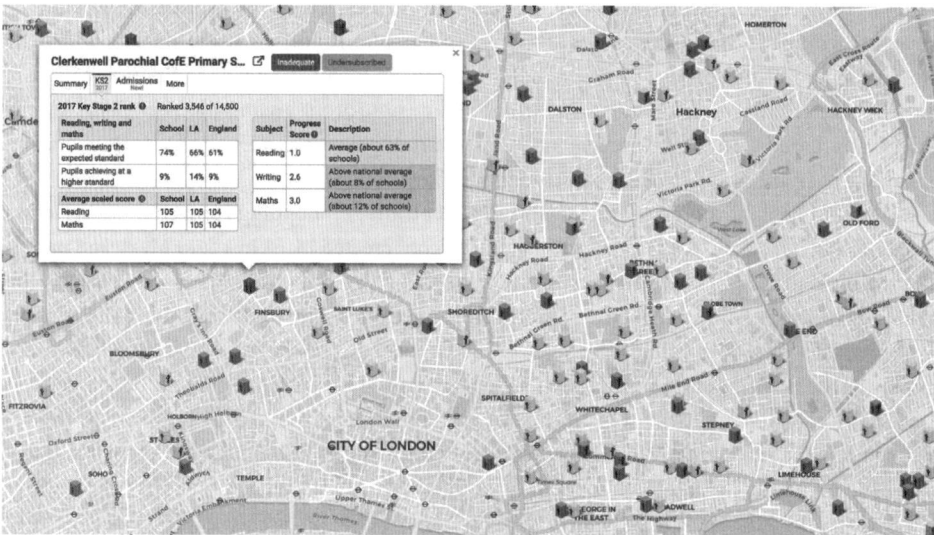

Figure 4:   Examples of school information platforms
Source: Locrating, A to Z of Schools, https://www.locrating.com/all_schools.aspx

Both examples offer an illustration of how the quality of education can be portrayed, but, even with contextual data, there is a risk that such information could stigmatise pupils from schools rated as inadequate or in low-income areas. We need to consider critical ethical questions when making data available about schools or, at the very least, ensure performance data is accompanied by contextualised information about the socioeconomic challenges faced by the relevant community, such as poverty, integration, and inclusion.

While school information portals are popular and may support more informed decision-making by learners faced with a complex mix of educational opportunities, there is limited empirical evidence to date on whether they ultimately improve education as much as advocacy-oriented efforts aimed at holding governments accountable or at ensuring proper funding for quality education for the most vulnerable in our society. When it comes to data on educational institutions, we have both ample open data supply and demand, as well as active intermediaries who are able to sustain their platforms. While there may be cases of individual impact for particular learners, the net social impact is difficult to determine.

Open data as an open educational resource

The final application of open data in education is its direct use in the development, or as part, of OER. OER are defined by UNESCO[25] as "any type of educational materials that are in the public domain or introduced with an open license". Open data used as OER can allow students to learn and experiment by working with the same raw data researchers, governments, civil society, international organisations, and policy-makers generate and use. They can form a key component in research- and scenario-based learning activities, and in supporting students to develop informational, statistical, scientific, media, political, and critical-thinking skills. By working with real-world data, students can develop storytelling and research skills, and can apply analytical, collaborative, and citizenship skills in using data to solve real-world problems.

This idea of using open data in education is recognised in the sixth principle of the Open Data Charter[26] on open data for inclusive development and innovation, which states that it is key to "[e]ngage with schools and post-secondary education institutions to support increased open data research and to incorporate data literacy into educational curricula." Although it is not clear how much emphasis has been placed to date on this point by countries and cities adopting the Charter, the groundwork to support the use of open data as OER has been laid in a number of projects.

In 2015, the Open Education Working Group of the Open Knowledge Foundation, established in 2013, published *Open data as Open Educational Resources: Case studies of emerging practice*[27] in which a series of authors presented activities that could be adopted by educators at schools and universities to promote the use of open data in research-related activities. The book provides examples and best practices, showcasing how to use real data from research and from national and international data projects to foster educational activities to develop data literacies and critical thinking through collaborations among students, researchers, and academics. One of the practices portrayed in the book is A Scuola di OpenCoesione in Italy,[28] an educational challenge, designed for Italian high school students. It was funded under the open government strategy on cohesion policy in partnership with the Ministry of Education and the Representation Office of the European Commission in Italy.

Other practical examples of the use of open data as OER[29] can be found at the Open Data School in Russia, which provides a series of lectures and seminars from experts on open data topics. The Open Linked Data project at the Universidad Técnica Particular de Loja in Ecuador presents the results of a study on Linked Data technology for students, researchers, and educators, and Data Science Fundamentals in Palestine offers an online tool to enable students to follow the

Foundations of Data Science training course developed by students and academics from Birzeit University. Finally, Monithon, also from Italy, offers an example of applied learning through open data, which citizens and university students, alongside researchers and policy-makers, use to monitor development projects. However, even with these notable successes, many initiatives focused on the use of open data as OER have been relatively short-lived, and the connections between the open education and the open data communities are still relatively weak with only a few points at which the communities intersect.

Supporting use of open data as OER is closely linked to work on data literacy (see Chapter 19: Data literacy). Recently, the Latin American Initiative for Open Data (ILDA) has developed a training programme for academics in the use of open data for teaching and learning[30] to support them in developing the capacities needed to live and work in the datafied society, including learning to construct knowledge and analysing information critically from a wide range of data sources.[31]

Following Uhlir and Schröder's argument[32] that "[s]tudents may be less effectively educated and trained if they are unable to work with a broad cross-section of data", and Davies'[33] assertion that "there will be greater need in future for capacity both in state and society to be able to debate the meaning of data, and to find responsible ways of using open data in democratic debate", we consider that the inclusion of open data in curricular activities is key to ensuring that both educators and learners acquire the skills they need to participate in contemporary society.

Conclusion

Over the last ten years, open data availability has grown, including data about education and data that can be used within education. Looking for school performance information may have involved using tables published once a year in newspapers ten years ago, but now many countries have interactive websites offering analysis and visualisation: ranging from official government sites to private sector-managed portals. Schools and post-secondary education institutions no longer need to rely on tables in textbooks, but can go to real-world updated datasets for teaching and learning; however, many challenges remain.

Although open data can provide evidence about problems that need to be addressed at the policy level, it can also be a key component in the development of the literacies needed in a datafied society, as well as in enhancing and promoting civic participation and understanding of the media and the sciences. However, it cannot be considered as the panacea for all educational problems.

Data is never neutral and it is ultimately a political instrument. Data and the algorithms used to analyse it can prompt stigmatisation, segregation, and discrimination. Mainstream narratives may place the blame for poor quality education on the children that perform poorly on standardised tests based on their economic or social background, instead of pointing at the authorities who have failed to provide the policies, programmes, and funding needed to improve the schools those children attend.

Arguments for opening data in education have tended to focus simply on the importance of access to data. Such arguments can gloss over the non-neutrality of data and the potential threats inherent in data-driven decision-making, where the context for data collection and presentation is opaque or where data "consumers" lack the critical thinking skills needed to interpret the data. They often also ignore the impact of trends toward the marketisation of education. We do not believe that it helps to approach open data as innocuous and benign per se. As Kitchin[34] states, "if open data merely serves the interests of capital by opening public data for commercial re-use and further empowers those who are already empowered and disenfranchises others, then it has failed to make society more democratic and open". However, as we have seen above, with examples like SchoolCuts.org, it is not only private interests that can deploy data for implicit or explicit political ends and there is potential for critical action.

Ultimately, while there are many challenges around the use of open data for education, it is through wider education about the creation and use of open data that these risks can be best addressed. The wealth of open data on all topics that could be applied to OER can be part of this. In conclusion, we recommend that:

- In the use and development of education indicators, it is important to prevent analysis exclusively through the use of algorithms as these may reflect biases and can foster the stigmatisation of vulnerable students.

- When governments open up educational data, they must ensure that it is anonymised to prevent the identification of individuals and collectives and, in addition, consider the potential uses of this data by public and private stakeholders to prevent this data from being used unethically.

- When institutions, civil society, and private sector organisations build tools using educational data, they need to consider the potential impact and use for students, educators, and educational communities.

- And finally, to foster data and citizenship literacies, the open education, open data, and open science communities must collaborate to develop educational materials and curricula to support educational institutions and programmes at all levels, including training for educators and educational communities.

Further reading

Atenas, J. & Havemann, L. (Eds.). (2015). *Open data as Open Educational Resources: Case studies of emerging practice*. London: Open Knowledge, Open Education Working Group. https://s3-eu-west-1.amazonaws.com/pfigshare-u-files/2396976/BookOpenDataasOpenEducationalResources.pdf

Mandinach, E.B. & Gummer, E.S. (2013). A systemic view of implementing data literacy in educator preparation. *Educational Researcher, 42(1)*, 30–37. https://journals.sagepub.com/doi/abs/10.3102/0013189x12459803

Schafer, M.T. & Van Es, K. (Eds.). (2017). The datafied society: Studying culture through data. Amsterdam: Amsterdam University Press. http://www.oapen.org/search?identifier=624771

About the authors

Javiera Atenas is the Education Lead at the Latin America Open Data Initiative (ILDA) and co-coordinator of the Open Knowledge Open Education Working Group. She holds a PhD in Education and her research focuses on educational policies, open educational practices, data ethics, and data literacies. She is an active researcher and advocate of open practices. You can follow Javiera at https://www.twitter.com/jatenas.

Leo Havemann is a Digital Education Advisor at University College London and a postgraduate researcher at the Open University. His interests focus on the use of technology in higher education, open educational practices, and learning literacies. Follow Leo at https://www.twitter.com/leohavemann.

How to cite this chapter

Atenas, J. & Havemann, L. (2019). Open data and education. In T. Davies, S. Walker, M. Rubinstein, & F. Perini (Eds.), *The state of open data: Histories and horizons* (pp. 91–102). Cape Town and Ottawa: African Minds and International Development Research Centre. http://stateofopendata.od4d.net.

This work is licensed under a Creative Commons Attribution 4.0 International (CC BY 4.0) licence. It was carried out with the aid of a grant from the International Development Research Centre, Ottawa, Canada.

Endnotes

1. UN (United Nations). (2018). Sustainable Development Goals: 4. Education. https://www.un.org/sustainabledevelopment/education/
2. Schafer, M.T. & Van Es, K. (Eds.). (2017). *The datafied society: Studying culture through data*. Amsterdam: Amsterdam University Press. http://www.oapen.org/search?identifier=624771
3. Kitchin, R. (2013). Four critiques of open data initiatives. *LSE Impact Blog*, 27 November. http://blogs.lse.ac.uk/impactofsocialsciences/2013/11/27/four-critiques-of-open-data-initiatives/
4. Davies, P. (1999). What is evidence-based education? *British Journal of Educational Studies, 47(2)*, 108–121. https://www.tandfonline.com/doi/abs/10.1111/1467-8527.00106
5. Niemi, H. (2007). Equity and good learning outcomes. Reflections on factors influencing societal, cultural and individual levels – the Finnish perspective. *Zeitschrift für Pädagogik, 53(1)*, 92–107. https://www.pedocs.de/volltexte/2011/4389/pdf/ZfPaed_2007_1_Niemi_Equity_good_learning_D_A.pdf
6. Burns, T. & Köster, F. (2016). *Educational research and innovation: Governing education in a complex world*. Paris: Organisation for Economic Co-operation and Development Publishing. http://dx.doi.org/10.1787/9789264255364-en
7. European Commission/EACEA/Eurydice. (2017). *Support mechanisms for evidence-based policy-making in education*. Eurydice report. Luxembourg: Publications Office of the European Union. https://eige.europa.eu/resources/206_EN_Evidence_based_policy_making.pdf
8. UNESCO. (2013). UNESCO handbook on education policy analysis and programming. Volume 1: Education policy analysis. Bangkok: United Nations Educational, Scientific and Cultural Organization. http://unesdoc.unesco.org/images/0022/002211/221189E.pdf
9. Motivans, A. (2015). Improving education statistics systems: Challenges and opportunities. Presentation at *World Statistics: Sustainable Data for Sustainable Development, 20–22 October 2015, Xi'an, People's Republic of China*. Montreal: UNESCO Institute for Statistics. https://unstats.un.org/sdgs/files/meetings/sdg-seminar-xian-2015/Presentation--3.4-Sustainable-Data-for-Sustainable-Development--UNESCO.pdf
10. http://kenya.opendataforafrica.org/gallery/Education, http://www.statssa.gov.za/?cat=16, https://educacion.gob.ec/estadisticaseducativas/, and http://www.mpin.gov.me/en/ministry
11. Sandefur, J. (2018). The case for global standardized testing. *Center for Education Innovations* [Blog post], 5 May. https://educationinnovations.org/case-for-global-standard-testing
12. See the OECD's PISA test data http://www.oecd.org/pisa/data/
13. https://ffteducationdatalab.org.uk/
14. Van Schalkwyk, F., Willmers, M., & McNaughton, M. (2016). Viscous open data: The roles of intermediaries in an open data ecosystem. *Information Technology for Development, 22(1)*, 68–83.
15. Van Schalkwyk, F. (2017). Open data on universities: New fuel for transformation. *University World News*, 14 July. http://www.universityworldnews.com/article.php?story=20170710104034491
16. UK Data Service. (2019). National pupil database. https://beta.ukdataservice.ac.uk/datacatalogue/series/series?id=2000108
17. https://en.unesco.org/themes/education/caped
18. https://es.datachile.io/geo/chile#education
19. McAuley, D., Rahemtulla, H., Goulding, J., & Souch, C. (2011). How open data, data literacy and linked data will revolutionise higher education. In L. Coiffait (Ed.), *New thinking about the future of higher education* (pp. 88–93). London: Pearson. https://www.academia.edu/1945211/The_Open_Data_Revolution_and_Data_Literacy_in_Higher_Education
20. Guy, M. (2016). The Open Education Working Group: Bringing people, projects and data together. In D. Mouromtsev & M. d'Aquin (Eds.), *Open data for education: Linked, shared, and reusable data for teaching and learning* (pp. 166–187). Cham: Springer International Publishing. https://doi.org/10.1007/978-3-319-30493-9_9

21. http://identicole.minedu.gob.pe/, http://www.mime.mineduc.cl/mvc/mime/portada, https://jedeschule.de/, https://www.conozcasuescuela.ac.cr/, http://www.scholenkeuze.nl/, and https://www.scholenopdekaart.nl/, respectively.
22. http://www.mejoratuescuela.org/
23. http://www.schoolcuts.org.uk/
24. Whittaker, F. (2018). NUT spent £326k on general election campaign. *Schools Week*, 19 March. https://schoolsweek.co.uk/nut-spent-326k-on-general-election-campaign/
25. UNESCO (United Nations Educational, Scientific and Cultural Organization). (2017). Open Educational Resources (OER). https://en.unesco.org/themes/building-knowledge-societies/oer
26. Open Data Charter. (2015). Principles: International Open Data Charter. https://opendatacharter.net/principles/
27. Atenas, J. & Havemann, L. (Eds.). (2015). *Open data as Open Educational Resources: Case studies of emerging practice.* London: Open Knowledge, Open Education Working Group. http://dx.doi.org/10.6084/m9.figshare.1590031
28. http://www.ascuoladiopencoesione.it/about-opencohesion-school/
29. http://opendataschool.ru/anketa/, http://data.utpl.edu.ec/, https://github.com/abedkhooli/ds1, and http://www.monithon.it/
30. https://idatosabiertos.org/en/investigaciones-2/modelo-docente-y-datos-abiertos/
31. Atenas, J., Havemann, L., & Priego, E. (2015). Open data as Open Educational Resources: Towards transversal skills and global citizenship. *Open Praxis, 7(4)*, 377–389. http://dx.doi.org/10.5944/openpraxis.7.4.233
32. Uhlir, P.F. & Schröder, P. (2007). Open data for global science. *Data Science Journal*, *6*, OD36–OD53, p. 201. https://www.jstage.jst.go.jp/article/dsj/6/0/6_0_OD36/_pdf
33. Davies, T. (2010). Open data, democracy and public sector reform: A look at open government data use from data.gov.uk. Master's Thesis. University of Oxford, UK, p. 5. http://www.opendataimpacts.net/report/
34. Kitchin, R. (2013). Four critiques of open data initiatives. *LSE Impact Blog,* 27 November. http://blogs.lse.ac.uk/impactofsocialsciences/2013/11/27/four-critiques-of-open-data-initiatives/

007

Environment

Selwyn Willoughby

Key points

- Data and information underpinning environmental knowledge is recognised as a form of power.
- Vast quantities of environmental data are available online through many dedicated local, regional, and international data portals. This reflects long-established norms and practices of data-sharing within the environmental research community.
- Emphasis must be placed on increasing the volume and geographic coverage of open water and air quality data.
- Making connections between datasets across borders and thematic silos is essential to support greater understanding of a changing climate, to address air quality, to manage water resources, and to sustain biodiversity. However, there is often a disconnect between academic and official data initiatives and open-source, grassroots/citizen-science open data projects.
- Context-aware open data approaches and well-resourced data infrastructures are crucial to avoid loss of data, missed opportunities, and duplication of effort.
- As the amount of environmental data from sensor networks increases, there will be major inequalities in global data coverage to address with developing countries often being more poorly represented.

Introduction

Since the early 1960s, we have seen an increasingly vocal response to unmitigated anthropogenic impacts on the environment.[1] Although there were earlier activists and movements, the 1960s marked the period when disparate voices started to coalesce. Environmental activists started conceptualising environmental problems as political matters, and, in doing so, using scientific knowledge as part of their armament. This led to a significant change in policy-making with regard to the use of scientific outputs and knowledge as supporting evidence. Data and information have become forms of power that are used to drive or change political discourse on issues affecting the environment. Knowledge derived from science, coupled with activism, played a major role in getting governments to endorse the Declaration of the United Nations Conference on the Human Environment in Stockholm in June 1972.[2] It was at this conference that governments accepted that anthropogenic impacts on the environment were a reality and that more research was needed to understand the causes, impacts, and mitigation measures. Since that time, we have had subsequent international environmental engagements that rely on scientific knowledge to guide activism, decision-making, and policy development.

The 1990s brought the digital revolution. Data generation and exchange became easier, and, by 1996, the internet had become mainstream, allowing for easy digitisation and the dissemination of data. Environmental data became easier to acquire and to share. Although access to environmental data, information, and knowledge is not a recent phenomenon, over time the emphasis for open access has shifted from information and knowledge as products to include the underlying elements: the data that comprises these products.

Environmental concerns are all-encompassing, ranging from microbial research through to large planetary weather systems research. Open data provides an opportunity to promote review, transparency, accountability, participation, and the identification of knowledge gaps. The growth in environmental open data portals to support research, advocacy, decision-making, and communication indicates the importance of sharing data on a range of environmental issues.

Earth, air, and water

The following sections present an overview of the progress on open data in relation to four key environmental domains: climate change, air quality, biodiversity, and water resources.

Open data and climate change

Known research into climate change can be traced back to 1824, when Joseph Fourier[3] noted the warming of the Earth. In the 1890s, Swedish scientist Svante Arrhenius[4] made the connection between carbon dioxide and rising temperatures, the "greenhouse effect". It took another century of research, publications, and advocacy before the issue secured global attention.

The Intergovernmental Panel on Climate Change (IPCC) has achieved great success in putting climate change on the international political agenda and ensuring that almost every national government is paying attention to the issue. The data underpinning IPCC research comes from various open sources, and there are robust processes in place to ensure data integrity. The transformation of statistical climate data into easily digestible visuals through data visualisation, such as maps, also helped convey the importance of the issue to the general public (see Figure 1). The IPCC Fourth Assessment Report provided credible evidence to gain the necessary political traction;[5] however, the identification of "major errors" in the main report had some sceptics questioning its veracity. The greatest error related to the incorrect referencing of 2035 as the date by which the Himalayan glaciers will have melted; however, a correction was made after a review of the source data, and the date estimate was changed to 2350.[6] Other perceived "errors" were not actual errors, but rather questions regarding the validity of including content that had not been peer reviewed.

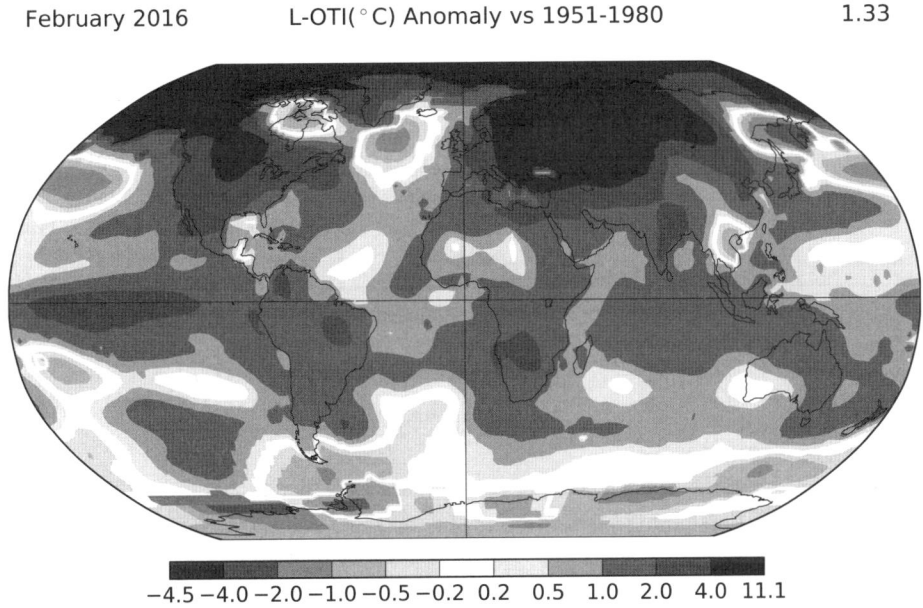

Figure 1: Data visualisation is a powerful tool to interpret complex climate data and make it accessible to a wider audience. In this image, NASA uses visualisation to illustrate temperature departures from the average during February 2016.
Source: IMAGE:NASA GISS

The 4th IPCC Assessment Report

The main criticism of the 4th IPCC Assessment Report has been that errors can be attributed to the referencing of non-peer reviewed literature, such as a World Wide Fund for Nature report, as well as various grey literature. The outcome of the criticism has had two positive effects: 1) the correction of the errors and 2) refinement in the process and structures to review data to support any claims the IPCC makes. In an open data environment, robust and well-documented data management processes are essential for credibility.

Due to the political, economical, and social visibility, as well as the importance of climate change research, a number of open data platforms have been created as detailed in Table 1, which also demonstrate various levels of open data licensing.

Table 1: Open data platforms to access climate-related data

Name	Year launched	Core focus	Data licence
IPCC Data Distribution Centre http://www.ipcc-data.org	1998	To facilitate the timely distribution of a set of consistent up-to-date scenarios of changes in climate and related environmental and socio-economic factors for use in climate impact and adaptation assessment.	OECD Principle of "openness"
World Bank Climate Change Knowledge Portal http://sdwebx.worldbank.org/climateportal/	2010	Hub for climate information	Various CC licences
Southern African Science Service Centre for Climate Change and Adaptive Land Management http://www.sasscal.org/	2012	To host, safeguard, and make data and information resources available openly, yet ensure the integrity and ownership of the contributing parties.	Open access to data (incl. climate change and weather data) for southern Africa.
European Union Copernicus Climate Data Store https://climate.copernicus.eu	2018	The Copernicus Climate Change Service (C3S) will combine observations of the climate system with the latest science to develop authoritative, quality-assured information about the past, current, and future states of the climate in Europe and worldwide.	Free of charge, worldwide, non-exclusive, royalty free, and perpetual.

Climate change open data portals present one of the best case studies of how open access to data, and the resulting scientific and advocacy collaborations, has led to a major shift in public understanding of science-backed policy and to large financial investments in further research and mitigation. Although data on the monetary investment and outcomes of mitigation measures is more limited, highlighting a gap still to be filled, a number of projects are now tracking climate-related financing. The National Determined Contributions Explorer aims to publish national climate change mitigation plans and data on progress as the means to hold governments accountable.[7] Transparency International (TI) also publishes data on the use of global funds to tackle climate change impacts,[8] noting that the amount pledged by national governments will be running at USD 100 billion per year by 2020, and set to increase over time. TI has also been exploring the adoption of the Open Contracting Data Standard to ensure transparency and accountability in the contracting chain for climate-related finances.[9]

Open data and air quality

Air pollution has been an historical concern since the industrial revolution. However, it was only in the 1970s that scientists made the link between air pollution and its impact on human health. It was also during this decade that the United States and the United Kingdom started to implement regulations to curb air pollution. Today, policy-makers rely heavily on air quality data to inform policy review and development.

Air quality monitoring requires the implementation and management of monitoring stations, which may take the form of real-time digital instrumentation or manually monitored diffusion tubes. While governments often collate and publish this data, the 2016/2017 Global Open Data Index ranks the openness of air quality data by national governments as very low with only 8% of governments sharing air quality data as accessible open data.[10] However, several initiatives are now working to aggregate and analyse air quality monitoring from around the world.

The World Air Quality Index (WAQI), created in 2007 by a team in Beijing, provides access to open air quality information from more than 10 000 stations in 800 cities from 70 countries.[11] Only data on particulate matter of PM2.5/PM10 and greater from official government or professionally maintained measuring stations is published.[12] This data is validated through neighbourhood and historical comparisons. The data from this platform conforms to the data requirements for reporting on the Sustainable Development Goal (SDG) health-related indicators,[13] and is, therefore, able to inform government policy and support SDG reporting obligations.

The OpenAQ initiative also aggregates data from government monitoring stations and is exploring the inclusion of data from citizen-run low-cost sensors. With a strong open source and open data ethos, and an emphasis on permanently archiving data, the project is a key example of data being used to influence people's behaviour and government action.[14]

Both OpenAQ and WAQI offer maps of the sensor networks they draw upon. A cursory glance at these reveals a dearth of measuring stations in Africa. This is supported by research conducted by Wetsman[15] that notes South Africa is the only country in Africa with an air-quality monitoring programme. The map (Figure 2) below illustrates the global distribution. The lack of data collection and open data in certain regions will, therefore, negatively impact research and mitigation-related actions. Future work in this sector will have to focus on extending measures to collect data from more locations in developing countries.

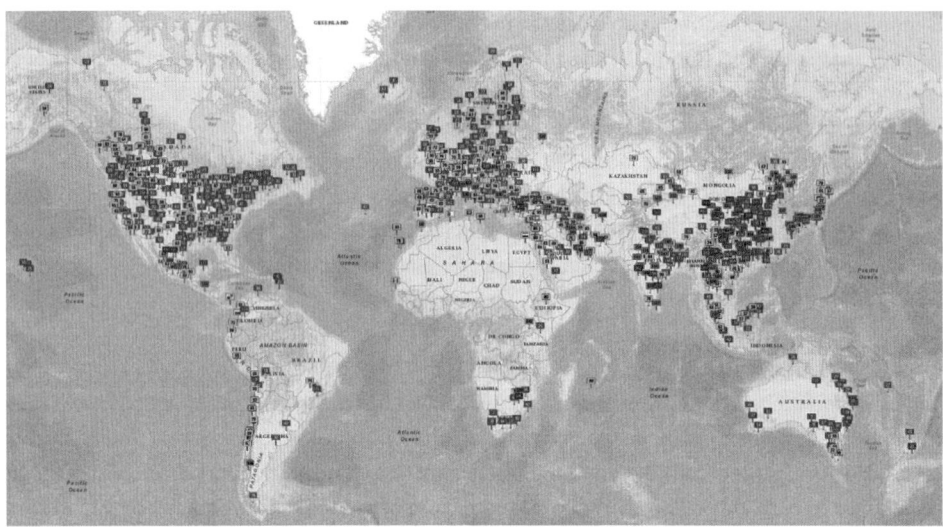

Figure 2: Distribution of air quality monitoring stations sharing data via the WAQI portal
Source: https://waqi.info/

Open data and biodiversity

Biodiversity is about the variety of life on earth. Typically, biodiversity data covers genetics through to landscapes and all the floral and faunal species in between. Many open data sources exist, ranging from the Biodiversity Heritage Library (BHL) and the Encyclopaedia of Life (EoL) to the Global Biodiversity Information Facility (GBIF). As an example, GBIF collates and shares over 1 billion biodiversity records from more than 1 400 institutions, covering the globe.[16] Figure 3 illustrates an extract from the GBIF portal of the available open biodiversity data for Niger where the 83 449 recorded occurrences contribute toward this resource. The general conclusion is that data collections on biodiversity held at the local, regional, and international level are vast and very often made available under open access licences.

While these datasets may be valuable at a local level or thematic scale, it is in the connectedness of this data that the true value is found. The ultimate goal of this data is to answer overarching questions on ecological interactions and interdependencies within the biotic and abiotic environment at different scales. This can create major challenges for data-sharing infrastructures, requiring systems, standards, and collaborative mechanisms to enable the discovery of data and to manage information on provenance. Many initiatives, such as the Biodiversity and Protected Areas Management Programme (BIOPAMA),[17] are now actively integrating the collation and collection of data into their project designs to encourage open data sharing. Funders are also playing an important role in creating funding conditions to share data. For example, the JRS Biodiversity Foundation[18] and many other grant-making agencies are including conditional clauses to enforce the free sharing of data collected as the result of grant funding.

Generally, the biodiversity community has self-organised to limit the overlap in data collection and management. Accordingly, organisations, such the Internal Union for the Conservation of

Nature, BirdLife, and the World Conservation Monitoring Centre, have adopted specific focus areas for the type of biodiversity data collected as part of their project work, assessments, and other related activities. These organisations also play a very important role in supporting national reporting obligations toward the Aichi Biodiversity Targets[19] and the SDGs.[20] It is important to note that not all biodiversity data is considered to be open data. BirdLife International, for example, has protocols that restrict access to certain bird data that it deems sensitive, such as nesting sites. The aim is to protect species from local or even global extinction as a result of poaching, illegal hunting, collection, or intrusive behaviour.

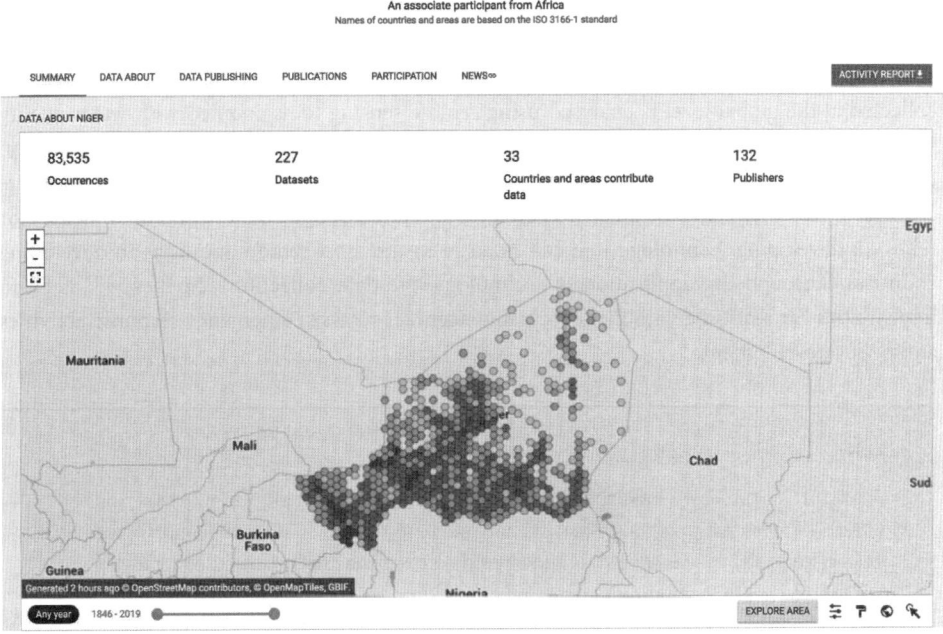

Figure 3:   An example of a biodiversity dataset available on the GBIF portal. Data is aggregated from many different sources and openly shared.
Source: https://www.gbif.org/country/NE/summary

Open data and water

Water is a basic human need, and access to clean water is becoming a major global concern. Climate change has had a significant impact on rainfall patterns, most notably in Sub-Saharan Africa. Changing rainfall patterns, coupled with poor management of existing water supplies, pose major livelihood challenges to millions of people. Those most affected by the lack of clean water are women and children in developing countries.[21]

The water sector has a fair number of dedicated data portals. The United Nations Educational, Scientific and Cultural Organization (UNESCO) has recently launched[22] the Water Data Quality

Portal to provide access to related global datasets.[23] The Global Environment Monitoring System for freshwater (GEMS/Water) provides data on fresh water quality intended to support scientific assessments and decision-making related to water management.[24] Sharing Water-related Information to Tackle Changes in the Hydrosphere - for Operational Needs (SWITCH-ON), a European Union (EU) initiative, provides access to water-related information to assist in managing water in a sustainable manner.[25] The International Water Management Institute's Water Data Portal provides access to global water-related information.[26] The European Commission, using Google Earth Engine, has developed the Global Surface Water Explorer, which maps the location and temporal distribution of surface water for the period 1984–2015.[27] Given the many available data portals, it is interesting to note that the Global Open Data Index[28] still ranks the openness of water quality data from national governments as very low with just 1% of index surveys able to access open data on water quality direct from governments.

Access to clean water is an immediate and critical concern. This is especially true in rural areas, where water contamination can affect human lives, livestock, and crops. The data currently collected at the global level is analysed using remote sensing tools coupled with water quality information obtained from available sensors. The challenge ahead will be to expand the collection of water quality information, using the power of technology to immediately communicate changes in water provision or quality. Therefore, the future of open data within the water sector relies on developing technology that can be used in the most remote locations in developing countries. Through the application of technology, the data collection activities will need to improve to near real-time with higher levels of accuracy to assist emergency response activities and policy development.

Cape Town drought

Since 2015, Cape Town has experienced an unprecedented drought, leading to serious water shortages. Although many causes have been postulated, and blame apportioned, defensible evidence was sought to understand whether the crisis was caused by less rainfall, increased evaporation, increased agricultural and urban use, or poor management. A study by the Climate Systems Analysis Group at the University of Cape Town, using open data, found the main cause of the water crisis to be a result of low rainfall between 2015 and 2017.[29,30]

Open datasets were used to create two separate maps to analyse the temporal levels of the Theewaterskloof Dam, the largest water source in Cape Town. Figure 4 shows that the dam levels were fairly constant for the period 1984–2015. Figure 5 illustrates the rapid decline of water volumes between 2016 and 2018. These two different datasets, using different visualisation techniques, complement the UCT study that found exceptional low levels of rainfall since 2015 had resulted in the water crisis.

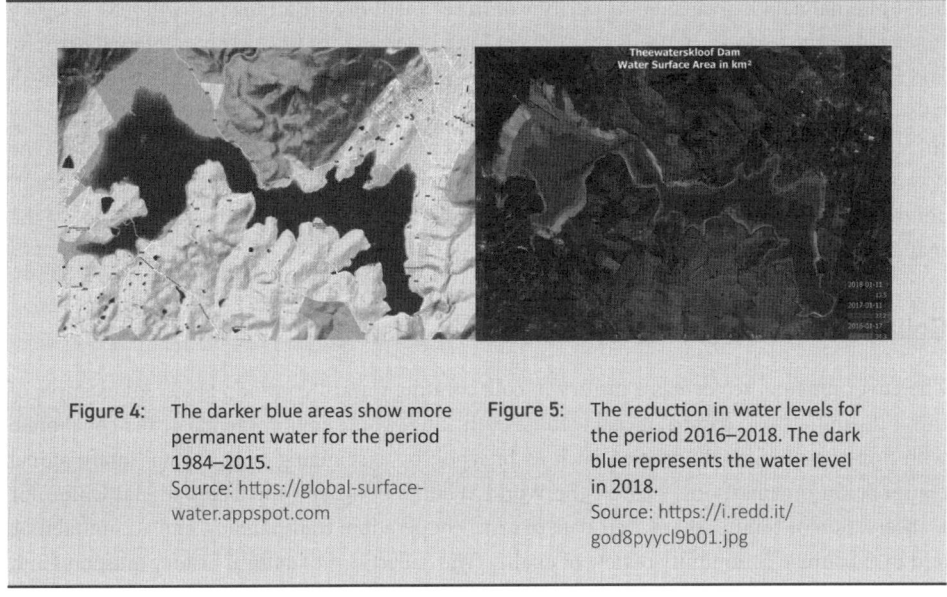

Figure 4: The darker blue areas show more permanent water for the period 1984–2015.
Source: https://global-surface-water.appspot.com

Figure 5: The reduction in water levels for the period 2016–2018. The dark blue represents the water level in 2018.
Source: https://i.redd.it/god8pyycl9b01.jpg

Opportunities and challenges

Stakeholders and sustainability

Governments, civil society, business, and academia are the four major groups driving the environmental open data agenda. Governments have been changing policies and legislation to support open data,[31] mostly as the result of pressure from civil society and academia. Traditionally, business is an active user of open data, but is not widely known for the release of open data.

Keeping open data portals open requires resources. Wealthier countries typically fund their own environmental open data initiatives; however, for developing countries, continuous access to open data is very much dependent on available funding to generate, curate, and publish datasets. Typical major funding sources include the World Bank, the United Nations, the Global Environmental Facility (GEF), bilateral foreign aid, and many private donors. This presents a particular challenge for emerging economies, where data management is linked to project-based funding and the data becomes "lost" or "orphaned" after a project has been completed. Therefore, the true value of the new data is not realised and the investment is not able to generate ongoing value. New projects then re-invest in data collection, often collecting the same or similar data, and the cycle repeats itself.

The pathway to sustainable data management practices must be multi-pronged and not rely on any single approach. To be successful in the long-term, the management of open datasets will require investment from host agencies in the form of money or in-kind resourcing, such as staff, infrastructure, or content. It is also important that donor funding be moulded to support the needs of the specific country or agency and to ensure that data collection and management is not responding solely to short-term donor agendas. The funding model used must be structured to build internal data management capacity within recipient organisations that will have a legacy impact after the temporary needs of a project have been met. In this manner, internal capacity and resources can be developed over time as the result of donor support. Importantly, a fresh take on the role of the private sector is also needed in order to evaluate how it can enhance the shared value of public datasets used by business as a means to contribute to the public good. One way is for private sector data users to return enhanced datasets to governments for publication; another approach is for the private sector to provide expertise and infrastructure to support the management and publication of data.

Collaboration, cooperation, and benefit sharing

The environmental sector has a history of collaborating toward common goals. An example of this is the initiative to combat illegal wildlife trafficking, where environmental actors collaborate with non-environmental agencies, such as Interpol, by exchanging critical data. International conservation organisations, such as the World Wildlife Fund and the International Union for Conservation of Nature, share their data to drive cooperation, transparency, and accountability, and to encourage community review of quality. The collections of natural history museums and herbaria are being digitised and placed in the public domain with the aim of the data being used to aid conservation and management.

Collaborations like these can also be extended to the management of open data. The Atlas of Living Australia[32] is an international leader in publishing collated open biodiversity data with more than 76 million records made freely available from 311 different data providers. Citizen science is becoming very popular and it is also adding volumes of data to established scientific collections. Through collaboration, environmental organisations are able to secure a range of benefits, including shared skills, experts, and infrastructure.

Innovation: Cybertracker

The award winning Cybertracker[33] app was created to provide the indigenous Kalahari San with technology to capture complex field data. The technology has been developed to be intuitive and to allow non-literate people to record data and knowledge for scientific conservation and management applications.

Source: http://www.sablenetwork.com/inspirations/classic/8

Indigenous knowledge, knowledge passed on from one generation to the next, can advance scientific research and improve the public image of science. However, this type of knowledge is often viewed as "unscientific" although it is the basis upon which we built our existing scientific knowledge. Ironically, we have seen the appropriation and exploitation of Indigenous knowledge on the use of plant-based natural resources by multinational corporations: a phenomenon known as biopiracy.[34] The World Intellectual Property Organization is currently working on international legal instruments to protect Indigenous knowledge and ensure appropriate benefit sharing.[35]

Many new companies have been established using public open data. As noted earlier, the private sector is an active user of public data, and the potential exists to create valuable public–private partnerships to further advance the private sector as a contributor of open data. Recognising the value of sharing data as the means to stimulate innovation and build positive public relations, the private sector is becoming more transparent. While the overall open data market value is projected to be in the region of € 286 billion by 2020,[36] the exact potential value of open environmental data is not known. However, it is reasonable to assume that the value of this open data is significant. In 2013, the Climate Corporation, a private company built on open climate data to support farming decisions, was sold for USD 1.1 billion to Monsanto, a multinational agricultural company.

Further evidence on the use of environmental data in the private sector comes from the Open Data 500 project,[37] which provides information on private companies using government open data through studies in six countries. The project seeks to map the economic and social impact of government open data by looking at the businesses using it. Figure 6 illustrates the number of businesses per country in the environment and weather sector. Canada tops the list with 45 businesses, followed by Italy (24) and Korea (16).

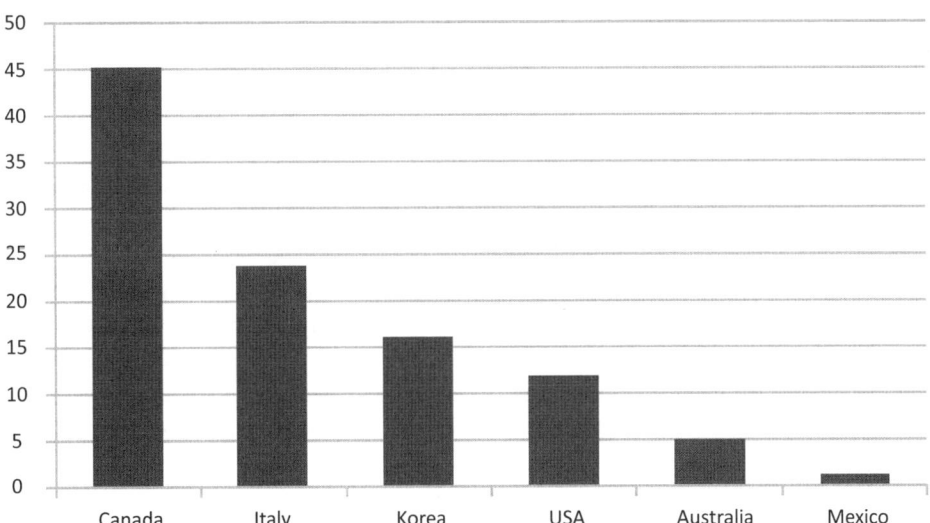

Figure 6: Number of private companies in the environment and weather sector using open access government data as an integral part of their business model and as a tool to generate new business
Source: www.opendata500.com. See the Open Data 500 website for more details.

Standards

Standards are necessary to define acceptable quality metrics for data, ensure consistent use, and to facilitate data sharing. The lack of common standards negatively impacts the credibility, use, and exchange of data across the environmental sector.

While environmental data collection has become easier, the development and maintenance of metadata has become increasingly laborious; however, without metadata, the value of the data erodes and data interoperability becomes extremely difficult. Making environmental data interoperable creates the capacity to share data and important indicators across systems regardless of geographic boundary, vendor, or organisation, but this requires consistent adherence to standardised metadata, ontologies, and vocabularies for the description and organisation of the data. The Committee on Data (CODATA) of the International Council of Science, established in 1966, is actively working toward coordinating data standards among scientific unions at the international level and has made major steps in embedding open data principles in their work.[38]

Capacity

The lack of skills, expertise, and equipment within governments needed to meaningfully exploit the vast quantities of available environmental open data is also a major constraint in addressing environmental challenges, especially in developing countries. It is widely noted that developing countries will be the most impacted by climate change with one (proprietary) index of climate change vulnerability identifying the Central African Republic, the Democratic Republic of the Congo, Haiti, Liberia, and South Sudan as facing the greatest risks.[39] Many developing countries are also home to vast natural resources that are under the pressure of exploitation or destruction. These very countries are under social and political pressure to protect their natural resources while simultaneously under economic pressure to grow their economy.

Providing capacity building for developing countries has been on the developmental agenda for many years and has taken the form of institutional, individual, and infrastructural interventions. Very often, capacity development has been focused on the needs of donor-funded projects, limited to the funding period or conditions and not structured around government-led interventions that can sustain impact. Linked to this technical capacity constraint are the political challenges that face institutions intending to make environmental data openly accessible. For example, the Government of Tanzania has recently withdrawn from the Open Government Partnership.[40] The systemic impact of this decision is to further limit disclosure of data into the public domain, restricting capacity development in publishing data, hindering innovation in using open data, and limiting potential private sector expansion using open data.

Generally, although substantial expertise exists within the research community, the broader environmental sector, including government and civil society actors, is lagging behind in terms of applied data management expertise. This has a profound effect on the quality, quantity, access, and frequency of data that can be released as open data, and further frustrates attempts to use data to mitigate environmental damage and the negative impacts of climate change.

Conclusion

Open data plays a crucial role in advancing our collective efforts to ensure sustainable management of all our natural resources. It has fostered collaboration that would not have been possible 30 years ago. It has allowed scientists to review the veracity of their work and hold them accountable for their conclusions, as it does politicians for their decisions. Furthermore, it has also supported instances of greater civil participation in the public and private sector spheres with the potential to give poor and marginalised people greater power through knowledge. Open data has also helped to drive the development of innovative products and services, not only in developed countries, but also in developing countries, addressing issues of environmental conservation, skills development, and economic growth. Overall, open data has shown revolutionary potential, although the measurement of impact remains difficult.

However, there is still much effort needed to ensure that environmental data becomes fully accessible to address environmental challenges. The advancement of the environmental open data agenda must happen at both the macro and micro levels. At the macro level, changes are necessary on an institutional scale to challenge closed governments to open their data. The collaboration between thematic sectors must be encouraged to avoid data duplication and gaps, as well as to maximise the value of open data. A coherent and collaborative approach must be adopted to address data gaps, specifically in developing countries. These gaps can be filled through adopting vendor and 'donor agnostic' data management systems, integrating data sharing agreements for funded programmes, and establishing formal data sharing programmes with the private sector without compromising personal information or trade secrets. The development of case studies is a powerful mechanism to encourage sharing as it can illustrate effective processes and the value of open data.

At the micro level, institutions should develop formal or structured data management strategies that can proactively lead to open data. Data management strategies must always be focused on organisational needs and address standards, quality, applications, and capacity building.

Environmental open data has helped shape national and international policies and decisions. Notwithstanding the challenges of getting governments and private sector entities to share data, the volume of open data is increasing. Our task is to ensure that the release of environmental open data is needs-based, user friendly, and of sufficient quality to address the local, regional, and global challenges in developing a sustainable future.

Further reading

EC (European Commission). (2013). Sharing water-related information to tackle changes in the hydrosphere – for operational needs. https://cordis.europa.eu/project/rcn/110496/factsheet/en

Hobern, D., Apostolico, A., Arnaud, E., Bello, J.C., Canhos, D., Dubois, G., Field, D., Alonso Garcia, E., Hardisty, A., Harrison, J., Heidorn, B., Krishtalka, L., Mata, E., Page, R., Parr, C., Price, J., & Willoughby, S. (2013). *Delivering biodiversity knowledge in the Information Age*. Copenhagen: Global Biodiversity Information Facility. http://orca.cf.ac.uk/71243/1/GBIO.pdf

Schmidt, B., Gemeinholzer, B., & Treloar, A. (2016). Open data in global environmental research: The belmont forum's open data survey. *PLOS ONE, 11(1)*. https://doi.org/10.1371/journal.pone.0146695

Transparency International. (2018). Climate Adaptation Finance Governance Standards: A new approach piloted in the Maldives and Bangladesh. Berlin: Transparency International. https://www.transparency.org/whatwedo/publication/climate_adaptation_finance_governance_standards

Wetsman, N. (2018). Air-pollution trackers seek to fill Africa's data gap. *Nature, 556*, 284. https://www.nature.com/magazine-assets/d41586-018-04330-x/d41586-018-04330-x.pdf

About the author

Selwyn Willoughby is an international information strategist with over 20 years of experience in the environment and conservation sector. He is the Director of the data advisory company, Information by Design, and a Fellow of the South African National Biodiversity Institute (SANBI). You can follow Selwyn at https://www.twitter.com/selwynwill and get more information about his work at https://www.infobydesign.co.za.

How to cite this chapter

Willoughby, S. (2019). Open data and the environment. In T. Davies, S. Walker, M. Rubinstein, & F. Perini (Eds.), *The state of open data: Histories and horizons* (pp. 103–118). Cape Town and Ottawa: African Minds and International Development Research Centre. http://stateofopendata.od4d.net

This work is licensed under a Creative Commons Attribution 4.0 International (CC BY 4.0) licence. It was carried out with the aid of a grant from the International Development Research Centre, Ottawa, Canada.

Endnotes

1. PBS (Public Broadcasting Service). (2014). A fierce green fire: Timeline of environmental movement and history. *American Masters*, 15 April. http://www.pbs.org/wnet/americanmasters/a-fierce-green-fire-timeline-of-environmental-movement/2988/
2. UN (United Nations). (1972). Declaration of the United Nations Conference on the Human Environment. Stockholm, 5–16 June 1972. http://www.un-documents.net/unchedec.htm
3. Bell, A. (2014). A very short history of climate change research. *Road to Paris*, 5 September. http://roadtoparis.info/2014/09/05/history-climate-change-research/
4. Pralle, S.B. (2009). Agenda-setting and climate change. *Environmental Politics*, 18(5), 781–799. http://www.tandfonline.com/doi/full/10.1080/09644010903157115
5. Nuccitelli, D. (2013). IPCC model global warming projections have done much better than you think. *The Guardian*, 1 October. https://www.theguardian.com/environment/climate-consensus-97-per-cent/2013/oct/01/ipcc-global-warming-projections-accurate
6. RealClimate. (2010). IPCC errors: Facts and spin. 14 February. http://www.realclimate.org/index.php/archives/2010/02/ipcc-errors-facts-and-spin/
7. Rateng, B. (2017). Using data visualisation to track climate change. *OpenLearn*, 1 August. https://www.open.edu/openlearn/nature-environment/environmental-studies/using-data-visualisation-track-climate-change
8. TI (Transparency International). (2015). Clean finance for a clean planet. https://www.transparency.org/whatwedo/activity/clean_finance_for_a_clean_planet
9. TI. (2018). *Safeguarding climate finance procurement: National-level procurement of the Green Climate Fund*. Nairobi: Transparency International. http://files.transparency.org/content/download/2236/13961/file/2018_Report_NationalProcurementGCF_English.pdf
10. https://index.okfn.org/dataset/emissions/
11. http://aqicn.org/sources/
12. http://aqicn.org/here/
13. Lim, S.S., Allen, K., Bhutta, Z.A., Dandona, L., Forouzanfar, M.H., Fullman, N., Gething, P.W. et al. (2016). Measuring the health-related Sustainable Development Goals in 188 countries: A Baseline analysis from the global burden of disease study 2015. *The Lancet*, 388(10053), 1813–1850. https://doi.org/10.1016/S0140-6736(16)31467-2
14. https://openaq.org
15. Wetsman, N. (2018). Air-pollution trackers seek to fill Africa's data gap. *Nature*, 556, 284. https://www.nature.com/magazine-assets/d41586-018-04330-x/d41586-018-04330-x.pdf
16. GBIF. (2018). Big data for biodiversity: GBIF.Org surpasses 1 billion species occurrences. *Global Biodiversity Information Facility* [News post], 6 July. https://www.gbif.org/news/5BesWzmwqQ4U84suqWyOQy/big-data-for-biodiversity-gbiforg-surpasses-1-billion-species-occurrences
17. http://www.biopama.org/
18. http://jrsbiodiversity.org/
19. CBD (Convention on Biological Diversity). (2010). Aichi biodiversity targets. https://www.cbd.int/sp/targets/
20. Brooks, T.M., Butchart, S.H.M., Cox, N.A., Heath, M., Hilton-Taylor, C., Hoffmann, M., Kingston, N., Rodríguez, J.P., Stuart, S.N., & Smart, J. (2015). Harnessing biodiversity and conservation knowledge products to track the Aichi targets and sustainable development goals. *Biodiversity*, 16(2–3), 157–174. https://doi.org/10.1080/14888386.2015.1075903
21. http://wholives.org/our-mission/mission/
22. UNESCO (United Nations Educational, Scientific and Cultural Organization). (2018). UNESCO launches a pioneering tool to monitor water quality. https://en.unesco.org/news/unesco-launches-pioneering-tool-monitor-water-quality
23. http://www.worldwaterquality.org/

24 https://gemstat.org/
25 http://www.water-switch-on.eu/
26 http://waterdata.iwmi.org/
27 https://global-surface-water.appspot.com
28 https://index.okfn.org/dataset/water
29 Wolski, P. (2018). Drivers of Cape Town's water shortage. *Climate Systems Analysis Group* [Blog post], 18 July. http://www.csag.uct.ac.za/2018/07/18/drivers-of-cape-town-water-shortage/
30 CPI (Centre for Public Impact). (2018). Impact insight: Cape Town water crisis. https://www.centreforpublicimpact.org/impact-insight-cape-town-water-crisis/?gclid=EAIaIQobChMI-L36IKb13wIVRbnACh1xuQGnEAAYASAAEgJjT_D_BwE
31 High-level Group for Partnership, Coordination and Capacity-Building for Statistics. (2017). Cape Town Global Action Plan for Sustainable Development data. United Nations Data Forum, 15 January. https://undataforum.org/WorldDataForum/wp-content/uploads/2017/01/Cape-Town-Action-Plan-For-Data-Jan2017.pdf
32 https://dashboard.ala.org.au/
33 https://www.cybertracker.org
34 IPW. (2016). Drawn out battle over genetic resources dampens Africa's hopes. *Intellectual Property Watch* [News post], 27 April. http://www.ip-watch.org/2016/04/27/drawn-out-battle-over-genetic-resources-dampens-africas-hopes/
35 WIPO. (2015). *The WIPO Intergovernmental Committee on Intellectual Property and Genetic Resources, Traditional Knowledge and Folklore: Background Brief*. Geneva: World Intellectual Property Organization. https://www.wipo.int/edocs/pubdocs/en/wipo_pub_tk_2.pdf
36 UrbanTide. (2016). Open data – is the open private sector the next frontier? *UrbanTide* [Blog post], 24 October. https://urbantide.com/fullstory2/2016/10/24/open-data-is-the-open-private-sector-the-next-frontier
37 http://www.opendata500.com
38 http://www.codata.org
39 Maplecroft. (2016). Climate Change Vulnerability Index 2017. World (Infographic). *ReliefWeb,* [Report], 14 November. https://reliefweb.int/report/world/climate-change-vulnerability-index-2017
40 Open Government Partnership. https://www.opengovpartnership.org/participants

008

Extractives

Anders Pedersen

Key points

- During the last decade, data has rapidly become more available across the extractives sector. Civil society, researchers, and journalists have responded by finding new ways to examine natural resource revenues, locations, production statistics, and corporate filings, drawing on data which, until recently, was only available to the companies involved or locked up in databases of proprietary data providers.

- The Extractives Industry Transparency Initiative (EITI) adopted an Open Data Policy in 2015 and has since introduced a database of revenue payments for its 51 members, demonstrating a shared view that open data can serve as an enabler of accountability.[1]

- Open data principles have also been gaining traction within government-led extractive industry reporting regimes, including requirements to submit structured and standardised data. However, experience shows that unless reporting as data is made mandatory, companies prefer to provide unstructured PDFs.

- New extractives open data has, in some cases, allowed for vibrant and timely evidence-based debate on taxation in resource-rich countries, offering a public space for review of various public policy options. However, it is important that analysis, journalism, and evidence-based advocacy reaches policy-makers in order for it to achieve lasting impact.

Introduction

Since the 1990s, academics, civil society organisations (CSOs), and multilateral institutions have paid increasing attention to the impact of oil, gas, and mining operations on human development in resource-rich countries. The apparent paradox that abundant natural resources have not, in many countries, translated into economic growth and human development[2] has sparked considerable work toward shining a light on how extractive industries operate. Questions of policy and taxation, of the local impact of extractive operations, and of governance and corruption, have all found their way onto the agenda.

At the start of this millennium, substantial international advocacy efforts toward greater transparency for the extractives sector started to make up ground with the creation of the Extractives Industry Transparency Initiative (EITI), Revenue Watch Institute (RWI), which later merged with the Natural Resource Charter to form the Natural Resources Governance Institute (NRGI) in 2013, and the Publish What You Pay (PWYP) global coalition among others. A focus on the disclosure of information about payments made from extractives companies to governments and on contracts and concessions have led, over the last 15 years, to a number of new legal disclosure requirements, national-level multi-stakeholder partnerships, and voluntary disclosure schemes. In the last few years, these reforms have started to yield new flows of documents, and, in some cases, open data.

However, persistent problems of unequal access to data and poor data quality in the extractives sector are far from solved, and it has long been acknowledged that a lack of accessible data affects everyone from grassroots civil society groups and national anti-corruption watchdogs through to multilateral institutions engaged in economic planning. This chapter will examine how stakeholders in the extractives sector have engaged with open data over the last decade, working in parallel to secure incremental policy change on data publication and to put the data that is already available to use. It will also explore how the broad community of practice around open extractives data has supported a cross-pollination of ideas and research methods, helping to break down silos between different development disciplines and to more rapidly facilitate informed and evidence-based debate.

Driving context-specific use: Open Jade Data Myanmar

OpenJadeData.org[3] is a public data portal launched by the Natural Resource Governance Institute (NGRI) in May 2018. The site, available in English and Burmese, aims to support engagement with new datasets on Myanmar's Jade trade. It has three main objectives: provide clean, collated data on jade to be used for further analysis; allow users to visualise the information with an online tool; and help users to dive deeper into some of the prevalent issues related to the jade industry through original "data stories". Each feature was developed with input from users in Myanmar and developed with different audiences and skills levels in mind, including researchers, journalists, and interested members of the general public.[4]

So far, the portal features stories re-examining estimates of the size of the Jade industry, highlighting the lack of accurate data on the scale of the sector with estimates ranging from USD 5 to USD 31 billion.[5,6]

Another clear goal of the portal is to support ongoing efforts of the government and civil society groups to increase transparency and conduct regular analysis of the jade sector. NRGI describes the portal as "focused on jade, at the moment, since it has become one of the symbols of Myanmar's inextricable political-economic situation which links a precious natural resource worth billions of dollars annually – and characterised by illegal trade and a huge amount of uncollected potential state revenues – with domestic conflicts and the peace process; as well as environmental and social disasters and unregulated, mass migration of workers with no safety regulations. Addressing the multiple challenges faced by the jade sector could be one of the best proofs that the 2015 elections and the consecutive National League for Democracy government are really ushering in a new era for Myanmar's politics and economy."[7]

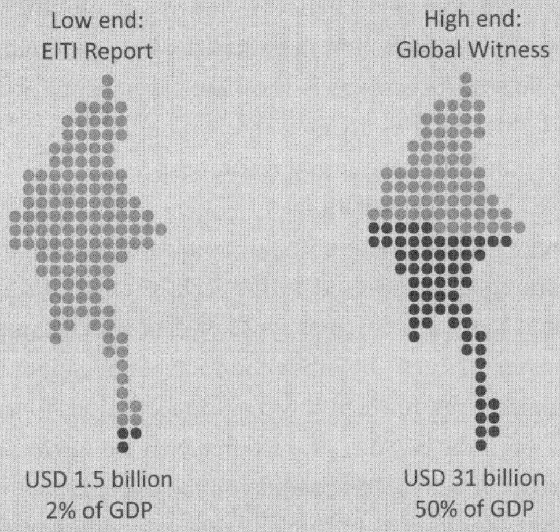

Low end: EITI Report	High end: Global Witness
USD 1.5 billion 2% of GDP	USD 31 billion 50% of GDP

Figure 1: Data story showing estimates of the size of the Jade trade in Myanmar
Source: https://openjadedata.org/Stories/how_much_jade_worth.html

Improving disclosure: Toward open data by default

Understanding the extractive sector requires data. A country's fiscal regimes provide detailed rules on how oil and minerals can be extracted, how extracted resources will be priced, the deductible costs for extractors, and how revenues are to be collected.[8] Further rules and environmental regulations regarding where and how extraction can take place are mapped through mining cadastre datasets. Information on the companies, corporate structures, the public–private partnerships involved, and the mechanisms through which they are financed, can only be understood through data analysis. Global commodity traders manage the transfer of oil, gas, and minerals around the world using complex data systems.

Although transparency efforts in the extractives industry in the early 2000s were focused primarily on the publication of documents ready to be checked and reconciled through an audit process, by the start of this decade, there was an increasing emphasis on disclosure in the form of data. This coincides with the emergence of the open data movement on the global stage, marking the extractives transparency sector as an early adopter of open data methodologies.

Notably, work on transparency in the extractives sector has focused as much on requiring the private sector to open up data as it has on opening up government data. PWYP has described how this framing was a strategic choice, noting that "At the time of the launch [of PWYP] there was little recourse at the global level to push for disclosure of revenues by resource-rich developing country governments", but "mechanisms to require disclosure by companies which are listed on stock exchanges and subject to accounting regulations were available and could be amended".[9] There is, within this work, an ambitious programme of re-imagining how a global market should function, with concerted work to rebalance the line between public and proprietary information. For some, this is simply a corrective action in a market where governance has not kept up with the globalised industry. For others, such as Berlin-based social enterprise OpenOil, launched in 2011 and operating under the tagline "imagine an open oil industry …",[10] there may be a deeper vision at play of transforming the way natural resources are managed and the role that policy-makers and citizens have in their exploitation.

As government agencies gain new data, both public and private, from companies, the attention of civil society and researchers has turned to the lack of cross-agency data sharing. Various government agencies tend to obtain different types of data which can all be of value when, for example, assessing tax payments and the other contractual obligations of companies. But if the data from different agencies is not brought together, opportunities to use it may be missed. In a survey of government officials in African resource-rich countries, OpenOil identified, in particular, that project costs, reserves, and production data were identified as areas where the gap between the perceived need for joined-up data and data availability was the most pronounced.[11] More research is necessary in order to determine the appropriate limits for how much data should be made public, but, in the meantime, models for data sharing between trusted agencies could be further advanced. In support of this, recent research in the mining sector noted that "Revenue authorities could improve their analysis of risks through sharing production data, findings from cost audits, mining agreements, and information on beneficial owners as a matter of course rather than just before a tax audit."[12] Concretely, the African Tax Administration Forum has indicated that such work is being explored.[13]

Putting mandatory disclosure data in action

In 2010, President Obama signed into law the Dodd-Frank Act[14] with a provision (Section 1504) which requires extractives companies to report on their project-level payments to governments as part of official security filings. The European Union followed suit with the 2013 Accounting and Transparency Directive that was subsequently transposed into national law across Europe,[15] and, in Canada, the Extractive Sector Transparency Measures Act (ESTMA) was passed at the end of 2014.[16] Although a decision by the United States (US) Congress, under President Trump, to vacate the rules for Section 1504 of the Dodd-Frank Act means that disclosure from US-listed extractives companies is currently on hold, other countries are pushing forward with disclosure. Fifty-one EITI member countries have now agreed to provide project-level disclosure for the 2018 financial year in open data formats.[17]

Experiences to date demonstrate that the implementation of these mandatory disclosure regulations and processes have a large impact on how far the disclosures lead to machine-readable and user-friendly open data. In Canada, where more than 500 companies have disclosed payments data, companies can choose under the regulations to either publish machine-readable data in XLS format or to publish PDF documents which place a heavy processing burden on anyone wanting to carry out detailed analysis of the reports. For the fiscal year 2016–2017, only 27 company reports were provided in machine-readable XLS format, while 687 reports were provided in PDF format.[18] According to PricewaterhouseCoopers Canada (PwC), an auditing company, the share of company reports submitted with one or more deficiencies in company reports fell from 80% in the first year to 46% in the second year.[19] In the United Kingdom (UK), the company register, Companies House, has developed an application programming interface (API) for the digital submission of reports, attracting structured data reports from 115 companies for the financial year 2015–2016.[20] Working with this released data, PWYP has noted that "Despite its value and importance, [...] the quality of mandatory extractive company reporting to date indicates that improvement is needed in several areas",[21] highlighting the impact that definitions and disclosure formats defined in the regulations has on the data output. Gaining an agreement on global standards and infrastructures for joined-up extractives reporting to improve quality will be no small task.

Demonstrating the value of data

One of the key ways in which mandatory disclosure can be improved is by different actors making use of, and providing feedback on, data disclosures. This enables civil society to provide detailed technical feedback that can strengthen implementation of new disclosure processes during their critical early years. High-profile use cases demonstrating the value of disclosures are also important to overcome resistance to ongoing publication. For example, in 2017, PWYP France, Oxfam France, ONE, and Sherpa analysed payments from the uranium mining company, Areva, to the Government of Niger. They concluded that a contract renegotiated in 2014 had led to a substantial reduction in government revenue.[22] The same year, NRGI published an analysis of oil revenues in Ghana[23] and in Nigeria[24] demonstrating how, with better access to data, civil society can ask more precise questions of both national oil companies and the government.

It is important that data use can be sustained and that potential users of data are supported in navigating a complex data landscape. In 2018, PWYP in the UK conducted a detailed study of extractives disclosures,[25] and, Global Witness and Resources for Development Consulting published a guide for using mandatory disclosure data, highlighting both sources of data and the "red flags" to look for.[26] To facilitate the use of disparate data, NRGI also pioneered the development of the ResourceProjects.org data platform which collects, processes, and standardises mandatory disclosure data across jurisdictions, taking some of the hard work out of data access. At the time of writing, the ResourceProjects.org platform contains mandatory disclosures covering more than 18 000 payments from 747 reporting companies with payments worth more than USD 537 billion. The platform allows users to navigate disclosure data either by reporting by company or by country. By collating disclosures from across reporting jurisdictions, the platform reduces the complexity of acquiring the data for local civil society users, thus lowering barriers to using the data.

There is also evidence that governments are beginning to consider how to better engage citizens as data users, applying open source and human-centred design principles to support the dissemination of data. In the US, the US Digital Service helped to develop the US EITI data platform. Although the US withdrew from EITI in 2017,[27] EITI Multi-Stakeholder Group (MSG) of Germany adopted the same open source developed platform.[28] In the Philippines, the government has pursued local workshops to stimulate the use of data collected through the EITI process.[29]

The wider data landscape

Disclosures secured by regulations are not the only source of data becoming available on the extractives sector. There exists a much wider landscape of data collection with increasing efforts to standardise and align data. Data ranges from high-level economic statistics from institutions like the World Bank and International Centre for Tax and Development (ICTD)[30] to extractives data on revenues and contracts published by companies and governments. In some cases, the data narrowly focuses on extractives; however, in other cases, extractives-relevant data is drawn from wider data sources, such as corporate registries (see Chapter 3: Corporate ownership), satellite data (see Chapter 9: Geospatial), and trade statistics.

A key source of comparable data about extractives is EITI. Through its implementation in 51 countries, EITI has established multi-stakeholder-led processes for regular data collection on several topics, such as the production of extractives, revenues paid to governments, and licences issued. In the past, this information was largely captured in PDF reports, but EITI has, since 2016, maintained a database of country-level data. In 2018, this was followed by the release of a public API that provides a feed of more than 300 reporting years from EITI member states and USD 2 trillion in revenue payments.[31] In December 2015, EITI had already adopted an Open Data Policy, which, a year later, became part of the EITI Standard. This encourages the development of open-by-default systems and the use of unique identifiers to link data between years and reporting sources.[32] As a sign of growing interest, the World Bank published a comprehensive study in 2016 on how the extractives sector could leverage existing open data standards for new disclosures.[33]

Aligned reporting requirements are key to mapping revenue flows between datasets. Between 2014 and 2017, the International Monetary Fund (IMF) engaged in a series of country pilots to examine how revenue in resource-rich countries could be matched to their Government Finance Statistics Manual. Beyond the studies themselves, the result of this has been a crosswalk between EITI and IMF standards and a new standard data collection template for resource revenue data.[34]

EITI has also developed a strategy for "mainstreaming" transparency requirements within country data systems, recognising the importance of having government agencies in charge of collecting disaggregated revenue data and sketching out how new and existing information systems, including financial systems and cadastres, can be oriented toward the development of standardised open data using case studies from Kazakhstan, Timor-Leste, Norway, and Mongolia.[35]

Contracts, licences, and information on fiscal terms are increasingly recognised as critical building blocks for analysing the public long-term benefits of extractives projects. During the past few years, substantive improvements have occurred in the publishing practices of both major companies and governments.[36] A focus on contracts has also helped build links to other complex sectors, such as land, infrastructure, and private–public partnerships, and has offered opportunities to work systematically on improvements to open contracting.[37] However, key standards, such as the Open Contracting Data Standard (OCDS), are yet to be fully adapted to capture structured data on concessions and extractives contracts, meaning that extracting data from disclosed contract documents continues to rely heavily on civil society and researchers.

Commercial data providers have, during recent years, also served as key actors in the rapid digitisation of extractives records management within government, thanks, in particular, to international donor funding. Yet open data principles have often failed to materialise within these projects. For example, among funded mining cadastres in 15 Sub-Saharan African countries, none have, to date, published the underlying licensed data in open formats. These constraints make it more difficult for civil society to scrutinise the data.

However, one example of progress on open data among ICT system providers can be found in the Revenue Development Foundation (RDF), which facilitates the publication of mining licences and revenue data for government ministries with plans to provide a public API in the future.[38] RDF reports 5 000 registered users, of which 65% are from mining companies and investors, 8% are researchers, and another 8% are from civil society. To date, RDF has launched four public data portals across Sierra Leone, Liberia, Mali, and Ghana, tracking a total of 17 000 mining licences and 30 000 payments.[39]

In some cases, countries are going beyond the minimum requirements for disclosure. In Mexico, for example, the EITI MSG developed a data portal with input from civil society, making contracts, production data, and revenue data available to the public. In Myanmar, the EITI MSG expanded its disclosure of disaggregated data on the Jade trade, thus enabling new analysis which has achieved coverage in national media.[40] In the coming years, implementation of beneficial ownership registers will be a new critical data priority, following commitments made by members of EITI to include the publication of beneficial ownership information as open data by 2020.[41] In several countries, reforms are currently underway to establish the legal frameworks that will mandate beneficial ownership disclosure.

In looking at extractives, we should also not ignore forestry and agriculture. In 2017, the World Resources Institute (WRI) examined the transparency of logging, mining, and agricultural concession data in 14 countries. The WRI concluded that, while data disclosure varies significantly by country and sector, its quality is limited by the absence of internationally agreed upon data standards, stating that "civil society can be a significant source of concessions information where official data are unavailable".[42] The forestry sector has also been a major user of satellite data, working in partnership with academia to process global landsat data to detect changes in land use.[43]

Although there is a long way to go before all relevant extractives-related data is well-structured, standardised, and open by default, the sector can no longer be considered data-poor as NRGI's mapping of the data supply ecosystem illustrates, identifying over 35 repositories and databases for extractive sector open data.[44] The ways in which the sector has engaged with the available data is instructive both to understanding what can be done even when data gaps persist and also to identifying the most crucial areas for advocacy to further improve data supply.

> ### Measuring extractives governance
>
> Neither the Open Data Barometer, Open Data Index, nor the Open Data Inventory measure specific variables on extractives governance. However, a number of sector-specific projects are now tracking data availability and offer the chance to continuously monitor trends in the future.
>
> In 2017, the **Resource Governance Index (RGI)** launched the most comprehensive measurement of extractives governance to date, including assessments of 81 countries (accounting for 82% of the world's oil production and a significant proportion of mineral extraction).[45] A number of the questions assess availability and machine-readability of key disclosures, and the index itself has published raw data across all its 149 questions. The RGI has also provided almost 10 000 supporting documents.[46]
>
> Launched in 2018, the **Responsible Mining Index (RMI)** has developed "an evidence-based assessment of mining company policies and practices on economic, environmental, social, and governance issues", including assessments at the company and mine-site level. The RMI examines the extent to which companies are supplying open data on a number of aspects of their operations.[47]

Working with what is available

Critical to the use of extractives data is an emerging ecosystem of platforms, infomediaries, and capacity-building activities.[48] Organisations, such as OpenOil, have deployed the Aleph platform that enables the search of security exchange filings from extractives companies, which helps data users to find the needle in the haystack of disclosure. In 2016, PWYP, in partnership with OpenOil, launched a global Data Extractors programme dedicated to building skills among CSOs working on extractives accountability issues,[49] and the WRI has released mapping platforms, Global Forest Watch and Resource Watch, which provide access to raw data and visualisations from public domain mining datasets.[50] All these activities are illustrative of the comparatively (to other sectors) well-resourced environment for data use in extractives. The following sections outline four different ways in which data is being put into use.

Going deeper: Running the numbers

With the increasing availability of contract information, information on revenue payments, and other key data points, a growing community of CSOs and consultants have engaged in financial modelling to help the public understand how different policies can lead to vastly different outcomes from resource extraction. OpenOil describe their modelling as "building an Excel-based model that recreates the past and forecasts the future cashflows of a specific mining or petroleum (oil and/or gas) project, and evaluates how these cashflows are shared between the resource owner – usually the government – and the investor – usually a mining or oil company – over the life of the project, under the fiscal rules (the fiscal regime) that apply to the project".[51]

So far, OpenOil has modelled eleven oil and mining projects across several countries, including Indonesia,⁵² Mongolia, and Brazil.⁵³ Similarly, the Columbia Center for Sustainable Investment (CCSI) has produced an analysis of gold mines,⁵⁴ and NRGI has used modelling to offer quantitative analysis on sector-wide fiscal regimes in order to contribute to national policy debates in many countries, such as Ghana, Kyrgyzstan, Uganda, Mongolia, and the Democratic Republic of Congo (DRC). In addition, the IMF released details on its modelling in 2015 following calls by civil society for transparency around how their models were built.⁵⁵

Modelling has proven effective at closing the gap between disclosure and discussion by taking advantage of improvements in data availability, and the work of a critical audience of infomediaries, to increase public scrutiny and debate. This was evident in Guyana, where the publication of the contract for the Stabroek project led to OpenOil publishing a financial model three months later which assessed that the government take from the project (52% at today's prices) was "low even for frontier provinces".⁵⁶ As another example, in the US, the Project on Government Oversight (POGO) used auction data to analyse how the price per acre for extracting oil in the Gulf of Mexico had "declined by 95.7 percent from $9,068 to $391".⁵⁷ Among multilateral institutions, the IMF has also contributed to this emerging open community of modelling practitioners with the publication of its official IMF model and methodology.⁵⁸

Besides the modelling of individual extractives projects, a range of actors are using available data for long-term forecasting. For example, in 2018, NRGI published a tool for visualising IMF forecasting data from the World Economic Outlook "to assess how countries have been coping with resource sector volatility and uncertainty".⁵⁹ In several countries, improved access to revenue data has also provided input for improved macro-economic analysis and revenue forecasting with implications relevant to open budget communities. In one example from Mongolia, revenue forecasts from five of the largest mines were used to feed into an openly licensed macro-economic analysis.⁶⁰

The disruption of black box data services

While civil society may, until recently, have referred to the extractives sector as data poor, the private sector has long benefitted from proprietary data provided by highly valued business intelligence companies, one of which was recently sold in a multi-billion dollar deal.⁶¹ Companies, such as S&P Global, Rystad Energy, and Wood Mackenzie,⁶² all produce commercial databases for oil and mining production, which, due to the high subscription fees, are rarely accessible to civil society, journalists, or even governments. Some have hoped that mandatory disclosure data, data from EITI reporting and contract information, will, over time, make these proprietary databases redundant and level the playing field between governments and CSOs on one side and companies on the other. However, government data releases to date have, to some extent, provided a sobering moment. Mandatory disclosure data does not, for example, provide the reserve and cost figures which are often needed for developing financial models. While some governments have, for a considerable period, had processes for obtaining independently produced data on cost and reserves that can be utilised for monitoring costs by operating companies, others have only more recently begun considering these options.⁶³

In the area of oil shipping, there are signs that new types of analytical products are emerging which could improve scrutiny of the commodity trading sector. The TankerTrackers platform has been publishing analysis based on open or public data on production and shipping since 2016, generating regular coverage in major news outlets.[64] This success highlights how incumbent commercial data providers may have left a number of users unserved due to high subscription costs for data services and the lack of data provenance within proprietary databases.

Looking ahead, the development of new business models across the extractives business intelligence market could play an important role in addressing data gaps created by the current unaffordable commercial databases, which often lack transparent methodologies and have limited coverage in developing countries. An analysis by the Organisation for Economic Co-operation and Development (OECD) of privately provided datasets for use in transfer price analysis underscores that often these proprietary sources have major limitations, leaving substantial gaps in the market for data products better oriented toward government and multilateral needs.[65] As yet, it is not clear whether the combination of entrepreneurs and investors needed to fill these gaps will emerge.

Use of microtasking to uncover oil spills

The limited extent of open data standardisation for extractives can sometimes mean that it can be difficult to use data to advance accountability. In Nigeria, the National Oil Spill Detection and Response Agency (NOSDRA) began providing online data for oil spill reports reported by companies operating in the country in 2014.[66] When approaching the data, Amnesty International was, however, faced with thousands of PDF documents without any standardised information. They turned to their Amnesty Decoders online community of human rights volunteers, working with them to deliver 1 300 hours of data cleaning and generating the structured data needed in order to analyse the track record of different companies' oil spill reports.

The investigation showed that figures reported by companies were vastly different from those of the Nigerian government. The Decoders helped identify massive delays in resolving spills with some spills continuing for months after they were reported. The investigation earned widespread media mentions and illustrated how "microtasking" can leverage volunteers to expand the investigative reach of CSOs.[67]

Telling the story: Investigations and journalism

Collaboration between civil society and investigative journalists working with new sources of data has helped with the scrutiny of extractives companies and corruption in resource-rich developing countries. Journalists used the Panama Papers to report how the Panama-based law firm, Mossack-Fonseca, served as "a major provider of secrecy to companies involved in extractive industries" in countries such as Algeria,[68] and Global Witness has leveraged company register data to report on how former generals in Myanmar benefitted from the opaque jade trade.[69] In fragile states, established and new media outlets have worked side-by-side to leverage satellite imagery and open datasets in order to uncover the role of natural resources in conflict.

During the rise of the Islamic State in Syria, the *Washington Post* mapped makeshift oil refineries using satellite imagery from Digital Globe,[70] and the *Financial Times* covered the political economy of conflict in Iraq using local oil price data.[71] In Libya, Al Jazeera has mapped oil fields in order to contextualise coverage of the ongoing civil war.[72]

In reporting with data, civil society and journalists both surface stories for wider public attention and demonstrate what could be done with data on a more systematic basis. The citizens' journalism collective, Bellingcat, for example, has noted that their "open-source research is only a small attempt to demonstrate that much more work can be undertaken to identify conflict pollution and improve humanitarian response and post-conflict reconstruction work" and have provided workshops and training to humanitarian organisations and UN agencies. They used satellite imagery to examine oil pollution in Syria during the civil war.[73] In Peru, the Amazon Conservation Association, a CSO, has documented deforestation from illegal gold mining. Lastly, a civil society-initiated project in Indonesia explored how community-based drone mapping could reveal land grabs related to mining.[74]

Research: Data, information, and action

There is a well-developed research community around extractives governance with signs of growing interest in the potential of quantitative and experimental research methods to generate policy-relevant knowledge from new data sources. Pioneering work by AidData, which combines geo-referenced concession data with remote sensing satellite data in order to look at connections between natural resource concessions and local economic development in Liberia, is illustrative of the new kind of approach researchers are exploring.[75] This research does not wait for perfect open data but rather brings together data in new configurations to rigorously generate new insights. International institutions are also heavily embedded in the research community, engaging with new data flows. For example, the IMF has explored the potential to monitor real-time fiscal data[76] which could be particularly useful for countries with volatile extractives revenues.

Central to the goal of turning research into action are strong connections between researchers, policy-makers, and non-governmental organisations (NGOs). The recently launched Project on Resources and Governance (PRG) describes how it is working to address the scant evidence about effective interventions in the extractives sector by bringing together a "network of social scientists, policy-makers, NGOs, and industry representatives dedicated to finding policies that promote welfare, peace, and accountability in resource-rich countries".[77] In the Disclosure to Development (D2D) programme, led by the International Finance Corporation, a message emerging from research so far is "that data needs to connect to policy and accountability within both government and the private sector",[78] and that this requires local voices and citizen participation. It is the combination of rigorous data analysis and local insight that can ultimately move the sector from being "data rich and information poor" to having actionable know-how for securing better impacts.[79] The initiative Leveraging Transparency to Reduce Corruption, headed by the Brookings Institution, released an annotated bibliography in 2018 which "reviewed more than 650 books, papers, and other resources in the transparency, accountability, and participation and/or natural resource space".[80]

Ultimately, as this chapter has sought to demonstrate, one of the key roles that increased data accessibility has played is to break down the silos of the different actors, enabling collaboration, knowledge transfer, and creative development of new methods and approaches.

Looking ahead: Future frontiers

In this chapter, we have highlighted trends in data collection and use which are starting to have an impact at both a global and country level. We see more robust analysis, more data-driven experimentation, and improved cross-sectional work to build skills among extractives-focused NGOs.

The extractives sector remains a highly volatile and capital-intensive sector. While there are different opinions on the pace, there is broad agreement that the sector will continue to invest heavily in new technologies, digitisation, and automation in the future.[81] The World Economic Forum has also identified a wide area of technologies which could impact the extractives value chains, including artificial intelligence, robotics, privately owned trading platforms drawing on distributed ledgers (blockchain technology), and automation across the supply chain.[82] This indicates that, while progress has been made in the last decade on data openness, private sector investments in data collection and management across extractives operations is likely to expand. At this stage, however, it is unclear how CSOs, activists, journalists, and policy-makers will be able to keep up with the pace of change to maintain access to data and to scrutinise a rapidly changing market.

As the extractives transparency movement heads into its third decade, and extractives open data enters its second, there is a need to draw on learning so far to sharpen our focus on clearly defined problems. Improvements are needed in providing reliable data, generating analysis which can address timely policy challenges, and finally getting the analysis and policy recommendations into the hands of broad-based civil society campaigns, journalists, and, ultimately, policy-makers. There are major benefits to be sought from linking up the sector with other "Follow the Money" efforts,[83] building alliances to trace funds across extractives, budgets, contracting, aid, and service delivery. While substantive research is yet to emerge beyond initial mapping,[84] there are opportunities here to go beyond breaking down silos in a single sector and to build bridges between groups concerned with fundamental questions of how public resources are managed. There is also a need to strengthen links with sustainability and climate change networks. Notable efforts are being made to connect analysis of extractives revenues, fiscal policy, and implications for climate change, for example, in areas such as fossil fuel subsidies[85] and through the Green Fiscal Policy Network.[86] Lastly, the emergence of the Task Force on Climate-related Financial Disclosures has led to the development of a framework for company disclosure of climate risks with commitments from 1 800 major companies.[87] Moving forward, these climate disclosures will be an important source for analysis.

As this chapter has shown, when machine-readable open data is available, infomediaries, civil society, and governments can leverage it to develop analysis and evidence-based policy recommendations. Yet, it is important to recognise that the road from data acquisition to analysis and policy impact remains highly complex and dependent on many factors, such as the political context, the capacity of civil society and other potential users, and opportunities for decision-making based on the results of analysis. The extractives sector will be able to continue to learn from peer research across the open government space.[88] Scaling up the use of extractives data is not necessarily about building mass-movements or substantially increasing investment in open data, but it does involve supporting the development of specialist skills among key stakeholders and leveraging those skills effectively, for example, by expanding work on fiscal modelling, which, if enabled by open data, would bring extensive domain expertise to bear on specific weaknesses in extractives governance. The future of open data in extractives will also rest on how well regulations for disclosure are implemented in practice by national agencies and how far multi-stakeholder initiatives advance interoperable disclosure requirements. The importance of getting the technical definitions and details right cannot be underestimated, and this will demand much deeper collaboration between open data and standards specialists, policy advocates, and policy-makers.

Overall, if the multi-stakeholder approach that has characterised extractives governance work over recent years can be sustained, and open data specialists can be further integrated into the process, then the next decade should see open data become an unprecedented tool for extractives governance.

Further reading

Natural Resource Governance Institute. (2017). *2017 Resource Governance Index*. https://resourcegovernanceindex.org/about/global-report

Ray, N., Lacroix, P.M.A., Giuliani, G., Upla, P., Rajabifard, A., & Jensen, D. (2016). Open spatial data infrastructures for the sustainable development of the extractives sector: Promises and challenges. In D. Coleman, A. Rajabifard, & J. Crompvoets (Eds.), *Spatial enablement in a smart world* (pp. 53–69). Quebec City: Global Spatial Data Infrastructure Association Press. https://archive-ouverte.unige.ch/unige:90248

Saavedra, S. & Romero, M. (2017). *Local incentives and national tax evasion: The response of illegal mining to a tax reform in Colombia*. Job Market Paper. Stanford, CA: Stanford University. http://web.stanford.edu/~santisap/Saavedra_JMP.pdf

Srivastava, N., Agarwal, V., Bhattacharjya, S., Gopalakrishnan, T., Meenawat, H., Nayak, B., & Soni, A. (2014). *Open government data for regulation of energy resources in India*. New Delhi: The Energy and Resources Institute. http://opendataresearch.org/sites/default/files/publications/Full%20-%20TERI%20OGD%20and%20energy%20resources%20July%202014-print.pdf

World Bank. (2016). *Options for data reporting – EITI Standard, 2016: The good, the better and the best*. Washington, DC: World Bank. http://documents.worldbank.org/curated/en/793601469102170609/pdf/107171-WP-P152662-PUBLIC.pdf

About the author

Anders Pedersen is a Senior Open Data Officer at the NRGI. At NRGI, Anders has overseen the development of global data platforms and technical assistance on open data and data-driven decision-making in more than a dozen countries across Asia, Latin America, and Africa. He has engaged with global stakeholders, such as IMF, Open Contracting Partnership, the World Bank, and IETI, on interoperability, data standards, and open licensing. Before joining NRGI, Anders worked for more than a decade in the field of open data, international development, and journalism at the Open Knowledge Foundation.

How to cite this chapter

Pedersen, A. (2019). Open data and extractives. In T. Davies, S. Walker, M. Rubinstein, & F. Perini (Eds.), *The state of open data: Histories and horizons* (pp. 119–136). Cape Town and Ottawa: African Minds and International Development Research Centre. http://stateofopendata.od4d.net.

This work is licensed under a Creative Commons Attribution 4.0 International (CC BY 4.0) licence. It was carried out with the aid of a grant from the International Development Research Centre, Ottawa, Canada.

Endnotes

1. https://www.resourcedata.org/organization/eiti
2. Humphreys, M., Sachs, J.D., & Stiglitz, J.E. (2007). *Escaping the resource curse*. New York, NY: Columbia University Press.
3. http://openjadedata.org/
4. Kyithar Swe, A. & Salomon, M. (2018). New data demystify Myanmar's jade sector. *Myanmar Times*, 2 August. https://www.mmtimes.com/news/new-data-demystify-myanmars-jade-sector.html
5. Global Witness. (2015). Jade: Myanmar's "big state secret": The biggest natural resources heist in history? *Global Witness*, 23 October. https://www.globalwitness.org/en/campaigns/oil-gas-and-mining/myanmarjade/
6. Dapice, D. (2018). *A grand bargain: What it is and why it is needed*. Cambridge, MA: Ash Center for Democratic Governance and Innovation, Harvard Kennedy School. https://ash.harvard.edu/files/ash/files/20160815_a_grand_bargain_eng_oct_24.2016.pdf
7. Author's interview with key informant.
8. IMF. (2012). *Fiscal regimes for extractive industries: Design and implementation*. Washington, DC: Fiscal Affairs Department, International Monetary Fund. https://www.imf.org/en/Publications/Policy-Papers/Issues/2016/12/31/Fiscal-Regimes-for-Extractive-Industries-Design-and-Implementation-PP4701
9. Van Oranje, M. & Parham, H. (2009). *Publishing what we learned: An assessment of the Publish What You Pay Coalition*. London: Publish What You Pay, p. 30. https://eiti.org/document/publishing-what-we-learned-assessment-of-publish-what-you-pay-coalition
10. http://openoil.net/about-openoil/
11. African Natural Resources Center, African Development Bank, and OpenOil. (2017). *Running the numbers: How African governments model the extractive projects*. African Natural Resources Center, African Development Bank, and OpenOil. https://www.afdb.org/fileadmin/uploads/afdb/Documents/Publications/anrc/Running_the_Numbers_Analytical_report.pdf

12. Readhead, A. (2016). *Preventing tax base erosion in Africa: A regional study of transfer pricing challenges in the mining sector*. New York, NY: Natural Resource Governance Institute. https://resourcegovernance.org/sites/default/files/documents/nrgi_transfer-pricing-study.pdf
13. https://www.ataftax.org/Exchange-of-information
14. Security and Exchange Commission. (2010). *Dodd-Frank Wall Street Reform and Consumer Protection Act of 2010*, 24 May. http://legcounsel.house.gov/Comps/Dodd-Frank%20Wall%20Street%20Reform%20and%20Consumer%20Protection%20Act.pdf
15. https://eur-lex.europa.eu/legal-content/EN/NIM/?uri=celex:32013L0050
16. https://laws-lois.justice.gc.ca/eng/acts/E-22.7/page-1.html
17. EITI. (2017). *Project-level reporting guidance note 29 – Requirement 4.7*. Oslo: Extractive Industries Transparency Initiative. https://eiti.org/sites/default/files/documents/guidance_note_29_on_project-level_reporting.pdf
18. Author's calculation based on available reports on Natural Resources Canada's disclosure site, Links to ESTMA reports, at https://www.nrcan.gc.ca/mining-materials/estma/18198
19. PwC Canada. (2017). *The Extractive Sector Transparency Measures Act – Year 1 reporting highlights*. Ottawa: PricewaterhouseCoopers LLP. https://www.pwc.com/ca/en/energy-utilities/publications/pwc-energy-canada-estma-year-1-reporting-highlights-July%2014,2017-EN.pdf and author's review of PwC Canada's 2018 review.
20. Litvinoff, M. (2017). *Submission to UK government review of the reports on payments to governments regulations 2014*. London: Publish What You Pay UK, p. 7. http://www.publishwhatyoupay.org/wp-content/uploads/2017/11/2017.11.17-PWYP-submission-to-UK-review-final.pdf
21. Ibid., pp. 2–4.
22. Alliot, C., Cortin, M., Kurkjian, M., Lemaître, S., Ly, S., & Parrinello, Q. (2017). *Beyond transparency: Investigating the new extractive industry disclosures*. Paris: PWYP France, One, Oxfam France, and Sherpa. https://www.oxfamamerica.org/explore/research-publications/beyond-transparency-investigating-the-new-extractive-industry-disclosures/
23. Malden, A. & Osei, E. (2018). Ghana's gold mining revenues: An analysis of company disclosures. *Natural Resource Governance Institute*, 11 September. https://resourcegovernance.org/analysis-tools/publications/ghanas-gold-mining-revenues-analysis-company-disclosures
24. Malden, A. (2017). *Nigeria's oil and gas revenues: Insights from new company disclosures. Natural Resource Governance Institute*. https://resourcegovernance.org/sites/default/files/documents/nigeria-oil-revenue.pdf
25. Litvinoff, M. (2018). *Comparing UK EITI and mandatory payments to governments data for 2016: Assessment report*. London: Publish What You Pay UK. www.publishwhatyoupay.org/wp-content/uploads/2018/09/Comparing-UK-EITI-mandatory-data-assessment-report-PWYP UK Sept18.pdf
26. Global Witness & Resources for Development Consulting. (2018). *Finding the missing millions: A handbook for using extractive companies' revenue disclosures to hold governments and industry to account*. https://www.globalwitness.org/en/campaigns/oil-gas-and-mining/finding-missing-millions/#chapter-0/section-0
27. Simon, J. (2017). US withdraws from extractive industries anti-corruption effort. *Reuters*, 2 November. https://www.reuters.com/article/us-usa-eiti/u-s-withdraws-from-extractive-industries-anti-corruption-effort-idUSKBN1D2290
28. https://revenuedata.doi.gov/
29. Palawan News. (2018). PH-EITI Roadshow 2018 pushes for extractives transparency in local development. *Palawan News*, 13 July. https://palawan-news.com/ph-eiti-roadshow-2018-pushes-for-extractives-transparency-in-local-development/
30. The International Centre for Tax and Development (ICTD) has developed the Government Revenue Dataset (GRD), which serves as a key source for government revenues in resource-rich countries. The dataset is hosted by UN Wider. https://www.wider.unu.edu/project/government-revenue-dataset
31. https://eiti.org/explore-data-portal
32. Extractive Industries Transparency Initiative. (2016). *EITI Open Data Policy*. https://eiti.org/document/eiti-open-data-policy

33. World Bank. (2016). *Options for data reporting – EITI Standard, 2016: The good, the better and the best*. Washington, DC: World Bank. http://documents.worldbank.org/curated/en/793601469102170609/pdf/107171-WP-P152662-PUBLIC.pdf
34. IMF. (2017). *Update on the standard template to collect data on government revenues from natural resources*. Washington, DC: International Monetary Fund. https://www.imf.org/en/Publications/Policy-Papers/Issues/2017/04/27/update-on-the-standard-template-to-collect-data-on-government-revenues-from-natural-resources
35. EITI. (2016). *Towards mainstreaming action plan*. Oslo: Extractive Industries Transparency Initiative.
36. For disclosing companies, see Oxfam. (2018). *Contract disclosure survey 2018: A review of the contract disclosure policies of 40 oil, gas and mining companies*. Oxfam Briefing Paper. Oxford: Oxfam. https://oxfamilibrary.openrepository.com/bitstream/handle/10546/620465/bp-contract-disclosure-extractives-2018-030518-en.pdf;jsessionid=9F7A2330301E95422B0426167E88B854?sequence=4. For disclosure practices among governments, see Hubert, D. & Pitman, R. (2017). *Past the tipping point? Contract disclosure within EITI*. New York, NY: Natural Resource Governance Institute. https://resourcegovernance.org/sites/default/files/documents/past-the-tipping-point-contract-disclosure-within-eiti-web.pdf
37. Pitman, R., Shafaie, A., Hayman, G., & Kluttz, C. (2018). *Open contracting for oil, gas and mineral rights: Shining a light on good practice*. New York, NY: Open Contracting Partnership & Natural Resource Governance Institute. https://resourcegovernance.org/sites/default/files/documents/open-contracting-for-oil-and-gas-mineral-rights.pdf
38. Revenue Development Foundation. (n.d.). The RDx Data Exchange Standard & API Service: Piloting and ongoing case studies. https://revenuedevelopment.org/page/rdx-data-exchange
39. Written interview, Aasmund Andersen, Revenue Development Foundation, August 2018.
40. https://www.mmtimes.com/news/new-data-demystify-myanmars-jade-sector.html
41. EITI. (2017). *2017 Progress report: Ending company anonymity – The key to fighting corruption*. Oslo: Extractive Industries Transparency Initiative, p. 14. https://eiti.org/sites/default/files/documents/eiti_progress_report_2017.pdf
42. Webb, J., Petersen, R., Moses, E., Excell, C., Weisse, M., Cole, E., & Szoke-Burke, S. (2017). *Logging, mining, and agricultural concessions data transparency: A survey of 14 forested countries*. Washington, DC: World Resources Institute. http://wriorg.s3.amazonaws.com/s3fs-public/Logging_Mining_and_Agricultural_Concessions_Data_Transparency_A_Survey_of_14_Forested_Countries.pdf
43. Hansen, M.C., Krylov, A., Tyukavina, A., Potapov, P.V., Turubanova, S., Zutta, B., Ifo, S., Margono, B., Stolle, F., & Moore, R. (2016). Humid tropical forest disturbance alerts using Landsat data. *Environmental Research Letters*, 11(3). https://doi.org/10.1088/1748-9326/11/3/034008
44. http://apps.resourcegovernance.org/supply-ecosystem/
45. The Economist. (2017). Resource Governance Index. *The Economist*, 1 July. https://www.economist.com/economic-and-financial-indicators/2017/07/01/resource-governance-index
46. Natural Resource Governance Institute. (2017). 2017 Resource Governance Index. https://resourcegovernanceindex.org/
47. https://responsibleminingindex.org/en/downloads
48. Van Schalkwyk, F., Willmers, M., & McNaughton, M. (2016). Viscous open data: The roles of intermediaries in an open data ecosystem. *Information Technology for Development*, 22(1), 68–83. https://www.tandfonline.com/doi/pdf/10.1080/02681102.2015.1081868?needAccess=true
49. https://www.pwyp.org/pwyp-news/qa-mining-new-company-data-with-pwyps-open-extractors/
50. https://data.globalforestwatch.org/datasets/26a457ee3b584824bb930f2ec791b60d_0
51. OpenOil. (n.d.). Financial Modeling Program. http://openoil.net/contract-modeling/financial-modeling-program/
52. http://openoil.net/wp/wp-content/uploads/2014/09/OO_id_batuhijau_narrative_v1.0_161109.pdf
53. http://openoil.net/wp/wp-content/uploads/2014/09/OO_br_Libra_narrative_1.0_161104.pdf
54. http://ccsi.columbia.edu/work/projects/open-fiscal-models/

55 Cust, J. & Mihalyi, D. (2015). IMF's Open FARI Model Release an Important First Step. *Natural Resource Governance Institute* [Blog post], 9 October. https://resourcegovernance.org/blog/imfs-open-fari-model-release-important-first-step

56 West, J. (2018). *Stabroek Oil Field, Guyana: Narrative report*. Berlin: OpenOil. http://openoil.net/wp/wp-content/uploads/2018/03/oo_gy_stabroek_narrative_v1.0_180315_1025_jw.pdf

57 Hilzenrath, D.S. & Pacifico, N. (2018). Drilling down: Big oil's bidding. *Project On Government Oversight (POGO)*, 22 January. http://www.pogo.org/our-work/articles/2018/drilling-down-big-oils-bidding.html

58 Luca, O. & Mesa Puyo, D. (2016). *Fiscal Analysis of Resource Industries (FARI) methodology*. Washington, DC: Fiscal Affairs Department, International Monetary Fund. https://www.imf.org/external/pubs/ft/tnm/2016/tnm1601.pdf

59 Mihalyi, D. & Morrison, T. (2018). World Economic Outlook Forecast Tracker. *Natural Resource Governance Institute*. https://resourcegovernance.org/analysis-tools/tools/world-economic-outlook-forecast-tracker

60 Mihalyi, D., Baksa, D., & Romhanyi, B. (2017). Mongolia Macro-Fiscal Model. *Natural Resource Governance Institute*. https://resourcegovernance.org/analysis-tools/tools/mongolia-macro-fiscal-model

61 Kent, S. (2015). Verisk analytics to buy Wood Mackenzie for $2.8 Billion. *Wall Street Journal*, 10 March. https://www.wsj.com/articles/verisk-analytics-to-buy-wood-mackenzie-for-2-8-billion-1425981462

62 See https://www.spglobal.com/en/, https://www.rystadenergy.com/, and https://www.woodmac.com/, respectively.

63 Readhead, A., Mulé, D., & Op de Beke, A. (2018*). Examining the crude details: Government audits of oil and gas project costs to maximize revenue collection. Ghana case study*. Oxfam Briefing Paper. Oxford: Oxfam. https://oxfamilibrary.openrepository.com/bitstream/handle/10546/620595/bp-examining-the-crude-details-ghana-131118-en.pdf

64 Tanker Trackers. (2018). Iran, September 2018 with oil production calculation. https://tankertrackers.com/news/crude-oil-exports-report/iran-september-2018

65 For a rare discussion on the quality, coverage, and cost of commercial databases, see pp. 22–24 of OECD & World Bank Group. (2017). *A toolkit for addressing difficulties in accessing comparables data for transfer pricing analyses*. The Platform for Collaboration on Tax Discussion Draft. Paris: Organisation for Economic Co-operation and Development. https://www.oecd.org/tax/discussion-draft-a-toolkit-for-addressing-difficulties-in-accessing-comparables-data-for-transfer-pricing-analyses.pdf

66 https://oilspillmonitor.ng/

67 Carstens, P. (2018). Amnesty says Shell, Eni negligent on Nigeria oil spills, *Reuters*, 15 March. https://www.reuters.com/article/us-oil-nigeria/amnesty-says-shell-eni-negligent-on-nigeria-oil-spills-idUSKCN1GS00A

68 Fitzgibbon, W. (2016). Secret offshore deals deprive Africa of billions in natural resource dollars. *International Consortium for Investigative Journalists*, 25 July. https://www.icij.org/investigations/panama-papers/20160725-natural-resource-africa-offshore/

69 https://www.globalwitness.org/jade-story/

70 Warrick, J. (2016). Satellite photos show Islamic State installing hundreds of makeshift oil refineries to offset losses from airstrikes. *Washington Post*, 7 July. https://www.washingtonpost.com/news/worldviews/wp/2016/07/07/satellite-photos-show-isis-installing-hundreds-of-makeshift-oil-refineries-to-offset-losses-from-air-strikes/?utm_term=.fdcf81ae44a9

71 Solomon, E., Kwong, R., & Bernard, S. (2016). Inside Isis Inc: The journey of a barrel of oil. *Financial Times*, 29 February. https://ig.ft.com/sites/2015/isis-oil/?

72 Raymond, P.A. & Haddad, M. (2015). The battle for Libya's oil: Fighting over Libya's oil resources is placing the country's future in jeopardy. *Al Jazeera*, 19 February. https://www.aljazeera.com/indepth/interactive/2015/02/battle-libyas-oil-150219124633572.html

73 Zwijnenburg, W. (2018). Nefarious negligence: Post-conflict oil pollution in Eastern Syria. *Bellingcat*, 9 April. https://www.bellingcat.com/news/mena/2018/04/09/nefarious-negligence-post-conflict-oil-pollution-in-eastern-syria/

74 Radjawali, I. & Pye, O. (2015). Counter-mapping land grabs with community drones in Indonesia. Paper presented at *Land Grabbing, Conflict and Agrarian–Environmental Transformations: Perspectives from East and Southeast Asia, 5–6 June 2015, Chiang Mai University, Bangkok*. https://www.iss.nl/sites/corporate/files/CMCP_80-Radjawali_and_Pye.pdf

75 Bunte, J.B., Desai, H., Gbala, K., Parks, B., & Runfola, D.M. (2017). *Natural resource sector FDI and growth in post-conflict settings: Subnational evidence from Liberia*. AidData Working Paper 34. Washington, DC: AidData. http://docs.aiddata.org/ad4/files/wps34_natural_resource_sector_fdi_and_growth_in_post-conflict_settings.pdf

76 Olden B., Poplawski-Ribeiro, M., & Kejji, L. (2017). *Nowcashing: Using daily fiscal data for real-time macroeconomic analysis*. Washington, DC: International Monetary Fund. http://www.imf.org/en/publications/wp/issues/2017/11/06/nowcashing-using-daily-fiscal-data-for-real-time-macroeconomic-analysis-45372

77 https://projectrg.org/

78 Kharma, S. & Crist, L. (2018). Data rich and information poor: Increasing the effectiveness of data disclosure in the natural resource sectors. *CommDev*. https://www.commdev.org/data-rich-and-information-poor-increasing-the-effectiveness-of-data-disclosure-in-the-natural-resource-sectors/

79 Ibid.

80 Eisen, N., Kaufmann, D., & Heller, N. (2018). *Annotated bibliography: Transparency, accountability, and participation along the natural resource value chain*. Washington, DC: Brookings Institution. https://www.brookings.edu/about-the-leveraging-transparency-to-reduce-corruption-project/

81 http://ccsi.columbia.edu/files/2015/07/mining-a-mirage-CCSI-IISD-EWB-2016.pdf

82 https://www.weforum.org/agenda/archive/fourth-industrial-revolution

83 http://followthemoney.net/

84 https://www.opengovpartnership.org/stories/share-love-share-data-follow-money

85 Ross, M., Hazlett, C., & Mahdavi, P. (2015). *The politics of petroleum prices: A new global dataset*. https://www.sscnet.ucla.edu/polisci/faculty/ross/papers/working/IPES_final.pdf

86 http://greenfiscalpolicy.org

87 https://www.fsb-tcfd.org/publications/final-recommendations-report/#

88 Berdou, E. & Shutt, C. (2017). Shifting the spotlight: Understanding crowdsourcing intermediaries in transparency and accountability initiatives. *Making All Voices Count*, 22 February. https://www.makingallvoicescount.org/publication/shifting-spotlight-understanding-crowdsourcing-intermediaries-transparency-accountability-initiatives/

009

Geospatial

Renée Sieber

Key points

- Approximately 80% of all government data contains some reference to location.

- Opening up geospatial data was a key early driver of open data advocacy, and there has been significant progress in opening up this type of data. However, much of government geospatial data remains under restrictive intellectual property agreements.

- Work on open geospatial data technology and infrastructure pre-dates the concept and implementation of open data, yet there are relatively weak links between the open geospatial and other open data communities. Stronger links could build critical capacity for spatial analysis within open data communities.

- Mapping visualisations are a popular way of presenting open data, yet the spatial analysis carried out is often unsophisticated. Relationships that appear on a map may not be statistically significant. It is important to recognise that geographic relations can be shown in other forms, such as tables and charts.

Introduction

Fifteen years ago, most users experienced online maps much as they might their paper counterparts: flat non-interactive images for browsing geography. In 2005, Google Maps changed that, giving rise to enthusiasm for the mapping mash-up, where data (often taken from public datasets) is located on an interactive scrollable and zoomable map. A year later, OpenStreetMap was launched, providing a platform for the collection and display of mapping data, unencumbered by intellectual property (IP) restrictions, and launched in response to ongoing frustration at the lack of open geographic data in the United Kingdom (UK).[1] The move from large proprietary desktop Geographic Information Systems (GIS) to increasingly open access to geospatial[2] data appeared to be underway.

Mapping visualisations have been strategic assets in the popularity of open data and they remain one of the public entry points to engage with open data. A typical mapping portal from the City of Phoenix[3] in the United States (US) demonstrates the type of geospatial data (and prepared maps) available through a typical North American municipal data portal, including property boundaries, zoning information, traffic volumes, and recreation areas (see Figure 1). A similar site can be found for Manchester, England,[4] although geospatial data and map access come with terms and conditions that restrict how that data can be used.

Both the potential demonstrated by mapping mashups and user interfaces and the desire for access to valuable geospatial datasets held by governments and government agencies can be seen as driving forces in the development of the open data movement. But what of geospatial data today? Is the data now widely open, accessible, and used? And what progress has been made in unlocking the potential of geospatial data for analysis and improved policy-making?

While much progress has been made in the availability of data, and in the development of tools to visualise it, substantial work is needed to better connect geospatial and open data communities, to equip creators and users of geospatial data with the critical skills (and technical platforms) needed to move beyond simply mapping, and to gain the full benefits of geospatial data analysis. There also are significant risks from the wider use of geospatial data that need to be more directly addressed. Ultimately, advances made in terms of sheer data availability and infrastructures are currently counterbalanced by significant stalemates in terms of analytical approaches to geodata, as well as ownership and privacy risks.

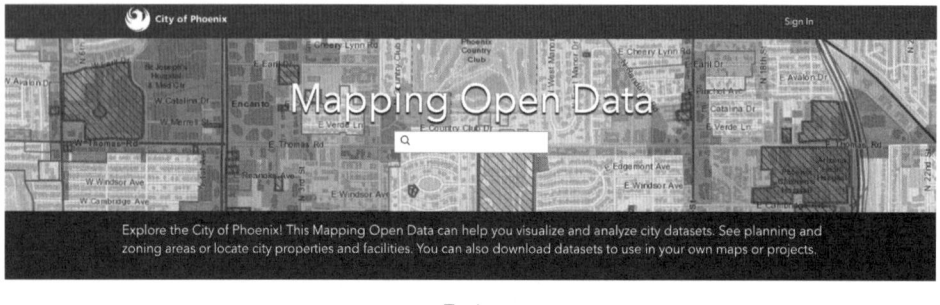

Figure 1: Screenshot of the City of Phoenix – Mapping Open Data platform
Source: https://mapping-phoenix.opendata.arcgis.com/

Primer: An overview of open geospatial data

It is estimated that 80% of all government data has some reference to location.[5] Almost every chapter in this volume touches upon geospatial data in some form. Geospatial content can be found in datasets on subjects as diverse as parks, refugee camps, financial transactions, natural resource distributions, and socioeconomic statistics. Many uses of open data rely on being "mapped" (i.e. attached) to basic geographic framework data.[6] For example, socioeconomic statistics, like population, may be mapped on top of administrative boundaries. Data on soil quality may be attached to digital elevation models to model erosion, and that same soil data may be compared to geographically intersecting data on land ownership and land subsidies. Without their geospatial component, many open datasets would have much reduced impact.

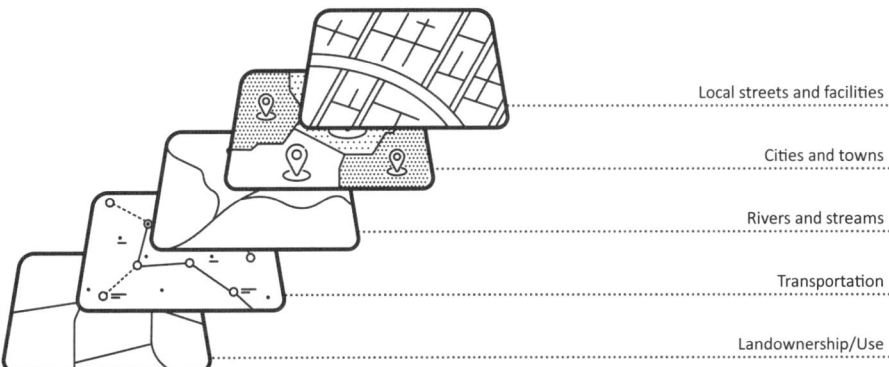

Figure 2: Simple illustration of geographic layers
Source: Author

Mapping generally involves presenting geospatial data alongside a geographic layer. Geographic layers are datasets that are essentially outlines and may or may not be open data themselves. These layers include jurisdictional boundary files (e.g. country, city, school catchment areas, and watershed districts) or linear features like rivers or roads. For completeness sake, there also are geographic point layers, such as centres of cities or locations of known elevation like mountain peaks. Geographic layers may also include remote sensed imagery. Imagery can function as a backdrop onto which geospatial data is overlaid (e.g. logging operations in forested areas). Like other geospatial data, remote sensed imagery can be analysed alone or in combination with other open datasets to identify areas of drought, land use, or pollution.

Many practitioners working with open data consider geography primarily in terms of x and y coordinates, usually expressed as latitude and longitude, respectively. It is important to recognise that there are numerous types of "coordinates". These include direct location references such as latitude/longitude, postal addresses, or GPS traces. There also are indirect references to location, such as place names (e.g. colloquial neighbourhood names, or official country or region names) that can be turned into a set of coordinates using a gazetteer or a lookup database.

The vast diversity of geospatial data may be more or less open along a number of dimensions. Data may be free to browse but not to download. Or data may be free to download but provided under restrictive licences that limit reuse. Or data may be openly licensed but only available in formats that require proprietary software or that use proprietary referencing systems. To understand open geospatial data, we need to ask: What kind of data is this? and How open is it?

> **Many kinds of geospatial data in terms of structure, representation, and analysis**
>
> There are many different kinds of geospatial data, and for any geographic feature, choices are made about how to represent it. The same feature might be represented using points, lines, polygons, or pixels. This choice impacts the kind of analysis that is possible, the technologies that can be used in analysis, and the biases to watch out for when drawing conclusions from the data.
>
> Figure 3 shows how a feature might be represented as a vector (a collection of linked points) or a raster (a collection of pixels scaled to a particular resolution with each individual pixel encoding information from its immediate area).
>
>
>
> Figure 3: Different ways to represent the same geographic feature
> Source: Author

Figure 4 illustrates how information is linked to geography for presentation (mapping) and analysis. Geographic layers are usually not directly accompanied by geospatial data. Instead, to a polygon (e.g. a country boundary), one could add (join) datasets, such as population data, information on political control, or catchment areas for particular service provision, and to a point (e.g. lat, lng) one could add details of public services provided at that location.

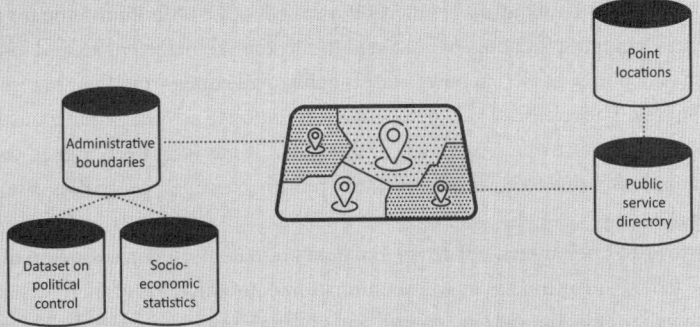

Figure 4: How information can be linked to geography for mapping and analysis
Source: Author

However, geospatial analysis does not require pre-existing boundaries like countries or cities. This can be useful when the boundaries are not available or when mapping onto those boundaries would be misleading (e.g. mapping incidences of crime onto areas with very different populations). Hexbinning, shown in Figure 5, is an approach to handle point data in these cases, creating a new geographic layer of arbitrary shapes into which the points can be aggregated.

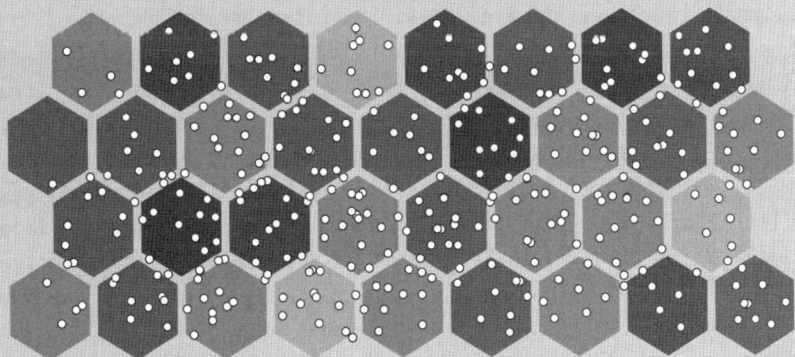

Figure 5: Hexbinning creates a new layer that allows data points to be mapped when boundaries are unavailable or when mapping the available boundaries could mislead.
Source: Author

Progress: Open geospatial data availability and infrastructure

The last decade has seen substantial strides in opening up geospatial datasets. Evidence suggests this has brought significant social and economic value. For example, in 2013, the Government of Denmark, through their Basic Data programme, released digital mapping data free under an open licence. A follow-up study in 2017 estimated that this had led to DK 3.5 billion (approx USD 495 million) in socioeconomic value in the preceding year.[7] It is estimated that making the US LandSat satellite imagery freely available in 2009 accrued USD 1.8 billion annual value to the economy; whereas, charging for access would lead to substantial inefficiencies and loss of value.[8] In the UK, open data policy has led to new datasets being made open from their mapping agency, the Ordnance Survey. The release of geospatial data responded to advocacy that focused on gains to the economy from a more open approach to this data.[9] It has long been argued that Canada suffered significant losses due to government's early reticence to open geospatial data,[10] which is being remedied.

In the US, efforts to open up federal geospatial data pre-date most consideration of open data worldwide. The federal government, as well as subnational jurisdictions of the US (states, cities), tends to publish geographic datasets as integral parts of their open data portals. The reason that geospatial data is arguably the first open (government) data is due to the establishment of national or subnational spatial data infrastructures (NSDIs), the first one being the Australian Land Information Council in 1986.[11] NSDIs are outgrowths of "the technology, policies, standards, and human resources necessary to acquire, process, store, distribute, and improve utilisation of geospatial data".[12] Geospatial data infrastructures tend to require high levels of interoperability in terms of standardisation to function. These datasets likely originate in different agencies with varying practices of data collection, update schedules, and definitions. Full standardisation requires geospatial data to be at the same geographic projection with the same coordinate system, spatial extent, updates, and data definitions. It is by no means easy to coordinate data so that layers "lie on top" of each other in alignment.

Spatial data infrastructures did not necessarily originate as open platforms. Many were designed as government-to-government data sharing platforms, although several promoted the idea that the data should be accessible to a range of applications and support economic development. Openness of geospatial data remains uneven across the world. The latest Open Data Index[13] identifies just 12 countries where governments provide fully open national geospatial data, and only one (Brazil) is not in the World Bank's "High-Income Economies" category. There is movement among numerous countries to increase openness (e.g. Indonesia's widely discussed One Map initiative). Progress has been slow and mostly focused on rationalisation of geospatial data management. Opening up geospatial data is not simply a matter of applying a licence to existing datasets, but also involves the adoption of policies, standards, and human resources specific to geospatial data.

Encouraged by the International Open Data Charter, and noting the value of an "open by default" approach, the Group on Earth Observation adopted open data principles in 2016,[14] seeing this as the natural step forward from their existing data sharing regime (established in 2006) and justifying this shift on the basis of the economic, social, governance, education, research, and innovation value.[15] The European Union's (EU) INSPIRE[16] directive has driven the inclusion of geospatial data features in a number of national data portals and extensions for geospatial data to the open source CKAN software.[17] Many NSDIs have had little integration into the open data landscape. However, the EU's initiative demonstrates how governments may integrate parallel tracks of activity between the open data and geospatial communities.

Gaps in geospatial data are increasingly addressed through the use of cross-border satellite imagery available on digital earth mapping platforms. Some of this data is sourced from government. The launch of the Africa Regional Data Cube in May 2018 resembles many features of an NSDI in terms of standardisation and provides access to free satellite imagery for Kenya, Senegal, Sierra Leone, Ghana, and Tanzania. It builds on an open source "data cube" platform that compresses pre-processed imagery to reduce the otherwise prohibitive costs of data transfer, storage, and analysis.[18]

Government data also is being augmented by the private sector and civil society, and some of these new geospatial datasets could become open data. Firms like DigitalGlobe provide imagery derived from commercial satellites. Whereas satellite coverage may be universal, street mapping remains limited by either the availability of non-proprietary street-mapping data or volunteer contributions. Much of this data is licensed to proprietary platforms like Google Maps. Users can zoom into most places on Earth and see road layouts or satellite imagery. To access the same data on other platforms to support applications or analysis can often be prohibitively expensive. For instance, software application programming interfaces (APIs) may be available but based on per-access pricing,[19] or sudden price changes may leave data out of reach of users seeking to map open data coordinates or build open data-related applications and businesses.[20] It is important to remember that free to use, but non-open, platforms are subject to prevailing business models of tech industries. Parts of Microsoft's Bing mapping division were sold to Uber in 2015, and Google increased prices for its mapping APIs up to fourteenfold in 2018. There is a precariousness to basing one's mapping applications on a specific non-open platform. Fortunately for data consumers, the last decade also has seen the emergence of tools like Leaflet,[21] which enable digital mapping using a variety of geospatial data providers. Companies like MapBox[22] provide a commercial offering but are committed to building on top of open source tools and data.

Open geospatial data also is being created through crowdsourcing. The largest platform, OpenStreetMap, "is built by a community of mappers that contribute and maintain data about roads, trails, cafés, railway stations, and much more, all over the world".[23] By comparing CIA World Factbook data on road length in a country with OpenStreetMap data, Maron and Channell found that some countries have 100% coverage of major roads.[24] In Asia and China coverage is more limited. In India, for example, only 21% of the road network has been digitised on OpenStreetMap.[25]

Use of private or crowdsourced data reflects the costs of collection and maintenance of geospatial data and related infrastructures. When geospatial data is funded directly from government budgets, rather than through cost-recovery (i.e. charging users for use of the data as a method of supporting government data collection and maintenance), access is at greater risk of budget cuts.[26] This can lead to pressure from agencies working with geospatial data to develop or retain financing regimes. The cost of data collection has led a few governments, particularly in North America, to explore partnerships with private sector firms to collect data through projects, such as Google Waze, Strava Metro, and Uber Movement.[27] Ironically, these datasets frequently originate from civil society or individual citizens, but ownership is claimed by the firms providing the platforms for data collection. This can introduce new sources of proprietary data in spatial data infrastructures at the same time that other aspects of those infrastructures may be opening up. Additionally, the inclusion of privately sourced or crowdsourced data invariably shifts control from government in terms of data accuracy, coverage, and timeliness of edits and updates. This will increase the risk to governments (real or perceived), particularly if that data is central to government operations.[28]

> ### Four examples of open geospatial data
>
> Thousands of examples of open geospatial data projects exist. These include:
>
> - **Crime Maps** presenting data from the police and justice system (see Chapter 4: Crime and justice) for individuals to see recorded crime incidents and rates in their communities.
> - **Community assets mapping** such as the MySociety.org "Keep it in the Community" project that is mapping an England-wide register of community assets and exploring issues around ownership of community buildings and land.
> - **Disaster relief and resilience initiatives** such as the work of Humanitarian OpenStreetMap Team (HOT) which mobilises volunteers to remotely map disaster-hit areas in support of responders. The OpenDRI (Open Data for Resilience Initiative) seeks to reduce vulnerability to natural hazards and impacts of climate change.[29]
> - **Aid mapping** including work to understand patterns of aid distribution and the geopolitics of aid.[30]

Challenges: IP, privacy, and standards

For all the progress that has been made in terms of data openness, four issues present notable challenges for work with open geospatial data.

First, numerous countries face challenges in opening key datasets due to IP restrictions. The UK's mapping agency, the Ordnance Survey, and postal service, Royal Mail, have long been restricted in how they can open up their geospatial data due to Crown Copyright. Ownership of all or part of the IP was further complicated when the management of the postcode database was outsourced to a private firm. The situation shows signs of improvement with a 2015 open data policy supporting a "presumption to publish".[31] However, efforts to create an open address register for the UK have been put on hold, which places this critical lookup dataset out of the reach of many open data projects.[32] CanadaPost has maintained strict IP protections on its postal code database. In Canada, a one-person firm, Geolytica, built an application that would reverse engineer Canadian postal code boundaries using computational geometry and crowdsourcing. It was done as a proof-of-concept, but the database was also opened up to the public. Geolytica's efforts led to it being sued by CanadaPost for violating the latter's ownership of the phrase "postal code" and the underlying content.[33]

The value of spatial data as IP means that firms are often interested in acquiring exclusive rights to it. Another example from Canada illustrates this. The Ontario-based firm, Teranet, purchased the rights to land registries (cadastres) around the world. In exchange for those rights, the firm maintains the registry datasets and then licenses access back to local and regional governments.[34] This represents not just private provision of the service but private ownership of the data. There is a paucity of reliable data on how many countries have substantial private ownership of IP in their spatial data infrastructure, yet this is likely to be an important area to track over the coming decade if further gaps are to be avoided in the open geospatial data landscape.

A second key challenge relates to privacy and security. When it concerns data about individuals, location data can often pierce privacy protections and enable surveillance. A combination of just three variables (i.e. gender, birthdate, US zip code) has been found sufficient to identify individuals by name in the US.[35] Individuals increasingly leave geographic data traces on the web through their use of fitness trackers, location-stamped photographs, or a myriad of other location tracking apps. The existence of this data can jeopardise the anonymity of other datasets that might contain coinciding location and timestamps. Methods exist to maximise privacy while preserving the ability to analyse data (e.g. through geographic masking).[36] However, the ability to deanonymise data will only improve as artificial intelligence and machine learning are applied to open data.[37] Whereas open datasets generally do not describe individual persons, the growing availability of geo-indexed data needs to be accounted for when creating, sharing, and using open datasets.

Standardisation presents a third major challenge for greater interoperability in the world of geospatial data. The most commonly used standard for geography is the "atomic standard" of the coordinates, latitude and longitude. Multiple alternatives exist to lat/long (e.g. polar coordinates are better for people near the poles). Considering coordinate systems requires contemplating standards in geographic projections. Inconsistent projections prevent one dataset from correctly being overlaid onto other data layers and may inhibit other operations like calculating travel distances. Polygons like jurisdictional boundaries also generate complexity related to standards. The schema.org standards for place, which contain at least ten different relationships of containment, overlapping, intersection, and equality between areas, provides a sense of how complicated it is to structure geometries beyond simple point locations.[38] Maintaining the quality of geographic data and ensuring standards are adopted correctly is not trivial. Unlike other sectors, the problem is not the availability of standards (e.g. the Open Geospatial Consortium maintains over 30 open standards for geographic data).[39] We need an educated understanding about their adoption. Instead of creating an integrated world of geospatial data, open data initiatives could lead to a soup of misaligned points and polygons that are difficult to distinguish.

This leads to the last challenge: the lack of interaction between open data communities and the communities that traditionally work with geographic data. Open geospatial data (via WAIS servers, NDSIs, and Al Gore's articulation of a Digital Earth[40]) predate the concept and implementation of open data. Open data advocacy in several countries was sparked by a desire for geospatial data as in the UK FreeOurData campaign[41] and Canada's DataLibre.[42] Nonetheless, there has been a gulf between the early open data movement with its focus on quantity over quality and the geography/geomatics community, which by 2010, was already well established and considering issues of standardisation and data management. We have seen plenty of missed opportunities to bridge the gulf, which has resulted in a bifurcation in skills for geospatial data handling that impedes both the opening, and the effective use, of geospatial data. In particular, this has led to the open data world's focus on mapping but very little focus on geographical analysis. There remains considerable potential for increased interaction between the two communities to enhance skills and analysis.

Pitfalls and potential: From mapping to analysis

Mapping is undoubtedly important, but visualisation of data is just one strategy of many. There has been a tendency among open data practitioners to map and make inferences based on visual inspection of geospatial datasets. However, these ostensible relationships are often not statistically significant. The ability to map open data in the absence of the critical skills to analyse it correctly can lead to problems and even incorrect policy prescriptions. Expanding skills for detailed spatial statistics and analysis, to allow conclusions to be drawn from open datasets and to create new, improved maps based on the results of that analysis, should be a high priority in the open data community. General data literacy capacity has grown, but the availability of tools, resources, and outreach to promote geospatial data literacy is much more limited. The current lack of analytical capacity represents a critical bottleneck to the effective use of open geospatial data.

For example, one large part of open geographic data handling concerns what is known as "feature geometry". Most open data containing geospatial attributes is point-based. That is, an entity's location (e.g. a park, a government transaction, a building project, or a refugee settlement) is represented by a single x, y coordinate. The choice of which points to use is not always obvious. Should the location be a headquarters of a local relief agency or the location where activities are occurring? Many of these points reflect what is called a central tendency or the centroid (a geometric centre of an area). Depending on the shape of the area (e.g. a crescent), a centroid could actually appear outside the area. The simple consideration of which location is mapped can affect the message a map communicates.

Numerous forms of analysis should not rely on point location at all. Many features, such as the geographic distribution of poverty or of crop types, are not natural distributions, easily interpreted through the use of latitude and longitude, but are shaped by politics. Such features are more appropriately described by areal measures. For example, poverty should be reported by the political boundary of a township. Unlike geographic points, working with jurisdictional data can be difficult because boundary file availability and discoverability are limited and there may be disputes over borders. Tools for working with containment (polygons) are less user-friendly, in many cases, than those for generating point-based online maps. Similar issues exist for raster datasets (e.g. satellite imagery), which are especially important for rural areas.[43] Working with raster data, whether it is satellite data or drone data, generally requires more extensive experience and expensive software than other types of data.

A common alternative to mapping by jurisdiction is through aggregation and clustering. Two popular aggregation methods are hexagonal binning (hexbins) and rectangular grids, which rely on the use of regular artificial areas into which points are counted. A different approach is clustering points through hotspot analysis, which infers the geospatial extent of a phenomenon (e.g. a cluster of disease outbreaks) and differentiates statistically significant clusters from non-significant clusters. Many tools can now automate aggregation and clustering, but tools need to be accompanied by a critical understanding of the way the choice of approach affects analysis. Geographers have widely discussed the modifiable areal unit problem (MAUP)[44] whereby aggregation units are understood as definitionally artificial and the results of data aggregation depend on the choice of the unit. Results (e.g. counts, rates, densities, and correlations) are influenced by the shape and orientation of the unit (e.g. slight tilting or enlarging of a rectangular grid), as well as by the way the units are combined (scale). O'Loughlin et al. (2014), for example, use open data on a rectangular grid to map violence, heat, and precipitation across the African continent.[45] They note limits in the data and its aggregation, even as they perform analyses at a finer aggregation than previously conducted to better understand climate conflicts. Tools exist to improve data literacy with regard to problems introduced by spatial aggregation.[46] The challenge is promoting their adoption outside the geography community and within the much wider community of open data users who may otherwise adopt naive analytical strategies. No aggregation is perfect, including those using jurisdictional boundaries. It is important to broaden critical understanding of the malleability of aggregations in the results they deliver.

This noted, we must be aware that improving the quality of analysis of geospatial open data can be knowledge and resource intensive. For example, AidData's infrastructure for sophisticated geospatial analysis of international aid patterns is expensive to maintain and requires substantial annual resources.[47] Although Google has instituted a business model for Google Maps, organisations like AidData cannot rely on similar mechanisms of support.

As we look to the future, opportunities lie in better connecting the open data and geospatial data communities. The latter has been working on improving open source geospatial data tooling for many decades. Even though much of this work has been focused in particular professional contexts, critical and community geographers have long been working on ways to open up access to, and support popular engagement with, geospatial data. The extensive learning and thinking within this field should not be ignored in the rush to open up data and excitement over the latest commercial tools and simplified mapping platforms.

Conclusion

Major advances have been made in open geospatial data. However, numerous gaps remain related to IP, standardisation, privacy, and analytical capacity. In the next decade of open data, we need to ensure greater coordination between the geomatics/GIS and the open data communities so better maps can be produced and greater value can be demonstrated from the wealth of geographic content within the open data released in the last decade.

More than anything, anyone working with geographic open data should approach it with a critical eye and ask two questions. Which choices have been made in creating this data? What lessons might there be from the existing geospatial data community to help with the analysis of this data?

Further reading

Armstrong, M. & Ruggles, A.J. (2005). Geographic information technologies and personal privacy. *Cartographica: The International Journal for Geographic Information and Geovisualization, 40(4)*, 63–73.

Johnson, P., Sieber, R., Scassa, T., Stephens, M., & Robinson, P. (2017). The cost(s) of geospatial open data. *Transactions in GIScience, 21(3)*, 434–445.

MacEachren, A.M. & Kraak, M.J. (2001). Research challenges in geovisualization. *Cartography and Geographic Information Science, 28(1)*, 3–12.

Monmonier, M. (2018). *How to lie with maps*. 3rd edition. Chicago, IL: University of Chicago Press.

Openshaw, S. (1983). *The modifiable areal unit problem*. Norwick: Geo Books.

About the author

Renée Sieber is an Associate Professor at McGill University in the Department of Geography and School of Environment, where she researches the use and value of geospatial information for social change. Renée examines applications in GIS for and by poor communities, social movements (particularly the environmental movement), and Indigenous groups. You can follow Renée at https://www.twitter.com/re_sieber.

How to cite this chapter

Sieber, R. (2019). Open data and geospatial. In T. Davies, S. Walker, M. Rubinstein, & F. Perini (Eds.), *The state of open data: Histories and horizons* (pp. 137–150). Cape Town and Ottawa: African Minds and International Development Research Centre. http://stateofopendata.od4d.net.

This work is licensed under a Creative Commons Attribution 4.0 International (CC BY 4.0) licence. It was carried out with the aid of a grant from the International Development Research Centre, Ottawa, Canada.

Endnotes

1. Haklay, M. & Weber, P. (2008). OpenstreetMap: User-generated street maps. *IEEE Pervasive Computing*, *7(4)*, 12–18.
2. GIS specialists tend to refer to data containing a geographic reference as "geospatial" instead of "geographic" or "locational" to suggest how geographic/locational data allows us to ask spatial questions, like "What is statistically near this location?" or "How many of these items are within this boundary?"
3. https://mapping-phoenix.opendata.arcgis.com/
4. https://mappinggm.org.uk/
5. Hahmann, S. & Burghardt, D. (2013). How much information is geospatially referenced? Networks and cognition. *International Journal of Geographical Information Science*, *27(6)*, 1171–1189.
6. The US Federal Geospatial Data Committee argued that all communities should have seven datasets: land ownership (cadastre), digital orthoimagery, elevation, geodetic control, jurisdictional and other government unit boundaries, hydrography, and transportation.
7. PwC. (2017). *The impact of the open geographical data: Follow up study*. PwC Danmark. https://sdfe.dk/media/2917052/20170317-the-impact-of-the-open-geographical-data-management-summary-version-13-pwc-qrvkvdr.pdf
8. Loomis, J., Koontz, S., Miller, H., & Richardson, L. (2015). Valuing geospatial information: Using the contingent valuation method to estimate the economic benefits of landsat satellite imagery. *Photogrammetric Engineering & Remote Sensing*, *81(8)*, 647–656. https://doi.org/10.14358/PERS.81.8.647
9. Yates, D., Keller, J., Wilson, R., & Dodds, L. (2018). *The UK's geospatial data infrastructure: Challenges and opportunities*. London: Open Data Institute. https://theodi.org/wp-content/uploads/2018/11/2018-11-ODI-Geospatial-data-infrastructure-paper.pdf
10. Klinkenberg, B. (2003). The true cost of spatial data in Canada. *The Canadian Geographer*, *47(1)*, 37–49.
11. Masser, I. (1999). All shapes and sizes: The first generation of national spatial data infrastructures. *International Journal of Geographical Information Science*, *13(1)*, 67–84.
12. https://www.fgdc.gov/nsdi/nsdi.html
13. https://index.okfn.org/
14. http://www.earthobservations.org/open_eo_data.php
15. Uhlir, P.F. (2015). *The value of open data sharing*. Geneva: Group on Earth Observations. http://www.earthobservations.org/documents/dsp/20151130_the_value_of_open_data_sharing.pdf
16. https://inspire.ec.europa.eu
17. https://docs.ckan.org/en/ckan-1.7.4/geospatial.html
18. Melamed, C. (2018). The Africa Regional Data Cube: Harnessing SATELLITES for SDG progress. *United Nations Foundation*, 4 June. https://unfoundation.org/blog/post/the-africa-regional-data-cube-harnessing-satellites-for-sdg-progress/
19. See, for example, https://platform.digitalglobe.com/maps-api
20. ProgrammableWeb. (2018). Time to challenge Google Maps pricing. *ProgrammableWeb*, 26 August. https://www.programmableweb.com/news/time-to-challenge-google-maps-pricing/elsewhere-web/2018/08/26
21. https://leafletjs.com/
22. https://www.mapbox.com/
23. https://www.openstreetmap.org/about
24. Maron, M. & Channell, T. (2015). How complete Is OpenStreetMap? *Mapbox*, 18 November. https://blog.mapbox.com/how-complete-is-openstreetmap-7c369787af6e
25. https://www.mapbox.com/data-platform/country/#india

26 Lee, T. (2018). Open data, and how we preserve it. *Medium*, 30 October. https://medium.com/@thomas.j.lee/open-data-and-how-we-preserve-it-4db836f354fc

27 Marzloff, L., Hamonic, A., & Rieg, J. (n.d.). *Quelles coopérations public-privé à l'ère de la Data ?* [Public–private partnerships in the age of data]. *Le Lab*. https://www.le-lab.org/enquetes/2-quelles-cooperations-public-prive-a-lere-de-la-data

28 Johnson, P.A. (2017). Models of direct editing of government spatial data: Challenges and constraints to the acceptance of contributed data. *Cartography and Geographic Information Science, 44(2)*, 128–138.

29 See https://www.hotosm.org and https://opendri.org/about/

30 http://aiddata.org/

31 https://www.ordnancesurvey.co.uk/business-and-government/public-sector/news/2015/presumption-publish.html

32 ODI (Open Data Institute). (2015). Creating the UK's first free and open address list. https://theodi.org/project/creating-the-uks-first-free-and-open-address-list/

33 https://cippic.ca/en/news/canada_post_settles_postal_code_geolytical_lawsuit

34 Sangiambut, S. (2017). Geospatial open data: Reshaping citizens and governments, roles and interactions. Master's Thesis, McGill University. digitool.library.mcgill.ca:8881/dtl_publish/1/145408.html

35 Sweeney, L. (2000). *Uniqueness of simple demographics in the US population*. Technical Report LIDAP-WP4. Pittsburgh: Carnegie Mellon University, School of Computer Science.

36 Armstrong, M. & Ruggles, A.J. (2005). Geographic information technologies and personal privacy. *Cartographica: The International Journal for Geographic Information and Geovisualization, 40(4)*, 63–73.

37 https://privacyinternational.org/blog/54/privacy-international-launches-surveillance-industry-index-new-accompanying-report

38 http://schema.org/Place

39 http://www.opengeospatial.org/

40 Foresman, T.W. (2008). Evolution and implementation of the Digital Earth vision, technology and society. *International Journal of Digital Earth, 1(1)*, 4–16. https://www.tandfonline.com/doi/full/10.1080/17538940701782502

41 http://www.freeourdata.org.uk/

42 http://datalibre.ca/

43 Sieber, R.E. & Parfitt, I. (2019). The future of open data is rural. In P. Robinson and T. Scassa (Eds.), *The future of open data*. Ottawa: University of Ottawa Press.

44 Openshaw, S. (1983). *The modifiable areal unit problem*. Norwick: Geo Books.

45 O'Loughlin, J., Linke, A.M., & Witmer, F.D.W. (2014). Effects of temperature and precipitation variability on the risk of violence in sub-Saharan Africa, 1980–2012. *Proceedings of the National Academy of Sciences, 111(47)*, 16712–16717.

46 See Amelia McNamara and Aran Lunzer's site at https://tinlizzie.org/spatial

47 Custer, S., DiLorenzo, M., Masaki, T., Sethi, T., & J. Wells. (2017). *Beyond the tyranny of averages: Development progress from the bottom up*. Williamsburg, VA: AidData at the College of William & Mary, p. 2.

010

Government finances

Cécile Le Guen

Key points

- Opening up data on government finance has been a major focus of open data advocacy with projects like OpenSpending bringing a data-driven approach to work on fiscal transparency.

- Opening up public finance data requires a whole set of conditions for success, including government capacity, access to technical platforms and standards, and in-depth engagement from civil society, to help make sense of complex financial data.

- When better connected to grassroots advocacy, open data approaches to government finance can help re-energise global budget transparency work.

Introduction

Working to ensure the transparency of government finances has a long history. By 1850, many countries in Europe had already enacted constitutional requirements that government budgets or accounts be published, leading to what Irwin[1] refers to as an "avalanche of data" that was sparked, in part, by "rulers' need to persuade creditors to lend and taxpayers' representatives to approve new taxes". However, this avalanche of annual accounts, published in printed paper reports, seems miniscule when compared to the data on government finances that could be made available today. When the East Asian financial crisis hit in 1997, fiscal transparency was firmly placed on the global agenda, and principles were put forward calling for disclosure of information across government operations, not just budgets.[2] And as the open data movement has developed over the last decade, it has brought a particular focus on transparency in government finances, adding a particular digital spin to advocacy and calling not only for data but for machine-readable data that is ready for public analysis.

Public finances are ultimately at the heart of government activity, constituting one of the main levers of public action through which governments shape society. The study of public finance may historically have been regarded as a question of simply determining the income and expenditures of governments. However, since the middle of the 20th century, this has expanded to recognise the role that taxes and spending play in shaping the wider economy (e.g. taxing activities that may have negative consequences and spending that may stimulate economic development and trade, including research grants or development aid). As such, citizen scrutiny and a clear understanding of all aspects of public finances is crucial. Debt, taxation, contracting, grants, and subsidies are all topics to be covered within the context of fiscal transparency, alongside more obvious themes of budgets and expenditures. With the right mechanisms in place, improved citizen understanding of the state's fiscal behaviour can encourage greater civic participation and oversight, can promote public accountability, and, most importantly, can potentially enhance the effectiveness and efficiency of public budgets and spending.[3,4]

From the start, the open data movement has placed an emphasis on government finances with projects such as the 2007 "Where Does My Money Go" prototype (see box below) that demonstrated the potential of open data in this sector. Over the last decade, civil society and government-led projects around the world have sought to make public finance data more accessible with initiatives on almost every continent. However, the latest findings from the Open Data Index[5] and Open Data Barometer illustrate that just 10% of surveyed governments publish fully open budget data (12 countries in total) and only 3% publish disaggregated open spending data (just 4 countries).[6] In some countries, such as the United Kingdom (UK), an early publisher of spend data, reliable data availability has not been sustained, and it is not clear how far citizens have engaged with the data that has been made available.[7]

A decade into the new wave of open data-driven financial transparency, it is important to take stock of progress and to ask whether efforts to open up financial data have delivered results or whether activity is beginning to stall. This chapter takes a look at the arc of activity since 2005, taking stock of the state of initiatives, issues, and communities related to open government finance data.

The new wave of fiscal transparency: From documents to datasets

"Fiscal transparency – the comprehensiveness, clarity, reliability, timeliness, and relevance of public reporting on the past, present, and future state of public finances – is critical for effective fiscal management and accountability. It helps ensure that governments have an accurate picture of their finances when making economic decisions, including of the costs and benefits of policy changes and potential risks to public finances. It also provides legislatures, markets, and citizens with the information they need to hold governments accountable."[8]

What counts as "public reporting" depends on your perspective. For much of the history of fiscal transparency, the focus has been on access to information being provided through the publication of government reports on budget formation and execution (including spending). These reports are generally static documents prepared by selecting, analysing, and summarising data from one or more "live" financial information systems. Governments may, in some cases, provide interactive tools to support the user's ability to "drill-down" into the contents of those reports. However, with documents, there is a limit on how far users can dig into the data or remix the information to present it in different ways.

This is where calls for "raw data" come in: asking not just for reports and documents about budgets, taxes, and spending, but also for the underlying granular data. Where a row in a published document might represent hundreds of individual budget allocations, an open dataset could include a row for every allocation, along with detailed classification information. Where a spending report might contain an aggregated figure on payments by a particular agency, spending data could contain a row for each payment with details on the suppliers paid in each case and information on the timing of those payments. The move from documents to data provides for both increased **granularity** (or disaggregation) of information and increased **flexibility** in how users can work with it (see Figure 1). With access to data, rather than documents alone, it becomes possible for a wider range of users to create a wider range of visualisations, interfaces, and analysis, although such applications are very dependent on the quality of the raw data and on the metadata to provide context.

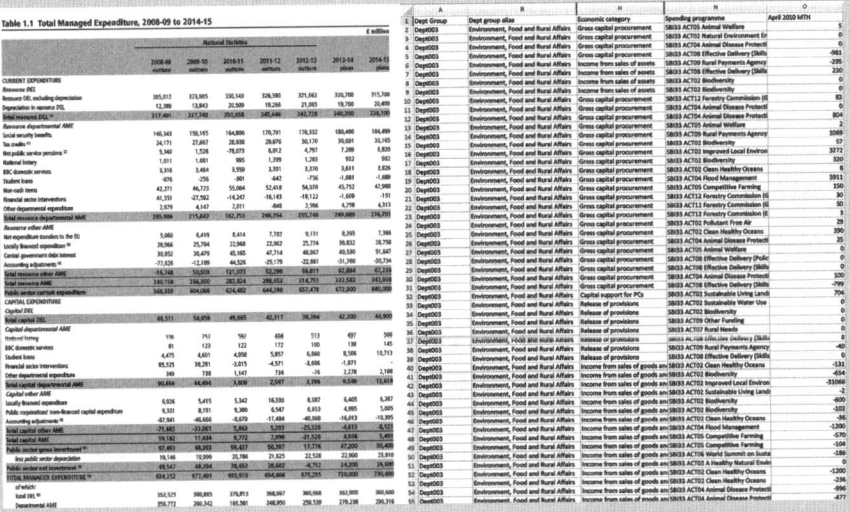

Figure 1: From documents to data: An example of the "Public Expenditure Statistical Analysis" document on the left, and the COINS public spending dataset to illustrate the difference in granularity between the two.
Sources: PESA document: HM Treasury. (2013). Public Expenditure: Statistical Analyses 2013, p. 19. https://assets.publishing.service.gov.uk/government/uploads/system/uploads/attachment_data/file/223600/public_expenditure_statistical_analyses_2013.pdf; COINS dataset: HM Treasury. (2010). COINS 2010–11 Q1 Dataset (coins_sept10_3.csv). data.gov.uk. https://data.gov.uk/dataset/3266d22c-9d0f-4ebe-b0bc-ea622f858e15/combined-online-information-system

The pioneers: Early steps to open financial data

In 2005, a trio of data journalists launched FarmSubsidy.org with the goal of facilitating access to information on the subsidy payments under the European Union (EU) Common Agricultural Policy (CAP). The platform, constructed with data accessed via freedom of information (FOI) requests to governments across Europe, made structured data accessible to search and explore, providing detail not only on subsidy payments, but also the details of the companies who receive subsidies. Danish journalists were able to use this information to challenge the dominant political narrative that the CAP supported primarily the poorest farmers by showing that it was actually large landowners and agri-businesses that received the most funds.[9] By 2009, EU member states were mandated to publish their subsidy data, removing the need for FOI requests, although, even now, the data is not always available in machine-readable formats. The growth of the project played a key role in demonstrating the value of data-driven public finance journalism and attracted interest from a range of funders, including the Hewlett Foundation.[10]

In 2007, the Open Knowledge Foundation's Jonathan Gray developed the idea for "Where Does My Money Go"[11] as a visual breakdown of the UK budget, tapping into a growing appetite for both data visualisation and open data ideas (see Figure 2). In 2008, the project was a winner of the UK Government's "Show Us A Better Way" competition and had soon secured grant funding from government to develop a working prototype.[12] Further funding from a UK state broadcaster (4IP), the Open Society Foundation, the Knight Foundation, the Hewlett Foundation, and the Omidyar Network enabled the evolution of the project into the global Open Spending platform,[13] which now hosts elements of fiscal data from at least 70 countries. The nascent community related to the project was not comprised of accountants or public finance experts but rather civic hackers and citizens interested in making complex government finance more accessible and supporting wider citizen engagement.

By 2010, more governments were starting to explore the direct publication of machine-readable budget data, reducing the need for citizens, organisations, and projects to manually scrape data out of documents and PDFs. The United States (US) government's USASpending.gov, originally created in response to legislation passed in 2006 requiring all "federal contract, grant, loan, and other financial assistance awards of more than $25,000 to be displayed on a publicly accessible and searchable website to give the American public access to information on how their tax dollars are being spent",[14] went through a number of relaunches in 2009 and 2010 with increasing emphasis placed on the availability of downloadable open data and enhanced granularity. Although the site had provided an application programming interface (API) since 2007, it was the addition of downloadable open data in subsequent versions that gained it an increased profile.

Intense policy competition between the UK and US during this period may be behind the UK government's 2010 publication of the COINS (Combined Online INformation System) dataset,[15] providing detailed "fact tables" that presented disaggregated spending data from across the public sector. *The Guardian* newspaper was one of the early users of this data, creating a public data explorer interface to help citizens search the large dataset and working with Open Knowledge Foundation to use citizen research and FOI requests to fill gaps in the data, particularly around individual supplier names.[16] *The Guardian* went on to write a number of stories based on their

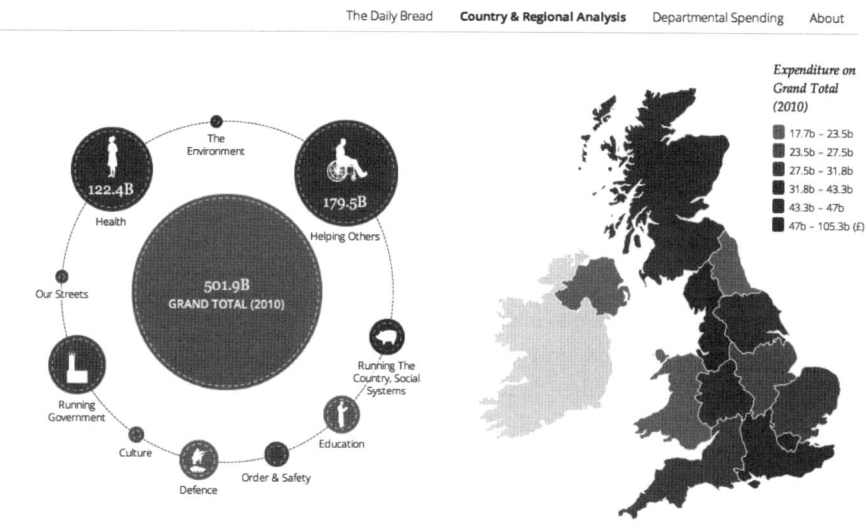

Figure 2:   WhereDoesMyMoneyGo
Source: http://app.wheredoesmymoneygo.org/about.html

analysis of the COINS data and used its release to explore gaps in the quality of public financial management in the UK.[17] In parallel, government departments and local authorities were asked in a letter from Prime Minister David Cameron on 31 May 2010 to publish details on all expenditures over GBP 25 000. The letter also committed to the online publication of information on all new central government contracts and all international development project spending over GBP 500 from January 2011 onward.[18]

Latin American governments also took a lead during this early wave of government activity. In Mexico, the first budget dataset was published in 2011 by the Ministry of Finance as part of a project under Mexico's Open Government Partnership (OGP) action plan.[19] The portal that was created published basic information about federal programmes with quarterly updates on the money spent, information on external evaluations, and a matrix illustrating progress toward planned and achieved goals. The intent of this project was to provide a place where both citizens and decision-makers could find government finance data in a unified format. An OGP case study credits the portal with generating "commitments from the Federal Public Administration to make progress on public projects and initiatives which [had] fallen behind".[20] Although such portals could theoretically be created without using open data, taking an open data approach helped to provide Mexico with a common format for aligning data from different departments and agencies, supporting the integration of information that originated from many different IT systems.

Although Brazil launched a National Transparency Portal in 2004, Beghin and Zigoni (2014) documented[21] that it was not until the passage of an Access to Information Act in 2011, establishing procedures for federated entities to follow in the disclosure of information, that access to government finance data increased. However, they note that, in 2014, there was still a long way to go before all budget and spending data would be accessible in machine-readable form.

It is no surprise then that a World Bank study in 2013 cited the UK, Mexico, and Brazil as members of a small pioneering group of countries working to provide good access to reliable open budget data from financial management information systems.[22] The full list of countries noted included Brazil, Germany, South Korea, Mexico, New Zealand, Spain, Sweden, the UK, and the US. They all have a high Open Budget Index score (above 60)[23] and OGP commitments to promote fiscal transparency in common.[24]

In this pioneer phase, we can see how the interaction between select journalists, civil society, and governments spurred action to make more granular and machine-readable data available on government finance. But whether or not this data can be used to answer questions like "where does the money go?" and whether these early publication projects are sustainable depends on a much wider network of actors and activities.

A growing community: Creating tools and capacity

While many of the most prominent actors working in the area of open budgets are intergovernmental organisations, international NGOs, and multi-stakeholder initiatives, according to Gray's analysis of the open budget data landscape, the active grassroot community is composed of a myriad of international and local CSOs involved in open government, government transparency, aid transparency, open data, and related topics.[25] The way these groups are making use of public finance data is innovative and ingenious and reflects a limited but dedicated citizen interest in understanding how public money is spent. For example, in Nigeria, BudgIT[26] has worked since 2011 on creating infographics that explain elements of the budget and, since 2014, has used Tracka to crowdsource information on the progress of development projects in local communities. Communicating through social media, mainstream media, and community outreach, BudgIT reports reach over 4 million Nigerians with their information.[27]

In an effort to help scale up innovations, equip organisations with open source tools, and improve data literacy around spending data, the Open Knowledge Foundation launched the OpenSpending project in 2011.[28] Its vision was to provide a central database of budget and spending data, as well as to build a community of groups and individuals who could work together to acquire, use, and add their contributions to the platform. From its launch, the resources made available increased substantially as the project grew, including a spending data handbook,[29] an open-source CKAN data portal with extensions,[30] a visualisation library based on Where Does My Money Go,[31] and a data specification called the Fiscal Data Package.[32] As of November 2018, OpenSpending contains government finance datasets from over 80 countries, although at varying levels of granularity and timeliness.

The tools provided by OpenSpending have been used by different civil society projects and platforms to provide citizens with accessible and user-friendly budget information (e.g. the

German project Offener Haushalt, the budget explorer tool in Kosovo, and the Open Budget platform in Ukraine).[33] Many other organisations have developed their own technology and visualisations. This is the case for the Open Key project in Israel, the Open Spending portal in the Netherlands, the Vuleka Mali project in South Africa, and the Dónde van mis impuestos platform in Spain.[34] A key driver for the editorial and technological choices of these projects has been the goal of building visualisations that reflect the needs of citizens and a desire to embed data within a pedagogical context that provides education on government finance.

Between 2013 and 2017, as the community grew, many more projects and platforms emerged from civil society organisations (CSOs), some of them with the specific objectives of using public finance data for investigation in journalism or to enhance civic participation. One notable data journalism project using public finance data is Spending Stories, a project by the former data journalism agency J++ that was developed in 2013 to allow comparisons between big and small amounts of money to give users a context to understand how money is being spent while referencing original news stories.[35] The Farmsubsidy.org network has also continued to play an important part in building data journalism capacity related to open financial data, giving rise to the annual European investigative journalism Dataharvest Conference that now brings together as many as 400 journalists, coders, and scholars from all over Europe each year.[36]

As Gray's map of the linkages between open budget data-related websites from 2015 suggests (Figure 3), it is also important to recognise different sub-communities working in the open finance data domain. As well as local groups, there are a number of overlapping global communities of practice, some with specific thematic areas of focus. Examples are the International Aid Transparency Initiative (IATI), the Extractives Industry Transparency Initiative (EITI), and others looking at particular sources of data, such as the Open Contracting Partnership which has, since 2015, developed a global network of governments, civil society organisations, and companies working with data on public procurement to enable a different way to "follow the money" that complements budget and spending data. Gray's 2015 mapping does not, however, capture groups working in the area of tax justice. Since 2017, the Open Data for Tax Justice network has sought to put more focus on companies reporting the tax payments they make to government,[37] which, once again, fills in another part of the complex government finance picture.

Although they do not feature heavily in Gray's mapping, we should also not ignore private sector actors. Firms like SpendNetwork[38] clean and re-package government spending data for firms interested in securing government contracts, and there is some evidence to suggest government spending data feeds into a range of other private sector products. This said, more could be done to understand the role of the private sector in this field.

It should be clear from the examples above that there is widespread interest in, and engagement with, open data on government finances. Networks like the FollowTheMoney network[39] host regular community calls to connect organisations working on different parts of the governance finance puzzle, and groups like the Global Initiative for Fiscal Transparency (GIFT)[40] place an emphasis on open data as part of wider fiscal transparency reforms. Yet there remain many shared practical challenges that mean the vision of timely, accessible, and accurate open data on government finances is far from fully realised.

The State of Open Data

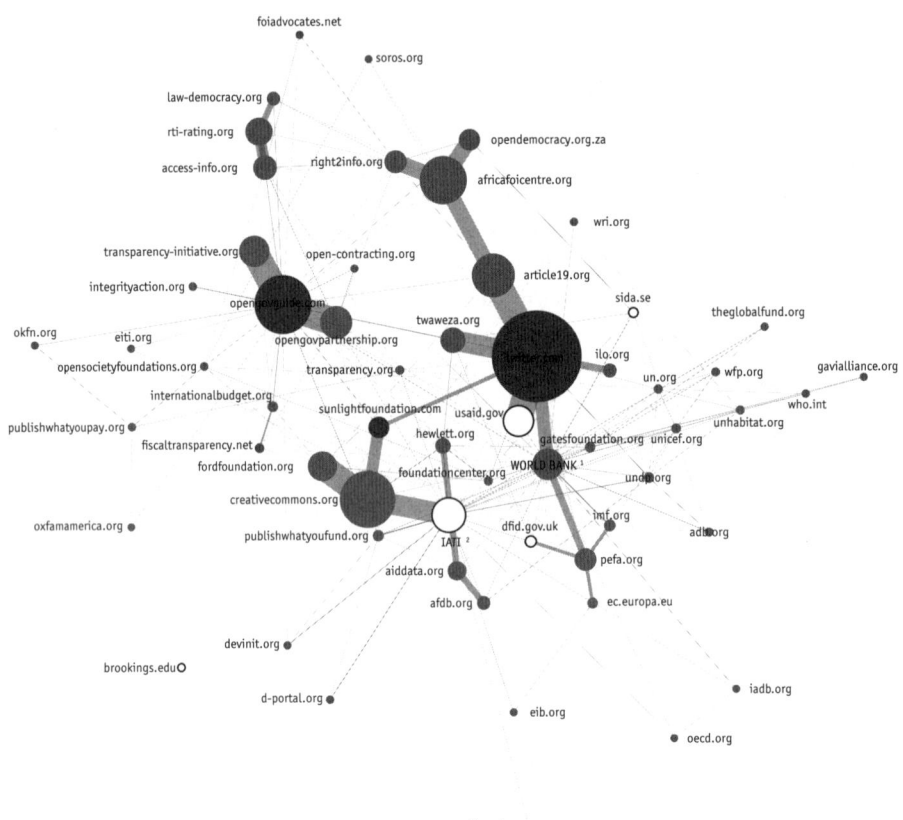

Figure 3: Open budget data: Mapping the landscape
Source: Gray, J. (2015). *Open budget data: Mapping the landscape*. Washington, DC: Global Initiative for Fiscal Transparency. http://www.fiscaltransparency.net/resourcesfiles/files/20150902128.pdf

Ongoing challenges and developments

Even though much progress has been made in opening public finance data, some gaps remain, including those related to policy and high-level commitments, technical platforms for data, linking data to decision-making, and challenges in encouraging the use of data.

Data quality

In 2009, the Sunlight Foundation in the US started the Clearspending[41] project to generate an annual report on the consistency, completeness, and timeliness of federal data published on USASpending.gov. The project discovered over USD 1.3 trillion worth of missing or inaccurate data.[42] *The Guardian* similarly reported problems with the accuracy and coverage of the early UK COINS datasets,[43] and monitoring of UK government departments' compliance with requirements to publish expenditures over GBP 25 000 indicates that many are failing to publish the required data on time.[44] When data quality is low, it becomes hard for citizens to use and interpret data or to draw conclusions from it. This can be addressed by providing documentation that explains how the data was created and its limitations. In other cases, independent monitoring of data quality can provide an impetus for governments to improve their data. However, it is difficult for civil society (and even governments themselves) to sustain a quality control over published data. For example, the Clearspending project in the US only ran until 2012, and a number of other projects that have sought to monitor the quality of data in specific countries or localities are now defunct.

One of the key barriers to improving data quality has been the lack of a legislative basis for open data publication. In the US, the Digital Accountability and Transparency Act of 2014 (DATA Act)[45] has addressed this in part, setting out standards for data publication and leading to the creation of detailed standards and procedures that apply quality assurance in stages as data is collated. Yet, in many countries, legislation or regulations supporting the transparency of government finance, even where they exist, have stopped short of providing enough detail to allow quality requirements to be enforced.

Standards and interoperability

The OpenBudgets.eu project looked at the standardisation of budget and spending datasets across the EU in 2016 and concluded that there were a "plethora of budget and spending data models which reflect ... fine-tuned differences in the legislative design of political entities",[46] although they also recognised the need for common approaches to data publication. One standard that has been put forward to address this gap, developed by a consortium of global organisations, including GIFT, the World Bank, and Open Knowledge International,[47] is the Open Fiscal Data Package (OFDP). Rather than impose a particular structure on source data, the latest iteration of the OFDP allows datasets coming from countries with different fiscal and accountability structures to be published in any tabular form and then subsequently annotated to explain how data should be interpreted and visualised.

Adoption of the OFDP remains limited at present; however, the way in which data standards can facilitate global collaboration around government finance data has already been demonstrated through the adoption of more mature standards for aid flows (IATI) and contracting data (the Open Contracting Data Standard (OCDS)), and with the right backing, there are opportunities for the OFDP to support a step-change in the accessibility and re-use of budget and spend data.

As noted in the introduction to this chapter, to construct a full picture of government finances, more than budget and spend data is needed. This calls for interoperability between standards. There has been some recent progress on this with extensions to the OCDS (Figure 4) being designed to provide interoperability with the OFDP, although this work is currently untested.

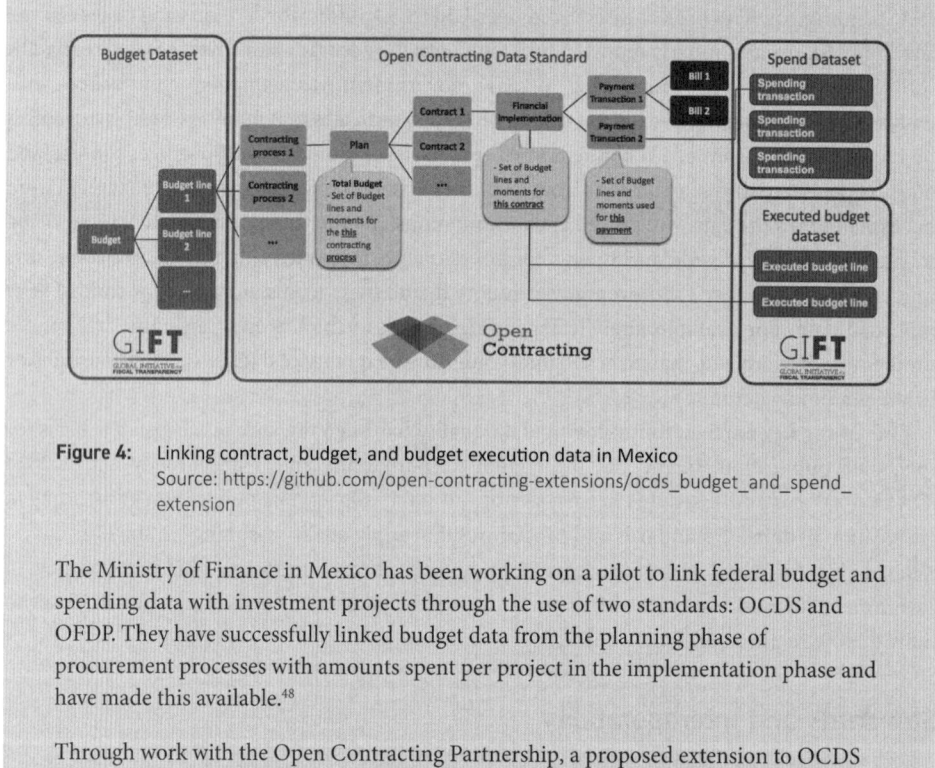

Figure 4: Linking contract, budget, and budget execution data in Mexico
Source: https://github.com/open-contracting-extensions/ocds_budget_and_spend_extension

The Ministry of Finance in Mexico has been working on a pilot to link federal budget and spending data with investment projects through the use of two standards: OCDS and OFDP. They have successfully linked budget data from the planning phase of procurement processes with amounts spent per project in the implementation phase and have made this available.[48]

Through work with the Open Contracting Partnership, a proposed extension to OCDS has been developed to describe how other governments could make similar linkages.[49]

Policy commitments

The greatest challenges (and opportunities) to increased adoption and impact from open data activities related to government financial transparency ultimately relate to policy. In 2017, the International Budget Partnership's Open Budget Survey (OBS) of 115 countries suggested that progress on opening up budgets had stalled for the first time in a decade.[50] Although the OBS does not look specifically at open data publication, its findings suggest that the global political will to increase financial transparency may be at a low ebb. There have also been long-standing challenges to securing public attention on open government finance data, as noted by Carter in 2013 that "budget transparency has still not captured global attention in the way that other related movements have".[51]

Regardless, in some noteworthy countries, open data regulations and legislative frameworks are being used successfully to enforce either the publication of public finance data[52] or to make finance data a priority within wider programmes of open data release across government.[53] The OGP has also provided a key forum for increasing the disclosure of contracting data in recent years with many commitments secured to adopt the OCDS.[54] This suggests that the current wave of interest in open data and data standards could still be used to help advance the financial transparency agenda. Crucially, getting to joined-up data that presents a full picture of government finances means overcoming silos in government and securing data across agencies. For this, the importance of political leadership cannot be underestimated.

User-engagement and capacity

Government finances are undoubtedly complex. Increasing the use of available data requires accessible technical platforms, skilled intermediaries, and capacity building for citizen-users of data. As a whole, the last decade has seen an increase in resources to support the development of data literacy skills which enable users to work with public finance data through digital tools, and many resources are still improving based on cases studies, user involvement, stakeholder feedback, and innovations in technology. However, continued capacity building will be needed for increased data availability to drive new models of citizen engagement around government finances.

Conclusion: Looking to the future

In the years ahead, the key challenge will be to better connect the current wave of the open data-driven transparency movement with other grassroots advocacy networks and government decision-makers. When it comes to securing impactful results from open government finance data, the evidence suggests that projects will require unique partnerships between technologists, CSOs, and government. This is the model followed in South Africa with the Vuleka Mali project, a partnership between the National Treasury and a coalition of CSOs called Imali Yethu to make government budget data and processes accessible to all citizens and interested parties. Their motto, "We aren't interested in transparency for transparency's sake",[55] should be one that more organisations place at the heart of their thinking. Technical work on government financial data also needs to connect with wider social agendas. For example, Carter notes that the potential exists to apply a gender lens to budget analysis;[56] however, we have not yet found open data projects that directly apply a gender lens to open budget data creation and sharing.

Given the long history of work on opening up government finance, we should not expect a complete transformation in less than 15 years of open data activity. The vision of current advocates for open government finances is an ambitious one – to provide more granular data than ever before. There are signs, however, that when data is used, and governments are willing to open up, substantial progress can be made. In their brief history with the DATA Act, Sunlight Foundation has described how "reporting bad data drove reform" to secure new legislation, better processes, and ultimately improved data.[57] Rather than waiting for perfect data, it is possible to publish data and then improve it with subsequent iterations.

The foundations laid in the last decade in terms of technology platforms and data standards, and in terms of networks and communities, is impressive. Long-term, opening up and securing the use of government finance data will require significant resources in terms of technology, financial and human capacities, as well as time and strong political support. Not all the organisations explored in this chapter will have the resources they need for sustainability, but all have demonstrated what could be possible in their local contexts, and they have collectively re-imagined ways to engage citizens on governance finances.

Government finance data has played a key role in shaping the early development of the open data movement. The challenge for the decade ahead is to see how far, and to what end, open data advocates and practitioners can shape a sustainable ecosystem of open government finance data.

Further reading

Beghin, N. & Zigoni, C. (2014). *Measuring open data's impact of Brazilian national and sub-national budget transparency websites and its impacts on people's rights*. Brasilia: Institute for Socioeconomic Studies (INESC). http://www.opendataresearch.org/sites/default/files/publications/Inesc_ODDC_English.pdf

Carter, B. (2013). Budget accountability and participation. *GSDRC Helpdesk Reports*, 15 July. London: Department for International Development. http://www.gsdrc.org/docs/open/hdq973.pdf

Dener, C. & Min, S.Y. (2013). *Financial management information systems and open budget data: Do governments report on where the money goes?* Washington, DC: World Bank. http://documents.worldbank.org/curated/en/659821468152725669/pdf/81332-REVISED-ENGLISH-PUBLIC-WB-Study-FMIS-and-OBD-eng.pdf

Gray, J. (2015). *Open budget data: Mapping the landscape*. Washington, DC: Global Initiative for Fiscal Transparency. http://www.fiscaltransparency.net/resourcesfiles/files/20150902128.pdf

Tygel, A.F., Attard, J., Orlandi, F., Campos, M.L.M., & Auer, S. (2015). "How much?" is not enough: An analysis of open budget initiatives. *Cornell University*, 7 April. https://arxiv.org/pdf/1504.01563.pdf

About the author

Cécile Le Guen is an associate of Datactivist, a French cooperative that provides open data services, strategies, research, and consulting to CSOs and the public and private sector. Datactivist is conducting projects in France and internationally, with a focus on data literacy, open data standards, and open government policies. You can follow Cécile at https://www.twitter.com/cecileLG and learn more about Datactivist at https://datactivist.coop/.

How to cite this chapter

Le Guen, C. (2019). Open data and government finances. In T. Davies, S. Walker, M. Rubinstein, & F. Perini (Eds.), *The state of open data: Histories and horizons* (pp. 151–165). Cape Town and Ottawa: African Minds and International Development Research Centre. http://stateofopendata.od4d.net

This work is licensed under a Creative Commons Attribution 4.0 International (CC BY 4.0) licence. It was carried out with the aid of a grant from the International Development Research Centre, Ottawa, Canada.

Endnotes

1. Irwin, T. (2013). *Shining a light on the mysteries of state: The origins of fiscal transparency in Western Europe*. IMF Working Papers 13–219. Washington, DC: International Monetary Fund. pp. 27 and 1, respectively. http://www.imf.org/en/Publications/WP/Issues/2016/12/31/Shining-a-Light-on-the-Mysteries-of-State-The-Origins-of-Fiscal-Transparency-in-Western-41012
2. International Monetary Fund. (2018). Fiscal transparency. https://www.imf.org/external/np/fad/trans/index.htm
3. GIFT. (2015). *The time is now: Advancing public participation in government fiscal policy and budget-making*. Washington, DC: Global Initiative for Fiscal Transparency. http://www.fiscaltransparency.net/resourcesfiles/files/20150729123.pdf
4. Carter, B. (2013). Budget accountability and participation. *GSDRC Helpdesk Reports*, 15 July. London: Department for International Development. http://www.gsdrc.org/docs/open/hdq973.pdf
5. https://index.okfn.org/
6. Web Foundation. (2017). *Open Data Barometer – Global report*. 4th edition. Washington, DC: World Wide Web Foundation. https://opendatabarometer.org/4thedition/report/
7. Worthy, B. (2015). The impact of open data in the UK: Complex, unpredictable, and political. *Public Administration*, 93(3), 788–805. https://doi.org/10.1111/padm.12166
8. International Monetary Fund. (2018). Fiscal transparency. https://www.imf.org/external/np/fad/trans/index.htm
9. Léchenet, A. (2014). *Global database investigations: The role of the computer-assisted reporter*. Fellowship Papers. Oxford: Reuters Institute for the Study of Journalism. https://reutersinstitute.politics.ox.ac.uk/our-research/global-database-investigations-role-computer-assisted-reporter
10. FarmSubsidy.org. (2017). Farmsubsidy.Org at a glance. Open Knowledge Foundation Deutschland. https://farmsubsidy.org/about/
11. http://app.wheredoesmymoneygo.org/about.html
12. https://webarchive.nationalarchives.gov.uk/20100807004350/http://www.showusabetterway.co.uk/
13. https://openspending.org/

14. US Congress. (2006). S.2590-109th Congress (2005–2006): Federal Funding Accountability and Transparency Act of 2006. https://www.congress.gov/bill/109th-congress/senate-bill/2590
15. HM Treasury. (2010). Combined online information system. https://data.gov.uk/dataset/3266d22c-9d0f-4ebe-b0bc-ea622f858e15/combined-online-information-system
16. Rogers, S. (2010). COINS data release: The 10 things we found out. *The Guardian*, 14 June. https://www.theguardian.com/news/datablog/2010/jun/14/coins-data-results-10-things
17. https://www.theguardian.com/news/datablog+politics/coins-combined-online-information-system
18. Cameron, D. (2010). Letter to government departments on opening up data. *GOV.UK*, 31 May. https://www.gov.uk/government/news/letter-to-government-departments-on-opening-up-data
19. Government of Mexico. (2011). *Alianza Para El Gobierno Abierto – Plan de Acción de México*, 20 September [Open Government Partnership - Mexico Plan of Action]. New York, NY: Open Government Partnership. https://www.opengovpartnership.org/sites/default/files/Mexico_Action_Plan_0.pdf
20. OGP. (2013). *Mexico: The budget transparency portal*. Washington, DC: Open Government Partnership. https://www.opengovpartnership.org/sites/default/files/Inspiring%20Story%20-%20Mexico.pdf
21. Beghin, N. & Zigoni, C. (2014). *Measuring open data's impact of Brazilian national and sub-national budget transparency websites and its impacts on people's rights*. Brasilia: Institute for Socioeconomic Studies. http://www.opendataresearch.org/sites/default/files/publications/Inesc_ODDC_English.pdf
22. Dener, C., & Min, S.Y. (2013). *Financial management information systems and open budget data: Do governments report on where the money goes?* Washington, DC: World Bank. http://documents.worldbank.org/curated/en/659821468152725669/pdf/81332-REVISED-ENGLISH-PUBLIC-WB-Study-FMIS-and-OBD-eng.pdf
23. IBP. (2017). *Open budget survey 2017*. Washington, DC: International Budget Partnership. https://www.internationalbudget.org/wp-content/uploads/open-budget-survey-2017-report-english.pdf
24. http://www.opengovpartnership.org/explorer/all-data.html
25. Gray, J. (2015). *Open budget data: Mapping the landscape*. Washington, DC: Global Initiative for Fiscal Transparency. http://www.fiscaltransparency.net/resourcesfiles/files/20150902128.pdf
26. http://yourbudgit.com/
27. http://yourbudgit.com/about-us/
28. Chambers, L. (2011). OpenSpending goes live. *Open Knowledge International Blog*, 26 June. https://blog.okfn.org/2011/06/26/openspending-goes-live/
29. OpenSpending. (2013). *Spending data handbook*. London: Open Knowledge International. http://community.openspending.org/resources/handbook/
30. Björgvinsson, T. (2015). Presenting public finance just got easier. *Open Knowledge International Blog*, 20 March. https://blog.okfn.org/2015/03/20/presenting-public-finance-just-got-easier/
31. https://github.com/openspending-archive/openspendingjs
32. Walsh, P., Pollock, R., Björgvinsson, T., Bennet, S., Kariv, A., & Fowler, D. (2018). *Fiscal data package* (version 1.0rc1). London: Open Knowledge International. https://frictionlessdata.io/specs/fiscal-data-package/
33. See https://offenerhaushalt.de/, http://www.institutigap.org/spendingsEng/, and http://openbudget.in.ua/, respectively.
34. See https://next.obudget.org/, http://www.openspending.nl/, https://vulekamali.gov.za/2017-18/national/departments/women, and https://dondevanmisimpuestos.es/, respectively.
35. Pedersen, A. (2013). Launching spending stories: How much is it really? *Open Knowledge International Blog*, 21 November. https://blog.okfn.org/2013/11/21/launching-spending-stories-how-much-is-it-really/
36. https://dataharvest.eu/
37. Cobham, A., Gray, J., & Murphy, R. (2018). *What do they pay? Towards a public database to account for the economic activities and tax contributions of multinational corporations*. #OD4TJ. http://datafortaxjustice.net/what-do-they-pay/
38. https://spendnetwork.com/
39. http://followthemoney.net/

40 http://www.fiscaltransparency.net/
41 https://web.archive.org/web/20110802165935/http://sunlightfoundation.com/clearspending/
42 Carr, A. (2010). The curious case of USASpending.Gov's missing $1.3 trillion. *Fast Company*, 7 September. https://www.fastcompany.com/1687410/curious-case-usaspendinggovs-missing-13-trillion
43 Evans, L. (2010). What was coins missing? The mystery of the government's hidden spending data. *The Guardian*, 14 July. https://www.theguardian.com/news/datablog/2010/jul/14/whole-government-accounts-coins-data
44 Freeguard, G., Campbell, L., Cheung, A., Lily, A., & Baker, C. (2018). *Whitehall Monitor 2018: The general election, Brexit and beyond*. London: Institute for Government. https://www.instituteforgovernment.org.uk/publications/whitehall-monitor-2018
45 US Congress. (2014). S.994 – DATA Act. https://www.congress.gov/bill/113th-congress/senate-bill/994
46 Dudáš, M., Klímek, J., Kučera, J., Mynarz, J., Sedmihradská, L., Zbranek, J., & Seeger, B. (2016). *The Openbudgets data model and the surrounding landscape*. OpenBudgets.eu. Berlin: OpenBudgets, p. 8. http://openbudgets.eu/assets/resources/Report-UEP-The-Open-Budgets-Data-Model-and-the-Surrounding-Landscape.pdf
47 http://www.fiscaltransparency.net/ofdp/
48 https://www.gob.mx/contratacionesabiertas/home#!/
49 Davies, T. & Pane, J. (2018). Open contracting budgets and spend extension. https://github.com/open-contracting-extensions/ocds_budget_and_spend_extension
50 IBP. (2017). *Open budget survey 2017*. Washington, DC: International Budget Partnership. https://www.internationalbudget.org/wp-content/uploads/open-budget-survey-2017-report-english.pdf
51 Carter, B. (2013). Budget accountability and participation. *GSDRC Helpdesk Reports*, 15 July. London: Department for International Development. http://www.gsdrc.org/docs/open/hdq973.pdf
52 Dulong de Rosnay, M. & Janssen, K. (2014). Legal and institutional challenges for opening data across public sectors: Towards common policy solutions. *Journal of Theoretical and Applied Electronic Commerce Research, 9(3)*, 1–14.
53 Lucchesi, L. (2016). Digital Republic Bill: France's first open bill. *Open Government Partnership Blog*, 28 January. https://www.opengovpartnership.org/stories/digital-republic-bill-frances-first-open-bill
54 https://www.open-contracting.org/why-open-contracting/worldwide/#/
55 https://imaliyethu.org.za/
56 Carter, B. (2013). Budget accountability and participation. *GSDRC Helpdesk Reports*, 15 July. London: Department for International Development. http://www.gsdrc.org/docs/open/hdq973.pdf
57 Rumsey, M. (2017). A brief history of the DATA Act. *Sunlight Foundation*. https://sunlightfoundation.com/2017/05/08/a-brief-history-of-the-data-act/

011

Health

Mark Irura

Key points

- There is relatively limited awareness of open data in the health sector, where, given the focus on patient data, the idea of "open by default" does not resonate. It is important for initiatives to understand that data exists on a spectrum from personal and closed to non-sensitive and open.

- Privacy concerns, a lack of fresh data, disjointed source systems, and usability problems have all hindered nascent open data initiatives in health. Initiatives have often failed to identify the high-priority use cases, driven by demand from multiple stakeholders, that would sustain the attention and investment necessary to help them overcome early challenges.

- Open data that originates from health facilitates as feedback from service users can be used to improve performance or support researchers as input into policy; however, if feedback is not connected to action or if input meets political and resource constraints, it is hard to create a virtuous cycle of data publication and reuse.

Introduction

The development of large public databases by government ministries, departments, and agencies (MDAs) has been ongoing in earnest in many countries around the world since at least the 1990s. The most basic of these government data systems are registers, supporting a range of government services, such as health insurance, social security, vehicle and business registration, and census-taking among many others. These registers form the basis of numerous vital public services whether the services are delivered electronically or not. Other systems are layered on top of these registers in order to support decision-making, planning, and policy-related research. To function well, many of these systems reside behind rigid security and multi-level authentication and authorisation protocols as they regularly contain very sensitive personal information about citizens.

Data about health is often considered some of the most sensitive information collected and held by governments and institutions. Yet over the last decade, there have been a number of initiatives focused on open data in the health sector. Broad et al. describe open data as "data made available by governments, businesses, and individuals for anyone to access, use and share".[1] Clearly this should not apply to the detailed personal information within health registers. So, when it comes to open data and health, it is paramount to understand the particular data held within each system, to think carefully about the levels of access that different stakeholders may want or need, and to determine how, or whether, the data may be safely anonymised prior to publication as open data. To do this, it is useful to consider a data spectrum for health, to enumerate the different stakeholders creating and using data, and to consider the challenges they must overcome before open data in the health sector can evolve from being a minor sub-community and enter the mainstream.

The spectrum of stakeholders and data access

Keen et al. (2013) state that government MDAs and private firms coexist, often exhibiting a dichotomous relationship between public and private interests in the national health system and the data therein. The following broad categories of actors can be identified within the national health system: the state, private-sector firms, citizens/patients, doctors and other health professionals, researchers, and a broader diaspora of interested parties, including health charities and journalists. All these actors, as illustrated in Figure 1, have the potential to generate data that could be accessed and used within the health sector, and all may also be users of data generated by other actors.

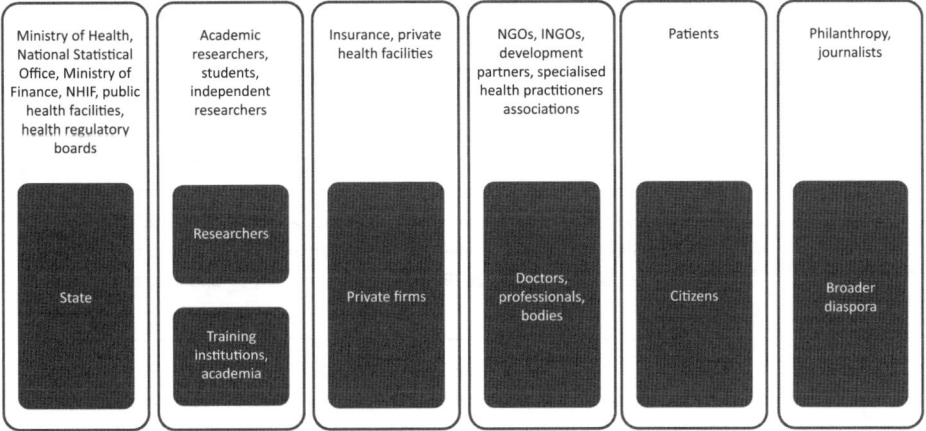

Figure 1: Spectrum of health data stakeholders
Source: Authors

Different actors seek to use data for a variety of purposes. In particular, users seek the data from registers, for example, to access and update information about individuals. They also look for data to support operational requirements, such as organisational planning and decision-making, and to improve efficiency and effectiveness of services, as well as to analyse for research purposes to inform policy and practice development. Data may also be used by patients to locate and access health services.

By examining how different uses of data are currently regulated, it is possible to identify a spectrum of data openness ranging from closed data with highly restricted access through to data that is openly published in reusable formats. Between these two ends of the spectrum can be found planning and decision-support data with ranging levels of restriction on access and reusability as illustrated in Figure 2.

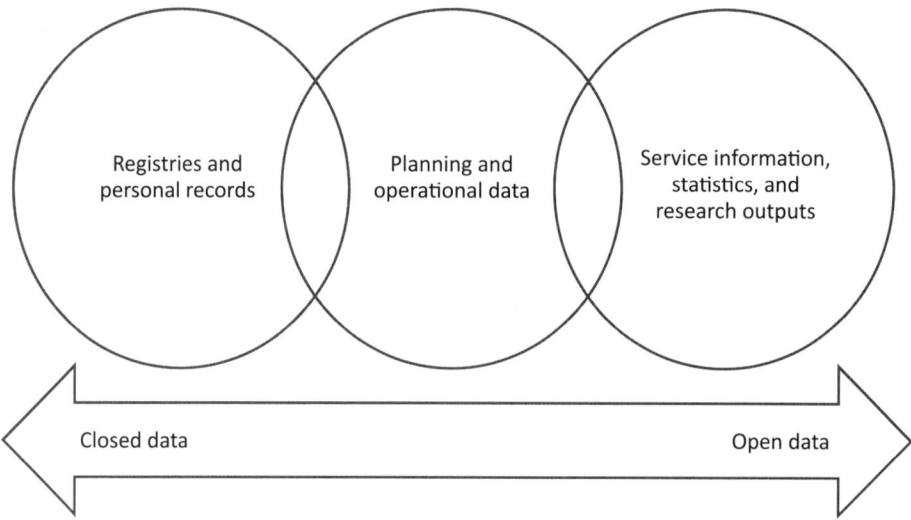

Data type	Registries and personal records	Planning and operational data	Service information, statistics, and research outputs
Used for	Searches and real-time access by clinicians, in-depth research analysis.	Improving efficiency and effectiveness of service delivery.	Access to services, learning, policy-making, and long-term planning.
Openness	**Closed** Sensitive personal data only released if adequately anonymised.	**Various degrees of openness** Dependent on context and sensitivity. May be shared across institutions, but not openly.	**Open** Public data in most cases. May include aggregated information from individual records.

Figure 2: Openness of data based on type and intended use
Source: Authors

The level of openness of data, who it is shared with, and in what level of detail, should also vary according to circumstances. For example, it may become vital to understand who and where patients are located in the case of an outbreak of a deadly disease epidemic, but detailed information may not be necessary when citizens engage civic leaders to mobilise resources for local health centres to be established.

This chapter will examine how to ensure health data is effectively placed on this continuum depending on its intended use. While the focus of this chapter is on the open data end of the spectrum, where individual records are generally only available in anonymised or aggregated form as Figure 2 indicates, the potential uses for open data often overlap with the needs of stakeholders who might also have access to shared or even closed data. This is an important point to be made as it affects the politics behind the open publication of health data. The challenge of working out where certain datasets should fall on this data spectrum is further compounded by advances in computing technologies that could potentially enable the deanonymisation of sensitive data on individuals.

The state of (open) health data

Data availability and use: Laying the foundations

Information technology has been the key process automation enabler in government, which has led to more and better data, and has dictated areas for integration in order to bolster efficiency in service delivery.[2] E-government both improves the quantity and veracity of data. Examples of e-government in health services include, but are not limited to:

- National health insurance schemes.
- Health registries (births, deaths, treatments).
- Electronic health records (patient records inputted at facilities by medical personnel).
- Electronic prescriptions.

Progress toward implementation of these systems has varied, but in Estonia, for example, 99% of all prescriptions are now electronically issued by doctors,[3] creating a potential wealth of data about prescribing practices.

The different political landscapes from country to country have an influence on which health programmes are prioritised by governments and the stage of development of the supporting data systems. For example, in Kenya, the health sector has been devolved so as to be able to offer more resources for better services to citizens at the subnational county level. However, this does not necessarily have to lead to poor data integration. In Kenya, the Health Data Collaborative,[4] established in 2015, provides a framework that stipulates how partners (international agencies, the United Nations, governments, civil society organisations, philanthropies, donors, and academics) engage and align data initiatives with the common aim of improving health data. Similar health data collaboratives exist in Tanzania, Malawi, and Cameroon.

The World Health Organization (WHO) hosts the Global Health Observatory,[5] which is a one-stop portal initiative where countries share both their health data and health priorities. Various countries are moving to implement their own national health data observatories or portals, and the scientific community is moving toward the adoption of common open data principles as evidenced by a number of platforms making clinical trials data available[6] and scientific journals, such as the *British Medical Journal*, campaigning for more open data publication.[7]

In many countries, the health sector has seen significant investment in capacity building over several years. For instance, the District Health Information System 2 (DHIS2)[8] is used in many countries as the national Health Management Information System (HMIS) to collect, manage, and analyse health data. At the time of writing, the open source DHIS2 software is used in over 40 countries in Africa, Asia, and Latin America, and countries that have adopted DHIS2 as their national HMIS software include Kenya, Tanzania, Uganda, Rwanda, Ghana, Liberia, and Bangladesh. The core development activities of the DHIS2 platform are coordinated by the Department of Informatics at the University of Oslo,[9] supported by the North American Aerospace Defense Command (NORAD); the President's Emergency Plan for AIDS Relief (PEPFAR); the Global Fund to Fight AIDS, Tuberculosis and Malaria; United Nations International Children's Emergency Fund (UNICEF); and the University of Oslo.

The introduction of HMIS software does not, however, automatically lead to good data quality. Processes often require data to be manually transcribed from paper into computer terminals at the health facility level before it can be captured and collated in the HMIS, where regional and national health management teams review data for quality. A review stage can impact the timeliness of data and its availability for operational decision support, with some delays of up to six months before data is made available at the local facilities where it originated.[10]

When data is keyed in by health workers solely for the purpose of reporting to administrative agencies, there may be limited local ownership of the data and, as a result, limited investment in its accuracy. There can be tension between the creation of systems that support doctors and clinicians in their day-to-day localised work and systems that emphasise centralised reporting. Arguably, a focus on open data availability can place extra emphasis on centralised reporting, with MDAs pushing healthcare providers to enter as much standardised information as possible. However, if system architectures do not give local stakeholders access to the information they need for planning and prioritisation, they can ultimately lead to expensive, error-prone, and patchy data.[11] One remedy for this comes through the use of automated data collection systems, relying on data created at source from digital keypads, mobile devices, and user interfaces that eliminate the need to transcribe from paper in the first place.

In summary, initiatives at the international, national, and subnational levels are actively encouraging health programmes to improve data management. These initiatives cover not just the creation of data, but also focus on strengthening the use of data by targeting monitoring and evaluation processes. This suggests that, although there may be a long way to go in terms of data quality in some settings, the right steps are being taken toward a strategic approach to establish a conducive environment for leveraging data (UNECA et al., 2016) as evidenced by:

- Legislative and policy reforms that will allow for harnessing data.
- Significant investments in information technology, tools, and infrastructure.
- Greater collaboration and coordination among health stakeholders.
- Investments in administrative data collection and use at the subnational level.
- Supporting and resourcing national statistical offices as key facilitators and drivers of national data ecosystems in their respective countries.

However, much of the focus here is on data use within a single stakeholder group or the use of data shared securely between two particular stakeholders. When it comes to opening up data for wider use, a number of gaps and challenges emerge.

Available but not accessible: (Missed) opportunities

Data from the 2016 edition of the Open Data Barometer indicates that health sector performance statistics exist in 98% of countries surveyed and are available in some form (such as aggregate tables in print or via PDFs) in 85% of countries, but only 7% of countries had openly licensed and machine-readable datasets.[12]

To allow for the maximum range of use when datasets are made open, they should be disaggregated to the lowest levels of administrative geography possible and split by gender, age, income, disability, and other categories. Many governments have made commitments to opening up datasets via their own open data portals, often included in the National Action Plans submitted under their membership in the Open Government Partnership. However, often data that exists in national HMIS remains locked away in countries where they are deployed, and few portals host statistical datasets on health that contain full details. When health data is published, it often does not meet the level of detail demanded or it is too outdated to meet the needs of users.[13] Although platforms like DHIS2 could be configured to generate regular, anonymised exports of data by using application programming interfaces (APIs), it appears this is only rarely the case (Tanzania's HMIS portal being an interesting exception[14]). For example, while the DHIS2 demo shows the location of all health clinics in Sierra Leone, the national open data portal gives no clue that such data even exists, nor does it provide links to the regularly updated dataset.[15]

For academia, particularly in Africa, the use of data to generate scientific output has remained very low (overall scientific research output is less than 1% of global research), limiting key opportunities for locally driven research that could address key development challenges.[16] Alongside the limited quantity of open data, the usability of open data platforms also limits discovery and the uptake of data. In the example of the Kenya Open Data Initiative Platform, usability experiments revealed that more than half of the users found it difficult to navigate and could not find the information they were looking for via the platform.[17] Where data is found and used for research in Africa, there are further challenges related to the ecosystem for knowledge dissemination, with much of the research published in non-indexed journals or left in unpublished dissertations.[18] Although there is more data being generated inside public and private health services than they can analyse themselves, the potential for external stakeholders to get involved in working with this data is currently almost entirely lost.

Increasingly, there is a push from data communities, including the open data community, to engage with policy-makers and other stakeholders to ensure that decision-making is driven by data and research. There have been successes in this regard; however, much remains to be done as evidence is often not a driving factor in decision-making. Many governments will grapple with other considerations, such as budgets, politics, and development partner priorities when it comes to resource allocation,[19] and these decisions can be as basic, as, for example, "Do we buy SMS bundles to disseminate information to patients, pay our staff, or buy additional hospital beds?"

As already noted, the lack of a supply of fresh data, especially from government as the key source of official statistics and operational information, has led to limited progress in developing open data initiatives in health. To date, many seem to have fallen short on scalability and sustainability. This can be attributed in part to failures in identifying high-priority use cases for health data that are driven by demand from multiple stakeholders, which will serve to embed open data initiatives within the wider data ecosystem. The integrated approaches illustrated through the examples in the box on what happens when health data is open are, at present, the exception rather than the rule. As a result, projects have often failed to actualise value through visible results that could lead to continued investment and development.[20] To make sure more opportunities related to open health data are realised, policy-makers, practitioners, and funders will need to address three key challenges.

What happens when health data is open?

The following examples illustrate the potential of open health data:

- Maternal mortality in Mexico: working with the Government of Mexico, the Data Science for Social Good programme at the University of Chicago has explored how available datasets can be leveraged to support reductions in maternal mortality, a key target of the Sustainable Development Goals (SDGs). Researchers, working with a combination of open and shared data, explored how analysis at the regional level could present a more granular picture of how current interventions may be working.[21]

- In Uruguay, A Tu Servico has taken data on healthcare provider performance and made this accessible to citizens, supporting them to make better decisions during the annual one-month window when Uruguayans can choose whether or not to switch healthcare providers.[22] Data made accessible through the site has been used by politicians, media, and by over 35 000 citizens (more than 1% of Uruguay's population).

> - During the Ebola outbreak in Sierra Leone, responders made use of HDX, the open data Humanitarian Data eXchange platform, to bring together up-to-the-minute data from different stakeholders, visualising the results through open mapping tools.[23] The Ministry of Health and Sanitation released geocoded data on health facilities, while others released data on ebola cases and current organisational responses. Multiple stakeholders used the data to identify the regions that needed the most urgent medical supplies. Using an open data approach reduced the friction on data exchanged during this crisis situation.

Ready for impact? Three key challenges

As explored in the previous sections, technology has been a key driver of e-government and has resulted in substantial growth in the amount of health data available. The coming decade could see further dramatic developments in the use of technology in healthcare, and, consequently, the rapid expansion of data availability, especially with the trend toward big-data enabled healthcare. Potential open data users must be prepared for this expansion, while also ready to address the critical need for information governance. Most importantly, the orientation of open data projects must move from analysis to action to create an evidence base that can reveal the different components needed to secure meaningful impact on the health system.

Working with big data

The potential for big data to improve health outcomes and create new revenue streams and complementary services has often been acknowledged.[24] One of the trends emerging as the healthcare community recognises the potential value of the data generated by advanced medical equipment is "servitisation". In commercial circles, servitisation describes the trend in the business of companies moving from selling goods to selling "bundles" of goods, services, support, self-service, and knowledge. These hybrid product-services place the emphasis on the service component and have a much heavier reliance on data,[25] creating new potential opportunities, including economic, social, and environmental efficiencies. In this new world, for example, expensive MRI scanners are constantly monitored and repaired by a service firm, while older models can be acquired by health systems with smaller budgets, such as MDAs in developing countries. Consumer technologies also now collect a wealth of data that may be of value to healthcare stakeholders with mobile phones and fitness trackers recording countless data points every day.

However, before healthcare stakeholders can realise the benefits of big data (including large anonymised open datasets), there are a number of prerequisites:

1. Infrastructure that can handle the required storage and analytics as managing large datasets can be complex and expensive. This infrastructure also needs to allow stakeholders to determine how and when data should be disposed of when it is no longer of value.

2. Access to data for external stakeholders, recognising it is often not the government agency which collects it, but other stakeholders who have the skills and resources to create new value from data.

3. Integration of data from multiple systems, including the ability to connect new streams of big data with systems that are still using brittle legacy architectures.

4. Connectivity to high-capacity internet. This has a huge impact for the developmental potential of health data in environments with poor connectivity.

Even if open data approaches enable access to data that is generally more evenly distributed, the capacity to use it may not be. More attention must be given to who ultimately benefits and whether healthcare inequalities might be challenged or reinforced. As a result of servitisation and the other broad trends in the delivery of healthcare, private firms (hospitals, banks, insurance) and civil society organisations are increasingly in possession of data that can also contribute to national or government healthcare objectives, even though the data may not be of great utility to the organisations that have collected it.[26] This draws attention to the non-state actors who are collecting important data that could be used to complement state data. Discussions about legal reforms that could allow privately generated data to contribute to official statistics have already begun but are mostly ongoing, and major advances have not yet been realised.[27] However, some of the recent literature has expressed concerns that this kind of public–private data sharing may reinforce relationships between state and private sector actors and weaken the power and positions of both citizens/patients and professionals.[28] Working out what should be shared beyond the private–state axis and how more data should be open to researchers and citizens to use remains a vital task. The success or failure of open data in health may largely depend on how the question of trust between organisations is addressed as big data flows continue to develop. This is ultimately a question of information governance.

Information governance and regulatory frameworks

Open data is not just about technology. It involves a mesh of people (with newer technologies implemented mostly in a piecemeal fashion), processes (policies and guidelines), culture (changes in attitudes, behaviours, and practices), and legacy systems (including existing IT infrastructures).[29] This "ecosystem" produces complex dynamics around data. For example, published data does not remain static. It can keep changing continuously with new fields introduced or integration with other related datasets, including those from non-health sectors, which also bring new challenges, namely the potential negative consequences from privacy breaches or from unethical research.

Many health problems are highly personal and patients need to be confident that their conversations with doctors and other professionals are confidential. While the data is important for treating the patient (primary use at administrative or operational levels at the facilities), secondary uses, such as medical research or planning health services, may pose a challenge. Striking a balance between primary and secondary uses of data is increasingly difficult because modern technology makes it possible to combine data and identify individuals through statistical inference.[30] This provides one of the regulatory paradoxes of open data in health: the more details a dataset contains, the more valuable it is (for example, to detect patterns of health inequality), but also the greater the likelihood of identifying individuals and disclosing sensitive personal information.

The European Union's General Data Protection Regulations and the data provisions of the United States Health Insurance Portability and Accountability Act (HIPAA) try to provide frameworks to address the security and reuse of data on individuals, but many countries still lack suitable legal frameworks (see Chapter 23: Privacy), and questions still remain around the appropriate reuse of personal experimental data in research-like activities.[31] When there is a lack of clarity between closed, shared, and open data, citizen trust may be undermined. This was evident when the Government of the United Kingdom proposed a data-sharing framework in 2013 for medical records from the National Health Service (care.data) using the language of "open data" even though the scheme would not have published individuals' information under an open licence.[32] After a backlash from citizens, the scheme was cancelled, and awareness and opinions about open data were also tainted.[33,34]

From use to action

Even in the absence of the socio-technical infrastructures and governance frameworks needed to identify what and how increased health-related data can be made open to academic and citizen stakeholders, there have been, as noted above, cases where health data has been available, accessible, and used; however, these cases have not always led to long-term change.

There is need to move from just data release to action. Although open health data may build transparency, if there is no real commitment and accountability for the use of evidence in decision-making within government, then effective adoption and use of data will not occur. For example, when citizens report on poor service delivery at a health facility and feedback is not acted upon, enthusiasm for data understandably wanes. The converse is true when data is visibly acted upon. In Swaziland, UNICEF's U-Report platform is used by the quality assurance teams within government to perform customer satisfaction surveys using a free short message service (SMS). Given the cultural context, a client might not provide clear feedback on what the problem was with the services they have obtained from a facility, but, with SMS, they are anonymous, and they might even mention names of those who have caused problems at the facility. Actions undertaken in response to this information are clearly evident to the client, and as a result, they are even willing to pay for the SMS.[35]

Getting from data use to action requires relationship building and the development of products that can scale and be adapted to different healthcare environments. As the Prescribing Analytics case shows (see box), it can be a long journey between discovering the potential for change in health services using open data and seeing that change realised at scale. At present, few initiatives outside of academia may have access to the funding needed to pursue these longer-term programmes. Expanding the number of stakeholders (funders, academia, technology innovators, medical charities, governments, etc.) who are able to invest the necessary resources, and work collaboratively to take open data initiatives from proof-of-concept to full implementation, is vital.

Case study: Prescribing Analytics

The Prescribing Analytics website[36] was created by a group of open data enthusiasts, companies, and researchers at a 2012 "NHS Hack Day" event. The project used newly released prescribing data from doctors to look for potential cost savings from prescribing cheaper drugs, identifying GBP 27 million a month potential savings from changing the approach for one drug alone.[37] Unsurprisingly, this single finding did not change doctor behaviour. Indeed, the problem of expensive drug use had been reported as early as 2006 using other data sources; however, the project team has gone on to develop the Evidence-Based Medicine DataLab[38] at Oxford University, as part of the Open Prescribing project,[39] which provides data, tools, and email alerts to doctors to help them find clinic-level cost savings and prescription improvements. This journey from idea to implementation of a platform tailored to the needs of key stakeholders highlights the movement from data release to impact and the need for longer-term research on the potential impacts of open data in health.

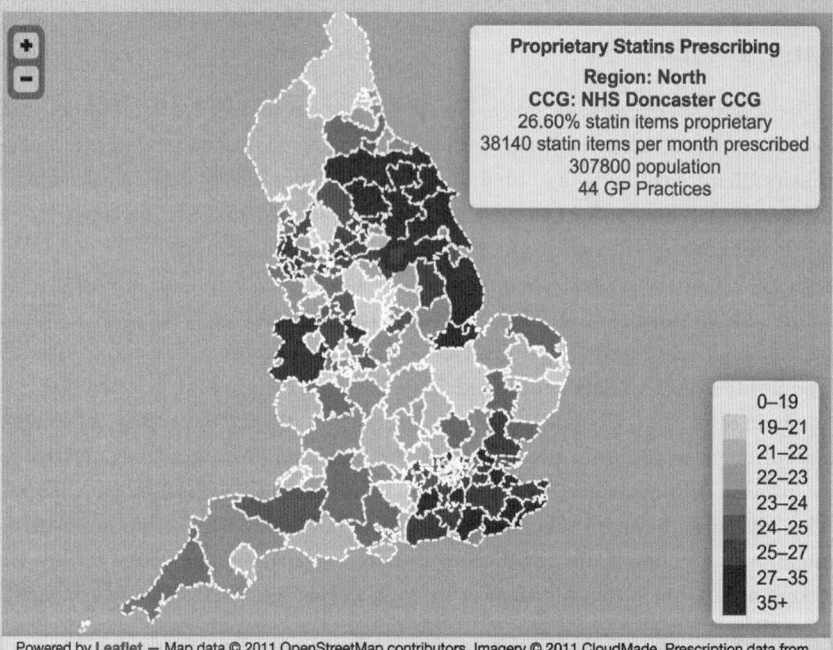

Figure 3: Percentage of proprietary statin prescribing by CCG September 2011 to May 2012
Source: www.prescribinganalytics.com

Conclusion

The International Open Data Conference (IODC) brings together a few thousand people every two years. Major healthcare conferences may have ten times that many attendees to discuss research, products, and innovations, most of which have a data component. Over the last decade, open data has made some inroads into the medical science community; however, concerns over privacy, infrastructure, and the challenges of creating trust and sustainable projects based on open health data have made limited progress. Yet, there is much for the open data field to learn from the health sector as it forces continuous engagement with issues related to personal data, ethics, and the interaction of different stakeholder groups.

This chapter has started to sketch out distinctions between different stakeholders and the different approaches to data sharing, as well as to highlight challenges arising from a private–public nexus of data sharing that could exclude citizen access to data. However, much more needs to be done to bring clarity to the health and open data discussion. Lumping together administrative data for decision-making and longitudinal data for research purposes can frustrate progress. This is because the goals of the stakeholders are different: some are focused on health planning and policy improvements, whereas health facility managers are mostly interested in day-to-day patient management. Building infrastructure capacity will be an ongoing issue as the technical foundations to produce and use open data vary substantially around the world even if all regions are heading toward increasingly digitised healthcare.

Perhaps when we look back on open data and health in the next decade, we will have a much clearer framework available to understand the different potential applications from policy and epidemiological research through to enabling decision-making by patients. Ultimately, the search for innovation should continue with a broader view of real-use cases and examples of stakeholders that have been able to access health data, build services, or develop policy, and then make the impact sustainable.

Further reading

Kostkova, P., Brewer, H., De Lusignan, S., Fottrell, E., Goldacre, B., Hart, G., Koczan, P. et al. (2016). Who owns the data? Open data for healthcare. *Frontiers in Public Health*, 4, 7. https://www.ncbi.nlm.nih.gov/pmc/articles/PMC4756607/

Tambo, E., Madjou, G., Khayeka-Wandabwa, C., Tekwu, E.N., Olalubi, O.A., Midzi, N., Bengyella, L., Adedeji, A.A., & Ngogang, J.Y. (2016). Can free open access resources strengthen knowledge-based emerging public health priorities, policies and programs in Africa? *F1000Research*, 5 (9 May). https://www.ncbi.nlm.nih.gov/pmc/articles/PMC4955019/

Verhulst, S., Noveck, B.S., Caplan, R., Brown, K., & Paz, C. (2014). *The open data era in health and social care: A blueprint for the national health service (NHS England) to develop a research and learning programme for the open data in health and social care*. Brooklyn: GovLab. http://www.thegovlab.org/static/files/publications/nhs-full-report.pdf

About the author

Mark Irura has extensive experience heading end-to-end digital implementations for bilateral and multilateral development agencies, government ministries, and the private sector. With a decade of experience across East and Southern Africa at both national and subnational levels, Mark has implemented and managed large-scale platforms, assessed scalable technical tools, and designed comprehensive data models. He previously studied at the University of Cape Town and at Strathmore University and is presently pursuing doctoral studies at the University of Eastern Finland.

How to cite this chapter

Irura, M. (2019). Open data and health. In T. Davies, S. Walker, M. Rubinstein, & F. Perini (Eds.), *The state of open data: Histories and horizons* (pp. 166–180). Cape Town and Ottawa: African Minds and International Development Research Centre.
http://stateofopendata.od4d.net

This work is licensed under a Creative Commons Attribution 4.0 International (CC BY 4.0) licence. It was carried out with the aid of a grant from the International Development Research Centre, Ottawa, Canada.

Endnotes

1. Broad, E., Smith, F., Duhaney, D., & Carolan, L. (2015). *Open data in government: How to bring about change – The ODI*. London: Open Data Institute. https://theodi.org/article/open-data-in-government-how-to-bring-about-change/

2. InfoDev & Center for Democracy and Technology. (2002). *The e-government handbook for developing countries*. Washington, DC: Center for Democracy & Technology. http://www.infodev.org/sites/default/files/resource/InfodevDocuments_16.pdf

3. Rivera, A.M.A. & Vassil, K. (2015). *Estonia – A successfully integrated population-registration and identity management system: Delivering public services effectively*. Washington, DC: World Bank. https://doi.org/10.1596/28077

4. https://www.healthdatacollaborative.org/

5. http://www.who.int/gho/en/

6. For example, Krumholz, H.M. & Waldstreicher, J. (2016). The Yale Open Data Access (YODA) Project: A mechanism for data sharing. *New England Journal of Medicine, 375(5)*, 403–405. https://doi.org/10.1056/NEJMp1607342

7. https://www.bmj.com/open-data

8. https://www.dhis2.org/

9. https://www.mn.uio.no/ifi/english/research/networks/hisp/

10. Development Gateway. (2016). *Development Gateway 2016 Annual Report: Turning data into action*. Washington, DC: Development Gateway.

11. Keen, J., Calinescu, R., Paige, R., & Rooksby, J. (2013). Big data + politics = open data: The case of health care data in England. *Policy & Internet, 5(2)*, 228–243. https://doi.org/10.1002/1944-2866.POI330

12. Web Foundation. (2017). *Open Data Barometer – Global report*. 4th edition. Washington, DC: World Wide Web Foundation. https://opendatabarometer.org/4thedition/report/

13. Mutuku, L. & Mahihu, C. (2014). *Open data in developing countries: Understanding the impacts of Kenya open data applications and services*. Nairobi: iHub Research. https://idl-bnc-idrc.dspacedirect.org/handle/10625/56300
14. See https://hmisportal.moh.go.tz/. Please note that data visualisation was not working at the time of our research in November 2018.
15. Based on a comparison of https://www.dhis2.org/demo and http://opendatasl.gov.sl/ in November 2018.
16. Francescon, D. (2017). Research without borders: Sharing expertise in Africa. *Elsevier Connect*, 13 January. https://www.elsevier.com/connect/research-without-borders-sharing-expertise-in-africa
17. Mutuku, L. & Mahihu, C. (2014). *Open data in developing countries: Understanding the impacts of Kenya open data applications and services*. Nairobi: iHub Research. https://idl-bnc-idrc.dspacedirect.org/handle/10625/56300
18. UNECA, United Nations Development Programme, Open Data for Development & World Wide Web Foundation. (2016). *The Africa Data Revolution Report 2016: Highlighting developments in African data ecosystems*. Addis Abba: United Nations Economic Commission for Africa Printing and Publishing Unit. http://www.africa.undp.org/content/rba/en/home/library/reports/the_africa_data_revolution_report_2016.html
19. Bhatia, V., Stout, S., Baldwin, B., & Homer, D. (2017). *Results Data Initiative: Findings from Tanzania*. Washington, DC: Development Gateway. https://www.developmentgateway.org/sites/default/files/2017-02/RDI-Tanzania.pdf
20. Mutuku, L. & Mahihu, C. (2014). *Open data in developing countries: Understanding the impacts of Kenya open data applications and services*. Nairobi: iHub Research. https://idl-bnc-idrc.dspacedirect.org/handle/10625/56300
21. Eng, N. (2014). Making our moms proud: Reducing maternal mortality in Mexico. *Data Science for Social Good*, 4 August. Center for Data Science and Public Policy at the University of Chicago. https://dssg.uchicago.edu/2014/08/04/making-our-moms-proud-reducing-maternal-mortality-in-mexico/
22. Sangokoya, D., Clare, A., Verhulst, S., & Young, A. (2016). *Uruguay's A Tu Servicio: Empowering citizens to make data-driven decisions on health care*. Brooklyn, NY: GovLab. http://odimpact.org/case-uruguays-a-tu-servicio.html
23. Young, A. & Verhulst, S. (2016). *Battling Ebola in Sierra Leone: Data sharing to improve crisis response*. Brooklyn, NY: GovLab. http://odimpact.org/case-battling-ebola-in-sierra-leone.html
24. Veale, M. (2016). *Data management and use: Case studies of technologies and governance*. London: British Academy and the Royal Society. https://royalsociety.org/~/media/policy/projects/data-governance/data-governance-case-studies.pdf?la=en-GB
25. Vandermerwe, S. & Rada, J. (1988). Servitization of business: Adding value by adding services. *European Management Journal*, *6(4)*, 314–324.
26. Veale, M. (2016). *Data management and use: Case studies of technologies and governance*. London: British Academy and the Royal Society. https://royalsociety.org/~/media/policy/projects/data-governance/data-governance-case-studies.pdf?la=en-GB
27. UNECA, United Nations Development Programme, Open Data for Development & World Wide Web Foundation (2016). *The Africa Data Revolution Report 2016: Highlighting developments in African data ecosystems*. Addis Abba: United Nations Economic Commission for Africa Printing and Publishing Unit. http://www.africa.undp.org/content/rba/en/home/library/reports/the_africa_data_revolution_report_2016.html
28. Harvey, D. (2005). *A brief history of neoliberalism*. New York, NY: Oxford University Press.
29. Buttles-Valdez, P., Svolou, A., & Valdez, F. (2008). A holistic approach to process improvement using the People CMM and the CMMI-DEV: Technology, process, people, & culture, the holistic quadripartite. In Software Engineering Institute, *SEPG 2008 Conference*, Tampa, FL.
30. Ohm, P. (2010). Broken promises of privacy: Responding to the surprising failure of anonymization. *UCLA Law Review*, *57*, 1701. https://papers.ssrn.com/abstract=1450006

31 Veale, M. (2016). *Data management and use: Case studies of technologies and governance*. London: British Academy and the Royal Society. https://royalsociety.org/~/media/policy/projects/data-governance/data-governance-case-studies.pdf?la=en-GB

32 Wolf, A. (2014). Thanks to care.data, your secrets are no longer safe with your GP. *Wired UK*, 7 February. https://www.wired.co.uk/article/care-data-nhs-healthcare

33 Boiten, E. (2016). Care.data has been scrapped, but your health data could still be shared. *The Conversation*, 12 July. http://theconversation.com/care-data-has-been-scrapped-but-your-health-data-could-still-be-shared-62181

34 Kostkova, P., Brewer, H., De Lusignan, S., Fottrell E., Goldacre, B., Hart, G., Koczan, P. et al. (2016). Who owns the data? Open data for healthcare. *Frontiers in Public Health, 4(7)*. https://www.ncbi.nlm.nih.gov/pmc/articles/PMC4756607/

35 UNICEF. (2016). *UNICEF Annual Report 2016: Swaziland*. New York, NY: United Nations International Children's Emergency Fund. https://www.unicef.org/about/annualreport/files/Swaziland_2016_COAR.pdf

36 http://www.prescribinganalytics.com/

37 The Economist. (2012). Beggar thy neighbour: Open data and health care. *The Economist*, 8 December. Print Edition. https://www.economist.com/britain/2012/12/08/beggar-thy-neighbour

38 https://ebmdatalab.net/

39 https://openprescribing.net/

012

Land ownership

Tim Davies and Sumandro Chattapadhyay

Key points

- Global availability of land ownership and land deals data is patchy, but, when available, it has been used by individual citizens, entrepreneurs, civil society, and journalists.

- Over the last decade, a number of responsible data lessons have been learned. These lessons can provide guidance on how to balance transparency and privacy and on how to draw research conclusions from partial data.

- In spite of large donor investments in land registration systems, few resources are currently made available to enable open data related to these projects. There are untapped opportunities as a result.

- Lessons from the land ownership field highlight the political nature of data, and illustrate the importance of politically aware interventions when creating open data standards, infrastructure, and ecosystems.

Introduction

Open data is often described as a non-rival good and inexhaustible resource. If I take a digital copy of a dataset, it doesn't leave less data for you. This effectively costless sharing of open data is central to the logic that it should be made freely available and reusable, rather than treated as a finite resource to be hoarded. Land as a resource, however, is very different. Each use of land precludes use by others. Land is finite, and there is competition to control and exploit it. Potential users of land are often excluded by distance, physical, and legal barriers. Data also plays into this competition over land. Effective access to land data for one user may lead to significant first-mover's advantage and, thus, preclude other users from taking action vis-a-vis a parcel of land, even if they eventually have access to the same data.

When we also consider the natural resources that land provides from the minerals underneath to the soil and crops on top, we can see that land can be managed well or can become degraded through over-exploitation. Unlike a digital dataset, where each different use can bring cumulative benefits, with land, there is a much more delicate balance to be struck. Yet, when it comes to understanding who owns or holds rights over land, the transactions that affect it, or how it is being managed, the word most often used is "murky".[1] Comprehensive and detailed information about land ownership is scarce.

Some of this is unsurprising. Land ownership patterns have developed over many centuries with overlapping systems of tenure, and, in many countries, these can involve feudal structures, traditional rights, common lands, leaseholds, and freeholds. The first registers of titles to land only emerged in the 1850s under colonial administrative predicaments, and many countries still lack centralised registers, let alone systems that have digitised full country-wide records. Unlike many other government databases that might be born-digital, such as those created by electronic monitoring of the distribution of welfare services, land (ownership) data is often stored in legacy, pre-digital, information systems. Digitisation and verification of such legacy data is a significantly expensive and extensive undertaking, especially in larger countries still migrating from a paper-based land records system. This implies, among other things, that land ownership data is costly to produce and maintain, even though relatively costless to share once digitised. Further, across the world, owners, custodians, and communities have a wide range of, often complex and overlapping, rights and responsibilities in relation to land, which are often not automatically captured by simplified data representations used when land information systems are migrated from paper-based to digital records.

However, over recent decades, markets for land have globalised, and land has increasingly become a valuable asset class. This has led to vast, and often secretive, land deals taking place across the world with much remaining unknown about their scale and scope.[2] At the same time, national and local debates over land rights have been unfolding, with local communities often fighting similar battles in parallel geographic silos. National-scale debates and movements have also brought into focus the importance of understanding land and land ownership. For example, the Constitutional Court of South Africa has recently declared two landmark judgments upholding the land rights of women and communities affected by mining activities.[3]

Ultimately, the lack of transparency on land deals and the fragmented information landscape around land ownership presents problems felt by government, citizens, civil society organisations, and the private sector. For example, without clear information, governments are unable to identify and evaluate policy interventions to stimulate housing development, developers cannot locate land to build on, and communities cannot monitor whether environmental protections are being upheld or claim their rights over geographical areas inhabited for generations. Taken together, all these challenges have fed into calls for increased openness about land ownership, and they bring focus to the idea that open data can be used as a critical tool to address the land ownership transparency gap.

Land ownership and open data already have a history. When, in 2011, Michael Gurstein wrote his widely cited paper, "Open data: Empowering the empowered or effective data use for everyone?", it was the release of land ownership information he turned to in order to ask his critical questions.[4] Drawing on the account by Solomon Benjamin et al. (2007) of the Bhoomi land reform project in Bangalore, he described how "the digitization and related digital access to land title had the direct effect of shifting power and wealth to those with the financial resources and skills to use this information in self-interested ways".[5] Although Gurstein was cautious not to frame this as an argument against open data, but as one about the complementary interventions needed alongside it, the Bhoomi case has become iconic in open data discourse, frequently used to introduce the potential downsides of openness.

How far then have open data ideas progressed in relation to land ownership and governance? What is the current state of the art? And what lessons has the last decade provided? In the following sections, this chapter explores these questions through four lenses: first, with a look at cadastres and land registers, then at data on land deals and transactions, followed by data on land use, and finally, at how the land governance community is engaging with open data. In doing so, the chapter seeks to highlight how the topic of land ownership and open data provides a unique perspective on the challenges of building open data infrastructures and ecosystems in the context of unequally distributed power and wealth and how the power dynamics around data cannot be ignored.

Cadastres and land registers

Understanding land ownership generally relies upon two types of data: cadastres, which record the boundaries (formal or informal) of land parcels, and land registries, which record property rights and interests, and the details of ownership of particular parcels of land.[6] While some countries have unified systems, in others, there are separate systems for each function, different systems at each level of government, or distinct cadastres and registries maintained by individual agencies, such as government departments related to natural resources and mining.

Since they started tracking land ownership data, both the Open Data Index[7] and the Open Data Barometer[8] have reported it to be one of the least available categories of data. This has remained a consistent finding, even after the Open Data Index dataset definition was updated in 2016 to remove the requirement that open land ownership data should include identifiable property owners.[9] This revision, based on work with Cadasta Foundation, represented a more mature understanding in the open data community of the complex power dynamics and administrative structures around property ownership in different countries and the careful balance to be struck between privacy and transparency when it comes to land ownership records.

For example, in New Zealand, a detailed cadastre showing plots and the tenure type of each plot has been available since 2011 under Creative Commons licensing,[10] but access to data that includes ownership information requires users to agree to a separate licence for personal data.[11] In the United Kingdom (UK), individual title information can only be accessed for individual plots by purchasing title deeds, but a unified dataset of land held by commercial, corporate, and government owners was made available for free as bulk data in 2017, albeit under restrictive licensing terms that emphasise it should only be used for personal and non-commercial use, effective management of land, and prevention of crime.[12] Apart from transparency needs and privacy concerns, the significant commercial value of land data, especially of disaggregated data that incorporates ownership and land use information, shapes the decisions by land administration authorities regarding the opening of data as the New Zealand and UK cases illustrate.

While Rufus Pollock's arguments support the view that the model of charging users for access to land titles is economically inefficient and leads to a loss of societal benefits (as well as leading to inequality between those who can afford to build their own plot-by-plot view of land ownership and those who cannot),[13] others see selling access to data plot-by-plot as a reasonable restriction, judging that open access to the full dataset would be harmful in a way that selective access to records is not. Cadasta Foundation's analysis of open land ownership data suggests, however, that the level of land ownership transparency that is appropriate is likely to be context dependent from country to country, noting that "the UK is a highly developed and relatively equitable country with a 150 year old land administration system that holds 24 million titles. Opening up data on property owners' names in this context has very different risks and implications than in a country with less formal documentation, or where dispossession, kidnapping, and or death are real and pervasive issues."[14]

Who uses land data?

United States (US) real-estate platform Zillow draws upon US housing transaction data to provide housing purchase and rental valuations and provides an open application programming interface (API) of government records it has digitised and converted into structured data. The business was valued at USD 540 million at the time of its IPO in 2011.[15]

In New Zealand, wind farm developers have taken advantage of machine-readable cadastral and land ownership data to speed up the process of identifying and planning new sites.[16]

Investigations by the *New York Times* uncovered the true owners of expensive New York apartments purchased through anonymous shell companies. The investigation helped lead to actions by the US Government to seize assets suspected to have been bought with money stolen from Malaysia's sovereign wealth fund in the 1MDB scandal.[17]

Note: current use of land data is greatly limited by availability. A number of the cases illustrating what could be done with land data in this chapter have sourced their data through Right to Information (RTI) requests or other research, rather than having direct access to open land datasets. Of the 17 countries with more than a 0% score for open publication of land ownership data in the latest Open Data Index, five are from Asia, 11 from Europe, and one from the Caribbean region.[18]

Privacy and security issues aside, one of the biggest hurdles to increasing the availability of land ownership records is the fact that many have still not been digitised. For many decades, development banks, including the World Bank, have provided extensive financial support to national and subnational efforts to develop cadastres and land registries in developing and middle-income countries. It is notable, however, that none of these projects, even those recently established, appear to have any explicit open data component, talking at best only about online portals.[19] It is also worth noting that many digital land titling projects have taken decades longer than planned to complete and have struggled to overcome the considerable technical and logistical challenges of converting millions of paper records into digital forms.

Large-scale land digitisation projects also face critical questions about their tendency to adopt narrow ontologies, and to represent land in terms of simple ownership, rather than as a complex web of rights.[20] Studies report that digitisation initiatives restructure not only data but the bureaucracy around it.[21,22] It is primarily this concern with the way digitisation took place, ignoring traditional land usage in favour of only a limited class of documented land rights and centralising power over land decisions within higher levels of government, that was arguably at the root of the Bhoomi case,[23] with open access in situations of low literacy or low capacity of users to effectively use the digitised data presenting a secondary, albeit critical, complication.

For the millions of people around the world without secure title to their land, the official datasets and data structures used to judge land disputes represent a major source of power. But if open data is understood as more than a one-way flow of data from governments, and instead, as a means to allow citizens to create and publish data about their land ownership, opportunities exist to shift that balance of power and create records that can be used to support land claims. For example, tools developed by Cadasta Foundation support communities to document their own land use and rights data, adopting flexible data models and offering fine-grained control of what is, or is not, shared openly.[24] Where such systems are compatible with local legal regimes, they can give communities more control of land ownership evidence and offer a route to greater empowerment.

There have also been a number of announcements in the last few years of blockchain or distributed ledger-based alternatives to, or add-ons for, government land registry systems. Although these might, in theory, provide access to cryptographically secured and open land data,[25] they do not escape the need to determine the provenance of the information added to the ledger, and evidence of any blockchain-based land registers in operation, or achieving impacts on the ground, is vanishingly thin.[26]

Even when land registry data is collected and kept updated, three further barriers to open data access are commonly found: cost, infrastructure, and discoverability. In South Africa, for example, it is possible to browse a detailed cadastral map of property boundaries and tenure types online through a free portal,[27] but access to detailed data requires the payment of fees for each 100 or 200 parcels.[28] Renee Sieber, in Chapter 9: Geospatial, also notes the increasing presence of private businesses in providing cadastral services, sometimes in return for exclusive rights to monetise the resulting data. In Europe, the 2007 INSPIRE Directives on geospatial data (see Chapter 32: European Union) have led to some progress on making cadastral records available as standardised open data,[29] although users seeking to bring together data across countries are likely to be met with numerous technical errors, incompatible metadata, and broken APIs. The technical complexity of both producing and consuming cadastral data may also help explain why spot checks of Open Data Index and Open Data Barometer assessments reveal weaknesses in the accuracy of their measurements with respect to land ownership and with their researchers apparently struggling to consistently locate and assess the openness of cadastral data.[30]

In summary, open data ideas are relatively new within the long-established and politically charged field of land registration. While in some higher-income countries an early balance appears to have been struck between making cadastral data "open by default" and protecting the privacy rights of individual owners, there is a long way to go before the balance is struck for most countries, particularly when capacity to use data is also unevenly distributed. While the possibility of open data approaches allowing marginalised groups to take control of the representation of their own land rights is worthy of more focused research, the key technological need right now appears to be skills for grassroots data collection and management as opposed to innovations in specific database technology, such as blockchain or other distributed ledger solutions.

Land deals

Data on land ownership is not only captured through static registries. Over the last decade, there has also been considerable interest in transaction data related to the buying and selling of land. This kind of data can reveal the value of land, show changing patterns of land ownership and use, and highlight risks related to money laundering and corruption.

Sources of land deal data range from national government records, such as the UK Land Registry Price Paid Dataset that lists residential property transactions,[31] to crowdsourced datasets, such as GRAIN[32] and Land Matrix,[33] created by a network of researchers drawing on crowdsourcing and media reports to provide a partial global view of prospective or completed land deals. This latter class of data has become the subject of some controversy, illustrating the tensions that can exist when creating datasets to support research and advocacy.

Founded in 2009 by a group involving the International Land Coalition (ILC), among others, LandMatrix.org launched a beta dataset of "land grabs" in April 2012, offering a downloadable list of locations and investors, along with the anticipated size of the area to be bought. This, along with data from GRAIN, helped to spark a number of academic papers and media reports on the phenomena of land deals with a particular emphasis on deals in Africa. However, Oya (2013) has argued that the crowdsourced data lacked methodological rigour, and a focus on generating "killer facts" through rapid research could ultimately undermine the work of researchers and advocacy organisations seeking to understand deals, providing "false precision" and generating data that would not be trusted by governments and businesses.[34] Scoones et al. (2013) have described this as the "politics of evidence".[35] By 2013, revisions to the LandMatrix methodology and dataset structure to more clearly illustrate source information had responded to some of these critiques, suggesting a reasonably tight feedback loop between academic and activist communities. Although it appears work on open data around land deals peaked in 2012–13, both GRAIN and LandMatrix have continued data collection. LandMatrix, in particular, is preparing for a new version to be released with updated data and features, working through a network of regional focal point institutions, including the University of Pretoria in South Africa, the Asian Farmers' Association for Sustainable Rural Development (AFA) in Asia, and the Foundation for Development in Justice and Peace (FUNDAPAZ) in Latin America.[36]

Oya's critique of land grab databases also questioned the reliance on datasets alone and called for more mixed-methods and in-depth research. One tool responding to this has been

OpenLandContracts.org,[37] which was launched in October 2015 by the Columbia Center on Sustainable Investment (CCSI) and builds on a platform created for extractives contract monitoring. This tool provides full text land deal documents and allows their annotation to create additional structured data. Szoke-Burke (2016) writes that the platform can encourage "more sustainable land-use practices and fresh opportunities for public participation in decision-making on [land] investments".[38]

It is notable, however, that while the systematic publication of government procurement contracts has received considerable international attention (see Chapter 1: Accountability and anti-corruption), there has been much less policy focus on proactive publication of government land deals, even in light of substantial programmes of government land disposal in a number of countries. The UK, for example, has required local government agencies to prepare and publish open data on their land holdings, identifying surplus land which might be sold off for housing or property development. Yet there is no corresponding requirement to publish data on the land that has been sold off, who it was sold to, and how it is subsequently developed.[39] This fits with an emphasis in government policy on using data to support an emerging PropTech (Property Technology) sector,[40] rather than supporting public ownership of land.[41] In seeking to take a global look at this issue, we could not locate any sources indicating the extent to which different countries provide structured data on government land holdings, their purchases, and disposals.

Ultimately, when it comes to land deals, crowdsourced open data has been instrumental in generating debate. However, its use has also brought into relief the politics of data, leading organisations to seek a balance between rapid data-driven research and rigorous data collection that combines quantitative and qualitative perspectives. Data on government land deals is of particular interest; however, there appears, at present, to be few coordinated calls for its proactive publication.

Private Eye - Land deals data and offshore ownership

In 2015 and 2016, British satirical and current affairs magazine, *Private Eye*, investigated ownership of UK property through offshore companies using a mix of land registry and land transaction data, albeit obtained through Freedom of Information requests, taking advantage of journalistic privilege to draw on some copyright protected information. The magazine published an interactive map showing GBP 170 billion of UK property acquired by companies registered offshore over a ten-year period, highlighting how these structures were used for large-scale tax avoidance or provided secrecy vehicles that could facilitate money-laundering.[42]

The investigation helped spark plans to require foreign companies buying UK property to declare their beneficial owners[43] and the open release of the UK's Overseas Company land ownership dataset.

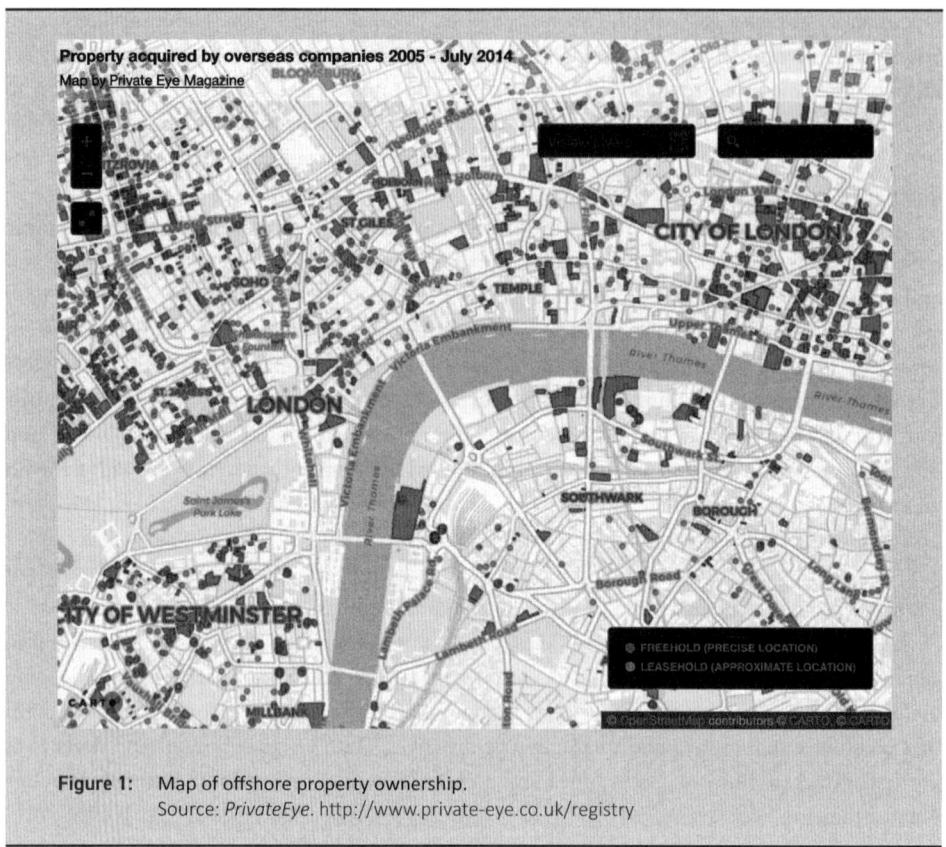

Figure 1: Map of offshore property ownership.
Source: *PrivateEye*. http://www.private-eye.co.uk/registry

Land use

From a sustainable development perspective, it is not so much land ownership that matters per se, but rather the use to which land is put (albeit noting that ownership has a big impact on the equitable or distorted distribution of benefits from that use). In recent years, there has been a step-change in the global availability of remote sensing data on land quality and its use. This has been accompanied by a number of local projects making use of geospatial tools to layer together land rights and land use information, guiding policy design and supporting community action. We also note promising examples that show how open data can be used to support citizens in accessing and enjoying the use of public lands.

Two sources have been instrumental in making it possible to zoom to any square mile on earth and access visualisations and open data on estimated soil quality, land cover, and land use. Openly licensed satellite data is the driver for platforms like soilgrids.org[44] that provides downloads under the Open Data Commons Open Database License (ODbL). However, recent experiments have also turned to crowdsourced OpenStreetMap data to generate land use maps, combining this with satellite data to offer usable land-use classifications across the world.[45,46,47] Although there are still some methodological challenges in reconciling figures from crowdsourced and remote sensing datasets with national records, this data has the potential to be used in both planning and measuring development interventions, including by tracking the impact of development activity on soil health and land productivity.

The East West Management Institute's (EWMI) Open Development Initiative (ODI) in the Mekong region[48] also draws on geospatial tools and a number of base maps as the background for curated datasets on concessions, oil and gas blocks, and registered Indigenous lands, supporting research into the relationship between different land users. Through the ODI, EWMI acts as a paradigmatic "infomediary"[49] with goals to "change public perceptions about information and build demand for more transparency, shift dynamics from debates over basic data, encourage independent analysis, and level the playing field in regard to information access".[50] The breadth of scholarly literature citing ODI sources suggests this goal is being met. Notably, however, the data available on different ODI maps across the Mekong region varies with detailed government-sourced land use only available for Cambodia, while sites for Laos, Myanmar, Vietnam, and Thailand have to fall back on international sources. When it comes to concessions, data gaps are a global problem with the 2017 Resource Governance Index[51] finding that over 50% of the countries surveyed lacked any public cadastre of oil, gas, or mining concessions and licences.[52]

Along with land allocated for resource extraction, many countries have land allocated for national parks, reserves, and recreation areas. In the US, an online platform for finding campsites (hipcamp.com), a mass membership environmental charity (the Sierra Club), and Code for America have come together with over 50 other partners to advocate for US National and State parks to adopt an open data approach within their park reservation system.[53] Active since 2014, the group has proposed model language for Parks Services to include in contracts with third-party vendors and has offered to broker introductions between national park staff and open data experts.[54] The AccessLand.org project hopes to encourage all parks to create open APIs that will allow a variety of civic and entrepreneurial platforms to hook into their data to discover available facilities and facilitate the booking of park spaces.[55]

This last case draws attention once again to the interactive opportunities of open data about land by creating systems that not only present information but also support two-way engagement through data.

The land governance community

As the introductory section of this chapter describes, land governance debates often play out in very local contexts, leading to the creation of many grassroots communities, activist networks, and stakeholder groups. However, the land governance sector has a track record of organising internationally with multi-stakeholder networks such as the ILC[56] and Global Land Tools Network (GLTN)[57] that emerged in 1995 and 2006, respectively.

In 2009, ILC and the consortium behind the experimental landtenure.info database[58] launched plans for the Land Portal to be a clearinghouse for land governance information and data.[59] The Land Portal quickly evolved to have a strong focus on open data and semantic linked open data standards, aggregating and repackaging existing indicator data and developing LandVoc as a flexible vocabulary for describing land governance documents and data.[60] Active in advocacy for open data in the land governance sector,[61] the Land Portal has taken a particular stance in its approach to both the sources of its data and the audience for the information that results from it.[62] In their 2014 business plan, the Land Portal describes a focus on "supporting the efforts of the rural poor to gain equitable access to land by addressing a fragmentation of information resources on land, which makes it difficult and often prohibitively expensive to draw together reliable evidence in support of programs, advocacy campaigns or policy formulation, especially for grassroots organisations".[63] One of the datasets made available through the site is the Property Rights Index (Prindex), launched in 2016 and now covering 36 countries with measures to represent citizen perceptions of how secure their land rights are and to complement or challenge more formal technical measures of national tenure systems.[64] Through a series of partnerships with grassroots groups in Latin America, Africa, and Asia, the Land Portal has also explored approaches to filling gaps in available information and data, seeking to redress the imbalance of an information ecosystem where the majority of data remains the product of powerful global players.[65]

Since the Sustainable Development Goals (SDGs) were established in 2015, the land governance community has been tracking the quality and availability of data required to measure progress against land-relevant targets and indicators. As of December 2018, of the 12 land-related indicators, only three have both an established methodology and regular data collection, with six indicators still lacking an established methodology. Of the "tier 2" indicators (methodology established, but no regular data collection), two relate to gender and one to inclusive access to public space for people of all ages, genders, and disabilities.[66]

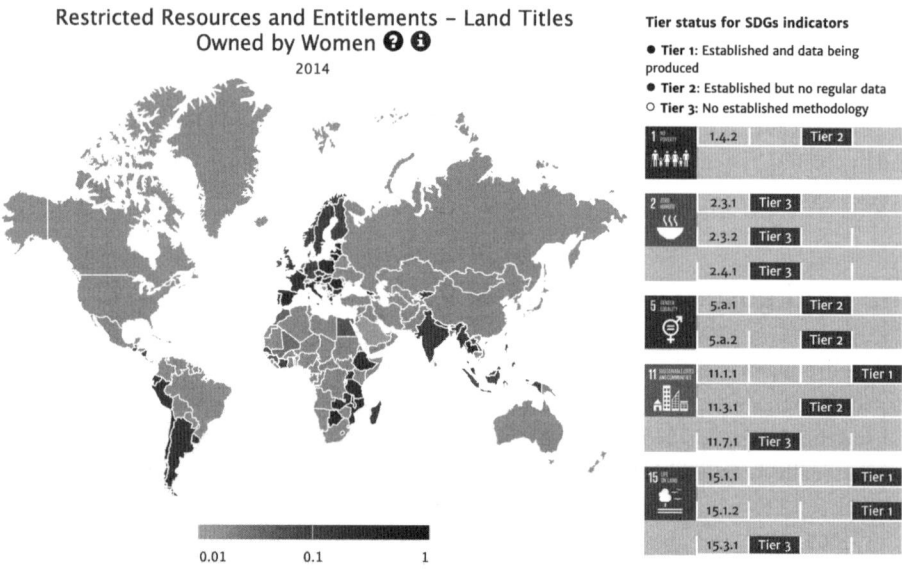

Figure 2: LandPortal.org mapping of SDG indicator status and visualisation showing the current limited number of countries covered by data that can be used to report against indicator 5.a.1.
Source: https://landportal.org/book/sdgs

Most recently, funding for the work of the Land Portal (and a number of other land governance data projects) has predominantly come from the UK Department for International Development's LEGEND (Land: Enhancing Governance for Economic Development) programme,[67] from Omidyar Network,[68] and from partnerships with GODAN (Global Open Data for Agriculture and Nutrition: see Chapter 2: Agriculture). However, compared to the levels of support for specific open data initiatives in other sectors, such as agriculture or anti-corruption, resourcing for open data in land remains comparatively limited at present.

Overall, open data appears to still be a relatively niche issue within the land governance community. An increasing number of organisations in the sector have adopted open licences for their data and publications, and, in 2017, a number signed onto a Land Information Ecosystem Declaration,[69] yet broad mainstream recognition of the role of open data still appears limited. This may be because of the particular political slant adopted by advocates of open land data, or simply because data issues still feel distant from the concerns of actors involved in fighting local land governance battles.

Conclusion

When it comes to land ownership data, we are confronted by a transparency gap and a messy reality of patchy and overlapping recordkeeping and data systems. However, where data is available, solid foundations have been laid for a responsible data[70] approach to be taken, recognising that, where ownership records include personal data, "open by default" does not automatically apply. Ultimately, both data collection and data publication need to account for the political context and power dynamics in which they are undertaken, and recognise the way in which remote sensing and crowdsourcing can rapidly transform the overall data landscape.

Over the last decade, numerous examples have made it clear that when better land ownership and use data is made available in appropriate ways, and when it is connected with data on company ownership, agricultural practices, or Indigenous rights, it can generate substantial value realised through investigative journalism, community action, academic research, and by informing government strategies. Continued development of the critical and multi-method research skills needed to use land data effectively will be vital to unlocking further value in the future.

Looking ahead, there are three key areas for action. First, we need continued work to understand and create the conditions under which marginalised and disadvantaged groups are empowered to access and use data on land ownership to secure their property claims, to seek justice, and to address corruption. Not only is capacity building vital to make the most of land ownership data, but without capacity building to level the playing field between developers, PropTech firms, and existing land users, just outcomes from increasing openness cannot be taken for granted.

Second, donors and governments investing in the technical infrastructures for land governance should be incorporating open data terms into all their project plans, funding agreements, and contracts. This does not mean all data must be open by default, but rather that systems must be open data ready, and the proprietary control of land ownership and use data must be ruled out. Directing just a small percentage of the millions invested in land registry systems every year toward open data approaches could be transformative.

Lastly, we need to see much better baseline and monitoring data on current levels of openness around the world for cadastre, land registry, and land deal data. Current open data studies lack the depth and geographic coverage needed to allow accurate monitoring of progress. At a minimum, studies need to distinguish between data that covers all forms of tenure and data that is restricted to only corporate or government-owned land. With a better baseline, it should also be possible to foster stronger advocacy, calling for land registry and land deal open data to be published with purpose.

In closing, the key lesson to take away from looking at open data and land ownership is that political struggles over the collection, curation, and release of data are now part and parcel of political struggles related to land ownership and use. Although this is brought into sharp relief in the case of land, open data in each sector is equally likely to possess its own complex politics, and advocates taking a stand on open data should always consider the wider political context within which it is pursued.

Further reading

Cadasta Foundation. (2017). *Towards a more open future: Increasing accountability and transparency through open land data*. https://cadasta.org/resources/white-papers/accountability-transparency-open-land-data/

Hetherington, K. (2012). Promising information: Democracy, development, and the remapping of Latin America. *Economy and Society, 41(2)*, 127–150. https://www.tandfonline.com/doi/abs/10.1080/03085147.2011.607365

Pierce, C.J., Tagliarino, N., MacInnes, M., Daniel, P., & Jaitner, A. (2018). *Towards transparency in land ownership: A framework for research on beneficial land ownership*. Berlin: Transparency International. https://www.transparency.org/whatwedo/publication/towards_transparency_in_land_ownership_a_framework_for_research

About the authors

Tim Davies has been researching the power dynamics around open data since 2009. He has worked with the Land Portal on strategy development and has an interest in UK land policy reform.

Sumandro Chattapadhyay is Research Director at the Centre for Internet and Society in Bangalore. He was a member of the founding team at the MOD Institute, Bangalore, and led a data analysis and visualisation project at the Azim Premji University, Bangalore. Sumandro was formerly a research associate at the Sarai programme, Centre for the Study of Developing Societies, Delhi, and was a member of the IDRC Open Data in Developing Countries research network. You can follow Sumandro on Twitter at https://www.twitter.com/ajantriks.

How to cite this chapter

Davies, T. & Chattapadhyay, S. (2019). Open data and land ownership. In T. Davies, S. Walker, M. Rubinstein, & F. Perini (Eds.), *The state of open data: Histories and horizons* (pp. 181–195). Cape Town and Ottawa: African Minds and International Development Research Centre. http://stateofopendata.od4d.net

This work is licensed under a Creative Commons Attribution 4.0 International (CC BY 4.0) licence. It was carried out with the aid of a grant from the International Development Research Centre, Ottawa, Canada.

Endnotes

1. Hogge, B. (2015). *Open data: Six stories about impact in the UK*. London: Omidyar Network. https://www.omidyar.com/sites/default/files/file_archive/insights/Open%20Data_Six%20Stories%20About%20Impact%20in%20the%20UK/OpenData_CaseStudies_Report_complete_DIGITAL_102715.pdf
2. Cotula, L. & Berger, T. (2017). *Trends in global land use investment: Implications for legal empowerment*. Land, Investment and Rights Series. London: Institute for Environment and Development. http://pubs.iied.org/pdfs/12606IIED.pdf
3. Mavhinga, D. (2018). South Africa's Constitutional Court protects land rights. *Human Rights Watch*, 6 November. https://www.hrw.org/news/2018/11/06/south-africas-constitutional-court-protects-land-rights
4. Gurstein, M.B. (2011). Open data: Empowering the empowered or effective data use for everyone? *First Monday, 16(2)*. https://doi.org/10.5210/fm.v16i2.3316
5. Benjamin, S., Bhuvaneswari, R., Rajan, P., & Manjunatha, P. (2007). *Bhoomi: "E-governance" or an anti-politics machine necessary to globalize Bangalore?* CASUM–m Working Paper. https://casumm.files.wordpress.com/2008/09/bhoomi-e-governance.pdf
6. Cadasta Foundation. (2016). An overview of property rights data. https://cadasta.org/open-data/overview-of-property-rights-data/
7. https://index.okfn.org/
8. https://opendatabarometer.org/
9. https://web.archive.org/web/20170508074348/https://index.okfn.org/methodology/
10. https://data.linz.govt.nz/layer/50804-nz-property-titles/
11. https://www.linz.govt.nz/data/licensing-and-using-data/linz-licence-for-personal-data
12. https://data.landregistry.gov.uk/data_pub/terms-of-use/read/ccod
13. Pollock, R. (2009). *The economics of public sector information*. Working Paper. Cambridge: University of Cambridge. https://doi.org/10.17863/CAM.5635
14. Cadasta Foundation. (2016). An overview of property rights data. https://cadasta.org/open-data/overview-of-property-rights-data/
15. Zillow. (2016). Data for good: Zillow's open data collaborations. https://www.zillow.com/research/data/
16. Land Information New Zealand. (n.d) Using LINZ data to develop wind farms. https://web.archive.org/web/20161201133406/https://www.linz.govt.nz/using-linz-data-develop-wind-farms
17. https://www.nytimes.com/news-event/shell-company-towers-of-secrecy-real-estate
18. https://index.okfn.org/dataset/land/
19. Author's research from International Aid Transparency Data. https://github.com/timgdavies/land-governance-open-data-research/

20. Ferris, L., Pichel F., & Sorensen, N. (2016). *Report: Debate on open data and land governance*. Land Portal and Cadasta Foundation. https://landportal.org/pt/library/resources/report-debate-open-data-and-land-governance

21. Hetherington, K. (2012). Promising information: Democracy, development, and the remapping of Latin America. *Economy and Society, 41(2)*, 127–150. https://doi.org/10.1080/03085147.2011.607365

22. Hetherington, K. (2011). *Guerrilla auditors: The politics of transparency in neoliberal Paraguay*. Durham, NC: Duke University Press.

23. Benjamin, S., Bhuvaneswari, R., Rajan, P., & Manjunatha, P. (2007). *Bhoomi: "E-governance" or an anti-politics machine necessary to globalize Bangalore?* CASUM–m Working Paper. https://casumm.files.wordpress.com/2008/09/bhoomi-e-governance.pdf

24. Pichel, F. & Weber, M. (2018). Strengthening land tenure in informal settings: A fit-for-purpose approach. *African Journal on Land Policy and Geospatial Sciences* (Special Issue, October 2018): 16–21. https://revues.imist.ma/index.php?journal=AJLP-GS&page=article&op=view&path%5B%5D=13368

25. Vos, J. (2016). *Blockchain based land registry: Panacea, illusion or something in between?* European Land Registry Association. https://www.elra.eu/wp-content/uploads/2017/02/10.-Jacques-Vos-Blockchain-based-Land-Registry.pdf

26. Burg, J., Murphy, C., & Pétraud, J.P. (2018). Blockchain for international development: Using a learning agenda to address knowledge gaps. *MERL Tech* [Blog post], 29 November. http://merltech.org/blockchain-for-international-development-using-a-learning-agenda-to-address-knowledge-gaps/

27. https://csg.esri-southafrica.com/

28. http://csg.dla.gov.za/fees_spatial.htm

29. http://inspire-geoportal.ec.europa.eu/overview.html?view=themeOverview&theme=cp

30. Author's research.

31. https://www.gov.uk/government/collections/price-paid-data

32. GRAIN. (2012). GRAIN releases data set with over 400 global land grabs. *GRAIN* [Article], 22 February. https://www.grain.org/article/entries/4479-grain-releases-data-set-with-over-400-global-land-grabs

33. https://landmatrix.org/

34. Oya, C. (2013). Methodological reflections on "land grab" databases and the "land grab" literature "rush". *The Journal of Peasant Studies, 40(3)*, 503–520. https://doi.org/10.1080/03066150.2013.799465

35. Scoones, I., Hall, R., Barros Jr, S.M., White, B., & Wolford, W. (2013). The politics of evidence: Methodologies for understanding the global land rush. *The Journal of Peasant Studies, 40(3)*, 469–483. https://doi.org/10.1080/03066150.2013.801341

36. https://landmatrix.org/region/

37. https://www.openlandcontracts.org/

38. Szoke-Burke, S. (2016). Here's the deal. *RICS Land Journal, October/November*. https://issuu.com/ricsmodus/docs/land_oct_nov_16_interactive_pdf/20

39. DCLG. (2015). *Local government transparency code 2015*. London: Department for Communities and Local Government. https://www.gov.uk/government/publications/local-government-transparency-code-2015

40. https://web.archive.org/web/20190104134543/https://digital-land.github.io/

41. Christophers, B. (2018). *The new enclosure: The appropriation of public land in neoliberal Britain*. London: Verso.

42. Private Eye. (2016). *Tax havens: Selling England by the offshore Pound – The story so far*. London: Pressdram Ltd. http://www.private-eye.co.uk/pictures/special_reports/tax-havens.pdf

43. Private Eye. (2016). *Selling England (and Wales) by the Pound*. London: Pressdram Ltd. http://www.private-eye.co.uk/registry

44. https://soilgrids.org/

45. Schultz, M., Voss, J., Auer, M., Carter, S., & Zipf, A. (2017). Open land cover from OpenStreetMap and remote sensing. *International Journal of Applied Earth Observation and Geoinformation, 63*, 206–213.

46 https://osmlanduse.org/

47 Yang, D., Fu, C.-S., Smith, A.C., & Yu, Q. (2017). Open land-use map: A regional land-use mapping strategy for incorporating OpenStreetMap with earth observations. *Geo-Spatial Information Science, 20(3)*, 269–281. https://doi.org/10.1080/10095020.2017.1371385

48 https://opendevelopmentmekong.net

49 Magalhaes, G., Roseira, C., & Strover, S. (2013). Open government data intermediaries: A terminology framework. *Proceedings of the 7th International Conference on Theory and Practice of Electronic Governance*, Seoul, Korea, 22–25 October, pp. 330–333. New York, NY: Association for Computing Machinery. https://doi.org/10.1145/2591888.2591947

50 Open Development Initiative. (n.d.). EWMI-ODI and the open movement. *Open Development Mekong*. https://opendevelopmentmekong.net/background/ewmi-odi-and-the-open-movement/

51 NRGI. (2017). *2017 resource governance index*. New York: Natural Resource Governance Institute. https://resourcegovernance.org/sites/default/files/documents/2017-resource-governance-index.pdf

52 https://www.resourcegovernanceindex.org/data/both/issue?category=1&indicator=2&region=global&subcategory=1

53 AccessLand Coalition. (2014). Whitepaper: Recreation.gov as a platform – How to inspire the next generation of conservationists, reach diverse audiences, and connect more Americans to their land. https://docs.google.com/document/d/1f6qNofxPHVWtywYavv-mTT4wkQaa0lZfrTemx55RkEM/edit?usp=embed_facebook

54 http://accessland.org/

55 Ravasio, A. (2014). Open data for open lands. *Medium*, 20 October. https://medium.com/@alyraz/open-data-for-93af9d3d30aa

56 http://www.landcoalition.org/

57 https://gltn.net/

58 https://web.archive.org/web/20101014014449/http://www.landtenure.info:80/

59 LandPortal.info. (2014). *Land portal development 2014–2017: Business plan*. https://landportal.org/sites/landportal.info/files/LandPortal_BusinessPlan_Sept2014-Web.pdf

60 https://landportal.org/voc/landvoc

61 Ferris, L., Pichel, F., & Sorensen, N. (2017). Towards a more open future: Increasing accountability and transparency through open land data. *2017 World Bank Conference on Land and Poverty*, Washington DC, 20–24 March 2017. https://www.conftool.com/landandpoverty2017/index.php/11-09-Pichel-661_paper.pdf?page=downloadPaper&filename=11-09-Pichel-661_paper.pdf&form_id=661&form_version=final

62 PDD. (2019). *Overcoming land data silos: The role of data ecosystems in achieving global development goals*. PDD Case Study: Land Portal. Principles for Digital Development. https://digitalprinciples.org/wp-content/uploads/PDD_CaseStudy-LandPortal_v4.pdf

63 LandPortal.info. (2014). *Land portal development 2014–2017: Business plan*. https://landportal.org/sites/landportal.info/files/LandPortal_BusinessPlan_Sept2014-Web.pdf

64 https://www.prindex.net

65 https://landportal.org/about/vision

66 https://landportal.org/book/sdgs

67 https://devtracker.dfid.gov.uk/projects/GB-1-204252

68 https://www.omidyar.com/investees/land-portal

69 Land Portal. (2017). Land information ecosystem declaration. https://landportal.org/news/2017/05/land-information-ecosystem-declaration

70 https://responsibledata.io/

013

National statistics

Shaida Badiee, Caleb Rudow, and Eric Swanson

Key points

- For national statistical offices (NSOs) and their partner agencies, open data provides a route to engage with a larger world of data-driven innovation and to demonstrate their relevance and value to the public.

- Progress on making official statistics openly available has been slow and fraught with quick wins missed and a lack of long-term investment.

- Greater engagement between open data and NSO communities is needed to drive cultural and practical changes, recognising the strengths that each bring to the data ecosystem in support of the Sustainable Development Goals.

Introduction

Data has the power to save lives, end poverty, protect the planet, and transform our world, but only if it is open and well used. This chapter is concerned with open, official statistics, which include some of the most important datasets that decision-makers need to create policies, design programmes, and monitor results. They are derived from data produced by governments as part of their official function. They provide a quantitative record of the country's social, economic, and environmental condition.[1] Collected through censuses, surveys, and administrative records, official statistics are the product of national statistical systems, which are confederations of official agencies that in most countries are coordinated by a national statistical office (NSO).

Since they are produced by public bodies using public funds, official statistics should be considered public goods, capable of being used and reused for many purposes without diminishing their value to others, and available to be copied or reproduced by anyone. In economists' terms, they are non-rivalrous and non-excludable. Making official statistics openly available is, therefore, economically efficient. Beyond satisfying economic theory, making official statistics openly available can stimulate innovative applications, encourage citizen engagement, and increase confidence in the statistical system as a whole.

Although their responsibilities differ from country to country, NSOs generally have the authority to set statistical standards, to design and implement large-scale data collection programmes, and to ensure the quality, reliability, and availability of official statistics. Through their links to other NSOs and to international statistical agencies, they contribute to, and benefit from, new techniques and common standards. Because of their centrality and the importance of statistics for setting policies and measuring outcomes, NSOs and national statistical systems should be at the forefront of the data revolution and the open data agenda. Where they lack explicit authority, they can, and should, lead by example. For NSOs and their partner agencies, open data is more than a dissemination strategy; embracing the principles of open data is an opportunity to engage with the larger world of data-driven innovation and to demonstrate their relevance to their own governments, the private sector, and the public at large.

There is an emerging, international consensus on the principles of open data, and much advice is available on how to make data open, but implementation of these principles has been difficult. Measurement of the availability of open data from official sources reveals slow progress at best. There are relatively low-cost actions that could make official statistics more open: providing data in machine-readable formats, making metadata available, and publishing open terms of use. However, producing larger and more complex datasets in response to the demands of the Sustainable Development Goals (SDGs) will require increasing the capacity of national statistical systems and securing additional resource commitments from governments to support robust, effective, independent, and open statistical systems.

National statistical offices, official statistics, and open data

As the coordinating body for a country's national statistical system, NSOs are charged with identifying, collecting, processing, analysing, and disseminating official statistics on behalf of the government. NSOs are a part of government, but should be independent of partisan activities. Their independence is critical to their position as information brokers that need to build trust and remain free from influences that might bias their data or analyses. NSOs and the larger statistical system should, however, be responsive to the demands of policy-makers, who finance their budgets to meet their own, and the public's, need for reliable information. These demands are not fixed. They grow and change as new challenges and opportunities present themselves.

National statistical systems are the repositories of two kinds of data: microdata, which are the unit records of censuses, surveys, and administrative datasets, as well as aggregate data or indicators. Microdata contains identifiable information about people, businesses, or other entities. Before this data can be made openly available, it must be anonymised or aggregated into public-use data and indicators. Access to the underlying microdata must be strictly controlled.

Guidance for NSOs is provided by the United Nations *Fundamental principles of official statistics*, a set of ten principles that set out the professional and scientific standards for NSOs.[2] The first principle, which arguably incorporates the remaining nine and embraces the core principle of open data, says that "official statistics that meet the test of practical utility are to be compiled and made available on an impartial basis by official statistical agencies to honour citizens' entitlement to public information". The sixth principle states that data on individuals "is to be strictly confidential and used exclusively for statistical purposes". Balancing the public's right to information with the possible privacy risks for certain microdata sets is a balancing act that all NSOs work to maintain.

As the data ecosystem expands, NSOs are expected to take a stronger coordinating role, encompassing new data sources, producers, and users, including both public and private actors. NSOs must also engage with a diverse set of stakeholders, including academic institutions, non-governmental organisations (NGOs), and bilateral and multilateral agencies in support of their research, development projects, and applications of open data. But many NSOs still lack the human, physical, and financial resources needed to perform even their traditional role. A report on the World Bank's Statistical Capacity Indicators Database found that 39% of the 131 countries studied had a low statistical capacity. They lack a recent census, survey, complete civil registration and vital statistics system, or general statistical capacity.[3] The global community needs to be conscious of the varying capacities of NSOs, and create space for a variety of approaches based on technical capacity and country-level compatibility. There is no one-size-fits-all approach to building open data practices in NSOs around the world.

By lowering the transaction costs for disseminating data, open data can reduce the operational costs for NSOs, who will have an increasing role in coordinating and managing the data ecosystem. There are greater economic benefits to governments through the more efficient management of programmes, and to individuals and businesses through the use of data to create new products and services. In one of the earliest studies of the benefits of open data, Rufus Pollock estimated welfare gains to opening data that were previously sold by the British government to be from GBP 1.6 to 6 billion.[4] A study of the European Union's open data portal predicted a total of Euro 1.7 billion will be saved in efficiency gains from open data for the public sector in the year 2020 alone.[5] Research on the opening of Landsat satellite data in the United States (US) points to similar financial benefits. Annual savings from the open Landsat data for NGOs, Federal Government, and the private sector is estimated at between USD 350 and 436 million per year.[6]

The degree of engagement with open data among NSOs varies widely. Some are leading, such as Mexico, Jamaica, and the Philippines. They are embracing open data by establishing open data portals, reviewing access to information laws and policies, and including open data in national budgeting and planning processes. Others have been slower to implement even the simplest open data policies.

International progress on open data

At the international level, there have been important steps taken toward open data. New standards, principles, and operating guidelines have been created; Open Knowledge International[7] and the Open Data Charter[8] have established a working definition of open data. The *Cape Town global action plan for sustainable development data*,[9] adopted at the first United Nations World Data Forum in 2017, includes open data among its key actions for innovation and the modernisation of national statistical systems. Open data was subsequently addressed at the

48th and 49th annual meetings of the United Nations Statistical Commission (UNSC), a meeting of chief statisticians from UN member states and the highest decision-making body on statistical activities. The UNSC discussions on open data from the 49th meeting, held in March 2018, showed that countries are starting to treat open data as a priority and trying to integrate it into their national strategies and budgeting processes, as well as seeking international support for technical and financial assistance. Further, discussions from the 49th UNSC resulted in the designation of a subgroup to recommend changes to incorporate open data concepts in the Fundamental Principles of Statistics.

Beyond international advocacy for open data, practical steps to implement open data have been taken. A network of regional open data hubs has been developed by Open Data for Development (OD4D).[10] PARIS21 now includes open data in its recommendations on National Strategies for the Development of Statistics (NSDS)[11] and in its training programmes. The World Bank's Open Data Readiness Assessment (ODRA)[12] helps countries identify gaps and opportunities for implementing open data. And NSOs are increasingly involved in international open data events, such as the International Open Data Conference (IODC). These are important advances that empower local actors to choose their own paths towards statistical development and learn from a growing network of open data actors.

The national and international policy developments are encouraging, but results must be measured by their impact on the availability and openness of official statistics. There is a consensus among projects measuring open data implementation that many countries have not fully adopted open data policies and practices and that implementation has been slow.[13] To accelerate progress, additional financial resources are needed to build capacity and modernise national statistical systems in low- and middle-income countries. Further, the value of data needs to be demonstrated to strengthen popular and political support for open data.

Key issues and challenges

Current state of open data for national statistics?

There are several quantitative indexes that measure the openness of government data. Among these are the Open Data Inventory (ODIN), the Open Data Barometer (ODB), and the Global Open Data Index (GODI). ODIN is designed to measure the openness of official statistics produced by national statistical systems and is the most appropriate index for this paper. The ODB and GODI both include "national statistics" among the types of public information they evaluate, but they are more concerned with non-statistical datasets, such as government budgets, voting records, transportation timetables, weather information, and maps.[14] Despite the differences in the data incorporated in their assessments, all these indexes employ a similar definition of open data, based on the principles of the Open Data Charter[15] and the Open Definition.[16] The indexes also point to similar conclusions: there is a large gap between the success of some countries regarding open data and the failure of others. Many of the datasets that users seek are unavailable or not provided on open terms, and there has been little improvement in open data scores over the last four years.

The ODIN scores highlight the large differences in open access to official statistics between countries. The highest scoring country in the ODIN 2017 report, Denmark, scored 80 (out of 100), while the lowest scoring country, Chad, scored 3. The median score was 37. Similar disparities between high and low-to-middle income countries' open data scores were found in the ODB.[17] Scores are typically correlated with a country's GDP, but there are examples of relatively poor countries that provide open data on a large set of official statistics. In ODIN 2017, Rwanda, for example, had a higher score for data openness than one-third of the OECD countries. A few countries have made significant improvements. In 2017, Bulgaria's ODIN score increased by 14 points, placing it in the top ten globally, because the NSO made more data available in machine-readable and non-proprietary formats, and revised its terms of use to make them more open.

Despite widespread support for open data, the open data indexes have not, on average, registered a significant improvement in the last few years. Figure 1 shows the average open data scores from the ODB, ODIN, and GODI indexes. To make these indexes more comparable, only countries that had a score in every year of the index's study period were used. Small changes in methodology limit comparability over time,[18] but a general pattern is clear: there is no clear upward trend in average scores; if anything, there appears to be a levelling off of progress toward open data.

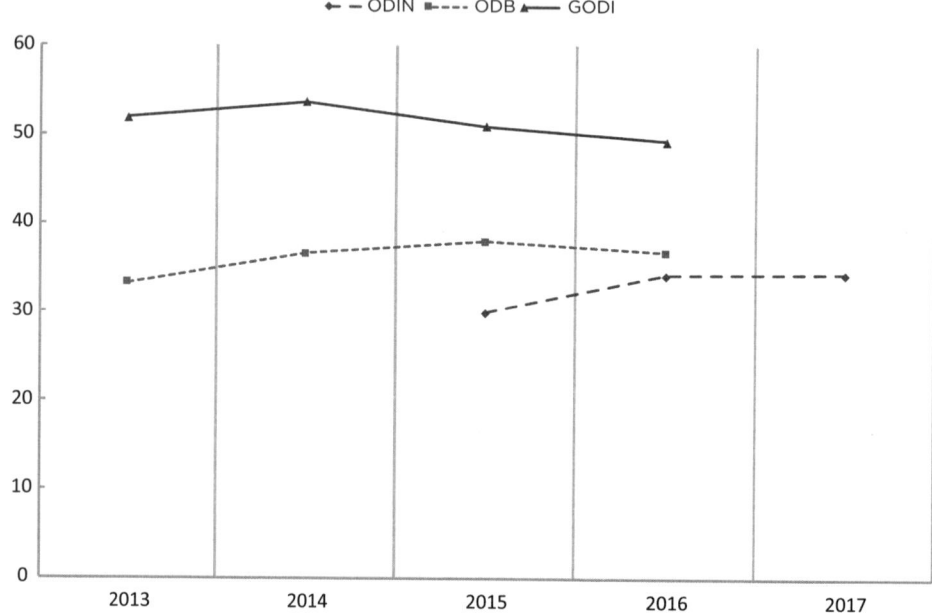

Figure 1: Measuring open data index scores over time
Source: Data taken from the ODB, ODIN, and GODI indexes

To have open data, you first need data. Without open data, it is difficult to demonstrate the value of data to policy-makers, and, without recognition of the value of data, progress toward complete and open data will remain slow. For many countries, this defines a nexus of problems: lack of focus on the demand side, lack of commitment, and, lack of resources. There continues to be a mismatch in countries between data demand and supply. Like all service providers, NSOs must understand their clients. If members of government, businesses, and citizens cannot access the data they need, then they will go elsewhere or do without.[19] Beyond simply publishing data on their website or through a dedicated data portal, NSOs must engage with their clients, demonstrate the relevance and value of data, and provide tools and information that make the data more accessible. User surveys, feedback options, and monitoring web traffic are some of the methods that can be used to understand client needs.

The SDGs have increased the demands on NSOs as they require a comprehensive set of data from social, economic, and environmental sectors to measure progress toward the 2030 targets. This presents an opportunity for closing the gap between supply and demand since much of the data required for monitoring the SDGs depends upon the work of the national statistical system. But the 2017 ODIN report finds that critical datasets on the environment and gender are absent from some national data portals.[20] The lack of gender data is a particular obstacle to the SDG commitment to "Leave no one behind",[21] which focuses on making disaggregated data available on gender, age, income, disability, and other important factors to make sure that the SDG targets are met for all segments of society. NSOs have an important role to play in closing these data gaps and meeting the demands of the SDGs.

Additional resources are needed for national statistical systems

Many national statistical systems are underfunded and lack the modern data infrastructure and statistical capacity necessary to meet the demands of the 2030 SDG Agenda. The *Development co-operation report 2017*[22] and *The state of development data funding*[23] report find that funding levels for statistics are insufficient. Both recommend that the donor community (including multilateral, bilateral, and philanthropic organisations) adopt new financing strategies to provide more resources for data production and statistical capacity building. It is not just a matter of how much financing is given, but how it is given. As PARIS21's project on Capacity Development 4.0 makes clear, better allocation of resources and coordination of donors' programmes can increase the effectiveness of capacity-building programmes. The amounts needed are not large. Properly allocated and well used, an increase in support for statistics from 0.30 to 0.45% of official development assistance is needed to increase the statistical capacity to support the SDGs. National statistical systems with strong open data practices will have a positive effect on capacity-building efforts.

Increasing political support for open data

The countries that outperformed expectations in the open data indexes can provide important lessons on best practices. Countries like Rwanda, which has the highest ODIN score of any low-income country, or Mexico, which has developed a strong culture of support for open data and is consistently ranked highly in measures of open data, are good examples. Because many of the actions needed to make data open (e.g. open licensing and providing machine-readable formats) do not require large investments and are achievable with simple policy changes, it is often leadership and politics that keep data from being open.

NSOs are, by their design, supposed to be apolitical government organisations. Politics, however, often becomes entangled in NSO activities because official statistics can be used to justify funding from donors[24] or defend a politician's governing record,[25] or because census statistics can be used for taxation and other functions of state power.[26] Because of NSOs' apolitical nature, the leadership in the organisations often lack or do not want to use their political capacity to push for an open data agenda.[27] Successful national movements for open data require a high-level commitment on behalf of the government (often at the head of state level), long-term planning to create continued political support in transition, and guiding political frameworks. With this political support, minor changes in policy and better dissemination tools could open data in many countries.

A rising open data star: Mexico

The Instituto Nacional de Estadística y Geografía (INEGI) in Mexico is opening data and leading the way in its region with high-level support from the Office of the President.[28] INEGI's hard work prompted the country to move into the top-ten most open countries in ODIN 2017, passing the United States (US). Mexico also consistently outperforms other countries in its region and other middle-income countries as measured by the ODB and GODI indexes. As a result, impactful open data programmes can be seen across the country, like Mejora Tu Escuela, a programme that displays school data and rankings to spur educational improvements by holding schools accountable.[29]

Demonstrating the value of data

The impact of open data on the economy, good governance, and democracy needs to be measured and communicated to the public, decision-makers, and politicians. If the value can be demonstrated, a virtuous cycle of data use can begin. People who use data will make better decisions. Data-based decisions will have more positive outcomes, and this will lead to greater data use and encourage additional funding for data and statistics. Broader use of data can also help NSOs improve the quality of their data. The more statistics are compared, contrasted, and combined with other data and information, the more light is shed on quality issues that may not have been identified previously.

The results from research studies on the use of open data on development are mixed and show that data has the capacity to generate economic impacts, but decision-makers often have difficulty incorporating data into their decision-making process. The Results Development Initiative[30] and the *Avoiding data graveyards* report[31] point to low use of data and open data platforms by decision-makers. Conversely, a survey from the United Nations Economic Commission for Europe finds there is a rising perception of the importance of data use and an increase in the citations of data in the countries surveyed.[32] More research is needed to understand the obstacles to, and incentives for, making better use of development data for public decision-making.

> ### Leading the pack on open data in Africa: Rwanda
>
> Rwanda has proven that, with a commitment to open data and some practical steps, low-income countries can open data. Rwanda has strategically invested in funding for statistics and open data.[33] As a result, the country earned the highest ODIN 2017 ranking for a low-income country. As a champion of open data, the country has also seen societal benefits like the open data land use portal that promotes land rights in the country. It especially benefits women, who are often cheated in land deals due to lack of access to land documentation.[34]

Conclusion

Taking stock of the state of open data for official statistics, we see that much progress has been made but that more is needed. International financial support for NSOs and a global push to demonstrate the value of open data for development could have dramatic effects on changing popular and political support for open data. However, there are also actions that NSOs can take to support open data in their own countries.

An important first step is to secure political and institutional support for open data within the government and to obtain the support of other stakeholders. This effort should be coordinated with a government-wide open data initiative, if possible. Legal frameworks and access to information policies should be reviewed and revised as necessary to support open data policies. Open data should be incorporated in countries' NSDS, as well as in the planning and implementation of SDG national reporting platforms. For countries that have not already done so, an ODRA can be used to identify a roadmap for implementing open data. NSOs should champion open data in their own countries. Their perspectives and voices are needed at international discussions around open data, such as the IODC and United Nations World Data Forum.

Implementing open data programmes for existing datasets need not be expensive, and countries do not need to wait for additional funding to make progress. Data in PDF or image files can be converted to non-proprietary and machine-readable formats at little or no cost. Current production processes should be updated to go directly to machine-readable files, which will reduce costs over the long run. Metadata should be assembled and made available. And all data should be published under an open licence, such as a Creative Commons Public Domain (CC0) or Attribution Only (CC-BY) licence. These steps only require the political will to open data and few additional resources.

Just as it is important to make the case for the value of data at the international level, it is also important at the country level. Open data expands the reach and influence of the national statistical system, increasing the value of official statistics to the government and to the public. Data that is open can be used and reused without diminishing its value, for mobile phone applications, analyses, and other applications. By following the "Leave no one behind" movement, NSOs can also build a broad coalition of all segments of society to make sure all people are included and can benefit from this data. Most NSOs are more focused on the technical aspects of running their organisations, but effort should also be put into spreading data success stories to the public to increase support for open data. Overall, open data can raise the profile of data and the profile of NSOs as trusted organisations that are responsive to national and international demands.

When these steps at the international and national levels are taken, the open data index scores will begin to improve, and, more importantly, citizens will start to see the promised benefits of open data and much needed movement toward the 2030 SDGs.

Further reading

Badiee, S., Jütting, J., Appel, D., Klein, T., & Swanson, E. (2017). The role of national statistical systems in the data revolution. In *Development Co-operation report 2017*. Paris: Organisation of Economic Co-operation and Development Publishing. https://doi.org/10.1787/dcr-2018-en

High-level Group for Partnership, Coordination and Capacity-Building. (2017). *Cape Town global action plan for sustainable development data*. Cape Town: United Nations Statistical Division. https://unstats.un.org/sdgs/hlg/Cape-Town-Global-Action-Plan/

Open Data Watch. (2019). *Open data inventory 2018/19 annual report*. Open Data Watch. http://odin.opendatawatch.com/report/pressReport

UN Statistical Commission. (2018). *Open data: Report of the Secretary-General*. New York, NY: United Nations Economic and Social Council. https://doi.org/10.1787/dcr-2018-en

About the authors

Shaida Badiee is a co-founder of Open Data Watch, where she directs the strategic planning, partnership, and fund-raising work. She is a Senior Advisor on gender data to Data2X, a co-chair of the SDSN TReNDS group, part of the Technical Advisory Group for the Global Partnership on Sustainable Development Data, a member of the PARIS21 board, and serves on a number of other boards. To follow Shaida, go to https://twitter.com/ShaidaBadiee.

Caleb Rudow is a Research and Data Analyst at Open Data Watch and conducts research on open data funding, patterns of data use, and technical issues around open data policy.

Eric Swanson is a co-founder of Open Data Watch, where he is the Director of Research. He is a globally recognised economist with a passion for analysing the most effective ways to use data for development. More information on Eric can be found at https://twitter.com/EricVSwanson and details on Open Data Watch are available at https://opendatawatch.com/about/.

How to cite this chapter

Badiee, S., Rudow, C., & Swanson, E. (2019). Open data and national statistics. In T. Davies, S. Walker, M. Rubinstein, & F. Perini (Eds.), *The state of open data: Histories and horizons* (pp. 196–206). Cape Town and Ottawa: African Minds and International Development Research Centre. http://stateofopendata.od4d.net

This work is licensed under a Creative Commons Attribution 4.0 International (CC BY 4.0) licence. It was carried out with the aid of a grant from the International Development Research Centre, Ottawa, Canada.

Endnotes

1. OECD. (2017). *Development co-operation report 2017: Data for development*. Paris: Organisation for Economic Co-operation and Development Publishing. https://doi.org/10.1787/dcr-2017-en
2. UNSC (United Nations Statistical Commission). (2018). *Fundamental principles of official statistics*. New York, NY: United Nations. https://unstats.un.org/unsd/dnss/gp/FP-Rev2013-E.pdf
3. World Bank. (2017). Statistical capacity indicator dashboard. http://datatopics.worldbank.org/statisticalcapacity/SCIdashboard.aspx
4. Pollock, R. (2010). Welfare gains from opening up public sector information in the UK. https://rufuspollock.org/papers/psi_openness_gains.pdf
5. Capgemini Consulting. (2015). *Creating value through open data study on the impact of re-use of public data resources*. Luxembourg: European Data Portal. https://www.europeandataportal.eu/sites/default/files/edp_creating_value_through_open_data_0.pdf
6. Landsat Advisory Group. (2018). *The value proposition for Landsat applications*. NGAC Landsat Economic Value Paper – 2014 update. Reston, VA: National Geospatial Advisory Committee. https://www.fgdc.gov/ngac/meetings/december-2014/ngac-landsat-economic-value-paper-2014-update.pdf
7. Open Knowledge International. (n.d.). Open definition 2.1. http://opendefinition.org/od/2.1/en/
8. Open Data Charter. (2015). Principles: International Open Data Charter. https://opendatacharter.net/principles/
9. High-level Group for Partnership, Coordination and Capacity-Building for Statistics for the 2030 Agenda for Sustainable Development. (2017). *Cape Town global action plan for sustainable development data*. New York, NY: United Nations Statistical Commission. https://unstats.un.org/sdgs/hlg/Cape-Town-Global-Action-Plan/
10. http://od4d.net/
11. PARIS21. (n.d.). NSDS (National Strategies for the Development of Statistics) guidelines: Open data. http://nsdsguidelines.paris21.org/node/530
12. World Bank. (2015). Readiness Assessment Tool. http://opendatatoolkit.worldbank.org/en/odra.html
13. Web Foundation. (2017). *Open Data Barometer – Global report*. 4th edition. Washington, DC: World Wide Web Foundation. https://opendatabarometer.org/4thedition/report/
14. Open Knowledge International. (n.d.). Global Open Data Index. https://index.okfn.org.
15. Open Data Charter. (2015). Principles: International Open Data Charter. https://opendatacharter.net/principles/
16. Open Knowledge International. (n.d.). Open definition 2.1. http://opendefinition.org/od/2.1/en/
17. Web Foundation. (2017). *Open Data Barometer – Global report*. 4th edition. Washington, DC: World Wide Web Foundation. https://opendatabarometer.org/4thedition/report/

18. For a discussion of the ODIN methodology, see Open Data Watch. (2017). *Open data inventory: 2017: Methodology report*. Washington, DC: Open Data Watch. https://opendatawatch.com/reference/open-data-inventory-2017-methodolgy-report/
19. Young, A. & Verhulst, S. (2016). *When demand and supply meet: Key findings of the open data impact case studies*. Brooklyn, NY: GovLab. http://odimpact.org/files/open-data-impact-key-findings.pdf
20. Open Data Watch. (2017). *Open data inventory 2017: Annual report*. Washington, DC: Open Data Watch. http://odin.opendatawatch.com/Downloads/otherFiles/ODIN-2017-Annual-Report.pdf
21. United Nations Statistics Division. (2016). Leaving no one behind. https://unstats.un.org/sdgs/report/2016/leaving-no-one-behind
22. OECD. (2017). *Development co-operation report 2017*. Paris: Organisation for Economic Co-operation and Development Publishing. https://doi.org/10.1787/dcr-2017-en
23. Global Partnership for Sustainable Development Data. (2016). *The state of development data funding*. Washington, DC: Open Data Watch. https://opendatawatch.com/wp-content/uploads/2016/09/development-data-funding-2016.pdf
24. Sandefur, J. & Glassman, A. (2014). *The political economy of bad data: Evidence from African survey & administrative statistics*. CGD Working Paper 373. Washington, DC: Center for Global Development. https://www.cgdev.org/publication/political-economy-bad-data-evidence-african-survey-administrative-statistics-working
25. Custer, S. & Sethi, T. (Eds.). (2017). *Avoiding data graveyards: Insights from data producers and consumers*. Washington, DC: Aid Data at the College of William and Mary. http://docs.aiddata.org/reports/avoiding-data-graveyards-report.html
26. Krätke, F. & Byiers, B. (2014). *The political economy of official statistics: Implications for the data revolution in Sub-Saharan Africa*. ECDPM Discussion Paper 170. Maastricht, Netherlands and Brussels, Belgium: European Centre for Development Policy Management, in partnership with PARIS21. http://www.ecdpm.org/dp170
27. World Bank. (2018). *World Bank support for open data 2012–2017*. Washington, DC: World Bank. http://opendatatoolkit.worldbank.org/docs/world-bank-open-data-support.pdf
28. Web Foundation. (2017). *Open Data Barometer: Latin America regional report*. (3rd edition). Washington, DC: World Wide Web Foundation. https://opendatabarometer.org/3rdedition/regional-report/latin-america/
29. Young, A. & Verhulst, S. (2016). *Mexico's Mejora Tu Escuela: Empowering citizens to make data-driven decisions about education*. Brooklyn, NY: GovLab. http://odimpact.org/case-mexicos-mejora-tu-escuela.html
30. Development Gateway. (2017). *Increasing the impact of results data*. Policy Brief. Washington, DC: Development Gateway. https://www.developmentgateway.org/sites/default/files/2017-02/RDI-PolicyBrief.pdf
31. Custer, S. & Sethi, T. (Eds.). (2017). *Avoiding data graveyards: Insights from data producers and consumers*. Washington, DC: Aid Data at the College of William and Mary. http://docs.aiddata.org/reports/avoiding-data-graveyards-report.html
32. https://www.unece.org/statistics/networks-of-experts/task-force-on-the-value-of-official-statistics.html
33. UNECA et al. (2016). *The Africa data revolution report 2016*. Addis Ababa: United Nations Economic Commission for Africa. https://www.uneca.org/sites/default/files/uploaded-documents/ACS/africa-data-revolution-report-2016.pdf
34. Crompton, S. (2016). *Success stories: Issue 1*. Wallingford, UK: Global Open Data for Agriculture and Nutrition. https://www.godan.info/sites/default/files/documents/GODAN_Success_Stories_Brochure_Issue_1.pdf

014

Telecommunications

Stephen Song

Key points

- Although open data relies upon connectivity, the telecoms sector has been overlooked as an area of focus for open data initiatives.

- Good practices exist for open data in telecommunications from providing details of cell towers and spectrum allocation to publishing pricing data; however, these good practices are not yet widely adopted.

- Open data enabled transparency for telecommunications network infrastructures and pricing could spur innovation, improve accountability, and help track the social impact of investments in connectivity.

Introduction

The value of being connected to a communication network is steadily rising. More than a decade ago, researchers established that simple proximity to a communication network was directly correlated[1] to a reduction in the probability of dying from malaria. Today, with smartphones delivering powerful generic services like group and personal messaging and more specific apps aimed at critical sectors like education, agriculture, and health, communication networks are approaching the status of essential infrastructure for a modern economy.

And yet, mobile subscriber growth is slowing[2] as current mobile network operators struggle to find viability in markets with subsistence-level incomes and/or sparsely populated regions. Attempts to address this problem through universal service strategies/funds have met with limited success.

This presents a conundrum for policy-makers and regulators where value continues to accrue to those with affordable access to communication infrastructure, while the unconnected fall further and further behind by simply staying in the same place. Those who most desperately need support are cut off from access to opportunity, to social and health safety nets, to education, to information that can improve lives, and to platforms to demand change. It is ironic, or perhaps tragic, that the voices of the unconnected are not heard on this issue for the very reason that they are unconnected.

In order to address this issue, fresh thinking is required. Previously, solving connectivity challenges could only be tackled by entire governments investing vast resources in state-owned networks. The mobile phone revolution opened the door to private sector investment in telecommunications, and new business models like pay-as-you-go services have extended sustainable communication services further than anyone could have imagined. However, becoming a mobile network operator still involves millions of dollars, creating a high barrier to market entry.

There are a number of factors that suggest that the telecommunications landscape is shifting once again.

- The value chain of telecommunications networks is becoming disaggregated. Previously, in order to enter a market, an operator needed to invest in international, national, middle mile, and last mile infrastructure. Now, we are beginning to see competition in each of those segments.

- The spread of fibre optic infrastructure, both undersea and terrestrial, is changing the access market. While there is no question that fibre optic networks are increasing the ability of existing operators to deliver broadband, those same networks are opening up possibilities for new players who now can deliver more targeted, localised, and affordable solutions to unserved populations.

- Changes in last mile technology are opening up new possibilities. The spread of WiFi as an access technology is empowering commercial, government, and community access initiatives to offer local services. Dynamic spectrum technology also shows promise as an alternative access technology.

- Finally, the meteoric growth of access and mass manufacturing has brought down the cost of access technologies to the point where they are within the reach of small-scale operators. Low-cost solar-powered open source GSM (Global System for Mobile Communications) base stations can be deployed for a fraction of the cost models of existing mobile network operators.

All of these changes represent genuine cause for optimism that it is possible to sustainably connect everyone on the planet. However, in order for that to happen, changes in access policy and regulation are required. And those changes need to be informed by accurate data on existing telecommunication infrastructure and its use. This includes data on the extent and uptake of fibre optic networks, towers used by mobile operators, broadcasters, and ISPs, as well as the wireless spectrum assignments that are assigned to operators. The pricing of wholesale networks is also an important data point, especially from the point of view of regional benchmarking.

To date, public access to any of the above information has been through communication regulators who collect some or all of this information from licensed operators. Some of this information may be passed on to the public through the regulator's website. In some cases, the operators themselves may release portions of this information. What is evident from an examination of the websites of communication regulators is that there is no consistency as to what information is made publicly available and how detailed that information is.

In the early days of mobile networks (and fibre networks), there was not that much emphasis on accurate mapping of network infrastructure, partially because operators were expanding so rapidly at the time. Now, as subscriber growth is slowing and the challenge of providing affordable access in more difficult regions becomes more evident, it is essential to have more accurate information on the state of network growth and the resources in use.

It is also essential that this data be made available to the public as open data. There are several reasons for this.

- Since a wider range of actors from community networks to wireless ISPs to municipalities have the potential to address access gaps in a sustainable manner, we need public access to telecom infrastructure data in order to open the doors to collective, community, and entrepreneurial approaches to infrastructure deployment. Open data on telecommunications infrastructure would enable the identification of infrastructure gaps and opportunities.

- Transparency is essential in any industry where hundreds of millions of dollars are invested by both private and public sector organisations. Public data will provide an important reality check.

- There is an ongoing need for comparative analysis. Telecommunications infrastructure varies dramatically from country to country and within countries, yet there is very little comparison of physical infrastructure, spectrum assignments, and backhaul costs. Having common public standards for telecommunications data will enable these comparisons and help to identify outliers both good and bad.

- Telecommunications infrastructure is enabling the profound social and economic impact that we see as a result of the spread of voice and data networks. The opportunity to compare telecommunications infrastructure development with other social and economic indicators represents a significant opportunity to understand more about their impact.

The open data movement in government has been growing for over a decade. It contributes to more accountable and democratic institutions, and is one way that governments can meet their obligation to provide access to information. The open data principle of providing timely, accessible, complete, affordable, and non-discriminatory access to data is ideal for the telecommunications sector, which stands to benefit with respect to both transparency and innovation. While blanket approaches to open data in government have not always been successful, there is substantial evidence to suggest that more targeted, bottom-up approaches can have very positive outcomes. Some examples include OpenSpending's work on government finance, Publish What You Pay's work on extractive industries, and work on transport data by organisations such as London Transport.

The rest of this chapter looks at specific aspects of the telecommunications sector and attempts to show why transparency is essential for it. Further, it demonstrates that good practices do exist for open data in telecommunications but they are not widespread. Promoting open telecommunications data is not about doing something new, but rather about normalising the examples of good behaviour that already exist and aligning with the principles of the open data movement.

The potential of open data

Fibre

The spread of undersea fibre optic cables around Africa since 2009, followed closely by the rapid spread of terrestrial fibre optic infrastructure, is nothing short of a revolution. It has spread far faster than anyone would have imagined possible. There are perhaps only two or three countries in Africa that do not have a national fibre optic backbone currently. Many countries have several. Fibre optic networks are the deep water ports of the internet; they enable orders of magnitude greater broadband capacity than any other kind of access technology and at very low latency. For terrestrial networks in particular, the capacity of this infrastructure is so great that it is effectively a non-rival resource: access for one service provider does not diminish opportunity for other providers.

However, operators are often reluctant to share information about their fibre networks. This reluctance betrays an apprehension that it may somehow compromise their competitive edge, but, in many cases, operators have simply not considered the issue from a strategic perspective. While the majority of operators decline to publish detailed information about their fibre networks, their response stands in stark contrast to companies like Dark Fibre Africa[3] in South Africa, and regional operator, Liquid Telecom,[4] who readily publish maps of their fibre networks. Dark Fibre Africa stands out in the detail and ease-of-use of their maps.

Taking this information from the narrow group of stakeholders within which it resides and opening it up to public input and discussion as open data can have multiple benefits. For example, a small rural municipality might determine from a public fibre map that it is in their interest to invest in 50 kilometres of fibre network to connect to a nearby network. A province or state might determine that their region is suffering due to a lack of fibre infrastructure investment. A school or a hospital could fundraise for better access if they can show that a fibre optic cable is within a reasonable distance. From a national strategic perspective, fibre optic infrastructure is now comparable in terms of importance with other basic infrastructure like roads, railways, and bridges. The public needs to be aware of its existence in order to identify opportunities to connect to it and to identify gaps where more investment is needed. Making this data public can also be good for operators who can use the scope of their investment in fibre infrastructure to market their services.

Spectrum

Once the end of the fibre network is reached, it is wireless technologies that typically deliver the last mile of connectivity to citizens. Wireless technologies are dependent on national regulatory authorities that grant specific permission to use any given set of radio frequencies. To become a wireless network operator, a licence to operate radio equipment within a given set of frequencies is typically required. The exceptions to this are the industrial, scientific, and medical (ISM) bands, or licence-exempt bands (used by technologies like WiFi, Bluetooth, etc.), which do not require a specific licence. Twenty years ago, when mobile networks were just getting off the ground and most of the internet was carried over copper wires, obtaining a spectrum licence was effectively a simple administrative process. Now that demand for wireless spectrum has significantly increased, spectrum licences have become valuable assets that are often sold at auction for millions of dollars.

It is essential that the public has access to information about which organisations have been assigned a given frequency band, that is, given a licence to operate in a given frequency and on what terms that licence has been granted. A few national regulators publish this information on their websites, but most do not. In Africa, Nigeria stands out for their diligence in publishing spectrum assignments.[5] Kenya and South Africa are also relatively good; however, not only do most national regulators not publish this information but some will also refuse a public request for this information.

Why is public access to information on spectrum assignments important? Because there are often opportunities to take better advantage of existing spectrum availability. In Mexico, a non-profit[6] is using low-cost GSM technologies to deliver affordable access[7] in the state of Oaxaca. The Mexican regulator has set aside a small amount of GSM spectrum specifically to enable rural access. This inspiring model deserves to be replicated elsewhere; however, without publicly available information on spectrum assignments, it is a challenge to understand where those opportunities are available.

Towers

Public access to data on mobile tower locations is also essential. Why? In terms of understanding who has network coverage, we currently must rely on mobile network operator coverage maps. Mobile network operators do not have the best incentives to be completely rigorous in ensuring the accuracy of their network maps. As it becomes more strategically important to connect every citizen, it becomes equally essential to understand exactly who does and who does not have network coverage. The simplest way to validate network coverage claims is to know where the towers are, which operators are on them, and what technologies (i.e. 2G, 3G, LTE) they are using on that tower.

A common push back to this suggestion is that publishing tower information would compromise the security of the networks. In fact, tower locations are already reasonably well-known. First, they are easily visible to the naked eye, therefore, not hard to locate. Second, many, if not most of them, can be identified through online services like OpenCellID[8] or Mozilla's Location Service.[9] These two resources are invaluable, but a limitation of their crowd-sourced approach is that they depend on someone (who has their software installed on their phone) being near a tower in order to detect it. To date, this approach has been successful in picking up a large percentage of the towers in many countries; however, the more remote towers (where populations are sparse) tend not to get picked up by these services. It is exactly in these more remote areas (where operators have the least incentive to provide coverage) that we want to know more about access conditions. Therefore, having open data on public tower locations would be extremely valuable from the point of view of mapping the unserved, and in terms of identifying opportunities for new business models to provide services.

Like fibre maps and spectrum charts, good practices already exist with regard to tower information. The Canadian government publishes open data via a Comma Separated Value (CSV) file[10] with the location of every tower in Canada together with information about the operator(s) on the tower, as well as the type of equipment, power output, antenna orientation, etc. This is all you would need to build a comprehensive map of towers across Canada, and indeed someone has done so. Steven Nikkel has imported that data into an online map that provides a detailed picture of mobile infrastructure in Canada.[11] This is essential information for the average citizen trying to choose a service provider in any region outside of a major urban centre, where coverage varies significantly between operators. There is no reason not to do this sort of mapping everywhere, but it will be necessary to explode a few myths and change the norms around publishing tower data.

It is not just the Canadian government that has seen the value of publishing tower data. In India, veteran operator, Airtel, has published a new website, Open Network,[12] where all of their towers for both 2G and 4G networks are mapped. They also identify where towers are being upgraded and where they are still needed. The website goes by the slogan "Because you have a lot to say. And we have nothing to hide". This is strong evidence to illustrate how transparency, far from being a liability, can actually be a powerful tool for marketing. This is the first instance of a commercial operator publishing tower location data.

Backhaul pricing

Demand for broadband is increasing exponentially in Africa with the result that backhaul networks are fast becoming the critical bottleneck in affordable access to broadband. As noted previously, there is a lot of fibre across Africa, but the cost of terrestrial fibre networks is often so high that it makes operator expansion impractical. This is not a problem if you happen to own the fibre (as many incumbent operators do), but it can be a significant obstacle for new operators. This is not a simple challenge to address, but a step in the right direction would be to introduce more transparency through open data on network backhaul pricing. The cost per Mbps varies dramatically across regions. Regulators may be unaware of how their country stacks up in terms of national backhaul pricing. A little transparency would go a long way. This is not to suggest that operators must reveal their business agreements, only their basic rate card. Among other things, this would have the result of establishing a ceiling for costs.

Once again, some good practices do exist. The regulator in Botswana (BOCRA) publishes a public rate card[13] on access to the national fibre optic backbone. Granted this is a state-owned network, which removes the complication of negotiating with the private sector, but even if we just succeeded with state-owned networks, it would be a big leap forward. The practice of publishing backhaul and interconnection pricing is more common in West Africa thanks to a directive in 2006 from the West African Economic and Monetary Union (UEMOA),[14] the West African regional economic community.

Conclusion

Affordable access to communication is now such a valuable social and economic enabler that it is no longer appropriate to talk about strategies that connect "most" of the population. We need strategies that can embrace all levels of society and all regions. Fortunately, market and technological trends have created new possibilities for the development of affordable access solutions; however, in order to have a meaningful conversation about those options, we need better data on current telecommunications network development. Governments across the world have seen the potential of open data to increase both transparency and innovation in specific sectors and to better meet the needs of their citizens. Open data policies contribute to more efficient and accountable governance, and facilitate the enjoyment of human rights. Telecommunications has been overlooked as a sector to which open data policies might be applied. This is not a question of massive change for either regulators or operators, but is more of a case of socialising and normalising the good practices that already exist for making telecommunications data public, whether fibre, spectrum, towers, or pricing.

To counteract the inertia of the status quo, a coalition of civil society and research organisations is needed. This group can come up with a simple, convincing campaign to get policy-makers, regulators, and operators to see the value of open telecommunications data with an initial set of data standards, descriptors, and tools that can help early adopters to start opening their data.

Further reading

Song, S. Open telecom data – moving forward. *Many Possibilities*, 25 May. https://manypossibilities.net/2018/05/open-telecom-data-moving-forward/. Note that this article was the basis for this chapter.

About the author

Stephen Song is a researcher, entrepreneur, and advocate for cheaper, more pervasive access to communication infrastructure in Africa. He is a 2018 Fellow at the Mozilla Foundation, a Research Associate with the Network Startup Resource Center (NSRC), and the founder of Village Telco, a social enterprise that manufactures low-cost WiFi mesh VoIP technologies to deliver affordable voice and internet service. Learn more about Steve and telecommunications in Africa through his blog at http://manypossibilities.net.

How to cite this chapter

Song, S. (2018). Open data and telecommunications. In T. Davies, S. Walker, M. Rubinstein, & F. Perini (Eds.), *The state of open data: Histories and horizons* (pp. 207–214). Cape Town and Ottawa: African Minds and International Development Research Centre. http://stateofopendata.od4d.net

This work is licensed under a Creative Commons Attribution 4.0 International (CC BY 4.0) licence. It was carried out with the aid of a grant from the International Development Research Centre, Ottawa, Canada.

Endnotes

1. Mozumder, P. & Marathe, A. (2007). Role of information and communication networks in malaria survival. *Malaria Journal, 6, 136–144.* https://doi.org/10.1186/1475-2875-6-136
2. Rizzato, F., Giles, M., & San Martin, M.C. (2018). *Unique subscribers and mobile internet users: Understanding the new growth story.* GSMA Intelligence, 15 February. https://www.gsmaintelligence.com/research/2018/02/unique-subscribers-and-mobile-internet-users-understanding-the-new-growth-story/653/
3. http://www.dfafrica.co.za/network/coverage/
4. https://www.liquidtelecom.com/about-us/network-map.html
5. See, for example, https://www.ncc.gov.ng/docman-main/spectrum-frequency-allocation-tables/756-frequency-assignments-900mhz/file
6. https://www.rhizomatica.org/
7. Lakhani, N. (2016). "It feels like a gift": Mobile phone co-op transforms rural Mexican community. *The Guardian* [World news], 15 August. https://www.theguardian.com/world/2016/aug/15/mexico-mobile-phone-network-indigenous-community
8. https://www.opencellid.org/
9. https://location.services.mozilla.com/
10. http://sms-sgs.ic.gc.ca/eic/site/sms-sgs-prod.nsf/eng/h_00010.html
11. https://www.ertyu.org/steven_nikkel/cancellsites.html
12. https://www.airtel.in/opennetwork/
13. http://www.bocra.org.bw/sites/default/files/documents/Telecommunications%20and%20ICT%20Prices.pdf
14. http://www.uemoa.int/

015. Transport

Pieter Colpaert and Julián Andrés Rojas Meléndez

Key points

- Public transport has been a poster-child of the open data movement with a variety of route planning applications used by millions of people every day. Transport data can also be used to analyse policy and advocate for service improvements.

- Tensions exist between centralised route planning services and distributed, open data-driven approaches to transport data. Only a fraction of the data used to drive mobility apps is truly open, and current technical architectures risk holding back a next wave of innovation.

- Data-driven transport tools have been developed worldwide; however, established standards need to be more flexible in order to accommodate semi-structured and informal transport networks in the developing world.

- The future success of "Mobility as a Service" will depend on a much greater range of open transport data and application programming interfaces (APIs).

Introduction

How far do you live from your place of work? Was your answer a distance or was it a duration dependent upon a specific mode of transport? The question of how far you can go, and how long it takes to go from one location to another, is key to identifying the opportunities you and your family can take advantage of. The amount of data an application could use to support an answer to this question is beyond imagination. Details of road networks, live public transport timetables, and even wheelchair accessibility of public buildings, are just a few of the applicable datasets.

Urban planners, real estate developers, travel application developers, and even manufacturers of autonomous vehicles, all need this kind of information to make their services better. For some, the availability of this data is even a primary condition for operation. Take the Dutch company, GoOV,[1] for example, which aids people with a mental disability to get home safely and autonomously using public transport. Without access to live transport tables, they would not be able to offer these services.

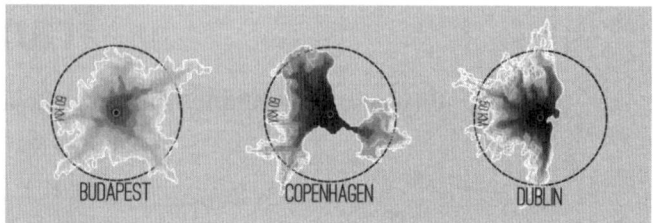

Figure 1: The shape of capitals of Europe – How far can you travel in 1 hour by car?
Source: Created by Topi Tjukanov (used with permission) https://static1.squarespace.com/static/5a25370fc027d841ff016862/5a76d9da53450ac90957f6bd/5a76d9f071c10bcbf-b7264af/1517738518899/isochronesv3.png?format=1000w

Transport apps have served as a poster child for the open data movement, with route planning apps, such as CityMapper, Transit App, or Google Maps often appearing in presentations on the benefits of open data. In 2014, the International Association for Public Transport (UITP) made open data the main subject of a focus paper,[2] and the association featured open data talks in its IT-Trans conference. A year later, the American Public Transport Association (APTA) published a Policy Development and Research Paper on embracing open data.[3] Although these developments indicate significant traction to date on open transport data, gaining the disclosure of transit data has not been straightforward. As pointed out in studies by Rojas[4] and Colpaert et al.,[5] many cultural, technical, and legal obstacles have had to be overcome.

While transport data is hard to define, this chapter will focus on data that can be used by route planners and on three main challenges:

1. Route planning – determining who does what and how transport data is licensed.
2. The accessibility and availability of datasets.
3. Emerging technologies such as Mobility as a Service (MaaS) and autonomous driving.

From schedule data to advice on route planning

Route or trip planner apps advise consumers on how to get to a specific destination. Travel information is displayed using a plethora of interfaces from in-car navigation systems to the website of a local bus company or a third-party travel app. In-car navigation systems may weight data elements differently when providing route planning advice when compared with an application from a municipal transit agency, yet both of them need access to the same data.

The data needed to create these types of applications resides inside the organisations that manage and operate public transport networks, and, due to the high degree of heterogeneity that can be found from one organisation to another in terms of how they manage data, opening and using this data can be a big challenge. To address this issue, several standardisation efforts have arisen around the world to support public transport operators in openly sharing their data in an interoperable fashion. Standards, such as the General Transit Feed Specification (GTFS),[6] the European Network Timetable Exchange (NeTEx),[7] the Standard Interface for Real-time Information (SIRI),[8] or the American Transit Communications Interface Profiles (TCIP),[9] provide mechanisms to model and describe scheduled services and real-time updates from transport networks, including arrival predictions, vehicle positions, and service advisories in machine-readable formats.

Some operators also offer route planning application programming interfaces (APIs), which function as open innovation tools, encouraging the creativity of partners who need access to route planning information quickly. However, offering a public route planning API comes at a cost. API providers need to consider whether they are able to respond to all queries with the consequent server bill for each request. As a consequence, route planning APIs are often only available via registration, API keys, and rate limiting. Open data advocates would not call this truly open data as data users are not in control of the algorithms that modify, filter, and operate on the data that is finally exchanged via the API. In a truly open transport data ecosystem, everyone would be able to create their own specific route planning API based on all data being published as open data first.

> **Transport for London**
>
> Transport for London is the local government body responsible for the transport system in Greater London, England, and is commonly cited as a source of open data success stories. When Transport for London began opening up data and offering public APIs, the economic growth potential was estimated at GBP 130 million,[10] with more than 600 apps created and more than 500 people directly employed in the reuse of public transport data. Transport for London now focuses primarily on publishing the data and not on building their own route planning apps.[11] However, they still publish both the raw timetable data as well as a unified API. Read more at https://tfl.gov.uk/info-for/open-data-users/.

The manner in which data is published also reflects legal constraints. In 2016, Scassa and Diebel[12] published a paper in which they, from a legal perspective, argued that publishing real-time data as open data is troublesome. Indeed, when a route planning API is offered, a Service Level Agreement (SLA) is needed, guaranteeing the up-times of an expensive but free service. When, however, the raw data is published via downloads or file updates, the effort required by the publisher is lower and, thus, easier to guarantee.

Public authorities and non-governmental organisations (NGOs) also play a key role regarding open data in the public transport ecosystem. Public authorities provide the legal framework and regulations that drive public transport organisations to pursue open data strategies. They also may provide technical and standardisation guidelines for data publishing that help to achieve greater interoperability. NGOs are avid users of public transport open data, which they use for different kinds of studies and data analysis that aim to shed light on social issues and potential solutions. For example, a study[13] conducted by the non-profit organisation, Despacio, on the current status of, and trends in, bike mobility in Bogotá (Colombia) relied on open data provided by the Secretaría de Movilidad of Bogotá to highlight the main challenges and gaps in terms of security and infrastructure for the growing number of bike users in the city. They also used this data, together with the public transportation routes information, to generate a mobility coverage map of the city. Another example is the study performed by the Public Knowledge Workshop, an Israeli NGO that facilitates open data initiatives, which used schedule and live update data from Israeli railway and bus companies to verify their operational synchronisation.[14] They revealed that despite the presence of an official government plan requiring joined-up scheduling, there was little synchronisation in practice between the trains and the corresponding buses that were supposed to deliver and pick up passengers to and from their trains. These open data-based studies provide a vital resource for urban planners to better design and plan the development of cities and for social organisations that work toward improving living conditions in cities.

Emerging technology

In 2015, Linked Connections was put forward as a middle-ground route planning solution, moving beyond the false dichotomy between data dumps and route planning APIs.[15] With Linked Connections, route planning happens on the infrastructure of the data user, but data is already prepared for the purpose of route planning by the provider. At the basis of the technology lies the same idea as behind Content Delivery Networks (CDN). By creating small fragments of data about the departures of public transport vehicles in cacheable documents, the raw data needed by users is published cost efficiently. The goal of the framework is to enable a new open source route planning ecosystem based on web querying. Further information is available at https://linkedconnections.org.

Toward global coverage: The need for accessible data

Although there have been major steps in opening up transit data in the last decade, building a global route planner that includes all public transport modes in the world remains close to impossible. The amount of effort and money required for such an endeavour exceeds what governments and companies are willing to invest. The obstacles are diverse, including technical, legal, and financial barriers, but the availability and accessibility of the required data is paramount.

The majority of public transport companies in the world still do not provide their schedules as open data, and even fewer publish live transit updates in machine-readable formats. Therefore, it is not possible to automatically include such data in a global route planning application. One approach to tackling this data gap might be the use of applications that crawl through transport provider websites and scrape schedule information. This kind of approach demands a high effort, as for every company, there must be an ad hoc implementation of the scraper to extract data. Furthermore, there are often legal uncertainties as to whether scraping transport websites is legal in a particular jurisdiction.

Despite the relatively low availability of data and legal uncertainties around scraped data, there are still some entrepreneurs and established businesses that have been addressing this titanic challenge. The most famous, and notorious, is Google Maps. Google uses the GTFS specification that they maintain, together with a global community of developers in order to import data on different transport modes and networks into their route planner. They encourage public transport companies to generate and deliver their data in this format, but Google does not require the data to be openly published. Sometimes they will work out a direct arrangement with the public transport operators as is the case for the urban bus company, Transmilenio in Bogotá (Colombia), where the operator hires an external company to generate and deliver the GTFS feed to Google without publishing it for public access. According to the Google Transit website, they currently support 5 640[16] different transport companies within their route planning application that covers over 18 000[17] different cities around the world.

There are several other examples of applications and services that reuse transport open data and that seek to provide a global route planner, such as CityMapper, Transit App, Ally, Moovit, among others. Some of them even try to generate their own data to include cities and transport networks that do not publish their own data (e.g. CityMapper and their work on Mexico City and Istanbul).[18] Navitia[19] makes an API available that currently contains 434 transport datasets from around the world from which developers can use route planning features, generate maps of time/distances, and access timetables. They take advantage of publicly available open data and encourage users to provide new data sources. However, Transitland is potentially the largest catalogue of open transit data,[20] which reports 945 open GTFS feeds, covering 2 377 different public transit operators at the time of writing.

Mexico City

In Mexico, a GTFS feed was introduced to take advantage of the collection of GPS data throughout its transit systems. In a matter of weeks, this mega-city with several different transit providers was able to introduce a fully functional GTFS feed and obtain the benefits of work done on route planning tools elsewhere. A range of free or low-cost customer-facing applications and planning tools were able to immediately capitalise on this data.

Problematic, however, is the fact that part of the public transit system in Mexico is only semi-structured, meaning that some services do not have fixed stops, nor a defined timetable. The project revealed an important limitation of GTFS in its current form as it is unable to easily accommodate the kind of semi-structured public transit services that operate in many developing world cities.

Eros et. al (2014) have detailed the experience in a full paper for the Transportation Research Board.[21]

By providing a standardised way to model and describe public transport time schedules in machine-readable formats, GTFS has become one of the most important tools to increase the amount of available open data in the transport sector. However, it has some notable limitations when working toward global coverage of transport data. It was originally designed to model structured networks that define a set of fixed stops for vehicles and that run on predefined time schedules that are often specified down to the second. But this is not the case for most of the public transportation services offered in the major cities of the Global South, where operators may define a set of routes that are followed by a set of vehicles but without predefined fixed stops. This type of limitation in the modelling capabilities of the available standards adds difficulty to both standards and open data adoption in these parts of the world. Moreover, public transport operators in developing countries often have few incentives to provide data about their operation, and public authorities may lack the necessary regulatory framework and resources to drive or support these organisations in publishing open data.

To address these shortcomings, and to promote the wider implementation of open data initiatives, a number of different approaches have arisen. For instance, the GTFS-flex[22] specification, created and maintained by the independent developer community, is a proposed extension for GTFS that aims to provide the capabilities for modelling semi-structured public transport and demand-responsive transportation services. In Kenya, the Digital Matatus project[23] has made use of mobile communication and geolocation technologies to map and generate a GTFS data source for the semi-structured public transport service in Nairobi, which has proven to be a feasible mechanism to fill the gap when data on these types of transport networks is not available from official sources. Following this initiative, the Digital Transport for Africa community was created, which has supported open data generation projects for public transport services in Cairo, Maputo, Accra, and Abidjan.[24] Similarly, the World Bank began offering a course to empower participants to create, manage, and use GTFS feeds in resource-constrained environments.[25] It is important to note that these types of initiatives help to increase available open data for the transport sector, but they still require significant investment and political will from the public authorities in the developing world.

Today, there is evidence that disclosing public transport data can generate many benefits for different actors, including developers, entrepreneurs, users, and transport companies, and the discussion is no longer centred on whether data should or should not be openly published. The resistance still encountered around the world to engaging with open data is attributed more to a matter of the political will of organisations. Policies promoted at the national, regional, and local levels can play an important role in increasing the implementation of open transport data initiatives. One clear example of such promotion is the Intelligent Transport System (ITS) Directive[26] of the European Union. The directive aims to accelerate the deployment of innovative transport technologies across Europe, and the public accessibility of data is one of its main requirements, indicating that both policy and research discussions about open data in the public transport sector have now moved to a technical and a legal level. The key questions to address in scaling coverage relate to how transport data should be published to improve interoperability, while keeping costs to a minimum, as well as how to address legal considerations to protect the interests of involved parties, without limiting open data benefits.

> **World-wide and open source – Transportr**
>
> Open source route planning software exists today, such as Open Trip Planner, OSRM, Navitia, or RRRR, and many companies, like Plannerstack, Conveyal, Digitransit, and Kisio Digital, make use of this open source software to provide services to their clients. Navitia.io, based on the Navitia code-base, is a freemium SaaS solution for route planning. Transportr reuses this service to create a fully open source and free app with the data available via the web-services. Read more at https://transportr.grobox.de/.

Mobility as a service: An emerging challenge

Mobility is always a core point of discussion in urban planning. Ever since its introduction in the early 20th century, cities have been adapting to, or have been "taken hostage by", as some would proclaim, the car as the primary means of transport. The continued dominance and density of cars, and their negative environmental and social impacts within urban environments, has created a sense of urgency around the need to diversify the way we move from one place to another. Yet statistics on car use will not trigger a worldwide change by themselves. In order to change dominant behaviour, mobility activists and entrepreneurs have coined the term Mobility as a Service (MaaS). This new idea tries to activate people to leave their cars behind and diversify their mobility choices by means of an app. Instead of having to use multiple apps to find routes and buy tickets for each different mode of transport, an ecosystem for all-in-one solutions must be built.

In order to grow a MaaS ecosystem in a certain region, three requirements need to be fulfilled. The first is that the data needs to be available on where and when specific services can be used. Given the low availability of open transport datasets today, the MaaS movement is also an important advocacy force for open data, arguing that every mobility player, whether public or private, needs to publish their data in order to create a truly level playing field for MaaS.

In Belgium, for example, an Open Data Charter was created in 2018 by local governments and regional governmental institutions[27] that lays out 20 principles for open data, including the 19th principle stating that data resulting from a government concession should be open as well. Local governments adopting such a principle may push forward the agenda of open data and MaaS worldwide.

The second requirement for MaaS is that an open ticketing API must be in place. The more you allow third parties to sell your tickets, the more integration can happen with other mobility solutions. An open ticketing API may allow tickets to be granted to users in various ways (e.g. per hour, per km, etc.). As evidenced by the low availability of fare data in general, it is certainly early days, yet this is an area that is currently rapidly evolving. In Finland, for example, an API for ticketing has been created that can be used by anyone to buy tickets without signing complicated contracts. This allows apps created by vendors, such as MaaS global,[28] to start selling tickets as a third party.

Finally, open data and open ticketing alone are not going to create a seamless travel experience for end-users. As a third condition, a city needs to prepare itself for multimodality. Infrastructures need to be better aligned with public and private transport offerings. Different enablers exist for brainstorming solutions in this area, such as Open Transport Camp in Australia[29] and TransportationCamp in the US,[30] or initiatives such as the MaaS alliance,[31] Fabrique Mobilité,[32] or Mobihubs[33] in Europe. Ultimately, it will take multiple data communities to output the policy, planning, and programmes of action that will truly reshape public space and mobility.

Conclusion

There is evidence worldwide that transport data is being released as open data, whether it is through crowdsourcing initiatives as in Mexico City or through official public transport or governmental organisations. In the US, thanks to the APTA, and in European countries, thanks to the ITS, Public Sector Information (PSI), and INSPIRE directives, policies are pushing the agenda for open transport data forward.

Now that the benefits of sharing public transport data openly are becoming visible through apps that can immediately turn these datasets into route planners, the way data is shared needs to evolve technically. The current de facto standard for sharing data via GTFS still requires a big investment from users before the data can be used in a route planner, and only a fraction of the data that exists in GTFS format is publicly available as open data. The true potential of open transport data is yet to be unlocked, although as the integration costs of transport data decrease and more data is made available, there is scope for substantial progress to be made.

Open data alone is not going to create a big change in how people move from one place to another. Advancement of MaaS will need to combine concepts of open data, support for open ticketing, and work on infrastructure investments in order to diversify the availability of transport options. It is up to policy-makers to create the right environment and infrastructure to properly prepare cities for the mobility of the future.

Further reading

Colpaert, P., Compernolle, M.V., Walravns, N., Mechant, P., Adriaenssens, J., Ongenae, F., Verborgh, R., & Mannens, E. (2017). Open transport data for maximising reuse in multimodal route planners: A study in Flanders. *IET Intelligent Transport Systems, 11(7)*, 397–402. https://ieeexplore.ieee.org/abstract/document/8061184

Eros, E., Mehndiratta, S., Zegras, C., Webb, K., & Ochoa, M.C. (2014). Applying the General Transit Feed Specification to the Global South: Experiences in Mexico City, Mexico – and beyond. *Transportation Research Record, 2442(1)*, 44–52. https://doi.org/10.3141/2442-06

Hogge, B. (2016). *Transport for London: Get set, go! Open data's impact.* GovLab and Omidyar Network. http://odimpact.org/files/case-studies-transport-for-london.pdf

Rojas, F.M. (2012). *Transit transparency: Effective disclosure through open data.* Transparency Policy Project. Cambridge, MA: Ash Center for Democratic Governance and Innovation. http://www.transparencypolicy.net/assets/FINAL_UTC_TransitTransparency_8%2028%202012.pdf

About the authors

Pieter Colpaert is a Researcher at Ghent University's Internet and Data Research Lab. His research focuses on enabling route planning at a large scale, using linked data. He is a board member of the Belgian chapter of Open Knowledge and a community coordinator of the open transport working group at Open Knowledge International. You can learn more about Pieter's work at http://pietercolpaert.be.

Julián Andrés Rojas Meléndez is a Researcher at the University of Ghent working on interoperable open data publishing strategies on the Web and decentralised route planning with open data. You can follow Julián at https://www.twitter.com/julianr1987.

How to cite this chapter

Colpaert, P. & Rojas Meléndez, J.A. (2019). Open data and transportation. In T. Davies, S. Walker, M. Rubinstein, & F. Perini (Eds.), *The state of open data: Histories and horizons* (pp. 215–224). Cape Town and Ottawa: African Minds and International Development Research Centre. http://stateofopendata.od4d.net.

This work is licensed under a Creative Commons Attribution 4.0 International (CC BY 4.0) licence. It was carried out with the aid of a grant from the International Development Research Centre, Ottawa, Canada.

Endnotes

1. http://go-ov.nl/
2. UITP. (2014). *Action points for the public transport sector. The benefits of open data*. Brussels: Union Internationale des Transports Publics. https://www.uitp.org/sites/default/files/cck-focus-papers-files/AP%20-%20Benefits%20of%20open%20data%20EN.pdf
3. APTA. (2015). *Public transportation embracing open data*. Washington, DC: American Public Transport Association. https://www.apta.com/resources/reportsandpublications/Documents/APTA-Embracing-Open-Data.pdf
4. Rojas, F.M. (2012). *Transit transparency: Effective disclosure through open data*. Transparency Policy Project. Cambridge, MA: Ash Center for Democratic Governance and Innovation. http://www.transparencypolicy.net/assets/FINAL_UTC_TransitTransparency_8%2028%202012.pdf
5. Colpaert, P., Van Compernolle, M., Walravens, N., Mechant. P., Adriaenssens, J., Ongenae, F., Verborgh, R., & Mannens, E. (2017). Open transport data for maximising reuse in multimodal route planners: A study in Flanders. *IET Intelligent Transport Systems*, 11(7), 397–402. https://ieeexplore.ieee.org/abstract/document/8061184
6. http://gtfs.org
7. http://netex-cen.eu/
8. http://www.transmodel-cen.eu/standards/siri/
9. http://www.aptatcip.com/
10. Deloitte. (2017). *Assessing the value of TfL's open data and digital partnerships*. London: Deloitte. http://content.tfl.gov.uk/deloitte-report-tfl-open-data.pdf
11. Hogge, B. (2016). *Transport for London: Get set, go! Open Data's Impact*. GovLab and Omidyar Network. http://odimpact.org/files/case-studies-transport-for-london.pdf

12. Scassa, T. & Diebel, A. (2016). Open or closed? Open licensing of real-time public sector transit data. *JeDEM – EJournal of EDemocracy and Open Government*, *8(2)*, 1–20. https://jedem.org/index.php/jedem/article/view/414
13. Verma, P., López, J.S., & Pardo, C. (2015). *Bicycle account: Bogota 2014*. Bogotá: Despacio. http://www.despacio.org/wp-content/uploads/2015/01/Bicycle-Account-BOG-2014-20150109-LR.pdf
14. See the OpenTrain project at http://otrain.org/ and Open Bus project details at http://www.hasadna.org.il/en/projects/
15. Colpaert, P. (2017). Publishing transport data for maximum reuse. PhD Thesis, Ghent University, Belgium. https://phd.pietercolpaert.be
16. https://maps.google.com/landing/transit/cities/
17. https://maps.google.com/help/maps/mapcontent/transit/participate.html
18. Citymapper. (2015). Building a city without open data. https://medium.com/citymapper/building-a-city-without-open-data-124356672deb
19. https://www.navitia.io/
20. https://transit.land/feed-registry/
21. Eros, E., Mehndiratta, S., Zegras, C., Webb, K., & Ochoa, M.C. (2014). Applying the General Transit Feed Specification to the Global South: Experiences in Mexico City, Mexico – and beyond. *Transportation Research Record*, *2442(1)*, 44–52. https://doi.org/10.3141/2442-06
22. https://github.com/MobilityData/gtfs-flex
23. Williams, S., White, A., Waiganjo, P., Orwa, D., & Klopp, J. (2015). The Digital Matatu Project: Using cell phones to create an open source data for Nairobi's semi-formal bus system. *Journal of Transport Geography*, *49*, 39–51. http://www.sciencedirect.com/science/article/pii/S0966692315001878
24. http://digitaltransport4africa.org/
25. https://olc.worldbank.org/content/introduction-general-transit-feed-specification-gtfs-and-informal-transit-system-mapping
26. https://ec.europa.eu/transport/themes/its/road/action_plan_en
27. Smart Flanders. (2018). Open Data Charter. https://smart.flanders.be/
28. https://maas.global/
29. http://www.transportcamp.org.au/
30. http://transportationcamp.org/
31. https://maas-alliance.eu/
32. http://wiki.lafabriquedesmobilites.fr/wiki/Ev%C3%A9nements
33. https://mobihubs.eu/

016

Urban development

Jean-Noé Landry

Key points

- Open data in the context of urban development is increasingly linked with "smart cities" and "urban resilience" agendas.

- There has been a shift from an early emphasis on hackathons, seen as a potential mechanism for co-production of public services with external experts, toward working on data standards, infrastructure, and in-house analytical capacity within city governments.

- Intermediaries, including public-funded organisations such as libraries, have an important role to play helping citizens gain value from urban open data.

- Without further work crafting practitioner communities and clear agendas, open data is likely to be seen primarily as a tool to be selectively used in smart cities, rather than as the central element of a comprehensive approach to achieve more open urban development.

Introduction

Since 2008, more than 50% of the world's population has resided in cities.[1] Estimates suggest this figure will be over 66% by 2050,[2] with much of this urbanisation taking place in the developing world. The ongoing growth of the urban environment and of urban density brings with it both opportunities and challenges. Creating vibrant communities, maintaining mobility, delivering essential services, and creating low-carbon development depend on a mix of planned and emergent action, all of which has come to rely more and more upon data. However, there are differing visions of effective urban development from centralised and highly technical "smart city" narratives that envisage a city organised using predominantly proprietary and commercial technology[3] to "smart citizen" viewpoints that stem more from an ad hoc bottom-up model of urban development based on open technology and open data.[4] The reality for many cities will likely lie somewhere between these extremes, and, over the last decade, open data has played a critical role in creating the space for dialogue about the future of the city and in providing a platform for various urban innovations.

To some extent, the template for the wider open data movement was originally set at the city level. In 2007, Vivek Kundra (who later became chief information officer for the United States (US) government and the architect of data.gov) launched the Washington, DC data portal, opening up datasets that had previously driven the government's own CitiStat dashboard.[5] Recognising the limited capacity of the city bureaucracy to develop new solutions with its own data, the driving goal was to harness ideas and energy from outside government. Today, hundreds of cities have their own open data portals (although this appears to be much more common in North America and Europe than in other parts of the world),[6] and many have hosted events to spur on use of this data to support engagement with independent developers, researchers, and municipal open data champions.

More recently, as the Sustainable Development Goals (SDGs) and the debate around resilience have become key elements of the mainstream development agenda, questions on how open data can play a role in urban sustainability and urban resilience have received increasing attention.[7] In many cities, a lack of data can hamper efforts to plan and coordinate development or lead to certain populations ending up "invisible" with their needs neglected as city leaders push forward with major infrastructure and construction projects. On the other hand, the innovative use of open data has provided the means for citizens to get involved in local government, using statistics, data visualisation, and storytelling to engage in debates about shared urban futures.

In this chapter, we explore these themes through four lenses: innovation, infrastructure, measurement and management, and resilience. We also identify some of the principles, interventions, and attitudes that will be required for open data-enabled urban development in the years ahead.

Innovation: From experimentation to institutionalisation

The concept of innovation is often a contested one because of the ambiguity around determining what is, or is not, innovative. However, since the earliest open data app competitions, the idea that releasing open data can unlock innovative capacity for urban development and local economic growth has been compelling for community-minded developers and service providers.[8] Open data has been framed as a tool to engage a wider range of actors in solving municipal problems, harnessing "innovative ideas" from academics, citizens, and the private sector. Sandoval-Almazan et al. describe this as creating new forms of citizen empowerment,[9] and Hielkema and Hongisto have argued that app competitions based on open data are important venues to bring together stakeholders (including government, developers, and users) to initiate collaborative projects and enable the private sector to tailor products to the public.[10]

Hundreds of urban open data hackathon events have taken place over the last decade, providing new points of connection between city officials and technically skilled communities who want to engage with them. When organised by government, they demonstrate a clear recognition of the fact that open data initiatives require more than just data release.[11] The hackathon model has been used across the world and, in many cases, framed as a catalyst for urban and economic development.[12] Building on a "government as a platform" premise, many early hackathons were based on the belief that innovation could only come from outside government. Over time, there has been a shift to recognise that effective co-production through hackathons requires a more strategic approach, with officials taking a more active role in defining problems and in finding, preparing, and using relevant datasets.[13]

Although popular, hackathons have also been subject to critique. Researchers have questioned their ability to produce meaningful social impact and citizen engagement, noting that there is scarce evidence of the link between hackathons and economic growth.[14] Johnson and Robinson have further argued that open data, particularly when delivered as part of a hackathon-model, may promote a particular model for outsourcing government functions with potentially negative outcomes for urban development.[15] City governments have also struggled with how to partner with, or procure from, civic entrepreneurs who will work with their open datasets. This has led to many hackathons focusing more on acting solely as demonstrators of what could be possible, rather than on the development of active tools to transform urban governance or city living. A number of studies have looked at identifying how cities can better design innovative competitions and events and how best to secure lasting impact from them.[16,17]

> ### Linking open data and urban governance in Jakarta
>
> In 2014, the Southeast Asia Technology and Transparency Initiative, the Web Foundation, and Government of Jakarta worked with a range of partners to host "HackJak", a two-day hackathon, where more than 100 participants worked on 53 different projects. Organisers took advantage of Indonesia's upcoming role as government co-chair of the Open Government Partnership to secure interest and participation in the event, which resulted in several prototypes, including an application that provided live feedback on public transport shelters and tools for navigating and engaging with the city budget.[18,19]
>
> In 2016, Jakarta's Provincial Disaster Management Agency, the National Indonesian Disaster Agency, the World Bank, Humanitarian OpenStreetMap Team (HOT), and other partners convened another hackathon to explore how technology, data, and open collaboration could be marshalled to address challenges around flooding. Five teams developed prototypes, including designs for tools that would keep citizens informed during flooding and provided an analysis on the areas of the city most vulnerable to flooding.[20]

Over time, city engagement with open data has become professionalised. Numerous cities now have internal innovation labs, connecting work on open data with wider themes of data-science, service design, and technology innovation. One of the early examples, Boston's Office of New Urban Mechanics, operates as a cross-departmental unit focused on addressing specific city challenges.[21] In the City of Buenos Aires, open data, open government, and smart city activities have been placed under the same directorate, the Innovation and Smart City Undersecretariat (Subsecretaría de Innovación y Ciudad Inteligente).[22] This integration of "openness" (open data and open government) into urban development, or "smart city" work, is becoming more common. In Montreal, the recently established Urban Innovation Lab[23] has absorbed all staff previously working on open data, mirroring a pattern seen in a number of cities, where external civic hackers and entrepreneurs were hired by government and then given a wider set of responsibilities that incorporate, but do not entirely centre around, open data.

This blending of open data into broader technology-driven urban development agendas has both benefits and risks. With the application of consistent values and principles, it can help drive an "open by default" approach to work on innovation and co-production. However, it can also lead to the importance of openness being downplayed or to less engagement with the kinds of experimental citizen engagement spaces that characterised early work on open data. A focus on instrumental and institutionalised use of open data may also orient work solely toward service delivery and away from transparency and accountability as is suggested in the framing of the 2013 Code for America book *Beyond transparency: Open data and the future of civic innovation*.[24]

While many new ideas and approaches have emerged from urban planners and service providers engaging with open data, in many cases, cities are facing similar challenges and, therefore, looking at similar solutions. For example, public transit apps, 311-reporting systems, city dashboards, and resource directories, although once innovative, have become open data initiatives more commonly adopted by cities whenever the data infrastructure exists to drive them. However, when it comes to the availability of data infrastructure, the picture is much more mixed across the globe.

Data infrastructure: Ownership and interoperability

Centrally coordinated management of the physical infrastructure of a city (electricity grids, water supply and waste disposal, transport networks, city services, etc.) requires a substantial data infrastructure. This data infrastructure relies, in turn, on a telecommunications infrastructure to connect sensors, staff, and systems together.[25] In the context of "smart cities", this infrastructure is usually built by private firms and offered as a package that may give corporate platform providers considerable control of the hardware, software, and data involved in city operations, and which may bring long-term dependency on specific vendors. Alternatively, some cities are piecing together legacy systems, or working with a mixed ecology of public, private, and citizen-generated data, laying the foundations for a more open model of the "smart city". Regardless, central to interoperability of these systems will be the continued development of open standards.

Over the last decade, open data standards development has been an area of considerable focus. Standards and API (application program interface) specifications, such as Open311 (initially developed as an API on top of Washington, DC's existing "311" public request system),[26] have helped facilitate the creation of open data via crowdsourcing and opening up existing issue-reporting systems.[27] Services built on top of Open311, such as SeeClickFix[28] and FixMyStreet,[29] have provided new avenues for citizen participation and co-production, as well as demonstrating a range of business models for civic technology. However, although its potential and impacts have been widely discussed, Open311's own dashboard suggests full adoption has been limited, with just 25 city deployments identified at the time of writing.[30] There is also evidence that individual implementations of 311 have undergone semantic and ontological divergence.[31] Similarly, the roughly 60 city-relevant standards listed by GovEx and GeoThink in their datastandards.directory[32] project have only been adopted by a minority of cities.

> **Case study: Open311**
>
> In 1996, the City of Baltimore launched a simple non-emergency phone number, 311, to relieve pressure on the emergency 911 service. By 2001, a number of US cities had taken up the idea, providing access to a wide range of services via 311 call centres. Subsequently, the first experiments with web-based 311 contacts started in Chicago. In 2008, SeeClickFix, a product that enables US cities to accept 311-style reports, was launched by a for-profit firm[33] in parallel with a similar platform, FixMyStreet, that was launched in the United Kingdom by MySociety.[34] The growth of 311, and of digital 311 platforms, meant increasing amounts of data on issues facing cities but also led to increased risks that different cities would be collecting fragmented data that was locked into proprietary systems.
>
> In 2009, the Open311 project was launched to develop an open API specification that would support both data collection and retrieval on reported issues,[35] turning 311 services from a one-way communication to government into a conversation between government and citizens about pressing issues at the neighbourhood level. Open311 specifications, created through an open community process, have now been implemented for both FixMyStreet and SeeClickFix, as well as custom systems in a number of municipalities. The presence of a standard has also given new cities a head-start in developing their own systems.

One urban data standard that has achieved widespread adoption is the General Transit Feed Specification (GTFS) for public transport schedules, which originated as a project between Google and the City of Portland.[36] While implementations of data standards in developed countries are often intended to digitise and extend existing analogue services provided by government, implementations in the Global South may focus on the development of new services not originally provided by government. One such example, Digital Matatus, a university collaboration in Nairobi, has mapped Nairobi's matatus (minibus) transit routes, which dominate the public transit environment, using a citizen science approach and GTFS to improve local trip planning.[37]

The ultimate impact of open data infrastructures on urban planning is often indirect. For example, third-party transit apps based on GTFS data can improve the ability of residents, including those with disabilities and the elderly, to navigate urban environments, [38] while the data on how and when people are travelling can be used for research and urban mobility planning by local government.[39]

Whether the pace of development and adoption of open data standards is enough to ensure urban environments run on open infrastructures is a critical question requiring further research. Similarly, further work is required to track how far standards have progressed in making data shareable between cities as evidence to date suggests that data interoperability across cities and regions remains a major challenge. A lack of open and interoperability infrastructures will impact governments' ability to undertake collaborative urban development initiatives at a broader scale. However, within individual cities, governments are certainly looking at how they can make more use of their existing data through new models of data presentation.

Measurement and management: Seeing the city

Over the last decade, many cities have opened up hundreds of datasets that provide both a real-time and an historic view on the urban environment, and numerous projects have taken place to create urban dashboards driven by that data. The underlying idea that open data can be analysed and visualised in a simple interface (e.g. dashboard) is a key driver for municipal government,[40] linking open data with other fields connected to e-government,[41] urban data analytics, big data, and government data infrastructures,[42] all of which have explored mechanisms to combine and display multiple streams of data. One iconic example is the Rio de Janeiro Operations Centre,[43] which combines multiple streams of data, including open data, for predictive modelling of development and disaster scenarios. Such systems may not necessarily require data to be open in order to function, and the concept of a government operations centre has been around for a while,[44] but the addition of open data brings greater transparency to the calculation and presentation of city performance measures.

Open data-powered dashboards have become key public-facing instruments to demonstrate city performance on select indicators[45] and have often been deployed to support citizen engagement. Many examples, such as the City of Edmonton's Citizen Dashboard,[46] reflect a new approach to city performance measurement over the past few years, transforming data into information through simple charts and web maps. It is a model adopted both by cities and by cross-city collaborations. For example, in a project framed specifically around open data, the InterAmerican Development Bank has supported the creation of an Urban Dashboard platform for 50 cities in Latin America, providing access to benchmark indicators and survey data for individual cities and allowing for performance comparisons between cities.[47]

While performance dashboards can still be manipulated by governments to present higher levels of performance (including performance on transparency indicators) than the reality,[48] open data approaches add an extra level of traceability and accountability by publicly linking data visualisations back to source data and the data owner responsible. Engaging effectively with open data can require high levels of data literacy. This has led to the rise of infomediaries who can help citizens to engage with flows of data.[49,50,51] However, dashboards and performance metrics can only visualise data if it is available and, in many cases, relevant datasets are not available[52] or simply do not exist. If available, it is also critical to ensure they do not contain biased information about the urban environment that can contribute to the marginalisation of certain populations.

A recognition of the importance of shaping not only decisions made with data, but also the stock of urban data that supports decisions, has driven the work of groups, such as Transparent Chennai in India, who have deployed small teams of researchers to work with grassroots communities to generate new datasets on issues ranging from public toilets to road safety. By using their own dashboards, Transparent Chennai is able to present a different view on the city and to support citizens in making a case for change to government officials. The initiative seeks to establish a bottom-up model of the "transparent city" and enable "smart citizens" to overcome top-down models of traditional citizenship.[53] Similar models of bottom-up data creation can be seen in action, working on open data for urban resilience.

Resilience: Embracing citizen-generated urban data

The Rockefeller Foundation describes resilience as "the capacity of individuals, communities, institutions, businesses, and systems within a city to survive, adapt, and grow no matter what kinds of chronic stresses and acute shocks they experience".[54] The Rockefeller Foundation's 100 Resilient Cities (100RC) initiative has helped to establish urban resilience as a major topic in mainstream discourse. Resilience has often been framed as a problem of infrastructure,[55,56] while open data has usually been linked to the urban context as an issue for data infrastructure.[57] As a result, open data is now viewed as a key element of city infrastructure that can help to predict and ameliorate stresses and shocks.[58] This is increasingly important in the developing world, where open data[59] and open source software[60] are presented as tools for international development.

The Open Data for Resilience Initiative (OpenDRI) under the World Bank Group's Global Facility for Disaster Reduction and Recovery (GFDRR) was created specifically to incorporate open data into urban resilience projects through data collection, data portals, and data analytics.[61] With a focus on risk data, OpenDRI incorporates key open data principles, such as open by default, and has supported numerous urban (and rural) community mapping initiatives in the developing world. The programme has developed a field guide[62] and a guide to creating OpenDRI Open Cities Projects.[63]

Urban resilience has become closely tied to crowdsourced mapping efforts in countries of the Global South as it can help governments fill in the gaps in their spatial data collection, especially in the mapping of urban infrastructure.[64] OpenStreetMap (OSM) has become a dominant platform for crowdsourcing geospatial open data and has been adopted by many programmes, including OpenDRI. This work originated from crisis responses to large natural disasters, such as the Haiti earthquake of 2010[65] and the Nepal earthquake of 2015.[66] The Humanitarian OpenStreetMap Team (HOT), an entirely volunteer-driven community focused on disaster mapping around the world, was established in the immediate aftermath of the Haiti earthquake.[67] Mapping of urban environments in cities struck by disaster has allowed humanitarian workers to target their services more accurately. However, OSM as a crowdsourcing platform was recognised to have greater benefits beyond short-term mapping needs. Humanitarian organisations, such as the Red Cross, have recognised the potential of OSM to support development activities, map infrastructure, and form the backbone of government geospatial data infrastructure traditionally provided by the private sector. This is reflected in financial and data contributions from the Red Cross[68] and the Red Cross Missing Maps initiative.[69] OpenDRI has actively pursued the use of OSM for its own projects. Other organisations have used OSM for their own initiatives. For example, the Kathmandu Living Lab has been able to map large sections of Kathmandu and Nepal, leading to support activities, such as mapping literacy workshops to sustain local OSM mapping and data currency. HOT has since partnered with the Red Cross, the World Bank, and the US State Department, providing one indicator that the international development community has begun to embrace open data production as a core element of their activities.

Just as the release of government data created a space for citizens to explore new models of engagement with city governance, the rise of citizen-led data generation to support urban resilience has opened up new possibilities for co-production. Sustaining the participatory dimensions of these efforts over the longer term will be an important challenge to meet.

Taking stock and looking forward

In some ways, open data is a golden thread running through modern urban development work. Development needs data, and the open sharing of that data is clearly an effective strategy to support collaboration between different stakeholders. But, in many ways, open data is still peripheral to other, more integrated, data-related work within the urban environment. Mainstream urban development literature is more likely to talk about big data, sensor networks, and APIs than it is to talk about "open" data. There are established networks working on open "smart" cities, international collaboration on standards, and strong indications of support from major institutions, yet, even though urban open data initiatives have been successful in pioneering new models of collaboration and co-production, excitement for citizen–government collaboration based on a foundation of open data has often waned, and it is not clear how many cities have truly embedded a culture of openness through data into their organisational DNA.

To keep openness on the urban development agenda, it will be vital to maintain and visibly demonstrate the value of open data as other emerging technologies, particularly big data and artificial intelligence, start to take over the spotlight. Building on existing events, such as the bi-annual Open Cities Summit, will help, but much wider outreach will be necessary. There are also challenges ahead for both research and practice. Much more sustainable investment is needed in shared and scalable open data infrastructures if the potential of an open marketplace for urban development solutions is to be realised. The strong and consistent adoption of existing and new data standards will be paramount to increasing interoperability and reuse. In parallel, work is needed at the grassroots to promote a vision of open data as a powerful tool for urban development and co-production with opportunities for development that can be initiated by both government and citizens. This requires building connections between existing civil society groups working to support urban communities and the technical intermediaries who can help them to make the most of open data. Crafting these practitioner communities around open data will be an ongoing challenge, but, if successful, it will result in the knowledge sharing and effective data-driven problem-solving needed to address the challenges of modern urban development.

Further reading

Beckwith, R., Sherry, J., & Prendergast, D. (2019). Data flow in the smart city: Open Data versus the commons. In M. de Lange & M. de Waal (Eds.), *The hackable city* (pp. 205–221). Singapore: Springer Singapore. https://link.springer.com/chapter/10.1007%2F978-981-13-2694-3_11

Goldsmith, S. & Crawford, S. (2014). *The responsive city: Engaging communities through data-smart governance.* Hoboken, NJ: John Wiley & Sons.

Goldstein, B. & Dyson, L. (Eds.). (2013). *Beyond transparency: Open data and the future of civic innovation.* San Francisco, CA: Code for America Press. http://beyondtransparency.org/pdf/BeyondTransparency.pdf

Landry, J.-N., Webster, K., Wylie, B., & Robinson, P. (2016). *How can we improve urban resilience with open data?* Ottawa: Open Data for Development. https://drive.google.com/file/d/0B739vUevKlPgYjJweC1NMElDaVk/view

Sadoway, D. & Shekhar, S. (2014). (Re)Prioritizing citizens in smart cities governance: Examples of smart citizenship from urban India. *Journal of Community Informatics, 10(3)*. http://ci-journal.org/index.php/ciej/article/view/1179

About the author

Jean-Noé Landry is a social entrepreneur and Executive Director of OpenNorth, Canada's leading not-for-profit organisation specialising in open data, civic technology, and smart cities. As an open data expert, he convenes data stakeholders, promotes data standardisation, and connects governments to their data constituents. You can follow Jean-Noé at https://www.twitter.com/jeannoelandry and learn more about Open North at https://www.opennorth.ca.

How to cite this chapter

Landry, J.-N. (2019). Open data and urban development. In T. Davies, S. Walker, M. Rubinstein, & F. Perini (Eds.), *The state of open data: Histories and horizons* (pp. 225–236). Cape Town and Ottawa: African Minds and International Development Research Centre.http://stateofopendata.od4d.net

This work is licensed under a Creative Commons Attribution 4.0 International (CC BY 4.0) licence. It was carried out with the aid of a grant from the International Development Research Centre, Ottawa, Canada.

Endnotes

1. World Bank. (2018). Urban population (% of total). https://data.worldbank.org/indicator/SP.URB.TOTL.IN.ZS
2. UN DESA (). (2018). 68% of the world population projected to live in urban areas by 2050, says UN. *United Nations Department of Economic and Social Affairs* [News post], 16 May. https://www.un.org/development/desa/en/news/population/2018-revision-of-world-urbanization-prospects.html
3. Rabari, C. & Storper, M. (2015). The digital skin of cities: Urban theory and research in the age of the sensored and metered city, ubiquitous computing and big data. *Cambridge Journal of Regions, Economy and Society, 8(1)*, 27–42. https://doi.org/10.1093/cjres/rsu021
4. Sadoway, D. & Shekhar, S. (2014). (Re)Prioritizing citizens in smart cities governance: Examples of smart citizenship from urban India. *Journal of Community Informatics, 10(3)*. http://ci-journal.org/index.php/ciej/article/view/1179
5. Tauberer, J. (2014). *Open government data: The book.* 2nd edition. (pp. 7–28). https://opengovdata.io/2014/history-the-movement/
6. https://www.opendatasoft.com/a-comprehensive-list-of-all-open-data-portals-around-the-world/

7   Landry, J.-N., Webster, K., Wylie, B., & Robinson, P. (2016). *How can we improve urban resilience with open data?* Ottawa: Open Data for Development. https://drive.google.com/file/d/0B739vUevKlPgYjJweC1NMElDaVk/view

8   Lee, M., Almirall, E., & Wareham, J. (2015). Open data and civic apps: First-generation failures, second-generation improvements. *Communications of the ACM, 59(1)*, 82–89. http://dl.acm.org/citation.cfm?doid=2859829.2756542

9   Sandoval-Almazan, R., Gil-Garcia, J.R., Luna-Reyes, L.F., Luna, D.E., & Rojas-Romero, Y. (2012). Open Government 2.0: Citizen empowerment through open data, web and mobile apps. In *Proceedings of the 6th International Conference on Theory and Practice of Electronic Governance* (pp. 30–33). New York, NY: Association for Computing Machinery. http://doi.acm.org/10.1145/2463728.2463735

10 Hielkema, H. & Hongisto, P. (2013). Developing the Helsinki Smart City: The role of competitions for open data applications. *Journal of the Knowledge Economy, 4(2)*, 190–204. https://doi.org/10.1007/s13132-012-0087-6

11 Kamariotou, M. & Kitsios, F. (2017). Open data hackathons: A strategy to increase innovation in the city. In *Proceedings of International Conference for Entrepreneurship, Innovation and Regional Development* (pp. 231–238). Thessaloniki, Greece. https://artionce-my.sharepoint.com/personal/iceird_artion_com_gr/Documents/ICEIRD2017-ProceedingsBook.pdf?slrid=f85ca99e-80f7-7000-a716-e87e89251c73#page=231

12 Khan, A. (2016). An incredible weekend for civic hacking in Islamabad! *Code for Pakistan*, 8 August. http://codeforpakistan.org/blog/2016/08/08/an-incredible-weekend-for-civic-hacking-in-islamabad/

13 Kamariotou, M. & Kitsios, F. (2017). Open data hackathons: A strategy to increase innovation in the city. In *Proceedings of International Conference for Entrepreneurship, Innovation and Regional Development*, 231. Thessaloniki, Greece. https://artionce-my.sharepoint.com/personal/iceird_artion_com_gr/Documents/ICEIRD2017-ProceedingsBook.pdf?slrid=f85ca99e-80f7-7000-a716-e87e89251c73#page=231

14 Johnson, P. & Robinson, P. (2014). Civic hackathons: Innovation, procurement, or civic engagement? *Review of Policy Research, 31(4)*, 349–357. https://doi.org/10.1111/ropr.12074

15 Ibid.

16 Kamariotou, M. & Kitsios, F. (2017). Open data hackathons: A strategy to increase innovation in the city. In *Proceedings of International Conference for Entrepreneurship, Innovation and Regional Development*, 231. Thessaloniki, Greece. https://artionce-my.sharepoint.com/personal/iceird_artion_com_gr/Documents/ICEIRD2017-ProceedingsBook.pdf?slrid=f85ca99e-80f7-7000-a716-e87e89251c73#page=231

17 Lee, M., Almirall, E., & Wareham, J. (2015). Open data and civic apps: First-generation failures, second-generation improvements. *Communications of the ACM, 59(1)*, 82–89. http://dx.doi.org/10.1145/2756542

18 McKenzie, J. (2014). #HackJak: Jakarta's first gov-sponsored open data hackathon tackles budget and public transportation. *TechPresident*. http://techpresident.com/news/wegov/24972/hackjak-jakartas-first-gov-sponsored-open-data-hackathon-tackles-budget-and-public

19 Lukman, E. (2014). Jakarta government held its first hackathon, here are the winners. *Tech in Asia*, 29 April. https://www.techinasia.com/jakarta-hackathon-hackjak-winners

20 Sutton, T. (2016). FloodHack 2016. *InaSAFE*, 8 April. http://inasafe.org/floodhack-2016/

21 Goldsmith, S. & Crawford, S. (2014). *The responsive city: Engaging communities through data-smart governance*. Hoboken, NJ: John Wiley & Sons.

22 http://www.buenosaires.gob.ar/innovacion/ciudadinteligente/proyectos

23 https://www.facebook.com/mtlvi/

24 Goldstein, B., & Dyson, L. (Eds.). (2013). *Beyond transparency: Open data and the future of civic innovation*. San Francisco, CA: Code for America Press. http://beyondtransparency.org/pdf/BeyondTransparency.pdf

25 Goldsmith, S. & Crawford, S. (2014). *The responsive city: Engaging communities through data-smart governance*. Hoboken, NJ: John Wiley & Sons.

26 Ashlock, P. (2015). Highlights from the Open311 Ecosystem. *Open311*, 21 June. http://www.open311.org/2015/06/highlights-from-the-open311-ecosystem/

27 Steinberg, T. (2013). Open311: What is it, and why is it good news for both governments and citizens? *MySociety*, 10 January. https://www.mysociety.org/2013/01/10/open311-introduced/

28 https://seeclickfix.com/

29 https://www.fixmystreet.com/

30 Based on https://status.open311.org/

31 Nalchigar, S. & Fox, M. (2017). Achieving interoperability of smart city data: An analysis of 311 Data. *Journal of Smart Cities, 3(1)*, 1–13. http://eil.mie.utoronto.ca/wp-content/uploads/2015/06/nalchigar-jsc17.pdf

32 http://datastandards.directory

33 Goodyear, S. (2015). The invention of 3-1-1 and the city services revolution. *CityLab*. https://www.citylab.com/city-makers-connections/311/

34 mySociety. (2018). The UK's street fault reporting website. FixMyStreet.com. https://www.mysociety.org/community/fixmystreet-in-the-uk/

35 Ashlock, P. (2009). Open311.org launches. *Open311*, 23 June. http://www.open311.org/2009/06/open311-launches/

36 McHugh, B. (2013). Pioneering open data standards: The GTFS story. In B. Goldstein & L. Dyson (Eds.), *Beyond transparency: Open data and the future of civic innovation* (pp. 125–136). San Francisco, CA: Code for America Press. http://beyondtransparency.org/pdf/BeyondTransparency.pdf#page=136

37 http://www.digitalmatatus.com/about.html

38 Mirri, S., Prandi, C., Salomoni, P., Callegati, F., & Campi, A. (2014). On combining crowdsourcing, sensing and open data for an accessible smart city. In *2014 Eighth International Conference on Next Generation Mobile Apps, Services and Technologies* (pp. 294–299), 10–12 September 2014. https://doi.org/10.1109/NGMAST.2014.59

39 Dong, J., Ma, C., Cheng, W., & Xin, L. (2017). Data augmented design: Urban planning and design in the new data environment. In *2017 IEEE 2nd International Conference on Big Data Analysis* (pp. 508–512), 10–12 March 2017. https://doi.org/10.1109/ICBDA.2017.8078685

40 Kitchin, R. (2014). *The data revolution: Big data, open data, data infrastructures and their consequences*. London: SAGE Publications.

41 Baumgarten, J. & Chui, M. (2009). E-Government 2.0. *McKinsey Quarterly*, July. https://www.mckinsey.com/industries/public-sector/our-insights/e-government-20

42 Ganapati, S. (2011). *Use of dashboards in government*. Fostering Transparency and Democracy Series. Washington, DC: IBM Center for the Business of Government. http://www.businessofgovernment.org/sites/default/files/Use%20of%20Dashboards%20in%20Government.pdf

43 Matheus, R., Vaz, J.C., & Ribeiro, M.M. (2014). Open government data and the data usage for improvement of public services in the Rio De Janeiro city. In *Proceedings of the 8th International Conference on Theory and Practice of Electronic Governance* (pp. 338–341). Guimaraes, Portugal, 27–30 October 2014. New York, NY: Association for Computing Machinery. https://doi.org/10.1145/2691195.2691240

44 Medina, E. (2011). *Cybernetic revolutionaries: Technology and politics in Allende's Chile*. Cambridge, MA: MIT Press. https://99percentinvisible.org/episode/project-cybersyn/

45 Kitchin, R., Lauriault, T.P., & McArdle, G. (2015). Knowing and governing cities through urban indicators, city benchmarking and real-time dashboards. *Regional Studies, Regional Science, 2(1)*, 6–28. https://doi.org/10.1080/21681376.2014.983149

46 http://dashboard.edmonton.ca/

47 http://www.urbandashboard.org/

48 Peled, A. (2011). When transparency and collaboration collide: The USA Open Data Program. *Journal of the American Society for Information Science and Technology, 62(11)*, 2085–2094. https://doi.org/10.1002/asi.21622

49 Van Schalkwyk, F., Chattapadhyay, S., Cañares, M., & Andrason, A. (2015). Open data intermediaries in developing countries. Working Paper. Washington, DC: World Wide Web Foundation. http://hdl.handle.net/10625/56288

50 Magalhaes, G., Roseira, C., & Strover, S. (2013). Open government data intermediaries: A terminology framework. In *Proceedings of the 7th International Conference on Theory and Practice of Electronic Governance* (pp. 330–333). New York, NY: Association for Computing Machinery. http://dx.doi.org/10.1145/2591888.2591947

51 Wolff, A., Gooch, D., Cavero, J., Rashid, U., & Kortuem, G. (2019). Removing barriers for citizen participation to urban innovation. In M. de Lange & M. de Waal (Eds.), *The hackable city* (pp. 153–168). Singapore: Springer Singapore. http://link.springer.com/10.1007/978-981-13-2694-3_8

52 Fox, M.S. & Pettit, C.J. (2015). On the completeness of open city data for measuring city indicators. In *2015 IEEE First International Smart Cities Conference* (pp. 1–6). 25–28 October 2015. http://dx.doi.org/10.1109/ISC2.2015.7366147

53 Sadoway, D. & Shekhar, S. (2014). (Re)Prioritizing citizens in smart cities governance: Examples of smart citizenship from urban India. *Journal of Community Informatics*, *10(3)*. http://ci-journal.org/index.php/ciej/article/view/1179

54 Rockefeller Foundation. (n.d.). 100 resilient cities: Resources. *100 Resilient Cities*. https://www.100resilientcities.org/resources/

55 Leichenko, R. (2011). Climate change and urban resilience. *Current Opinion in Environmental Sustainability*, *3(3)*, 164–168. https://doi.org/10.1016/J.COSUST.2010.12.014

56 Muller, M. (2007). Adapting to climate change: Water management for urban resilience. *Environment and Urbanization*, *19(1)*, 99–113. https://doi.org/10.1177/0956247807076726

57 ODI. (2016). Principles for strengthening our data infrastructure. *Open Data Institute* [Article], 31 August. https://theodi.org/article/principles-for-strengthening-our-data-infrastructure/

58 Landry, J.-N., Webster, K., Wylie, B., & Robinson, P. (2016). *How can we improve urban resilience with open data?* Ottawa: Open Data for Development. https://drive.google.com/file/d/0B739vUevKlPgYjJweC1NMElDaVk/view

59 Linders, D. (2013). Towards open development: Leveraging open data to improve the planning and coordination of international aid. *Government Information Quarterly*, *30(4)*, 426–434. https://doi.org/10.1016/j.giq.2013.04.001

60 Hartung, C., Lerer, A., Anokwa, Y., Tseng, C., Brunette, W., & Borriello, G. (2010). Open data kit: Tools to build information services for developing regions. In *Proceedings of the 4th ACM/IEEE International Conference on Information and Communication Technologies and Development*. London, 13–16 December. New York, NY: Association for Computing Machinery. http://doi.acm.org/10.1145/2369220.2369236

61 https://opendri.org/about/

62 GFDRR (Global Facility for Disaster Reduction and Recovery). (2014).*Open Data for Resilience Initiative: Field guide*. Washington, DC: World Bank. https://www.gfdrr.org/sites/gfdrr/files/publication/opendri_fg_web_20140629b_0.pdf

63 GFDRR. (2014). *Open Data for Resilience Initiative: Planning an open cities mapping project*. Washington, DC: World Bank. https://opendri.org/wp-content/uploads/2014/12/Planning-an-Open-Cities-Mapping-Project_0.pdf

64 Goodchild, M.F. (2007). Citizens as sensors: The world of volunteered geography. *GeoJournal*, *69(4)*, 211–221. https://doi.org/10.1007/s10708-007-9111-y

65 Zook, M., Graham, M., Shelton, T., & Gorman, S. (2010). Volunteered geographic information and crowdsourcing disaster relief: A case study of the Haitian earthquake. *World Medical & Health Policy*, *2(2)*, 7–33. https://doi.org/10.2202/1948-4682.1069

66 Poiani, T.H., dos Santos Rocha, Castro Degrossi, L., & d'Albuquerque, J.P. (2016). Potential of collaborative mapping for disaster relief: A case study of OpenStreetMap in the Nepal earthquake 2015. In *2016 49th Hawaii International Conference on System Sciences (HICSS)* (pp. 188–197). Koloa, HI, 5–8 January. https://doi.org/10.1109/HICSS.2016.31

67 Soden, R. & Palen, L. (2014). From crowdsourced mapping to community mapping: The post-earthquake work of OpenStreetMap Haiti. In C. Rossitto, L. Ciolfi, D. Martin, & B. Conein (Eds.), *COOP 2014 – Proceedings of the 11th International Conference on the Design of Cooperative Systems* (pp. 311–326). Nice, France, 27–30 May. Cham: Springer International Publishing. https://doi.org/10.1007/978-3-319-06498-7_19

68 Exel, M.V. (2017). OpenStreetMap receives $25,000 grant from American Red Cross. *OpenStreetMap Blog*, 8 September. https://blog.openstreetmap.org/2017/12/08/openstreetmap-receives-25000-grant-from-american-red-cross/

69 http://www.missingmaps.org

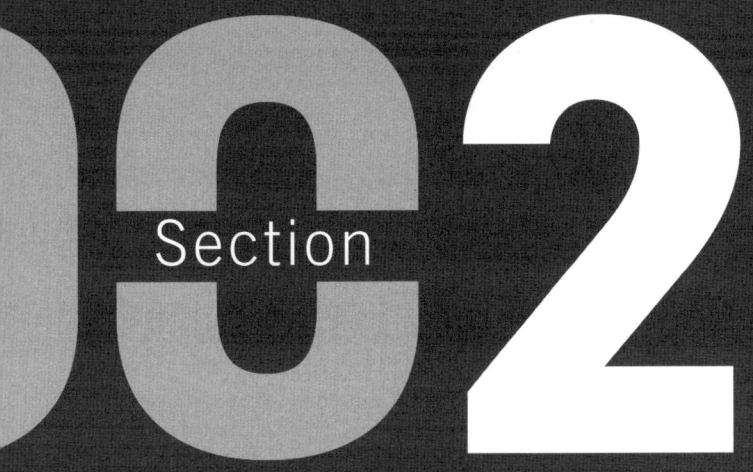

Section 2: Issues in Open Data

CONTENTS

Introduction	238
Chapter 17. Algorithms and artificial intelligence	243
Chapter 18. Data infrastructure	260
Chapter 19. Data literacy	274
Chapter 20. Gender equity	287
Chapter 21. Indigenous data sovereignty	300
Chapter 22. Measurement	320
Chapter 23. Privacy	339

The chapters in this section address a number of cross-cutting issues that shape the current state of open data.

From raw data now to publishing with purpose

In 2009, while giving a TED Talk on "The next web" and invoking an earlier talk by Hans Rosling[1] on the potential of data, Sir Tim Berners-Lee invited the audience to chant "Raw data, now".[2] That message was highly influential in early open data work. Coupled with the argument that government-collected data has already been paid for by taxpayers and so should, by rights, be available for them to reuse, the mantra of "raw data, now" led to a focus on getting as much data as possible, as quickly as possible, on to open data portals. Notably, although the open government data movement initially sought to draw a clear line between data about individual people and non-personal government data, focusing only on the latter, Berners-Lee's speech covered the whole spectrum of data from official government datasets to social network data, research data, and crowdsourced citizen-generated data. His argument was that access to raw data was the first step toward building a web of interlinked data, noting that "there's not an immediate return on the investment", but that "it will only really pay off when everybody else has done it".[3] "Raw data, now" was both a political call to remove the gatekeepers restricting the flow of data to skilled users and a strategic move, seeking to pre-emptively challenge the "data hugging" and organisational inertia that might prevent the potential benefits of data sharing from being realised.

In the decade that has followed, that idea of "raw data, now" has faced a number of critical issues and open data advocacy has had to adapt in response. First, the line between public and private data has turned out to not be so easily drawn. As early as 2010, governments attempted to balance open data and privacy concerns, although, as Chapter 23 (Privacy) explores, it was not until 2015 that privacy principles started to be widely incorporated into the international discourse on open data. As the chapter notes, considerable work has now gone into developing tools and resources to support governments and civil society in addressing privacy risks related to open data efforts. Because new technologies can transform older documents published by governments into searchable data, these risks relate to more than just the publication of new datasets. Although anecdotes of open data-related privacy breaches are relatively few and far between, it has become clear that with very different legal frameworks, cultural practices, and risk profiles across the world, providing raw data on demand may not always be possible. Instead, a more intentional approach has to be taken, weighing the potential public benefits of opening data against the privacy rights of individuals included in the data or even of third-parties who may be affected by the data.

Chapter 23 also introduces the Open Data Institute's data spectrum, situating open data on a continuum from closed to open. This, alongside a range of other conceptual innovations, such as "data stewardship"[4] and "responsible data",[5] may serve to blur (artificially) the neat boundaries of open data, presenting open data programmes with the choice of maintaining a narrow focus on data availability or considering the consequences, positive and negative, of broader data accessibility and use.

This leads to the second critical issue. Data use requires users with the technical and analytical capacity to transform data to information, knowledge, and action. As per Chapter 19 (Data literacy), data literacy has moved up on the agenda of funders, governments, and civil society networks, but capacity to make the most of open data remains scarce, and training and capacity building delivered to date is woefully inadequate. Calls for more investment in this area are well warranted and should be matched by a continued shift in open data measurement work to look not only at the supply of, and the demand for, data but also examine data use (Chapter 22: Measurement). However, when it comes to enabling open data use, there is also an interaction that exists between the "rawness" of data and data literacy building. Chapter 19 describes how lower-quality data requires users with relatively advanced technical skills, not to mention relevant domain knowledge. The "rawer" the data, the higher the investment needed in data literacy to enable use, which brings us to the third critical issue: systematically improving data quality requires concurrent work to build better data infrastructures.

In Chapter 18 (Data infrastructure), the authors describe data infrastructure using a comparison to the physical infrastructure of road networks in order to bring focus to the problems caused by "potholes" in our data and the inconsistent quality of data infrastructures around the world. More specifically, they describe the need for shared identifiers, standards, and registers that, along with guidance, policies, and organisations, will support the realisation of joined up data and help to meet the Sustainable Development Goals (SDGs). Governments have to shift from simply throwing raw data over the wall to working collaboratively to build shared spaces around open data. The most difficult challenge will be to find the resources, and funding models, to support a "step change in investment and in the level of effort put into creating data infrastructures" (Chapter 18). The current web of documents has broadly been funded by advertising and the investments of millions of individual publishers. Funding the more complex work to maintain (inclusive and open) infrastructures for a web of data requires new approaches.

Together, concerns about privacy, questions of data literacy, and visions of data infrastructure, all contribute to a shift toward a new framing of open data, which was captured in the strategy announced by the Open Data Charter in 2018, signalling a shift from "open by default" to "publishing with purpose".[6] At its best (and the way in which it is undoubtedly intended), this new mantra highlights the need to understand that all datasets, and the programmes of engagement around them, embed certain values and potentiality, and that responsible open data practices involve going beyond raw data to co-create datasets, data infrastructure, and opportunities for reuse with a wide range of stakeholders. However, at its worst, the idea of publishing with purpose may risk governments acting more as gatekeepers, making their own self-interested political and strategic decisions about what, or what not, to release, instead of acting primarily in a stewardship role to protect privacy, promote inclusion, and maximise data reusability. The three chapters (Privacy, Infrastructure, Data literacy) argue for embedding rights, inclusion, equity, and a culture of openness in any updated strategies for advancing open data, but the degree to which this may be achieved in the coming years is an outstanding question.

Re-constructing data and openness

Chapters on gender equity (Chapter 20) and Indigenous data sovereignty (Chapter 21) also pick up on issues of inclusion and rights, calling for a focus on the ways in which government data (mis-)represents marginalised groups and on how data divides can reinforce marginalisation. Although principles of gender equity have been recognised in international law for decades and Indigenous community rights have risen in prominence, taking major steps forward with the UN Declaration on the Rights of Indigenous People (UNDRIP) in 2009, both chapters note that these issues have only started to appear on the open data agenda since 2015.

In the case of gender equity, Chapter 20 describes a growing space for discussion of gender, as new groups have emerged and built strong women-led networks of support. The authors reflect on anecdotal evidence that suggests the stereotypical open data organisation is no longer exclusively young, urban, and male, but also note that there is little systematic evidence available to track progress on gender equality in open data. Furthermore, simply counting who is present in the field can hide disparities that require women to work much harder than their male colleagues to be heard and recognised. The chapter also identifies the potential for bias within datasets, highlighting how a lack of gender-disaggregation in data or the non-collection of data of relevance to women's lives will frustrate efforts to monitor progress on the SDGs. As the authors state, "as long as gender data gaps persist, any open datasets created based on raw data that does not adequately represent women will have limited potential to support transformative action on gender equity" (Chapter 20: Gender equity).

A similar challenge exists for Indigenous communities. In Chapter 21 (Indigenous data sovereignty), the authors describe how national statistical systems often render Indigenous populations invisible or introduce biases that fail to reflect community needs, priorities, and self-conceptions. However, they go further than simply arguing for better representation of Indigenous communities within government datasets to promote Indigenous data sovereignty, staking the claim of Indigenous populations to collective ownership and self-governance of data resources generated by or about them. They critique "Eurocentric conceptualisations of privacy and licensing", arguing that Indigenous communities need to be able to exert more control over how their data is used to protect against exploitation, misinterpretation, and misuse. Indigenous data sovereignty is offered as more than just a critical perspective. Through a series of case studies in the chapter, the authors illustrate how it offers practical principles and tools, and, ultimately, a source of deep wisdom that can direct more sensitive governance of data.

For some readers, these chapters may make for challenging reading. They call into question many issues that have been taken for granted in the past when planning open data projects or carrying out research into the dynamics of open data. They challenge a traditional reliance on schematic definitions of openness and question neo-colonial biases, encouraging readers to consider how far their own biases or positions of privilege may affect their perspectives and calling on them to confront a much more multi-layered world. These chapters call for both an individual and collective response, reflecting the position of the authors of Chapter 20 (Gender equity, p. 296) that "This need for self-reflection is a part of a larger cultural challenge that needs to be addressed actively in both professional and personal capacities".

At the more systemic level, Chapter 22 (Measurement) explores the role that the measurement of progress and impact plays in shaping the state of open data, noting that, here again, issues of inclusion are currently poorly addressed. Rethinking open data measurement tools to better consider gender equity and Indigenous data issues, as well as the complex realities of administrative geography, still needs attention. However, the potential consolidation of existing measurement tools in the coming years may provide opportunities to improve methodologies, as well as the communication of results.

New frontiers and lessons learned

The scoping of topics to cover in our examination of the state of open data began in mid-2017. Since then, a number of issues have started to take up more space within both policy and academic debates around data, offering potential new frontiers for open data. In the case of a number of these issues, such as the rise of data collaboratives (private–public partnerships for data sharing)[7] and data trusts (governance frameworks for managing data),[8] discussions remain at an early stage, and, therefore, the decision was made not to address them in this volume. In other cases, such as with blockchain and distributed ledger technologies, we chose to let coverage emerge from sectoral and regional chapters, rather than addressing them in specific cross-cutting issue chapters. However, the rapid growth of debates around algorithms and artificial intelligence (AI) led us to the decision to add a chapter in order to survey how this growing field might shape the future state of open data.

As Chapter 17 (Algorithms and artificial intelligence) explores, since 2015, an increasing number of governments have published AI strategies, frequently turning to open data as a "raw material" to fuel the growth of their AI industries. At the same time, machine-learning techniques are able to create new sources of data from unstructured inputs, changing the landscape of data availability, particularly for developing countries. However, as Chapter 17 argues, the rise of AI in the form of both enthusiasm and concerns should not be regarded simply as a new hook for selling the idea of open data, nor simply as a source of tools for data analysis. Instead, many forms of AI represent a distinct form of data power, tending toward centralisation of control and toward black box data analysis in ways that run counter to the decentralising logic of many open data initiatives. Lessons from the open data movement related to equity, inclusion, privacy, data infrastructure, and data literacy all have important contributions to make in shaping the future of AI.

One of the great successes of open data has been that it opened the black box of government data, bringing into view their processes for data collection and use that were previously hidden from the public. In doing so, as many questions have been raised and answered, leading to the identification and exploration of a number of cross-cutting issues for open data. For those who view open data solely as a resource for innovation or for improving the efficiency of business processes, it may be possible to side-step some of these issues and simply reuse data when it is profitable and useful. For those who see open data as part of a wider social and political movement, the encouraging message from the chapters that follow is that there are many people already working to address these issues that will shape the future of open data, and solid progress is being made on the construction of a critically aware field of practice.

Endnotes

1. Rosling, H. (2019) The best stats you've ever seen. https://www.ted.com/talks/hans_rosling_shows_the_best_stats_you_ve_ever_seen
2. Berners-Lee, T. (2019). *The next Web*. https://www.ted.com/talks/tim_berners_lee_on_the_next_web
3. Ibid.
4. https://datastewards.net/
5. https://responsibledata.io/
6. Open Data Charter. (2019). *Bringing power into the open – 2019 strategy*. https://drive.google.com/file/d/1fY6EBrXfal1e289FzPlaqhJBalZ6MPuU/view?usp=sharing&usp=embed_facebook
7. http://datacollaboratives.org/
8. O'hara, K. (2019). *Data trusts: Ethics, architecture and governance for trustworthy data stewardship*. Monograph. http://dx.doi.org/10.5258/SOTON/WSI-WP001

017

Algorithms and artificial intelligence

Tim Davies

Key points

- Open data has long been recognised as an important asset to boost artificial intelligence (AI) research and practice. Although governments often recognise open data supply as a key lever to stimulate the domestic AI industry, open data communities have been relatively slow to engage with AI.

- Many current high-profile uses of AI and algorithms rely on proprietary data. Work is needed to track the use of open data in AI systems and to develop approaches that address the potential bias or opacity of algorithms through the strategic release of open data and the careful creation of inclusive open data infrastructures.

- AI approaches often rely on centralising big datasets and seeking to personalise services through the application of black-box algorithms. Open data approaches can offer an important counter-narrative to this, focusing on both big and small data and enabling collective responses to social and developmental challenges.

Introduction

Artificial intelligence (AI) involves machines taking on tasks that previously required human intelligence to complete. Smith and Neupane describe AI as "an area of computer science devoted to developing systems that can be taught or learn to make decisions and predictions within specific contexts", adding that "AI applications can perform a wide range of intelligent behaviours: optimization (e.g. supply chains); pattern recognition and detection (e.g. facial recognition); prediction and hypothesis testing (e.g. predicting disease outbreaks); natural language processing; and machine translation".[1] The AI models that carry out these tasks often require, and generate, vast quantities of data. In many cases, open datasets provide key inputs to AI systems.

Although AI research goes all the way back to the early days of computing, the last few years have seen substantial renewed interest in the topic. Companies, governments, and non-profit organisations have all joined the new wave of AI, looking to mine their existing stocks of data or to process ever increasing data flows. As Figure 1 suggests, interest in AI far outstrips interest in open data *per se*. While searches for information on open data have flatlined since 2016, interest in AI is on an upward curve. This is also reflected in funding with one report citing over USD 500 million invested by United States (US) philanthropists into AI research in 2018 alone[2] (quite possibly more than the total sum of philanthropic investment in open data over the entire decade), and numerous governments are developing strategies and funding programmes to boost AI development to gain national competitive advantage in the AI space.[3]

However, the current wave of AI interest has not been without controversy. Concerns about bias and exclusion, the loss of jobs through automation, human rights impacts of automated decision-making, centralisation of power (and wealth), surveillance through mass data collection, hidden environmental damage, and the safety of AI systems have all been expressed by a growing number of AI institutes, think tanks, and other stakeholders.[4] This has led to a search for strategies to promote the positive outcomes of AI, while mitigating the potential hazards. Open data has a key role to play in this regard.

This chapter will examine where open data and AI meet, exploring their historic relationship and the ways in which data may be shaped by, and may shape, the future of AI applications. Although open data communities have been relatively slow to engage with AI, the chapter will also explore the pivotal role they can play in making safe and effective use of emerging AI technologies and in providing critical scrutiny to determine when AI approaches are the right answer or when alternative grass roots 'small data' strategies should be preferred.

Interest over time

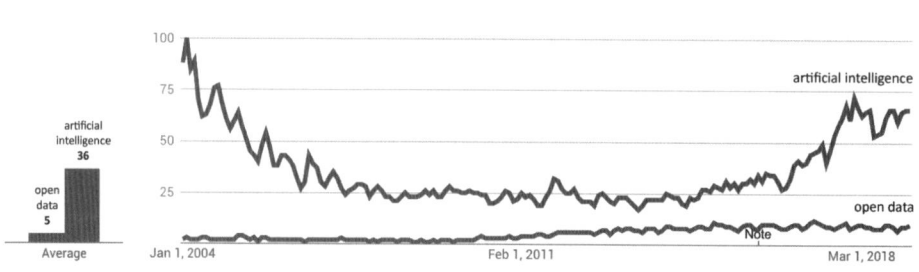

Figure 1: Google Trends analysis of global searches for "open data" and "artificial intelligence"

> **Primer: AI, algorithms, and machine learning**
>
> AI relies on applying algorithms to data. An algorithm is simply a set of instructions that can take an input and generate some sort of output.
>
> Some algorithms are manually written. In such cases, it should be theoretically possible to read the algorithm and trace a comprehensible path from input to output. However, many modern algorithms are also based on machine learning, a process by which the output of the algorithm is "trained" by being repeatedly fed data and judged on its outputs. Over time, a machine-learning algorithm adapts to better provide the required output even without the presence of explicit instructions that cover all steps from input to output.
>
> Many ongoing discussions use AI as a shorthand for machine learning, although AI is a broader field including many other areas of focus, such as knowledge representation, planning, and reasoning. There are hundreds of different machine-learning methods and algorithms now available, some of which are specialised for particular problem spaces (e.g. image or speech recognition) and others which are more general purpose. Deep learning (sometimes called deep neural network) models take advantage of vast computing power to create layered learning systems with a structure inspired by the human brain.
>
> Beside method choice and tuning, the quality of a machine-learning model depends largely on three things: the quantity of training data available, the quality of training and input data, and the amount of computing power used to build the model.

Linked histories: Shaping data inputs, outputs, and environments

Many histories trace the birth of AI to a workshop at Dartmouth College in the US in 1956. Research at the time promised the creation of automated general intelligence and captured the imagination of science fiction writers. Yet, when it proved much more complex than anticipated to deliver, funding was rapidly reduced leading to what has been termed the first "AI Winter".[5] The late 1980s and early 1990s saw subsequent episodes of AI investment boom and bust, attributed in part by AI advocates not to failures of the technology but to a loss of confidence by governments and companies when AI technologies, far from failing, became so commonplace as to be unremarkable.[6] This experience may be instructive for open data communities as they reach the end of their first decade, and early innovations are soon taken for granted. As of today, however, AI is experiencing a substantial and sustained boom, traced by many to the widespread adoption of deep learning methods from 2010 onward[7] and buoyed by widespread (albeit shallow) public awareness of the concept from literature and media coverage.

It is notable that a number of open data pioneers had roots in the AI community, or, more specifically, in Semantic Web research.[8] In 2001, Web inventor Tim Berners-Lee and colleagues outlined a vision for a Semantic Web as the "evolution of a Web that consisted largely of documents for humans to read to one that included data and information for computers to manipulate".[9] Revisiting that vision in 2006, Shadbolt, Hall, and Berners-Lee discussed the "increasing need and a rising obligation for people and organizations to make their data available [...] driven by the imperatives of collaborative science, by commercial incentives such as making product details available, and by regulatory requirements".[10] Two years later, a number of the same authors also reported on their efforts to bootstrap the Semantic Web with public sector information (PSI).[11]

AKTive PSI: Semantic Web and open data

In 2005, the United Kingdom (UK) Office of Public Sector Information (OPSI) initiated a project with the Advanced Knowledge Technologies (AKT) group at the University of Southampton to develop a range of Semantic Web demonstration applications, drawing on different sources of PSI. Shadbolt et al. (2011) describe how the "small-scale success of AKTive PSI in 2006–2008 paved the way for the more ambitious data.gov.uk[12] site, which followed in 2009–2010".[13]

The project built on semantic data extraction tools and involved the creation of vocabularies and ontologies for modelling PSI as Linked Open Data (LOD), seeking to lay the groundwork for more advanced "software agents" to intelligently make connections between government services and support greater interoperability.

When in 2009, Tim Berners-Lee and Nigel Shadbolt had the opportunity to shape the development of the UK's open data portal, data.gov.uk, they placed a particular emphasis on structuring data according to Semantic Web principles, strongly influenced by AI, knowledge representation, and research work on ontologies, vocabularies, and identifiers.[14] A number of other countries also incorporated Semantic Web and "linked data" principles and practices into their early open data work, although there is little evidence of how far this has been sustained. This is perhaps because, although a desire for structured data to feed data-hungry and university-led AI research was a key driver for early open government data advocacy, the current wave of AI interest has quite distinct origins.

ImageNet is a database of annotated images first published by Princeton University in 2009. Since 2010, an annual challenge has invited machine-learning researchers to compete to provide software that outperforms humans in recognising what the images contain. By 2012, the improving accuracy and speed of the submissions sparked renewed industry interest in AI and in the deep learning methods being used.[15] It was not the analysis of structured data which sparked this new wave of AI but rather the creation of structured data out of a wealth of unstructured inputs. As a result, the AI methods now widely deployed to extract data from images, sounds, and video, and to make probabilistic connections between data points in different datasets, appear, at first, to sidestep the complex and expensive labour of standardising and structuring every row of a dataset. Yet, these AI models still rely on structured data for training as with ImageNet, where the annotations were as important as the pictures. Although some applications of AI do draw upon open government datasets both to train models and as part of their operation, some of the largest applications of AI today draw on big data gathered by private companies that firms are able to tailor for their machine-learning needs by gathering millions of inputs from user and customer interactions every day. Many modern applications of AI bypass government data for the most part and operate on personal data inside corporations rather than from an open web of public data, which has led to an active debate on the need for improved data governance, including through stronger articulation of data ownership,[16] data rights,[17] and regulation of AI use.[18]

In short, algorithms and open data connect in three main ways. First, at the input level, open data can be an input for machine-learning models (or to develop improved non-AI algorithms), and these models can turn unstructured information into structured open data. Second, at the output level, advanced algorithms can be used to analyse open data in ways that would be far too time consuming to do manually. Suitably designed algorithms can find patterns, supporting decisions and informing actions based on the contents of open datasets. As we will see later, it may also be appropriate for algorithms and machine-learning models themselves to be output as open data. Third, at the level of the wider data landscape or environment, the availability of open data may shape who has access to the data they need to carry out AI research or to adopt algorithmic techniques within their business or projects. Equally, the potential power of AI, and the unequal distribution of access to its power, challenges the (contested)[19] idea that opening data will inevitably level the playing field of democratic discourse, innovation, or social action. The ability of machines to draw connections between datasets increases the salience of privacy concerns and raises new ethical issues about data publication, as well as concerns that AI systems risk reinforcing systemic biases and patterns of discrimination.

Open data and algorithms in action

It is notable that few other chapters in this volume specifically discuss examples of AI applied to open data, yet a deeper look reveals numerous cases where elements of machine-learning algorithms are being applied to gain economic and social value from open datasets or simply to further research. Moreover, there are signs that governments are increasingly recognising the important relationship between open data and the development of AI, particularly for countries without a predominance of large private sector data-rich businesses.

Policy: Open data as an engine for AI growth

In October 2016, in the last days of the Obama administration, a report from the Office of Science and Technology Policy on "Preparing for the future of Artificial Intelligence" included among its leading recommendations the idea of an "Open Data for AI" initiative with the objective of releasing a significant number of government data sets to accelerate AI research and galvanise the use of open data standards and best practices across government, academia, and the private sector".[20] Similar ideas are found in a 2017 report from the UK Royal Society that called for "continued efforts [...] to enhance the availability and usability of public sector data" in order to provide "open data for machine learning",[21] in calls for the Government of India to release more public data to AI developers,[22] and in recommendations from the University of Pretoria that stakeholders in Africa should "adopt open data initiatives as a way of using technology to support distributed innovation and to make AI development more participatory and transparent",[23] as well as in AI strategies under development in Uruguay and Argentina, to name just a few. Oxford Insight's 2017 Government AI Readiness Index also draws on the Open Data Barometer and Organisation for Economic Co-operation and Development (OECD) OURdata index to assess the quality of digital infrastructure available for AI innovation.[24] Simply put, open data is seen as a resource governments can use to lower barriers to entry to AI research and to support domestic AI industries to develop.[25] Government company registers, for example, are often used as a reliable source against which to reconcile data extracted from unstructured documents and filings. However, while these arguments for open data appear in a number of AI-focused policy papers, there is less evidence that open data communities have used policy engagement and commitments around AI as an additional "sales pitch" to overcome flagging engagement in open data policy initiatives.

Alongside recognition of open data as a resource for AI innovation, there is generally strong recognition that this is not just a case of releasing data that exists. Rather, with awareness of the problems that biased data can create, a study from the University of Pretoria describes the deeply political problems associated with data supply and the insufficiency of data about marginalised communities or data covering informal economies. The study suggests that addressing these challenges may require substantial changes to government data ecosystems, as well as efforts to open data from publicly funded academic institutions and to incentivise the sharing of non-proprietary data from the private sector.[26]

This question of how to incentivise, or provide regulatory mandates for, private sector actors to share their data is increasingly salient in the context of AI. Tennison (2018) argues that while open data approaches remain a net positive overall, ultimately "more data disproportionately benefits big tech".[27] As long as large firms have both the computational resources and the access to proprietary datasets to combine with open data, they are likely to maintain a competitive advantage. This can create monopoly and competition issues that require new regulatory responses. One emerging voluntary solution, appropriate when the data in question might involve commercially sensitive information or personal data, involves the creation of data trusts: practical and legal mechanisms for sharing datasets and supporting data use that can protect data subjects and ensure good data governance.[28] For some, attempts by open data organisations to engage with this agenda represent a dilution of commitments for openness and presents a risk to the future coherence of the open data agenda. For others, it represents a necessary development, recognising that to shift the balance of market and government power created by data requires a wider range of approaches to data openness and sharing.[29]

Analysis: Algorithms unlocking open data value

The McKinsey Institute has developed a library of over 160 AI use-cases and has found that AI is being applied in relation to each of the 16 key Sustainable Development Goals (SDGs).[30] They identify the greatest number of use-cases are associated with Health, Peace, Justice and Strong Institutions, and Education. Although it is not clear how many of the surveyed cases directly use or generate open data, given that deep learning on structured data is the most common AI capability deployed, it is reasonable to assume that open data is a component for many of them.

Although McKinsey is focused heavily on examples from the US, cases of algorithmic and machine-learning approaches to open data can be found across the world. For example, since 2013, the Data Science Africa[31] initiative has provided a hub for machine-learning research on the continent, and labs such as Makerere University's AI Research Group[32] are among a number on the continent exploring traffic models, air quality assessment, and crop diseases surveillance using AI-driven systems.[33] In Asia, a public–private partnership, the Centre of Excellence on Data Science and Artificial Intelligence established by the State Government of Telangana in India, is just one example of numerous university and private sector programmes building capacity to work with both public and private data.[34] And in Latin America, researchers and civil society groups are deploying algorithmic analysis to find patterns in data and promote government accountability (see, Serenata.ai: Case study). Crucially, the way algorithms and machine learning are currently applied reflects the availability of structured data in different regions. At Makerere University, for example, applications focus on generating structured data from images, addressing challenges of data scarcity prior to analysis. This points to the possibility that machine learning may allow some countries to leapfrog over the requirement for governments to collect particular structured datasets by adopting different strategies to address operational and policy-making data needs by turning unstructured data into structured data.

Serenata.ai: Case study

Figure 2: Screenshot of serenata.ai

"Operação Serenata De Amor" [Operation Serenade of Love] is a crowdfunded project hosted by Open Knowledge Brazil using algorithms and AI to audit public spending and politicians expenses.[35,36] The system uses a popular machine-learning toolkit for the open source python language to classify incoming expense records and identify outliers that it flags for human investigation. To date, the tool has identified over 8 000 suspicious payments, totalling BRL 3.6 million. During 2017, the project ran a hackathon event to carry out a "citizens' audit" of suspicious expense claims and generated over 200 reports to the official auditing body.[37] In total, the tool has processed more than 1.5 million expense claims.

Alongside their role in data extraction and the filtering needed to find the signal in the noise of large datasets, it is the predictive power of certain algorithms and machine learning that holds a particular attraction. Rather than simply visualising data for humans to interpret, algorithmic analysis holds the promise of constructing models that can find patterns and guide future action. As illustrated below (see Dengue fever: Training decision trees in Paraguay), such predictive models can provide data that might guide health decision-making. However, perhaps the most widely discussed predictive AI applications relate to crime and justice, both in terms of predictive policing and algorithmic sentencing decisions. AI models using open data to predict future crimes have been developed by researchers in the UK,[38] US,[39] India,[40] and a number of other countries, although there is little to suggest that these public models have moved beyond proof-of-concept. There is evidence, however, of police forces and courts making use of proprietary systems to guide their decision-making from the allocation of police resources[41] through to sentencing and bail decisions.[42] How far such systems are able to draw upon data from other parts of government as a result of open data policies is an area that warrants further investigation.

AI-enabled interfaces have also been explored as a means to make particular open datasets more accessible. Potential users of open data are often only interested in one specific fact,[43] but knowing how to search for it can be challenging. Responding to the need for new interfaces to open data, Porreca et al. (2017) made use of IBM's Watson platform and a dataset of Italian infrastructure projects to create an experimental Facebook Messenger chatbot that could answer questions about infrastructure spending.[44] In a similar vein, in 2016, Taiwanese firm, DSP, ran a challenge to create a "procurement chatbot" that could use public data on contracting to answer questions from potential bidders.[45] In other settings, machine-learning-based approaches have the potential to overcome the language barriers to use global open datasets, improving the accessibility of open data and supporting greater inclusion in the work to address SDGs.

However, for all the potential of machine learning, it is often neither necessary nor sufficient to support the effective use of open data. The World Wide Web Foundation has reported on a case in Uruguay, where the Ministry of the Interior, following a trial of a predictive policing algorithm, abandoned it and turned instead to the use of retrospective statistical analysis methods.[46] When the potential downsides of AI are taken into account, then it becomes clear that beyond experimentation, the full application of AI requires a high degree of data literacy and also requires AI solutions to be assessed alongside other less technologically advanced, but potentially more appropriate, methods of data analysis and use.

Dengue fever: Training decision trees in Paraguay

Dengue fever is endemic in Paraguay and a growing public health concern along with other mosquito-borne diseases, including Zika and Chikungunya. In 2016, using data on past dengue fever outbreaks collected by national health surveillance systems and converting published data to a common standard, researchers at the Universidad Nacional de Asunción in Paraguay were able to train and test a decision tree-based machine-learning model to predict future dengue cases based on climate, geographic, and demographic variables drawn from additional open datasets.[47] Care was taken in the project design to consider the privacy of individuals who have recorded dengue cases.

The research, which resulted in an open source web application, demonstrated the potential of machine learning to generate new insights from data. Because the machine-learning method chosen uses decision trees rather than deep learning neural networks, it generates a more legible model which aids interpretation of how different variables influence the predictions generated. Writing about the case in 2017, GovLab noted that the ultimate impact of the new predictive model would be based on how far it could influence strategy within the government agency responsible for responding to disease epidemics.[48]

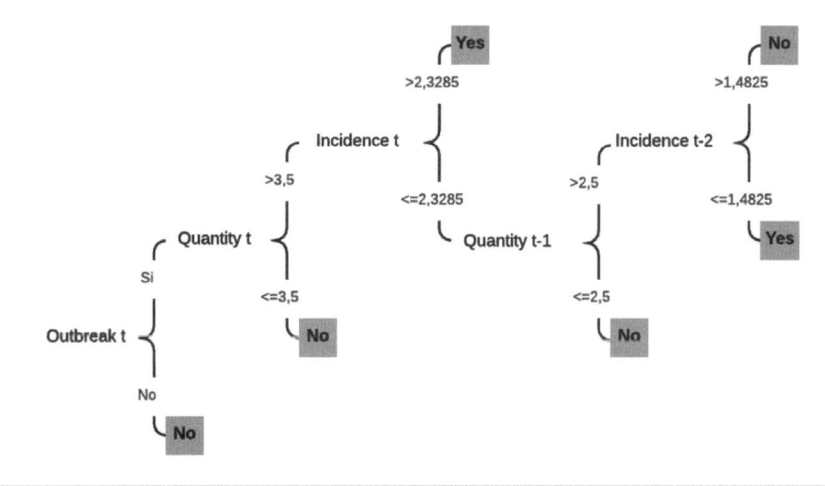

Figure 3: Example of a decision tree from a test run of dengue outbreak prediction algorithms, illustrating the relative legibility of decision-tree machine-learning methods.
Source: Pane et al. (2016)[49]

Adverse impacts: Addressing the data environment

Concerns have been widely raised about the potential for algorithmic discrimination, when biases in the data on which machine-learning models are trained is then reflected in the outcomes from their operation. This can reinforce patterns of social exclusion. When the datasets used to train these models are open, it becomes possible to scrutinise both whether particular populations are underrepresented in the data and whether particular fields are missing or collected using biased classifications. Where models are failing to take into account key variables, providing new open datasets to fill that gap has the potential to improve AI applications. This is particularly relevant in a development context, where there is a risk that models optimised for the data available in developed economies might be applied to developing countries where limited data flow renders them much less effective. As the Web Foundation argues, "Opening key datasets will help identify potential biases, lead to more competition between potential service providers, ensure better public services, and increase citizen trust in government."[50] However, given many applications of AI involve making decisions about individuals, there are inevitably difficult privacy challenges to navigate in many instances,[51] and the potential use of AI to connect up disparate databases may turn data that did not previously have privacy risks into sensitive data.[52]

As yet, there are few identifiable cases of projects engaging in the strategic creation, publication, or suppression of open data with AI specifically in mind. However, as the following section illustrates, there is a growing critical community around AI where such issues may need to be addressed in future.

Open data and AI: Critical friends?

Over the last three years, there has been an explosion of work looking at the potential risks of AI, developing ethical frameworks for AI, and creating partnerships to carry out public interest research and advocacy on AI development. A number of organisations active in open data, such as the Web Foundation,[53] Iniciativa Latinoamericana por los Datos Abiertos (ILDA),[54] and the Open Data Institute (ODI),[55] have developed programmes of work around AI. The International Development Research Centre (IDRC) has initiated an Artificial Intelligence for Development (AI4D) programme,[56] building on their experience with open data for development, and many more organisations have been established with an AI focus. The Fairness, Accountability and Transparency in Machine Learning (FATML) community,[57] for example, has grown steadily since its first meetings in 2014, although questions of how to make algorithms truly accountable and transparent remain technically and politically challenging. Transparency may not refer to disclosure of the full contents of datasets, but could involve providing more detailed and standardised metadata that describes why and how the data was collected and covers issues relevant to decisions about whether to use the data for machine learning.[58] The multi-stakeholder Partnership for AI talks of accountability in terms of "systems that can explain the rationale for inferences" that they draw,[59] and, more recently, the AI Commons has brought together the AI community to explore the concept of a data commons.[60]

For some, bringing openness to algorithms and AI involves not just open data, but also open source. However, while many AI frameworks are available as open source software, having access to complex source code often does little to support the auditing of the algorithm against expected outputs,[61] and where a model has been training at least partially on proprietary or sensitive data, copyright[62,63] or privacy issues may act as a block to fully opening the black box. In New York, the creation of a task force on "Automated Decision Making"[64] in 2018 led to early proposals that agencies using algorithmic systems should also accept user-submitted datasets to be processed by the agencies' algorithms with the outputs provided back to the user to allow them to assess whether the system is drawing fair and legitimate conclusions.

ODI has looked beyond data and source code to argue that engagement with AI needs an "open culture",[65] hinting at the kinds of organisational change needed to maintain legitimacy when using systems that may produce useful outputs but are less amenable to simple explanation. The Web Foundation's publication on AI in Latin America operationalises some of these ideas by summarising the kinds of transparency, public engagement, and accountability activities needed for each element of an algorithmic system from data collection through model set-up to execution and interpretation of output, as well as in relation to the socio-legal frameworks against which algorithms are deployed.[66] Lepri et al. point to "living labs" as a potential testing ground for algorithmic systems.[67]

Overall, open data ideas are clearly at play in shaping responses to AI, albeit with a focus on public sector applications of AI in most cases. Yet there may also be a case for exploring open data strategies not as a fix for the weak points of AI but as distinct and different response to the challenges of governance and decision-making in the modern world. When Lepri et al. (2017) describe the "tyranny of data", they point to the kind of technocratic and top-down decision-making that comes from large centralised data systems. However, contrary to the theoretical ideals of a distributed Semantic Web inherent in much early open data advocacy, modern AI systems, almost by definition, rely upon the centralisation of large quantities of data on cloud computing platforms that are only accessible to those with adequate financial and technical resources, not to mention the high energy costs of continually refining machine-learning models.[68] When algorithms are proprietary, then the market structure around AI-based data analysis may also be very different from that around open data (e.g. giving startups easier access to capital, but making it more difficult to align social goals with the commercial objectives of the platforms).

It may be as important to defend "small data" and to promote accessible methods of data literacy and data analysis as it is to critically engage with big data, AI, and algorithms. As ALLDATA, the International Conference on Big Data, Small Data, Linked Data, and Open Data recognises, different kinds of data require different analytical approaches, and not all data is big data.[69] While machine-learning techniques are often biased toward personalisation and granular decision-making, many applications of open data seek to surface societal problems and to support collective action and empowerment to address sustainable development challenges.

Conclusion

Open data work has already had a powerful and positive influence on the development of AI. Policy interest in supporting domestic AI development has the potential to support both the release of government data and regulatory action to encourage private sector data disclosures. Open data is one of the tools that concerned observers of AI are turning to in order to sketch out ways to make machine learning fair, accountable, and transparent. At the same time, a realisation of what AI can do is starting to change the privacy conversation around open data.

There is a risk that open data work is seen just as the infrastructural labour required to provide the raw material for AI rather than as a distinct area of activity with a much broader role and, at times, divergent set of values. Contemporary AI has much to learn from the last decade of open data, including the need to be problem, rather than data or technology, led and the need for nuance in sector-by-sector approaches rather than the simple application of broad brush principles. The challenges of going from proof-of-concept or prototype to sustainable products that influence policy and practice are also shared by AI and open data communities.

In response to the current state of AI and open data, three specific actions are needed:

1. Address machine learning within wider open data literacy building. To make sure the use of AI is led by the need to solve a problem and not by the technology, data literacy and other capacity building should cover machine learning, addressing it as an analytical tool and as a social phenomenon affecting the data environment in which we live. This should support learners in choosing between algorithms and other analytical approaches when identifying the best tools for their own data analysis needs, as well as in improving their capacity to critically understand the impacts of AI on their work and their communities. Support for critical literacy among policy-makers in the Global South is particularly important, so that effective decisions can be made about when to use data derived from machine learning and when to continue to invest in state-led structured data collection and disclosure.

2. Track machine learning and open data cases across the world. There is a pressing need for baseline data in order to better understand what is really happening with AI and open data,[70] cutting through the hype and assessing the depth and breadth of open data practice in work on AI. Work by the ILDA on AI addresses the data infrastructure of each AI use-case,[71] and the Web Foundation's work on AI in Latin America includes a case study variable to identify whether inputs to AI projects were open data.[72] It will be important for other larger scale AI studies to do the same and for open data studies to incorporate variables that can identify where machine-learning methods are in use.

3. Consciously create open data infrastructures. Smith and Neupane (2018) describe how "AI leverages existing infrastructure", but that when we are operating from a starting point of stark inequality, there is no reason to assume that the outputs will be ethical or equitable.[73] This makes it all the more important to bring data infrastructures into view by opening them and to actively work to create more equitable open data infrastructures in terms of the datasets, standards, and governance that they are made up of.

Addressing these issues will require deeper collaboration between the AI and open data communities and will undoubtedly benefit from the critical understanding of the messy reality of government data that has been developed by open data practitioners over the last decade.

Further reading

Access Partnership. (2018). *Artificial intelligence for Africa: An opportunity for growth, development and democratisation*. Pretoria: University of Pretoria, South Africa. https://www.up.ac.za/media/shared/7/ZP_Files/ai-for-africa.zp165664.pdf

Lepri, B., Staiano, J., Sangokoya, D., Letouzé, E., & Oliver, N. (2017). The tyranny of data? The bright and dark sides of data-driven decision-making for social good. In T. Cerquitelli, D. Quercia, & F. Pasquale (Eds.), *Transparent data mining for big and small data* (pp. 3–24). Cham: Springer International Publishing. https://arxiv.org/pdf/1612.00323.pdf

Ortiz Freuler, J. & Iglesias, C. (2018). *Algorithms and artificial intelligence in Latin America: A study of implementation by governments in Argentina and Uruguay*. Washington, DC: World Wide Web Foundation. http://webfoundation.org/docs/2018/09/WF_AI-in-LA_Report_Screen_AW.pdf

Scrollini, F. (2018). *Automatizar con cautela. Datos e Inteligencia Artificial en América Latina* [Automate with caution. Data and artificial intelligence in Latin America]. Montevideo: Iniciativa Latinoamericana por los Datos Abiertos. https://idatosabiertos.org/automatizar-con-cautela-datos-e-inteligencia-artificial-en-america-latina/

Smith, M. & Neupane, S. (2018). *Artificial intelligence and human development: Toward a research agenda*. Ottawa: International Development Research Centre. http://hdl.handle.net/10625/56949

About the author

Tim Davies has been researching the social impacts of open data for the last decade. He is a co-editor of *The state of open data: Histories and horizons*.

How to cite this chapter

Davies, T. (2019). Issues in open data: Algorithms and artificial intelligence. In T. Davies, S. Walker, M. Rubinstein, & F. Perini (Eds.), *The state of open data: Histories and horizons* (pp. 243–259). Cape Town and Ottawa: African Minds and International Development Research Centre. http://stateofopendata.od4d.net

This work is licensed under a Creative Commons Attribution 4.0 International (CC BY 4.0) licence. It was carried out with the aid of a grant from the International Development Research Centre, Ottawa, Canada.

Endnotes

1. Smith, M. & Neupane, S. (2018). *Artificial intelligence and human development: Toward a research agenda.* Ottawa: International Development Research Centre, (pp. 25 & 28, respectively). http://hdl.handle.net/10625/56949

2. Gose, B. & Di Mento, M. (2019). Billionaire philanthropists make bold investments that reflect hope, and worry, about the future. *The Chronicle of Philanthropy*, 12 February. https://www.philanthropy.com/article/Billionaire-Philanthropists/245658/

3. Dutton, T. (2018). An overview of national AI strategies. *Politics + AI*, 28 June. https://medium.com/politics-ai/an-overview-of-national-ai-strategies-2a70ec6edfd

4. Whittaker, M., Crawford, K., Dobbe, R., Fried, G., Kaziunas, E., Mathur, V., Myers West, S., Richardson, R., Schultz, J., & Schwartz, O. (2018). *AI now report 2018.* New York, NY: AI Now Institute, New York University. https://ainowinstitute.org/AI_Now_2018_Report.pdf

5. Crevier, D. (1994). *AI: The tumultuous history of the search for artificial intelligence.* New edition. New York, NY: Basic Books, p. 203.

6. Kurzweil, R. (2005). *The singularity is near: When humans transcend biology.* New York, NY: Viking Penguin.

7. Parloff, R. (2016). Why deep learning is suddenly changing your life. *Fortune*, 28 September. http://fortune.com/ai-artificial-intelligence-deep-machine-learning/

8. Halpin, H. (2004). The Semantic Web: The origins of artificial intelligence Redux. In *Proceedings of the Third International Workshop on the History and Philosophy of Logic, Mathematics, and Computation,* Donostia San Sebastian, Spain. http://citeseerx.ist.psu.edu/viewdoc/summary?doi=10.1.1.134.6799

9. Berners-Lee, T., Hendler, J., & Lassila, O. (2001). The Semantic Web. *Scientific American, 284(5)*, 34–43.

10. Shadbolt, N., Berners-Lee, T., & Hall, W. (2006). The Semantic Web revisited (p. 100). *IEEE Intelligent Systems, 21(3)*, 96–101.

11. Alani, H., Chandler, P., Hall, W., O'Hara, K., Shadbolt, N., & Szomszor, M. (2008). Building a pragmatic Semantic Web. *IEEE Intelligent Systems, 23(3)*: 61–68.

12. https://data.gov.uk/

13. Shadbolt, N., O'Hara, K., Salvadores, M., & Alani, H. (2011). EGovernment. In J. Domingue, D. Fensel, & J.A. Hendler (Eds), *Handbook of Semantic Web technologies* (pp. 839–900). Berlin: Springer-Verlag, p. 866. https://core.ac.uk/download/pdf/1511395.pdf

14. Ibid.

15. Parloff, R. (2016). Why deep learning is suddenly changing your life. *Fortune*, 28 September. http://fortune.com/ai-artificial-intelligence-deep-machine-learning/

16. Scassa, T. (2018). Data ownership. *SSRN.* https://papers.ssrn.com/abstract=3251542

17. Tisne, M. (2018). It's time for a bill of data rights. *MIT Technology Review*, 14 December. https://www.technologyreview.com/s/612588/its-time-for-a-bill-of-data-rights/

18. Scherer, M.U. (2015). Regulating artificial intelligence systems: Risks, challenges, competencies, and strategies. *SSRN.* https://papers.ssrn.com/abstract=2609777

19. Gurstein, M.B. (2011). Open data: Empowering the empowered or effective data use for everyone? *First Monday, 16(2).* https://doi.org/10.5210/fm.v16i2.3316

20. Office of the President of the United States. (2016). *Preparing for the future of artificial intelligence.* Washington, DC: National Science and Technology Council, p. 14. https://obamawhitehouse.archives.gov/sites/default/files/whitehouse_files/microsites/ostp/NSTC/preparing_for_the_future_of_ai.pdf

21. Royal Society (UK). (2017). *Machine learning: The power and promise of computers that learn by example.* London: Royal Society, p. 8. https://royalsociety.org/~/media/policy/projects/machine-learning/publications/machine-learning-report.pdf

22. Srivastava, S.K. (2018). Artificial intelligence: Way forward for India. *Journal of Information Systems and Technology Management, 15(0)* (July 24). http://www.jistem.fea.usp.br/index.php/jistem/article/view/2965

23 Access Partnership. (2018). *Artificial intelligence for Africa: An opportunity for growth, development and democratisation*. Pretoria: University of Pretoria, South Africa, p. 36. https://www.up.ac.za/media/shared/7/ZP_Files/ai-for-africa.zp165664.pdf

24 Stirling, R., Miller, H., & Martinho-Truswell, E. (2017). Government AI Readiness Index. *Oxford Insights*. https://www.oxfordinsights.com/government-ai-readiness-index

25 See, for example, European Union. (2018). EU Member States sign up to cooperate on artificial intelligence. https://ec.europa.eu/digital-single-market/en/news/eu-member-states-sign-cooperate-artificial-intelligence

26 Access Partnership. (2018). *Artificial Intelligence for Africa: An opportunity for growth, development and democratisation*. South Africa: University of Pretoria. https://www.up.ac.za/media/shared/7/ZP_Files/ai-for-africa.zp165664.pdf

27 Tennison, J. (2018). Doesn't open data make data monopolies more powerful? *Jeni's Musings*, 14 January. http://www.jenitennison.com/2018/01/14/data-monopolies.html

28 O'Hara, K. (2019). Data Trusts: Ethics, architecture and governance for trustworthy data stewardship. *Web Science Institute White Papers*, 13 February. http://dx.doi.org/10.5258/SOTON/WSI-WP001

29 Omidyar Network/Dalberg. (forthcoming). Retrospective assessment – Open Data. Omidyar Network's Governance & Citizen Engagement initiative.

30 Chui, M., Harryson, M., Manyika, J., Roberts, R., Chung, R., Van Heteren, A., & Nel, P. (2018). *Notes from the AI frontier: Applying AI for social good*. San Francisco, CA: McKinsey Global Institute. https://www.mckinsey.com/~/media/mckinsey/featured%20insights/artificial%20intelligence/applying%20artificial%20intelligence%20for%20social%20good/mgi-applying-ai-for-social-good-discussion-paper-dec-2018.ashx

31 http://www.datascienceafrica.org/

32 http://air.ug/

33 Brandusescu, A., Ortiz Freuler, J., & Thakur, D. (2017). *Artificial intelligence: Starting the policy dialogue in Africa*. Washington, DC: World Wide Web Foundation. http://webfoundation.org/docs/2017/12/Artificial-Intelligence-starting-the-policy-dialogue-in-Africa.pdf

34 Iyengar, V. (2018). Complete overview of the AI startup ecosystem in India. *Medium*, 25 September. https://medium.com/datadriveninvestor/ai-startups-in-india-1c49e71a1ce5

35 https://serenata.ai/

36 Internet Health Report. (2018). In Brazil, a bot in the public interest. *Internet Health Report 2018*. https://internethealthreport.org/2018/in-brazil-a-bot-in-the-public-interest/

37 Pazzim, B. (2017). Como Está Acontecendo a Hackaton de Denúncias Da Operação Serenata de Amor? [How is the Hackaton of Denunciations of Operation Serenata de Love happening?] *Medium*, 12 January. https://medium.com/data-science-brigade/como-est%C3%A1-acontecendo-a-hackaton-de-den%C3%BAncias-da-opera%C3%A7%C3%A3o-serenata-de-amor-a8bd193e0c76

38 Gakrelidz, N. (2017). Predicting London crime rates using machine learning. *Data iku*, 14 January. https://blog.dataiku.com/predicting-london-crime-rates-using-machine-learning

39 McClendon, L. & Meghanathan, N. (2015). Using machine-learning algorithms to analyze crime data. *Machine Learning and Applications: An International Journal (MLAIJ), 2(1)*, 1–12.

40 Deepak, K.K. & Vinod, S. (2018). Crime analysis in India using data mining techniques. *International Journal of Engineering &Technology, 7(2.6)*, 253–258. http://doi.org/10.14419/ijet.v7i2.6.10779

41 Brayne, S., Rosenblat, A., & Boyd, D. (2015). Predictive policing. *Data & Civil Rights: A New Era Of Policing And Justice*, 27 October. http://www.datacivilrights.org/pubs/2015-1027/Predictive_Policing.pdf

42 Raso, F., Hilligoss, H., Krishnamurthy, V., Bavitz, C., & Kim, L. (2018). *Artificial intelligence and human rights: Opportunities & risks*. Cambridge, MA: Berkman Klein Center. https://cyber.harvard.edu/sites/default/files/2018-09/2018-09_AIHumanRightsSmall.pdf?

43 Davies, T. (2010). Open data, democracy and public sector reform. Master's Thesis. University of Oxford. http://www.opendataimpacts.net/report/

44 Porreca, S., Leotta, F., Mecella, M., & Catarci, T. (2017). Chatbots as a novel access method for government open data. *SEBD*. http://ceur-ws.org/Vol-2037/paper_19.pdf

45 Liu, C.-K. (2016). Taiwan's challenge: Making contracting smarter with data. *Open Contracting Partnership*, 11 November. https://www.open-contracting.org/2016/11/11/taiwans-challenge-making-contracting-smarter-data/

46 Ortiz Freuler, J. & Iglesias, C. (2018). *Algorithms and artificial intelligence in Latin America: A study of implementation by governments in Argentina and Uruguay*. Washington, DC: World Wide Web Foundation. http://webfoundation.org/docs/2018/09/WF_AI-in-LA_Report_Screen_AW.pdf

47 Pane, J., Paciello, J., Ojeda, V., & Valdex, N. (2016). Enabling dengue outbreak predictions based on open data. *Open Data Research Symposium 2016*, 5 October, Madrid, Spain. https://drive.google.com/file/d/0B4TpC6ecmrM7Q1lpQ0xoNlJnZlU/view?usp=drive_open&usp=embed_facebook

48 McMurren, J., Young, A., & Verhulst, S. (2017). *Paraguay: Predicting dengue outbreaks with open data*. Open Data for Developing Economies Case Studies. Brooklyn, NY: GovLab. http://odimpact.org/files/case-paraguay.pdf

49 Pane, J., Paciello, J., Ojeda, V., & Valdex, N. (2016). Enabling dengue outbreak predictions based on open data. *Open Data Research Symposium 2016*, 5 October, Madrid, Spain. https://drive.google.com/file/d/0B4TpC6ecmrM7Q1lpQ0xoNlJnZlU/view?usp=drive_open&usp=embed_facebook

50 Ortiz Freuler, J. & Fagan, C. (2018). How open data can save AI. *World Wide Web Foundation*, 11 January. https://webfoundation.org/2018/01/how-open-data-can-save-ai/

51 Angwin, J., Larson, J., Mattu, S., & Kirchner, L. (2016). Machine bias. *ProPublica*, 23 May. https://www.propublica.org/article/machine-bias-risk-assessments-in-criminal-sentencing

52 Smith, M. & Neupane, S. (2018). *Artificial intelligence and human development: Toward a research agenda*. Ottawa: International Development Research Centre. http://hdl.handle.net/10625/56949

53 http://webfoundation.org

54 https://idatosabiertos.org/

55 http://theodi.org

56 http://www.idrc.ca/ai4d

57 http://www.fatml.org

58 Gebru, T., Morgenstern, J., Vecchione, B., Vaughan, J.W., Wallach, H., Daumeé III, H., & Crawford, K. (2018). Datasheets for datasets. *Proceedings of the 5th Workshop on Fairness, Accountability, and Transparency in Machine Learning*, Stockholm, Sweden. https://arxiv.org/pdf/1803.09010.pdf

59 https://www.partnershiponai.org/

60 Goldstein, E., Gasser, U., & Budish, R. (2018). Data Commons Version 1.0: A framework to build toward AI for good. *Medium, Berkman Klein Center*, 21 June. https://medium.com/berkman-klein-center/data-commons-version-1-0-a-framework-to-build-toward-ai-for-good-73414d7e72be

61 Rieke, A., Bogen, M., & Robinson, D.G. (2019). *Public scrutiny of automated decisions: Early lessons and emerging methods*. Upturn and Omidyar Network. https://www.omidyar.com/sites/default/files/file_archive/Public%20Scrutiny%20of%20Automated%20Decisions.pdf

62 Fjeld, J. & Kortz, M. (2018). Art that imitates Art. *Berkman Klein Center*, 22 May. https://cyber.harvard.edu/events/2018/luncheon/05/Fjeld_Kortz

63 Sobel, B. (2017). Artificial intelligence's fair use crisis. *SSRN*. https://papers.ssrn.com/abstract=3032076

64 City of New York. (2018). Mayor De Blasio announces first-in-nation task force to examine automated decision systems. *The Official Website of the City of New York*, 16 May. http://www1.nyc.gov/office-of-the-mayor/news/251-18/mayor-de-blasio-first-in-nation-task-force-examine-automated-decision-systems-used-by

65 Thereaux, O. (2017). Using artificial intelligence and open data for innovation and accountability. *The ODI* [Article], 20 December. https://theodi.org/article/using-artificial-intelligence-and-open-data-for-innovation-and-accountability/

66 Ortiz Freuler, J. & Iglesias, C. (2018). *Algorithms and artificial intelligence in Latin America: A study of implementation by governments in Argentina and Uruguay*. Washington, DC: World Wide Web Foundation. http://webfoundation.org/docs/2018/09/WF_AI-in-LA_Report_Screen_AW.pdf

67 Lepri, B., Staiano, J., Sangokoya, D., Letouzé, E., & Oliver, N. (2017). The tyranny of data? The bright and dark sides of data-driven decision-making for social good. In T. Cerquitelli, D. Quercia, & F. Pasquale (Eds.), *Transparent data mining for big and small data* (pp. 3–24). Cham: Springer International Publishing. https://arxiv.org/pdf/1612.00323.pdf

68 Al-Jarrah, O.Y., Yoo, P.D., Muhaidat, S., Karagiannidis, G.K., & Taha, K. (2015). Efficient machine learning for big data: A review. *Big Data Research, 2(3)*, 87–93. https://arxiv.org/pdf/1503.05296.pdf

69 http://www.thinkmind.org/index.php?view=instance&instance=ALLDATA+2018

70 Smith, M. & Neupane, S. (2018). *Artificial intelligence and human development: Toward a research agenda*. Ottawa: International Development Research Centre. http://hdl.handle.net/10625/56949

71 Scrollini, F. (2018). *Automatizar con cautela. Datos e Inteligencia Artificial en América Latina* [Automate with caution. Data and artificial intelligence in Latin America]. Montevideo: Iniciativa Latinoamericana por los Datos Abiertos. https://idatosabiertos.org/automatizar-con-cautela-datos-e-inteligencia-artificial-en-america-latina/

72 Ortiz Freuler, J. & Iglesias, C. (2018). *Algorithms and artificial intelligence in Latin America: A study of implementation by governments in Argentina and Uruguay*. Washington, DC: World Wide Web Foundation. http://webfoundation.org/docs/2018/09/WF_AI-in-LA_Report_Screen_AW.pdf

73 Smith, M. & Neupane, S. (2018). *Artificial intelligence and human development: Toward a research agenda*. Ottawa: International Development Research Centre. http://hdl.handle.net/10625/56949

018

Data infrastructure

Leigh Dodds and Peter Wells

Key points

- Understanding data infrastructure by using an analogy to physical infrastructure like roads and rail helps us to see the range of components that make up data infrastructure: from datasets and servers to standards, policies, rules, and governance mechanisms.

- Just as the quality of physical infrastructure, and the capacity of governments or the private sector to maintain it, varies across the world, access to high quality data infrastructure is unequally distributed. This leaves some countries much less able to secure the benefits of open data.

- Open standards, identifiers, and registers (reference data) are the essential building blocks of data infrastructure, yet they often lack investment and see limited adoption.

- In the future, data infrastructures will need to accommodate both open data and more restricted datasets. It will be important to build both trust and openness into our data infrastructures to maximise their social and economic value.

Introduction

Infrastructure powers our societies. It provides the fundamental services and systems that enable our economies to function, allow us to communicate, and support our daily activities. When we think of infrastructure, we first think of roads, bridges, water supplies, and electrical grids, but infrastructure also takes less tangible forms, such as ideas, basic research, and the internet.[1]

In this chapter, we discuss why data should be treated as infrastructure. It is a public good that enables the creation of a wide range of products and services. All sectors of our economies, at the local, national, and global level, rely on it. Roads help us to navigate to a destination; data helps us to navigate to a decision.

Just as societies and sectors strategically plan, invest in, and protect the physical infrastructure they rely on, we must also begin to do the same with our data infrastructure. Having a strong data infrastructure will become more vital as our populations grow and our economies and societies become ever more reliant on getting value from data to meet a range of needs.[2]

Good infrastructure is there when we need it, but, at the moment, too much of our data infrastructure is unreliable, inaccessible, siloed, or can only be used if you can afford access. Data innovators struggle to get hold of data and to work out how they can best use it, while individuals do not feel that they are in control of how data about them is used or shared.

Data infrastructure should be as easy to use as our road networks. The time and effort that goes into working around poor data infrastructure, due to the equivalents of potholes, toll booths, and missing intersections, would be better spent building services that improve our lives. To maximise value from data, we need data infrastructure to be high quality, and as open as possible, while protecting privacy, national security, and commercial confidentiality.

The rapid development and adoption of technologies that help us to collect and process data in new ways, and in ever-increasing volumes, is creating new data infrastructure in sectors such as health, transport, and agriculture. It is important that we make conscious decisions about how these sector-specific data infrastructures are designed,[3] so that, over time, they are interoperable and form a connected data infrastructure (with appropriate measures in place to build and maintain trust). We must ensure that data is used ethically, that people are engaged in decisions about the data that impacts them, and that there is equitable access to, and benefits from, that data.

Defining data infrastructure

Describing data as infrastructure is more than just an analogy. In his exploration of the social value of infrastructure, Brett Frischmann defines infrastructural resources as resources that are consumed non-rivalrously, are required as inputs to support downstream activities, and are used to create a variety of goods and services.[4] This definition clearly applies to data. Consumption of data is non-rivalrous: the same data can simultaneously be used by many different users. Data is a necessary input for making better decisions and a raw material for new products and services. Data is also used to create a wide variety of goods and services from commercial products[5] to art.[6]

By understanding data as infrastructure in this way, we can begin to apply existing analysis and other insights that have been developed for "traditional" infrastructure to the management and supply of data. For example, we can start to acknowledge the level of planning, investment, and maintenance that is required to support that infrastructure in order to deliver benefits for the public good. We can also better appreciate that data infrastructure should be designed to support and enable a variety of uses, just as our roads support multiple modes of transport, in order to maximise benefits for all.

However, we also need to identify the individual building blocks of data infrastructure. Road infrastructure consists of more than physical assets. In addition to the physical assets like roads and traffic signals, the infrastructure also includes the standardised road markings and symbols that help us to safely and fairly use the roads, the policies and guidance that define how and where roads are built, and the organisations that maintain them. Similarly, data infrastructure also consists of more than just physical assets like servers and networks. A useful definition of data infrastructure must recognise more than just the technical infrastructure that we use to collect and store data.

The quality and connectivity of road infrastructure across different countries and even within countries can vary considerably (e.g. roads may be well-developed networks in cities and of poorer quality in rural areas). We should be able to assess the quality of our data infrastructure and define ways to strengthen it.

We provide a suggested definition of data infrastructure below. This broad definition reflects that used by the geospatial data community in their definition of spatial data infrastructure.[7,8]

Defining data infrastructure

Data infrastructure consists of:

- Data assets, such as datasets, identifiers, and registers.

- Standards and technologies used to curate and provide access to data assets.

- Guidance and policies that inform the use and management of data assets and the data infrastructure itself.

- Organisations that govern the data infrastructure.

- The communities involved in contributing to or maintaining it, and those who are impacted by decisions that are made using it.

Infrastructures may be local, regional, national, or international. For example, to deliver the Sustainable Development Goals (SDGs), numerous sector-specific networks have been working to develop standards, guidance, and organisational structures that can capture comparable indicator data to measure progress toward the goals. This involves identifying existing sources of data that might be brought within the SDG "data infrastructure", establishing new flows of data and thinking about how they will be maintained.

Data infrastructure at all levels might be maintained or used by government, private, or third-sector organisations. In developing countries, road infrastructure is being built through foreign investment, which raises questions about who benefits from that infrastructure. Similarly, we should understand who controls our data infrastructure[9] and recognise that there is an evolving variety of governance models. The right model for the governance of a given element of data infrastructure might vary across sectors, nations, or communities.

Aspects of data infrastructure

Identifying and describing data infrastructure

Reflecting on the nature of data infrastructure can help the open data community to achieve a number of goals that are outlined below.

Firstly, our definition of data infrastructure clearly highlights the importance of the variety of actors that play a role in designing, managing, and governing data infrastructures, or in creating value from the data assets that they provide. This systems-related thinking can help us to publish data in ways that will enable a variety of long-term impacts. For much of the last decade, open data initiatives focused on encouraging the creation of data portals to help data stewards publish data and to support people in finding the data they need to create things. OpenDataSoft now lists over 2 600 open data portals around the world[10] with the highest concentration in Europe and North America, where cities, government agencies, and national governments have created their own portals. Where portals are being used as a means to creating ecosystems of applications and services, we should invest appropriately in making them sustainable,[11] ensure they are appropriately governed, and encourage the adoption of open standards to provide access to data.

Secondly, defining data infrastructure effectively can help us to recognise and describe existing gaps or deficiencies in data infrastructure.[12] We can ask meaningful questions about whether that data infrastructure is as open as possible and advocate for practical interventions to help unlock additional value, such as through the creation of open standards or improved governance.

> ### Examples of infrastructure: CrossRef and ORCID
>
> Over the last decade, the research community has improved the data infrastructure for scholarly research. This has involved the creation of a range of data assets, organisational models, and policies mandating open access and licensing to enable better discovery and use of research outputs.
>
> CrossRef and DataCite are not-for-profit membership organisations that provide unique identifiers for papers and datasets. Another not-for-profit, ORCID, provides similar identifiers for researchers. CrossRef is currently leading projects to create identifiers for other parts of the research ecosystem, including organisations and grants. They have also negotiated the licensing of open data from social media platforms[13] to support analysis of the debate around scholarly research.
>
> Each of these organisations plays a role in the research data infrastructure. They each support a wide variety of organisations, including established publishers, startups, and research institutions in developing a range of applications and services that support the research ecosystem.

There are many existing examples of data infrastructure. Some are provided by governments, while others are supported by sector or community initiatives. For example, CrossRef and ORCID (see box, Examples of infrastructure: CrossRef and ORCID) support the research and publishing sectors, while Europeana[14] is enabling the cultural heritage sector to exchange and archive data, and initiatives like MusicBrainz[15] and Discogs[16] are providing data about music to support a variety of commercial and non-commercial projects.[17] Projects like Wikidata[18] and OpenStreetMap (see box, Examples of infrastructure: OpenStreetMap) are also best understood and evaluated as examples of data infrastructure.

Efforts to describe and document government information infrastructures predate the open data movement, often focusing on the internal interoperability of data within government. Open data initiatives have helped to refocus this work, so that government data is recognised as part of a wider open data infrastructure that is of benefit to businesses and society, as well as to government for its internal use. However, many early open data initiatives and advocacy campaigns encouraged governments to release a standard list of discrete datasets and to upload them to central data portals,[19] rather than adopting tailored approaches to discussing, releasing, and supporting the use of data that met the needs of local communities.

Adopting more of a systems-thinking approach to documenting and mapping[20] existing infrastructures helps us to better understand the specific challenges and pressures they face. For example, the increasing collection of data by commercial organisations is impacting our national and global data infrastructures for geospatial,[21] transport,[22] and weather data.[23] Similarly, the increasing use of commercial data sources in national statistics[24] or local government policy-making[25] raises questions about the quality of those data assets and how well they represent the communities impacted by their use.

Finally, by understanding the shape and design of existing data infrastructures, we can identify common patterns that will help us to identify principles[26,27] to inform the design of stronger infrastructure. New data infrastructure is being created in a number of sectors. Examples include the Open Banking Initiative in the United Kingdom (UK)[28] and Mexico,[29] OpenActive,[30] GODAN in agriculture,[31] and the DFID Digital Strategy in global development.[32]

In 2018, the Open Data Charter updated its strategy, moving from a focus on "high value datasets" to a focus on "publishing with purpose".[33] In line with this shift, it will be important to supplement our existing understanding of how data supports change with insights into successful patterns for delivering better services using data,[34,35] and further, how these patterns can be replicated in other contexts nationally and internationally when the right data infrastructure exists to support them.

Examples of infrastructure: OpenStreetMap

OpenStreetMap (OSM) illustrates how an open, collaborative process can produce a global data infrastructure. Over the last 12 years, OSM has grown from a project supported by only individual contributors to one that now routinely receives contributions from a wide range of community groups, as well as commercial organisations like Mapbox and Facebook in addition to government agencies.

> Supported by the provision of aerial imagery from a number of commercial sources, the OSM community has created more than just a global geospatial dataset. They have also constructed the necessary governance framework that supports its use in the creation of a wide variety of products and services. These uses include community-led mapping projects to support the investigation of land rights, humanitarian mapping, as well as a number of commercial applications.
>
> For more detail, see Chapter 9: Geospatial.

The role of standards, identifiers, and registers

Open standards for data are reusable agreements that make it easier for people and organisations to publish, access, share, and use better quality data.[36] When data is published using open standards, it can be used with off-the-shelf tools that support those standards, reducing the time and effort required to unlock value from the data.

Early open data efforts focused on "raw data", and then pushed more for use of open file format standards (e.g. CSV rather than PDF). Where data has become available in standard formats, emphasis is now increasingly being placed on the creation or publication of data that uses common open standards for field names and definitions, identifiers, and classifications. The challenge this presents should not be underestimated as the vast majority of data published through open data portals makes limited use of open standards beyond file format, and, in many countries, data is still predominantly only available in PDF format.

Open standards are created using open, collaborative processes[37] that enable many different stakeholders to create a useful agreement. Standards for data are essential whenever we want to consistently collect and exchange data. Some standards help to define shared vocabularies, while others define how we exchange data or capture best practices and guidance. We can also combine simple standards to create complex standards and workflows.

Creation and adoption of open standards can generate a variety of technical, economic, and policy impacts. Examples include the Open Contracting Data Standard, which is helping to create transparency around public spending in Paraguay and Nigeria,[38] and the General Transit Feed Specification, which is supporting the publication of transport data for cities around the world and can be consumed using a variety of tools and services.[39]

Open standards for data that have been developed, however, are often not adopted. There are many reasons for this, including a lack of engagement with stakeholders and potential users, which can often lead to poorly defined standards, as well as difficulties in finding existing standards.[40] Governments can also overlook their ability to encourage adoption by building requirements to support standards into the procurement and delivery of public services. As of 2018, the Open Data Institute (ODI) and others are working to develop new guidance and tools to support the creation and adoption of standards.[41]

To enable the consistent exchange and use of data, we often need to standardise specific elements within our data assets. For example, we may need standard identifiers for the organisations, places, and products referenced in our data assets. Standard identifiers help to link together datasets from multiple sources. They are the means through which we create the "junctions" between and within data infrastructures. Simply listing valid identifiers is seldom useful. Registers[42] are datasets that provide consistent, accurate, and up-to-date lists of information that can also help to improve the quality of data collection and linking. Registers typically consist of identifiers and some basic reference data. Examples of registers include lists of countries and government departments, companies, and food types (see box, An example: UK government registers).

Openly licensed standards, identifiers, and registers are vital building blocks for data infrastructure.[43] There is still a great deal of work to be done to support the adoption of existing standards, and to create new standards to help improve data collection and use in specific sectors. If the open data community is to create impact through the purposeful release of specific datasets, we must ensure that we are considering opportunities to improve our data infrastructure by creating openly licensed reference data.

Figure 1: What can we standardise?
Source: http://standards.theodi.org/introduction/

> ### An example: UK government registers
>
> The UK government has long been a leader in open data and digital government. The UK's Government Digital Service (GDS) recognises the importance of making better use of data, while the National Infrastructure Commission has noted data emerging as a form of infrastructure.[44] In 2015, GDS started exploring how to build a series of registers: authoritative lists that people can trust.[45]
>
> The list of registers published by GDS includes the list of countries recognised by the UK government and lists of local authorities, schools, and job centres. The content of the registers vary with what is being listed. For example, the list of local authorities includes two name variants and the start and end date for the entry, while the register of schools includes an address and the name of the head teacher. Each register is governed by a single government employee known as the custodian.
>
> The GDS registers are driven primarily by the needs of government data users, but they are open for anyone to use. External organisations, such as MySociety and Transparency in Supply Chains (TISC), use them in their work.
>
> The documentation for registers, including the list of registers, how to use them, how they are governed, and who maintains them, is publicly available. This is in line with the GDS commitment to working in the open.[46] There are currently 34 live registers with 36 more in the process of being developed.

Governance and trust

With the ever-increasing use of data comes questions about governance and trust. People, communities, businesses, and governments must have trust in data if we are to maximise its social and economic value. This is particularly important for personal data. If we do not have trust in how personal data is used, then people will refuse to consent to data collection or withdraw from initiatives that share and use data. Much of open data is derived from personal data. For example, data collected by national censuses is used to produce official statistics, and data collected on passengers' use of transport is used to create timetables. Meanwhile, some societies have decided that some personal data should be published openly like the names and addresses of the directors of corporations.

To increase levels of trust, the whole data ecosystem will need to build ethical considerations into how data is collected, managed, and used in order to ensure equity around who can access and use data and how the benefits are distributed. This will only be possible through meaningful engagement with the people and organisations potentially affected by the data. Within the context of data infrastructure, some of these activities will be performed by data stewards, who may create tools and services using data or draw on data to make decisions. Good data governance mechanisms are needed at every stage.

Data ethics is a branch of ethics that evaluates data practices with the potential to adversely impact people and society – through data collection, sharing, and use.[47] Ethical issues are not limited to personal data. A number of organisations have published tools to help organisations make more ethical decisions about data,[48] while others are publishing practices for ethical service design.[49] Complying with legal obligations (e.g. supporting the rights granted by the European Union General Data Protection Regulation) is just one aspect of treating data ethically. Data-related activities can be unethical but still lawful; therefore, putting good regulations in place also helps to create ethical social norms.

The World Wide Web Foundation, in a review of low- and middle-income countries, has found that progress on introducing appropriate safeguards and regulations is mixed, and affected communities are not always engaged in shaping these interventions.[50] As more countries and sectors contribute to data infrastructure, we must ensure that people are actively engaged and can contribute to both the data and its governance.

It will be particularly critical in the coming years to address issues of equity, ethics, and cultural diversity emerging from cross-border data transfers and the increasing use of data within service delivery. Many low- and middle-income countries lack the ecosystems to use data and build competitive data-enabled services like those provided by firms from high- and upper-middle income countries such as the United States, the UK, and China. Making data infrastructure as open as possible with the appropriate safeguards can help create a fair, competitive, and more level playing field,[51] but it will also need other interventions, such as capacity building and better tax regimes,[52] to create an effective systemic response and avoid either a future dominated by data monopolies or a future where our data infrastructure has only limited utility.

People, processes, and progress

It is also worth reflecting on the work required to develop and maintain data infrastructures, as well as the people and processes required to make them successful. Data and information infrastructures have historically been developed by a range of organisations, including governments and the private sector. Key infrastructure components like data policies, legislation, and standards for data exchange have been developed by national and international bodies that convene expert groups to help with the necessary work.

Participation in these processes has often been limited to those people and organisations that can invest time and money in contributing or can see the immediate value in contributing. Like many aspects of infrastructure development, the significant investment and work required is easily overlooked. This can lead to lack of investment in the creation of the infrastructure required to deliver on policy goals or to help to create more open markets. The need for significant investment can also unintentionally exclude some organisations and communities from participation in the creation of data infrastructure. This may lead to the creation of infrastructure that is less optimal because of the lack of consideration of different or diverse perspectives and needs.

The ability to work online, using a variety of agile collaboration tools, is creating more opportunities for communities to collaborate in the creation of standards and other aspects of data infrastructure. The adoption of open government initiatives, like open policy-making and the OpenStand principles,[53] reflects a conscious effort to work more openly, include more views, and produce better outputs.

Greater sharing of insight through case studies, peer networking, and other activities will also help to highlight the investment required to develop data infrastructure, to build skills, and to cement an understanding of successful approaches. Initiatives like the Interoperability Data Collaborative[54] and the African Regional DataCube,[55] both part of the Global Partnership for Sustainable Development Data, reflect this approach to creating stronger data infrastructure.

The rise of Wikipedia and OpenStreetMap reflects another aspect of how data infrastructures are evolving. For these examples, the work of curating and maintaining data infrastructure falls to a community of volunteers and supporting organisations, reflecting a more networked, collaborative approach to the stewardship of data. We are at the early stages of understanding how to develop and maintain data infrastructure in this way. These initiatives offer opportunities for communities around the world to participate in the collection and maintenance of data about their local area and lives; however, there is also a risk that a lack of resources, skills, engagement, and investment may lead to the creation of infrastructure which excludes or does not reflect the needs of specific communities that are unable to participate.

Future directions

Data standards only made it onto the agenda of the International Open Data Conference in 2015, and, as yet, there has been little focus on the other aspects of data infrastructure. The open data community should recognise that after more than a decade of open data initiatives, we are not just releasing datasets, we are actively creating data infrastructure. The choices we make about licensing, technology, access, and governance will help to shape the ecosystems that this infrastructure enables.

Data exists across a spectrum. Not all data can be open. We need to design data infrastructures that support both open data and data shared in more restricted ways. The organisations that contribute to data infrastructure and use it will come from the public, private, and voluntary sectors, so we need to design for, and engage with, this mixed economy much more than we are doing now. We need to avoid treating open data as a special case by designing openness into any and all broader approaches to data sharing.

We will also need a step change in investment and in the level of effort put into creating data infrastructures. This requires a commitment to longer-term projects and support for the key infrastructural work required to make them successful. Embracing systems thinking, and exploring existing work on the social and economic impacts of infrastructure, as well as focusing on commons-based approaches, will help us move forward on key questions related to measurement, impact, and adoption.

We must also recognise the role that other organisations working on other aspects of the open movement have in helping to create stronger data infrastructures. In the last few years, the open source movement has also been discussing their outputs as infrastructure,[56] particularly in recognition of how vulnerable large parts of the open source ecosystem are when key components are not maintained. We need to work with those promoting open cultures and digital rights, because they can help us understand how to retain trust while creating openness. Working together as a community, and in collaboration with other parts of the open movement, will help us maximise our impact.

We must continue to emphasise the importance of open standards, identifiers, and registers as the building blocks of data infrastructure, but we also need to ensure that we are placing enough emphasis on governance and the policies and legislation that help to create ethical and equitable access to the benefits of data. We need both trust and openness in our data infrastructure to maximise its social and economic value. If we get this right, then when we write about the state of open data and data infrastructure ten years from now, we will be able to tell the story of sound theory put effectively into practice.

Further reading

Bilder, G., Lin, L., & Neylon, C. (2015). Principles for open scholarly infrastructures. *Figshare*, 23 February. http://dx.doi.org/10.6084/m9.figshare.1314859

Dodds, L., Longden, A., McLellan, S., & Smith, A. (2017). The state of weather data infrastructure. *Open Data Institute* [Article], 20 April. https://theodi.org/article/4021/

Frischmann, B.M. (2013). *Infrastructure: The social value of shared resources*. Oxford and New York, NY: Oxford University Press.

ODI (Open Data Institute). (2016). Principles for strengthening our data infrastructure. https://theodi.org/article/principles-for-strengthening-our-data-infrastructure/

ODI (Open Data Institute). (2018). Open standards for data. https://standards.theodi.org/

About the authors

Leigh Dodds is an open data practitioner with experience working with a variety of sectors and organisations, developing and promoting the adoption of best practices for publishing and consuming data. Leigh can be found on Twitter at https://twitter.com/ldodds. More information on ODI is available at https://theodi.org.

Peter Wells is focused on data policy and helping people, organisations, and communities around the world to use data to make better decisions while being protected from harmful impacts. You can follow him on Twitter at https://twitter.com/peterwells. Learn more about ODI at https://theodi.org.

How to cite this chapter

Dodds, L. & Wells, P. (2019). Issues in open data: Data infrastructure. In T. Davies, S. Walker, M. Rubinstein, & F. Perini (Eds.), *The state of open data: Histories and horizons* (pp. 260–273). Cape Town and Ottawa: African Minds and International Development Research Centre. http://stateofopendata.od4d.net

This work is licensed under a Creative Commons Attribution 4.0 International (CC BY 4.0) licence. It was carried out with the aid of a grant from the International Development Research Centre, Ottawa, Canada.

Endnotes

1. Frischmann, B.M. (2007). Infrastructure commons in economic perspective. *First Monday,12(6)*. https://firstmonday.org/ojs/index.php/fm/article/view/1901
2. Tanaka, H. & Takagi, S. (2016). Open data as an infrastructure: Impact of availability of government data as open data on the Japanese economy. *Public Policy Review, 12(1)*, 23–46. https://www.mof.go.jp/english/pri/publication/pp_review/fy2015/ppr012_01b.pdf
3. ODI (Open Data Institute). (2016). Principles for strengthening our data infrastructure. https://theodi.org/article/principles-for-strengthening-our-data-infrastructure/
4. Frischmann, B.M. (2013). *Infrastructure: The social value of shared resources*. Oxford, New York: Oxford University Press. https://global.oup.com/academic/product/infrastructure-9780199975501
5. Shadbolt, N. (2015). Open data means business. *Open Data Institute* [Article], 31 May. https://theodi.org/article/open-data-means-business/
6. https://theodi.org/service/data-as-culture/
7. Esri. (2010). *GIS best practices: Spatial data infrastructure*. Redlands, CA: Environmental Systems Research Institute . http://www.esri.com/library/bestpractices/spatial-data-infrastructure.pdf
8. United States Government. (1994). Coordinating geographic data acquisition and access: The National Spatial Data Infrastructure (Executive Order 12906). *Federal Register, 59(71)*, 17671–17674 https://www.epa.gov/sites/production/files/2014-08/documents/nationalspatialdatainfrastructure_executiveorder_12906_2.pdf
9. ODI (Open Data Institute). (2016). Who owns our data infrastructure? https://theodi.org/article/who-owns-our-data-infrastructure/
10. OpenDataSoft. (2018). A comprehensive list of 2600+ open data portals around the world. https://www.opendatasoft.com/a-comprehensive-list-of-all-open-data-portals-around-the-world/
11. Fawcett, J., Whitworth, G., Chauvet, L., & Ibáñez, L.-D. (2018). *Ensuring the economic sustainability of open data portals: Understanding impact and financing*. Luxembourg: European Data Portal. https://www.europeandataportal.eu/sites/default/files/s3wp4_sustainability_recommendations_ii.pdf
12. OECD. (2013) *Strengthening health information infrastructure for health care quality governance*. OECD Health Policy Studies. Paris: Organisation for Economic Co-operation and Development. http://www.oecd-ilibrary.org/social-issues-migration-health/strengthening-health-information-infrastructure-for-health-care-quality-governance_9789264193505-en
13. CrossRef. (2017). Event data. https://www.crossref.org/services/event-data/
14. https://www.europeana.eu/portal/en
15. https://musicbrainz.org/doc/About
16. https://www.discogs.com/about
17. Dodds, L. (2016). Discogs: A business based on public domain data. *Lost Boy* [Blog post], 4 November. https://blog.ldodds.com/2016/11/04/discogs-a-business-based-on-public-domain-data/
18. https://en.wikipedia.org/wiki/Wikidata [accessed 4 January 2019].
19. Davies, T. (2014). Open data policies and practice: An international comparison. *SSRN* [Article], 8 September. https://papers.ssrn.com/abstract=2492520
20. Champion, I. (2018). Creating ecosystem maps for open data. *Open Data Institute* [Article], 23 March. https://theodi.org/article/creating-ecosystem-maps-for-open-data/
21. Wellenstein, A. (2017). Reversing the geospatial digital divide – one step, or leap, at a time. *Sustainable Cities* [Wold Bank blog post], 12 June. https://blogs.worldbank.org/sustainablecities/reversing-geospatial-digital-divide-one-step-or-leap-time
22. Campbell, P. (2017). UK urged to clarify data rules from connected cars. *Financial Times*, 2 July. https://www.ft.com/content/0ebdd2aa-5dc5-11e7-9bc8-8055f264aa8b
23. Dodds, L., Longden, A., McLellan, S., & Smith, A. (2017). The state of weather data infrastructure. White paper. *Open Data Institute* [Article], 20 March. https://theodi.org/article/4021/

24 Government of the United Kingdom. (2017). *Digital Economy Act 2017*. http://www.legislation.gov.uk/ukpga/2017/30/section/80/enacted

25 See, for example, https://metro.strava.com/ and https://movement.uber.com/cities

26 Bilder, G., Lin, L., & Neylon, C. (2015). Principles for open scholarly infrastructures. *Figshare*, 23 February. http://dx.doi.org/10.6084/m9.figshare.1314859

27 ODI (Open Data Institute). (2016). Principles for strengthening our data infrastructure. https://theodi.org/article/principles-for-strengthening-our-data-infrastructure/

28 https://www.openbanking.org.uk/

29 Espejo, S. (2018). Mexico financial technology law passes final hurdle in Congress. *Reuters*, 1 March. https://www.reuters.com/article/us-mexico-fintech-idUSKCN1GD6KX

30 https://www.openactive.io/

31 Allemang, D. & Teegarden, B. (2016). *A global data ecosystem for agriculture and food*. Wallingford, UK: Global Open Data Agriculture and Nutrition. https://www.godan.info/sites/default/files/documents/Godan_Global_Data_Ecosystem_Publication_lowres.pdf

32 DFID. (2018). *DFID digital strategy 2018 to 2020: Doing development in a digital world*. DFID Policy Paper. London: Department for International Development. https://www.gov.uk/government/publications/dfid-digital-strategy-2018-to-2020-doing-development-in-a-digital-world/dfid-digital-strategy-2018-to-2020-doing-development-in-a-digital-world

33 Open Data Charter. (2018). Publishing with purpose: Introducing our 2018 strategy. *Medium* [Blog post], 29 January. https://medium.com/@opendatacharter/publishing-with-purpose-introducing-our-2018-strategy-ddbf7ab46098

34 Parkes, E., Karger-Lerchi, T., Wells, P., Hardinges, J., & Vasileva, R. (2018). Using open data to deliver public services. *Open Data Institute* [Article], 2 March. https://theodi.org/article/using-open-data-for-public-services-report-2/

35 Sunlight Foundation. (2017). *A guide to tactical data engagement: Version 1.0*. Washington, DC: Sunlight Foundation. https://sunlightfoundation.com/tde/guide

36 ODI (Open Data Institute). (2018). Open standards for data. https://standards.theodi.org/

37 OpenStand. (2012). The modern standards paradigm: Five key principles. https://open-stand.org/about-us/principles/

38 Open Contracting Partnership (2019). Impact stories. https://www.open-contracting.org/impact-stories/

39 ODI. (2018). *Exploring the development and impact of open standards for data*. London: Open Data Institute. https://docs.google.com/document/d/1Sab5YMVj4PVqLjZD35hX8FTnMeeP6gLGG0xszuRMIaM/view

40 ODI. (2018). *Open standards for data: User-experience*. London: Open Data Institute. https://docs.google.com/document/d/1E5uARrZf5AJUIF_DJz-42_793EY_Dwk7n7B3bMn3x5A/view

41 https://theodi.org/article/documenting-the-development-of-open-standards-for-data/

42 Miller, D. & Roe, S. (2018). Registers and collaboration: Making lists we can trust (report). *Open Data Institute* [Article], 3 May. https://theodi.org/article/registers-and-collaboration-making-lists-we-can-trust-report/

43 Dodds, L., Phillips, G., Hapuarachchi, T., Bailey, B., & Fletcher, A. (2016). *Creating value with identifiers in an open data world*. London: Thomson Reuters and Open Data Institute. https://innovation.thomsonreuters.com/content/dam/openweb/documents/pdf/corporate/Reports/creating-value-with-identifiers-in-an-open-data-world.pdf

44 National Infrastructure Commission. (2017). Data for the public good. https://www.nic.org.uk/publications/data-public-good/

45 Farrant, G. & Bracken, M. (2015). Building on the steel thread. *Government Digital Service* [Blog post], 24 July. https://gds.blog.gov.uk/2015/07/24/building-on-the-steel-thread/

46 https://registers.cloudapps.digital/using-registers.html

47. Broad, E., Smith, A., & Wells, P. (2017). *Helping organisations navigate ethical concerns in their data practices*. London: Open Data Institute. https://www.scribd.com/document/358778144/ODI-Ethical-Data-Handling-2017-09-13
48. See, for example, AI Now, https://ainowinstitute.org/AI_Now_2017_Report.pdf; Accenture, https://www.accenture.com/gb-en/insight-data-ethics; The Engine Room, https://www.theengineroom.org/projects/responsible-data/; and the Open Data Institute, https://theodi.org/article/data-ethics-canvas/
49. See, for example, IF data permissions catalogue, https://catalogue.projectsbyif.com/
50. Web Foundation. (2017). *Personal data: An overview of low- and middle-income countries*. Washington, DC: World Wide Web Foundation. http://webfoundation.org/docs/2017/07/PersonalData_Report_WF.pdf
51. Tennison, J. (2018). Doesn't open data make data monopolies more powerful? *Jeni's Musings* [Blog post], 14 January. http://www.jenitennison.com/2018/01/14/data-monopolies.html
52. Tennison, J. (2018). Getting paid for personal data won't make things better. *Open Data Institute* [Blog post], 29 March. https://theodi.org/article/jeni-tennison-getting-paid-for-personal-data-wont-make-things-better/
53. OpenStand. (2012). The modern standards paradigm: Five key principles. https://open-stand.org/about-us/principles/
54. http://www.data4sdgs.org/index.php/initiatives/interoperability-data-collaborative
55. http://www.data4sdgs.org/initiatives/africa-regional-data-cube
56. Eghbal, N. (2016). *Roads and bridges: The unseen labor behind our digital infrastructure*. New York, NY: FordFoundation.https://www.fordfoundation.org/about/library/reports-and-studies/roads-and-bridges-the-unseen-labor-behind-our-digital-infrastructure

019

Data literacy

Mariel Garcia Montes and Dirk Slater

Key points

- The release of open data has outpaced open data use. A key cause has been low levels of data literacy among individuals and organisations who could benefit from open data.
- There is a lack of evidence on data literacy baselines, a dearth of systemic interventions to build data literacy, and limited research on what works. Existing initiatives face funding or organisational challenges in working out how to scale an effective training response.
- When organisations have access to a range of data skills, they can be more effective in making use of open data. Understanding "data as a team sport" can help move from a perspective on individual data literacy to an understanding of organisational data maturity.
- Realising the full potential of open data will require continued work on building wide-ranging capacities to create, understand, analyse, and use data.

Introduction

One of the central premises of open data for development is the potential for transformation that can be realised when people use open data. Open data proponents have often made assumptions about the interest and abilities of citizens as potential end users; however, programmes to increase the amount of open data available rarely contemplate the resources needed to promote the use of that data once released. Accounting for the gap between data release and actual use is one of the goals of data literacy advocates.

What is (open) data literacy?

Contemporary academic literature puts forward many literacies needed for the modern world (numeracy, information literacy, statistical literacy, technology literacy, etc.), yet, until recently, data literacy was primarily discussed in the context of the skills needed by students and researchers. Frank et al. (2016) argue that the rise of the web and, in particular, open data, has helped to change this, putting data literacy on the agenda for a far more extensive range of organisations and individuals.[1] They also note that many different definitions of data literacy have been proposed.

School of Data,[2] an international network of individuals and organisations promoting skills for the effective use of data, interviewed civil society practitioners in 2016[3] about their understanding of data literacy. The research focused mainly on the abilities they strive to develop among their audiences through their work (such as being able to use data to advance one's goals or to know how to find information). Practitioners expressed resistance to descriptions of data literacy they felt were widespread but of limited use. They argued that data literacy should not be seen as the result of a linear learning process nor as a binary in which one is either illiterate or literate. In addition, data literacy should not be promoted solely as an individual capacity without accounting for groups and communities.

The Data-Pop Alliance[4] has proposed that data literacy as a term does not adequately account for the need to adapt and update our understanding of the role of (open) data in the modern world, particularly as machine learning and other technologies change the use of data. They suggest that we should not refer to a sub-type of literacy (i.e. data literacy) but rather to the broader idea of "literacy in the age of data".[5] Gray et al.[6] build on this idea by introducing the concept of "data infrastructure literacy", calling for efforts that "make space for collective inquiry, experimentation, imagination and intervention around data in educational programmes and beyond, including how data infrastructures can be challenged, contested, reshaped and repurposed to align with interests and publics other than those originally intended". Open data literacy is not only about working with data. It also involves strategic efforts to shape the data environment within which we work.

While acknowledging the ongoing discussions around how best to define or conceptualise data literacy, this chapter considers "data literacy" primarily from the perspective of the pedagogies and organisational processes used to promote and acquire the skills needed to utilise open data. For the purposes of this chapter, we start from a working definition from Bhargava and D'Ignazio,[7] who describe data literacy as "the ability to read, work with, analyze, and argue with data".

Matthews[8] offers a catalogue of core competencies (see Figure 1) discussed across different sources on data literacy, highlighting the mix of capacities required related to data consumption, data creation, and data ethics, as well as a broad range of common competencies needed to manage data. Work on "open" data literacy has tended to focus more specifically on skills relating to data discovery and acquisition, data cleaning, and working with data in open data formats (CSV, JSON, etc.), using a particular set of common open data tools, as well as data visualisation, presentation, and storytelling. There is a further challenge for open data literacy in that the landscape of data availability, digital tools, analytical methods, and linkability between datasets is rapidly evolving. Moreover, understanding the significance of the term "open" when applied to data literacy implies an additional set of competencies and skills that focus on interoperability. Work on open data literacy in general aims to promote an understanding of, and commitment to, openness.

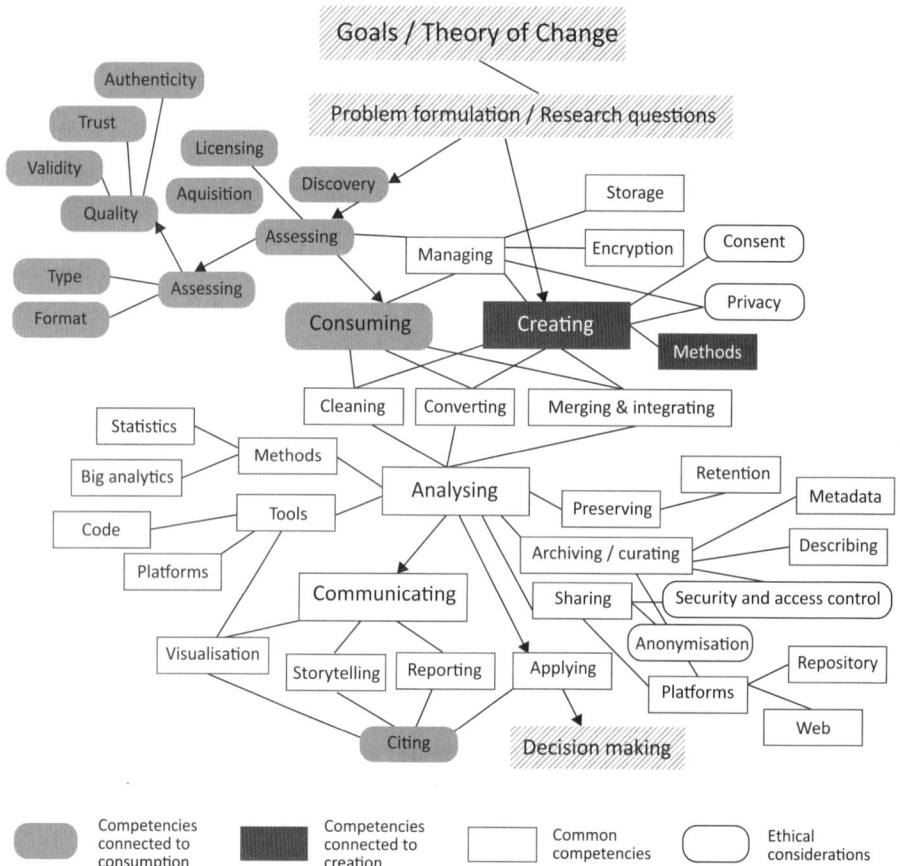

Figure 1: Generalised conceptual model of data literacy activities. Starting point Koltay (2015)[9].
Source: http://ci-journal.org/index.php/ciej/article/view/1348/1222

As we will see in the following sections, while initiatives focused on the broad topic of data literacy have developed their practice over the last decade, a lack of definitional clarity has, at times, frustrated efforts to establish baselines and to measure progress, and limited the development of an evidence base on what works.

Building open data literacy around the world

Over the last decade, as attention has shifted from just securing the release of "raw data" to the actual use of data, a variety of initiatives focused on spreading skills and methodologies related to data use have been implemented. Civil society organisations, as well as governments and international organisations, have promoted several data literacy capacity-building models, ranging from short-term efforts, such as workshops, community events, and datathons, to medium-term efforts, such as multi-week "lab" models and training programmes, and further, to long-term initiatives, such as fellowship programmes, research initiatives, and other longer-term projects.[10]

> ### Data is a team sport
>
> In 2017, the "Data is a team sport" podcast broadcast a series of conversations with data literacy practitioners to capture lessons learned and examine how methodologies are shifting and adapting in the wake of an ever-evolving data literacy ecosystem. As political and economic forces become more adept at using data, we enter a new era of data literacy where just being able to understand information is not enough.[11]

Organisations rely on different frameworks and pedagogies for their short-, medium-, and long-term efforts. For the School of Data, working with real data is central to the "data expedition" learning model. They note that on an expedition, learners may "go in circles, get lost, make mistakes, and sometimes, not reach [their] goal. But that's fine! This is the best way to get familiar with working with data."[12] Data expeditions are structured along a data pipeline, an approach focused on "working with data from beginning to end".[13] Moreover, participants adopt different roles based on their skills to work in teams that work through the pipeline.

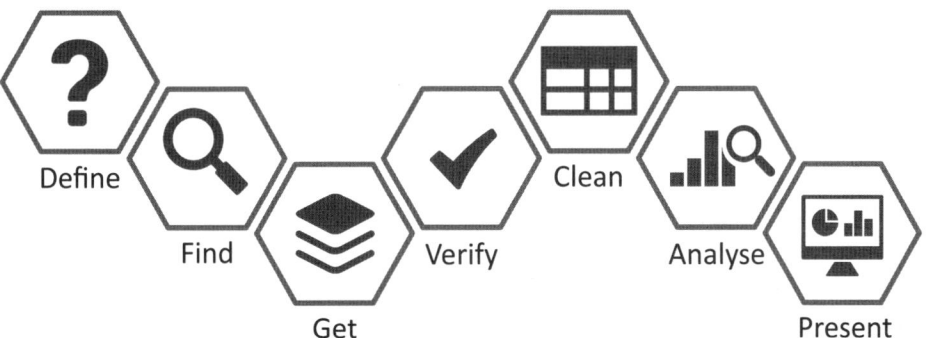

Figure 2: The School of Data's data pipeline
Source: https://schoolofdata.org/methodology/

The recognition that much real-world open data is low quality, and that working with it may require quite advanced skills, has fed into the design of Global Integrity's "Open Data Treasure Hunt" approach, which is also informed by the data expedition model. In an open data treasure hunt, participants are encouraged to assess the quality and integrity of data and identify how to put it to use. The hunt establishes realistic expectations of data use and identifies data issues that can be sent to the data creators and curators to make the data more accessible to work with in the future.[14]

The Open Data Institute (ODI), founded in London in 2012 and now distributed worldwide through a franchised "nodes" model, has emphasised creating training oriented toward organisations and governments on creation and publication, as well as the use of data. The ODI training menu has expanded from courses initiated in 2013, such as "Open Data in a Day" focused on basic concepts, including data formats and licences, and the three-day "Open Data in Practice" (2013) course that covers data publication, discovery, and business models, through to the "Open Data Science" course launched in 2016 and "Introduction to Data Ethics" launched in 2018. ODI courses have reached over 17 000 people, including approximately 2 000 attending in-person public courses, 5 500 via e-learning, and a further 4 750 face-to-face and 5 000 online through in-house courses.[15]

The School of Data and ODI have also emphasised a "Training the Trainers" model, including School of Data fellowships, as well as specific work in Tanzania that sought to develop in-country capacity both to understand open data and to deliver practical training to others.[16] This model relates to curriculum development for open data educators, an area where the work of the Investigative Reporters and Editors Network is notable.[17]

Building open data capacity in Tanzania[18]

ODI and the World Bank have collaborated with the Tanzania Open Data Initiative to improve data publication and use in the country. Through in-person visits to Tanzania, they have trained 222 people and reached another 127. Their efforts have also resulted in four e-learning modules.

DataBasic[19] is an online learning platform created by Rahul Bhargava and Catherine D'Ignazio, data literacy researchers and facilitators at the Center for Civic Media at the MIT Media Lab. Their scan of existing online data tools led them to the conclusion that available tools were "designed for users, not learners, and privilege the production of quick visuals at the expense of supporting a learning process". Instead, they set out to design tools that respond to pedagogical goals, rather than being designed around particular data outputs. Their designs draw on Paulo Freire's empowerment-focused pedagogy with its emphasis on critical thinking and consciousness, creating tools that are "focused, guided, inviting, and expandable".[20]

It is notable that, in absolute terms, these generalist data literacy-building efforts have reached a relatively small audience (in the tens rather than hundreds of thousands of people trained). Market research by data analysis firm Qlik in 2017 and 2018, looking at data skills within businesses, put levels of data literacy in Europe at just 17% of workers[21] and in Asia[22] and America at around 20%[23] with the majority of workers surveyed interested in improving their skills. While the methodology for these studies is unpublished and the results should be approached critically, they are indicative of a significant gap between the potential to use data and the skills to use it. This raises important questions about what it would take to fill these skills gaps. One promising approach has been to work with open data literacy as a capacity of communities and organisations rather than one of individuals.

DataKind UK[24] and Data Orchard,[25] charities based in the United Kingdom that advocate for the use of data and research for good, have championed an approach that looks at the use of data well beyond individual data literacy. Aimed at the organisational level, "data maturity" is defined by the ability to manage data-driven projects. This approach to achieving organisational data literacy recognises that workshops or training will succeed in raising awareness, but do not necessarily support the deeper engagement or skills building needed for an organisation to achieve self-sufficiency in running data projects. To help organisations better understand their progression toward data maturity, DataKind UK and Data Orchard have developed a framework that looks at seven key themes and plots out a five-stage journey to reach data maturity,[26] while also matching organisations with mentors who can provide support in implementing data projects.

Also aimed at the organisational level, projects like Internews' fellowships, which have been embedded in newsrooms for several weeks in places like Palestine[27] and Kenya,[28] offer a longer-term model for building capacity by changing the processes of organisations to promote the use of data in everyday work. Another initiative using the fellowship model to promote data literacy within a team, the Caribbean Open Institute fellowship in Ayitic, aimed to help young women to find employment in the digital economy in Haiti.[29]

Three other responses to the practical challenge of building data literacy are worth noting. First, a focus on infomediaries, actors who analyse and create outputs based on open data to make it more accessible and useful for end-users.[30] Data journalists, in particular, have been playing this role in the open data and data literacy ecosystem by finding and presenting relevant data to citizens as in stories like the Panama Papers,[31] which used vast quantities of data and had a global impact, as well as more local efforts that seek to uncover facts and explore causes of societal problems.[32] Networks like Exposing the Invisible[33] and Visualizing Impact[34] have included data literacy components in their work to build capacity for investigative journalism.

Second, we have seen other initiatives that seek to embed data literacy components within wider programmes. For example, Publish What You Pay (PWYP) ran a "Data Extractors"[35] programme that provided support for individuals embedded in PWYP chapters to "dig for data" and find new ways to use it. The International Federation of the Red Cross (IFRC) has developed an in-house data literacy program for staff called "The Data Playbook" that is a collection of "social" learning exercises meant to drive a deeper understanding of the role of data in supporting effective humanitarian responses.[36]

Third, additional initiatives have been developed to address ethical considerations around the use of data. The Responsible Data Forum[37] is an initiative stewarded by The Engine Room that works to "identify the unintended consequences of using data in this kind of work, and bring people together to create solutions". The Responsible Data Forum has explored the implications of the publication and use of data in the fields of public health, violence, and humanitarian response.

What works? Where are the gaps?

The critical question then is whether all these interventions are helping to close the gap between the potential benefits of open data and their realisation. Although funders have made significant investments in data literacy-related interventions, often as part of other programmes, the empirical evidence on what works when it comes to open data literacy is surprisingly scant. We were not able to locate any published pre- and post-intervention data from data literacy-building programmes, or established measurement tools to monitor progress. While the literature describing pedagogic principles suggests some context-specific best practices and highlights challenges in improving data literacy, the lack of a coherent and generally accepted definition of data literacy and requisite skill set leaves us without a real quantification of progress on open data literacy. Without better measurement, it will remain challenging to secure ongoing investment instead of ad hoc programming.

A study by the School of Data that interviewed organisations involved in data literacy building noted that while effective programmes require long-term engagement, the majority of organisations are only engaged in short-term efforts (workshops that last from two hours to ten days, community events, and datathons). Funding for medium-term training and longer-term initiatives is rare.[38]

A podcast episode for Data is a Team Sport, entitled "Government Priorities and Incentives",[39] recently explored the challenges facing governments in producing open data. Ania Calderon from the Open Data Charter and Tamara Puhovski, an open government consultant based in Croatia, reflected

> *that for governments to develop and maintain open data programs, there needs to be an ecosystem of data literate actors. This includes knowledgeable civil servants and incentivised elected officials being held to account by a critical thinking citizenry supported by smart, open data advocates. Once elected officials are elected, it's too late to educate and motivate them to push for open data programs as they have too many other priorities and pressures. A level of data literacy is required before they are elected to provide enough knowledge, motivation, and commitment.*

They also maintained that the connection between the existence of open data to data literacy efforts interwoven into the very fabric of society is not enough.

> *A government's incentivisation for open data can't be based on budgetary or monetary savings alone. They need to be motivated to use data to improve the effectiveness of their programs. Access to government produced open data is critical for healthy functioning democracies, but the government's ability to release open data is heavily dependent on their capacities to produce and work with data. There is currently not enough technical support for most public officials tasked with implementing open data projects.*

This reality is confirmed by the World Bank, one of the international organisations that supports governments in the development of national statistical systems. The World Bank acknowledges that its own current support models have focused more on data production rather than data sharing and use, with only 27 of the 201 projects evaluated including support for activities to build capacity for data use.[40]

In understanding the gaps in open data literacy building, it is also important to pay attention to issues of language, geography, and gender. Many resources and tools are available only in English, and networks like Open Heroines[41] have drawn attention to gender-based disparities in the open data movement, which may have an impact on who has access to data literacy opportunities.

Efforts to build capacity within marginalised communities to help them collect and use data to prove injustices that are occurring within their communities have had varying degrees of success. A multi-year project initiated by Tactical Technology Collective supported sex workers in collecting and using data to prove the impact of police violence in their communities in Kolkata, India and Phnom Penh, Cambodia.[42] The benefits for the advocacy groups involved included the development of skills applied to the effective collection and use of data for advocacy, new skills in analysing data to deliver a clearer understanding of the threats faced by the community, and significant improvement to their ability to conduct advocacy for their human rights. Since the data they collected had a focus on violence against women, they received requests from other advocacy groups to make use of the data. Community-based groups need to be supported to produce and use open data to strengthen their advocacy efforts. If more public data was open, more grassroots groups could learn to make use of it to contextualise their advocacy activities across the social justice spectrum.

Turning to qualitative evidence on what works, we do have some clues as to where future efforts should be focused. A group of researchers at Dalhousie University examined data literacy efforts in higher education in Canada and proposed a set of best practices in a knowledge synthesis report. They recommend a focus on hands-on learning in workshops and labs, module-based learning, project-based learning, the inclusion of real-world data that is relevant to the students' interests, and an engaging context, as well as integrating data literacy teaching into existing subjects that make use of some element of data.[43]

The future of open data literacy

Gray et al. have illustrated[44] how the rise of open data has played an essential part in increasing awareness of data in general and in bringing the history and context of datasets into question. In addition, as awareness of machine learning and the use of data by corporations has grown, new themes have arisen in the data discourse, including issues of privacy and the ethical use of data.

The Data-Pop Alliance proposes that the only way to harness the potential of open data through data literacy is by conceptualising data literacy "as a significant means and metrics for social inclusion".[45] They also point to big data as one of the areas where the power dynamics of data are most evident, especially concerning personal data. Even though open data advocates appeal for the clear distinction between public-interest data (government or corporate) and personal information, initiatives like the Responsible Data Forum are pointing to the difficulty of sustaining that distinction in practice. As a result, it may be less and less sustainable to treat open data literacy in isolation from wider critical data literacy building.

In writing this chapter, we have focused on documented data literacy efforts; however, it is important to recognise that efforts are currently underway around the world, and the Open Data Barometer's (ODB) visualisation of support for use helps make sense of the status of data literacy at a global scale. The ODB asks "To what extent is training about open data available for individuals or businesses who want to increase their technical skills or develop businesses to use (open) data?" In Figure 3, the map used to visualise results indicates scores between 0 (no training available) to 10 (widespread access to high-quality training).

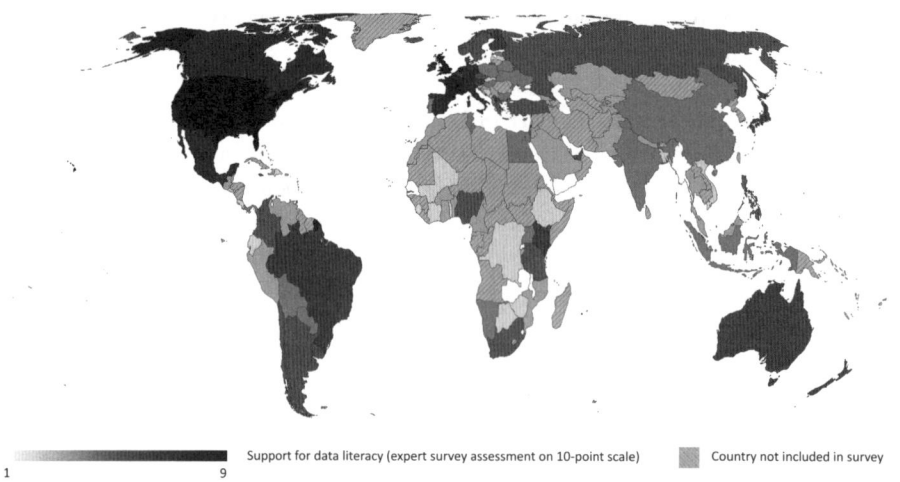

Figure 3: Support for use of data all over the world
Source: https://opendatabarometer.org/?_year=2017&indicator=ODB

Conclusion

The success of open data efforts is heavily dependent on the existence of an ecosystem of actors focused on driving the use of data through all aspects of society. There are strong traditions within civil society to build and learn from existing efforts. Through the development of networks that are openly sharing research and learnings regarding effective and less effective practices, we are developing a deeper understanding of how to achieve data literacy. However, we need to put a greater focus on understanding how class, gender, and race impact access to data and training on data use or we risk data literacy activities becoming another means of increasing inequality.

As data literacy practitioners ourselves (the authors of this chapter), we advise organisational or institutional data literacy programmes to integrate long-term capacity building, social learning exercises, awareness-raising on the collaborative nature of data projects, support for "Open Data Literacy" networks of practice, and a greater focus on the value of openness.

Long-term capacity building should provide mentoring and counselling which aim for self-sufficiency in running data-driven projects, rather than continuing to fund isolated events with the hope of increasing the number of beneficiaries through single interventions. Internews' newslab model provides a good example in this regard.

Organisations should use social learning exercises and activities to bring individuals, teams, and projects together to discuss their contexts and challenges to understand how the data will be used versus focusing entirely on technical skills. DataBasic[46] provides a good example of learning tools that contemplate social learning.

Open data literacy programming should raise awareness of the different skills and actors needed to undertake data projects, as well as the importance of distributing labour across teams and fostering collaboration. Individualistic efforts on data literacy do not suffice. School of Data's division of roles as part of data expeditions provides an example of the way this collaboration can be fostered through short-term efforts.

A focus should be placed on the value of openness in fighting inequality versus focusing solely on the value of data analysis. Equity must be placed at the centre of data analysis, and practitioners must actively push for reflection on the inclusion gaps in the data and the harm these gaps can bring. Communities like the Responsible Data Forum and Open Heroines foster continuing conversations that are relevant to this exercise.

Finally, to recognise and further the efforts that already exist on the ground, organisations should strengthen "Open Data Literacy" networks of practice to provide opportunities for peers to dialogue and discuss shared challenges and lessons learned.

Further reading

Bohman, S. (2015). Data visualization: An untapped potential for political participation and civic engagement. In A. Kő & E. Francesconi (Eds.), Electronic government and the information systems perspective. *Lecture Notes in Computer Science, 9265*, 302–315. Cham: Springer.

Journal of Community Informatics, 12(3) Special Issue on Data Literacy: http://ci-journal.org/index.php/ciej/issue/view/59

Letouzé, E., Noonan, A., Bhargava, R., Deahl, E., Sangokoya, D., & Shoup, N. (2015). *Beyond data literacy: Reinventing community engagement and empowerment in the age of data*. Cambridge, MA: Data-Pop Alliance (Harvard Humanitarian Initiative, MIT Media Lab and Overseas Development Institute) and Internews. https://datatherapy.files.wordpress.com/2015/10/beyond-data-literacy-2015.pdf

About the authors

Mariel Garcia Montes is a practitioner and researcher in the field of technology with the Center of Civic Media at the Massachusetts Institute of Technology (MIT). You can follow Mariel at https://twitter.com/faeriedevilish.

Dirk Slater is the founder of FabRiders, a consultancy focusing on utilising data and technologies to strengthen social change efforts. FabRiders leads and facilitates participatory events, designs and develops network-centric resources, and mentors capacity-building expertise. Follow Dirk at http://www.twitter.com/fabrider.

How to cite this chapter

Montes, M.G. & Slater, D. (2019). Issues in open data: Data literacy. In T. Davies, S. Walker, M. Rubinstein, & F. Perini (Eds.), *The state of open data: Histories and horizons* (pp. 274–286). Cape Town and Ottawa: African Minds and International Development Research Centre. http://stateofopendata.od4d.net

This work is licensed under a Creative Commons Attribution 4.0 International (CC BY 4.0) licence. It was carried out with the aid of a grant from the International Development Research Centre, Ottawa, Canada.

Endnotes

1. Frank, M., Walker, J., Attard, J., & Tygel, A. (2016). Data literacy: What is it and how can we make it happen? *The Journal of Community Informatics*, *12(3)*. http://ci-journal.org/index.php/ciej/article/view/1347
2. https://schoolofdata.org/
3. Slater, D. & Garcia, M. (2016). Our data literacy research findings. *School of Data*, 8 January. https://schoolofdata.org/2016/01/08/our-data-literacy-research-findings/
4. http://datapopalliance.org
5. Letouzé, E., Noonan, A., Bhargava, R., Deahl, E., Sangokoya, D., & Shoup, N. (2015). *Beyond data literacy: Reinventing community engagement and empowerment in the age of data*. Cambridge, MA: Data-Pop Alliance (Harvard Humanitarian Initiative, MIT Media Lab and Overseas Development Institute) and Internews. https://datatherapy.files.wordpress.com/2015/10/beyond-data-literacy-2015.pdf
6. Gray, J., Gerlitz, C., & Bounegru, L. (2018). Data infrastructure literacy. *Big Data & Society*, *5(2)*, 1–13. https://doi.org/10.1177/2053951718786316
7. Bhargava, R. & D'Ignazio, C. (2015). *Designing tools and activities for data literacy learners*. Oxford, UK: Web Science – Data Literacy Workshop. https://dam-prod.media.mit.edu/x/2016/10/20/Designing-Tools-and-Activities-for-Data-Literacy-Learners.pdf
8. Matthews, P. (2016). Data literacy conceptions, community capabilities. *The Journal of Community Informatics*, *12(3)*. http://ci-journal.org/index.php/ciej/article/view/1348
9. Koltay, T. (2015). Data literacy: In search of a name and identity. *Journal of Documentation*, *71(2)*, 401–415. https://doi.org/10.1108/JD-02-2014-0026
10. Slater, D. & Garcia, M. (2016). Research results part 2: The methodologies of data literacy. *School of Data*, 14 January. https://schoolofdata.org/2016/01/14/research-results-part-2-the-methodologies-of-data-literacy/
11. https://schoolofdata.org/teamsport/

12 School of Data. (n.d.). Methodology. https://schoolofdata.org/methodology/
13 Ibid.
14 Global Integrity. (n.d.). What is a 'treasure hunt'? https://www.globalintegrity.org/treasure-hunts/
15 Figures from correspondence with the Open Data Institute.
16 ODI (Open Data Institute). (2018). Building open data capacity in Tanzania. https://theodi.org/project/building-open-data-capacity-in-tanzania-the-story-of-two-years-of-training-and-support/
17 IRE (Investigative Reporters and Editors). (2018). Educators' Center. https://ire.org/resource-center/educators-center/
18 ODI (Open Data Institute). (2018). Building open data capacity in Tanzania. https://theodi.org/project/building-open-data-capacity-in-tanzania-the-story-of-two-years-of-training-and-support/
19 http://databasic.io
20 D'Ignazio, C. & Bhargava, R. (2016). DataBasic: Design principles, tools and activities for data literacy learners. *The Journal of Community Informatics*, *12(3)*. http://ci-journal.org/index.php/ciej/article/view/1294
21 The Campaign for Data Equality. (n.d.). Research. http://dataequality.org/research
22 Pani, P. (2018). India pips Singapore, China in data literacy. *The Hindu Business Line*, 6 March. https://www.thehindubusinessline.com/info-tech/india-pips-singapore-china-in-data-literacy/article22951784.ece
23 The Campaign for Data Literacy. (n.d.). Research. http://www.dataliteracy.info/research
24 http://datakind.org/chapters/datakind-uk
25 http://dataorchard.co.uk
26 Data Evolution. (2017). The data maturity framework. http://dataevolution.org.uk/the-framework/
27 Constantares, E. (2014). Using data journalism to probe economics in the West Bank. *School of Data*, 27 August. https://schoolofdata.org/2014/08/27/using-data-journalism-to-probe-economics-in-the-west-bank/
28 Jooste, I. (2016). Data journalism: The new normal in Kenya. *Internews*, 15 June. https://www.internews.org/story/data-journalism-new-normal-kenya
29 http://www.ayitic.net/en/index.html
30 Janssen, M. & Zuiderwijk, A. (2014). Infomediary business models for connecting open data providers and users. *Social Science Computer Review*, *32(5)*, 694–711.
31 ICIJ (International Consortium of Investigative Journalists). (2018). The Panama Papers: Exposing the rogue offshore finance industry. https://www.icij.org/investigations/panama-papers/
32 Slater, D. (2017). Data is a team sport: Data-driven journalism. *School of Data*, 20 June. https://schoolofdata.org/2017/06/20/data-driven-journalism/
33 http://exposingtheinvisible.org/
34 http://visualizingimpact.org
35 http://www.publishwhatyoupay.org/our-work/using-the-data/the-data-extractors/
36 Slater, D. & Leson, H. (2018). Data playbook (Beta). International Federation of Red Cross and Red Crescent Societies Global Disaster Preparedness Center. https://www.preparecenter.org/toolkit/data-playbook
37 http://responsibledata.io/
38 Slater, D. & Garcia, M. (2016). Research results part 5: Improving data literacy efforts. *School of Data*, 5 February. https://schoolofdata.org/2016/02/05/research-results-part-5-improving-data-literacy-efforts/
39 Slater, D. (2017). Data is a team sport: Government priorities and incentives. *School of Data*, 13 August. https://schoolofdata.org/2017/08/13/team-sport-government/
40 World Bank. (2017). *Data for development: An evaluation of World Bank support for data and statistical capacity*. Washington, DC: Independent Evaluation Group, World Bank. http://documents.worldbank.org/curated/en/705581506620506441/pdf/120111-WP-REVISED-PUBLIC.pdf
41 http://openheroines.org

42 Ganesh, M., Martini, B., & Slater, D. (2015). Leave your potatoes at home. *TheFabBlog* [Blog post], 28 April. https://www.fabriders.net/potatoes/

43 Ridsdale, C., Rothwell, J., Smit, M., Ali-Hassan, H., Bliemel, M., Irvine, D., Kelley, D., Matwin, S., & Wuetherick, B. (2015). *Strategies and best practices for data literacy education: Knowledge synthesis report*. Halifax, Canada: Dalhousie University. http://dalspace.library.dal.ca/bitstream/handle/10222/64578/Strategies%20and%20Best%20Practices%20for%20Data%20Literacy%20Education.pdf

44 Gray, J., Gerlitz, C., & Bounegru, L. (2018). Data infrastructure literacy. *Big Data & Society*, *5(2)*, 1–13. https://doi.org/10.1177/2053951718786316

45 Letouzé, E., Noonan, A., Bhargava, R., Deahl, E., Sangokoya, D., & Shoup, N. (2015). *Beyond data literacy: Reinventing community engagement and empowerment in the age of data*. Cambridge, MA: Data-Pop Alliance (Harvard Humanitarian Initiative, MIT Media Lab and Overseas Development Institute) and Internews. https://datatherapy.files.wordpress.com/2015/10/beyond-data-literacy-2015.pdf

46 http://databasic.io

020

Gender equity

Ana Brandusescu and Nnenna Nwakanma

Key points

- Work on gender equity is an important new frontier for open data communities, drawing on, and connecting to, many decades of wider work on feminist advocacy and action.

- Gender impacts issues of access and infrastructure, representation within datasets, and labour and leadership within open data communities.

- A commitment to gender equity must address both gender bias in data collection and publication, as well as in patterns of exclusion.

- Action is required to challenge embedded patriarchal attitudes and norms and practical steps must be taken to create better data, adopt clear policies, and promote opportunities and safe spaces for women.

Introduction

Gender is on the open data agenda and Sustainable Development Goal (SDG) 5 directly commits governments to "achieve gender equality and empower all women and girls", specifically targeting the use of "communications technology to promote the empowerment of women".[1] Groups like Data2X have expressed the need for more attention to be given to gender when data is collected, so that progress toward these goals can be tracked, and, since late 2017, the #MeToo movement has drawn global attention to the threats that women face in many professional settings. However, in the open data field, gender equity is still an emerging issue, often contextualised as a new frontier for progressive work. This chapter will explore the early movement to embed gender considerations in open data policy and practice and look at the challenges to be addressed in the years ahead.

Gender equity is defined as "fairness of treatment for women and men, according to their respective needs. This may include equal treatment or treatment that is different, but which is considered equivalent in terms of rights, benefits, obligations, and opportunities."[2] Although "gender equity" differs from "gender equality", the two concepts are inherently linked. Gender equity involves practices and processes that contribute to attaining gender equality as an end goal.[3] This involves challenging and changing socioeconomic mechanisms around us on a day-to-day basis. On the other hand, gender equality as an end goal has been rooted in constitutional provisions, women's rights, and the labour movement ever since the principle was first recognised in international law in the 1948 Universal Declaration of Human Rights.[4]

Given that the foundational principles of open data involve the promotion of accessibility and usability for all, gender equity should be an integral element in making this a reality. However, like gender-related work in many other spaces at present, gender data efforts are often siloed within the open data field. Although work to mainstream gender considerations within the open data space has already been a long process, encountering many institutional challenges and norms that stifle progress, it is still early days. The open data community has much to learn from pre-existing and long-standing movements for gender equality, as well as from the broader feminist literature, particularly with regard to its collective understanding of its approach to data, and how data collection and use relates to social justice and equity.[5,6] While this chapter focuses more on contemporary debates, we encourage readers to engage with the wider scope of literature when reflecting on gender and open data in the coming decade.

A note on limitations

The chapter does not explore issues beyond the binary. Our focus on the gender binary is not meant to be at the expense of, or to overlook, the non-binary. It is rather an effort to find initial avenues to open up political and institutional acknowledgement of the marginalised. We do, however, acknowledge this limitation of the chapter. Moreover, gender (even in binary terms) is viewed in this chapter as a separate issue from other factors that may marginalise the role of women, such as race.

From invisibility to awareness

At the start of this decade, it would not have been uncommon to attend major open data events and experience all-male panels or to observe that very few women were attending, let alone participating as speakers. Gender was rarely, if ever, discussed as a topic at these events. However, over the last few years, gender awareness and discussions of gender issues have become more central to the agenda of forums, conferences, workshops, and sessions around the world.

In 2016, the TechMousso (TechWoman)[7] open gender data competition was held in Abidjan, Cote d'Ivoire, organised by the Millennium Challenge Corporation, Data2X, and the World Wide Web Foundation (Web Foundation) to highlight the difficulties of obtaining data on gender and on women's organisations. During that same year, the first dedicated open data and gender session was held at the 4th International Open Data Conference (IODC) in Madrid, Spain. It was followed by sessions at the Open Government Partnership (OGP) Summit in Paris, France, where the Web Foundation held a workshop on why gender equality matters for open government[8] and the Open Heroines network of women in open data, open government, and civic tech held their first Open Gender Monologues session.[9]

> ### Creating spaces for gender discussions
>
> The growth of formal and informal networks working to advocate for, and support, women's representation and participation in data and, at times, open data debates and discussions has been a positive sign over the past few years. While open data is the explicit focus of some of these networks, it is implicit or indirect in others.
>
> **Open Heroines** (https://openheroines.org/) was launched in January 2016. Organised around a Slack team (instant messaging), the Open Heroines network was established to provide "a safe virtual space where women can meet like-minded women, share their experiences, and get advice and words of encouragement".[10] The network has hundreds of members around the world and was recently able to access funding to provide travel grants to IODC 2018.
>
> **GeoChicas** (https://geochicas.org/) is an initiative that aims to close the gender gap in the OpenStreetMap community through collaborative and participatory projects in Latin America. Currently, women are substantially underrepresented among those who contribute to collaborative online projects like OpenStreetMap, and GeoChicas is one of a number of grassroots projects aiming to create balanced representation.
>
> **Data2X** (https://www.data2x.org/) is housed at the United Nations Foundation and is an alliance "dedicated to improving the quality, availability, and use of gender data in order to make a practical difference in the lives of women and girls worldwide".[11] Created in 2012, Data2X has established a range of partnerships, focusing on issues related to big data, data on displaced populations, SDG monitoring, financial inclusion, and women's work and employment. To date, they have not developed a specific open data partnership.
>
> **EQUALS** (https://www.equals.org/) is a global partnership of corporate leaders, governments, non-profit organisations, communities, and individuals around the world working to bridge the gender divide in technology. Founded in 2016 by the International Telecommunications Union (ITU), UN Women, the International Trade Centre, Global System for Mobile Communications (GSMA), and the United Nations University, the partnership focuses on capacity building, political leadership, and action projects across four areas: access, skills, leadership, and research.

In 2017, the UN World Data Forum in Cape Town, South Africa, held important sessions on gender-disaggregated data. This was followed by the ATGENDER (European Institute for Gender Equality) Spring Conference on gender mainstreaming and gender budgeting[12] in Vilnius, Lithuania, and the "Open Data Brussels goes gender-smart" hackathon[13] in Belgium. Also in 2017, at the Africa Open Data Conference in Ghana, a panel was held to discuss building an African open data gender agenda,[14] and, in Wonolelo, Indonesia, women's groups discussed the importance of having access to women's development budgets as open data.[15]

In 2018, Article 19 Brazil hosted Dados y Feminicides (Data on femicides in Brazil) on Open Data Day, and the OGP launched the Feminist Open Government (FOGO) initiative to advance gender equity and hosted a high-level panel on the initiative at the OGP Summit in Tbilisi, Georgia. Additional events to incorporate gender and open data took place at IODC 2018 in Buenos Aires, Argentina, and at the UN World Data Forum in Dubai, UAE.

Taken together, these events indicate a gathering momentum with gender being increasingly addressed at key meetings of the open data field. However, it is notable that few other chapters in this volume are able to highlight sector-specific work on gender and open data, suggesting that global attention may not yet have filtered through to action in more specific sectors of open data work. This may reflect the reality that we are in the early stages of gender mainstreaming in open data, although it also highlights the risk that gender could become a sub-field separated from other major focus areas rather than an integrated strand within all open data action.

In preparing this chapter, the authors sought community input to identify stakeholders involved in supporting and championing efforts to bring a gender focus to work on big data, data for development, open data, and civic technology, mapping out the main stakeholders geographically, their primary focus, and the programmes they are working on. The two graphics below provide a summary, and a full table with details of each programme can be found in the online version of this chapter. While not exhaustive, this mapping gives an indication of the breadth, and limitations, of work on gender and data. In analysing the list of programmes and organisations, it is important to note, in particular, that many organisations are also working on advancing data literacy, gender equality, sustainable development, and women's human rights. In addition, there are a range of funders supporting these activities, as well as a number of new organisations that have been established.

Figure 1: Regions and programmes working at the intersection of gender and data
(Programmes include the use of open data, big data, development data, and gender data)
Source: Authors

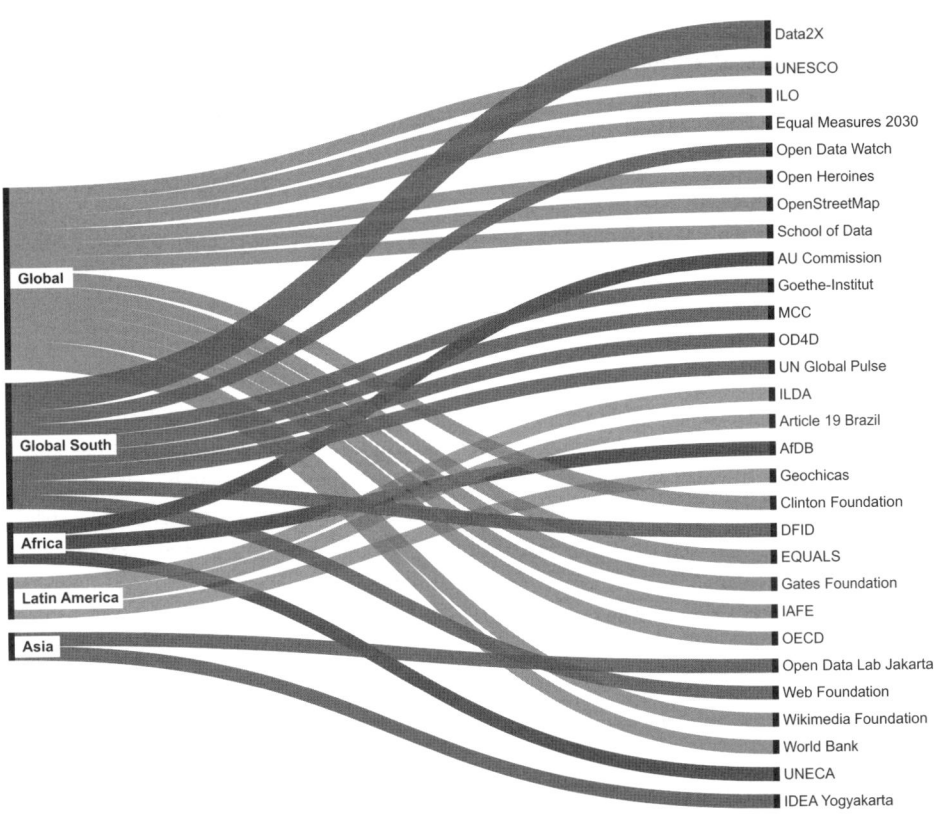

Figure 2: Regions and stakeholders working at the intersection of gender and data
Source: Authors

From awareness to action

There are three main challenges that organisations working on gender and data need to address: the capacity of women to contribute to and use data; the representation of women in data; and the representation of women in labour and leadership within open data organisations.

Access

Although open data advocacy often assumes that making data accessible equals putting data online, one cannot ignore the exclusions created by unequal access to technology. The digital world still has many gaps and limitations and is effectively inaccessible to the 50% of the world's population who are still offline.[16] Women are overrepresented among those without internet access. In 2015, women in poor urban communities of the Global South were 50% less likely to use the internet than men. In 2017, this finding was confirmed by ITU data that identified, on average, a 12% gap in internet access between men and women, particularly in Asia (17%) and

Africa (25%). This gender-based digital divide prevents women from making full use of the internet. Furthermore, research findings indicate that the dramatic spread of mobile phones is not enough to get women online,[17] as well as that many potential applications of open data are not optimised for mobile phones.

Given the dire reality of the disparity in infrastructure and access, it is no surprise that translating the availability of open data into meaningful applications and inclusive use has been an ongoing challenge.[18] The prerequisite to open data, digital connectivity, cannot be overlooked. Although, as Stephen Song suggests in Chapter 14: Telecommunications, open data on telecoms would help in advocating for better connectivity and addressing regional inequalities. Open data advocates also need to speak up more strongly on issues of internet access. Ultimately, many of the potential benefits of open data are available only to those who have access to internet-connected mobile and/or desktop technology. As a result, anyone developing an open data project needs to be able to answer questions related to who will be able to access its results, what consequences does unequal access have for the project, and whether they can be mitigated.

Even when access is present, alarming impediments to women's participation in digital spaces can be found in gender-based violence (GBV), personal data protection, and privacy concerns. Women worldwide experience higher levels of online harassment than men.[19,20] They may be deterred from contributing to data sources that could otherwise be used to surface and address policy issues because of fears about how personal data may be abused. Although the open data movement has generally focused on non-personally identifying information, many important datasets are derived from personal data, and, as a Web Foundation study conducted in Nigeria has shown, without strong data protection legislation, women may have little or no recourse when personal data breaches occur.[21] For gender data activities to be sustainable, women need to feel safe and secure online, as well as confident that their personal data will be handled safely. Companies, governments, and online communities must work together to stamp out hate speech and misogyny online, making the web a safer space for women.

A key consequence of present patterns of unequal access to internet and data technologies can be found in unequal representation of women within data itself. In the next section, we address the considerations that open data creators, intermediaries, and users need to take into account to work toward gender equity.

Representation

Data is never neutral:[22,23,24] neither politically, technologically, or socio-culturally.[25] Questions of what to collect, how to collect it, and which analytical framework to apply in order to present it, must acknowledge implicit and explicit gender dynamics. Opening up data for those with internet connectivity is a start and can challenge societal gender biases in terms of who controls access to data. However, opening up data should be about more than access. It needs to involve opening that data to scrutiny and bringing into focus questions of how it was created and shaped, and, in particular, how women and issues affecting women's lives are represented in the data upon which decisions may be based.

There are two main issues to be addressed here: data gaps and data distortions. Awareness of both is growing, although, to date, more has been done on addressing gaps in data than has been achieved in creating critical awareness of the way that datasets and their analysis, knowingly or unknowingly, present only a partial and politically loaded view of the world, inhibiting efforts to ensure gender equity.

A gender data gap exists when a dataset describing people, or phenomena affecting people, does not include gender disaggregation, or omits women entirely. Such gaps are often a result of an inherent lack of understanding of how problems affect different genders in different ways. For example, there are problems that women face that cannot be fully understood without specific data in areas such as land inheritance, wage discrimination, and maternal mortality. The Data4SDGs network has argued that "without data equality, there is no gender equality",[26] because when women are invisible in statistics, or statistics cannot tell a story of the comparative position of women and men, it is impossible to meaningfully track progress on gender equity and equality targets.

Data gaps may occur at the time of data collection or when data is aggregated for presentation. Data2X has mapped 28 critical gender data gaps faced in monitoring SDG performance on health, education, economic opportunities, political participation, and human security.[27] They found gender data lacked coverage in terms of countries and/or regular country production. Almost half of the topics reviewed lacked international standards and complexity (information that would allow patterns and determinants of variables to be understood), and more than half of them lacked granularity.[28]

Data2X findings show gaps were particularly pronounced in data relating to employment and entrepreneurship, access to childcare, connectivity, and participation in peace and security processes. While some gaps may exist because survey tools lack fields for disaggregation, others occur due to gender-biased assumptions. One of the most prominent examples of the latter can be found in household surveys that reference the primary activities of the "head of the household", who is often assumed to be male. This kind of bias is also illustrated by the lack of data on women's non-market activities.[29]

Femicide data case study

In Latin America, Article 19 has drawn on the open data agenda in their work to create the report "Data on femicide in Brazil – #InvisibilidadeMata".[30] The project, while it has produced a dossier on the problem, has called for better synchronisation between state datasets that address aspects of violence against women, demonstrating how when data is more open, citizens and NGOs can engage in advocacy for a better data infrastructure and for reliable sources of data on problems that are being ignored or side-lined by a patriarchal political system.

The Latin America Open Data Initiative (ILDA) has also developed a programme of work on data, gender, and security issues across the region with a goal of exploring the development of data standards that could be used to monitor femicides.[31]

As organisations explore complementing conventional data collection with use of private sector big data and citizen-sourced open data to monitor the SDGs in relation to women, approaches to identify data gaps will become more and more important.[32] Beyond the Global North, open data initiatives need to undergo major restructuring efforts in terms of participatory data collection, access, and use. To work toward advancing gender equity, it is critical that marginalised groups are consulted and have a say when new data collection or data release efforts are being designed. Moreover, inclusive design processes can help tackle existing institutional norms of discrimination and exclusion. As long as gender data gaps persist, any open datasets created based on raw data that does not adequately represent women will have limited potential to support transformative action on gender equity.

It is not only statistical data where women may or may not be represented. Connecting sex-disaggregated data to gender-responsive budgeting is another way that the gender data gap can be addressed. Although there have been a number of successful projects in this area, gender-responsive budgeting has not yet been widely adopted.

Data distortions occur when the classifications, categories, and instruments used to capture or analyse data embed certain gender biases; hence, technological affordances and choices play a significant role. Masters quotes Olson's work on library classification systems to illustrate this point.[33] Olson describes how the designer of 1904 library classification standards envisaged a "singular public" who share the same cultural, social, or political interests. Because of the hierarchical nature of the library classification scheme, the introduction of a subdivision in those standards for "relations with women" served to emphasise a social hierarchy, positioning women in relation to men. This marginalisation within data structures can create marginalisation in the real world, shaping the layout of the library, the discoverability of information on women's experience, and marginalisation of the marginalised within library spaces. We live surrounded by a myriad of examples like this within data politics, built up over centuries and continuing to be created today.

Masters calls for "feminist data structuring processes, with equality as the goal", noting that this "would involve a great amount of reflection, articulation, and collaboration".[34] This may seem demanding, but, over time, there have been efforts toward inclusive representation of women in data and classification, enabled and manifested by a shift away from hierarchical organisational technologies toward tagging systems. Open data can be transformed into new data structures, escaping the boundaries of the database within which it was originally collected. The legacy of prior bias is, nevertheless, hard to shift, as, for example, when tags for the writings of women authors still tend to be an expansion of traditional, male-centred classifications.[35] Importantly, while open data does allow some new opportunities for engagement and experimentation with how data is structured, statistical classifications and formal datasets often use rigidly defined structures that may be qualitatively different from the free-form tagging of literary texts. As a result, it is important to think about how women are represented within the bodies setting data collection standards and about the kinds of actions needed to undo decades of accrued bias.

In addressing the representation of women within data, there will also be work needed that goes beyond the limitations of this chapter, addressing other biased classification systems of race, disability, and other areas of inequality. Indeed, work to include non-gender binary groups within data, and to sensitively balance a desire for data minimisation with a desire to understand the gendered dynamics of social policy, will need considerable thought and a commitment to dialogue.

Labour and leadership

Access and representation are issues that affect the entire data landscape, but there are also issues closer to home to be dealt with by the open data community. One of the most important of these relates to the role of women within open data organisations and projects. At the start of this decade, the stereotypical open data organisation was young, urban, white, and male. Anecdotal evidence suggests that this has shifted substantially, but there are still many barriers to gender equity within the institutions that work on open data, and we lack good data on diversity and equity across open data organisations that could be used to benchmark progress.

One indicative dataset to draw upon is the speaker list from the IODCs. From 2015 to 2018, the percentage of women on the speaker list grew from around a third to reach 49%; however, further analysis has found that "women filled 173 (51%) of 337 slots in the schedule, while the men filled 164. In other words, each man spoke, on average, in 1.36 sessions, while each woman spoke in 1.56 sessions or 15% more."[36] As this short study states, "This means that if you were a woman speaking at IODC, you were working 15% harder on average, a number coincidentally matching the gender pay gap of OECD [Organisation for Economic Co-operation and Development] countries."[37] Bursaries, travel funding, and active outreach can all be important to help challenge the reproduction of systemic gender biases in leadership development.

Important barriers to women becoming active in the open data field also include the limited availability of learning opportunities and the structure of many open data projects that rely on gaining skills during "free time". Open data has parallels to open source, where researchers have argued that male participation is effectively "subsidised" by men's access to higher paid employment and a lack of contribution to domestic labour in their free time, increasing their availability to contribute volunteer labour to "open" projects.[38] This requires work on capacity building and data literacy for, and with, women, including raising awareness of the use of data for societal impact. Addressing such global imbalances will require increasing the resources allocated to building e-learning centres and tech hubs that women can use to gain access to internet and open data skills, especially in developing countries and rural areas.[39]

It does not just matter whether women are present in open data organisations. The distribution of labour and the way it is valued also matters. There has been growing recognition that sustaining open data projects, which are often cross-organisational and cross-cultural collaborations, requires a substantial investment of emotional labour.[40] This disproportionately falls to women and is often undervalued. Until the narratives around open data projects better account for the emotional labour and intellectual labour that makes for the success of projects, rather than focusing on solely technological innovation, recognition and reward is not likely to be equitably distributed.

When it comes to gender data projects specifically, women often work on and drive these projects alone. Ultimately, the issue of gender data work should not be solely placed on the backs of gender data organisations. Gender issues need to be better mainstreamed into the work of all open data organisations. There are promising signs of this in organisations such as ILDA which has sought to establish internal self-reflection processes around gender dynamics within a gender-mixed project team working on data and security. Building on this and working across organisations to create good practice resources and handbooks that can be used to improve organisational policy and practice may be a good starting point.

In 2018, the year of the #MeToo movement, we cannot ignore the civic technology sector's own challenges with respect to discrimination, harassment, and abuse. Events have revealed the need for change in individual attitudes and in organisational responses to harassment or abuse cases. More open data conferences now have codes of conduct in an effort to create safer spaces for women, but there is still a long way to go. Significant advances will only come with clear leadership within the open data field and critical reflection from everyone on how to create safe, inclusive, and empowering spaces. Gender is a personal issue; therefore, personal self-reflection among men is needed. This is especially true for men involved in technology and open data, who may see themselves as not contributing to the problem through direct discrimination, but who are contributing to the problem indirectly. This need for self-reflection is a part of a larger cultural challenge that needs to be addressed actively in both professional and personal capacities.

Conclusion

The chapter has explored key issues concerning gender equity in open data, including issues related to infrastructure and access, as well as the representation of women in datasets, open data labour, and open data leadership. It has also attempted to address where progress has been made to date and to sketch out key actions that need to be taken going forward. In particular, there is a need to build bridges between open data organisations and more specialised gender organisations. Action is needed at regional, national, and global levels. Datasets need to be generated, policies need to be adopted and implemented, opportunities need to be created and safe spaces need to be provided. As a community, open data stakeholders may want to consider a collective code of conduct against gender-based harassment that could be endorsed by organisations, governments, and companies. This would also strengthen any existing internal codes and policies and promote best practices.

The nature of empowerment must be explored by individuals and organisations in the attempt to better identify biases in current open data work and to understand what needs to be challenged, and, in turn, changed. Existing power dynamics in open data need to be actively addressed, especially those related to gender equity, race, and inclusion, in order to solve long-standing inequalities, or open data will continue to only empower the empowered.[41]

As the drivers of a movement, the open data community must track the gender impacts of its own activities. Ultimately, patriarchal norms must be confronted to realise the full potential of gender equity in open data. Targeted interventions to address access and the needs of women and girls is vital, but there is a foundational need to change the perception of norms and the way people think about gender. This is not simply about the technology or data per se, but about the fundamental way we think about gender and gender dynamics.

Further reading

Ada: A Journal of Gender, New Media, and Technology is an open-access peer reviewed journal featuring scholarship on gender, new media, and technology. http://adanewmedia.org

Gurumurthy, A. & Chami, N. (2016). "Data: The new four letter word". *GenderIT.org* [Article], 31 May. https://www.genderit.org/articles/data-new-four-letter-word-feminism

Masters, C.L. (2015). Women's ways of structuring data. *Ada: A Journal of Gender, New Media, & Technology*, 8. http://adanewmedia.org/2015/11/issue8-masters/

Ørnemark, C. (2017). Gender and open data: "Is there an app for that?" *ICTUpdate*, 84. http://ictupdate.cta.int/2017/03/01/gender-and-open-data-is-there-an-app-for-that/

About the authors

Ana Brandusescu researches and advocates for a more transparent, inclusive, and responsible use of existing and emerging technologies through data and policy projects. These include initiatives on open data, data governance, open government, and digital equality.

Nnenna Nwakanma advocates for open data, open government, and the open web across the world, bringing together local and international stakeholders to advance an open and inclusive development agenda. Speaker, mentor, and leader, she inspires women to aspire more, learn more, and achieve more through technology.

The authors would like to acknowledge the contributions to this chapter of Tina Appiah, Dhanaraj Thakur, Fabrizio Scrollini, Nancy Salem, Paulina Bustos, Mor Rubinstein, Noémie Girard, Martin Bader, Selene Yang, Kate Vang, Joshua Powell, James McKinney, Manuel Acevedo, David Sasaki, Ruba Ishak, Policy Ignite, Gabriela Rodriguez, Jonathan van Geuns, and Steven Adler.

How to cite this chapter

Brandusescu, A. & Nwakanma, N. (2019). Issues in open data: Gender equity. In T. Davies, S. Walker, M. Rubinstein, & F. Perini (Eds.), *The state of open data: Histories and horizons* (pp. 287–299). Cape Town and Ottawa: African Minds and International Development Research Centre. http://stateofopendata.od4d.net

This work is licensed under a Creative Commons Attribution 4.0 International (CC BY 4.0) licence. It was carried out with the aid of a grant from the International Development Research Centre, Ottawa, Canada.

Endnotes

1. https://sustainabledevelopment.un.org/sdg5
2. ILO. (2000). *ABC of women workers' rights and gender equality*. Geneva: International Labour Organization. http://www.ilo.org/global/publications/books/WCMS_080613/lang--en/index.htm
3. Mencarini, L. (2014). Gender equity. In A.C. Michalos (Ed.), *Encyclopedia of quality of life and well-being research* (pp. 2437–2438). Dordrecht: Springer. https://doi.org/10.1007/978-94-007-0753-5_1131
4. Connell, R.W. (2005). Change among the gatekeepers: Men, masculinities, and gender equality in the global arena. *Signs: Journal of Women in Culture and Society*, *30(3)*, 1801–1825.
5. See *Ada: A Journal of Gender, New Media, and Technology*. http://adanewmedia.org
6. Gurumurthy, A. & Chami, N. (2016). Data: The new four-letter word for feminism. *GenderIT.org* [Article], 31 May. https://www.genderit.org/articles/data-new-four-letter-word-feminism
7. http://techmousso.ci/
8. Web Foundation. (2016). Beyond gender commitments: OGP needs to "walk the talk". Washington, DC: World Wide Web Foundation. https://webfoundation.org/2016/12/beyond-gender-commitments-ogp-needs-to-walk-the-talk/
9. Open Heroines. (2016). Open gender monologues. *Open Heroines Blog*, 30 December. https://openheroines.org/open-gender-monologues-the-stories-of-women-in-the-open-government-movement-26f7766e3e9f
10. Open Heroines. (2016). Hello, we are Open Heroines. *Open Heroines Blog*, 16 May. https://openheroines.org/hello-we-are-open-heroines-8e7830e3b3a0
11. https://www.data2x.org/who-we-are/
12. https://atgenderconference2017.wordpress.com/
13. https://smartcity.brussels/news-187-the-results-are-in-of-the-open-data-brussels-goes-gender-smart-hackathon
14. http://africaopendata.net/
15. http://labs.webfoundation.org/projects-2/genderdevelopment/
16. ITU. (2017). *ICT facts and figures 2017*. Geneva: International Telecommunications Union. https://www.itu.int/en/ITU-D/Statistics/Documents/facts/ICTFactsFigures2017.pdf
17. Web Foundation. (2015). *Women's rights online: Translating access into empowerment*. Washington, DC: World Wide Web Foundation. https://webfoundation.org/research/womens-rights-online-2015/
18. Bezuidenhout, L.M., Leonelli, S., Kelly, A.H., & Rappert, B. (2017). Beyond the digital divide: Towards a situated approach to open data. *Science and Public Policy*, *44(4)*, 464–475. https://academic.oup.com/spp/article/44/4/464/3959654
19. Mozilla. (2018). Fighting online harassment with artificial intelligence. *Internet Health Report*. https://internethealthreport.org/2018/fighting-online-harassment-with-artificial-intelligence/
20. Web Foundation. (2015). *Women's rights online: Translating access into empowerment*. Washington, DC: World Wide Web Foundation. https://webfoundation.org/research/womens-rights-online-2015/
21. Izuogu, C. (2018). *Personal data protection in Nigeria*. Washington, DC: World Wide Web Foundation and Paradigm Initiative. https://webfoundation.org/research/personal-data-protection-in-nigeria/
22. Johnson, J.A. (2015). How data does political things: The processes of encoding and decoding data are never neutral. *LSE Impact Blog*. London: London School of Economics and Political Science. http://blogs.lse.ac.uk/impactofsocialsciences/2015/10/07/how-data-does-political-things/
23. Johnson, J.A. (2018). The political life of metrics. *Toward Information Justice: Technology, Politics, and Policy for Data in Higher Education Administration*, *33*, 83–105. Cham: Springer. https://doi.org/10.1007/978-3-319-70894-2_4
24. Gitelman, L. (2013). *Raw data is an oxymoron*. Cambridge, MA: MIT Press.

25 Brandusescu, A. (2017). Open data is about people, not just innovation. *SciDev.Net*, 8 June. https://www.scidev.net/global/data/opinion/open-data-people-innovation.html

26 Data2X. (2017). Without data equality, there is no gender equality. *Global Partnership for Sustainable Development Data*, 2 August. http://www.data4sdgs.org/news/without-data-equality-there-no-gender-equality

27 https://www.data2x.org/what-is-gender-data/gender-data-gaps/

28 Ibid.

29 Brandusescu, A. & Nwakanma, N. (2018), Is open data working for women in Africa? *World Wide Web Foundation* [News and blogs],13 July. https://webfoundation.org/2018/07/is-open-data-working-for-women-in-africa/

30 Article 19. (2018). Brazil: New research on open data and cases of femicide. *ARTICLE 19*, 8 March. https://www.article19.org/resources/brazil-new-research-on-open-data-and-cases-of-femicide/

31 https://idatosabiertos.org/en/algunas-novedades-de-nuestro-trabajo-sobre-datos-genero-y-seguridad/

32 http://www.unwomen.org/en/news/in-focus/women-and-the-sdgs

33 Olson, H.A. (2001). The power to name: Representation in library catalogs. *Signs*, *26(3)*, 639–668.

34 Masters, C.L. (2015). Women's ways of structuring data. *Ada: A Journal of Gender, New Media, and Technology*, *8*. https://adanewmedia.org/2015/11/issue8-masters/

35 Butler, T., Fisher, S., Coulombe, G., Clements, P., Grundy, I., Brown, S., Wood, J., & Cameron, R. (2000). Can a team tag consistently? Experiences on the Orlando Project. *Markup Languages*, *2(2)*, 111–125.

36 McKinney, J. & Brandusescu, A. (2018). #IODC18: How'd we do on gender balance? *Open Heroines Blog*, 14 November. https://openheroines.org/iodc18-howd-we-do-on-gender-balance-dbf2a9c8f648

37 Ibid.

38 Berry, D.M. (2008). *Copy, rip, burn: The politics of copyleft and open source* (pp.138–140). London: Pluto Press.

39 Kingboye, D. (2018). Women Economic and Leadership Transformation Initiative Open Data Event 2018. *Open Knowledge International Blog*, 18 April. https://blog.okfn.org/2018/04/18/women-economic-and-leadership-transformation-initiative-welti-open-data-event-2018/

40 Fessler, L. (2018). An extremely clear definition of emotional labor for anyone who still doesn't get it. *Quartz at Work Blog*, 24 May. https://qz.com/work/1286996/an-extremely-clear-definition-of-emotional-labor-from-adam-grants-podcast/

41 Gurstein, M.B. (2011). Open data: Empowering the empowered or effective data use for everyone? *First Monday*, *16(2)*. https://firstmonday.org/ojs/index.php/fm/article/view/3316

021

Indigenous data sovereignty

Stephanie Carroll Rainie, Tahu Kukutai, Maggie Walter,
Oscar Luis Figueroa-Rodríguez, Jennifer Walker, and Per Axelsson

Key points

- Indigenous Data Sovereignty (IDS) has emerged as an important topic over the last three years, raising fundamental questions about assumptions of ownership, representation, and control in open data communities.

- IDS refers to the right of Indigenous peoples to control data from and about their communities and lands, articulating both individual and collective rights to data access and to privacy.

- Ideas from IDS provide a challenge to dominant discourses in open data, questioning current approaches to data ownership, licensing, and use in ways that resonate beyond Indigenous contexts, drawing attention to the power and post-colonial dynamics within many data agendas.

- Growing IDS networks are working to shape open data principles to better respect the rights of Indigenous peoples.

Introduction

"Open data in the context of Indigenous peoples is a double-edged sword."[1]

Open data is a site of tension for Indigenous peoples. Open data provides opportunities for sustainable development according to Indigenous aspirations, yet also sits at the nexus of current and historic data challenges as a result of colonisation, bias, and a lack of knowledge of Indigenous rights. Indigenous data sovereignty (IDS) provides a framework for maximising the benefit of open data for Indigenous peoples and other users of Indigenous data and for affecting the stewardship of all data. Open data communities often assume many binaries, including a single government actor (nation-states), that data is open or not, and that open data is useful data (devoid of biases and relevance issues). In the context of Indigenous peoples, there are clear challenges for the mainstream open data movement around these binaries, as well as paths forward to assure the protection of Indigenous rights and data for development.

IDS refers to the right of Indigenous peoples to govern the collection, ownership, and application of data about Indigenous communities, peoples, lands, and resources. Indigenous data is defined here as data in a wide variety of formats inclusive of digital data and data as knowledge and information. It encompasses data, information, and knowledge about Indigenous individuals, collectives, entities, lifeways, cultures, lands, and resources.[2,3,4,5] Under IDS, the data governance rights of Indigenous nations apply regardless of where the data is held or by whom. This includes the right to the generation of the data that Indigenous peoples require to support nation rebuilding and governance. IDS concerns itself with binary digital data (e.g. scientific, administrative, corporate), as well as information and knowledge, meaning a somewhat broader scope than normally considered by the open data movement. However, all too often researchers, agency staff, and others digitise Indigenous knowledge and information and enter it into open data arenas without the express permission of Indigenous peoples.[6] While these acts may be well-intentioned, the result is the co-opting of Indigenous knowledge and the removal of Indigenous peoples from data governance processes. Therefore, IDS also comprises the entitlement to determine how Indigenous data is governed and stewarded, referred to as Indigenous data governance (IDG). IDS covers both data for governance and IDG.[7,8]

Over the past three years, during the first iteration of the Open Data Charter (ODC),[9] IDS became a global movement. The initial establishment phase, beginning in 2015, was primarily focused on raising awareness of IDS within Indigenous nations and nation-state data entities. As of 2018, IDG principles and protocols are now being conceptualised and operationalised across nation-states and across the broad terrain of Indigenous data realities. These actions notwithstanding, in the open data community, there remains a general lack of knowledge or understanding of IDS.

To date, open data policy and discussions have largely been framed around the needs and interests of nation-states and of open data advocates and users with minimal Indigenous engagement. This is unacceptable from an IDS perspective because of the potential conflicts between open data goals and the aspirations of Indigenous nations and peoples. For example, the ODC states that "Open data is digital data that is made available with the technical and legal characteristics necessary for it to be freely used, reused, and redistributed by anyone, anytime, anywhere."[10] This is a lofty goal, but the objective is in direct tension with the rights of Indigenous peoples to govern their data, including the right to decide what is shared or withheld, likely resulting from the ODC being developed without the involvement of Indigenous peoples. Articulating this fundamental tension, and how it can be addressed through Indigenous data governance and stewardship mechanisms, underpins this chapter.

Indigenous peoples

The United Nations (UN) estimated in 2009 that there were approximately 370 million Indigenous peoples living in 90 countries, with up to 5 000 different Indigenous cultures around the world.[11] Concern for many years about the rights of Indigenous peoples led to the establishment of the United Nations Permanent Forum on Indigenous Issues (UNPFII) in 2000.[12] This body is mandated to deal with Indigenous issues related to economic and social development, culture, education, health, and rights. The UNPFII defines Indigenous peoples as those who are

> *inheritors and practitioners of unique cultures and ways of relating to people and the environment. They have retained social, cultural, economic and political characteristics that are distinct from those of the dominant societies in which they live. Despite their cultural differences, Indigenous peoples from around the world share common problems related to the protection of their rights as distinct peoples.*[13]

As a means of setting a minimum standard to protect the rights of Indigenous peoples, the UN has developed the *UN Declaration on the Rights of Indigenous Peoples* (UNDRIP).[14] Adopted by the General Assembly of the United Nations in September 2007, it develops a cohesive set of Indigenous peoples' rights through 46 articles.[15] Article 18, in particular, is relevant to Indigenous data rights, stating that Indigenous peoples have the right to participate in decision-making in matters which would affect their rights in accordance with their own procedures. It is also important to note that in the context of Indigenous data, the UNDRIP specifically addresses the collective rights of Indigenous peoples.

Indigenous peoples and data

Data collection: Invisibility and bias

Indigenous nations need data about their citizens, communities, lands, resources, and culture to make informed decisions. Yet few official statistics agencies, researchers, and data collectors make any meaningful concession to Indigenous rights in relation to Indigenous data. Despite being the rights holders in relation to data about them or for them, Indigenous peoples across nation-states remain peripheral to the channels of power through which consequential decisions about Indigenous statistics are made.[16] This marginalisation continues within open data discussions, the open data community, and the ODC itself.

There are also numerous contexts in which Indigenous peoples are invisible in their national statistics systems. A recent study showed that in the global 2010 Census round (2005–2014), under half of the countries that encompassed at least one Indigenous people actually included an Indigenous identifier on their census form.[17] This is particularly a challenge in the Global South in regions such as Africa where Indigenous peoples are not counted or recognised.

In nations where Indigenous data is collected, federal, state, and local governments, as well as researchers, primarily collect data with limited input from the Indigenous nations, communities, and individuals described. The result is that Indigenous nations rely on external data that largely fails to reflect community needs, priorities, and self-conceptions. This data imbalance threatens self-determination, limits informed policy decisions, and restricts progress toward Indigenous aspirations for healthy, sustainable communities.[18,19,20] Likewise, reliance on this data by researchers and governments limits the robustness of data-driven research and the validity of policy decisions. The IDS movement has been critical to fostering discussions and actions to improve the quality and relevance of official statistics data to Indigenous peoples and other policy-makers.

Australia – Closing the gap

The Indigenous peoples of Australia are comprised of two separate groups, Australian Aborigines and people from the Torres Strait Islands. Torres Strait Islander people make up about 10% of the total. While conventionally combined for statistical purposes, the two populations are not homogeneous and have significant demographic, social, and cultural differences. Regardless of population, the collection of Indigenous data in Australia has a fraught history. Until amended by referendum in 1967, Section 127 of the Australian Constitution specifically excluded the "aboriginal race" from official population figures.[21]

The first Census of Population and Housing inclusion of Indigenous peoples was in 1971. The reliable collection of Indigenous data has developed only slowly since then and not always in positive directions. The importance of Indigenous data is increasingly recognised within official statistical agencies, policy areas, and public and private administrative entities, yet there remains a fixed focus on what the government wants to know about Aboriginal and Torres Strait Islander people and very little on what Aboriginal and Torres Strait Islander people need to know.

There is also very little true engagement with Aboriginal and Torres Strait Islander people on what data is collected, why that data is collected, or the data needs of Indigenous Australians. Not coincidentally, the primary Indigenous policy which identifies the *Closing the Gap* targets developed by national and state governments is now being refreshed. After ten years, no socioeconomic or health gaps have been closed and only a minority of targets have shown either absolute or relative improvement in that period.[22]

As a way of advancing Indigenous data governance in Australia, an Indigenous Data Sovereignty Summit for Aboriginal and Torres Strait Islander leaders across academia, peak bodies, and community organisations was held in June 2018 as a partnership between the Miaim nayri Wingari Indigenous Data Sovereignty Group and the Australian Indigenous Governance Institute, with the outcomes delivered in a Summit Communique.[23]

> ### Sweden – Absence of data
>
> The European Union General Data Protection Regulation (GDPR) replaced the Personal Data Act in Sweden in 2018 but maintained that the processing of data that reveals ethnicity or race is prohibited. This regulation was first introduced in the Data Act (1973:289) and has severely impaired discussions in relation to Indigenous data.
>
> Sweden is an example of a welfare state where health equity and equality are advanced, and where epidemiology and health statistics are cutting-edge, but also where laws surrounding data have resulted in Sweden being unable to provide any significant data to understand the health and social well-being of the Sámi, its Indigenous people. This circumstance also means that there is little official data produced by the state that Sámi people can take ownership of.
>
> Indigenous data is mainly produced by researchers and is guarded by Swedish ethical protocols that do not take Sámi ownership or control into account.[24] However, things have recently been moving forward due to increased pressure from Sámi society and non-governmental organisations (NGOs) that have called for a truth and reconciliation commission, ethical guidelines for Sámi research, a consultation order for Sámi issues, and enhancement of the Sámi Parliament's role in the collection of data. Together with the implementation of a Nordic Saami Convention, this may force the Swedish state to open up for discussions on ownership and governance of data.

Data access, use, and interpretation

There are multiple problems with the ways in which state agencies have collected, stored, analysed, and disseminated data about Indigenous peoples and their lands and resources, which have been well documented across a range of contexts and timeframes.[25,26,27,28,29] The information that Indigenous nations have access to is often unreliable, inaccurate, irrelevant, and fraught by a long-standing mistrust of data and data systems by Indigenous peoples.[30] Furthermore, statistics about Indigenous peoples often perpetuate a narrative of inequality, creating a dominant portrait of Indigenous peoples as defined by their statistically measured disparity, deprivation, disadvantage, dysfunction, and difference.[31] Data infrastructures are designed based on cultural assumptions that can lead to the systematic misrepresentation of Indigenous peoples (e.g. not allowing for the entry of names that do not conform to the dominant cultures naming conventions).[32] Further, conceptualisations of open data purely as digital data produce an area ripe for knowledge co-optation and the theft of Indigenous knowledge as, for example, in cases where researchers or others who collect Indigenous knowledge about the environment (as opposed to digital data) digitise that knowledge and then share it openly without consent or oversight from Indigenous peoples.[33]

Indigenous peoples and nations experience a number of challenges in accessing data. These difficulties are driven both by internal and external environments.[34,35,36] External challenges include inconsistent Indigenous identifiers, the siloing of data by sector, laborious or unclear data sharing and access protocols, low investments in Indigenous peoples' data science skills, and Indigenous nations' data infrastructures. Internally, for Indigenous nations and peoples, there are difficulties in accessing and paying for programmes to build data capacity and a general lack of access to digital hardware, software, connectivity, and funding for issue-specific capacities.

The inconsistencies and inadequacies of, and lack of access to, existing Indigenous data systems have led to researchers, data repositories, and data service operations being increasingly aware of the need to understand IDS. At the same time, few researchers, governments, or organisations are aware of the appropriate processes. Thus, the aim is for governments, researchers, funders, and others to choose data governance and stewardship mechanisms that better align with Indigenous rights and aspirations; to improve data quality, access, and value; and to invest in building data capacity and infrastructure.

Mexico – Data access

Mexico's Indigenous population (7.4 million) represents about 6% of the total population in the country. Most of Mexico's Indigenous peoples live under marginalised conditions (87.6%). Only 15% report having access to a computer, and only 10% report having access to the internet. This alone represents a big challenge for open data availability within Mexican Indigenous communities, despite the existence of a well-established government open data platform.[37] Furthermore, even if accessed, data interpretation and use is limited or irrelevant since there are limited capacities within Indigenous communities to make sense of data available from open data platforms.

The average education level for Indigenous people in Mexico is five years of school attendance, representing less than the completion of elementary school. Nevertheless, as a first step toward recognising IDS, an Indigenous consultation law has been drafted which will establish the right for Indigenous groups to be consulted regarding, among other topics, their natural resources and land use. Such consultation is to be prior to action, free, and informed. This last point implies the right to access information presented in a fashion understandable and relevant to Indigenous communities in advance of consultation.

Data ownership and appropriation

IDS derives from inherent sovereignty and finds its genesis in the oral traditions of Indigenous peoples and community roles and responsibilities.[38] The collection, storage, sharing, and use of data have been a strong part of Indigenous cultural knowledge throughout history[39] with data storage taking diverse forms, including art, painting, written records, oral traditions, and stories. Open data communities often solely consider data as digital. There is often a focus on quantitative information at the expense of qualitative information based on the lived experience. IDS constitutes a challenge to this narrow conception of data both by protecting knowledge and information that may be taken and digitised and by underscoring that there are other ways of knowing. IDS is then also a broader critique of the turn to digital data in governmental and societal "ways of knowing".

IDS also refers to a collective right to data.[40,41] While individuals may hold data and have data rights, Indigenous peoples as collectives (or nations) have the right to govern the data about their peoples, lands, and resources. This represents several implications for open data and big data: conceptualising collective rights for data linkage, sharing, and use; protecting data used to describe or compare Indigenous nations; and exploring collective rights of Indigenous nations to privacy and confidentiality. While these and other issue areas have been identified in relation to Indigenous peoples' collective rights to data, the IDG and data stewardship mechanisms and legal strategies have yet to be fully realised. However, some international standards, particularly those set by the UN, support Indigenous peoples' collective rights to govern data.

As previously noted, Article 18 of the UNDRIP stipulates the right to participate in decision-making in matters affecting Indigenous rights and to maintain and develop Indigenous decision-making institutions. As Kukutai and Taylor argue,[42] the UNDRIP raises urgent questions about the proper role of state machinery in gathering statistics on Indigenous peoples. The UNDRIP also clearly set outs the rights of Indigenous peoples related to data about them. As per Articles 3, 5, and 23, Indigenous peoples have the right to self-determination, inclusive of the right to control and determine what for them as Indigenous peoples constitutes economic, social, and cultural development. The functional planning and implementation of that development is reliant on data – data that Indigenous peoples currently do not have access to or does not exist.

The UN Sustainable Development Goals (SDGs) provide an example of engagement to support Indigenous rights and development according to Indigenous aspirations. The "Transforming Our World: The 2030 Agenda for Sustainable Development" resolution[43] refers to Indigenous peoples six times, underscoring the need for the participation of Indigenous peoples at the country level and calling for disaggregated data on Indigenous status on Indigenous peoples' terms, aligning with the UNDRIP and other human rights standards. Since the open data of nation-states plays a key role in tracking progress toward the SDGs, the engagement of Indigenous peoples and respect for Indigenous rights must be fundamental components of this process, as well as the open data principles of the ODC and practices.

In some cases related to the preservation and/or exploitation of natural resources, Indigenous rights are established in legal international protocols. Article 26 of The Cartagena Protocol on Biosafety regarding socioeconomic considerations, for example, establishes that parties "may take into account … the impact of living modified organisms on the conservation and sustainable use of biological diversity, especially with regard to the value of biological diversity to Indigenous and local communities".[44] With regard to the Nagoya Protocol on access to genetic resources and the fair and equitable sharing of benefits arising from their utilisation, Article 12 on traditional knowledge associated with genetic resources states that parties "shall in accordance with domestic law take into consideration Indigenous and local communities' customary laws, community protocols and procedures, as applicable, with respect to traditional knowledge associated with genetic resources".[45]

> ### Nagoya Protocol – Who benefits from data?
>
> Benefits stemming from access to data should be mutual among all actors involved, particularly data related to traditional knowledge from Indigenous communities. The Nagoya Protocol[46] serves as an important reference regarding three main issues:
>
> 1. **The importance of establishing proper mechanisms and legal grounds to achieve mutual benefits from data use.** Article 7 establishes that "In accordance with domestic law, each Party shall take measures, as appropriate, with the aim of ensuring that traditional knowledge associated with genetic resources that is held by Indigenous and local communities is accessed with the prior and informed consent or approval and involvement of these Indigenous and local communities, and that mutually agreed terms have been established" (p. 7).
>
> 2. **The relevance of raising awareness about data exploitation** regarding traditional knowledge in relation to genetic resources through education and training (capacity building) about data access, interpretation, and use. Article 21 paragraph (g) establishes the need to take measures to raise awareness regarding "education and training of users and providers of genetic resources and traditional knowledge associated with genetic resources about their access and benefit-sharing obligations" (p. 16). All this should be developed in a culturally sensitive fashion.
>
> 3. **The importance of maintaining an awareness of the delicate position of the least developed countries** which are inhabited by a number of Indigenous communities that generally have increased difficulty with accessing open data sources.
>
> These issues illustrate the importance of properly establishing common legal and operational grounds regarding data exploitation of any kind in relation to Indigenous knowledge and resources, including not only genetic resources but also cultural, demographic, and other types.

As political entities, Indigenous peoples and nations are more than mere "stakeholders" in data ecosystems.[47] They have the right to control data about their peoples, lands, and resources. That right is the fundamental difference in the relationship between Indigenous peoples and Indigenous data and other stakeholders' relationships with Indigenous data. Data stakeholders include nation-states and other governments, researchers, NGOs, Indigenous organisations, funders, and IDS networks. These stakeholders have diverse interests in Indigenous data and, at times, are in situations to govern or steward Indigenous data.

Increases in knowledge and awareness of IDS in Aotearoa/New Zealand, Australia, Canada, Sweden, and the United States (US) are occurring at multiple levels and among a variety of rights holders and stakeholders (e.g. Indigenous nations and peoples, nation-state and local governments, non-profits/NGOs, researchers). Although IDS is not currently an open data concern for most nation-states, incremental efforts to improve the standing of Indigenous peoples and nations in relation to open data are occurring.

Canada – Data governance and informing the nation-to-nation relationship

Canada's Open Government Plan with respect to Indigenous data has been evolving. The plan has gone from promoting programme access for First Nations people to recognition of the developing nation-to-nation relationship between Indigenous nations in Canada, including over 600 First Nations, Metis Nations, Inuit, and the federal Crown. Canada has made a commitment to reflect this renewed relationship in open government planning. It is expected that Canada's Open Government Plan will continue to evolve as these nations assert data sovereignty. Across Canada, the conversation about open data also involves provincial and territorial governments. For example, the Ktunaxa Nation asserts data sovereignty and will work with both the governments of Canada and British Columbia to determine the parameters for opening data related to their Nation or to their people.

Aotearoa/New Zealand – Embedding Māori data sovereignty across the government

Aotearoa/New Zealand is one of the world's most advanced digital nations.[48] Data is seen as a key national strategic asset, and several policy and legislative initiatives are underway to facilitate easier data sharing and linkage. The Integrated Data Infrastructure (IDI), a world-leading research database, contains de-identified data from more than 50 surveys and administrative datasets across the state, research, and NGO sectors. There is also increasing interest in how a "social licence" can enable more flexible data sharing without individual consent, and the government recently adopted the ODC. Missing, however, are robust, innovative models of data governance and ethics, value creation, and benefit-sharing.

Māori have well-tested "tikanga" (ethics, processes, principles) around the protection and sharing of knowledge for collective benefit that can be readily adapted to digital data environments. Māori Data Sovereignty (MDS) advocates are developing a number of tikanga-based solutions, including models of Māori/iwi (tribal) data governance for the IDI and wider government ecosystem, a "cultural license" as the "social licence" alternative for community acceptability of data use, and a Māori Data Audit Tool to assess organisational readiness to incorporate MDS principles. The potential benefits of embedding MDS principles across government data ecosystems extend beyond Māori to include the wider Aotearoa/New Zealand public.

Challenging the dominant data discourse

As the scale and scope of Indigenous peoples' economic, social, and cultural development accelerates, the demand for data is increasing. Indigenous nations also are seeking methods to protect and control their proprietary information, especially data stewarded by other governments, non-profits, and researchers. At the same time, non-tribal entities and individuals stewarding and using Indigenous data increasingly recognise the need to protect information about Indigenous nations and peoples. Often, this data collection and usage exists in a vacuum with little to no guidance from others, given the unique circumstances of Indigenous peoples' data. These are issues not just of IDS but also of IDG. These issues are crystallised when set against key principles and goals set out in the ODC.[49] This section addresses the ODC, discussing assumptions which underlie the movement, including assumptions around democracy and citizenship that are highly problematic for Indigenous peoples. It then presents a path forward for engaging with Indigenous peoples around open data at the nation-state and international levels through existing and nascent IDS networks.

Principle 1: Open by default

As the name suggests, this principle supports the open use of data as the norm, shifting the onus onto governments to justify why and when data should be kept closed (e.g. for security or data protection reasons). In general, the argument behind the open data movements has been that with data in the open, discussions to improve interpretation can then take place. This assumes particular positions of privilege in relation to access to public debate, but also in how that data is interpreted. The problem here is that very few governments have supported or incorporated IDG principles into the values and principles that guide open data practices. A lack of IDG principles results in the absence of processes aligned with Indigenous rights to guide decision-making for how and why Indigenous data should be shared and in the ethical use of that data. More fundamentally, opening Indigenous data by default bypasses entirely the rights of Indigenous peoples to decide what, if any, of their data should be shared, let alone issues of ownership. In the absence of such basic decision-making ability, there is a heightened risk of data misinterpretation and misuse.

While the ODC recognises the need to protect individual privacy and to adhere to domestic laws, it is silent on the issue of collective privacy. Yet this is a crucial factor for Indigenous peoples, especially with the move toward algorithmic decision-making and data mining. National privacy laws are increasingly being revised to strengthen the protection of personal data privacy and impose penalties for data breaches, but they have yet to grapple with more complex issues of collective privacy, and, thus, they offer minimal protection. Likewise, open data licensing regimes do not generally accommodate collective rights, and reuse often relies on use of permissive licensing with few restrictions. These Eurocentric conceptualisations of privacy and licensing challenge IDS collective rights to data and are also problematic in many other societies with imbalances in power, such as those with a post-colonial context.

Principle 5: Improved governance and citizen engagement

As data becomes available through open data portals, more sectors and individuals gain access. However, for Indigenous peoples, one of the key challenges to open data is the risk of interpreting results in the absence of historical, cultural, political, and social contexts. This risk could even further marginalise and stigmatise Indigenous peoples, ostensibly the opposite of what is intended. There will be unintended and pejorative consequences for Indigenous peoples if open data movements do not acknowledge the bias and values inherent in all data.

The choice of what is counted, the ways that people are categorised and grouped, and the methods of data collection all reflect decisions made by people who may not have the cultural or contextual knowledge to interpret data fairly. For example, findings may show that the prevalence of chronic disease is higher for Indigenous people living in cities than for those who are living in more remote traditional lands and communities. The data could be used to justify decreased resources to communities for chronic disease management; however, a key underlying reason for the difference may be the pre-existing lack of resources in the communities that force people to relocate to seek care.

As per inherent sovereignty rights underscored by UNDRIP, and recognition by nation-states, particularly Aotearoa/New Zealand, Canada, and the US, Indigenous peoples have the right to control the data about them. Additionally, Indigenous data histories are plagued by the misuse and misinterpretation of Indigenous data,[50,51] sometimes intentionally, sometimes not. Without Indigenous data ownership and control, data can inadvertently result in a perpetuation of marginalisation. But while results may be inadvertent, a lack of knowledge does not exonerate those who cause it. Only through engagement with, and active control over, data by Indigenous peoples can the inadvertent wrongs be righted, and, ultimately, the benefits of data be realised for governance.

Principle 6: Inclusive development and innovation

This principle recognises that open data can "help to identify social and economic challenges, and monitor and deliver sustainable development programs. Open data can also help meet global challenges such as poverty, hunger, climate change, and inequality." These goals are indeed laudable and highly relevant for Indigenous peoples who, through processes of colonisation and colonialism, incur systematic social, economic, and political disadvantage in most, if not all, national contexts.[52] For many decades, Indigenous peoples have often been the targets of policy interventions aimed at improving their socioeconomic position, but they have rarely been asked, let alone empowered, to contribute their own solutions. It is not uncommon for Indigenous values to clash with the development goals of national governments and, at times, even intergovernmental organisations and international NGOs, particularly in relation to environmental stewardship. The principle of inclusive development and innovation needs to be tempered with an appreciation of the fraught relationship that many Indigenous communities have experienced in the name of development, democracy, and citizenship, as well as an awareness of the systemic barriers that continue to make it challenging for Indigenous peoples to take leadership of solutions which support their own aspirations (including data-driven solutions).

Developing a new discourse

To date, three national-level IDS networks exist: Te Mana Raraunga Māori Data Sovereignty Network,[53] the United States Indigenous Data Sovereignty Network (USIDSN),[54] and the Maiam nayri Wingara Aboriginal and Torres Strait Islander Data Sovereignty Collective in Australia.[55] Similar initiatives are underway elsewhere, including in Scandinavia, where there is not yet an established network, but two Sámi research centres (Umeå University and UiT – The Arctic University of Norway) have recently started discussions on establishing a network. And while the use of IDS terminology is relatively new, the First Nations Information Governance Centre (FNIGC) in Canada has been a leading voice for the rights of Indigenous peoples in relation to their data for over two decades.[56]

The First Nations principles of OCAP® (standing for data Ownership, Control, Access, and Possession) are a set of standards that establish how First Nations data should be collected, protected, used, or shared and are now the *de facto* standard for how to conduct research with Canadian First Nations.[57] Building off the strong history of Indigenous rights in relation to data, a network focused on IDS is being incubated in Canada.

Currently, these networks are engaging in an informal, and somewhat ad hoc fashion, to share information and strategies, hold joint events, and collaborate on research. In the last three years alone, this spirit of collaboration has produced seven events, ten joint panel/workshop initiatives, and a co-edited book, *Indigenous data sovereignty: Toward an agenda*.[58] Freely available online, the book was downloaded more than 8 000 times in its first year, reflecting the very high level of international interest in IDS.

In 2017, the founders of the existing networks joined to create the International Indigenous Data Sovereignty Interest Group at the Research Data Alliance (RDA IDS Group).[59] This group is committed to expanding the IDS discussion beyond North America and Australasia to include the Global South, notably South America and Africa. The RDA IDS Group also supports the drafting of principles for the governance of Indigenous data for adoption and implementation by international research organisations.

IDS network engagement with other data actors has occurred both at the nation-state and international levels across a range of data topics, including privacy, ethics, research data, big data, open data, and many others. Open data is just one aspect of the larger data and Indigenous data sovereignty discussions. Open data agents and actors must recognise that Indigenous peoples and networks, which have already experienced bias, disregard, and limited investment in data capability and capacity, are operating across a range of topics. Of the almost unlimited amount of work still to be undertaken, open data is but one aspect.

The Canadian government has recognised the need to collaborate more closely with Indigenous peoples with respect to open data. First Nations have had input into Canadian open government discussions, and Canada's 4th Plan on Open Government 2018-20 includes Indigenous engagement activities.[60,61] Members of the RDA IDS Group also have participated in the third and fourth International Open Data Conferences, hosting a side event, the International Indigenous Open Data Summit, at the 2016 gathering in Madrid. The summit drew over 25 participants from Australia, Aotearoa/New Zealand, US, Africa, Taiwan, and other countries. Presentations and discussions focused on three elements: 1) how Indigenous peoples were or were not engaging with open data and why; 2) building connections and community at the intersection of IDS and open data; and 3) identifying the tensions between IDS and open data (and potential paths forward to ameliorate the tensions, while supporting useful data to meet development goals). In addition, members from Te Mana Raraunga and Maiam nayri Wingara

Indigenous Data Sovereignty collective presented at the 2018 UN Special Rapporteur on the Right to Privacy Consultation on Open Data-Big Data workshop held in Sydney.

Despite these efforts, there are ongoing resource and infrastructure constraints to advancing the shared goals and aspirations of IDS partners, including connecting with and expanding the IDS dialogue beyond the wealthy colonial settler states of North America and Australasia. Given the global scope of IDS, it is critical that the colonial and oppressive exclusion of Indigenous peoples in the Global South is not reproduced in IDS discourse and advocacy. To that end, a more robust and coherent international collaboration is needed to achieve impactful outcomes at the intersection of IDS, IDG, and open data. Currently there are no funders or investors driving activity at the nexus of these topics.

The RDA IDS Group and the nation-state network activities highlight three potential steps forward for the open data community in relation to Indigenous data and peoples. First, the necessity of engaging with Indigenous peoples, not merely in a consultative way, but rather as partners and knowledge holders at the table to inform how to steward Indigenous data. Second, the IDS networks need to provide a way forward for engagement with Indigenous peoples. The networks offer pre-existing contacts for non-Indigenous entities to begin working with in order to insert an Indigenous voice and vision into existing open data principles and practices. These networks can also connect non-Indigenous data actors with Indigenous leaders and communities. Finally, there needs to be progress related to research, exemplified by the desire of RDA to adopt and implement principles for the governance/stewardship of Indigenous data for researchers, and the opportunity for work on administrative open data to incorporate IDS.

United States – Generating principles of Indigenous data governance

The University of California Los Angeles (UCLA), the Native Nations Institute[62] at the University of Arizona, and the United States Indigenous Data Sovereignty Network, with funding from UCLA and the Stewart L. Udall and Morris K. Udall Foundation, hosted an "Indigenous Policy Forum: The Governance of Indigenous Data" in May 2017. The forum fostered discussion on IDS across four stakeholder groups, including tribal leaders, scholars, federal government officials, and non-profit organisations, as well as staff. The dialogue focused on drafting principles of IDG for use by tribes and other entities that govern and steward Indigenous data. Draft principles included recognition of inherent sovereignty and the right to self-determination. With respect to data, this has many implications for: control and access; the protection of Indigenous peoples and their data via ethics that ensure equal explanatory power of Indigenous ways of knowing and equitable outcomes; a focus on intergenerational collective well-being, understanding that data needs to align with Indigenous values for collective well-being across generations; the importance of relationships to the governance of Indigenous data, including respect, responsibility, and reciprocity between Indigenous peoples/nations and other stakeholders; and data governance and stewardship that serves to honour Indigenous knowledge, asserting that such knowledge is of the peoples and includes relationships to the non-human world. Since gathering at UCLA, the draft principles have been discussed at a number of events in order to finalise the principles and a format for sharing.

> **International Indigenous collaboration – Creating broad principles of Indigenous data governance for policy-makers, researchers, and others**
>
> The RDA IDS group, leveraging its "network of IDS networks", has been drafting principles of IDG for adoption and implementation by scientific organisations, international policy entities, and others. Conceptualised as a set of five to seven key words, each principle would have a brief descriptor statement and then one to three paragraphs placing the principle in context for the intended audience (e.g. researchers). The principles will be accompanied by a companion set of use cases to present the principles in practice. While the principles are currently being drafted, they are envisioned to be broad concepts akin to those in the Te Mana Raraunga Māori Data Sovereignty Network Charter, put forth in the Maiam nayri Wingara Indigenous Data Sovereignty Collective Communique, and recognised in the First Nations principles of OCAP®.

Conclusions

The concept of open data that is free to use, reuse, and share is laudable. But as we have described in this chapter, open data principles are in direct tension with IDS and the rights of Indigenous peoples to govern their data. This chapter has articulated, via a description of the history and current state of Indigenous data, case studies, and recommendations, that the path forward to addressing this fundamental tension between IDS and open data is through engagement with Indigenous peoples, both in the drafting of the next round of the ODC and the myriad open data contexts, and the inclusion of IDS and IDG principles within the ODC and in how open data is stewarded. All open data actors have a role in this path forward, including funders, national statistical offices, those building data infrastructures, and sector-specific communities like agricultural or environmental data groups.

Additionally, funder commitments are needed in order to support increased scholarship, action, and education about the issues at the intersection of open data and IDS and to bring Indigenous peoples into the conversations around open data. Such efforts could range from projects to increase Indigenous community data science capacity to encouraging engagement between nation-states and IDS networks in order to create open data policies around the stewarding of data in accordance with IDS and IDG.

This chapter also describes how government is more multi-layered than current open data governance assumes, and that data for governance requires a number of sources. Indigenous nations are political entities, and, as such, are another government actor in the open data world. This challenges the open data binary with one government actor, the nation-state. In addition, the history of Indigenous data and IDS illustrates that the data needed for governance (for Indigenous nations or other nation-states) requires information from more sources and perspectives than are currently available. As a result, IDS calls for more nuanced approaches to data than open data binaries often assume. Thus, the stewardship of open data arises as a key area of action requiring engagement with Indigenous peoples.

The ODC sits in a powerful seat to advocate for IDS and changes to data stewardship, as well as to facilitate investments in building Indigenous data capacity and capability. The ODC, now in a revision phase, must recognise IDS in its next iteration. Such recognition also should include the importance of IDG and the stewardship of Indigenous data by others, in partnership with Indigenous peoples. IDS can be seen as an anathema to open data, but acknowledgment of IDS and engagement with Indigenous peoples supports ethical open data that allows for development aligned with and benefitting Indigenous aspirations. Adoption and implementation of the principles of IDG emerging from the RDA IDS Group would strengthen the ODC. Engagement with Indigenous peoples during the next round of ODC revisions must include the IDS networks, but also Indigenous leaders, scholars, and community members. Particular care should be taken to include Indigenous rights holders from the Global South, including Africa and Central and South America. The existing IDS networks provide a launching point for establishing such relationships.

When creating open data stewardship policies and practices to make data open, nation-states, researchers, civil society, and others must abide by the rights of Indigenous nations to govern data. This requires engagement with the data's rights holders beyond mere consultation or advice. Indigenous peoples have the right to decide what is shared or withheld, ultimately affecting how others steward open data. Relationships are key and necessitate that open data actors reach out to Indigenous peoples and not just assume their involvement. While tension exists between IDS and open data, multiple paths forward exist as opportunities to diversify data types and improve sources, stewardship, access, and data quality.

Further reading

Kukutai, T. & Taylor, J. (Eds.). (2016). *Indigenous data sovereignty: Toward an agenda.* Canberra: Australian National University Press. See the editors' Introduction and Chapter 7.

Kukutai, T. & Walter, M. (2015). Indigenising statistics: Meeting in the recognition space. *Statistical Journal of the IAOS, 31(2),* 317–326.

Miaim nayri Wingara Indigenous Data Sovereignty Collective and the Australian Indigenous Governance Institute. (2018). Indigenous data sovereignty communique. *Indigenous Data Sovereignty Summit,* 20 June 2018, Canberra. http://www.aigi.com.au/wp-content/uploads/2018/07/Communique-Indigenous-Data-Sovereignty-Summit.pdf

National Congress of American Indians. (2018). *Resolution KAN-18-011: Support of US Indigenous data sovereignty and inclusion of tribes in the development of tribal data governance principles.* http://www.ncai.org/attachments/Resolution_gbuJbEHWpkOgcwCICRtgMJHMsUNofqYvuMSnzLFzOdxBlMlRjij_KAN-18-011%20Final.pdf

Rainie, S.C., Rodríguez-Lonebear, D., & Martinez, A. (2017). *Policy brief: Data governance for native nation rebuilding*. (version 2). Tucson: Native Nations Institute, University of Arizona. http://nni.arizona.edu/application/files/8415/0007/5708/Policy_Brief_Data_Governance_for_Native_Nation_Rebuilding_Version_2.pdf

Rainie, S.C., Rodríguez-Lonebear, D., & Martinez, A. (2017). *Policy brief: Indigenous data sovereignty in the United States*. Tucson: Native Nations Institute, University of Arizona. http://nni.arizona.edu/application/files/1715/1579/8037/Policy_Brief_Indigenous_Data_Sovereignty_in_the_United_States.pdf

Rainie, S.C., Schultz, J.L., Briggs, E., Riggs, P., & Palmanteer-Holder, N.L. (2017). Data as a strategic resource: Self-determination and the data challenge for United States Native Nation and Tribes. *International Indigenous Policy Journal, 8(2)*. http://ir.lib.uwo.ca/iipj/vol8/iss2/1. DOI: 10.18584/iipj.2017.8.2.1

Walter, M., Lovett, R., Bodkin Andrews, G., & Lee, V. (2018). *Indigenous data sovereignty*. Briefing Paper 1. Miaim nayri Wingara Data Sovereignty Group and the Australian Indigenous Governance Institute. https://static1.squarespace.com/static/5b3043afb40b9d20411f3512/t/5b70e7742b6a28f3a0e14683/1534125946810/Indigenous+Data+Sovereignty+Summit+June+2018+Briefing+Paper.pdf

About the authors

Stephanie Carroll Rainie is Ahtna (Alaska, US), and is Assistant Professor, Public Health Policy and Management, Mel and Enid Zuckerman College of Public Health; Assistant Research Professor, Udall Center for Studies in Public Policy; Associate Director, Native Nations Institute; and Co-Director, Center for Indigenous Environmental Health Research at the University of Arizona. She is the co-founder of the US Indigenous Data Sovereignty Network. You can follow Stephanie on Twitter at https://www.twitter.com/scbegonias.

Tahu Kukutai is from the Ngāti Tiipa, Ngāti Kinohaku, and Te Aupōuri tribes of Aotearoa/New Zealand and is Professor of Demography at the University of Waikato. She is a founding member of the Te Mana Raraunga Māori Data Sovereignty Network. You can follow Tahu on Twitter at http://www.twitter.com/thkukutai and learn more about her work at https://www.temanararaunga.maori.nz/.

Maggie Walter is Palawa (Tasmanian Aboriginal) and Professor of Sociology at the University of Tasmania, Australia. She is a founding member of the Maiam nayri Wingara Indigenous Data Sovereignty Collective. You can follow Maggie on Twitter at http://www.twitter.com/IDSovOz.

Oscar Luis Figueroa-Rodríguez is Associated Professor Researcher with the Rural Development Studies Program at the Colegio de Postgraduados Campus Montecillo, Mexico.

Jennifer Walker is a member of the Six Nations of the Grand River and holds a Canada Research Chair in Indigenous Health at Laurentian University. You can follow Jennifer on Twitter at http://www.twitter.com/jencandlish.

Per Axelsson is an Associate Professor at the Centre for Sámi Research and the Department of Historical, Philosophical and Religious Studies at Umeå University, Sweden.

How to cite this chapter

Rainie, S.C., Kukutai, T., Walter, M., Figueroa-Rodríguez, O.L., Walker, J., & Axelsson, P. (2019). Issues in open data: Indigenous data sovereignty. In T. Davies, S. Walker, M. Rubinstein, & F. Perini (Eds.), *The state of open data: Histories and horizons.* (pp. 300–319). Cape Town and Ottawa: African Minds and International Development Research Centre. http://stateofopendata.od4d.net

This work is licensed under a Creative Commons Attribution 4.0 International (CC BY 4.0) licence. It was carried out with the aid of a grant from the International Development Research Centre, Ottawa, Canada.

Endnotes

1   Smith, D.E. (2016). Governing data and data for governance: The everyday practice of Indigenous sovereignty. In T. Kukutai & J. Taylor (Eds.), *Indigenous data sovereignty: Toward an agenda* (pp. 117–135). Canberra: Australian National University Press, p. 132. http://press-files.anu.edu.au/downloads/press/n2140/pdf/book.pdf#page=141

2   De Beer, J. (2016). *Ownership of open data: Governance options for agriculture and nutrition.* Wallingford: Global Open Data for Agriculture and Nutrition. http://www.godan.info/sites/default/files/documents/Godan_Ownership_of_Open_Data_Publication_lowres.pdf

3   Kukutai, T. & Taylor, J. (2016). Data sovereignty for Indigenous peoples: Current practices and future needs. In T. Kukutai & J. Taylor (Eds.). *Indigenous data sovereignty: Toward an Agenda* (pp. 1–22). Canberra: Australian National University Press. http://press-files.anu.edu.au/downloads/press/n2140/pdf/book.pdf#page=25

4   Snipp, M. (2016). What does data sovereignty imply: What does it look like? In T. Kukutai & J. Taylor (Eds.), *Indigenous data sovereignty: Toward an agenda* (pp. 39–55). Canberra: Australian National University Press. http://press-files.anu.edu.au/downloads/press/n2140/pdf/book.pdf#page=63

5   Raine, S.C., Rodríguez-Lonebear, D., & Martinez, A. (2017). *Policy brief: Indigenous data sovereignty in the United States.* Tucson: Native Nations Institute, University of Arizona. http://nni.arizona.edu/application/files/1715/1579/8037/Policy_Brief_Indigenous_Data_Sovereignty_in_the_United_States.pdf

6   De Beer, J. (2016). *Ownership of open data: Governance options for agriculture and nutrition.* Wallingford: Global Open Data for Agriculture and Nutrition. http://www.godan.info/sites/default/files/documents/Godan_Ownership_of_Open_Data_Publication_lowres.pdf

7   Smith, D.E. (2016). Governing data and data for governance: The everyday practice of Indigenous sovereignty. In T. Kukutai & J. Taylor (Eds.), *Indigenous data sovereignty: Toward an* agenda (pp. 117–135). Canberra: Australian National University Press. http://press-files.anu.edu.au/downloads/press/n2140/pdf/book.pdf#page=141

8   Rainie, S.C., Rodríguez-Lonebear, D., & Martinez, A. (2017). *Policy brief: Data governance for native nation rebuilding (version 2).* Tucson: Native Nations Institute, University of Arizona. http://nni.arizona.edu/application/files/8415/0007/5708/Policy_Brief_Data_Governance_for_Native_Nation_Rebuilding_Version_2.pdf

9   Open Data Charter. (2015). International Open Data Charter: Principles. https://opendatacharter.net/principles/

10 Open Data Charter. (2015). International Open Data Charter, p 1. https://opendatacharter.net/wp-content/uploads/2015/10/opendatacharter-charter_F.pdf

11 United Nations Department of Economic and Social Affairs. (2009). *State of the world's Indigenous peoples.* New York, NY: United Nations Publications. https://www.un.org/esa/socdev/unpfii/documents/SOWIP/en/SOWIP_web.pdf

12. United Nations. (2019). Permanent forum. https://www.un.org/development/desa/indigenouspeoples/unpfii-sessions-2.html
13. United Nations. (n.d.). Indigenous peoples at the UN. https://www.un.org/development/desa/indigenouspeoples/about-us.html
14. Kukutai, T. & Taylor, J. (2016). Data sovereignty for Indigenous peoples: Current practices and future needs. In T. Kukutai & J. Taylor (Eds.), *Indigenous data sovereignty: Toward an agenda* (pp. 1–22). Canberra: Australian National University Press. http://press-files.anu.edu.au/downloads/press/n2140/pdf/book.pdf#page=25
15. United Nations. (2008). *Declaration of the rights of Indigenous peoples*. New York: United Nations. https://www.un.org/esa/socdev/unpfii/documents/DRIPS_en.pdf
16. Kukutai, T. & Walter, M. (2015). Recognition and indigenizing official statistics: Reflections from Aotearoa New Zealand and Australia. *Statistical Journal of the IAOS*, *31(2)*, 317–326. https://content.iospress.com/articles/statistical-journal-of-the-iaos/sji896
17. Mullane-Ronaki, M.-T.T.K.K. (2017). Indigenising the national census? A global study of the enumeration of Indigenous peoples, 1985–2014. Master's Thesis. University of Waikato, New Zealand. https://researchcommons.waikato.ac.nz/handle/10289/11175
18. Rainie, S.C., Rodríguez-Lonebear, D., & Martinez, A. (2017). *Policy brief: Data governance for native nation rebuilding (version 2)*. Tucson: Native Nations Institute, University of Arizona. http://nni.arizona.edu/application/files/8415/0007/5708/Policy_Brief_Data_Governance_for_Native_Nation_Rebuilding_Version_2.pdf
19. Rodríguez-Lonebear, D. (2016). Building a data revolution in Indian country. In T. Kukutai & J. Taylor (Eds.), *Indigenous data sovereignty: Toward an agenda*. Canberra: Australian National University Press. http://press-files.anu.edu.au/downloads/press/n2140/pdf/book.pdf#page=277
20. Smith, D.E. (2016). Governing data and data for governance: The everyday practice of Indigenous sovereignty. In T. Kukutai & J. Taylor (Eds.), *Indigenous data sovereignty: Toward an agenda* (pp. 117–135). Canberra: Australian National University Press. http://press-files.anu.edu.au/downloads/press/n2140/pdf/book.pdf#page=141
21. Chesterman, J. & Galligan, B. (1997). *Citizens without rights: Aborigines and Australian citizenship*. Melbourne: Cambridge University Press.
22. https://www.pmc.gov.au/indigenous-affairs/closing-gap
23. http://www.aigi.com.au/wp-content/uploads/2018/07/Communique-Indigenous-Data-Sovereignty-Summit.pdf
24. OECD. (2019). *Linking the Indigenous Sami People with regional development in Sweden*. Paris: Organisation for Economic Co-operation and Development Publishing. https://www.oecd-ilibrary.org/urban-rural-and-regional-development/linking-the-indigenous-sami-people-with-regional-development-in-sweden_9789264310544-en
25. Kukutai, T. & Walter, M. (2015). Recognition and indigenizing official statistics: Reflections from Aotearoa New Zealand and Australia. *Statistical Journal of the IAOS*, *31(2)*, 317–326. https://content.iospress.com/articles/statistical-journal-of-the-iaos/sji896
26. Ittmann, K., Maddox, G.H., & Cordell, D.D. (2010). Counting subjects: Demography and empire. In K. Ittmann, D.D. Cordell, & G.H. Maddox (Eds.), *The demographics of empire: The colonial order and the creation of knowledge* (pp. 1–21). Athens, OH: Ohio University Press.
27. Andersen, C. (2008). From nation to population: The racialisation of "métis" in the Canadian census. *Nations and Nationalism*, *14(2)*, 347–368.
28. Rowse, T. (2005). Towards a history of Indigenous statistics in Australia. In B.H. Hunter (Ed.), *Assessing the evidence on Indigenous socioeconomic outcomes: A focus on the 2002 NATSISS* (pp. 1–10). Canberra: Australian National University Press. http://press-files.anu.edu.au/downloads/press/p119431/pdf/ch0113.pdf
29. Snipp, M. (1989). *American Indians: The first of this land*. New York: Russell Sage Foundation.
30. Rainie, S., Schultz, J., Briggs, E., Riggs, P., & Palmanteer-Holder, N. (2017). Data as a strategic resource: Self-determination, governance, and the data challenge for Indigenous nations in the United States. *The International Indigenous Policy Journal*, *8(2)*. https://ir.lib.uwo.ca/iipj/vol8/iss2/1

31. Walter, M. (2016). Data politics and Indigenous representation in Australian statistics. In T. Kukutai & J. Taylor (Eds.), *Indigenous data sovereignty: Toward an agenda* (pp. 79–99). Canberra: Australian National University Press. http://press-files.anu.edu.au/downloads/press/n2140/pdf/book.pdf#page=103

32. McKenzie, P. (2010). Falsehoods programmers believe about names. *Kalzumeus Software* [Blog post], 17 June. https://www.kalzumeus.com/2010/06/17/falsehoods-programmers-believe-about-names/

33. De Beer, J. (2016). *Ownership of open data: Governance options for agriculture and nutrition*. Wallingford: Global Open Data for Agriculture and Nutrition. http://www.godan.info/sites/default/files/documents/Godan_Ownership_of_Open_Data_Publication_lowres.pdf

34. Australian Indigenous Governance Institute. (2016). *Indigenous data governance: Submission by the AIGI to the Australian productivity commission*. https://www.researchgate.net/publication/306118017_Indigenous_Data_Governance_Submission_by_the_AIGI_to_the_Australian_Productivity_Commission_2016

35. Rodríguez-Lonebear, D. (2016). Building a data revolution in Indian country. In T. Kukutai & J. Taylor (Eds.), *Indigenous data sovereignty: Toward an agenda* (pp. 253–272). Canberra: Australian National University Press. http://press-files.anu.edu.au/downloads/press/n2140/pdf/book.pdf#page=277

36. Raine, S.C., Rodríguez-Lonebear, D., & Martinez, A. (2017). *Policy brief: Indigenous data sovereignty in the United States*. Tucson: Native Nations Institute, University of Arizona. http://nni.arizona.edu/application/files/1715/1579/8037/Policy_Brief_Indigenous_Data_Sovereignty_in_the_United_States.pdf

37. www.datos.gob.mx

38. Kukutai, T. & Taylor, J. (2016). Data sovereignty for Indigenous peoples: Current practices and future needs. In T. Kukutai & J. Taylor (Eds.), *Indigenous data sovereignty: Toward an agenda* (pp. 1–22). Canberra: Australian National University Press. http://press-files.anu.edu.au/downloads/press/n2140/pdf/book.pdf#page=25

39. Rodríguez-Lonebear, D. (2016). Building a data revolution in Indian country. In T. Kukutai & J. Taylor (Eds.), *Indigenous data sovereignty: Toward an agenda* (pp. 253–272). Canberra: Australian National University Press. http://press-files.anu.edu.au/downloads/press/n2140/pdf/book.pdf#page=277

40. Kukutai, T. & Taylor, J. (2016). Data sovereignty for Indigenous peoples: Current practices and future needs. In T. Kukutai & J. Taylor (Eds.), *Indigenous data sovereignty: Toward an agenda* (pp. 1–22). Canberra: Australian National University Press. http://press-files.anu.edu.au/downloads/press/n2140/pdf/book.pdf#page=25

41. First Nations Information Governance Centre. (2016). Pathways to First Nations' data and information sovereignty. In T. Kukutai & J. Taylor (Eds.), *Indigenous data sovereignty: Toward an agenda* (pp. 139–155). Canberra: Australian National University Press. http://press-files.anu.edu.au/downloads/press/n2140/pdf/book.pdf#page=16

42. Kukutai, T. & Taylor, J. (2016). Data sovereignty for Indigenous peoples: Current practices and future needs. In T. Kukutai & J. Taylor (Eds.), *Indigenous data sovereignty: Toward an agenda* (pp. 1–22). Canberra: Australian National University Press. http://press-files.anu.edu.au/downloads/press/n2140/pdf/book.pdf#page=25

43. United Nations General Assembly. (2015). *Transforming our world: The 2030 agenda for sustainable development (A/RES/70/1)*. New York, NY: United Nations. http://www.un.org/ga/search/view_doc.asp?symbol=A/RES/70/1

44. Secretariat of the Convention on Biological Diversity. (2000). *Cartagena protocol on biosafety to the convention on biological diversity*. Montreal: Secretariat of the Convention of Biological Diversity. https://treaties.un.org/pages/ViewDetails.aspx?src=TREATY&mtdsg_no=XXVII-8-a&chapter=27&clang=_en

45. Secretariat of the Convention on Biological Diversity. (2011). *Nagoya protocol on access to genetic resources and the fair and equitable sharing of benefits arising from their utilization to the convention on biological diversity*. Montreal: Secretariat of the Convention of Biological Diversity, p. x. https://treaties.un.org/pages/ViewDetails.aspx?src=TREATY&mtdsg_no=XXVII-8-b&chapter=27&clang=_en

46. https://www.cbd.int/abs/

47 Banerjee, S.B. (2003). The practice of stakeholder colonialism: National interest and colonial discourses in the management of Indigenous stakeholders. In A. Prasad (Ed.), *Postcolonial theory and organizational analysis: A critical engagement* (pp. 255–279). New York: Palgrave Macmillan. https://link.springer.com/chapter/10.1057/9781403982292_11

48 Aotearoa is part of the D7 network of the world's most advanced digital nations. The others are Estonia, Israel, South Korea, United Kingdom, Canada, and Uruguay.

49 Open Data Charter. (2015). International Open Data Charter: Principles. https://opendatacharter.net/principles/

50 Rainie, S., Schultz, J., Briggs, E., Riggs, P., & Palmanteer-Holder, N. (2017). Data as a strategic resource: Self-determination, governance, and the data challenge for Indigenous nations in the United States. *The International Indigenous Policy Journal, 8(2)*. https://ir.lib.uwo.ca/iipj/vol8/iss2/1

51 Walter, M. (2016). Data politics and Indigenous representation in Australian statistics. In T. Kukutai & J. Taylor (Eds.), *Indigenous data sovereignty: Toward an agenda* (pp. 79–99). Canberra: Australian National University Press. http://press-files.anu.edu.au/downloads/press/n2140/pdf/book.pdf#page=103

52 Walker, J., Lovett, R., Kukutai, T., Jones, C., & Henry, D. (2017) Indigenous health data and the path to healing. *The Lancet, 390(10107)*, 2022–2023. https://doi.org/10.1016/S0140-6736(17)32755-1

53 http://temanararaunga.maori.nz

54 http://usindigenousdata.arizona.edu

55 http://maiamnayriwingara.org

56 http://fnigc.ca/

57 OCAP® is a registered trademark of the First Nations Information Governance Centre (FNIGC). http://fnigc.ca/ocapr.html

58 Kukutai, T. & Taylor, J. (Eds.). (2016). *Indigenous data sovereignty: Toward an agenda*. Canberra: Australian National University Press. http://press-files.anu.edu.au/downloads/press/n2140/pdf/book.pdf

59 http://rd-alliance.org

60 Treasury Board of Canada Secretariat. (2018). *Canada's action plan on open government 2014–2016 End-of-term self-assessment report*. Ottawa: Treasury Board of Canada Secretariat. http://publications.gc.ca/collections/collection_2017/sct-tbs/BT22-130-2017-1-eng.pdf

61 Treasury Board Secretariat of Canada. (2018). Creating Canada's 4th plan on open government 2018-20. https://open.canada.ca/en/4plan/creating-canadas-4th-plan-open-government-2018-20, /en/4plan/creating-canadas-4th-plan-open-government-2018-20

62 http://nni.arizona.edu

022

Measurement

Danny Lämmerhirt and Ana Brandusescu

Key points

- Measurement is critical to the future of open data because it provides a mechanism to track progress over time. Measurement has also played a role in securing improved engagement in open data work from some governments.

- There have been a range of initiatives to quantify open data readiness, implementation, and impact, using a variety of methods including expert surveys, crowdsourced data collection, and detailed dataset assessments. While each measurement initiative brings its own contribution, there is some duplication of effort, and opportunities for better coordination exist.

- Although open data measurements inform public policy, investments in open data and accountability efforts, more critical research is needed about the political dimensions of measurement methods. Research should further investigate how different methods lead to different ways of seeing return on investment, impact, high-value data, and the values underpinning such measurements, as well as how measurements inform policy, advocacy, and investments.

- There is significant untapped potential in the data gathered for measurement, which is mainly used for one-off reports rather than ongoing research. In particular, cross-pollination between research and management could be stronger, so that research methods and models inform management decisions, while theories of change, programme reports, and other documentation used for measurement could be reused as data by research organisations.

Introduction

This chapter focuses on measurement activities related to open data: the tools, history, stakeholders, as well as the strengths and weaknesses of the approaches to date. Moreover, the chapter addresses the roles of the many actors involved in the measurement of open data and their efforts to address not only the methodological but also the political opportunities and challenges inherent in evaluating the impact and progress of open data. We will conclude with recommendations on how best to leverage open data measurement activities in the future.

Open data has the potential to encourage citizen participation, support better public services, and uphold government accountability. One way to observe the effects of open data over time is through measurement tools, such as indices which observe phenomena over time, often using numerical indicators or qualitative assessments frequently grounded in empirical case studies. Measurement tools provide different mechanisms to track change over time, to understand progress (or the lack thereof), and to better assess the readiness, publication, use, and impact of data.

Indicators are used, in particular, in quantitative methodologies (e.g. rankings). They also define objects of study as variables that get assigned a numerical value to measure longitudinal developments of these objects against a baseline value. Found in different contexts, indicators are part of national benchmarking, scoring, and rankings. After World War II, indicators, such as the Gross Domestic Product (GDP), became tools for benchmarking countries, and progressively expanded to many other areas of society, such as university rankings.[1] Fast forward to 2015, the Sustainable Development Goals (SDGs) with their 230 global indicators that countries use to report against 17 overarching sustainability goals,[2] epitomise this process of country benchmarking, scoring, and ranking.

Individual organisations and programmes develop theories of change to understand whether invested actions and resources lead to desired outcomes.[3] Theories of change establish relationships between "input", "process", and "output" indicators, and are used for monitoring and evaluation (M&E). In M&E, ongoing and time-bound processes collect data for many purposes, including assessing how well a project is performing, and whether inputs and processes lead to desired outcomes.

Lastly, "impact case studies" have received increased attention in assessing the societal effects of higher education. These case studies provide descriptive accounts of how, for example, research output has led to societal benefits. It is noteworthy that the viability of "impact" research methods is controversially discussed not only in fields like higher education but also in open data.[4]

> **Glossary**
>
> - **Measurement:** In this chapter, we adopt a broad definition of "measurement", including all structured methods to gather quantitative and qualitative information about readiness, publication, use, and impact of open data.
>
> - **Measurements:** In general, techniques, methods, and methodologies used for quantitative or qualitative assessment.
>
> - **Measurement tools:** Indices (observing development of phenomena over time, often using numerical indicators) and/or qualitative assessments (e.g. context-based case studies), each with its own methodology. Examples include the Global Open Data Index (GODI), Open Data Barometer (ODB), Open Data Inventory, and the GovLab's impact case studies.
>
> - **Indicators:** Define objects of study as variables which often get assigned a numerical value (referred to as normalisation) to measure longitudinal development of these objects against a baseline value.
>
> - **Theories of change:** Models to understand the relationships between "input", "process", and "output" indicators. Theories of change are used for monitoring and evaluation.
>
> - **Monitoring and evaluation:** Ongoing and time-bound processes to collect data for many purposes, including how well a project is performing and whether inputs and processes lead to desired outcomes.

Brief history of measurement and open data

Since the 1980s, measurement has played an increasingly important role in public sector management through the rise of "new public management", managerialism,[5] and new institutional economics. In this climate, measurements have proliferated in many forms to support neoliberal governance schemes.[6,7] Measurements are applied across various types of institutions with different methodologies, analysing very different variables ranging from single organisations to entire countries. This "audit explosion" has been driven by numerous visions, including efficiency, value for money, managing for results, accountable government actions, and market-based incentives for improvement.[8]

Open data measurement tools are a continuation of this development. In 2007, the Sebastopol Principles[9] defined open government data as we know it. The establishment of the Open Government Partnership (OGP) in 2011 and the G8 Open Data Charter[10] have also played an important role in establishing the foundations of the open data movement. Open data then quickly became a popular open government commitment, garnering support for official open government initiatives (e.g. the United Kingdom (UK) and the United States (US)) that have transformed or evolved into many initiatives existing today.

In 2012, Open Knowledge International (OKI), formerly Open Knowledge Foundation, launched the Open Data Census.[11] In 2013, both the World Wide Web Foundation (Web Foundation) and OKI published their first editions of the Open Data Barometer (ODB)[12] and the Global Open Data Index (GODI).[13] In 2014, the Web Foundation and New York University's GovLab convened a workshop to define the Common Assessment Framework[14] for open data, a framework for measuring readiness, publication, use, and impact of open data.

Organisations have, over time, created a plethora of measurement tools to assess open data, including indices, such as the Open Data Inventory (ODIN), the Open Useful Reusable Government Data (OURdata) Index, the European Open Data Maturity Assessment (EODMA), the Open Data Readiness Assessment (World Bank), and impact case studies (Sunlight Foundation, GovLab, Web Foundation).

In 2015, the Open Data Charter Principles[15] were collaboratively drafted and later launched at the OGP Summit in Mexico City. The Open Data Charter's Measurement and Accountability Working Group (MAWG) currently convenes representatives of the largest open data indices. In 2018, MAWG developed the Measurement Guide,[16] inspired by the Common Assessment Framework, in an attempt to understand how open data indices are aligned or not aligned with the Open Data Charter Principles, including highlighting limitations and existing gaps.

Stakeholders

The section provides an overview of the stakeholders that engage with open data measurements, the basis for their interest in engaging and/or working with measurements, and how they put that interest into action.

The interest in open data measurement spans multiple stakeholder groups. One large group is government, which includes data publishers, open data champions, policy-makers, civil servants, and other agencies/task forces within government. Interest groups outside of government include non-profits working on open data, civil society groups, and academia. Governments and civil society use measurement tools to benchmark government performance on publishing, sustaining support, and making use of open government data. For example, some measurement tools, such as the GODI, anticipate a direct relationship between civil society (the auditor) and government (the auditee), which reflects normative assumptions that these are tools of "sousveillance" and data activism.

Sociologists of quantification have noted that groups of people engage with measurements, such as indices or rankings, in complex ways, often adjusting their behaviour to align with measurement tools by meeting measured targets.[17] Research findings highlight that measuring government performance may create unintended incentives and encourage undesired behaviour to meet targets (e.g. CompSTAT).[18] Others have critically examined evidence-based decision-making and have argued that the contemporary trend to "trust in numbers"[19] serves as a discursive device to cover up political arguments hidden in the numbers.

Contrary to the wealth of research from academia, evidence from within government on how open data measurement tools are used or impact interest groups is scarce. However, recent case study-based research conducted in the UK, Argentina, and Ukraine suggests that civil servants use measurement tools to assess whether their organisations deliver on targets.[20] The indicators wihin these tools provide open data agencies with a baseline for discussion and for developing strategies to improve open data publication. Rankings may also incentivise ministerial support or sustain momentum for open data in the absence of an official open data policy. Indicators are a discursive tool with which governments can demonstrate their openness, yet case studies suggest that open data may be confounded with open government at large or even create incentives for lowering commitments in other areas of transparency.[21] The implications of these findings for future research are discussed later in the chapter.

It is often noted that global indices may favour some world regions over others[22] by setting globally applicable targets and standards (see Strengths and weaknesses section below). As a response, some tailored regional assessments are being produced that use adjusted indicators designed to better detect the levers needed for open data readiness, publication, and impact (e.g. Africa).[23] Similar to the GODI and ODB's model, these assessments rely on partnerships with a small number of regional organisations who help decide what data should be analysed.

Noteworthy open data measurement producers include international non-profits (including Web Foundation, OKI, and Open Data Watch), government bodies (including the European Commission with support from consultancy firms such as CapGemini), multilateral organisations (including the Organisation for Economic Co-operation and Development (OECD) and the World Bank), academic research organisations and divisions (such as GovLab), and national civil society organisations (CSOs), civic groups, and non-profits (such as Article 19). In general, measurement tools are supported financially by funding from philanthropic donors or government institutions via commissioned contracts or supported through voluntary efforts via in-kind contributions by the open data community. There have been repeated discussions about resourcing the production of measurement tools, but also about providing resources for those being assessed, so that they can improve their policies and practices.

Funders engage differently with measurement of open data. Some provide funding for the development of measurement tools (e.g. Omidyar Network, Hewlett Foundation, and IDRC fund the GODI and the ODB). Others commission research on the impact of open data. If programmes are tied to external funding, organisations may be required to assess the impact of their programmes and agree on internal impact metrics with the respective funder. Measurements are not only relevant to assess open government data, but also to assess the capacity of organisations working with open government data to deliver impact.

Methodologies

An increasing number of measurement tools with their own indicators and methodologies are now available to better assess open government data. Quantitative open data indices (using indicators to measure progress against comparable phenomena and baselines) that produce a rank and score (see Table 1 below) are possibly the most prominent type of open data measurement; however, qualitative indicators are critical to the process. The ODB, OURdata, and EODMA use qualitative data sources (e.g. descriptive news articles and research articles). In addition, the ODB collects qualitative primary data (short answers via desk research and interviews) to assess policies and impact.

There are currently five prominent open data measurement tools (see Table 1) that assess a range of elements related to open government data. The GODI and ODIN focus on measuring data publication. The ODB and EODMA measure data publication and also provide cross-country metrics for readiness and impact. In 2016, the ODIN covered 173 countries, the ODB covered 115 countries, the GODI covered 94 countries, and OURData and EODMA covered mostly only OECD and European Union (EU) countries, respectively. These measurement tools apply different criteria and measure different aspects of open data, using more than 130 different indicators in total.

Measurement tools also exist for specific topics or regions, such as the National Democratic Institute's Legislative Openness Data Explorer,[24] Article 19's open data analysis on femicides (Brazil),[25] and Imaflora's environmental open data assessment (Brazil).[26] There are also subnational assessments, such as city rankings by Canada's Open Cities Index[27] and Sunlight Foundation's U.S. City Open Data Census.[28]

There are also qualitative approaches to measuring the outcomes and impact of open data (see Table 2). Qualitative studies can have different objects of study, including: 1) the types of impact generated; 2) pathways and enabling conditions of impact; and 3) the types of data use. Some studies provide narrative accounts of impact, while others develop analytical models and tools for practitioners. These analytical models are practice oriented, attempting to map out the enabling factors which support open data impact and relate these factors to one another.[29] Some exemplify use cases based on existing open data projects and suggest data sources for monitoring purposes.[30] Other studies identify typologies of impact[31] or attempt to model how open data use translates into behavioural changes within and across organisations by applying methods such as outcome mapping.[32]

To support research on data use and impact, organisations also built repositories of data use cases useful for follow-up analyses. For example, Open Data for Development's (OD4D) Open Data Impact Map[33] is a repository of organisations (e.g. companies, non-profits, and academic institutions) that use open government data for advocacy, to develop products and services, to improve operations, to inform strategy, and to conduct research.

Researchers do not, however, agree upon the best methods to capture outcomes and impact. Arguably, open data has not existed as a phenomenon long enough for substantive impacts to be observable. A common assumption is that, with time, evidence on impact will accrue, yet we note several challenges to capturing that impact. First, measurement tools that use indicators for longitudinal analyses (e.g. indices) may struggle to adequately capture change simply by observing changing indicators. This is partly because social context may change, which requires indicators to be attuned to these changes[34] and possibly prevents observing long-term changes solely based on indicators. Second, impact case studies may struggle to attribute impact specifically to open data release. Therefore, it is no surprise that there seems to be agreement that the causal connections between investments, outputs, and outcomes will be challenging to determine conclusively.

Table 1: Prominent measurement tools that assess open government data

Project	Methodology	Geographic coverage
ODB[35] opendatabarometer.org	Expert survey and secondary data. Assessment based on quantitative and qualitative data that combines contextual data, technical assessments, and secondary third-party indicators. Results are peer reviewed and have a QA process.	Focuses on national governments. Expanded coverage from 77 countries in 2013 to 115 countries in 2016.
GODI[36] index.okfn.org	Ongoing crowdsourcing with expert review to create an annual index. Discussions from survey and review displayed publicly. Checklist with qualitative justifications. GODI_methodology.	94 countries covered in 2016–2017 (focuses on national governments). Expanding coverage from 70 countries in 2013 to 94 countries in 2016–2017.
Open Data Inventory[37] odin.opendatawatch.com	Research carried out by trained researchers. Inputs from government officials taken into consideration. Two rounds of review conducted by Open Data Watch staff.	180 countries covered in 2017; subnational data assessed at administrative levels 1 and 2.
OECD OURdata Index[38]	Government survey completed by public sector officials from OECD countries and partners with analysis by OECD Secretariat. Includes secondary third-party indicators. A high-level overview of the report can be found in the OECD publication *Government at a Glance* 2017, Section 10, Open Government Data (p. 192). Note that OURdata methodologies are not publicly available online.	32 countries covered in the 2017 OURdata Index. 31 were OECD countries (focuses on national governments) and 1 was a country partner (Colombia).
European Open Data Maturity Assessment[39]	Government survey completed by officials with validation and analysis from the European Data Portal team in cooperation with government officials. The methodology is in Annex III of the 2017 report.	39 countries covered in 2017, including the 28 EU member states, Liechtenstein, Norway, Switzerland, and Iceland. Also, EU accession countries. Focuses on national governments.

Source: Open Data Charter Measurement Guide, 2018

Table 2: Ways of measuring the impact of open data

Organisation	Methodological approach	Advantages	Disadvantages
The GovLab research series on "The Impacts of Open Data"[40]	**Type:** Qualitative case studies **Description:** Each case study highlights descriptions of data use cases and consults various types of data sources (e.g. fiscal, electoral, educational data) to understand what aspects led to outcomes. **Data sources:** Interviews, government documents, academic papers, media reports	• Research series provides a taxonomy of open data impact. • Uses primary sources that help the reader gain contextual knowledge to understand the linkage between data use and outcomes.	• Reliance on interviewees and publicly accessible interviews can close off or bias certain evidence (e.g. it may be hard to reach the "right" interview partner in an organisation). • Assessment only provides a snapshot of impact and does not capture its dynamic nature.
The Web Foundation's Exploring the emerging impacts of open data in developing countries[41]	**Type:** Reports, academic papers, case studies **Description:** A multi-country, multi-year study to understand how open data is being put to use in different countries and contexts across the global South, informing the development of planned and ongoing open data initiatives and their emerging impacts. **Data sources:** Interviews, government documents, academic papers, media reports	• Uses primary sources that help the reader gain contextual knowledge to understand the linkage between data use and outcomes. • Investigates the mechanisms needed to address long-term challenges to achieve impact.	• Study captures impact as a snapshot in time and is limited by the timeframe in which the research was conducted.

Organisation	Methodological approach	Advantages	Disadvantages
The Web Foundation's Open Data Barometer[42]	**Type:** Survey **Description:** The ODB collects qualitative stories of impact across social, political, and economic dimensions. **Data sources:** Researchers collect "credible claims made in academic and scientific publications, mainstream media, or other accredited online sources". These reports need to demonstrate certain impacts to open data publication and use.[43]	• Reviews secondary data sources that are accredited to verify existence of outcomes. • Uses primary sources (e.g. interviews) that help the reader gain contextual knowledge to understand the linkage between data use and outcomes.	• Survey format focuses on any observable relationship between data use and outcomes. • Longer-term "impacts" are not considered. • Reliance on third-party reporting does not allow for in-depth exploration (e.g. perceived benefits for groups).
Sunlight Foundation's Social Impact of Open Data[44]	**Type:** Case studies **Description:** The study employs outcome mapping to understand how open data leads to behavioural changes in organisations. The objects of study are behaviour, relationships, activities, or actions of those people, groups, and organisations. **Data Sources:** Face-to-face interviews, workshops	• Tests hypotheses of logic models (e.g. does open data publication lead to desired changes in an organisation?) and provides a summary of behavioural changes in organisations. • Acknowledges that open data affects multiple organisational settings at once. • Focus on observable short- and mid-term outcomes to understand accuracy of logic models and theories of change.	• Less suited to investigate long-term changes. • Drawing conclusions on causality is challenging. The study acknowledges follow-up research is needed to refine the conclusions of the study.

Organisation	Methodological approach	Advantages	Disadvantages
European Open Data Portal's European Open Data Measurement Assessment[45]	**Type:** Survey **Description:** The European Open Data Portal evaluates evidence on the political, social, and economic impact of open data monitored by governments, and creates comparable metrics of impact across countries based on government's estimations of impact. **Data sources:** Impact reports issued by government, data use cases, applications, news articles	• Gathers self-assessments from government and allows for comparability of impacts by assigning normalised scores.	• Government self-assessments may be biased. The latest report edition acknowledges that governments find it challenging to assess the social impact of their work. • Assessment does not consider whether open data applications and use cases had beneficial effects. Therefore, the assessment of long-term societal impact is at risk of being confounded with the mere existence of open data case studies.
Open Knowledge International's reports on the effects of open data use: • Data and The City[46] • Changing What Counts[47] • From Evidence to Action[48]	**Type:** Qualitative case studies. **Description:** Each case study contains problem-centred descriptions of data use and how that data use can be enabled to alleviate a problem (problem-centred outcome). The cases cover fiscal and procurement data, crime statistics, air pollution statistics, and others. **Data sources:** Interviews, government documents, academic papers, media reports	• Uses primary sources that help the reader gain contextual knowledge to understand the linkages between data use and outcomes.	• Reliance on interviewees and publicly accessible interviews can close off or bias certain evidence.

Strengths and weaknesses of measurement tools

This section highlights the strengths and weaknesses of existing measurement tools, discusses the political and societal effects of rankings as the most prominent measurement tools, and reflects upon research replication, organisational learning, as well as on how inclusion can be measured and how to embed participatory processes into measurement tools.

Open data funders and governments[49] may commission impact research to understand their return on investment. Other groups interested in impact research include civic tech and data for development communities that intersect with open data.[50] Benefits of these groups working together include organisational learning and improving programme design for impact.

However, there are a number of potential challenges to using measurement tools. First, the resources required to develop, apply, and report on measurement tools, projects, and programmes are significant. Second, there is a very broad and diverse range of content that can be taken into consideration for measurement at various levels, both vertically (e.g. global, national, subnational) and horizontally (e.g. sectoral). Measurement processes can also be very time consuming for both civil society and governments. These challenges in achieving an impact on policy affect how the impact of open data is measured globally. In addition, indicators rely on the existence of secondary impact research, yet comparative accounts of impact are difficult to generate and tend to have a narrow focus on broader long-term, socioeconomic impact.

Rankings

Rankings have become a prominent tool for measurement as they simplify the interpretation of complex problems through categorisation and common metrics. Rankings are easy to understand and communicate, allow for comparison of performance, track progress over time, and are effective.[51] The use of measurement indicators to develop dashboards is also a common practice.

More substantive research is needed to understand how governments engage and respond to open data measurements. Such endeavours could address how the internal audit procedures of government and global open data measurement tools relate to one another. Even though measurement tools frequently measure the same phenomena, there are often no consistent criteria to define and measure readiness, publication, use, and impact of open data. More specifically, we refer to the type of impact that is being measured (e.g. economic, social, environmental) and the criteria for data to be considered timely, available, accessible, useable, and of good quality. In addition, given the existence of several global measurement tools, it is imperative to address how governments respond to different measurement tools. Do governments indeed discriminate and adjust their behaviour according to the tool that ranks them the highest as recent research on the effects of multiple rankings suggests?[52]

To understand how civil society that is not necessarily focused on open data engages with the GODI, an ethnographic study was conducted using the case of water advocates in South-East Asia. The study highlighted the issue that the GODI's definition of water data is too output-oriented (the GODI assesses water pollutant concentration), while water advocates may have more interest in process-related data (water management schemes), and that government data is usually not trusted or is considered to be low quality in the region.[53] This points to a tension that global indices apply proxy indicators to measure an entire sector based on a selection of representative indicators that do not reflect the complexity of a given sector. These findings are based on a small sample of interviewees, but they suggest that more research is needed to understand when open data measurement tools become relevant at local levels and for what types of organisations.

There are ongoing debates on whether global rankings are the best tools to assess open data in low- and middle-income countries, whether more contextual analysis is needed to detect levers to advance open data programmes, and on how existing rankings could be improved by using more relevant metrics to highlight the steps needed for low-ranking countries to improve. Some argue that metrics do not take into account all the levers necessary to improve scores in environments where enabling conditions for open data are scarce. Proponents of quantitative metrics argue that low scores mobilise commitment and action to improve scores, while critics argue that by applying a common standard, rankings tend to disadvantage or de-incentivise countries that are not in the top tier. Therefore, rankings tend to benefit governments and champions from countries in the Global North who have greater means to promote change around open data.[54]

Given the normative power relations that often exist in global measurements, there is a complicated history of measurement in the Global South as illustrated by the role of measurement in development planning[55] and in colonial and post-colonial development.[56] These experiences further echo concerns over the potential for creating unintended incentives, encouraging undesired behaviour to meet targets, and understanding who benefits and who loses. This also relates to literature that has the explored problematic aspects of development metrics.[57]

Furthermore, global rankings can apply criteria that penalise low-tier countries when new countries (often from the Global South) are added to a measurement index for assessment. Indicators operate with globally applicable baselines to incentivise progress in top-tier countries. It is challenging, if not impossible, to create indicators that are consistently meaningful across all low-, middle-, and high-income countries.

Measuring data use to understand demand and impact

Open data organisations do provide evidence of impact; however, when this evidence and information is reused by researchers and other stakeholders, open data measurement research is unevenly represented, especially with regard to concrete examples of data use and follow up on success stories, which is integral to achieving the measurement of impact. In order to enhance the measurement of progress on open data impact, organisations need to go beyond advocacy efforts and conduct participatory action research that complements global measurement assessments.

In accordance with the broader shift to user-centric open data or "publishing with purpose", measurement tools should consider data use with the goal of measuring the demand for, and impact of, open data. Quantitative metrics have experimented with data requests and data downloads to measure demand.[58] As the Sunlight Foundation discusses, these metrics may only provide fragmented insight into specific audiences and user groups. Furthermore, relevance, usefulness, and usability are data- and use case-specific.[59] This suggests that quantitative figures like requests or download metrics should be complemented by qualitative descriptions of data users. Case studies of data use and outcomes are part of researching impact and can provide additional descriptions of demand or justify the costs of data publication.[60] In addition, problem-focused research that explores what makes data fit for a specific purpose is encouraged to explore what makes data understandable, accessible, timely, or comprehensive enough for a given task.[61]

Partnerships, replication of research, and collaborative learning

Our review in support of this chapter suggests that there is an opportunity for measurement efforts to learn from one another and to conduct follow-up analyses to test their limitations. This issue may stem from a lack of collaboration and coordination between organisations and a lack of awareness about the different use cases of measurement methods and how they can inform many different audiences and use purposes. In addition, the replication of measurements is scarce with a few exceptions (e.g. the Open Data Survey[62]), and measurements do not tend to build on one another. Furthermore, impact studies remain one-off projects and are generally not replicated or tested again.

Case study-based impact research depends on the availability of reliable information to construct an account of how actions led to certain outcomes. As research by the GovLab notes, information on impact produced by open data organisations is aspirational, but without "concrete evidence [of] impacts at meaningful scale".[63] Such information lacks reflection on intention, implications, and impact. This points to a larger problem that open data initiatives might not systematically monitor and evaluate their work or that the incentives to provide nuanced accounts of what works and what does not are not evident. This situation seems to continue despite the rise of organisational learning and programme design for impact as recurring topics in the open data, civic tech, and data for development communities.[64]

However, quantitative methodologies, such as the ODB and GODI, are reused by the Natural Resource Governance Institute's Resource Governance Index[65] (gauging whether countries create an enabling environment for natural resource governance) and Blavatnik School's International Civil Service Effectiveness (InCiSE) Index (Oxford University). Others reuse significant parts of these methodologies, including the Canadian Open Cities Index and EODMA.

Partnerships can be used to clarify the expectations of measurement tool assessments. The Open Data Charter Measurement Guide identifies that it may be challenging to match existing measurements with aspirational or ambivalent principles and the commitments they represent. This may pose challenges for measuring the implementation of a number of policy commitments. A broader discussion needs to be had on what cannot be feasibly measured, which is an often overlooked topic in this space. However, there are signs of improvement with the work of the Open Data Charter's MAWG that intends to identify overlaps and differences across measurement tools.

Sustaining global measurement tools and the role of funders in supporting and refining this work is critical. There is an opportunity for funders to collaborate more on providing financial support for measurement tools and the sustainability of these products. Beyond the need to identify partners with whom to pool resources, it is necessary that measurement programmes and tools scope out to what extent they differ, as well as how different methodologies could build on each other to improve efficiency and complementarity.

Inclusion

One weakness of existing measurements of open data is that inclusion is not prominently measured by all tools. However, some progress can be noted in the methodologies of the ODB and ODIN, which test whether governments publish sex-disaggregated data. In addition, only the ODB measures the impact of open data on marginalised communities. Further investigation is needed into the evidence behind these measurements and the potential methodological drawbacks of solely relying on government self-assessments or secondary data sources like news articles.

Inclusion also refers to who has a say in defining what gets counted and measured. Before asking how local communities can participate in methodology development,[66] more research is needed to understand when and how open data measurement tools become relevant at the local level and for what types of organisations. Similarly, understanding how CSOs, researchers, and others engage with globally defined indicators and how open data measurement tools can provide a basis for new collaborations in which these topical experts can participate more strongly in the design of methodologies. This should be complemented by participatory governance models over measurement tools which ensure meaningful engagement opportunities during methodology design, data collection, analysis, publication, and use of results. There are initiatives that work to generate localised metrics from the Global South, such as the Open African Innovation research network,[67] but more can be done. We recommend addressing issues on whether measurement tool creators include multidisciplinary design teams with diverse backgrounds and whether these teams consult local communities in the design process to capture diverse perspectives.

Conclusion

Overall, progress has been made to create tools and methodologies for the measurement of open data. Over the last decade, the landscape has expanded with a proliferation of measurement tools; however, this does not necessarily lead to better measurement. To improve and continue the evolution of open data measurement, the expansion of collaborative efforts, such as the Open Data Charter's MAWG, is necessary. Beyond virtual working groups, it is paramount for measurement practitioners to consider the politics implicit in any measurement approach, to listen, and to include people from different geographies, prioritising diversity and gender balance in measurement conversations and practices. Measurement practitioners need to also engage with stakeholder groups that use, or could potentially use, open government data in real-world applications to guide investment or to support policy development.

A balance between quantitative and qualitative open data assessment is needed to fully understand open data impact as there currently seems to be an instinctive preference for quantitative assessments of open data, which may be due to the methodological benefits of indicators that enable ranking and comparisons (including historical comparability). Discussions need to continue on which measurement methods most contribute to authoritative knowledge about open data. Future work should focus more on the governance of measurement tools and the demand side of measurements, including what measurements are most useful for different organisations and how organisations are currently making use of measurement results to support impact tracking. Organisations and funders should be attentive to the effects of performance targets on organisational operations and consider more flexible or qualitative assessments for organisational impact.[68] Moreover, organisations should conduct independent audits of existing measurement tools to support future improvements.

Furthermore, concrete steps toward the reuse of measurement tools, methodologies, and results are needed but this will only be possible by addressing the current lack of transparency around existing metrics. Most methodologies, as well as the granular results of the assessments themselves (including justifications), are not public. Finally, it is vital to not consider any measurement as the final assessment. Policy-makers, practitioners, and programme managers need to be able to make use of results data as an essential component of further reviews, as well as to identify opportunities for qualitative follow-up research on the impact of open data.

Further reading

Brandusescu, A. & Lämmerhirt, D. (2018). *Open Data Charter measurement guide*. Open Data Charter. https://open-data-charter.gitbook.io/odcmeasurement-guide/. This guide includes the methodologies of existing measurement tools: Open Data Barometer, Global Open Data Index, Open Data Inventory, OURdata Index, and European Open Data Maturity Assessment.

Davies, T. (2014). Towards common methods for assessing open data. *World Wide Web Foundation Blog*, 12 June. https://webfoundation.org/2014/06/towards-common-methods-for-assessing-open-data/

Walker, J., Frank, M., & Thompson, N. (2015). *User centred methods for measuring the value of open data*. Open Data Research Network. http://www.opendataresearch.org/dl/symposium2015/odrs2015-paper60.pdf. The article discusses how open data indicators can be defined to assess criteria relevant to them, including trade-offs when designing broader and narrower indicators.

World Wide Web Foundation and GovLab. (2014). Common assessment framework. https://webfoundation.org/2014/06/towards-common-methods-for-assessing-open-data/

About the authors

Danny Lämmerhirt is an independent research consultant and PhD candidate at the University of Siegen. His research investigates how data infrastructures can work in the public interest, the design and governance of collaborative data projects, data activism, and the politics of metrics. His PhD studies emerging proposals of "data taxation", how value generation can be understood across data infrastructures, and the values and norms underpinning emerging proposals to quantify value and taxing approaches. Danny was research lead at OKI, has lead research for GODI, and co-chaired the MAWG at the Open Data Charter. You can follow Danny at https://www.twitter.com/danlammerhirt.

Ana Brandusescu is a researcher, advisor, and facilitator, who works for more transparent, inclusive, and responsible use of existing and emerging technologies through data and policy projects. These include initiatives on open data, data governance, open government, and digital equality. Previously, she has led research efforts on the ODB and co-chaired the MAWG of the Open Data Charter. You can follow Ana at https://www.twitter.com/anabmap.

How to cite this chapter

Lämmerhirt, D. & Brandusescu, A. (2019). Issues in open data: Measurement. In T. Davies, S. Walker, M. Rubinstein, & F. Perini (Eds.), *The state of open data: Histories and horizons* (pp. 320–338). Cape Town and Ottawa: African Minds and International Development Research Centre. http://stateofopendata.od4d.net

This work is licensed under a Creative Commons Attribution 4.0 International (CC BY 4.0) licence. It was carried out with the aid of a grant from the International Development Research Centre, Ottawa, Canada.

Endnotes

1. Davies, W. (2014). *The limits of neoliberalism*. Los Angeles CA: SAGE.
2. Ariss, A. & Manley, L. (2018). *Strategies for SDG national reporting: A review of current approaches and key considerations for government reporting on the UN Sustainable Development Goals*. Washington, DC: Centre for Open Data Enterprise. http://reports.opendataenterprise.org/CODE_StrategiesforSDGreporting.pdf
3. Roberts, D. & Khattri, N. (2012). *Designing a results framework for achieving results: A how-to guide*. Washington, DC: World Bank – Independent Evaluation Group (IEG). https://siteresources.worldbank.org/EXTEVACAPDEV/Resources/designing_results_framework.pdf
4. Power, M. (2015). How accounting begins: Object formation and the accretion of infrastructure. *Accounting, Organizations and Society, 47*, 43–55.
5. Rhodes, R.A.W. (1996). The new governance: Governing without government. *Political Studies, 44(4)*, 652–667. https://onlinelibrary.wiley.com/doi/abs/10.1111/j.1467-9248.1996.tb01747.x
6. Davies, W. (2014). *The limits of neoliberalism: Authority, sovereignty and the logic of competition*. Los Angeles: SAGE Publications.
7. Broome, A. & Quirk, J. (2015) Governing the world at a distance: The practice of global benchmarking. *Review of International Studies, 41(5)*: 819–841. http://wrap.warwick.ac.uk/76899/1/WRAP_1170063-pais-030216-broome__quirk_-_governing_the_world_at_a_distance_-_the_practice_of_global_benchmarking.df?fbclid=IwAR0yxx3oAKD84Bg96cgZhsKkFRWcLfFWuo9STBs6fC45Ba5QHag9sZrxOAM

8. Power, M. (1994). *The audit explosion*. London: Demos. https://www.demos.co.uk/files/theauditexplosion.pdf
9. Tauberer, J. (2014). Open government data definition: The 8 principles of open government data. In J. Tauberer (Ed.), *Open government data: The Book*. 2nd edition. https://opengovdata.io/2014/8-principles/
10. G8. (2013). G8 Open Data Charter and Technical Annex. *GOV.UK*, 18 June. https://www.gov.uk/government/publications/open-data-charter/g8-open-data-charter-and-technical-annex
11. Newman, L. (2012). Launching the Open Data Census 2012! *Open Knowledge International Blog*, 17 April. https://blog.okfn.org/2012/04/17/launching-the-open-data-census-2012/
12. Davies, T. (2013). *Open Data Barometer – 2013 global report*. Washington, DC: World Wide Web Foundation. http://opendatabarometer.org/doc/1stEdition/Open-Data-Barometer-2013-Global-Report.pdf
13. https://web.archive.org/web/20131101182955/https://index.okfn.org/
14. Caplan, R., Davies, T., Wadud, A., Verhulst, S., Alonso, J.M., & Farhan, H. (2014). *Towards common methods for assessing open data: Workshop report & draft framework*. New York, NY: World Wide Web Foundation and GovLab. http://opendataresearch.org/sites/default/files/posts/Common%20Assessment%20Workshop%20Report.pdf
15. https://opendatacharter.net/principles/
16. Brandusescu, A. & Lämmerhirt, D. (2018). *Open Data Charter measurement guide*. Open Data Charter. https://open-data-charter.gitbook.io/odcmeasurement-guide/
17. Espeland, W.N. & Sauder, M. (2007). Rankings and reactivity: How public measures recreate social worlds. *American Journal of Sociology, 113(1)*, 1–40. https://www.jstor.org/stable/10.1086/517897
18. Bruno, I., Didier, E., & Vitale, T. (2014). Statactivism: Forms of action between disclosure and affirmation. *Partecipazione E Conflitto, 7(2)*, 198–220. http://siba-ese.unisalento.it/index.php/paco/article/view/14150
19. Porter, T.M. (1996). *Trust in numbers: The pursuit of objectivity in science and public life*. Princeton, NJ: Princeton University Press.
20. Žuffová, M. (2017). Governing by rankings: How the Global Open Data Index helps advance the open data agenda. *Open Knowledge International*. https://research.okfn.org/governing-by-rankings/
21. Ibid.
22. Broome, A. & Quirk, J. (2015) Governing the world at a distance: The practice of global benchmarking. *Review of International Studies, 41(5)*: 819–841. http://wrap.warwick.ac.uk/76899/1/WRAP_1170063-pais-030216-broome__quirk_-_governing_the_world_at_a_distance_-_the_practice_of_global_benchmarking.pdf?fbclid=IwAR0yxx3oAKD84Bg96cgZhsKkFRWcLfFWuo9STBs6fC45Ba5QHag9sZrxOAM
23. http://opendatatoolkit.worldbank.org/en/odra.html
24. See the Legislative Openness Data Explorer at https://beta.openparldata.org/
25. Article19. (2018). Brazil: New research on open data and cases of femicide. *Article 19*, 8 March. https://www.article19.org/resources/brazil-new-research-on-open-data-and-cases-of-femicide/
26. Morgado, R.P. & De M. Bezerra, M.H. (2017). *Dados abertos em clima, floresta e agricultura: Uma análise da abertura de bases de dados federais* [Open data on climate, forest and agriculture: An analysis of the openness of federal databases]. *Imaflora*, 5 November. http://www.imaflora.org/downloads/biblioteca/5a1dad18c4364_perspectiva_dados_imaflora_aprovacao_2811.pdf
27. https://www.publicsectordigest.com/open-cities-index-oci
28. See US City Open Data Census from Open Knowledge International and Sunlight Foundation at http://us-cities.survey.okfn.org/
29. Verhulst, S. & Young, A. (2017). *Open data in developing economies: Toward building an evidence base on what works and how*. Cape Town: African Minds. http://www.africanminds.co.za/dd-product/open-data-in-developing-economies-toward-building-an-evidence-base-on-what-works-and-how/
30. Verhulst, S., Noveck, B.S., Caplan, R., Brown. K., & Paz, C. (2014). *The open data era in health and social care: A blueprint for the National Health Service (NHS England) to develop a research and learning programme for the open data era in health and social care*. Brooklyn, NY: GovLab. http://www.thegovlab.org/static/files/publications/nhs-full-report.pdf

31 http://www.odimpact.org
32 Keserű, J. & Chan, J.K. (2015). *The social impact of open data*. Washington, DC: Sunlight Foundation. http://assets.sunlightfoundation.com.s3.amazonaws.com/policy/SocialImpactofOpenData.pdf
33 http://opendataimpactmap.org
34 Uprichard, E. (2011). Dirty data: Longitudinal classification systems. *The Sociological Review, 59(2)*, 93–112.
35 https://opendatabarometer.org/4thedition/methodology/
36 https://index.okfn.org/methodology/
37 http://odin.opendatawatch.com/Downloads/otherFiles/ODIN-2016-Methodology.pdf
38 OECD. (2017). Open Government Data. In OECD, *Government at a glance 2017* (pp. 192–193). Paris: Organisation of Economic Co-operation and Development Publishing. https://www.oecd-ilibrary.org/governance/government-at-a-glance-2017/open-government-data_gov_glance-2017-68-en
39 Carrara, W., Radu, C., & Vollers, H. (2017). *Open data maturity in Europe 2017: Open data for a European data economy*. Brussels: European Data Portal. https://www.europeandataportal.eu/sites/default/files/edp_landscaping_insight_report_n3_2017.pdf
40 http://odimpact.org
41 Open Data Research Network. (2015). Exploring the emerging impacts of open data in developing countries. http://www.opendataresearch.org/emergingimpacts/
42 Brandusescu, A., Iglesias, C., & Robinson, K. (2017). *Open Data Barometer – Global report*. 4th edition. Washington, DC: World Wide Web Foundation. http://opendatabarometer.org/4thedition/data/
43 Iglesias, C. & Brandusescu, A. (2016). *Open Data Barometer* (4th edition)*: Research handbook v. 1.0*. Washington, DC: World Wide Web Foundation. https://opendatabarometer.org/doc/4thEdition/ODB-4thEdition-ResearchHandbook.pdf
44 Keserű, J. & Chan, J.K. (2015). *The social impact of open data*. Washington, DC: Sunlight Foundation. http://assets.sunlightfoundation.com.s3.amazonaws.com/policy/SocialImpactofOpenData.pdf
45 Carrara, W., Radu, C., & Vollers, H. (2017). *Open data maturity in Europe 2017: Open data for a European data economy*. Brussels: European Data Portal. https://www.europeandataportal.eu/en/highlights/open-data-maturity-europe-2017
46 Gray, J. & Lämmerhirt, D. (2017). Data and the city: New report on how public data is fostering civic engagement in urban regions. *Open Knowledge International Blog*, 9 February. https://blog.okfn.org/2017/02/09/data-and-the-city-new-report-on-how-public-data-is-fostering-civic-engagement-in-urban-regions/
47 Gray, J. (2016). New report: "Changing what counts: How can citizen-generated and civil society data be used as an advocacy tool to change official data collection?" *Open Knowledge International Blog*, 3 March. https://blog.okfn.org/2016/03/03/changing-what-counts/
48 Lämmerhirt, D., Jameson, S., & Prasetyo, E. (2017). *From evidence to action: Turning citizen-generated data into actionable information to improve decision-making*. Civicus and Open Knowledge International. http://civicus.org/thedatashift/wp-content/uploads/2017/03/from-evidence-to-action_brief.pdf
49 Carrara, W., Radu, C., & Vollers, H. (2017). *Open data maturity in Europe 2017: Open data for a European data economy*. Brussels: European Data Portal. https://www.europeandataportal.eu/en/highlights/open-data-maturity-europe-2017
50 Hudson, A. (2017). Learning and power: Or, whose learning and adaptation counts? *Global Integrity Blog*, 5 December. https://www.globalintegrity.org/2017/12/learning-and-power-or-whose-learning-and-adaptation-counts/; Hudson, A. (2017). Exploring how data can make a difference: A call for collective action. *Global Integrity Blog*, 6 July. https://www.globalintegrity.org/2017/07/exploring-how-data-can-make-a-difference-a-call-for-collective-action/; Carolan, L. (2017). *Mapping open data for accountability: The need for a new framework for open data for accountability*. Open Data Charter and Transparency and Accountability Initiative. http://www.transparency-initiative.org/wp-content/uploads/2017/06/taiodc_draft_data4accountabilityframework.pdf
51 Davis, K., Fisher, A., Kingsbury, B., & Merry, S.E. (2012). *Governance by indicators: Global power through quantification and rankings*. New York, NY: Oxford University Press.

52 Pollock, N., d'Adderio, L., Williams, R., & Leforestier, L. (2018). Conforming or transforming? How organizations respond to multiple rankings. *Accounting, Organizations and Society, 64*, 55–68. https://doi.org/10.1016/j.aos.2017.11.003

53 Thompson, N. & Lämmerhirt, D. (2017). How do open data measurements help water advocates to advance their mission? *Open Knowledge International Blog*, 23 November. https://blog.okfn.org/2017/11/23/how-do-open-data-measurements-help-water-advocates-to-advance-their-mission/

54 Ibid.

55 Darian-Smith, E. (2016). Mismeasuring humanity: Examining indicators through a critical global studies perspective. *New Global Studies, 10(1)*, 73–99.

56 Mitchell, T. (2002). Rule of experts: Egypt, techno-politics, modernity. Berkeley, CA: University of California Press. https://www.ucpress.edu/book/9780520232624/rule-of-experts

57 Ravallion, M. (2010). *Mashup indices of development*. Washington, DC: World Bank. https://elibrary.worldbank.org/doi/abs/10.1596/1813-9450-5432

58 See the Sunlight Foundation's analysis of data requests in American cities: Zencey, N. (2017). Who's at the popular table? Our analysis found which open data the public likes. *Sunlight Foundation* [Blog post], 11 September. https://sunlightfoundation.com/2017/09/11/whos-at-the-popular-table-our-analysis-found-which-open-data-the-public-likes/

59 Wand, Y. & Wang, R.Y. (1996). Anchoring data quality dimensions in ontological foundations. *Communications of the ACM, 39(11)*, 86–95. https://dl.acm.org/citation.cfm?id=240479

60 Noteworthy examples include the School of Data, DataKind, Reboot, or the Sunlight Foundation's Tactical Data Engagement programme.

61 Brandusescu, A. & Nwakanma, N. (2018). Is open data working for women in Africa? *World Wide Web Foundation*, 13 July. https://webfoundation.org/2018/07/is-open-data-working-for-women-in-africa/

62 OKI. (n.d.). The Open Data Survey Application. Open Knowledge International. https://github.com/okfn/opendatasurvey/

63 Verhulst, S.G. & Young, A. (2017). *Open data in developing economies: Toward building an evidence base on what works and how*. Cape Town: African Minds. http://www.africanminds.co.za/wp-content/uploads/2017/10/AM-OD-in-Developing-Economies-COMPLETE-R-WEB-10Nov2017.pdf

64 Hudson, A. (2017). Learning and power: Or, whose learning and adaptation counts? *Global Integrity Blog*, 5 December. https://www.globalintegrity.org/2017/12/learning-and-power-or-whose-learning-and-adaptation-counts/; Hudson, A. (2017). Exploring how data can make a difference: A call for collective action. *Global Integrity Blog*, 6 July. https://www.globalintegrity.org/2017/07/exploring-how-data-can-make-a-difference-a-call-for-collective-action/; Carolan, L. (2017). *Mapping open data for accountability: The need for a new framework for open data for accountability*. Transparency and Accountability Initiative. http://www.transparency-initiative.org/wp-content/uploads/2017/06/taiodc_draft_data4accountabilityframework.pdf

65 NRGI (Natural Resource Governance Index). (2017). 2017 Resource Governance Index. https://www.resourcegovernanceindex.org/

66 Gray, J. & D. Lämmerhirt (2019) *Making data public? The Open Data Index as participatory device*. In A. Daly, S.K. Devitt, & M. Mann (Eds.), *Good data*. Amsterdam: Institute of Network Cultures.

67 Open AIR. (2017). Metrics and policies. http://www.openair.org.za/metrics-and-policies/

68 See, for example, adaptive learning approaches, as discussed by the Overseas Development Institute, at https://www.odi.org/sites/odi.org.uk/files/resource-documents/10401.pdf.

023

Privacy

Teresa Scassa

Key points

- Privacy concerns are increasingly at the forefront of debates about data, and publishers of open data are struggling with identifying and addressing potential privacy issues.

- Privacy rights are complex and are not absolute. There is often a balance to strike between transparency and privacy when government information about individuals is involved.

- Striking this balance requires training, resources, and combined commitments to both respecting privacy and advancing openness.

Introduction

Open data programmes urge the release of government datasets in reusable formats under open licences. They also seek to make data findable and datasets interoperable with a view to maximising their reuse both alone and in combination with other datasets. Open data is meant to serve a broad range of purposes, including increasing transparency, enhancing government efficiency, empowering citizens, and stimulating innovation.[1] However, many government datasets also include data about identifiable individuals. Further, some of the most valuable government data is that which relates to citizens and their use of government services.[2] Privacy is, therefore, an important open data issue.

Privacy is treated as a human right in many countries, as well as under several international conventions, including the Charter of Fundamental Rights of the European Union,[3] the Universal Declaration of Human Rights,[4] and the American Convention of Human Rights.[5] Nevertheless, the legal protection available for privacy can vary significantly from one country to another.[6] Some countries have no data protection laws in place.[7] There is also a gap in terms of global data protection frameworks.[8]

Privacy is a broad concept and its normative content may vary from one country to another. Even within individual nations, concepts of privacy may vary considerably among different segments of the population and in different contexts. In the case of information, privacy is often viewed as a right to exercise some form of control over information about one's self.[9]

While the concept of privacy in the abstract may be difficult to encapsulate, many countries have laws that specifically address the obligation of governments to protect the personal information they collect from citizens. Borgesius et al. (2015) observe that around one hundred countries have some form of data privacy law that adopts fair information principles.[10] The General Data Protection Regulation (GDPR),[11] which took effect in the European Union (EU) in May 2018, provides a comprehensive framework for privacy across public and private sectors and may have an impact on privacy protection beyond EU borders.

Data protection laws aim to protect individuals from a range of different harms. These may vary depending on the nature and extent of the disclosure of personal information. A dataset containing information that links an individual to a particular location, workplace, or income bracket could expose that individual to security risks. The release of sensitive personal data (e.g. financial or health information) may have impacts on an individual's ability to gain employment, secure insurance, or other benefits. The disclosure of this type of data may result in more direct and more easily quantifiable harms than the release of less sensitive data.

An example: Gun permits in the United States

Following the tragic school shooting in Newtown, Connecticut, a newspaper used public registry data to create online interactive maps that showed the names and addresses of all registered gun owners in two New York counties.[12] Many individuals expressed outrage either at being identified as living in a household for which a gun permit had been issued or at being identified as one for which no permit had been issued. While the information had been acceptably public when contained in a registry accessible only through a government office or an access to information request, it was considered unacceptably public when represented on an online interactive map.

It is important to note, however, that privacy rights are not absolute, and they are balanced against other competing public interests. One of these is transparency. In many countries, "right to know" or "access to information" laws mandate the release of information in the hands of government, yet also contain limitations on disclosure that serve to protect privacy. In other words, there is a long-standing acknowledgement that there is a balance to be struck between the right to access government information and the privacy rights of citizens.[13] National/state laws may reflect different visions of privacy or may strike a balance between privacy and transparency differently according to prevailing values. The consequence may be that in a context of global, interoperable, government open datasets, the citizens of some countries may find their personal information more exposed than those in other countries (see Figure 1).

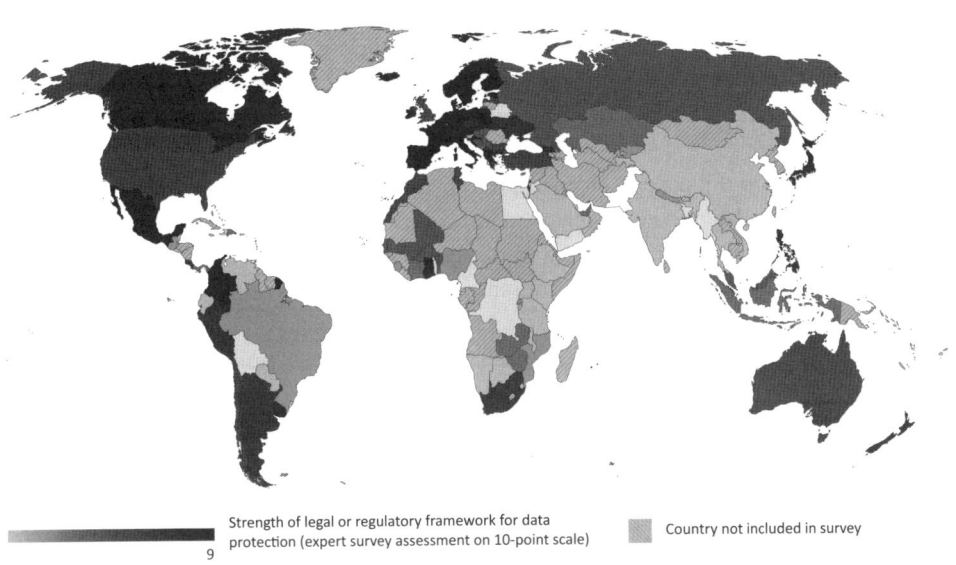

Figure 1:   The Open Data Barometer asks about the presence of robust legal or regulatory frameworks for data protection as part of assessing open data readiness. The results illustrate a global divide in the presence of suitable laws and regulations.
Source: https://opendatabarometer.org/?_year=2017&indicator=ODB

The shifting context for open data and privacy

Privacy concerns are at the forefront of the current context for big data analytics, artificial intelligence, and machine learning, all of which are technologies fuelled by data. Open government data can be used in these new technologies and processes,[14] making privacy concerns more acute. While the loss of control over one's personal information is on its own a harm, in our contemporary big data environment, the potential consequences of this loss of control are magnified. A very broad range of other data that can be associated with individuals through analytics could have impacts on decisions made about those individuals or the opportunities that are offered, or never offered, to them.[15] Adding to the privacy harms that may arise if open datasets inappropriately contain personal information, concerns over privacy could lead citizens to seek to share less data with governments.[16]

The 2013 G8 Open Data Charter[17] did not mention privacy, perhaps because earlier views on open data were that it involved only non-personal data, and therefore, did not raise privacy issues. The potential for reidentification of individuals from deidentified datasets using data from multiple sources (the mosaic effect) sharpened concerns about privacy and open data. The International Open Data Charter of 2015[18] specifically acknowledges that open data by default must involve appropriate anonymisation.

In addition to the issues about how data is used in the context of big data and artificial intelligence, it is important to note that governments are poised to collect even greater volumes of personal information as cities become increasingly sensor-laden and networked. The smart cities context also presents privacy challenges when the release of smart city sensor data is contemplated.[19]

While the focus of this paper is on open government data, it is important to keep in mind that the concept of open data is now broader than just government data. Open data now comes from many different sources, including open scientific data and data voluntarily published by various organisations. Still other data is open in the sense that it is published online and capable of being scraped or otherwise extracted (such as social media platform data).[20] The availability of all of this data contributes to the issues of identifiability of individuals as a result of the release of open government datasets, even in anonymised forms, because of the potential for combining these different sources of data to achieve reidentification. The combined use of data from all of these sources of "open" data in big data analytics and machine learning raises compelling privacy issues, as well as issues that go beyond privacy to social justice and equality.[21]

Key issues

The definition of personal information

Privacy in open government data tends to be addressed through a consideration of whether datasets identified for release contain personal information. As most public sector data protection laws deal with government treatment of personal information, this focus is not surprising. Therefore, the scope of privacy protection in open data depends on the definition of "personal information". Unique identifiers (i.e. names or numbers on official identification documents) are clearly personal information. Some approaches to open data simply consider this type of information to be unsuitable for release as open data. In other words, open data is, by definition, data that does not include personal information.[22] Nevertheless, the obligation to protect privacy generally goes beyond merely declining to release datasets that contain unique personal identifiers, such as names or identity numbers. Privacy is generally defined for data protection purposes as "information about an identifiable individual" or "personally identifiable information". Identifiability has been interpreted broadly by many data protection authorities. Thus, if an individual can be identified from a dataset when it is combined with other available data, regardless of the source of that data, then the dataset is said to contain personal information.[23] Notorious examples involving supposedly deidentified or anonymised private sector data include the reidentification of individuals from anonymised datasets of Netflix viewing habits,[24] or, more recently, from anonymised data used to create Strava heat maps.[25] As data analytics become more sophisticated, and as the volume of available "other" data grows exponentially, reidentification risks in anonymised datasets may be extremely high.[26] Ohm cautions that in a big data era, the effectiveness of anonymisation techniques may be considerably undermined.[27] If taken to a logical extreme, reidentification risks could lead to decisions not to release any government data that might be linked to identifiable individuals. This would significantly reduce the stock of available open data. Some researchers insist that remote and intangible risks should not drive policies around open data in light of strong anonymisation techniques, and they have designed and proposed anonymisation tools and techniques to support the release of useful data.[28]

Not all personal information necessarily has the same level of sensitivity. Some categories, such as health data or data about religious or ethnic identity, may be considered more sensitive than others.[29] The level of sensitivity may determine the degree of anonymisation required before a dataset can be released as open data.

Although not strictly personal information, "demographically identifiable information" (DII) or "community identifiable information" (CII) may also be sensitive information. DII is defined as "data that can be used to identify a community or distinct group, whether geographic, ethnic, religious, economic, or political".[30]

The privacy/transparency balance

When it comes to the relationship between citizens and the state, privacy is not an absolute. In many instances, privacy is balanced with transparency, permitting the public disclosure of some forms of personal information (e.g. political donations, permit applications, land titles registration, etc.). In some cases, this balance is defined within specific legislative instruments that determine how particular kinds of information are to be dealt with. In other cases, general principles are found in access to information/right to know laws. As Borgesius et al. (2015) note, the privacy/transparency balance was negotiated in the context of such laws for decades prior to the open data movement.[31]

It is sometimes difficult to separate information about institutions from information about individuals.[32] The balance between privacy and transparency may be struck differently in different countries, depending upon political and social contexts. For example, in some countries, battling corruption may be seen as a more urgent priority than protecting privacy. This does not mean that privacy is not respected, but it may mean that there is less privacy with respect to some kinds of information that is shared with government. Greater transparency may also serve goals of equity by exposing biases and inequality. Principles of transparency may mandate the disclosure of considerable amounts of quite personal information. For example, open court principles require trials to be open to the public, and mandate the publication of court and tribunal decisions.[33] Some governments require the publication of the salaries of public servants, identified by name and position. While it is possible to treat some of this information as open information and not open data (i.e. publishing it in tabular form on a website, rather than as a downloadable dataset), the technological reality is that once it is published in either form, it is available for extraction and reuse. Thus, although there is a distinction between open data and open information, it may be largely meaningless from a privacy perspective.

In cases where such data is shared publicly, their transparency value is considered to outweigh any privacy concerns. In many cases, however, these assessments may have been made in a pre-digital era or at least prior to our big data era. Where this is the case, the privacy impacts of the release of such data may have changed and may require reassessment.[34] Assessing privacy impacts throughout the life of a dataset, and not just upon its release, is now an open data best practice.[35] Recent struggles in Canada with the exploitation of personal information contained in court and tribunal decisions published online highlight these challenges.[36]

As noted earlier, different countries may set the balance between privacy and transparency differently, and open data is available without geographic restrictions. Its users may be found anywhere in the world. Therefore, while the transparency benefits of open data tend to be experienced within the jurisdiction releasing the data, the privacy risks may be global.

> ### An example: Court decisions in Canada
>
> Court and administrative tribunal decisions in Canada are published on the websites of the specific courts and tribunals, as well as on CanLII, a portal that aggregates and provides open access to these documents. These decisions often contain personal information, some of which might be quite sensitive. To balance the open court principle with privacy rights, the court, tribunal, and CanLII websites do not permit indexing by search engines. In 2013, the Office of the Privacy Commissioner of Canada began receiving complaints that a Romanian-based entity was scraping decisions from these websites and posting the decisions on its own fully indexed website. Individuals who complained to the Romanian website about the publication of their personal information were offered the option to pay in order to have this information deleted. A court case brought in Canada ruled that the Romanian site breached Canadian data protection law, ordering the site to remove all Canadian court and tribunal decisions that contained personal information.

Open data challenges

There are some features of open data that present particular challenges when it comes to addressing privacy issues. For example, the ideal of open data is data that "can be freely used, modified, and shared by anyone for any purpose".[37] This includes commercial purposes. The commercial reuse of open data, particularly in a big data environment, may increase privacy risks.[38] As noted earlier, some of the most useful and important datasets are ones that relate to citizen activities and their consumption of public services.[39] Data may, therefore, be more useful if it contains personal information.[40] It may also be less useful if anonymisation techniques substantially impact the data for certain purposes.[41]

Other challenges exist at the operational level. Identifying datasets that contain personal information and preparing them for release through anonymisation can be time and resource intensive. In some cases, available government resources may not be sufficient for the task.[42] Further, deciding whether datasets contain information capable of leading to the reidentification of individuals can be challenging, as can determinations of whether the anonymisation techniques applied are adequate, depending on the degree of sensitivity of the data. In many cases, civil servants are left to make judgement calls about whether certain datasets should be released. This can lead to variance from one government department to another in terms of willingness to release certain types of datasets. Further, a risk-averse government culture may lean toward non-release where any doubts arise.[43] Some have argued that open data requires a cultural shift within governments to overcome such barriers and hesitations.[44] In the case of privacy, that cultural shift might mean accepting some level of reidentification risk.

Privacy issues and preparing open data for release

A considerable amount of work has gone into the design and development of guidance for governments around how to open data while addressing privacy concerns. Some of this work has been led by governments involved in the release of open data and some by academics. Considerable attention has been paid to the development of tools, analytical frameworks, and other guidance documents.[45] These are meant to provide practical guidance to those who must decide whether a dataset that contains personal information should be opened, and then, if so, decide how the dataset should be dealt with in order to protect privacy.

One important privacy-protective measure is greater government awareness of the importance of limiting the collection of personal information to only that which is truly necessary.[46] Another measure is to conduct risk/benefit analyses or privacy impact assessments with respect to the release of datasets that may raise privacy concerns.[47] Given the rapidly changing technology and big data context, it is also advisable that privacy issues be considered at every stage of a dataset's life cycle and not just at the point leading up to its publication as open data.[48] Attention must also be paid to the various techniques that are available for removing personal information, including pseudonymisation (replacing names with unique identifiers) or anonymisation. Various anonymisation techniques exist, including aggregation and randomisation.[49]

Some have argued that the release of datasets that raise potential privacy issues might call for a different kind of licensing.[50] In other words, such datasets might be subject to licences that restrict their reuse to only certain contexts (e.g. non-commercial) or that prohibit activities aimed at reidentification. However, privacy protection through licensing terms depends on the licensor's ability to track and monitor reuse, as well as their willingness to take legal action in case of breach of terms.

Some now argue for a more nuanced approach to "open". For example, the Open Data Institute (ODI) proposes a spectrum of openness with different levels of access to data depending upon its nature, the identity of the user, and the proposed use (see Figure 2, overleaf).

Conclusion

There is no doubt that privacy is a key issue for open data. Not only does citizen trust depend on governments' abilities to appropriately protect the personal information that is shared with them, individuals can be exposed to privacy harms if personal information is inappropriately shared. Nevertheless, privacy rights are not an absolute. The need to balance privacy with transparency in relation to government information and data predates the open data movement. In some cases, public interest in transparency may justify the disclosure of personal information as open data. Privacy is a concept that can vary from one country to another and among subgroups within a given country. In addition, the privacy/transparency balance may be struck differently in different countries depending on the relative importance of either goal. It is important to note, however, that privacy impacts may now be experienced on a global scale.

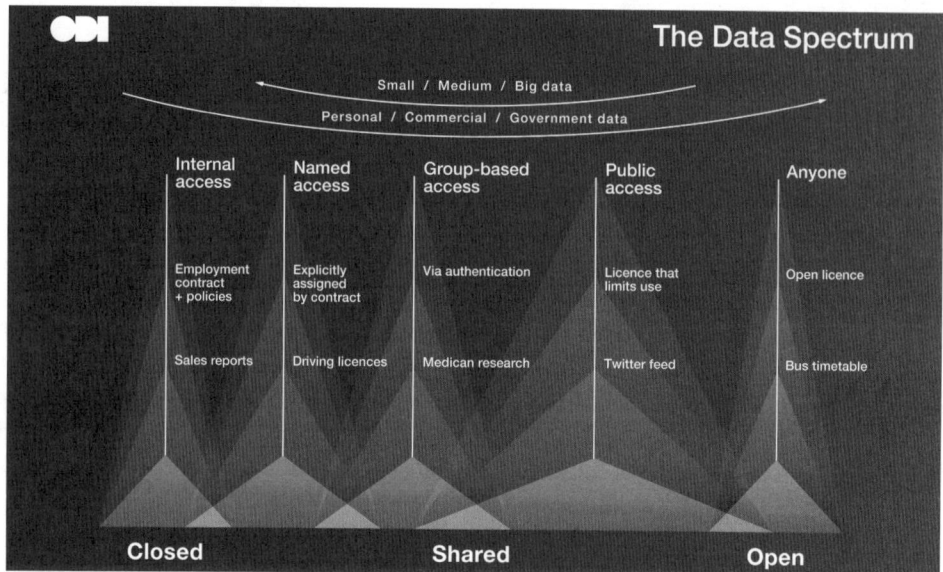

Figure 2: The Open Data Spectrum was published in 2016, consolidating a growing understanding in the open data field that ideas of "open by default" must be considered alongside a recognition of legitimate access control for some datasets.
Source: https://theodi.org/about-the-odi/the-data-spectrum/

The rapidly evolving era of big data and artificial intelligence has given rise to new uses for open government data. These technologies also increase the risk of reidentification of individuals through the matching of anonymised data from multiple different sources. This increased reidentification risk poses challenges for the release of useful open data, and requires a carefully balanced approach. Some reidentification risk may be acceptable, depending on the nature and value of the data at issue. Over the last few years, there has been a proliferation of tools to provide guidance to government agencies and departments struggling with open data privacy issues. These tools will be useful to those who want to open up data in other contexts as well.

At the same time as the publishers of open data struggle with identifying and addressing potential privacy issues, a large volume of often highly personal information is routinely published by governments based on policies developed prior to the big data era, and, in some cases, even prior to the internet. Publicly available personal information is found in multiple government registries, as well as in court and tribunal decisions, and it is published under various transparency laws and policies related to elections, procurement, public sector salaries, etc. The impacts of the digital environment and of big data on privacy in relation to these categories of government data will require a reassessment of how such data is made publicly available.

Balancing privacy and transparency in the release of open data will require training and resources, and the commitment of governments to provide these resources will have a significant impact on how the balance is struck. When datasets contain personal information, a simple refusal to disclose the datasets will limit access to the data for reuse. Instead, what is required is a process for determining whether the data can be adequately anonymised to protect privacy while furthering the release of open data.

Further reading

Borgesius, F.Z., Gray, J., & Van Eechoud, M. (2015). Open data, privacy, and fair information principles: Towards a balancing framework. *Berkeley Technology Law Journal*, *30(3)*, 2073–2130. http://btlj.org/data/articles2015/vol30/30_3/2073-2132%20Borgesius.pdf

Finkle, E. (2016). *Resources: Open data release toolkit*. Version 1.2. San Francisco, CA: Data SF. https://datasf.org/resources/open-data-release-toolkit/

Floridi, L. (2014). Open data, data protection, and group privacy. *Philosophy and Technology*, *27(1)*, 1–3. https://link.springer.com/article/10.1007/s13347-014-0157-8

Garfinkel, S.L. (2016). *De-identifying government datasets*. DRAFT NIST Special Publication 800-188. Washington, DC: US Department of Commerce, National Institute of Standards and Technology. https://csrc.nist.gov/csrc/media/publications/sp/800-188/archive/2016-08-25/documents/sp800_188_draft.pdf

Green, B., Cunningham, G., Ekblaw, A., Kominers, P., Linzer, A., & Crawford, S. (2017). *Open data privacy*. Cambridge, MA: Berkman Klein Center for Internet & Society Research Publication. https://cyber.harvard.edu/publications/2017/02/opendataprivacyplaybook

ODI (Open Data Institute). (n.d.). The data spectrum. https://theodi.org/about-the-odi/the-data-spectrum/

About the author

Teresa Scassa is the Canada Research Chair in Information Law and Policy at the University of Ottawa. She teaches and researches in the area of information law, including intellectual property and privacy law. More information about Teresa is available at https://www.teresascassa.ca.

How to cite this chapter

Scassa, T. (2019). Issues in open data: Privacy. In T. Davies, S. Walker, M. Rubinstein, & F. Perini (Eds.), *The state of open data: Histories and horizons* (pp. 339–350). Cape Town and Ottawa: African Minds and International Development Research Centre. http://stateofopendata.od4d.net

This work is licensed under a Creative Commons Attribution 4.0 International (CC BY 4.0) licence. It was carried out with the aid of a grant from the International Development Research Centre, Ottawa, Canada.

Endnotes

1. Davies, T.G. (2014). Open data policies and practice: An international comparison. *SSRN* [Article], 5 September. http://dx.doi.org/10.2139/ssrn.2492520
2. Simperl, E., O'Hara, K., & Gomer, R. (2016). *Analytical report 3: Open data and privacy*. Luxembourg: European Data Portal. https://www.europeandataportal.eu/sites/default/files/open_data_and_privacy_v1_final_clean.pdf
3. EU. (2000). *Charter of Fundamental Rights of the European Union*, 2000/C 364/01. Brussels, Belgium: European Union Parliament. http://www.europarl.europa.eu/charter/pdf/text_en.pdf
4. UN. (1948). *Universal Declaration of Human Rights*. General Assembly Resolution 217A. New York, NY: United Nations. http://www.un.org/en/universal-declaration-human-rights/
5. OAS. (1969). *American Convention on Human Rights*. Washington, DC: Organization of American States. https://www.cidh.oas.org/basicos/english/basic3.american%20convention.htm
6. See, for example, DLA Piper. (2018). Data protection laws of the world. https://www.dlapiperdataprotection.com/
7. UNCTAD (United Nations Conference on Trade and Development). (n.d.). Summary of adoption of e-commerce legislation worldwide. New York, NY: United Nations. http://unctad.org/en/Pages/DTL/STI_and_ICTs/ICT4D-Legislation/eCom-Global-Legislation.aspx
8. UNCTAD (United Nations Conference on Trade and Development). (2016). *Data protection regulations and international data flows: Implications for trade and development*. New York, NY: United Nations. http://unctad.org/en/PublicationsLibrary/dtlstict2016d1_en.pdf
9. Nissenbaum, H. (2016). *Privacy in context: Technology, policy, and the integrity of social life*. Stanford, CA: Stanford Law Books; Solove, D.J. (2008). *Understanding privacy*. Cambridge, MA: Harvard University Press.
10. Borgesius, F.Z., Gray, J., & Van Eeechoud, M. (2015). Open data, privacy, and fair information principles: Towards a balancing framework. *Berkeley Technology Law Journal*, *30(3)*, 2073–2130.
11. GDPR (General Data Protection Regulation). (2018). Regulation (EU) 2016/679, *OJ* L 119, 04.05.2016; cor. *OJ* L 127, 23.5.2018. Strasbourg: European Parliament and Council of the European Union. https://gdpr-info.eu/
12. Worley, D.R. (2012). *The gun owner next door: What you don't know about the weapons in your neighbourhood*. http://people.sju.edu/~ggrevera/se/privacyIssues/JournalNews-The-gun-owner-next-door.pdf
13. Janssen, K. (2012). Open government and the right to information: Opportunities and obstacles. *Journal of Community Informatics*, *8(2)*, 1–11.
14. Kitchin, R. (2014). *The data revolution: Big data, open data, data infrastructures & their consequences*. London: SAGE Publications Ltd.
15. Borgesius, F.Z., Gray, J., & Van Eechoud, M. (2015). Open data, privacy, and fair information principles: Towards a balancing framework. *Berkeley Technology Law Journal*, *30(3)*, 2073–2130; Citron, D.K. & Pasquale, F.A. (2014). The scored society: Due process for automated predictions. *Washington Law Review*, *89*, 1–34. https://ssrn.com/abstract=2376209
16. Borgesius, F.Z., Gray, J., & Van Eechoud, M. (2015). Open data, privacy, and fair information principles: Towards a balancing framework. *Berkeley Technology Law Journal*, *30(3)*, 2073–2130.
17. https://www.gov.uk/government/publications/open-data-charter/g8-open-data-charter-and-technical-annex
18. https://opendatacharter.net/
19. Borgesius, F.Z., Gray, J., & Van Eechoud, M. (2015). Open data, privacy, and fair information principles: Towards a balancing framework. *Berkeley Technology Law Journal*, *30(3)*, 2073–2130.
20. Scassa, T. (2017). Sharing data in the platform economy: A public interest argument for access to platform data. *University of British Columbia Law Review*, *50(4)*, 1017–1071. https://papers.ssrn.com/sol3/papers.cfm?abstract_id=3077996

21 Citron, D.K. & Pasquale, F.A. (2014). The scored society: Due process for automated predictions. *Washington Law Review*, *89*, 1–34. https://ssrn.com/abstract=2376209; Kim, P.T. (2017). Auditing algorithms for discrimination. *University of Pennsylvania Law Review*, *166*, 189–203.

22 Open Knowledge International. (n.d.). What is open data? In *The open data handbook*. Cambridge, UK: Open Knowledge International. http://opendatahandbook.org/guide/en/what-is-open-data/

23 Scassa, T. (2010). Geographic information as personal information. *Oxford University Commonwealth Law Journal*, *10(2)*, 185–214.

24 Porter, C.C. (2008). De-identified data and third party data mining: The risk of re-identification of personal information. *Shidler J.L. Com. & Tech*, *5(1)*. http://www.lctjournal.washington.edu/Vol5/a03Porter.html

25 Hsu, J. (2018). The Strava Heat Map and the end of secrets. *Wired*, 29 January. https://www.wired.com/story/strava-heat-map-military-bases-fitness-trackers-privacy/

26 Green, B., Cunningham, G., Ekblaw, A., Kominers, P., Linzer, A., & Crawford, S. (2017). *Open data privacy*. Cambridge, MA: Berkman Klein Center for Internet & Society Research Publication. https://cyber.harvard.edu/publications/2017/02/opendataprivacyplaybook; Ohm, P. (2017). Broken promises of privacy: Responding to the surprising failure of anonymization. *UCLA Law Rev*, *57*, 1701–1777; Sweeney, L. (2010). k-Anonymity: A model for protecting privacy. *International Journal on Uncertainty, Fuzziness and Knowledge-Based Systems*, *10(5)*, 557–570. https://epic.org/privacy/reidentification/Sweeney_Article.pdf

27 Ohm, P. (2017). Broken promises of privacy: Responding to the surprising failure of anonymization. *UCLA Law Rev*, *57*, 1701–1777.

28 See, for example, El Emam, K. (2013). *Guide to the de-identification of personal health information*. Boca Raton, FA: CRC Press.

29 ICO (Information Commissioner's Office). (n.d.). Special category data. https://ico.org.uk/for-organisations/guide-to-the-general-data-protection-regulation-gdpr/lawful-basis-for-processing/special-category-data/

30 NRC. (2017*). 510 Data Responsibility Policy*. Version 2.0, 8 November. The Hague: Netherlands Red Cross. https://www.510.global/wp-content/uploads/2017/11/510_Data_Responsibility_Policy_V.2_PUBLIC-1.pdf

31 Borgesius, F.Z., Gray, J., & Van Eechoud, M. (2015). Open data, privacy, and fair information principles: Towards a balancing framework. *Berkeley Technology Law Journal*, *30(3)*, 2073–2130.

32 Simperl, E., O'Hara, K., & Gomer, R. (2016). *Analytical report 3: Open data and privacy*. Luxembourg: European Data Portal. https://www.europeandataportal.eu/sites/default/files/open_data_and_privacy_v1_final_clean.pdf

33 Scassa, T. (2014). Privacy and open government. *Future Internet*, *6*, 397–413. www.mdpi.com/1999-5903/6/2/397/pdf

34 Ibid.; Borgesius, F.Z., Gray, J., & Van Eechoud, M. (2015). Open data, privacy, and fair information principles: Towards a balancing framework. *Berkeley Technology Law Journal*, *30(3)*, 2073–2130.

35 Green, B., Cunningham, G., Ekblaw, A., Kominers, P., Linzer, A., & Crawford, S. (2017). *Open data privacy*. Cambridge, MA: Berkman Klein Center for Internet & Society Research Publication. https://cyber.harvard.edu/publications/2017/02/opendataprivacyplaybook

36 Dobby, C. (2015). Canadians upset with Romanian website that exposes court case details. *The Globe and Mail*, 4 January. http://www.theglobeandmail.com/report-on-business/industry-news/the-law-page/canadians-upset-over-romanian-website-that-exposes-court-case-details/article22284367/; *A.T. v. Globe24h.com*, 2017 FC 114 (CanLII). http://canlii.ca/t/gx6bl

37 Open Knowledge International. (n.d.). The Open Definition. Cambridge, UK: Open Knowledge International. http://opendefinition.org; Ubaldi, B. (2013). *Open government data: Towards empirical analysis of open government data initiatives*. OECD Working Papers on Public Governance 22, p. 6. Paris: Organisation for Economic Co-operation and Development Publishing. http://dx.doi.org/10.1787/5k46bj4f03s7-en

38 Simperl, E., O'Hara, K., & Gomer, R. (2016). *Analytical report 3: Open data and privacy*. Luxembourg: European Data Portal. https://www.europeandataportal.eu/sites/default/files/open_data_and_privacy_v1_final_clean.pdf

39 Simperl, E., O'Hara, K., & Gomer, R. (2016). *Analytical report 3: Open data and privacy*. Luxembourg: European Data Portal. https://www.europeandataportal.eu/sites/default/files/open_data_and_privacy_v1_final_clean.pdf

40 Green, B., Cunningham, G., Ekblaw, A., Kominers, P., Linzer, A., & Crawford, S. (2017). *Open data privacy*. Cambridge, MA: Berkman Klein Center for Internet & Society Research Publication. https://cyber.harvard.edu/publications/2017/02/opendataprivacyplaybook

41 Garfinkel, S.L. (2016). *De-identifying government datasets*. DRAFT NIST Special Publication 800-188. Washington, DC: US Department of Commerce, National Institute of Standards and Technology. https://csrc.nist.gov/csrc/media/publications/sp/800-188/archive/2016-08-25/documents/sp800_188_draft.pdf

42 Johnson, P.A., Sieber, R.E., Scassa, T., Stephens, M., & Robinson, P.J. (2017). The cost(s) of geospatial open data. *Transactions in GIS, 21*, 434–445. http://onlinelibrary.wiley.com/doi/10.1111/tgis.12283/full

43 Huijboom, N. & Van den Broek, T. (2011). Open data: An international comparison of strategies. *European Journal of ePractice, 12*, 1–13. https://research.vu.nl/en/publications/open-data-an-international-comparison-of-strategies

44 See, for example, Davies, T. & Bawa, Z.A. (2012). The promises and perils of Open Government Data (OGD). *The Journal of Community Informatics, 8(2)*. http://ci-journal.net/index.php/ciej/article/view/929/926

45 See, for example, Green, B., Cunningham, G., Ekblaw, A., Kominers, P., Linzer, A., & Crawford, S. (2017). *Open data privacy*. Cambridge, MA: Berkman Klein Center for Internet & Society Research Publication. https://cyber.harvard.edu/publications/2017/02/opendataprivacyplaybook; Borgesius, F.Z., Gray, J., & Van Eechoud, M. (2015). Open data, privacy, and fair information principles: Towards a balancing framework. *Berkeley Technology Law Journal, 30(3)*, 2073–2130; Garfinkel, S.L. (2016). *De-identifying government datasets*. DRAFT NIST Special Publication 800-188. Washington, DC: US Department of Commerce, National Institute of Standards and Technology. https://csrc.nist.gov/csrc/media/publications/sp/800-188/archive/2016-08-25/documents/sp800_188_draft.pdf; Finkle, E. (2016). *Resources: Open data release toolkit*. Version 1.2. San Francisco, CA: Data SF. https://datasf.org/resources/open-data-release-toolkit/; Article 29 Data Protection Working Party. (2013). Opinion 06/2013 on open data and Public Sector Information ('PSI') reuse. http://www.gpdp.gov.mo/uploadfile/2014/0505/20140505062629657.pdf; Scassa, T. & Conroy, A. (2016). Strategies for protecting privacy in open data and proactive disclosure. *Canadian Journal of Law and Technology, 14*, 215–262.

46 Scassa, T. & Conroy, A. (2016). Strategies for protecting privacy in open data and proactive disclosure. *Canadian Journal of Law and Technology, 14*, 215–262; IPC. (2009). *Privacy and government 2.0: The implications of an open world*. Toronto: Information and Privacy Commissioner of Ontario. http://www.ontla.on.ca/library/repository/mon/23006/293152.pdf

47 Scassa, T. & Conroy, A. (2016). Strategies for protecting privacy in open data and proactive disclosure. *Canadian Journal of Law and Technology, 14*, 215–262; Green, B., Cunningham, G., Ekblaw, A., Kominers, P., Linzer, A., & Crawford, S. (2017). *Open data privacy*. Cambridge, MA: Berkman Klein Center for Internet & Society Research Publication. https://cyber.harvard.edu/publications/2017/02/opendataprivacyplaybook

48 Simperl, E., O'Hara, K., & Gomer, R. (2016). *Analytical Report 3: Open data and privacy*. Luxembourg: European Data Portal. https://www.europeandataportal.eu/sites/default/files/open_data_and_privacy_v1_final_clean.pdf

49 See, for example, Garfinkel, S.L. (2016). *De-identifying government datasets*. DRAFT NIST Special Publication 800-188. Washington, DC: US Department of Commerce, National Institute of Standards and Technology. https://csrc.nist.gov/csrc/media/publications/sp/800-188/archive/2016-08-25/documents/sp800_188_draft.pdf; Finkle, E. (2016). *Resources: Open data release toolkit*. Version 1.2. San Francisco, CA: Data SF. https://datasf.org/resources/open-data-release-toolkit/; Scassa, T. & Conroy, A. (2016). Strategies for protecting privacy in open data and proactive disclosure. *Canadian Journal of Law and Technology, 14*, 215–262.

50 Borgesius, F.Z., Gray, J., & Van Eechoud, M. (2015). Open data, privacy, and fair information principles: Towards a balancing framework. *Berkeley Technology Law Journal, 30(3)*, 2073–2130; Scassa, T. & Conroy, A. (2016). Strategies for protecting privacy in open data and proactive disclosure. *Canadian Journal of Law and Technology, 14*, 215–262.

Section 03

Open Data Stakeholders

CONTENTS

Introduction	352
Chapter 24. Civil society	355
Chapter 25. Donors and investors	367
Chapter 26. Governments	381
Chapter 27. Journalists and the media	395
Chapter 28. Multilateral organisations	406
Chapter 29. Private sector	418
Chapter 30. Researchers	430

The chapters in this section explore the various roles of the major stakeholders that have shaped the development of the open data ecosystem, including civil society, government, the private sector, journalists, researchers, donors, and multilateral agencies.

Mapping the stakeholders

For the most part, the authors that have contributed to this section offer their perspective as members of their respective stakeholder groups. The selection of chapters draws on discussions at recent events, such as the International Open Data Conference and Open Government Partnership Summit, where civil society, governments, researchers, and donors, among others, have all hosted their own side events, reflecting on their particular agendas, roles, and shared interests. As Wilson notes, the dividing line between different stakeholders is not always clear (Chapter 24: Civil society). In some contexts, private sector and civil society organisations (CSOs) may be competing to provide the same services, and, as Van Schalkwyk explores, the landscape of research often involves overlapping networks of academics, CSOs, and donor-backed projects (Chapter 30: Researchers). Open data itself is a contributing factor in blurring the boundaries between different stakeholder groups, creating what Hammer refers to as "the need for new paradigmatic thinking about the relationships among governments, civil society, the private sector, and citizens" (Chapter 28: Multilateral organisations, p. 413). For example, when relevant data is open, roles formerly carried out by governments might shift to the private sector, or the work of journalists might be carried out by civil society startups. In looking at different stakeholder groups, it is necessary to pay attention as much to their inter-relationships as to their distinctive roles.

Institutionalisation, engagement, and sustainability

One thing is clear in the chapters that follow. The work of all stakeholder groups has evolved over time. Chapters on governments (Chapter 26) and on multilateral organisations (Chapter 28) highlight an increase in the consolidation of supply-side arrangements for open data provision, and as part of this maturation of organisational approaches to open data, new institutional and governance arrangements are evolving to move from innovation and experimentation to long-term sustainability. The authors of these two chapters identify the need for open data to be further integrated into existing funding streams and policy agendas and for the creation of collaborative spaces, where governments and multilaterals can work with other stakeholders to align data supply and tools for reuse with external demands. This points to a key tension that may be prevalent in the years ahead between a desire to maintain the generative, collaborative, and silo-busting spirit of open data work, while, at the same time, making it more business-as-usual and less reliant on political leaders whose tenure is always temporary.

Making sure that potential users have the capacity to work with open data surfaces is a critical challenge for a number of the stakeholders discussed in this section. Chapter 24 (Civil society) describes international CSOs that have been able to hire data science specialists, adopting agile and user-centric development methodologies from the private sector. However, for most CSOs at the national level, as well as for small and medium-sized enterprises (SMEs) in the private sector, particularly in the Global South, the skills, experience, and intermediary support required to leverage open data remains scarce.

Chapter 27 (Journalists and the media) describes significant challenges associated with creating the business cases necessary to sustain data journalism. Although journalists are essential partners in turning national and local government open data into resources for transparency and accountability, the business models behind conventional journalism are collapsing and data journalism has not yet adequately refined new approaches that can fill this gap with a measure of stability. There is a very real risk that, just at the point when governments may be on track to make open data supply more reliable, potential users from civil society, journalism, and the private sector will exhaust their resources, and open data will remain unused.

The critical duality of the role of donors is explored in Chapter 25 (Donors and investors). Donors have not only provided much needed financial support for open data research and initiatives all over the world, they also play an important convening role, shaping the field through their interventions. The last decade has seen a number of efforts at consolidation and coordination of open data investments, and this chapter suggests a number of sectors have reached a level of resilience with access to funding from a diverse set of donors, while other sectors remain highly dependent on a smaller pool of funders and are vulnerable to a loss of funding. In outlining the risks moving forward, the chapter points to shifting donor priorities and the threat this may present to future work needed to improve interoperability and data infrastructures, as well as that required to increase collaboration and community linkages across the open data ecosystem.

Who's who?

Although each stakeholder group may possess its own structures and logic, there are, ultimately, individual stakeholders active in leading and shaping open data practice. Chapter 30 (Researchers) explores the composition of the research community, identifying particular biases toward Northern-led research, male authors, and a lack of inter-regional collaboration. The author also notes that the composition of the stakeholder group has a substantial impact on the areas of research explored and types of outcomes it produces. This is a theme that is also picked up in both the private sector (Chapter 29) and civil society (Chapter 24) chapters, where both geographical and gender biases are identified as issues to be addressed, and there is a common call to go beyond the "usual suspects" and to ensure greater inclusiveness of open data programmes and initiatives.

This points to another area of limited information with regard to open data activity. Although Chapter 25 (Donors and investors) offers us a view of those organisations with active open data projects, unlike the bibliometrics analysis carried out in Chapter 30 (Researchers), it is not easy to determine who makes up the network of individuals actually responsible for implementing these projects. Although a number of organisations have been involved, this may serve to obscure that a relatively small number of individuals moving between organisations, both as funders and implementers, make up the true support base for open data work. Providing pathways for new actors to engage with open data, and to expand that experience over time, is an important aspect of increasing diversity and sustainability.

Stakeholder horizons

The context for open data work is changing for all stakeholders. Chapter 28 (Multilateral organisations) sums up current technologically driven change as a "fourth industrial revolution", a source both of new opportunities but also new challenges, such as threats to privacy, structural job losses, and growing social dislocation. Chapter 27 (Journalists and the media) refers to the erosion of public trust and the centralisation of power in the hands of major internet platforms. Against this backdrop, governments, private sector firms, donors, CSOs, and researchers are all challenged to consider whether to maintain a full-time focus on open data or shift their limited resources to other potential tools for development, democratisation, or profit-making.

The authors in this section are largely in favour of maintaining a distinct emphasis on open data while also working to connect open data with other agendas. They recognise that the last decade has laid considerable groundwork, but that, in light of capacity gaps and unstable funding, it is only now that open data resources largely untapped to date might start to be put to greater use. The recommendations across these chapters are also remarkably well aligned: more investment in capacity building and data use; a focus on inclusion; continued work to align data supply and demand; support for mainstreaming open data into sectoral work, while retaining resources to work on core open data issues; and support for increasing engagement with data and open data in the Global South. Both the chapters on the private sector (Chapter 29) and civil society (Chapter 24) also place an emphasis on the need for more targeted and actionable project level metrics, as opposed to measurement that tries to estimate the state or value of the open data field in general.

The section as a whole puts forth grounds for both cautious optimism and concern. In light of reflective learning across a range of stakeholders, the required conditions to secure impacts from open data are closer than ever, but there are ongoing concerns that, in the majority of sectors, advances to date will be difficult to maintain if internal commitment and external investment are reduced in a more crowded and confusing data policy landscape.

024

Civil society

Christopher Wilson

Key points

- Civil society has been a driving force in advancing open data agendas, especially through standard setting, awareness raising, and defining public expectations.

- The conceptual ambiguity around open government data presents strategic challenges for civil society and can lead to competition for resources between civil society organisations and private sector startups.

- Smaller civil society organisations still lack the resources to develop the technical capacities they need to take advantage of open data.

- Future work should move beyond engagement with the "usual suspects" in the open data community to focus on developing the capacities of established national-level civil society organisations that are closer to grassroots activities.

Introduction

Civil society has been a key force in advancing the open data movement over the last ten years. Many of the most prominent milestones during that time have involved the setting of standards and expectations for open data globally. From the articulation of open government data principles in 2007[1] to agreement on the Open Definition and standards for open data licensing in 2012 and 2013 and the launch of the Open Data Charter in 2015, civil society actors have played a key role in convening stakeholders, framing agendas, and driving open data uptake across sectors and policy domains.

As a result of these efforts, open data has been widely accepted as a progressive civic norm,[2] a public policy resource,[3,4] an engine for generating economic wealth,[5] and an established field of practice and study.[6,7] However, this level of success has resulted in new challenges for civil society. As the open data movement gains salience among different stakeholder groups and in different sectors, civil society organisations have been called upon to play a wider role.

Civil society organisations regularly campaign for the release of open data and raise public awareness about open data availability. They provide technical consulting services to stakeholders and often build the online platforms that host open data. They facilitate interaction between government institutions and community groups, while also training other organisations as potential users and educating them on how open data can help to fulfil their mandates. Civil society organisations conduct user research but also conduct investigative research using open data to act as a democratic watchdog. When data is lacking, civil society often collects and publishes that missing data to drive advocacy and raise public awareness, fills gaps in government data, and supports policy-making. In one form or another in a multitude of countries across the world, civil society plays an intermediary role, making government data open and useful to the public.[8] Civil society, it seems, can do it all.

Civil society is often a sort of chameleon, picking up the slack and adapting to the strategic environments in which it needs to work. In the context of the open data movement, however, this capacity for adaptation has perhaps been civil society's most defining feature. As the movement has matured from statements of principle to the messy realities of open data implementation, things have become more complicated. Inflated expectations, ambiguous roles, strategic challenges, and unanticipated ethical dilemmas all pose new demands on civil society. Simultaneously, the capacities and resources required to meet these challenges are often unequally distributed. Despite all this, and notwithstanding the absence of clear evidence that open data is having any consistent impact on governance processes, civil society remains remarkably invested in advancing the open data movement and may well be the movement's greatest resource. To understand this potential and its limitations, this chapter presents four key trends in civil society engagement with open data over the last ten years.

Key trends

Fragmentation and ambiguity

One of the most remarkable trends in the development of the open data movement has been the proliferation of practical and rhetorical ambiguity as open data discourse has spread across sectors and fields of practice. Domain-level ambiguity in popular discourse is likely the most obvious example of this as evidenced by regular equivocation between open data, open government data, and open government. While conceptually distinct, these three terms are often muddied in use and in practice. For example, open government activities have been criticised for overemphasising open data,[9,10] and the presumption that open data is necessarily government data obscures the important role played by civil society organisations and the private sector in generating and opening data for public use.[11,12] Similarly, significant advances by the open data community have complicated collaboration between advocates for open data and advocates for freedom of information,[13] raising questions about compatibility and the competition for resources.[14]

Further ambiguity can be noted when considering the types of actors that participate in open data discourse. The open data movement can be considered as a Venn diagram in which one circle is populated by government accountability advocates and organisations working on civic technology and the other is populated by organisations focused on profit-making, either startups using data as part of a business model or investors and entrepreneurs who couple their financial objectives with social aims. Some organisations have blurred this line further by adopting a for-profit model in an effort to enhance their sustainability and reduce reliance on grant-makers, although some research suggests that this has an impact on the way organisations function and the projects they implement.[15]

Government actors can be seen engaging with open data to support accountability and to generate value, but not necessarily in equal measure. This dual engagement with two normatively distinct fields of practice is both an advantage and a challenge for open data advocates. While the "big tent" approach is advantageous for recruiting broad support,[16,17] a diversity in approaches to different types of activities can frustrate expectations and complicate agreement on objectives.

Similar strategic dilemmas are posed by open data's increased relevance across a broad swathe of policy areas. While salience in multiple sectors undoubtedly carries a rhetorical advantage for campaigning and lobbying activities, the demands and practicalities of mainstreaming meaningful open data practice vary significantly from sector to sector. This forces civil society organisations to build specific capacities if they wish to support open health data, open transportation data, open land data, etc. Given the capacity restraints experienced by many civil society organisations, this often forces a choice between sectoral specialisation and a more generalised, high-level advocacy. This trade-off is particularly noteworthy as pioneering open data initiatives move beyond early success, revealing the critical need for high-level policy engagement to address challenges of institutionalisation and sustainability.[18,19]

The increased standing of open data over the last decade has broadened and diversified the open data discourse. Likewise, this has dramatically increased the diversification of civil society organisations working with open data that today draw from a variety of sectors and organisational models. This diversification brings a nuts-and-bolts specificity to implementation (e.g. how to conduct open data user research in developing countries or best practices for securing consent for open health portals), while also increasing capacity and resource challenges for many civil society organisations. Overlap between communities and fields of practice muddy the waters for national and international collaborations, frustrate a clear narrative regarding open data's impact, and further complicate processes for accessing international resources and funding. Close association with profit-seeking initiatives can also put capacity-strapped civil society organisations in direct competition with a startup community that may enjoy investor backing and pursue significantly different objectives.

The capacity gap

The work of civil society organisations demands a wide variety of skills, resources, and capacities. Some of these are familiar. Running public messaging and awareness campaigns to support engagement and the uptake of open data is well within the wheelhouse of most advocacy organisations. Similarly, community research, training, and facilitating interaction between open data stakeholder groups require capacities familiar to most organisations. The hard technical capacities required to work directly with open data are often more challenging to secure.

They are often also essential not only for managing, cleaning, formatting, and porting data, but also to support meaningful training, research, engagement, and facilitation activities.

These demands are well recognised, and recent years have seen a dramatic investment in civil society's hard technical capacities to work with open data. This is most visible in the significant increase in data scientist hires by international organisations,[20] as well as in the proliferation of ad hoc, conference-based, and roving training mechanisms intended to boost the hard technical skills of advocates and civil society organisations working to advance open data in a national context.[21] Simultaneously, civil society-led training that targets open data producers has increasingly emphasised strategic approaches borrowed from the world of software development, such as "agile" and "user-centric" methodologies, suggesting that there has been at least some spillover of knowledge and capacity from the private sector into civil society.

There remains a pernicious gap between well-resourced international civil society organisations' levels of expertise, social capital, and access to financial resources and those of less-equipped national organisations, particularly those based in the Global South. This is likely due, in part, to the close alignment of open data goals with other efforts to support the private sector and generate economic value in developed countries[22] and the tendency of international civil society organisations working on open data to be based in those countries. As a result, less developed economies may receive less investment in open data-related social ventures, which may have a spillover effect on the level of support for national open data advocacy organisations.

This gap is also a function of the network dynamics that underpin funding mechanisms and capacity development within the open data community. Smaller organisations working at the national level often lack the resources to invest in long-term technical capacity, and they also lack the resources to engage in international networking activities. This is problematic when contact with international non-governmental organisations (NGOs) and civil society networks is the primary means by which many national-level civil society organisations in the developing world learn about technology and data.[23] Lack of fundamental digital skills is normally an indicator of other capacity limitations, including the inability to develop other "digital goods", such as digital infrastructure and digital network connections.[24] This can inhibit national NGOs from developing an international profile, further frustrating access to funding and networking resources.

There has been no definitive analysis of the capacity gap between civil society organisations operating at the global level and at the national level in developed and developing countries. However, it does not appear that investments in global networking and capacity development activities, such as sponsorship of the International Open Data Conference (IODC) or School of Data fellowships and training, are having a significant impact on civil society capacities in general. There simply does not seem to be enough resources. This dynamic only seems likely to increase as broader international advocacy initiatives, such as the Open Data Charter, gain normative traction with governments around the world, increasing the demand for civil society support without a corresponding increase in the financial and strategic resources available for organisations at the national level.

Unexpected challenges

Field-level ambiguities and capacity gaps are, in some ways, scaled and predictable consequences of the way in which the open data movement has developed and how it organises itself. However, the movement's significant progress has also faced more novel challenges. In particular, new technologies have introduced a wide array of unexpected ethical challenges, and the potential social benefits associated with open data have introduced challenges related to how governments approach collaboration and partnership. These new challenges require new ways of thinking and working in the context of open data.

Ethical dilemmas at the intersection of technology, development, and governance have generated a significant amount of attention. Privacy concerns have been prominent in this regard, especially relating to the opening of public data on individuals and vulnerable communities.[25] This has forced a rethinking of several seminal concepts, including personally identifiable information and anonymity.[26] The debate over whether or not privacy concerns warrant caveats to the mandate of "open by default" is particularly challenging and remains unresolved[27,28] despite a lack of documented instances in which open data releases have led directly to documented harm to individuals.

Other ethical dilemmas are also relevant in an open data context, including moral obligations to anticipate the way in which data might be repurposed or reused, concerns regarding the consent of individuals reflected in open data releases, and the question of whether open data is properly serving the communities from whose activities it is generated.[29] Some have framed this last point in terms of a moral obligation for policy-makers to collect and release more data on vulnerable groups in order to serve them better,[30] although there is also scepticism about the degree to which governments are able to do so.[31] While there is little agreement on the appropriate response to such challenges, civil society has proven remarkably proactive in advancing the debate by asking difficult questions as demonstrated by the efforts of the responsible data community[32] and organisations like the GovLab at New York University (NYU).[33]

The approach taken by governments to open data activities or to their collaboration with civil society has also generated ethical issues as illustrated by the spread of "openwashing". Originally coined in the context of the open software movement to describe efforts "to spin a product or company as open, although it is not",[34] the idea of openwashing has recently been adapted to open data and open government to describe instances where governments exploit excitement around the idea of openness in order to avoid meaningful reforms.[35] When governments and companies take superficial steps toward opening data, or take steps to open data that is not meaningful or useful for stakeholders, this poses strategic challenges for open data advocates who have worked hard to secure support for open data. The question of whether to condemn symbolic efforts or to use them to push for more progressive approaches can be challenging, particularly for international advocates and initiatives.[36,37,38] In some instances, collaboration between national-level civil society organisations and government or corporate partners has resulted in compromises that some describe as the "co-opting" of civil society organisations and the subversion of their missions.[39]

Open data organisations have also struggled with issues related to gender equity (see Chapter 20: Gender equity). The most effective calls to deal with gender labour and representation inequities in the open data movement have come not from prominent organisations, but from ad hoc and earnest voices at the periphery of the discourse, such as Open Heroines.[40] This suggests that perennial ethical challenges, like those related to privacy and consent, as well as those surrounding government collaboration, will require new thinking and creative solutions that may not come from the more established civil society organisations in the open data movement, although they can play a powerful role in facilitating the contributions of other actors.

Better governance: Never say die

Perhaps the most remarkable trend in the open data movement's last decade has been civil society's consistent investment in open data activities to improve the quality of governance and government. Of the many rationales and rhetorical frames used as the basis for arguments in support of open data,[41] its value in advancing democracy likely aligns best with the mandates of most civil society organisations. A review of the agendas for international networking events, like the IODC, and the rhetoric around initiatives like the Open Data Charter suggest that leveraging open data for more accountable and responsible government has never been far from the central rationale for open data in general, and, in particular, the rationale for civil society organisations directly involved in the movement.

Nevertheless, there remains no clear or consistent evidence of open data's impact on the quality of governance and government. Although scholarship on open data has expanded dramatically over the last ten years,[42] attention focused on the impact of open data on governance, in particular, has mainly come from organisations such as the GovLab at NYU, which has close ties to the civil society community through the formalisation of civil society activities like the Open Data Research Network and the Open Data Research Symposium. However, evidence that open data has contributed to improvements in the quality of governance in national contexts remains both sporadic and speculative.

The most comprehensive exploration of open data's impact on governance is likely provided by the GovLab's portal on Open Data's Impact, which suggests 27 contextual and design considerations that affect open data initiatives' potential to achieve impact and 14 case studies that demonstrate how open data has improved government.[43] A closer review of these open data cases illustrates the diversity of each case and its resulting impact, including inter-ministerial cooperation for the release of Brazilian spending data,[44] on health spending in the Burundi pharmaceutical industry,[45] and the coincidental access to postcode data which enabled meaningful parliamentary monitoring in the United Kingdom.[46] In short, when open data does improve governance, it takes a lot more than simply opening data, and what it requires will differ radically from country to country.

None of this is meant to assert that open data does not improve governance. The theories of change that underpinned initial optimism around open data have been complicated by recent lessons from implementation[47] but remain feasible. There is good reason to believe that open data can play a necessary, if not totally sufficient, role in improving the quality of governance in a variety of national contexts. However, that potential is not readily apparent, and there is not yet any convincing or systemic evidence to point to. This is what makes civil society's continued dedication to the cause so remarkable. In the face of all the challenges described above, including capacity gaps, insufficient resources, duplicitous partners, impossible competition, and no clear evidence that their efforts will bear fruit, civil society organisations continue to pioneer inspiring and unlikely efforts to leverage open data for gains in governance and democratic accountability.

There is enthusiasm evident in network initiatives aiming to "follow the money"[48] or facilitate "open contracting".[49] The energy that exists when such groups meet to address these challenges feels less like an uphill battle. It feels like a fresh push in a long struggle that is just on the precipice of success. There are colorful sticky notes and Silicon Valley facilitators with entertaining icebreakers. There are flashy websites and esoteric hacker personalities. There is a culture of creative solutionism, and it is inspiring. It focuses attention, and, in the end, this dogged optimism, creativity, passion, and resilience may be civil society's greatest contribution to the open data movement.

Conclusion

The trends described above provide a sketch of a dynamic landscape in which civil society advocates of open data have been forced to adapt and address a variety of challenges. Some of these challenges are systemic, such as the ambiguity and fragmentation that characterises open data's penetration into new sectors and policy domains or the resourcing and support obstacles increasingly faced by national organisations that are arguably best positioned to have an impact on open data ecosystems. Meaningfully addressing these challenges will require a clear strategic response from funding and capacity development organisations.

First, a better overview is required of who is receiving funds and support to work with open data at the national level. This need not be public or field-wide information, but funders and global organisations should map out how resources and capacity development efforts are distributed (see Chapter 25: Donors and investors). This may entail a review of many diverse programming channels, such as funding for data journalism training, funding for anti-corruption campaigns in an international aid context, and many more. Understanding how open data support is distributed across funder portfolios and the support networks of large organisations is a first step in addressing both coordination challenges and uneven access to resources.

Second, funders and support organisations should take concrete steps to increase the outreach and inclusivity of international support networks and activities. At the most pedestrian level, this simply implies allocating more funds to sponsor the participation of national civil society organisations in international events, such as the IODC. Funders should also consider additional investments in prominent capacity-building mechanisms, such as the School of Data or Internews data journalism training. Investment should seek to increase the scope and breadth of capacity development opportunities, but should also include resources earmarked specifically to increase inclusivity.

Moreover, efforts to increase the scope of international support should go beyond "the usual suspects" of the open data movement. International open data networks and events suffer from a reliance on a handful of particularly charismatic and articulate personalities and their organisations, especially in the Global South. Moving beyond such actors to engage with a broader group of civil society organisations at the country level that may not be connected with global networks is no small task; however, doing so would have immediate positive benefits for the organisations receiving support, as well as for the general health and diversity of the international open data community. It would also provide important insights that could benefit funders' longer-term strategies to provide support. One first step that would assist in such efforts would be to translate existing resources for civil society into multiple languages.

Third, it is worth acknowledging that the above efforts will be limited by the availability of funding and human resources, as well as by the level of interest from international donors and investors. Meaningful responses to the trends described above will require significant investment and coordination at the country level as well. International actors engaging with national governments to advocate for open data should encourage them to establish funding and networking resources for civil society organisations within their jurisdictions. Placing the importance of such investments on par with policy activities may have significant benefits at the country level. Initiatives like the Open Data Charter's demonstration activities with national governments[50] offer a unique opportunity to promote such investments.

Funders and global support organisations may wish to temper their interest in metrics for the impact of open data. To be sure, demonstrating open data's impact is a logical objective for open data advocates. To get governments and companies to open data, one wants to be able to show them what they will get out of it. However, measurement efforts need to be precise in their methods and with their objectives, and they should not be equivocated with either programme-level metrics or the viability and potential of open data as a field.

The pressure on civil society organisations to measure and report on their activities is, in many instances, exacerbated by a culture of results-based management in the aid and philanthropic sectors, as well as the often-latent expectation that anything using technology should have measurable outcomes. While open data initiatives do often support the use of metrics, these should be applied only to the degree that they are useful for adaptive management and when they measure outputs (the immediate results of an open data initiative) rather than impacts (the long-term, societal-level consequences of an initiative).[51]

Finally, civil society leaders should be mindful of the novel and collaborative ways in which solutions to these challenges might arise. Large and bureaucratic organisations should develop opportunities to facilitate the contributions of more flexible actors and networks. Smaller organisations should make deliberate choices about how they position themselves in a fragmented discourse marked by limited resources. Leaders of all types of organisations should remember the normative power civil society wields in many contexts. Increasing attention on eliminating "manels" (all male panels) at international conferences is an excellent example of how small and consistent interventions in the service of a clear change objective can support incremental changes in institutional culture.

These recommendations provide a clear, if ambitious, starting point for responding to the systemic trends and challenges discussed above. Though the organisations facing these challenges will, in many cases, be best suited to frame and develop effective responses, there is an untapped potential for creative collaboration between organisations that the open data movement is well positioned to exploit, and international support is critical as well. As the open data movement continues to mature, strategic thinking on civil society's role should focus more around the needs and potential of national organisations, and international support should be structured to better serve the diverse activities civil society organisations will undertake in a fragmented open data landscape.

Further reading

Bernholz, L., Cordelli, C., & Reich, R. (2013). *The emergence of digital civil society*. Stanford: Stanford Center on Philanthropy and Civil Society. https://pacscenter.stanford.edu/publication/the-emergence-of-digital-civil-society/

Gray, J., Lämmerhirt, D., & Bounegru, L. (2016). Changing what counts: How can citizen-generated data and civil society data be used as an advocacy tool to change official data collection? *Civicus/DataShift*. http://civicus.org/thedatashift/learning-zone-2/research/changing-what-counts/

Sieber, R.E. & Johnson, P.A. (2015). Civic open data at a crossroads: Dominant models and current challenges. *Government Information Quarterly, 32(3)*, 308–315. https://www.sciencedirect.com/science/article/pii/S0740624X15000611

Van Schalkwyk, F., Willmers, M., & McNaughton, M. (2016). Viscous open data: The roles of intermediaries in an open data ecosystem. *Information Technology for Development, 22(1)*, 68–83. https://www.tandfonline.com/doi/full/10.1080/02681102.2015.1081868

About the author

Christopher Wilson is a Research Fellow at the University of Oslo and the Beeck Center at Georgetown University. He previously co-founded The Engine Room and now provides research support to NGOs and blogs about civic tech research at https://methodicalsnark.org. You can follow Christopher at https://www.twitter.com/cosgrovedent.

How to cite this chapter

Wilson, C. (2019). Open data stakeholders: Civil society. In T. Davies, S. Walker, M. Rubinstein, & F. Perini (Eds.), *The state of open data: Histories and horizons* (pp. 355–366). Cape Town and Ottawa: African Minds and International Development Research Centre. http://stateofopendata.od4d.net

This work is licensed under a Creative Commons Attribution 4.0 International (CC BY 4.0) licence. It was carried out with the aid of a grant from the International Development Research Centre, Ottawa, Canada.

Endnotes

1. Public.Resource.Org. (2007). 8 Principles of Open Government Data. https://public.resource.org/8_principles.html
2. Sieber, R.E. & Johnson, P.A. (2015). Civic open data at a crossroads: Dominant models and current challenges. *Government Information Quarterly, 32(3)*, 308–315. http://www.sciencedirect.com/science/article/pii/S0740624X15000611
3. Johnston, E.W. (2015). *Governance in the information era: Theory and practice of policy informatics.* New York, NY: Routledge. https://www.routledge.com/Governance-in-the-Information-Era-Theory-and-Practice-of-Policy-Informatics/Johnston/p/book/9781138832084
4. Clarke, A. & Margetts, H. (2014). Governments and citizens getting to know each other? Open, closed, and big data in public management reform. *Policy and Internet, 6(4)*, 393–417. http://doi.wiley.com/10.1002/1944-2866.POI377
5. Manyika, J., Chui, M., Groves, P., Farrell, D., Van Kuiken, S., & Doshi, E.A. (2013). *Open data: Unlocking innovation and performance with liquid information.* New York, NY: The McKinsey Global Institute. https://www.mckinsey.com/business-functions/digital-mckinsey/our-insights/open-data-unlocking-innovation-and-performance-with-liquid-information
6. Charalabidis, Y., Alexopoulos, C., & Loukis, E. (2016). A taxonomy of open government data research areas and topics. *Journal of Organizational Computing and Electronic Commerce, 26(1–2)*, 41–63. http://www.tandfonline.com/doi/full/10.1080/10919392.2015.1124720
7. Hossain, M.A., Dwivedi, Y.K., & Rana, N.P. (2016). State of the art in open data research: Insights from existing literature and a research agenda. *Journal of Organizational Computing and Electronic Commerce, 26(1–2)*, 14–40. http://www.tandfonline.com/doi/full/10.1080/10919392.2015.1124007
8. Van Schalkwyk, F., Cañares, M., Chattapadhyay, S., & Andrason, A. (2015). Open data intermediaries in developing countries. *Journal of Community Informatics, 12(2)*, 9–25.
9. Bahl, A. (2012). So what's in those OGP action plans, anyway? *Global Integrity.* http://www.globalintegrity.org/2012/07/whats-in-ogp-action-plans/
10. Schwegmann, C. (2013). *Open data in developing countries.* European Public Sector Information Platform Topic Report no. 2013/02. Luxembourg: European Data Portal. https://www.europeandataportal.eu/sites/default/files/2013_open_data_in_developing_countries.pdf
11. Wilson, C. & Rahman, Z. (2015). *Citizen-generated data and governments: Towards a collaborative model.* Civicus/DataShift. http://civicus.org/thedatashift/frontpage-article/citizen-generated-data-and-governments-towards-a-collaborative-model-2/
12. Gray, J., Lämmerhirt, D., & Bounegru, L. (2016). *Changing what counts: How can citizen-generated data and civil society data be used as an advocacy tool to change official data collection?* Civicus/DataShift. http://civicus.org/thedatashift/learning-zone-2/research/
13. Fumega, S. (2015). *Understanding two mechanisms for accessing government information and data around the world.* Washington, DC: World Wide Web Foundation. http://webfoundation.org/about/research/understanding-two-mechanisms-for-accessing-government-information-and-data/
14. Piotrowski, S.J., Ingrams, A., & Berliner, D. (2018). Could the open government movement shut the door on freedom of information? *The Conversation.* https://theconversation.com/could-the-open-government-movement-shut-the-door-on-freedom-of-information-92724
15. Brabham, D.C. & Guth, K.L. (2017). The deliberative politics of the consultative layer: Participation hopes and communication as design values of civic tech founders. *Journal of Communication, 67(4)*, 445–475. https://doi.org/10.1111/jcom.12316
16. Goldstein, J. & Weinstein, J. (2012). The benefits of a big tent: Opening up government in developing countries. *UCLA Law Review Discourse, 178*, 178–208. http://dx.doi.org/10.2139/ssrn.2012489
17. De Blasio, E. & Selva, D. (2016). Why choose open government? Motivations for the adoption of open government policies in four European countries. *Policy and Internet, 8(3)*, 225–247. http://dx.doi.org/10.1002/poi3.118

18 Mungai, P., Van Belle, J.-P., & Sevilla, J. (2016). Mechanisms that are impacting the Kenya open data initiative. In *CONF-IRM 2016 Proceedings*, *35*. https://aisel.aisnet.org/confirm2016/35

19 Calderon, A., Carolan, L., Smith, F., Ong, I., Zarek, C., Tales, R., & Thigo, P. (2017). *Resilient reform in government: Lessons from open data leaders*. London: Open Data Charter, Open Data Institute. https://opendatacharter.net/resilient-reform-government-lessons-open-data-leaders/

20 Sample-Ward, A. (2017). The top three nonprofit jobs of the future. *Fast Company*, 2 February. https://www.fastcompany.com/3067922/the-top-three-nonprofit-jobs-of-the-future

21 See, for example, School of Data (https://schoolofdata.org/), as well as training offered by the Open Data Institute (https://theodi.org/service/courses-and-training/), Open Data Services (http://opendataservices.coop/), and Open Data Watch (https://opendatawatch.com/data-support/)

22 Knight Foundation. (2016). Trends in civic tech, 2016. https://knightfoundation.org/features/civictech/

23 Wilson, C. (2013). *TechScape module report*. The Engine Room. https://www.theengineroom.org/wp-content/uploads/2016/07/engnroom_TSnetworkreport_OxfamNovib_021213.pdf

24 Bernholz, L., Cordelli, C., & Reich, R. (2013). *The emergence of digital civil society*. Stanford, CA: Stanford Center on Philanthropy and Civil Society. https://pacscenter.stanford.edu/publication/the-emergence-of-digital-civil-society/

25 Carolan, L. (2016). *Open data, transparency and accountability: Topic guide*. Birmingham: GSDRC, University of Birmingham. http://www.gsdrc.org/topic-guides/open-data-transparency-and-accountability/

26 Walker, T. (2015). Who's responsible for checking how data is de-identified? *Responsible Data* [Blog post], 23 March. https://responsibledata.io/2015/03/23/whos-responsible-for-checking-how-data-is-de-identified/

27 Green, B., Cunningham, G., Ekblaw, A., Kominers, P., Linzer, A., & Crawford, S. (2017). *Open data privacy: A risk-benefit, process-oriented approach to sharing and protecting municipal data*. Cambridge, MA: Berkman Klein Center. http://nrs.harvard.edu/urn-3:HUL.InstRepos:30340010

28 See also online exchange in comments at https://responsibledata.io/responsible-data-in-open-contracting/

29 Carolan, L. (2016). *Open data, transparency and accountability: Topic guide*. Birmingham: GSDRC, University of Birmingham. http://www.gsdrc.org/topic-guides/open-data-transparency-and-accountability/

30 McGee, R., Anderson, C., Hudson, H., & Feruglio, F. (2018). *Appropriating technology for accountability: Messages from making all voices count*. Brighton: Institute of Development Studies. http://opendocs.ids.ac.uk/opendocs/handle/123456789/13452

31 Clarke, A. & Margetts, H. (2014). Governments and citizens getting to know each other? Open, closed, and big data in public management reform. *Policy and Internet*, *6(4)*, 393–417. http://doi.wiley.com/10.1002/1944-2866.POI377

32 http://responsibledata.io/

33 http://www.thegovlab.org/

34 Pomerantz, J. & Peek, R. (2016). Fifty shades of open. *First Monday*, *21(5)*. http://www.ojphi.org/ojs/index.php/fm/article/view/6360

35 Verhulst, S.G. & Young, A. (2017). *Open data in developing economies toward building an evidence base on what works and how*. Cape Town: African Minds. http://www.africanminds.co.za/dd-product/open-data-in-developing-economies-toward-building-an-evidence-base-on-what-works-and-how/

36 Brockmyer, B. & Fox, J.A. (2015). Assessing the evidence: The effectiveness and impact of public governance-oriented multi-stakeholder initiatives. *SSRN*. https://papers.ssrn.com/abstract=2693608

37 Villum, C. (2014). "Open-Washing": The difference between opening your data and simply making them available. *Open Knowledge International* [Blog post], 10 March. https://blog.okfn.org/2014/03/10/open-washing-the-difference-between-opening-your-data-and-simply-making-them-available/

38 Brandusescu, A. (2016). #openwashing...anyone? Washington, DC: World Wide Web Foundation. https://webfoundation.org/2016/10/openwashing-anyone/

39 Bates, J. (2012). "This is what modern deregulation looks like": Co-optation and contestation in the shaping of the UK's open government data initiative. *The Journal of Community Informatics*, *8(2)*. http://ci-journal.net/index.php/ciej/article/view/845

40 https://openheroines.org/

41 De Blasio, E. & Selva, D. (2016). Why choose open government? Motivations for the adoption of open government policies in four European countries. *Policy and Internet, 8(3)*, 225–247. http://dx.doi.org/10.1002/poi3.118

42 Van Schalkwyk, F. & Verhulst, S. (2017). The state of open data and open data research. In F. van Schalkwyk, S.G. Verhulst, G. Magalhaes, J. Pane, & J. Walker (Eds.), *The social dynamics of open data* (pp. 1–12). Cape Town: African Minds. https://doi.org/10.5281/zenodo.1117807

43 See http://odimpact.org

44 Graft, A., Verhulst, S., & Young, A. (2016). *Brazil's open budget transparency portal: Making public how public money is spent*. Brooklyn, NY: GovLab. http://odimpact.org/case-brazils-open-budget-transparency-portal.html

45 Graft, A., Young, A., & Verhulst, S. (2017). *Burundi's open RBF: Making health spending and performance transparent*. Brooklyn, NY: GovLab. http://odimpact.org/case-burundis-open-rbf.html

46 Hogge, B. (2016). *They work for you: Taking the long view*. Brooklyn, NY: GovLab. http://odimpact.org/case-united-kingdoms-theyworkforyou.html

47 Worthy, B. (2015). The impact of open data in the UK: Complex, unpredictable, and political. *Public Administration, 93(3)*, 788–805. https://doi.org/10.1111/padm.12166

48 http://followthemoney.net/

49 https://www.open-contracting.org/

50 Calderon, A. (2018). Publishing with purpose: Introducing our 2018 strategy. *Medium* [Blog post], 29 January. https://medium.com/@opendatacharter/publishing-with-purpose-introducing-our-2018-strategy-ddbf7ab46098

51 The Engine Room. (2014). *Measuring impact on-the-go: A users' guide for monitoring tech and accountability programming*. The Engine Room and WeGov. https://www.theengineroom.org/wp-content/uploads/2016/07/engnroom_monitoringguide_finalmay14.pdf

025

Donors and investors

Fernando Perini and Michael Jarvis

Key points

- Open data programming and funding is becoming more mainstreamed across sectors, but progress is uneven. Many donors have focused particularly on open data for anti-corruption initiatives, journalism and media, national statistics, extractives, international aid and disaster relief, government finance, and agriculture.

- Open data has become a global and diverse movement. Investments in open data have happened on multiple continents, targeting a variety of stakeholders, but more should be done to make their collective impact more coherent.

- A global infrastructure to support a somewhat fragmented open data community has begun to emerge, including elements of a global agenda, coordinated investment mechanisms, measurement, and global and regional events.

- There is a need for substantial new and joint investments among open data funders, and donors in general, especially to meet cross-cutting needs that are hard for any one project, organisation, or donor to address alone.

Introduction

Ever since government and civil society actors first started calling for greater openness in government data, donors have played an important role in supporting the expansion of the open data community. They have helped to convene a multiplicity of actors to explore how best to produce, publish, and use open data, and their contributions have provided seed funding for entrepreneurs to test the waters with riskier and more innovative initiatives. Some have even opened their own data and championed open data as part of government reforms. Donors have commissioned and supported research on open data that has helped to articulate emerging outcomes around the world and have supported the case for future investment, as well as more coordination among the range of donors interested in the advancement of open data.

That said, we should not overestimate the importance of donors. Public and private donors represent just one part of the financing ecosystem for open data. For-profit actors, governments, and civil society groups investing their own resources have been critical in scaling open data applications around the world. Nonetheless, donors can and must play a key role where there is a lack of incentive for the private sector to provide investment, most notably, in providing support for the development of public goods that often underpin open data impacts. This might include supporting standards development to enable interoperability and investing in the necessary guidance on how to use and manage open data to maximise its public use and value.

As the open data movement emerges from its first decade, it is an appropriate time to assess whether donors' contributions, using their money and influence, have succeeded in building a more resilient, inclusive, and coherent global open data movement. To that end, this chapter reflects on the role that international donors have played as stakeholders in developing the global open data ecosystem. Donors are frequently considered external actors to any cause, taking rational investment decisions based on clear evidence of impact. However, when we look back at the nascent open data movement, the causal relationship between open data and its intended benefits has rarely been well-defined, taking on instead what Weinstein and Goldstein have categorised as a "big tent approach".[1] What constitutes success is often only broadly articulated and evidence of impact is usually scarce. Donors have, therefore, had to take more of a leap of faith on the potential impact of open data when they invest in its many different agendas.

In order to substantiate this reflection, we have made a preliminary attempt to map the social network of donors supporting open data within specific communities or sectors. In addition to their financial resources, donors may also operate as knowledge brokers and connectors within sectors. Digging into this donor "view of the world" can also be useful in identifying some of the perceived achievements and challenges that may affect the broader community. Accordingly, we have extracted some lessons learned from several recent reports, as well as discussions with and among donors, in order to identify some of the challenges faced by donors and explore the potential for motivating ongoing support moving forward.

This chapter focuses on both public and philanthropic donors, particularly those that are internationally active (perhaps overly reflective of the missions of the authors' own institutions, an international development research organisation and a donor collaborative that prioritises effective data use).[2] This chapter does not attempt to cover the whole ecosystem of open data investment nor the data publishing activities of donors themselves.[3]

What are public goods that merit donor support and investment?

There is much talk currently of data infrastructure and the potential for confusion over terminology. For the purposes of this chapter, data infrastructure refers to "public goods" that would enable quality data to be easily shared, combined, and accessed by different users (see also Chapter 18: Data infrastructure). In particular, we refer to elements of data infrastructure that could and should be the focus of donor support and investment.

> The International Open Data Roadmap, the result of a community collaboration at previous International Open Data Conferences in 2015 and 2016 highlights many calls for action in the development of a global infrastructure.[4,5] Examples include:
>
> - Development of norms and data standards and their support systems, such as the reconciliation of organisational identifiers and open source data cleaning tools.
> - Innovative solutions and research on the state of open data, such as the Open Data Barometer and the Open Data Index.
> - Capacity-building activities in government and civil society, particularly in less developed economies, where the capacity for long-term investments is smaller and building initial human and social capital is crucial to sparking change.
>
> Investment in these foundational activities for effective data use may not generate sufficient revenue to attract private sector investment; therefore, public and philanthropic investments are needed to help build a more robust and open data ecosystem.

Exploring the network of funding and support

There is no comprehensive way to track all funding for open data initiatives. As just one small element of the investments made by government, not-for-profits, or the private sector, it is likely that most of the support for open data initiatives is invisible to traditional official indicators and international mechanisms that track funding. In recent analyses related to "data for development", such as the Organisation for Economic Co-operation and Development's (OECD) 2017 *Data for development* report[6] and the Global Partnership for Sustainable Development Data's (GPSDD) 2016 report on the state of development data funding,[7] investment in open data is acknowledged, but it is impossible to disentangle it from broader investments in statistical capacity building, information and communications technology (ICT), innovation, open science, and other categories. Investment "bundling" limits our understanding of which investments are dedicated specifically to open data efforts.

However, there are a few select tools to draw on that offer some useful detail. For example, grants data published to the 360Giving Standard can be searched by keyword. A search in the GrantNav database using the keywords "open data" reveals 51 grants provided by eight different funders based in the United Kingdom.[8] A search using the same keywords on the International Aid Transparency Initiative (IATI) database identifies 360 projects from 52 publishers.[9] However, it is unclear how many of these projects are explicitly open data projects or if they simply include "open data" in filenames or boilerplate text. As an investment in open data is not considered an explicit development area by the OECD or IATI, it is hard to track the amount invested in open data as part of larger investments. Digging into the data does highlight the different ways donors associate projects with open data, although the subset of real open data projects may be under one hundred records.

Thus, given the limited availability of quality data on open data investment, we turned to the environmental scans developed for each of the chapters in the State of Open Data project to try to understand how donors support the global open data community. These environmental scans have identified key funders for each sector, region, and stakeholder group. We have used this input, corrected the underlying data to create Figure 1, and complemented the analysis with interviews with key actors, a qualitative review of available IATI data, a review of recent programme evaluations, and a review of the initial drafts of other chapters in this book.

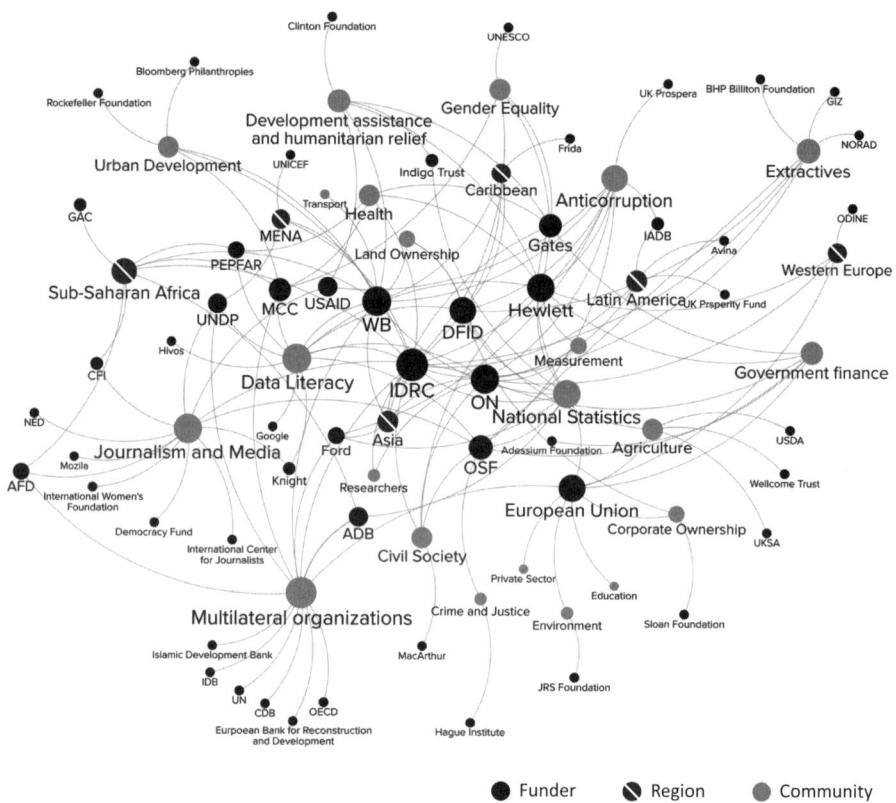

Figure 1: Network analysis based on State of Open Data environmental scans
Note: The graph above illustrates thematic areas, related funders, and the links between them identified by an analysis of State of Open Data environment scans.[10]

This approach builds on snowball sampling methodology[11] frequently used in social network analysis. While this may still be a limited view, this type of network topology can help to understand the community, offering some insight into the complex relationship dynamics in an emerging field. There are some limitations to this approach. For example, it does not provide information on the intensity (i.e. total dollar amounts) of the investment made. Thus, donors that make small investments in many sectors and regions are more likely to be central (more networked) than donors that make larger investments in specific countries or issue areas. The International Development Research Centre (IDRC) is an example of the first type of donor. The Millennium Challenge Corporation collaboration with the President's Emergency Plan for AIDS Relief (MCC-PEPFAR), a USD 21.8 million partnership that created the Data Collaboratives for

Local Impact programme, is an example of the latter. The analysis shown in Figure 1 offers only a partial view of the funding commitments made over the last decade, not a dynamic view of what is currently in play today. It does not tell us what constitutes core funding support to organisations or about project-specific funding. Being able to gauge core funding amounts would be useful in assessing the flexibility that open data-focused organisations might have in directing resources toward changing or evolving priorities.

So what can this network analysis tell us about resilience, diversity, and coherence within the open data ecosystem? Three key areas of insight are outlined below.

> ### Assessing the ecosystem: Potential metrics
>
> How can we assess resilience, diversity, and coherence of the open data ecosystem? In developing the analysis in this chapter, we have drawn upon the following outline metrics:
>
> - Resilience – an increase in the number of donors contributes to the resilience of a specific community.
>
> - Diversity – a diverse data ecosystem requires donors supporting different types of stakeholders and communities in different regions.
>
> - Coherence – the presence of central actors (donors and organisations with more connections) and established coordination mechanisms.

Resilience: Open data is becoming more mainstreamed into key sectors

Figure 1 shows a total of 55 donors funding 28 different communities of practice in the open data space. Funding covers a range of open data-related issues from standards development and capacity building by both government and civil society to work on strengthening ICT and data systems.

The network analysis shows that there have been some core players funding the open data community and ecosystem, including basic infrastructure and practice; however, there is also a growing list of new donors supporting open data as part of their specific sector programming. This is a positive sign in terms of creating a more sustainable financing base for open data.

If we hypothesise that a diversity of donors increases the resilience of a specific community at the international level, we can group the sectors according to three categories: low resilience (less than three donors), medium (three to five donors), and high resilience (more than five donors).

- The first group, with less than three donors, includes crime and justice, environment, education, and transport. Some communities could not identify any international donor support, as is the case of open data for Indigenous communities. While there are a range of examples and cases in these sectors, we could argue that donor support for these topics remains relatively weak.

- The communities working on open data in relation to gender equality, health, urban development, and corporate ownership were able to identify between three and five donors. Potentially, these sectors could be seen as emerging communities in the open data movement. Their modest but growing presence in international events, such as the International Open Data Conferences in Madrid and Buenos Aires, would support this claim.

- The sectors which could identify more than five donors include open data for anti-corruption, journalism and media, national statistics, extractives, international aid and disaster relief, government finance, and agriculture. As can be observed in international events and in the related chapters in this publication, these open data communities also tend to have better articulated priorities, existing or emerging standards, stronger community coalitions, and more evidence to date of effective results.

Across these different groups, there is much that donors and communities could learn about how to better mainstream open data into the different sectors, how progress has been achieved, and how it can be sustained. There is no question that many communities have developed specific partnerships and alliances to catalyse social change which are, in turn, more successful in attracting multiple donors (e.g. the Global Open Data for Agriculture and Nutrition (GODAN) and Open Contracting Partnership (OCP) networks).

Diversity: Open data is an increasingly global and diverse movement

In order to examine whether donors have supported open data with a specific emphasis on inclusiveness, we explored two dimensions: geographic presence and programmatic modalities.

There is some indication that there are emerging patterns for how donors and communities operate within the different global regions with at least three donors in each region and up to seven in Sub-Saharan Africa. Open data activities may target evidence-based policy-making to advanced democratic governance, economic development, and other objectives specific to particular sectors. This has allowed local, national, and regional open data communities to emerge with different priorities in order to serve multiple agendas and simultaneously adjust to cultural differences.

The data also indicates that there is a range of donors focusing on specific stakeholders. Many donors, particularly multilateral organisations, tend to target governments. Others focus on civil society organisations and broader data literacy efforts. A smaller number of donors fund researchers and standards development or have an explicit interest in private sector activities.

Preferences for funding particular stakeholders often align with donor modalities. Multilateral and bilateral donors are set up specifically to provide support to governments. Private philanthropic organisations are best structured to support civil society directly. All have ways to support specific research agendas. Finding ways to leverage the comparative advantages of different donors is important in considering the sustainability needs of the open data ecosystem as a whole.

While the overall picture may sound positive, it is important to note that there are plenty of blind spots and gaps in support in terms of geographies, themes, and sectors, reflecting the fact that donors have specific preferences and constraints in terms of the types of actors and modalities needed to deliver their particular programmes. For instance, some multilateral organisations have specific constraints related to time-bound support to governments in low-income countries. Too many development projects require longer-term support, leading to investment cycles, which cannot be sustained by one investor. The past decade has seen more than its fair share of funded initiatives that failed to gain traction, often leaving behind "white elephant" data portals which cannot be maintained or supported locally. Also, a focus on the creation of new global organisations has led to greater fragmentation within the broader open data community. Northern-based organisations have been involved in many donor-supported activities in the Global South, but, in most cases, the global expansion efforts of Northern open data organisations have failed to sustain long-term engagement in developing countries.

Like other funded movements, the open data field has not been immune to the effects of donor-skewed priorities and the potential duplication of efforts. Yet, there is still the potential to find smarter approaches. Clearly, lone actors cannot support the needs of the entire open data value chain. Therefore, rather than devolving toward a simplistic supply versus demand-side framing, there is a growing recognition that investment needs to be coordinated to create functioning data ecosystems.[12,13] Donors need to understand how open data interacts with contextual variables and be able to adjust their decision-making processes to specific sectors or regional settings.[14]

As the sector matures, funders, alongside other stakeholders, will play an important role in "connecting the dots" and even exploring what kind of consolidation might be useful and/or practical. They will also seek to clarify comparative advantages among different stakeholders focused on open data efforts. Leading open data and governance data groups began one such exercise in spring 2018 with support of the Hewlett Foundation and the Transparency and Accountability Initiative (TAI). Better coordination could increase effectiveness and free up donor funds to focus on those areas for which there is no market alternative, but which are still vital to the open data ecosystem.

Coherence: Key elements of the global open data infrastructure have emerged

In order to discuss coherence, we have reviewed reports and conducted interviews with the central actors identified in our network analysis. IDRC, Omidyar Network, the World Bank, and the Hewlett Foundation were identified as donors with more than ten connections to different sectors or communities of practice. Given their greater relative centrality, they are in a position to play a significant role in building an open data infrastructure that can spread good practices across regions, sectors, and stakeholder groups. See box, What are donors learning? A moment of introspection, which identifies some of the documents and processes reviewed during this research.

> ### What are donors learning? A moment of introspection
>
> Several funders of open data efforts have been providing support in the field for a decade, if not longer, and this has provoked some reflection on progress to date. Some have gone as far as to commission evaluations of their investments in open data:
>
> - The World Bank has been a key leader and investor at the multilateral level and recently published a review of its investments over the past five years.[15]
>
> - IDRC, the host of the Open Data for Development (OD4D) Network, a programme jointly funded by IDRC, the Department for International Development (DFID), the World Bank, and Global Affairs Canada, recently published an evaluation of the programme[16] and a management response.[17]
>
> - Omidyar Network is a leading investor in open data investment among philanthropic funders and recently commissioned an evaluation of its decade of investments in open data.
>
> - The Hewlett Foundation has not put out a specific publication reviewing its open data portfolio, but it is currently supporting a collective reflection by several open data organisations through the TAI. Arguably, Hewlett investments have been primarily thought of in terms of fiscal governance rather than open data, supporting global norm-setting bodies, including the Extractive Industries Transparency Initiative (EITI),[18] Global Initiative for Fiscal Transparency (GIFT),[19] the IATI,[20] and Open Contracting Partnership (OCP).[21]

Building the field?

Do steps toward resilience, diversity, and coherence of funding add up to field building around open data? In this section, we look back and look forward to assess progress to highlight the remaining challenges still to be addressed in establishing ongoing support for open data activities.

The need for greater coordination

As the open data community has grown and become more diverse, calls for coherence across fragmented efforts have mounted from donors and practitioners alike. Over the years, there have been a number of efforts to coordinate agendas and reduce duplication in the open data field. One indicator of this is the increasing popularity of global open data events, which focus on providing opportunities for networking and collaboration. For example, the first International Open Data Conference (called the Open Government Data Conference for its first edition) took place in 2010 with no more than 50 people, while the last edition, in 2018, brought together more than 1 600 participants.

Efforts toward greater strategic coordination across the regions and sectors that make up the open data community have increased over the last few years. For instance, in June 2013, a number of leading open data organisations announced the establishment of the Global Open Data Initiative (GODI),[22] which aimed at "developing, finding and sharing tools, guidelines and lessons relating to policy, institutions, and activities that governments can use to build successful open data initiatives".[23] While the aim was to become an authoritative voice for the sector, the initial plans for GODI did not receive funding support from donors and the initiative eventually disappeared.

A few months later, in September 2013, the World Bank announced the Partnership for Open Data,[24] a collaboration with the Open Data Institute[25] (ODI) and Open Knowledge International[26] through a grant from the World Bank's Development Grant Facility.[27] In October 2013, backed by a grant from IDRC's OD4D initiative, the World Wide Web Foundation, and the Government of Canada announced the establishment of the Open Government Partnership's (OGP) Open Data Working Group.[28]

In order to avoid duplication, the Partnership for Open Data merged into IDRC's OD4D Network, creating a multi-donor programme to support key initiatives for the open data community. The Network also became the host of the International Open Data Conference (IODC) and refined its programmatic strategies based on the Roadmap that was produced as a result of community engagement at the IODCs in 2015[29] and 2016.[30] The Roadmap ultimately led to OD4D support for the development of the Open Data Charter and the open data measurement initiatives, such as the Open Data Barometer and Open Data Index, as well as grassroots open data initiatives across the Global South that sought to build open data capacity and local expertise.

Activities organised by OD4D and by TAI have started to build fora to encourage more dialogue among donors; however, we have yet to see an effective donor coordination mechanism emerge that might help better address coordination gaps among key donors in the field.

Looking to the future, there are still some questions about the coherence of the global open data agenda. Has a lack of coordination among some of the core donors or a shared strategic long-term vision, led to a proliferation of pet donor-funded projects and concepts? Or are we simply seeing the results of a "let a thousand flowers bloom" approach? While specific donors have articulated their strategy, it can be argued that funding decisions are not made in the context of a coherent forward-looking vision for an efficient open data ecosystem or to meet the specific needs of a range of open data sectors and communities.

Taking into consideration the future priorities of key donors, we can observe some developing trends. For instance, IDRC, through OD4D, has emphasised the establishment of a network of regional initiatives with lighter coordination at the global level using the IODCs and regional events as key tools. The World Bank has increasingly prioritised their work with the OGP and GPSDD, which still touches open data in many different ways. Omidyar Network has backed the establishment of the Open Data Charter as a new organisation, which is focused on updating its principles based on emerging trends in open data.

Some argue that the amount of duplication among the main international actors is too significant, and, as donor funds have not increased, there is still room for further consolidation. The recent agreement established between OD4D and the OGP[31] to advance a more coordinated agenda should be welcome news to the open government and open data communities. The acid test, however, will be whether this unlocks more opportunities for coordinated support of the open data agenda or simply shifts donor coordination priorities yet again.

Amid mainstreaming, who funds cross-cutting open data issues?

Subsidising the cost sharing of field-wide public goods may not be feasible for a donor looking at leveraging open data in a particular sector or region. For example, if a donor wants to target an open data initiative to improve domestic resource mobilisation in Francophone West Africa, are they likely to assume a responsibility to fund the international infrastructure that enables the interoperability of the relevant datasets? Probably not, even if they come to realise the need for such interoperability.

Much of the progress that has been achieved in recent years in terms of global and regional coordination may be in jeopardy as donors look to mainstream open data into specific sectors and country operations. This trend will be exacerbated if open data is no longer the "shiny object" that attracts donor attention. New data-related issues will compete for funding, including big data, research data, data privacy, and data for the Sustainable Development Goals. Should funders try to align these competing themes? Will they each pick a different area to focus on or will they shift to a broader framing of "data funding" within which open data is just one integrated element?

Donor modalities: An orphaned donor agenda

Open data can be relevant to a whole host of programmatic objectives for donors, including evidence-based policy-making, democratic governance, economic development, and a range of social and/or sector issues. This potential to serve multiple agendas may lead to a real ownership challenge within donor organisations, as well as their grantees.

There is a risk that open data is everyone's agenda and, therefore, no one's. It is rare for donor organisations to have a programme officer or team lead explicitly for open data. Typically, engagement with open data-related issues gets spread across several different thematic units (e.g. agriculture units support GODAN, governance units support transparency and anti-corruption data initiatives, and science units support open research data). Sometimes, responsibility may be bundled with broader ICT infrastructure investment teams. This diversity of "homes" for open data within funder organisations may have hindered the sharing of tested donor approaches. It is harder to support development of a nascent field without a sufficient or coherent pool of champions on the donor side and among practitioners.

Conclusions

This chapter has provided some reflections on the impact of donors on the development of resilience, diversity, and coherence across the open data ecosystem as a result of their efforts over the past decade. Examining a network analysis of how donors fund different open data activities and communities, and taking into consideration recent reports from key donors, we can draw several conclusions.

- Open data is becoming more mainstreamed into sector-specific funding, but progress is uneven among sectors. A few sectors, such as anti-corruption, agriculture, and data journalism, have built a greater diversity of donors, while others experience challenges to secure ongoing support.

- Open data is increasingly a more global and inclusive movement, but much remains to be done. Different donors have supported different communities in different regions, and many programmatic modalities have been developed to accommodate the need to support different stakeholders. Nevertheless, many blind spots and coordination challenges exist due to the complexity of building a functioning global data infrastructure.

- Some of the core infrastructure for the open data field has been created, including a network of global, regional, and national events, common principles, capacity-building resources, peer networks, and measurement tools. However, donors may be moving away from open data in general to focus more on sectoral issues or other emerging issues that might more directly articulate impact. This can potentially jeopardise any achieved coherence to date within the global open data community.

What can donors do to build more resilience, diversity, and coherence in the open data community? There are a wide range of potential actions, such as better tagging open data grants through IATI or other reporting instruments or increasing the sharing of funding strategies and lessons learned at key events (e.g. the annual IODC and regional meetings) to create opportunities for donor collaboration. More substantive progress will require a shared sense of field needs and moving beyond the current "loose touch" approach to cross-donor coordination. There is a strong need for substantial new and joint investment among open data funders and donor organisations in general. Donors need to explore more targeted investments in the core building blocks of the data ecosystem, including civil registration and vital statistics systems (CRVS), censuses, surveys, and analytical and leadership capacity in the field. Considering the significant experience within the community and the range of open data projects and initiatives to date, there is now a foundation to build upon, but it may start to erode without new investment. Greater coherence among donors will support increased alignment with regional and country priorities, help to avoid duplication, fill funding gaps, and contribute to an overall strategic approach in consideration of different programme priorities and funding methodologies.

Further reading

Acevedo-Ruiz, M. & Peña-López, I. (2017). *Evaluation of the Open Data for Development program*. Ottawa: OD4D Network. http://od4d.net/wp-content/uploads/2017/05/OD4D-Final-evaluation-report-v2_31-May.pdf

Boyera, S. & Iglesias, C. (2014). *Open data in developing countries: State of the art*. Partnership for Open Data. https://docs.google.com/document/d/1FMyfLu-jouL7j7Pw0kEwUn_B07aZ9IX3vlFGqPO0gX0/edit

Carolan, L. (2017). *Mapping open data for accountability.* Washington, DC: Transparency and Accountability Initiative and the Open Data Charter. http://www.transparency-initiative.org/wp-content/uploads/2017/06/taiodc_draft_data4accountabilityframework.pdf

Global Partnership for Sustainable Development Data. (2016). *The state of development data funding.* Washington, DC: Open Data Watch. https://opendatawatch.com/wp-content/uploads/2016/09/development-data-funding-2016.pdf

World Bank Group. (2017). *World Bank support for open data – 2012–2017.* Washington, DC: World Bank. https://openknowledge.worldbank.org/bitstream/handle/10986/28616/120801-WP-P133276-PUBLIC.pdf?sequence=1&isAllowed=y

About the authors

Fernando Perini coordinates the Open Data for Development (OD4D) programme for Canada's International Development Research Centre. OD4D works with global open data advocacy organisations and a network of regional partners committed to the creation of locally driven and sustainable open data ecosystems in developing countries. You can follow Fernando on Twitter at http://www.twitter.com/fperini. Learn more about OD4D at http://od4d.net.

Michael Jarvis has over two decades of experience working on global good governance, openness, and corporate responsibility. He is the Executive Director of the Transparency and Accountability Initiative (TAI), which works specifically to help donors improve grant-making practices in order to boost collective impact. You can follow Michael on Twitter at http://www.twitter.com/michaeljarvisdc and learn more about the TAI at http://www.transparency-initiative.org.

How to cite this chapter

Perini, F. & Jarvis, M. (2019). Open data stakeholders: Donors and investors. In T. Davies, S. Walker, M. Rubinstein, & F. Perini (Eds.), *The state of open data: Histories and horizons* (pp. 367–380). Cape Town and Ottawa: African Minds and International Development Research Centre. http://stateofopendata.od4d.net

This work is licensed under a Creative Commons Attribution 4.0 International (CC BY 4.0) licence. It was carried out with the aid of a grant from the International Development Research Centre, Ottawa, Canada.

Endnotes

1. Weinstein, J. & Goldstein, J. (2012). The benefits of a big tent: Opening up government in developing countries. *UCLA Law Review, 60(38)*. https://www.uclalawreview.org/the-benefits-of-a-big-tent-opening-up-government-in-developing-countries/

2. The International Development Research Centre, https://www.idrc.ca/en and Transparency and Accountability Initiative, http://www.transparency-initiative.org/, respectively.

3. It should be noted that donors are also open data publishers and aggregators. They publish to dedicated portals and many support and adhere to the implementation of the International Aid Transparency Initiative and other data standards. In this chapter, we do not focus on donors as publishers. The focus is on how donors, particularly international donors, support different open data communities and priorities.

4. IDRC. (2015). *Enabling the data revolution: An international open data roadmap. Conference report*. Ottawa: International Development Research Centre. http://1a9vrva76sx19qtvg1ddvt6f.wpengine.netdna-cdn.com/wp-content/uploads/2015/09/IODC2015-Final-Report-web.pdf

5. OD4D (Open Data for Development) Network. (2016). *IODC 16: International Open Data Roadmap*. Ottawa: OD4D Network. http://od4d.net/roadmap/assets/files/report-iodc-2016-web.pdf

6. OECD. (2017). *Development co-operation report 2017: Data for development*. Paris: Organisation for Economic Co-operation and Development Publishing. https://doi.org/10.1787/dcr-2017-en

7. Global Partnership for Sustainable Development Data. (2016). *The state of development data funding*. Washington, DC: Open Data Watch. https://opendatawatch.com/wp-content/uploads/2016/09/development-data-funding-2016.pdf

8. http://grantnav.threesixtygiving.org/

9. http://d-portal.org/ctrack.html?search=open%20data#view=main. D-Portal provides a view of all IATI data by recipient country or publisher that is comparable with the latest OECD Development Assistance Committee's (DAC) Creditor Reporting System (CRS) data.

10. An interactive version of the network chart, with access to the underlying data, is available at http://bit.ly/2Qm5FT9

11. *Wikipedia*. (2018). Snowball sampling. https://en.wikipedia.org/w/index.php?title=Snowball_sampling&oldid=856893462 [accessed 27 December 2018].

12. Open Data Watch. (2018). The data value chain: Moving from production to impact. https://opendatawatch.com/publications/the-data-value-chain-moving-from-production-to-impact/

13. Carolan, L. (2017). *Mapping open data for accountability*. Washington, DC: Transparency and Accountability Initiative and the Open Data Charter. http://www.transparency-initiative.org/wp-content/uploads/2017/06/taiodc_draft_data4accountabilityframework.pdf

14. Davies, T. & Perini, F. (2016). Researching the emerging impacts of open data: Revisiting the ODDC conceptual framework. *The Journal of Community Informatics, 12(2)*. http://ci-journal.org/index.php/ciej/article/view/1281

15. World Bank Group. (2017). *World Bank support for open data – 2012–2017*. Washington, DC: World Bank. https://openknowledge.worldbank.org/bitstream/handle/10986/28616/120801-WP-P133276-PUBLIC.pdf?sequence=1&isAllowed=y

16. Acevedo-Ruiz, M. & Peña-López, I. (2017). *Evaluation of the Open Data for Development program*. Ottawa: Open Data for Development Network. http://od4d.net/wp-content/uploads/2017/05/OD4D-Final-evaluation-report-v2_31-May.pdf

17. Faruqui, N. & Federico, B. (2018). *Management response to the evaluation of the Open Data for Development program*. Ottawa: International Development Research Centre. https://idl-bnc-idrc.dspacedirect.org/handle/10625/56937

18. https://eiti.org/document/eiti-open-data-policy

19. http://www.fiscaltransparency.net/

20. https://iatistandard.org/en/

21. https://www.open-contracting.org/
22. http://globalopendatainitiative.org/
23. GODI (Global Open Data Initiative). (2013). Announcing the Global Open Data Initiative. https://web.archive.org/web/20140301110448/http://globalopendatainitiative.org/2013/06/12/announcing-the-global-open-data-initiative/
24. World Bank. (2013). New Partnership seeks to bring benefits of open data to developing countries. World Bank press release, 18 September. http://www.worldbank.org/en/news/press-release/2013/09/18/new-partnership-seeks-bring-benefits-open-data-developing-countries
25. https://theodi.org/
26. https://okfn.org/
27. http://documents.worldbank.org/curated/en/829141468329986040/World-Bank-support-for-global-and-regional-initiatives-under-the-Development-Grant-Facility-DGF-compendium-of-DFG-programs
28. https://www.opengovpartnership.org/
29. IDRC (International Development Research Centre). (2015). *Enabling the data revolution: An International Open Data Roadmap. Conference report*. Ottawa: IDRC. http://1a9vrva76sx19qtvg1ddvt6f.wpengine.netdna-cdn.com/wp-content/uploads/2015/09/IODC2015-Final-Report-web.pdf
30. OD4D Network. (2016). *IODC 16: International Open Data Roadmap*. Ottawa: Open Data for Development Network. http://od4d.net/roadmap/assets/files/report-iodc-2016-web.pdf
31. Perini, F. (2018). Open government partnership and the open data for development network join forces to support open data initiatives around the world. *Open Government Partnership* [News post], 10 May. https://www.opengovpartnership.org/stories/open-government-partnership-and-open-data-development-network-join-forces-support-open-data

026

Governments

Barbara-Chiara Ubaldi

Key points

- Over the last decade, many governments have moved from open data experimentation toward consolidation, making open data part of the public sector's way of doing business.

- There is growing awareness of the need to upgrade policies, institutional structures, programmes, and practices to produce, manage, and ensure the effective reuse of government data to secure long-term sustainability and continuity of open data initiatives.

- As open data-related initiatives become part of broader efforts to advance the digital transformation of government services across countries, it becomes essential to establish linkages between open data and other policy areas.

Introduction

A decade ago, many in the open data movement primarily viewed governments as the institutions hoarding data, and they felt it was the responsibility of open data advocates to access and unlock that data. In a simple supply and demand model of open data, the government role was primarily as the data supplier; however, over the last ten years, there has been a recognition that governments can play a much broader role in the open data ecosystem. Not only have a large number of governments embraced open data as part of broader reforms of their digital infrastructure, many have worked to identify and optimise institutional arrangements, as well as the hard and soft policy levers needed to shape the implementation and impact of open data activities within their jurisdictions. In recent years, governments have also had to integrate open data activities into a much wider range of data governance issues that need to be addressed, including privacy, security, and algorithmic governance.

Since the breakthrough of open data onto the international stage in 2009 with President Obama's Open Government Directive in the United States (US) and the initiatives subsequently launched by the United Kingdom (UK), France, Kenya, Canada, and many other countries, the leaders in power driving those activities have changed, more than once in most cases. The extent to which open data ideas have been sustained across different administrations provides evidence as to the strength of institutionalisation of open data policy within governments. There is evidence in many countries of mature coordination among institutions within and across levels of government, as well as beyond national borders, with work undertaken to sustain the implementation of open data commitments, drawing on initiatives such as the Open Government Partnership and the International Open Data Charter. Open data has also become central to wider agendas, such as monitoring the Sustainable Development Goals (SDGs)[1] or responding to the aftermath of the global financial crisis.[2] It is notable that government representatives have consistently made up the largest single stakeholder group at the International Open Data Conferences, demonstrating the significance of government officials and resources in popularising open data, as well as their own ongoing interest in exchanging ideas to create a shared global agenda.

In managing the development of (open) data ecosystems both domestically and internationally, clear governance frameworks are critical to supporting inclusive decision-making and the alignment of actions to implement policies which cross administrations and levels of government. Effective governance frameworks can enable the effective coordination of actors within the data ecosystem, including decision-makers, data producers, data users, data stewards, and intermediaries.[3]

This chapter will argue that clear governance helps provide greater transparency about the key stakeholders, their roles and responsibilities in the management of open data value chains, and who is accountable for open data decisions. This will sustain a more informed dialogue and better engagement across the entire ecosystem on the performance and impact of data publication and reuse.[4] Even if different contexts for action require different governance models as there is no one-size-fits-all option, the maturing of open data policies requires stable governance models in order to secure long-term continuity and sustainable results.

The following sections will outline how government's engagement with open data has developed over the last decade, explore common patterns of open data institutionalisation within government systems, set out ten elements of governance that governments need to address to fully realise social and economic value from open data, and consider which of these elements will need the most critical attention in the coming years.

The evolution of open data policy

There have been many strands and stages in the development of government open data policies and practices, starting long before the current wave of interest in opening government data. However, governments have generally had to navigate three main phases in the adoption and implementation of open data programmes, moving from an initial exploration of open data, through experimentation and consolidation, to, more recently, strengthening of international collaboration on common principles.

Initial exploration – making the case

The key drivers for open data have varied from country to country and over time.[5] In many countries, the Right to Information (RTI) movement, which aims to promote the public's right of access to information from a human rights and good governance perspective, has played a key role as the promoter of open data, and consequently has been reflected in various governance frameworks and priorities. For example, where open data policies have been driven primarily by RTI advocates, open data programmes have often emerged from building on or adapting access to information laws or equivalent normative instruments.[6] This has been the case in Mexico and Spain, and evidence from the Organisation for Economic Co-operation and Development (OECD) *Open government data report* indicates that most OECD countries (21 out of the 33 surveyed in 2018 for the OECD Open Useful and Reusable Data Index – OURData Index[7]) have used freedom of information and/or access to information laws as a legal basis to support the release of open government data. In particular, in most European countries, this approach was accelerated and supported through the transposition into national laws of the European Union Public Service Information (EU PSI) Directive[8] on the reuse of public sector information. Greece, for example, amended its existing law on the reuse of public sector information in 2014 based on the EU PSI Directive to include an open by default principle.[9]

This approach in Greece was in line with a general trend showing how, in response to open data advocacy, governments have adjusted existing legal and regulatory frameworks with the intent of progressively allowing access by the general public to an increasing amount and variety of data held by the state. For a number of years, the potential value of open data for improved good governance in terms of government transparency and accountability was the primary argument used to make the case for an open data agenda. This often resulted in a strong emphasis placed on the obligation of public bodies to respond to requests for information, rather than on creating the framework conditions, and the incentives necessary, for a proactive release of large volumes of data in ways that permit and encourage reuse.[10]

Although one could claim that the strong focus on open data as a tool for open government and public sector transparency meant that few countries initially explored its potential in other policy domains, such as open innovation or urban planning, more recently many public authorities have come to appreciate the relevance of accessible government data for producing social impact and stimulating data-driven economic growth. As a result, governments have started changing the way in which they value, manage, use, and share data both inside and outside their jurisdictions. This increasing focus on the potential economic and social value of open data has resulted in a growing emphasis on establishing conditions that can sustain the public accessibility of key datasets, representing a shift from only publishing reports, analysis, and documentation to substantially increasing the supply of machine-readable data.

A greater focus from the start of this decade on increasing open data availability has translated into efforts geared toward establishing and populating open data portals. Early in this decade, it was not uncommon for governments to benchmark their open data work against peers by comparing the number of datasets listed on their portals. The basic idea was to make as much data as possible accessible for technical users and to provide opportunities for less technical segments of the society to realise the value of data reuse through the provision of tools and guidance on data visualisation or by signposting applications created by third parties.

With time, governments started to understand the importance of going beyond just the release of datasets on data portals. With this recognition, they have increasingly focused on creating a critical mass of open data producers and users, often around specific datasets or particular sectors, in order to foster more sustainable value creation. By adopting and promoting common definitions and standards across the public sector, central units have built a wider common understanding of open data and increased the number of public sector organisations capable of releasing and working with open data. This has helped open data ideas and practices to gain momentum across government, rather than as something solely discussed within technology-focused or executive central departments. This has also been complemented by efforts to actively engage external actors and different communities across the ecosystem to raise awareness and spur reuse, working toward a critical mass of visible case studies of data reuse.[11,12]

This change in focus has contributed to strengthening a more mature open data culture both across governments and the whole ecosystem. As a result, with more stakeholders coming to rely on government data, governments have become more aware of the need to establish sound governance frameworks and to move from experimentation toward making opening data the public sector's regular way of doing business. Over the last few years, awareness has grown of the importance of creating or upgrading existing policies, institutional structures, and practices in order to produce, manage, and support the use of government data. This has resulted in a rapid maturation of open government data programmes in many countries that have moved from experimentation to consolidation.

From experimentation to consolidation

The 2018 United Nations (UN) E-Government Survey found that 139 countries (72% of UN member states) now have open government data portals, up from just 46 countries in 2014.[13] Although many of these portals do not yet host predominantly machine-readable data, with PDFs remaining a common information format for dissemination, this trend illustrates the extent to which providing access to data has become an important international norm for governments. However, there is substantial variation in approach and level of investment. For some countries, their open data programmes represent a relatively minor project focused mainly on the operation of a portal, whereas, for others, open data has moved from a small programme to a major policy initiative.

However, even where open data initiatives have become well established, beyond simply the provision of portals, gains made are by no means automatically secure and sustainable. Many initiatives are still vulnerable to changing government priorities or subsequent retrenchment into old business-as-usual models that could undo any progress made to date. Making the most of the opportunities that open data provides requires changes in the organisational structure of governments to avoid existing rules, routines, norms, and power relations that will otherwise leave the potential of open data unfulfilled. Counteracting the tendency of governments to be silo-based, and more prone to inertia than innovation, is a requirement for the successful implementation of open data. Structural changes and new forms of organisation that allow communities to link across organisational boundaries need to be enabled for open data to mature and contribute to public value creation.[14,15] In some cases, governments have managed to create new operational units to lead open data work, although not all such reforms have proven successful. For example, efforts at the wholesale reform of trading funds (government-owned companies responsible for key public datasets) in the UK, through the creation of a "Public Data Corporation" that was to facilitate public–private and civil society partnerships around strategic datasets, ultimately made little headway.[16]

> ### Creating focal points for open data activity
>
> In France, Etalab, the main public sector organisation in charge of open government data policies, was created to promote open government data release but also to enhance its reuse. Thus, among its numerous responsibilities, Etalab is in charge of engaging the open data ecosystem to promote data reuse both within and outside the public sector. It works toward this through initiatives aimed at promoting awareness of the benefits of open government data reuse, partnerships with civil society organisations and private sector actors, the organisation of hackathons, and building capacity related to open data reuse, such as open data literacy programmes.
>
> In Korea, according to Article 13 of the Open Data Law, the National Information Society Agency provides support to public sector organisations to both publish open government data and promote its reuse, including support for the development of open data-based startups. For example, the open data startup competition is a government contest that promotes the creation and development of startups using open government data. Different startups are encouraged to participate, and winners are offered government funding and assistance to fully establish and/or further develop their businesses.

Experience shows that consolidating open data progress requires support for data management across organisational silos, although without necessarily centralising ownership and responsibility for data within a single agency. This kind of governance framework is new for most governments around the world. Civil society activists and the private sector have not always realised the extent of institutional innovation required for government to respond to open data agendas effectively. Governments ultimately need a framework that can provide a friendly policy environment, adequate institutional structures and procedures, a solid and comprehensive legal framework, clear guidance on data licensing and standards, provision of incentives, and a solid commitment to define, steer, and support long-term action plans that include performance indicators and measures. These elements are recognised in World Bank research as critical to helping policy-makers create the enabling environment to move their open data initiatives from experimentation to consolidation.[17]

In order to embed new governance frameworks for open data, governments around the world have begun developing and implementing specific open data policies to facilitate data release and use, going beyond simple transparency agendas.[18] However, it is notable that efforts of this type have been more prevalent in developed than in developing countries[19] (e.g. the open data policies that first gained momentum in the UK and US with origins in the UK Power of Information

Review[20] and the 2009 US Open Government Directive from President Obama[21]). These set the pattern later followed by many other governments, including Kenya, where efforts in 2011 were framed in terms of the power of information,[22] and Mexico, where in 2015, the President published the Open Data Executive Decree.[23]

In a number of countries, policies have gone through a series of iterations, building open data concepts into government business operations. Open data policy is an essential element of the governance of data ecosystems as it defines a common vision and clarifies goals and expected results, such as increased efficiency, higher transparency, and improved quality of public services. The vision established through policy can also embed key milestones and can propose indicators to measure progress. Having this common vision defined by policy also helps to target efforts toward shared objectives, set expected benefits, monitor achievements at the institutional level, and exploit potential synergies. Where they have been adopted, open data policies have set a process in motion toward political awareness not only among national public authorities, but also within the broader ecosystem of national actors.

Relatively robust data on the consolidation of open data policies and initiatives exists for OECD countries,[24] yet there are substantial gaps when it comes to comparable data on the features and functioning of open data policy for other countries around the world. There is also relatively limited information, at present, on how open data policies relate to other policy areas. However, as open data-related initiatives become part of broader efforts to advance the digital transformation of the public sector, it will become essential to understand the linkages between open data and other related policy areas as part of sound data governance. An improved understanding of this could, for instance, help to advance the adoption and implementation of personal data management policies that ensure that data is consistently and properly handled across the public sector, improving data security while also promoting the overall efficiency of the data value chain. Even consolidation efforts are not a one-time thing and require renewal as the wider policy context changes. It is notable that one of the biggest barriers for open data adoption noted in OECD countries in 2018 was the uncertainty currently created by privacy legislation, which has often been developed on an entirely separate track of activity from work on open data.[25]

International efforts, shared policy, and common principles

The international community has been long aware of the critical value of a friendly policy context for both e-government and the handling of public sector information, although it is only comparatively recently that these elements have been framed in terms of open data. The European Commission (EC) formulated the foundations of open data policy via a Green Paper on Public Sector Information (PSI) in 1998,[26] acknowledging the fundamental role of accessible data for the proper functioning of the EU internal market and setting up the key framework conditions for successful open data policy within the EU. In 2003, with the aim of establishing the "systemic" prerequisites for effective use and reuse of data through legal and soft law measures, the EU adopted legislation to foster the reuse of open government data in member states via the PSI Directive 2003/98/EC.[27,28]

The European Directive established rules regarding availability, accessibility, and transparency of public sector datasets, and recommended that EU member countries both adopt a standard electronic licence for the reuse of data and provide tools to easily find relevant data sets. The PSI Directive was amended in 2013 by Directive 2013/37/EU,[29] which introduced the terminology of open data alongside PSI and the general principle that all information accessible under member state legislation should be, in principle, reusable, and that administrative charges should not exceed the marginal costs of making it available for such reuse.[30]

With a more global focus, on 18 June 2013, the G8 leaders, chaired by the UK, signed the G8 Open Data Charter,[31] which set out five strategic principles that all G8 members pledged to act on, including an expectation that all government data be published "open by default", alongside principles to increase the quality, quantity, and reuse of the released data. When adopting this Charter, the G8 members also identified 14 thematic areas – from education to transport and from health to crime and justice – for which they would release "high value" datasets with the expectation that these would help unlock the economic potential of open data, support innovation, and provide greater accountability for governments. This indicated a shift to a more focused approach on specific datasets that should be released at a minimum.

Building on the G8 Open Data Charter, a framework for wider engagement and alignment was established as a result of collaboration between governments and civil society organisations working on open data, leading to a shared set of principles under the banner of the International Open Data Charter.[32] This multi-stakeholder charter is intended to support the strengthening of open data around the world through its adoption by national, state, and municipal governments far beyond the G8. The International Open Data Charter, established in 2015, has ultimately proved to be a useful driver for the adoption of open data policies and the establishment of clearer governance frameworks. This is particularly true for countries that were latecomers in regarding government data as a valuable or vital resource for value creation. The Charter has also inspired the adoption of open data international commitments within policy specific global initiatives, such as the G20 Open Data Principles for Anti-Corruption.[33]

Institutionalising open data

As shared global principles and clear visions established through policy have matured as a basis for open data activity, governments have had to now grapple with how to institutionalise open data as an integrated practice, and a number of common elements have emerged. With open data policies and programmes continuing to expand, the necessary supporting operational and administrative systems and programmes have become more complex and sophisticated. Certainly, given the complexity and cross-cutting nature of government data, each government needs to establish an organisational set-up that can appropriately support coherence and convergence of the actions of multiple departments responsible for hundreds of lines of business and is aligned with overarching strategic decisions.[34] Institutional arrangements as part of the governance framework for data are essential to reinforce governmental capacity to steer strategies and their implementation, as well as to create a collective commitment to the open data agenda across the entire public sector. This kind of collective committee requires a shift in organisational culture that can only happen if individual institutions buy into a government-wide vision that has been clearly articulated and operationalised.[35]

Despite all the good initiatives underway to adopt policies aimed at improving open data availability, accessibility, and reuse, many countries still lack the internal coordination needed to move their open data agenda forward beyond simple data publication. As a result, many initiatives have been delivered as stand-alone projects, and the challenge remains of aligning the diverse efforts of multiple institutions so that governments can be as effective as possible in delivering public data for the benefit of citizens and businesses. This noted, the general trend across countries with more mature open data ecosystems is in the direction of establishing clearer governance frameworks that clarify responsibilities, capture the interests of all key actors, and respond to their demands (e.g. through the establishment of advisory groups).[36]

Increased transparency of these governance frameworks themselves is also seen as key to improving accountability and increasing public trust; however, in many cases, too little is known about how open data is governed, how accountable data holders are to both data consumers and policy-makers, how data producers ensure the quality of government data, and who is specifically tasked to make data open.[37] We do not just need governance of open data; we also need open governance of data. Getting a better understanding of open data governance is not only important from an accountability point of view. With better insights into the different decision-making models and structures, the implementation of open data principles, such as those advocated by the International Open Data Charter, can be accelerated across countries.

The institutional arrangements put in place to steer strategic decisions and coordinate actions across the public sector often reflect national administrative cultures. Observing over a decade of national experiences has indicated that this often begins with tasking a government body, often the centre of government (such as the Prime Minister's Office) or a line ministry, with responsibilities related to the government's digital agenda or public sector modernisation, to champion, coordinate, and provide support for implementing open data programmes. For example, in France the open data agenda is led by Etalab within Prime Minister Services, while in Mexico, the open data programme is under the President's Office, and in Canada, open data is led by the Treasury Board Secretariat. In Indonesia, the open data initiative is led by the President's "Delivery Unit".[38] The choice of a charismatic figure, or champion, to lead the coordinating institution also often plays a key role in creating the new mind-set required across the administration. As open data becomes institutionalised within governments, these organisations are increasingly becoming just one player in a new form of open-source governance and may often play the role of arbiter, coordinator, funder, or regulator for the activities of others in delivering public value through the use of open government data.[39] From this perspective, open data becomes the platform that can enable governments to establish new forms of collaborations and partnerships.

Embedding effective governance frameworks

How can governments move forward with institutionalising open data? In the box below, ten elements are set out that governments should consider in establishing long-term governance frameworks that can support the institutionalisation of open data activities. While many elements of a governance framework for open data are cross-cutting and intersect with agendas related to digital infrastructure, e-government, public engagement, data protection, and other emerging areas, such as artificial intelligence and algorithmic governance, it is vital for the future of open data that they also remain distinct within the open data governance framework. Without this, it will be challenging to sustain cross-border collaboration on open data into the future.

> ### Ten key elements of an effective governance framework
>
> An analysis of government experiences around the world suggests the following elements of an open data governance framework will be central to securing the resilience and sustainability of open data in the years ahead:
>
> 1. A strategic vision – defining and guiding actions, actors, and sector initiatives in pursuit of common strategic objectives. A shared strategic vision should be complemented by a roadmap or action plan for implementation and should be backed by clear public leadership.
> 2. Legal and regulatory framework – providing for required changes in the laws or regulations to support safe and effective release and reuse of open data.
> 3. Institutional and organisational leadership arrangements – providing a focal point for reforms, but distributing responsibilities for data release and use across government as far as is appropriate given capacity.
> 4. Technical infrastructure – providing for data searching, access, sharing, and reuse.
> 5. User engagement – increasing the value of data as a public good by meeting user requirements and identifying priority high-value datasets.
> 6. Partnerships – establishing partnerships both across government institutions and with other governments, civil society organisations, and the private sector. Established partnerships move beyond ad hoc interaction to have an ongoing model of engagement with clear, stable, and transparent processes for public administration officials to work together on publishing and using data.
> 7. Sustainable funding – identifying sustainable sources to resource the implementation of open data policy and related initiatives.
> 8. Capacity building – establishing programmes that ensure the necessary intellectual, human, and financial resources for ongoing provision and use of data.
> 9. Communication planning – ensuring broad communication of intentions, efforts, and results.
> 10. Measurement processes – assessing and publishing results of open data efforts in order to take corrective actions as needed to realise the strategic vision for open data, secure value creation, and ensure continuous support for reforms.

Although OECD surveys track many elements of an effective open data governance framework, to date, no government has every piece of the puzzle in place such that they can be assured of the sustainability and continuity of their open data work across time and changing political administrations. In particular, more work is needed to fully secure the right policy environments, the connection between data supply and demand, sustained funding for open data, and the mature organisational and partnership arrangements that support collaboration between stakeholders.

Even though, as this chapter argues, the most effective governance frameworks are those that focus on facilitating collaboration and the convergence and alignment of actors, in many contexts around the world, centralised and top-down decision-making processes still prevail. This provides limited mechanisms for different stakeholders to engage and strengthen the open data ecosystem. Notably, only around 40% of OECD countries currently have formal requirements for consultation with open data users to inform their open data planning,[40] and, as a result, open data is often still primarily supply, rather than demand, driven. The establishment of spaces and mechanisms as part of the overall governance framework that foster collaboration between governments and other stakeholders that leads to value co-creation needs increased emphasis.

When it comes to sustainable funding, there are some positive signs that governments are recognising its importance. Evidence shows that 20 out of the 36 OECD countries surveyed in 2018 for the OURData Index have assigned a distinct line of financing to open government data policies and strategies, and, in 16 of these countries, individual public sector organisations provide finance for their own specific open government data initiatives.[41] However, evidence to date does not indicate how funding is changing year-on-year, nor is there much information on the resources available for open data policy and strategy beyond OECD countries.

Although some governments are well advanced in establishing legal and regulatory frameworks for open data, often building, as noted above, on existing legislation and regulation, in other countries, this remains a pressing gap to fill.[42] Many developing countries taking part in Open Data Readiness Assessments appear not yet to have enacted and implemented the full range of necessary open data-related legislation, including access to information and data protection acts.[43] Even where laws and regulations are in place, training for relevant staff often remains ad hoc rather than part of normalised practices, and, in a number of cases, the independent commissioners required by their enacted legislation have not yet been appointed, creating a gap between the promise and the reality of the regulatory framework.

Similarly, many countries have not yet been able to take forward key policy reforms, such as establishing a clear fee regime for data access. These policies are frequently lacking in countries where open data efforts are led by institutions with limited political power, and the higher-level political leadership necessary to bring alignment and coherence across different data-related agendas is not present. Furthermore, in some countries, the institutionalisation of the responsibilities for coordinating open data activity has not yet been fully realised, creating strong risks for instability as a result of national elections.

In the years ahead, measurement and communications planning will also become increasingly critical parts of open data governance. Open data communities need to recognise shifting government priorities with global policy attention shifting away from open data. Having a clear way to communicate to stakeholders the value of open data in order to sustain awareness of a strategic open data vision will increase in importance. Communication is also vital to realising the benefits of making open data governance more transparent, allowing stakeholders to understand the touchpoints for engaging with government, and keeping track of the ongoing health of open data reforms.

Conclusion

For governments, open data is one of many reform agendas, yet it is one with the potential to transform policy-making and service delivery by fostering whole new models of collaboration. Through regular surveys, including OECD studies and the UN E-Government Report, government progress on open data has been tracked, and there are many promising signs of open data becoming more established and institutionalised. Institutionalisation requires clear and transparent frameworks for the governance of open data, making sure that open data is made integral to the business of government and that it can support engagement across traditional programming silos and stakeholder groups.

International collaboration among governments has made significant progress, especially in the development and adoption of shared principles. In the coming years, deeper collaboration on institutionalising open data will be critical around the development of shared or connected data infrastructures, capacity building, and the sharing of practices, knowledge, and tools.

Most importantly, governments need to continue to evolve more mature, consolidated, and embedded approaches to open data. Although open data reforms have proven reasonably resilient to shifts in political power, they are by no means automatically sustainable. Getting governance models right will be the key to ensuring we can still meaningfully discuss the state of open data for governments ten years from now.

Further reading

Davies, T. (2014). Open data policies and practice: An international comparison. *SSRN* [Article], 5 September. https://papers.ssrn.com/abstract=2492520

OECD. (2018). *Open government data report: Enhancing policy maturity for sustainable impact.* OECD Digital Government Studies. Paris: Organisation for Economic Co-operation and Development Publishing. https://doi.org/10.1787/9789264305847-en

Ubaldi, B. (2013). *Open government data: Towards empirical analysis of open government data initiatives.* OECD Working Papers on Public Governance. Paris: Organisation for Economic Co-operation and Development Publishing. https://www.oecd-ilibrary.org/content/paper/5k46bj4f03s7-en

About the author

Barbara-Chiara Ubaldi is a senior project manager at the OECD within the Division for Public Sector Reform, where she coordinates work on the use of emerging technologies, social media, and open data to enhance public sector openness, efficiency, and innovation.

How to cite this chapter

Ubaldi, B. (2019). Open data stakeholders: Governments. In T. Davies, S. Walker, M. Rubinstein, & F. Perini (Eds.), *The state of open data: Histories and horizons* (pp. 381–394). Cape Town and Ottawa: African Minds and International Development Research Centre. http://stateofopendata.od4d.net

This work is licensed under a Creative Commons Attribution 4.0 International (CC BY 4.0) licence. It was carried out with the aid of a grant from the International Development Research Centre, Ottawa, Canada.

Endnotes

1. United Nations Secretary General's Independent Expert Advisory Group (IEAG) on the Data Revolution for Sustainable Development. (2014). *A world that counts: Mobilising the data revolution for sustainable development.* http://hdl.handle.net/20.500.11822/20065

2. Couillault, B., Mizuguchi, J., & Reed, M. (2017). *Collective action: Toward solving a vexing problem to build a global infrastructure for financial information.* OFR Brief Series 17-01, 1–13. Washington, DC: Office of Financial Research. https://www.financialresearch.gov/briefs/files/OFRbr_2017_01_LEI.pdf

3. OECD. (2018). *Open government data report: Enhancing policy maturity for sustainable impact.* OECD Digital Government Studies. Paris: Organisation for Economic Co-operation and Development Publishing. https://doi.org/10.1787/9789264305847-en

4. Brandusescu, A., Lämmerhirt, D., & Verhulst, S. (2017). Mapping open data governance models: Who makes decisions about government data and how? *Open Knowledge International Blog*, 16 February. https://blog.okfn.org/2017/02/16/mapping-open-data-governance-models-who-decides-and-how/

5. Davies, T. (2014) Open data policies and practice: An international comparison. *SSRN* [Article], 5 September. https://papers.ssrn.com/abstract=2492520

6. Fumega, S. (2015). *Understanding two mechanisms for accessing government information and data around the world.* Tasmania, Australia. http://hdl.handle.net/10625/55344

7. OECD. (2018). *Background: The OECD Open Useful and Reusable Data (OURdata) Index.* Paris: Organisation for Economic Co-operation and Development Publishing. https://doi.org/10.1787/9789264305847-3-en

8. European Commission. (2019). *European legislation on the re-use of public sector information.* https://ec.europa.eu/digital-single-market/en/european-legislation-reuse-public-sector-information

9. OECD. (2018). *Open government data report: Enhancing policy maturity for sustainable impact.* OECD Digital Government Studies. Paris: Organisation for Economic Co-operation and Development Publishing. https://doi.org/10.1787/9789264305847-en

10. Ubaldi, B. (2013). *Open government data: Towards empirical analysis of open government data initiatives.* OECD Working Papers on Public Governance. Paris: Organisation for Economic Co-operation and Development Publishing. https://www.oecd-ilibrary.org/content/paper/5k46bj4f03s7-en

11 OECD. (2016). *Open government data review of Mexico: Data reuse for public sector impact and innovation.* OECD Digital Government Studies. Paris: Organisation for Economic Co-operation and Development Publishing. https://dx.doi.org/10.1787/9789264259270-en

12 OECD. (2018). *Open government data report: Enhancing policy maturity for sustainable impact.* OECD Digital Government Studies. Paris: Organisation for Economic Co-operation and Development Publishing. https://doi.org/10.1787/9789264305847-en

13 UN. (2018*). United Nations E-Government Survey 2018: Gearing e-government to support transformation towards sustainable and resilient societies.* New York, NY: United Nations. https://publicadministration.un.org/egovkb/Portals/egovkb/Documents/un/2018-Survey/E-Government%20Survey%202018_FINAL%20for%20web.pdf

14 Harrison, T., Pardo, T, Cresswell, A., & Cook, M. (2011). *Delivering public value through open government.* Albany, NY: Centre for Technology in Government. https://www.ctg.albany.edu/media/pubs/pdfs/opengov_pubvalue.pdf

15 OECD. (2018). *Open government data report: Enhancing policy maturity for sustainable impact.* OECD Digital Government Studies. Paris: Organisation for Economic Co-operation and Development Publishing. https://doi.org/10.1787/9789264305847-en

16 https://www.gov.uk/government/groups/public-data-group

17 World Bank Group. (2017). *World Bank support for open data 2012–2017.* Washington, DC: World Bank. http://hdl.handle.net/10986/28616

18 OECD. (2018). *Open government data report: Enhancing policy maturity for sustainable impact.* OECD Digital Government Studies. Paris: Organisation for Economic Co-operation and Development Publishing. https://doi.org/10.1787/9789264305847-en

19 World Bank Group. (2017). *World Bank support for open data 2012–2017.* Washington, DC: World Bank. http://hdl.handle.net/10986/28616

20 Mayo, E. & Steinberg, T. (2007). The power of information: An independent review. London: UK Cabinet Office. https://webarchive.nationalarchives.gov.uk/20100407163222/http://www.cabinetoffice.gov.uk/reports/power_of_information.aspx

21 Obama, B. (2009). Transparency and Open Government. Memorandum for the Heads of Executive Departments and Agencies, 21 January. Washington, DC: The White House. https://obamawhitehouse.archives.gov/the-press-office/transparency-and-open-government

22 Majeed, R. (2014). *Disseminating the power of information: Kenya Open Data Initiative, 2011–2012.* Princeton, NJ: Princeton University. https://successfulsocieties.princeton.edu/publications/disseminating-power-information-kenya-open-data-initiative-2011-2012

23 OECD. (2018). *Open government data in Mexico: The way forward.* OECD Digital Government Studies. Paris: Organisation for Economic Co-operation and Development Publishing. https://dx.doi.org/10.1787/9789264297944-en

24 OECD. (2018). *Open government data report: Enhancing policy maturity for sustainable impact.* OECD Digital Government Studies. Paris: Organisation for Economic Co-operation and Development Publishing. https://doi.org/10.1787/9789264305847-en

25 Ibid.

26 EC. (1999). *Public sector information: A key resource for Europe.* Green Paper on Public Sector Information in the Information Society. Brussels: European Commission. http://aei.pitt.edu/1168/1/public_sector_information_gp_COM_98_585.pdf

27 EU (European Union). (2013). Directive 2003/98/EC of the European Parliament and of the Council of 17 November 2003 on the re-use of public sector information. https://eur-lex.europa.eu/legal-content/EN/ALL/?uri=celex:32003L0098

28 See also https://ec.europa.eu/digital-single-market/en/policies/76010/3502

29 EU (European Union). (2013). Directive 2013/37/EU Amending Directive 2003/98/EC of the European Parliament and of the Council of 17 November 2003 on the Re-Use of Public Sector Information. http://data.europa.eu/eli/dir/2013/37/oj/eng

30. Morando, F., Lemma, R., & Basso, S. (2013). Is there such a thing as free government data? *Internet Policy Review, 2(4)*. https://policyreview.info/articles/analysis/there-such-thing-free-government-data
31. G8. (2013). G8 open data charter and technical annex. London: Government of the United Kingdom. https://www.gov.uk/government/publications/open-data-charter/g8-open-data-charter-and-technical-annex
32. For more information on this topic, see https://www.europeandataportal.eu/en/homepage
33. G20 ACWG. (2015). *G20 anti-corruption open data principles*. G20 Anti-Corruption Working Group. http://www.g20.utoronto.ca/2015/G20-Anti-Corruption-Open-Data-Principles.pdf
34. OECD. (2015). *Open government data review of Poland*. OECD Digital Government Studies. Paris: Organisation for Economic Co-operation and Development Publishing. https://dx.doi.org/10.1787/9789264241787-en
35. OECD. (2018). *Open government data report: Enhancing policy maturity for sustainable impact*. OECD Digital Government Studies. Paris: Organisation for Economic Co-operation and Development Publishing. https://doi.org/10.1787/9789264305847-en
36. Ibid.
37. Brandusescu, A., Lämmerhirt, D., & Verhulst, S. (2017). Mapping open data governance models: Who makes decisions about government data and how? *Open Knowledge International Blog*, 16 February. https://blog.okfn.org/2017/02/16/mapping-open-data-governance-models-who-decides-and-how/
38. World Bank Group. (2017). *World Bank support for open data 2012–2017*. Washington, DC: World Bank. http://hdl.handle.net/10986/28616
39. Ubaldi, B. (2013). *Open government data: Towards empirical analysis of open government data initiatives*. OECD Working Papers on Public Governance. Paris: Organisation for Economic Co-operation and Development Publishing. https://www.oecd-ilibrary.org/content/paper/5k46bj4f03s7-en
40. OECD. (2018). *Open government data report: Enhancing policy maturity for sustainable impact*. OECD Digital Government Studies. Paris: Organisation for Economic Co-operation and Development Publishing. Table 4.A.2. https://doi.org/10.1787/9789264305847-en
41. Ibid.
42. Ibid.
43. World Bank Group. (2017). *World Bank support for open data 2012–2017*. Washington, DC: World Bank. http://hdl.handle.net/10986/28616

027

Journalists and the media

Alex Howard and Eva Constantaras

Key points

- Data journalists have a key role to play as public interest watchdogs. The label "data journalism" can cover a wide range of practices from using data science to find stories to storytelling with data and creating interactive content and visualisations for articles.

- The costs and complexity of effective data journalism, combined with the time pressures common in reporting, make for a difficult business case. Finding sustainable models of data journalism is even more urgent at a time when traditional media outlets face competition from online journalists.

- The promise of "automated journalism" based on open data is largely unfulfilled; however, if more media houses focus on making open data an essential source, we may see more examples of automation tools in the future.

- This is a critical moment for public trust, and there is no clear template for how data journalism can contribute to society's response.

Introduction

The social impact of open data depends upon its use and reuse by different actors across society. For decades, journalists and media outlets have served and informed the public as a key infomediary for government statistics, academic and scientific research, business information, and their own analysis.

In the 21st century, data journalism is now an emerging field of practice around the world, but there is still no universally shared definition. Some practitioners consider data journalism to be thoughtful storytelling with data as the centrepiece. Others say it is including statistical data in stories, visualisations, interactive elements, or the application of data science to journalism.

Journalists who acquire, clean, analyse, report on, and, in some cases, create open data, now play a key role as public interest watchdogs. Reporters can transform the raw data into new insights, facilitate public engagement in the democratic process, inform consumers, and hold powerful institutions accountable. Journalists have made opaque financial transactions more visible, catalysing regulatory reform, such as with the International Consortium of Investigative Journalists (ICIJ)[1] collaborative reporting on massive leaks of data. Reporters at the *Washington Post* and *The Guardian* have created a database of undocumented killings by law enforcement,[2] raising awareness of racial injustice and shaming government agencies into keeping better statistics. In "Life in the camps",[3] Reuters journalists mapped the abhorrent living conditions of refugees, revealing the failures of global diplomacy.

History

The computer-assisted reporting of the last century, when the tools and methodologies of social science were first applied to journalism using mainframe and then desktop computers, has been transformed by the rapid public adoption of broadband internet connections, smartphones, open source software and frameworks, and the unprecedented scale of data generation and publication. While the data-driven journalism of 2019 is distinguished from what has come before by computers and the internet, journalists have been reporting on data as a source, the most basic definition for "data journalism", for centuries, printing statistics and tables in pamphlets, tabloids, and newspapers long before "open data" was an idea.

Around the world, a growing number of media organisations are downloading, analysing, and reporting on open data from multiple sources in ways that inform, engage, and empower the public. Over the past decade, pioneers in the global transparency movement have adopted and adapted principles and practices from the open source software world, where "showing your work" and collaborating around a shared code are important signals for both trust and transparency.

At their best, journalists are as appropriately sceptical of the open data published by corporations and governments online as they would be of the accounts from human sources.

Expanding horizons

The geographic reach of data journalism has grown over the past decade, driven by foundational investments, industry adoption, and grassroots organisations training reporters on the ground. The data journalism community, traditionally centred around the annual National Institute for Computer-Assisted Reporting[4] (NICAR) conference run by investigative reporters and editors, now hosts a much more cross-border conversation.

The Global Editors Network[5] and their annual Data Journalism Awards, the European Investigative Journalism & Dataharvest Conference,[6] the Global Investigative Journalism Conference,[7] and a plethora of smaller country-based data journalism events organised under the auspices of Hacks/Hackers or Schools of Data, are convening communities of data journalism around the world.

The growing diversity in the practice has opened new "scrappier" models for data journalism with a more explicit public interest mission in countries where small teams of data journalists expose blatant inequality and corruption.

Enduring challenges to the field

Like journalism that relies upon humans as a source, there is no global consensus that the purpose of data journalism is to inform the public about governance issues, reveal corruption, or hold powerful institutions accountable. Despite the extraordinary work produced by publications around the world, some recent research about the state of data journalism paints a grim picture of the field.

Google News Lab's *Data journalism in 2017*[8] found that data skills remain specialised and time-consuming to develop. Time pressures prevent aspiring journalists from producing the data-driven stories they believe need reporting. While some interactive features that engage readers have proven wildly popular, the business case for media houses to invest in data teams is still a hard sell in boardrooms.

The editorial decisions of organisations also determine where the lens of data-driven reporting is directed. When researchers at the University of Hamburg evaluated the projects that were nominated for the Global Editors Network's annual Data Journalism Awards, they found that most of the coverage is on political rather than social issues, and that most of the data used was disclosed by official sources rather than collected by reporting teams.

The failure of data journalism to become just journalism

The data journalism community has exploded in the last decade with more and more media houses now including at least one data journalist on their staff. Yet six years after Simon Rogers, founder of *The Guardian DataBlog*,[9] declared "Anyone can do it. Data journalism is the new punk",[10] everyone is *not* doing it. While every reporter now uses a computer and a smartphone in their reporting, the "nerds" have not taken over the newsroom.

Despite the potential of data journalism to harness open data to provide critical context, insight, and actionable information in times of information crisis, some media outlets are turning away because it is difficult, slow, and expensive.[11] Even after massive projects like the Panama Papers[12] prompted political upheaval and an examination of global financial oversight, some publishers remain reluctant to take the risk of investing in their own data team.

The unfulfilled promise of automation

A universal complaint among data journalists is the lack of quality, reliable, timely, and disaggregated open data, which, in turn, inhibits opportunities for its use in local journalism. Stakeholders emphasise that government failures to facilitate access to structured, high-quality open data make it onerous for journalists to keep datasets updated or to build relevant apps to monitor spending, performance, and government services. They also highlight governments' use of loopholes and grey areas in access to information laws being used to hide data, a strategy also employed by businesses. Still, in many countries, the data journalism community has not made use of the limited statistics that are made public, and only a few journalists have requested data through official Freedom of Information Act processes.

There have, however, been some encouraging developments. The Organized Crime and Reporting Project, for instance, provides an Investigative Dashboard[13] that centralises open data resources and helps reporters avoid repetitive scraping and cleaning. Reuters' Lynx Insights[14] guides reporters to relevant data sources by "surfacing trends, facts, and anomalies in data, that reporters can then use to accelerate the production of their existing stories or to spot new ones". If more media houses focus on making open data an essential source, we may see more automation tools in the future.

Making the business case for data journalism

The sustainability of data journalism is all the more urgent as more legacy media outlets struggle for survival in the digital age. Around the world, only a few newsrooms have made an effort to ensure reporters understand how the business model for their newsroom works. Some outlets need to produce in-depth, value-added investigations that are not available elsewhere in order to attract and retain subscribers. Media companies that rely upon advertising need to create compelling interactives, infographics, and visualisations that attract and retain large audiences.

Economic challenges within the industry have also led to competing priorities within newsrooms with editors emphasising urgency of delivery and data journalists seeking more time to produce complex investigations with statistical rigour. In that context, there is also an enduring debate about whether public interest journalism should move to a non-profit model entirely. If more publishers regarded data, and staff with the skill to report on it, as more of an asset and not as a resource drain, data journalism could fulfil an essential role in the transparency and accountability cycle.

While some outlets, such as ProPublica,[15] have established data stores to try to monetise the data that they have obtained and cleaned, this is still a nascent strategy. Other outlets are experimenting with offering personalised news apps with mainstream appeal to subsidise their work on longer-term investigations.

Many of the current challenges faced by stakeholders across the journalism world, including the financial pressures that have resulted from the massive disruption of the business model for traditional publishers and the dominance of tech companies in the online advertising markets, stem from a crucial failure to make data an essential, strategic resource for all the journalism produced by outlets.

Inclusion and accessibility for data-driven democracy

With the rise of nationalist, populist political movements in many countries, an increasing number of members of the global journalism community are exploring how to produce more accessible journalism by, about, for, and *with* marginalised communities.

OpenNews[16] has taken the lead in this work, proposing that "a diverse community of peers working, learning, and solving problems together can create the stronger, more representative ecosystem that journalism needs to thrive". These efforts include creating opportunities for journalists of colour and women within an industry that traditionally has been primarily white and male. It also means having a greater focus on supporting local media in rural areas to produce data-driven content relevant to their communities. ProPublica's Local Reporting Network[17] and the Bureau Local[18] are both relevant efforts to accelerate such content production.

In some developing countries, both legacy print and startup news organisations are experimenting with harnessing data to make injustice, inequality, and discrimination measurable, visible, and solvable. Data teams at La Nación Data[19] in Argentina, IndiaSpend[20] in India, and Nation Newsplex[21] in Kenya are devoting themselves almost exclusively to analysing open data to explain policy issues that affect ordinary citizens. Even much bemoaned technical obstacles like weak content management systems, low internet speeds, mobile display limitations, and low-quality data sources have not stopped these journalists from pushing for better socioeconomic policies and evidence-based decision-making.

Nation Newsplex: Inclusivity and an alternative lens

The Nation Newsplex, the data team of the *Daily Nation*, the highest circulation daily newspaper in Kenya, used data to focus its election coverage on policy not politics during the last presidential elections. Nation Newsplex has a rare combination: a public interest data-driven mandate and an audience with a diverse background. Whether fact-checking economic issues related to small business growth,[22] foreign direct investment,[23] and unemployment;[24] examining public services related to health[25] and food security;[26] or analysing compensation for internally displaced people,[27] the focus of reporting and analysis was on the welfare of citizens, not on the politicians involved or the populist rhetoric that dominated mainstream coverage.

Another common frustration expressed by data journalists in both Western and non-Western newsrooms is the dearth of professional growth opportunities and clear advancement paths. This may play a role in dissuading professionals from more socioeconomically diverse backgrounds from pursuing careers in the media, which, in turn, has negative effects on the industry and leads to errors or blind spots in the journalism itself.

While reporters with data skills continue to be in high demand in many newsrooms, peer-to-peer learning and online courses remain insufficient to meet the growing demand for more advanced data journalism skills. The soaring popularity of the annual NICAR conference in recent years, which features many hands-on workshops, speaks to the demand for skills development. Unfortunately, entry-level data journalists complain of being pigeonholed into roles such as simply creating visualisations for more senior reporters or managing websites instead of producing their own data journalism. Mid-career professionals bemoan the lack of a clear career ladder as many senior-level editors are typically selected from the traditional newsroom.

> ### Data-driven beat reporting
>
> In one of the poorest areas of Pakistan, where self-censorship is rampant, an online publication, *Balochistan Voices*, used data to take on a corrupt, inefficient government.[28] In "Balochistan government builds roads while people sink further into poverty",[29] Adnan Amir explored Balochistan's corrupt procurement process. He showed how siphoning off public funds had left Balochistan's citizens sicker, poorer, and less educated than their neighbours.
>
> In a follow up story, "In Balochistan, five times more people die in highway accidents than suicide blasts",[30] published in late February, he offered the government an easy way to save face and improve access to healthcare. Sure enough, the National Highway Authority signed a Memorandum of Understanding[31] on 18 March to establish five trauma centres along Balochistan's highways.

Reusability and archiving

An underreported challenge to measuring the evolution of data journalism over the last ten years is the lack of consistent archiving. Interactive journalism, created using a plethora of proprietary tools, technologies, and data formats across the industry, has been inconsistently stored and maintained by publishers, unlike the print and microfiche archives of traditional journalism.

Many data-driven interactives now no longer work or have even disappeared entirely. Archiving news apps and visualisations presents a particular challenge, because they depend on tools and systems that may be managed by external entities. Without a consistent conservation strategy, this first draft of history will be lost.[32]

In many newsrooms, data units are simply too short-staffed to address pressing issues like archiving or data reusability. The lack of developers or data scientists in the newsroom to clean and maintain key datasets, preserve projects, and ensure data reusability prevents many media houses from investing in the very systems that would make their journalism faster, more efficient, and more impactful.

Journalists have sought to harness open data to inform the public about institutionalised discrimination, inequality, and oppression in an attempt to uncover issues that were invisible before, and now, may become invisible again if journalists stop counting the causes, the victims, and the wasted funds, or if the projects disappear from the internet entirely. Consistent coverage driven by independent editors combined with effective archiving has the potential to foster systemic change.

> ### Data reusability
>
> In the United States, ProPublica was founded to "expose abuses of power and betrayals of the public trust by government, business, and other institutions, using the moral force of investigative journalism to spur reform through the sustained spotlighting of wrongdoing".[33]
>
> The independent non-profit's digital-first journalism not only uses data as a source in its narrative reporting, but publishes the data with the stories and the code that drives the news applications that make that data more understandable.
>
> ProPublica takes government information disclosed directly to the public online, sometimes as the result of a successful public records lawsuit and court-ordered disclosure under the federal Freedom of Information Act, cleans and structures it, and then publishes the open data, newsapps,[34] code, and stories online.
>
> Notably, ProPublica partners with other news organisations and the public online in collaborative reporting projects that then produce open data, like collecting political ads on social media platforms.
>
> A decade later, the social impact of the release of public records as open government data by federal agencies can be measured by the social impact of ProPublica's data-driven reporting.
>
> ProPublica's Local Reporting Network,[35] launched in early 2018, seeks to address the dearth of local investigative reporting by using its expertise in open data and investigative reporting to strengthen and amplify local reporting. Investigations lowered the barrier for accessing large national and state-level datasets on issues such as conflicts of interest, housing, mental healthcare, criminal justice, and workplace safety.
>
> The new project has a special focus on state government accountability reporting. Recent research by Poynter finds that the great majority of Americans trust their local news sources.[36] Making open data sources relevant to local communities is an emerging strategy for reinvigorating democratic participation at the local level through journalism.

Conclusion

In 2019, the journalism industry around the world is grappling with multiple challenges after quicksilver societal changes in how information is being created, shared, and discovered by humans everywhere.

Public trust in mass media is sinking to historic lows in the United States,[37] fuelled by the spectre of an American president decrying "fake news" and describing the press holding his administration accountable as the "enemy of the people". To close that deficit, editors and producers will need to "optimize for public trust", as New York University professor Jay Rosen has proposed,[38] prioritising verification, openness, listening, engaging, co-production, and diversity.

These principles echo many of the conversations and frustrations faced by data journalists who are navigating and shaping the many ways in which communities are consuming and engaging with the news.

Technology companies like Facebook, Google, and Amazon now dominate the markets for online advertising and information discovery, sharing, and distribution by operating vast digital platforms for billions of users around the world. Media companies face a dramatically different landscape for their work and its publication. News organisations need to find readers, viewers, and subscribers, and get their attention to inform and engage them. National, state, and city governments are publishing open data, usually driven by only a nominal desire to inform the public about public business.

It's a difficult historic moment for journalists and their publishers who face these challenges at a time when the industry itself has been so diminished. Tens of thousands of journalists have lost their jobs, leaving local governments without partners for their online disclosures. At the same time, far too many cities and states have engaged in "transparency theatre", engaging in openwashing with low quality data disclosures. Officials cloak themselves in the rhetoric of "open data" while denying freedom of information requests from the press.

Worse still, less democratic states have shown how open data programmes and policies can exist without open government, where disclosures are focused on driving economic impact or even weaponised against marginalised populations. The levels of press freedom, strength of access to information laws, and the capacity of the government institutions that exist in a given country heavily influence whether journalism based upon open data will lead to positive societal changes.

The transparency and accountability that governments publishing open data cite as a key goal will only occur when journalists do not face hazards from seeking information under the law, publishing reports that reveal corruption, or bearing witness to human rights violations or abuses of power. In that context, the local journalists who report on that data should be viewed as the community's guardians, ensuring that the rights of the governed are upheld by informing the public about the public's business.

Further reading

Ausserhofer, J., Gutounig, R., Oppermann, M., Matiasek, S., & Goldgruber, E. (2017). The datafication of data journalism scholarship: Focal points, methods, and research propositions for the investigation of data-intensive newswork. *Journalism*, 4 April. https://journals.sagepub.com/doi/10.1177/1464884917700667

Baack, S. (2018). Practically engaged: The entanglements between data journalism and civic tech. *Digital Journalism*, 6(6), 673–692. https://www.tandfonline.com/doi/full/10.1080/21670811.2017.1375382

Constantaras, E., Asad, J., Asma Usman, A., & Adil, M. (2018). *The promise and challenge of data journalism: Lessons from Pakistan. Reports and surveys*. Internews. https://www.internews.org/sites/default/files/2018-04/Internews_Pakistan_data_journalism_casestudy_public.pdf

Gray, J., Chambers, L., & Bounegru, L. (Eds.). (2012). *The data journalism handbook*. First edition. Sebastopol, CA: O'Reilly Media.

Howard, A.B. (2014). *The art and science of data-driven journalism*. New York, NY: Tow Center for Digital Journalism Publications.

Loosen, W., Reimer, J., & De Silva-Schmidt, F. (2017). Data-driven reporting: An ongoing (r)evolution? An analysis of projects nominated for the Data Journalism Awards 2013–2016. *Journalism*, 12 October. https://journals.sagepub.com/doi/abs/10.1177/1464884917735691

About the authors

Alex Howard is an independent writer, digital governance analyst, and open government advocate based in Washington, DC. He is the former deputy director of the Sunlight Foundation and the author of The art and science of data-driven journalism from the Tow Center for Digital Journalism at Columbia University and other publications. Follow Alex on Twitter at https://twitter.com/digiphile or on his blog on government information technology at https://e-pluribusunum.org/.

Eva Constantaras is an investigative data journalist specialised in establishing data units in mainstream media in developing countries. Her teams operate in Kenya, Afghanistan, Pakistan, and Central America, covering public interest topics ranging from extractive industries and access to justice to reproductive rights and food security. You can follow Eva on Twitter at https://twitter.com/evaconstantaras.

How to cite this chapter

Howard, A. & Constantaras, E. (2019). Open data stakeholders: Journalists and the media. In T. Davies, S. Walker, M. Rubinstein, & F. Perini (Eds.), *The state of open data: Histories and horizons* (pp. 395–405). Cape Town and Ottawa: African Minds and International Development Research Centre. http://stateofopendata.od4d.net

This work is licensed under a Creative Commons Attribution 4.0 International (CC BY 4.0) licence. It was carried out with the aid of a grant from the International Development Research Centre, Ottawa, Canada.

Endnotes

1. https://www.icij.org/
2. Tate, J., Jenkins, J., Rich, S., & Muyskens, J. (2018). Fatal force: 2018 police shootings database. *Washington Post*. https://www.washingtonpost.com/graphics/2018/national/police-shootings-2018/
3. Cai, W. & Scarr, S. (2017). Life in the camps. *Reuters*, 4 December. http://fingfx.thomsonreuters.com/gfx/rngs/MYANMAR-ROHINGYA/010051VB46G/index.html
4. https://www.ire.org/nicar/
5. https://www.globaleditorsnetwork.org/
6. https://europeanjournalists.org/blog/2018/02/20/eijc18-dataharvest-in-may-2018/
7. https://gijn.org/global-conference-2/
8. Rogers, S., Schwabish, J., & Bowers, D. (2017). *Data journalism in 2017: The current state and challenges facing the field today*. San Francisco, CA: Google News Lab. https://newslab.withgoogle.com/assets/docs/data-journalism-in-2017.pdf
9. https://www.theguardian.com/data
10. Rogers, S. (2012). Anyone can do it. Data journalism is the new punk. *The Guardian*, 24 May. https://www.theguardian.com/news/datablog/2012/may/24/data-journalism-punk
11. Rogers, S., Schwabish, J., & Bowers, D. (2017). *Data journalism in 2017: The current state and challenges facing the field today*. San Francisco, CA: Google News Lab. https://newslab.withgoogle.com/assets/docs/data-journalism-in-2017.pdf
12. ICIJ (International Consortium of Investigative Journalists). (2018). The Panama Papers: Exposing the rogue offshore finance industry. https://www.icij.org/investigations/panama-papers/
13. https://investigativedashboard.org/
14. Bilton, R. (2018). Reuters' new automation tool wants to help reporters spot the hidden stories in their data (but won't take their jobs). *NiemanLab*, 12 March. http://www.niemanlab.org/2018/03/reuters-new-automation-tool-wants-to-help-reporters-spot-the-hidden-stories-in-their-data-but-wont-take-their-jobs/
15. https://www.propublica.org/
16. https://opennews.org/
17. ProPublica. (2017). ProPublica local reporting network selects seven newsrooms across US. https://www.propublica.org/atpropublica/propublica-local-reporting-network-selects-seven-newsrooms-across-u-s
18. https://www.thebureauinvestigates.com/local
19. https://www.lanacion.com.ar/data
20. https://www.indiaspend.com/
21. https://www.nation.co.ke/newsplex
22. https://www.nation.co.ke/newsplex/state-of-nation-2016-fact-check/2718262-3852980-j0gsfw/index.html
23. https://www.nation.co.ke/newsplex/foreign-investment/2718262-3990224-ehbaunz/index.html
24. https://www.nation.co.ke/newsplex/mudavadi-high-unemployment/2718262-3995274-pbpw17/index.html
25. https://www.nation.co.ke/newsplex/Thika-Kiambu-hospitals-Uhuru-Kenyatta/2718262-3986010-ocrxmg/index.html
26. https://www.nation.co.ke/newsplex/weather-maize/2718262-3995278-pu22a7/index.html
27. https://www.nation.co.ke/newsplex/idp-compensation-funds/2718262-3975950-nc8j92/index.html
28. Aamir, A. (2017). Balochistan schools: Failing grade despite funding spike. *Balochistan Voices*, 26 May. http://balochistanvoices.com/2017/05/balochistan-schools-failing-grade-despite-funding-spike/

29 Aamir, A. (2017). Balochistan government builds roads while people sink further into poverty. *Balochistan Voices*, 26 December. http://balochistanvoices.com/2017/12/balochistan-government-builds-roads-people-sink-poverty/
30 Aamir, A. (2018). In Balochistan, five times more people die in highway accidents than suicide blasts. *Balochistan Voices*, 26 February. http://balochistanvoices.com/2018/02/balochistan-five-times-people-die-highway-accidents-suicide-blasts/
31 https://www.documentcloud.org/documents/4436283-NHA-MOU.html
32 Boss, K. & Broussard, M. (2017). Challenges of archiving and preserving born-digital news applications. *IFLA Journal, 43(2)*, 150–157. https://doi.org/10.1177%2F0340035216686355
33 ProPublica. (n.d.). About us. https://www.propublica.org/about/
34 https://www.propublica.org/newsapps/
35 https://www.propublica.org/local-reporting-network/
36 Guess, A., Nyhan, B., & Reifler, J. (2018). *All media trust is local? Findings from the 2018 Poynter Media Trust Survey*. St. Petersburg, FL: Poynter Institute. http://www-personal.umich.edu/~bnyhan/media-trust-report-2018.pdf
37 Swift, A. (2016). Americans' trust in mass media sinks to new low. *Gallup*, 14 September. https://news.gallup.com/poll/195542/americans-trust-mass-media-sinks-new-low.aspx
38 Rosen, J. (2018). Optimizing journalism for trust. *Medium: The Correspondent* [Blog post], 14 April. https://medium.com/de-correspondent/optimizing-journalism-for-trust-1c67e81c123

028

Multilateral organisations

Craig Hammer

Key points

- Multilateral organisations, such as the development banks, play a key role in promoting development outcomes in low- and middle-income countries. They do this through providing finance and connecting a wide range of public, non-government, and private stakeholders, as well as providing technical assistance and knowledge transfer.

- Since 2010, a number of multilaterals have deployed their considerable capacity to support open data initiatives.

- There is increasing understanding of how context affects open data interventions, initiating a move away from "copy and paste" to more context-sensitive and tailored intervention designs.

- Multilaterals also invest in many other aspects of the data ecosystem and could achieve substantial impact by mainstreaming open data work across their operations. This could maximise the return on their investments in projects that have a data component.

Introduction

Refugee crises, climate change, biodiversity losses, the threat of pandemics, significant gaps in sustainable infrastructure, and persistent fragility or armed conflict – the list of global challenges to social and economic development seems to get longer each day. Each successive challenge underscores the need for robust, flexible, and effective multilateral development banks and organisations (hereinafter referred to as multilaterals) to bring international partnership, financing, and expertise to bear on the world's most layered and complex challenges.

Multilaterals have played an important part in human development for generations. The Bretton Woods institutions, created in 1944, sought to rebuild both Europe and the global economic order after the horrors of World War II. Over the following decades, the multilateral system developed a sharpened focus on poverty reduction and post-colonial reforms to drive social and economic improvements, including through the formation of regional development banks. During the 1950s, nascent recognition of the role of private enterprise as an enabler of development by multilaterals subsequently placed greater emphasis on investment in high-risk sectors and on countries to create jobs and raise living standards. The 1960s saw the advent of interest-free loans, advice, and grants intended to boost growth, reduce inequalities, and improve conditions in the world's poorest countries. Following a stock market crash and global oil crisis in the early 1970s, multilaterals developed a broader recognition of their role in enabling better investment in the private sector across regions, and, by the 1980s, there was a focus on more and better insurance and guarantees to protect and spur foreign direct investments in developing countries. Toward the end of the last century, multilateral support for development began to broaden beyond work with just governments to direct work with, and support for, civil society, Indigenous communities, and non-governmental organisations. This work specifically looked to improve the quality and sustainability of social and economic development initiatives, to shine a light on corruption, and to give voice to demands for government transparency and accountability.[1] Throughout this period, the number of multilaterals has grown,[2] and over the last two decades, enabled by exponential changes in technology, they have evolved to include an increased focus on knowledge,[3,4] data, and, to some extent, open data.

There are a range of views concerning the comparative advantage of today's multilaterals versus bilateral organisations (e.g. national aid agencies, foundations, and other donors). This chapter will not explore these perspectives in detail; however, for the purpose of this chapter, these comparative advantages include:

- A focus on strengthening social and/or economic development outcomes in middle-income countries (MICs), low-income countries (LICs), and/or fragile and conflict-affected states.

- The twin abilities to convene and work with a spectrum of stakeholders, including actors from across the public and private sectors at the national, regional, and global levels, and combinations thereof.

- In-depth technical knowledge across key sectors and in country contexts.

- The ability to mobilise and bring (or leverage) significant financing and technical support to bear.

With these criteria in mind, this chapter will briefly set out insights gleaned from interaction with several multilaterals that provide programmatic support for open data. This chapter is not meant to be exhaustive, but rather a snapshot of issues currently relevant for multilateral stakeholders in the open data landscape. The analysis that follows aims to discern relevant issues, reflecting on key lessons learned from effective and ineffective open data interventions, and to look forward to surface priorities and recommendations regarding the near-, medium-, and long-term opportunities and challenges for open data. While drawn from the experience of multilateral institutions, the hope is that this may be collectively useful for a wide range of stakeholders either currently engaged with open data or developing plans for the future.

The evolution of multilateral support for open data

Within the last decade, a number of multilaterals have become increasingly seized of the role and importance of open data for development. Several multilaterals have been in the vanguard of this great global disruption by opening their vast data holdings for free with the launch of their own open data initiatives. The World Bank was an early adopter in 2010,[5] and open data portals have since been launched by the African Development Bank (2013),[6] the Inter-American Development Bank (2015),[7] and the Asian Development Bank (2018),[8] among others. These open data platforms have provided access not just to edited summary statistics but to detailed datasets. In itself, this has marked a significant departure from the way multilaterals previously operated, and concepts such as "open by default" and "as open as possible" have since gathered much momentum throughout the international development community. This has resulted in a dramatic increase in users accessing and using data up and down the development value chain, including the increased use of data by staff within their own institutions.

Following their own experiments with open data, several multilaterals began to assist LICs and MICs with opening government data. The earliest case, World Bank support for Kenya's open data initiative in 2010,[9,10] was swiftly followed by a range of work in countries across regions and at the subnational level, as well as the creation of the Open Data Readiness Assessment (ODRA) and its implementation in more than 45 countries as of 2017.[11] The Inter-American Development Bank, through the Open Government programme, has supported wide-reaching regional dialogue and knowledge sharing on open data, and has funded a number of thematic technical assistance projects, including work in 2015 on geospatial data[12] and open data for transparency applications.[13] The African Development Bank has supported countries in adopting open data practices by providing a shared data portal infrastructure and by bringing countries onto the "African Information Highway", building on pre-existing statistical capacity development programmes.[14]

While not all multilateral development banks have embraced open data as a high-profile theme in their work, many have engaged as contributors to the International Aid Transparency Initiative (IATI), and a number have adopted specific thematic open data interventions, such as the European Bank for Reconstruction and Development's support for Open Contracting (see Chapter 5: Development assistance and humanitarian action).[15] Other multilateral organisations have also been active in building networks around open data. For example, the Organisation for Economic Co-operation and Development (OECD) has provided backing for open data through regular studies, country reviews,[16] and expert meetings, and the United Nations Development Programme is a lead partner in the Open Data for Development Node in Europe and Central Asia (ODECA).[17]

Across these multilateral interventions, a range of approaches has been deployed, including technical assistance, capacity development, funding, the creation of knowledge products and tools, and the inauguration of international and global partnerships, communities of practice, and fora. Some of these interventions have helped to generate collaborations which have catalysed continuing initiatives, such as the International Open Data Conference (IODC). Others have been short-term interventions, such as online communities of expert consultants, set up to take advantage of the global convening power of multilaterals to rapidly identify potential partners for governments working on open data. Several examples of approaches are evident in the World Bank's review of its own open data activities between 2012 and 2017.[18]

This forward momentum did not occur in a vacuum. Awareness of the role and value of open data for social and economic development blossomed relatively quickly through a range of important events and engagements around the start of the last decade. Through a number of reports, conferences, and meetings, multilaterals both were influenced by, and influenced, national, regional, and global open data activities, helping to develop a model for open data initiatives and establishing open data as a concept that more than just a few higher-income countries could explore.

It is also relevant to note the financial and practical support that multilaterals have given to the Open Government Partnership (OGP), which has become a key forum for furthering the open data agenda.[19] Governments, such as the United Kingdom (UK) and United States (US), for whom open data has been a domestic priority, have also used their positions as chairs of multilateral fora, such as the G8, to push forward open data activities, including the G8 Open Data Charter[20] and the launch of the Global Open Data for Agriculture and Nutrition (GODAN) initiative.[21]

As with other activities undertaken by multilaterals in the past, an initial focus on supporting governments in engaging with open data was soon followed by efforts to provide support to non-government actors from corporations and mobile network operators to civil society organisations, media organisations, and more. This support has focused both on the use of open data and on assisting organisations in opening their own data in support of social and economic development objectives.

Ultimately, in just a few short years, many thousands of datasets have been opened as free digital public goods available to all interested users. A multiplicity of open data-driven tools, services, publications, diagnostics, and analyses have been developed from this data, and open data policies and initiatives have been launched and have flowered in regions across the world. Taken together, this progress has undoubtedly enabled more equitable access to information and digital data by users around the globe and has supported more accountable and efficient public administrations, contributing to social development and economic growth.

Lessons learned: Supporting open data ecosystems

As described above, multilaterals have a unique perspective from which to reflect on lessons learned from the global open data landscape, in particular, how furthering the advance of open data can support social and economic development in the 21st century. This is particularly true with respect to a hard-won understanding of different operational successes and failures and how the fundamental building blocks of an effective open data ecosystem vary from one context to another. The experience of multilaterals has also resulted in the development of insights on how to support the broader development community to engage with open data through international cooperation, access to expertise and funding, and the provision of a range of public goods. These public goods, ranging from knowledge projects and data standards to software tools and shared algorithms, are resources that multilaterals are particularly well placed to provide. The following section provides an indicative synopsis of key learning points and opportunities for the future.

Open data maturity through alignment with other priority agendas

From the perspective of many multilaterals, open data as an issue has clearly reached policy maturity in part due to efforts by several multilaterals to integrate open data with other important agendas, such as the Sustainable Development Goals (SDGs) and national development plans. In addition to high-level discussions about the role and value of open data, multilaterals are likewise increasingly encouraging discussions about, and support for, open data at the local level and in sector-specific contexts, including work on standards and best practices in contracting,[22] statistics,[23] transport,[24,25] urban resilience,[26] and a number of other areas. This "mainstreaming" of open data as a methodology in support of other agendas demonstrates an effort to move the agenda from dialogue to implementation. This is largely due to the recognition that while open data can be understood as a global public good, supporting the enabling environment for open data at different levels requires work focused on specific challenges, sources, and constituencies in the service of key social and/or economic development outcomes. Otherwise, securing engagement, and ultimately impact, is very difficult to achieve.

Multilaterals can provide the medium- and long-term support needed for social and economic development impacts from open data

While open data is showing signs of maturity in developed countries, success stories are still sparse in developing countries and the early sprouts of potential are very slow to grow. Advocates for, and practitioners of, open data initiatives in developing contexts need sustained financial, material, and human capital in order to bring together all the elements needed for open data impact.[27] Multilaterals are uniquely placed to provide such medium-to-long-term support by virtue of their clear mandates and deep engagement in developing contexts, including through their physical presence with on-the-ground experts who have established professional relationships among government and non-government actors. When used effectively, the funding modalities, presence, and physical infrastructure of multilaterals can enable authentically collaborative work, adding to momentum where it exists and ensuring context-sensitivity and tailored approaches that engender mutual trust to prioritise specific development outcomes. This does not necessarily include transplanting models that work in the developed world.

Sustaining political will requires a strategic approach

For long-term impact from open data, evangelism and short-term engagements are not enough. Institutionalising open data as a mechanism within larger sectoral initiatives requires ample political will up and down the value chain. Advocates and practitioners of open data need to discern what this means in practical terms and work to coordinate action. Multilaterals are often well-placed to support this, including leading or contributing to rigorous contextual analysis (drawing on in-country experts and practitioners) and mapping where key decision-makers and stakeholders fall on a spectrum of support/opposition. Building on this, multilaterals can help in identifying strategic entry points to achieve traction or can add to existing momentum over time. They are likewise well placed to deliver ODRAs and to further unpack the national and subnational enabling environment for open data.

Furthermore, it is clear that timing with respect to election cycles is important, as are connections between open data and related policy implementation and reform initiatives, such as Access to Information bills, management information system (MIS) implementations, procurement reforms, and OGP action plans. When multilaterals are able to draw on their cross-cutting work to ensure that the details and timing of open data interventions are strategically aligned, the foundations for impact can be strengthened. This requires the discipline to manage expectations and to balance a focus on relatively "low-hanging fruit", and otherwise attractive or high-visibility approaches, with complementary medium-to-long-term approaches that might deliver more sustainable value.

Working with National Statistical Offices (NSOs) is key to improving data quality in developing countries

NSOs are an important stakeholder group, particularly for developing countries, where they are often the primary (if not the only) source of high-quality, official statistics, which could be published as open data under the right circumstances, especially if enabled by an authorising environment characterised by amenable leadership and receptivity to new ideas. NSOs are uniquely situated to encourage and support innovation when opportunities arise to reform or update statistical legislation. Several multilaterals have strong, long-standing partnerships with NSOs across developing and developed countries, as well as existing system-wide approaches to support the strengthening of NSO technical capacity and infrastructure through financing, grant programmes, and technical assistance. Multilaterals also play a key role in the development and dissemination of statistical methods and standards. These are all effective points from which to help encourage prioritisation and implementation of open data initiatives in developing countries and at the subnational level.

Multilaterals also need to recognise the importance of experimentation and adaptation to support NSOs to modernise in order to play their part in a fast-changing data ecosystem. At a minimum, multilaterals should encourage NSOs to recognise that they are joining a plurality of data producers. This involves collaborating with NSOs to explore new or additional roles and responsibilities, such as quality control and validation of open data, as well as becoming "infomediaries" themselves.[28] Ultimately, as NSOs assume a stronger coordination role across an expanding constellation of data producers, multilaterals can share relevant experiences on new collaborations and methods of partnership. This does not mean, however, that multilaterals have all the answers, nor should they impose top-down solutions. Adopting strategies where multilaterals fund successes without prescribing specific tasks is the way ahead and involves living with the risk that some investments may fail.

Increased focus is needed on data use

Multilaterals have not been particularly effective in promoting the sustained use of open data by governments and citizens. Open government data use by citizens in developing economies (for good governance or improved accountability) is still low. Recent analyses indicate that the majority of people around the world either will not or cannot use opened government data.[29,30]

For multilaterals to help realise the potential of open data for decision-making at various levels and across country contexts, the challenges of promoting data use need to be overcome. This necessitates a concerted effort among multilaterals and partners to make open data and civic technologies work for everyone (not just elites) through the creation of tools for a broader audience (including the most vulnerable groups) and the development of more meaningful and coordinated efforts to tackle the root causes of human, financial, and technical challenges to sustained open data use. It includes addressing ubiquitous capacity gaps in data literacy, inadequate salaries for data scientists and practitioners, insufficient resources to launch and maintain permanent open data platforms, constraints on opening data in local languages, difficulty maintaining standards and quality of data, and challenges in identifying actionable data to be opened. Other chapters in this volume explore these challenges in more depth. However, with their broad portfolios, multilaterals have the opportunity to address these issues systemically, from technical infrastructure and connectivity through to scaling up inclusive data literacy investments and working to make sure open data projects listen to the needs and priorities of non-elite, non-users, including the poor, marginalised, and chronically underserved. To date, no multilateral has set out a comprehensive vision for how work across all their programmes can contribute to the foundations for, culture of, and impacts from, open data. This should be a priority.

Careful engagement with private sector investment can bring value, but risks of proprietary data should be addressed

Several multilaterals have either increased or entirely focused their efforts on support for private sector markets to help address development challenges. The general rationale for doing so is to augment multilateral-led development by drawing in both private sector solutions and financing, which typically helps to complement scarce public financing, to help ensure developing countries can avoid high levels of debt and contingent liabilities. In the context of support for open data, multilaterals should focus investment on the broader open data ecosystem, which may necessarily implicate private sector solutions or resources for infrastructure. However, deliberation and attention must be paid to the inherent risks, particularly where data, systems, and civic applications may become proprietary, rather than open. For example, as explored in Chapter 12: Land ownership, it may be appealing to accept private financial support to improve land registers, but if this comes at the cost of proprietary ownership of the cadastre and the systems for maintaining it, the short-term gain may come with a long-term cost. We do not know, at present, how common this kind of private investment-for-data-ownership engagement is across developing countries or in multilateral portfolios. Likewise, the extent of public–private partnerships focused on data-sharing agreements among multilaterals is also unclear. However, it is not difficult to imagine that such engagements will occur.

In any case, multilaterals must be deliberate and vigilant. Each individual engagement necessitates careful analysis and understanding of any and all personal data privacy protection issues, thorough and thoughtful deliberation about any potential ethical issues arising from entering into data-sharing licensing arrangements with private sector actors, and the assurance that multilaterals carefully safeguard their integrity and role as honest brokers in all circumstances.

Looking ahead: The fourth industrial revolution

The world is at the threshold of what has been called the Fourth Industrial Revolution.[31,32] Countries around the world are seeing exponential advances in artificial intelligence, disruptive technologies, and digital economies, which are occurring alongside mega-trends like climate change, globalisation, urbanisation, and the rise of social media. This combination of forces is rapidly transforming societies across the globe. In addition to the potential benefits of technological progress, there are also the spectres of structural job loss, income inequality, atomising of social consciousness, and loss of privacy – all factors with profound consequences for social and economic development across polities. Accompanying these trends is an increasing recognition of the need for new paradigmatic thinking about the relationships among governments, civil society, the private sector, and citizens, and the role of data, including open data, which underpins these relationships.

Moving forward, multilaterals could comprehensively integrate open data into what they do and how they operate in five key ways:

1. **Leading by example.** All multilaterals should make their own development and operational data "open by default", subject to key legal and privacy considerations. This includes incorporating open data requirements into operational procurement processes, such that where products or services involving the creation, acquisition, management, or publication of data are funded by the multilateral, the default provision should be for any resulting data to be made available as open data and deposited in an open data catalogue or in-country equivalent. This will help to maximise the impact of open data, since multilaterals would be taking a consistent approach to applying open data principles to all relevant aspects of their institutional work. This would also vest multilaterals with even more institutional credibility to build, share, and support digital public goods, such as tools and infrastructure, that encourage the creation, management, and use of high-quality open data, international standards, and principles for open data.

   As part of their leadership role, multilaterals should also endorse the International Open Data Charter and adopt positions consistent with it within other partnerships, activities, and business lines. Moreover, those multilaterals which are not yet signatories of IATI should sign up to ensure a comprehensive multilateral commitment to improving the quality, coverage, and timeliness of the data they publish in a consistent (IATI) format. They should likewise advocate for, participate in the development of, and adopt data standards which further the IATI vision for open data.

2. **Mainstreaming open data across development support.** Multilaterals should mainstream open data activities into their broader sectoral development operations. This would not only maximise the return on investments in data in general, it could enable more and better data discovery, access, and use, as well as provide a foundation for improvements across sectors, governance, and in citizen engagement. Building on a renewed recognition of the value of open source code and open knowledge, multilaterals should explore an "open by design" approach to programme development, considering

how various aspects of openness can be built-in, rather than bolted-on to their interventions. This involves a step change from early modalities for open data support, where open data components were often included as a supplementary component of programmes that had already been largely designed, to an approach where open data principles are incorporated much earlier in the scoping of projects.

While adopting open data approaches should not necessarily be an immediate requirement for all work with multilaterals, and there will be cases where open approaches are not yet proven, multilaterals should always explore such approaches where appropriate and advise clients on their potential benefits. Key lessons should be parsed from across these efforts to support iterative learning and to scale successes.

3. **Privacy.** Conversations about open data led by multilaterals would benefit from a far stronger focus on privacy and data security issues. It has been pointed out that datasets with microdata across sectors (such as healthcare, education, transportation, criminal justice, property registration/housing, and voter registration, among other areas) may include individual records that may threaten individual privacy if released openly. Multilaterals should either facilitate or be part of the larger conversation to help governments find a public interest balance between privacy risks and maximising accessibility and use of open data.[33]

4. **Fragile, conflict, and violence-afflicted states.** The majority of the world's poor live in fragile, conflict, and violence-affected states. Multilaterals have a particular role to play in these countries, where statistics and the generation of official data remain particularly neglected and under-invested areas. Due to a combination of factors, official statistics are often reported erratically, subject to quality issues, or not disseminated in a timely manner or a user-friendly format, limiting their role in decision-making. Truly open data in these contexts is rare, and efforts to provide systematic support for open data and to otherwise make that data which exists accessible for public analysis are often further complicated by the lack of political will and an enabling policy environment. Yet, accessible data may be key to coordinating action to address development challenges, and multilaterals must be careful to avoid contributing to a growing data-divide leaving these countries further disadvantaged. In particular, non-national holdings of government data (including those of multilaterals) may indeed be more robust than government holdings. When open, they can provide a useful stop-gap for analysis, capacity development, and development of knowledge products, although international provision of national data is not a sustainable long-term solution. As a result, multilaterals should explore how to shift resources to fragile, conflict, and violence-affected states, including resources for open data, comprehensive end-to-end data support, and data infrastructure which meets the particular needs of these states and, in particular, the poor and marginalised. This is especially critical in pursuit of global priorities, such as the SDGs and a range of poverty-alleviation priorities.

5. **Investing in open approaches to monitoring, knowledge sharing, and research.** Lastly, in order to help overcome the data use challenges outlined above, multilaterals should adopt a more coordinated, systematic approach to monitoring the use and impact of open data across their interventions, including the specific measurement of impact within sectors and for different types of open data. Effective impact measurement in the future cannot rely only on case studies and anecdotes. It will require well-resourced and rigorous research programmes that generate robust political economy analyses and data on returns on investment in open data interventions. Early open data advocacy made use of economic modelling to make the case for open approaches, and there is a need to bring back a stronger economics research focus on open data. Both the funding and convening power of multilaterals may be usefully deployed here.

If deployed effectively, multilateral contributions to the research base on what works in open data, and how open data works within specific sectors, have the potential to substantially advance the field over the next ten years, taking us far beyond the progress made already to date.

Conclusion

Every year multilaterals invest millions of dollars, considerable staff time, and political capital in supporting data-related projects, technical assistance, research, and knowledge sharing. It is only now, however, that they are starting to systematically track these data investments, laying the foundation for future research to understand how far they contribute to the open data landscape. While over the last decade, support for open data has become a small but established part of multilateral portfolios, the challenge for the decade ahead is to integrate open data approaches at the heart of wider data interventions to put "open by default" and "open by design" ideas into practice. This will require particular sensitivity to issues of privacy and security, as well as ongoing and in-depth research and learning to support constant improvement. However, as this chapter has explored, multilaterals bring a set of unique assets to this challenge and will undoubtedly continue to have a crucial role to play in taking open data into its next phase.

Further reading

Engen, L. & Prizzon, A. (2018). *A guide to multilateral development banks*. London: Overseas Development Institute. https://www.odi.org/sites/odi.org.uk/files/resource-documents/12274.pdf

World Bank Group. (2017). *World Bank support for open data 2012–2017*. Washington, DC: World Bank. http://hdl.handle.net/10986/28616

About the author

Craig Hammer is a Program Manager at the World Bank, and Secretary of the World Bank's Development Data Council. He specialises in evidence-based governance reforms, with a particular emphasis on open government and open data initiatives. His work at the World Bank has included strengthening institutions, laws, policies, and technical capacity, with a focus on data-driven decision-making in more than 30 countries in Africa, the Middle East, Latin America, South Asia, and Central Europe. He has published books and articles on topics including governance, data-driven policy reforms, and social development.

How to cite this chapter

Hammer, C. (2019). Open data stakeholders: Multilateral organisations. In T. Davies, S. Walker, M. Rubinstein, & F. Perini (Eds.), *The state of open data: Histories and horizons* (pp. 406–417). Cape Town and Ottawa: African Minds and International Development Research Centre. http://stateofopendata.od4d.net

This work is licensed under a Creative Commons Attribution 4.0 International (CC BY 4.0) licence. It was carried out with the aid of a grant from the International Development Research Centre, Ottawa, Canada.

Endnotes

1. Lindbaek, J., Pfeffermann, G., & Gregory, N. (1998). The evolving role of multilateral development banks: History and prospects. *EIB Papers*, 3(2), 60–81. http://hdl.handle.net/10419/44756
2. Engen, L. & Prizzon, A. (2018). *A guide to multilateral development banks*. London: Overseas Development Institute. https://www.odi.org/sites/odi.org.uk/files/resource-documents/12274.pdf
3. World Bank. (1998). *World development report: Knowledge for development*. New York: Oxford University Press. https://openknowledge.worldbank.org/handle/10986/5981
4. King, K. & McGrath, S.A. (2004). The World Bank or the Knowledge Bank?. In K. King & S.A. McGrath (Eds.), *Knowledge for Development?: Comparing British, Japanese, Swedish and World Bank aid* (pp. 55–98). London: Zed Books.
5. Howard, A. (2010). Widgets, maps and an API make World Bank data sing. *O'Reilly Radar*, 10 September. http://radar.oreilly.com/2010/09/widgets-maps-and-visualization.html
6. Wahlén, C.B. (2013). AfDB launches additional data platforms to support Africa Information Highway. *SDG Knowledge Hub*, 23 May. http://sdg.iisd.org/news/afdb-launches-additional-data-platforms-to-support-africa-information-highway
7. IDB. (2015). The Inter-American Development Bank launches its open data portal: Numbers for Development. *IDB Improving Lives*, 28 April. https://www.iadb.org/en/news/news-releases/2015-04-28/new-open-data-portal-numbers-for-development%2C11148.html
8. Asian Development Bank. (2018). ADB Data Library. https://www.youtube.com/watch?v=NxeoaUmWZZA
9. Rahemtulla, H., Kaplan, J., Gigler, B.-S., Cluster, S., Kiess, J., & Brigham, C. (2012). *Open Data Kenya: Case study of the underlying drivers, principal objectives and evolution of one of the first open data initiatives in Africa*. Open Development Technology Alliance (ODTA). https://www.scribd.com/document/75642393/Open-Data-Kenya-Long-Version
10. Majeed, R. (2012). *Disseminating the power of information: Kenya Open Data Initiative, 2011–2012*. Innovations for Successful Societies. Princeton University. https://successfulsocieties.princeton.edu/publications/disseminating-power-information-kenya-open-data-initiative-2011-2012

11. World Bank Group. (2017). *World Bank support for open data 2012–2017*. Washington, DC: World Bank. http://hdl.handle.net/10986/28616
12. https://www.iadb.org/en/project/RG-T2664
13. https://www.iadb.org/en/project/RG-T2709
14. https://www.afdb.org/en/knowledge/statistics/africa-information-highway-aih/
15. Emerging Europe. (2018). Municipal governments begin to see benefits of open government tools. *Emerging Europe*, 27 October. https://emerging-europe.com/news/municipal-governments-begin-to-see-benefits-of-open-government-tools/
16. http://www.oecd.org/gov/digital-government/open-government-data.htm
17. http://www.odecanet.org/about/
18. World Bank Group. (2017). *World Bank support for open data 2012–2017*. Washington, DC: World Bank. http://hdl.handle.net/10986/28616
19. https://www.opengovpartnership.org/multilateral-organizations
20. Shadbolt, N. (2013). G8 Open Data Charter: Why it matters. *The Telegraph*, June 18. https://www.telegraph.co.uk/news/worldnews/g8/10128266/G8-Open-Data-Charter-why-it-matters.html
21. GODAN (Global Open Data for Agriculture and Nutrition). (2018). Statement of purpose. https://www.godan.info/pages/statement-purpose
22. http://www.open-contracting.org/
23. http://www.data4sdgs.org/partner-listing?f%5B0%5D=type_of_organization_taxonomy_term_name%3AMultilateral%20Organization
24. World Bank. (2016). The World Bank launches new Open Transport Partnership to improve transportation through open data. *World Bank* [Press release], 19 December. http://www.worldbank.org/en/news/press-release/2016/12/19/the-world-bank-launches-new-open-transport-partnership-to-improve-transportation-through-open-data
25. http://opentraffic.io/
26. https://opendri.org/
27. Davies, T. & Perini, F. (2016). Researching the emerging impacts of open data: Revisiting the ODDC conceptual framework. *The Journal of Community Informatics*, *12(2)*, 148–178. http://ci-journal.org/index.php/ciej/article/view/1281
28. Giovannini, E. (2015). How data revolution and new policy demands create new requirements for capacity building and training official statisticians? In *Conference Proceedings of the High Level Forum on Partnership for Capacity in the context of the Data Revolution*. New York, NY: United Nations. https://unstats.un.org/unsd/statcom/statcom_2015/seminars/high_level_forum/default.html
29. Pew Research Center. (2015). Americans' views on open government data. *Pew Research Center*, 21 April. http://www.pewinternet.org/2015/04/21/open-government-data/
30. Web Foundation. (2015). *Open data agenda-setting for Africa 2015: Workshop report*. Washington, DC: World Wide Web Foundation. http://webfoundation.org/docs/2015/05/ODAfrica2015_WorkshopReport.pdf
31. World Economic Forum. (2015). *The fourth industrial revolution*, by Klaus Schwab. https://www.weforum.org/about/the-fourth-industrial-revolution-by-klaus-schwab/
32. Schwab, K. (2016). *The fourth industrial revolution*. New York: Crown Business.
33. World Bank. (2019). Data privacy & open data: Getting to coexistence? *World Bank Live*, 13 February. Washington, DC: World Bank. https://live.worldbank.org/data-privacy-open-data-getting-to-coexistence

029

Private sector

Joel Gurin, Carla Bonina, and Stefaan Verhulst

Key points

- Private sector actors play three key roles in open data: as data users, as data intermediaries, and as data providers through data collaboratives.
- Incubators and accelerators have supported hundreds of companies around the world in applying and using open data.
- Large and small businesses use open data for business operations and to create new products and services.
- Open data remains largely an untapped resource with much more work needed to support small and medium-sized enterprises (SMEs) to realise the benefits it can bring to drive business innovation.

Introduction

The open data movement launched a decade ago with a focus on transparency, good governance, and citizen participation. As other chapters in this collection have documented in detail, those critical uses of open data have remained paramount and are continuing to grow in importance at a time of fake news and increased secrecy. But the value of open data extends beyond transparency and accountability – open data is also an important resource for business and economic growth.

The past several years have seen an increased focus on the value of open data to the private sector. In 2012, the Open Data Institute (ODI) was founded in the United Kingdom (UK) and backed with GBP 10 million by the UK government to maximise the value of open data in business and government. A year later, McKinsey released a report[1] suggesting open data could help unlock USD 3 to 5 trillion in economic value annually. At around the same time, Monsanto acquired the Climate Corporation, a digital agriculture company that leverages open data to inform farmers for approximately USD 1.1 billion. In 2014, the GovLab launched the Open Data 500,[2] the first national study of businesses using open government data (now in six countries), and, in 2015, Open Data for Development (OD4D) launched the Open Data Impact Map,[3] which today contains more than 1 100 examples of private sector companies using open data. The potential business applications of open data continue to be a priority for many governments around the world as they plan and develop their data programmes.

The use of open data has become part of the broader business practice of using data and data science to inform business decisions, ranging from launching new products and services to optimising processes and outsmarting the competition. In this chapter, we take stock of the state of open data and the private sector by analysing how the private sector both leverages and contributes to the open data ecosystem. Readers should note that this chapter does not cover the release of open data *about* private sector companies and their operations. This is addressed in Chapter 3: Corporate ownership.

How does the private sector engage with open data?

Private sector organisations, ranging from small businesses to large corporations, participate in the open data ecosystem in three key ways: as data users, as data intermediaries, and as data providers.

The private sector as open data users

Companies use open government data to improve their operations and/or develop new products and services

There are now thousands of examples of companies having used open government data as a key business asset that have been documented by the Open Data 500,[4] the Open Data Impact Map,[5] the ExploraLatam,[6] and other studies. These projects have illustrated that companies use open government data for business optimisation, for developing new products and services, or for a combination of the two.

Businesses use open government data for business optimisation in a wide variety of ways, ranging from activities that have been established for decades to others that are more recent innovations. Large retail corporations, such as Starbucks and the Kellogg's Company, for example, are using sophisticated analytics to find correlations between open data on weather, demographics, and other factors and their own data on customer behaviour and buying patterns.[7] On a broader scale, companies of all sizes in all countries can use government data to improve their business in a number of ways:

- Marketing – using demographic data to identify new customers and reach them with more relevant and targeted messaging.
- Supply chain management – using transportation and GPS data to develop more efficient supply chain operations, including shipping.

Insights from the Open Data Impact Map

The Open Data Impact Map,[8] a project of the OD4D network, is a searchable, sortable database of organisations using open government data around the world. About two-thirds of those organisations, more than 1 050 of them, are for-profit companies. The two charts below indicate that these businesses include companies of all sizes, operating across many different sectors. Businesses with one to 200 employees, considered small to medium-sized enterprises (SMEs), make up 72% of this group.

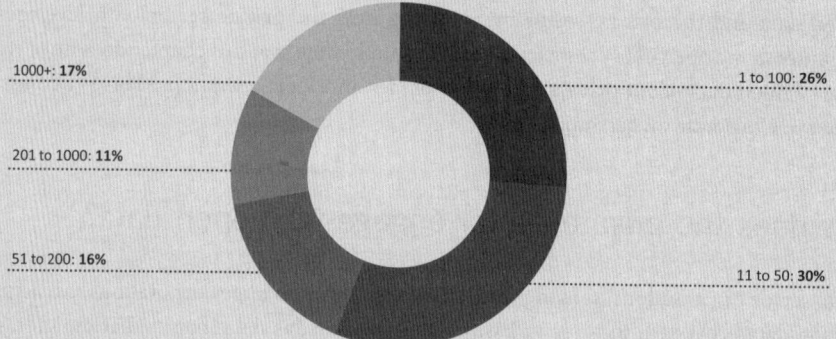

Figure 1: Size of companies using open data by number of employees
Source: Calculated from Open Data Impact Map data

Among the 13 sectors analysed, a third of the for-profit companies on the Impact Map fall into the IT and geospatial sector, while one in six are in the business, research, and consulting sector.

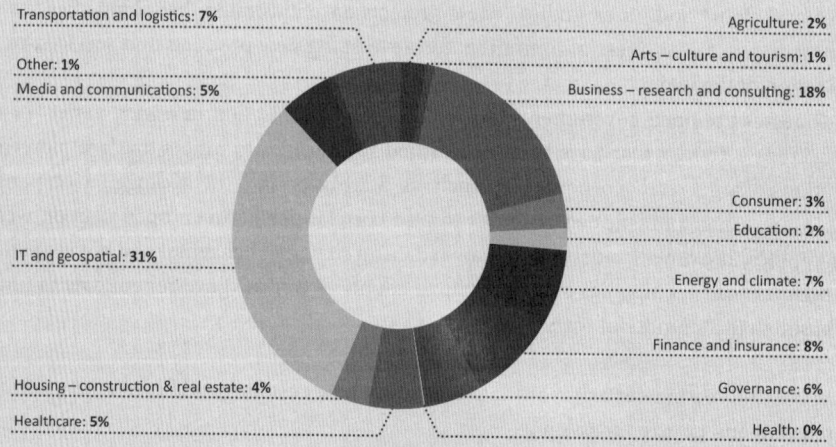

Figure 2: Sector of companies using open data
Source: Calculated from Open Data Impact Map data

- Strategic planning – using weather, economic, and other data to identify and manage business risks.

- Business intelligence – using economic, demographic, and other data to identify factors and trends that impact a company's business.

Many companies are also using open government data to develop new products and services either as extensions of their existing business or as entirely new entrepreneurial ventures. In the European Union (EU), a study on the European data economy has reported that when asked about the benefits open data brings to companies, innovation was by far the most mentioned benefit (47% of the surveyed companies), followed by reduced costs and increased efficiency (26%).[9] These innovations, which are emerging throughout the world in virtually all sectors of the economy, can benefit both business-to-business/government and business-to-consumer ventures.

These companies have developed a number of revenue sources[10] and business models, including freemium (advertising) and premium (subscription) models, or have developed an open source or platform-based approach. Other companies, including many that specialise in real estate data (such as Zillow[11] and Properati[12]), also earn revenue from lead generation (consumers who use their services may ultimately make purchases that result in payments back to the company).

Unlike large corporations, SMEs may not have the means to acquire or collect large amounts of their own data, impacting their ability to compete effectively with those that do. For that reason, SMEs are among the chief beneficiaries of open data. The rise of an open data ecosystem, which includes not only greater access to information but also a proliferation of tools (often cloud-based) to make sense of that information, opens new avenues and represents new business opportunities for smaller businesses. When the GovLab originally mapped 500 companies that were using open data, more than 70% (354 in total) were SMEs and startups (see box, A small sample of SMEs).[13] The Open Data Impact Map shows a similar pattern worldwide.

Despite the considerable promise of open data, SMEs also face a number of challenges in using this data. They often lack the human resources and sophisticated analytical tools necessary to process and analyse large datasets. These challenges highlight the need for data intermediaries as described further below.

A small sample of SMEs

Around the world, thousands of SMEs are demonstrating the business value of open data in a wide variety of economic sectors. Here is a small sampling of businesses operating in different countries:

- Mexico, Transportation, AutoChilango[14] – improves government services by helping licensed commercial drivers who use data on regulations, insurance, and more.

- Ukraine, Smart Cities, CityScale[15] – an information portal that empowers citizens and professionals by providing access to relevant data and statistics about their city, using open urban, transport, and crime data from various government sources.

- Ghana, Agriculture, Farmerline[16] – an SMS-based service that provides small-scale farmers with up-to-date agricultural information and advice, helping them to adopt new farming practices to increase crop yield, using data from the Ministry of Food and Agriculture and weather data from a number of sources.

- India, Engineering, Spageo[17] – a geospatial engineering, data management, and geoscience consulting company for government, utilities, and business, using floating vehicle, geospatial, infrastructure, and agricultural data from the Government of India.

- United States (US), Finance, Credit Sesame – a credit reporting and tracking service that helps users manage their credit, loans, and debt, using open government data from the Department of Commerce and the US Census Bureau.

The private sector as data intermediaries

Companies improve and repackage government data for public use and/or for business intelligence

While open government data has great potential value, potential users may not have the capacity to prepare or improve the data before they can use it, analyse it, or share the results. Data may be released in formats that are not initially machine-readable, are otherwise difficult to use, or may have quality problems relating to accuracy, completeness, timeliness, etc.

Different types of data intermediaries have emerged that view the existing gaps and challenges in the open data ecosystem as a business opportunity by making government data more usable as a resource for different audiences. These range from information giants like Thomson Reuters and Reed Elsevier, which work to improve the quality of large datasets, to companies operating in countries where just converting data from PDFs to more accessible formats is the priority.

Other companies operate as data brokers that aggregate and sell data from both government and non-government sources, analytics companies that add value to open government data for business clients, or data visualisation companies that make open government data easier to access, use, and understand.

Finally, there are companies like OpenDataSoft,[18] Junar,[19] and Socrata[20] that help governments and businesses to publish and share their data in open formats and offer data visualisation and analytics as services. These are usually cloud-based services, generating revenue using data-as-a-service models.

Open data incubators and accelerators

A number of open data companies have secured the funds they need from venture capital firms or other investors; however, it can be difficult for new companies to explain their business model to potential investors who are not familiar with open data and its value. To bridge that gap, several governments over the past few years have launched a number of programmes to help incubate and accelerate open data ventures:

- Canada's Open Data Exchange (CODX)[21] – a public–private partnership to accelerate the use of open data for commercial purposes.
- Data Pitch[22] – an EU-funded open innovation programme that matches startups with larger organisations to solve defined challenges with data.
- Future Internet Open Data Expansion (Finodex)[23] – a European virtual accelerator for commercial open data projects across Europe.
- Labora[24] – an open data incubator in Mexico run in partnership with the UK Open Data Institute (ODI).
- ASEAN Data Startup Accelerator[25] – an accelerator for data-driven startups in the ASEAN region.
- Open Data Incubator for Europe[26] (ODINE) – a 2016 incubator for open data entrepreneurs across Europe funded by the EU Horizon 2020 programme.

The private sector as data providers or collaborators

Companies seek to further public interests by sharing some of their own data or by collaborating with the public sector

In recent years, a number of data-driven companies, such as AirBnB, Properati, and Uber, have published at least some of their data as open data. They may choose to do so for several reasons, ranging from the public relations value of sharing their data to the opportunity to improve their own data through crowdsourcing. Most private sector companies have been reluctant to share their data openly as long as their competitors keep their data to themselves; however, a relatively new, collaborative approach is making it easier for different companies to work together to benefit from each other's data and simultaneously to benefit the public.

Data collaboratives[27] represent an emerging model of public–private partnership within which various actors across sectors exchange data and pool analytical expertise to help solve complex public problems. This model has become increasingly prevalent in recent years with several examples around the world. The practice will likely continue to increase following several recent developments such as Open Banking[28] and the implementation of the General Data Protection Regulation (GDPR) in Europe. Data collaboratives can take many forms and vary by sector or by the problem being addressed. (See box, Six kinds of data collaboratives.)

> ### Six kinds of data collaboratives
>
> The GovLab's Data Collaboratives Explorer[29] has identified six main types of data collaboratives.
>
> 1. Trusted intermediaries, where companies share data with a limited number of known partners through a third party. For example, the South African telecommunications company, Mobile Telephone Networks (MTN), has made anonymised call records available to researchers through a trusted intermediary.
>
> 2. Prizes or challenges, where companies make data available to qualified applicants that compete to develop new apps or discover innovative uses for the data. One example is the Orange Telecom Data for Development Challenge[30] in the Ivory Coast and Senegal, where Orange Telecom hosted a global challenge that allowed researchers to use anonymised, aggregated Call Detail Record (CDR) data to help solve various development problems related to transportation, health, and agriculture.
>
> 3. Research partnerships, in which corporations share data with universities and other research organisations to map weather patterns and natural resources, for example.
>
> 4. Intelligence products allow companies to share (often aggregated) data that provides general insight into market conditions, customer demographic information, or other broad trends.
>
> 5. Application Programming Interfaces (APIs) which allow developers and others to access data for testing, product development, and data analytics. Typically, third parties are asked to sign a terms of service agreement in exchange for which they receive corporate data that allows them to build applications.
>
> 6. Corporate data cooperatives or pooling, in which businesses and other data holders, such as government agencies, work together to create "collaborative databases" with shared data resources (e.g. databases containing medical data to promote drug development).

Challenges and recommendations

Despite the terabytes of data that have now been shared and the very evident potential of open data for the private sector, there is general recognition that the benefits of open data remain largely untapped. There are many reasons for this, as well as several possible solutions that would promote greater progress.

One key issue is a persistent mismatch between supply and demand or between the data being released by companies and governments and the data that potential data users actually need. In most countries, there are few established channels for the private sector to engage with government open data providers, and the demand for open data is often poorly understood or defined as a result. Different sectors, such as healthcare, agriculture, and finance, have different information needs and require different datasets to be released. A more demand-driven approach with public–private engagement would help to set priorities that would better serve the business community's needs. The Open Data for Business (OD4B) Assessment Tool,[31] developed for the World Bank, is one approach to this kind of engagement.

Data usability is as important an issue as data usefulness. The fourth edition of the Open Data Barometer has noted that "data is hard to use because there is no metadata or guidance documentation available. Less than a third (31%) of the published datasets have some supporting basic metadata or companion guidance documentation."[32] Usability is a particular concern in developing countries where technical capacity and financial means may be limited. There may also be problems with data released in proprietary formats or in formats that require significant technical expertise to process. Increasing the adoption of best practices in data release and documentation would help to ensure that useful data is also as usable as possible.

For government data to be truly open, it needs to be open both technically and legally. Companies will have difficulty using government data if it is not published in open, machine-readable formats or if it is not licensed for open use, reuse, and republication. The fourth edition of the Open Data Barometer also reported that only 7% of data released is fully open at a global scale, only one of every two datasets is machine-readable, and only one in four datasets is released under an open licence. In addition, legal and ethical limitations on the use of personal data can make it difficult to apply government data for business use. A number of strategies, including de-identification and data aggregation, could help balance privacy protection with potential data applications as a recent report describes.[33]

Finally, as with most open data initiatives, private sector organisations also face challenges in developing and applying reliable metrics to help guide their use of open data. Metrics are essential for deciding on financial and other investments, as well as for determining the efficacy of open data initiatives. Metrics can capture the direct value of open data to SMEs and other companies and the indirect value of open data to third-party organisations doing business with open data corporations, to consumers, and to the wider economy, as well as capture the wider societal impacts that can be attributed to open data. To date, most studies have based their metrics on ex-ante estimations, whether through surveys or indirect research. Better metrics and methods are needed. The EU Economic Benefits of Open Data[34] report of 2017 concludes "with a call for action for further evidence that needs to be gathered, at both the EU and country level".

Conclusion

While open government data has clear business value, it is not clear how much of that value is being realised. Many have questioned the 2013 McKinsey study's estimate that open data is worth USD 3 to 5 trillion annually.[35] It has been difficult to find concrete evidence to support that claim. At the same time, however, it has also become clear that the use of open data is so embedded in many companies' business operations that the benefits of open data, while very real, are difficult to quantify.

Although much attention has been paid to companies that are based entirely on open data, like those described in the box above on SMEs, most businesses that use open data do not identify themselves as an "open data company". Instead, they identify themselves using conventional sector or market terminology even though they may use open data to optimise their business operations or improve their profit margins. For example, they may use weather data to manage their inventory, demographic data to decide where to build a new retail outlet, or geospatial data to plan more efficient transportation. While these companies would exist without open data, their use of such data can make a huge difference to their efficiency, profitability, and overall success.

As the value of open government data is more widely understood, businesses and other non-government stakeholders can work together to develop new ways to apply it. Data and entrepreneurial communities can work together to enhance their awareness, skill levels, and utilisation of open data for innovation. The "smart cities" movement could be a major opportunity for this kind of engagement internationally as evidenced in the open data initiatives ongoing in cities from Singapore to Bristol. Universities and enterprise centres could also act as educators and mediators by training students to work with organisations (SMEs and social enterprises) to further practical applications of open data research.

Ultimately, the business use of open government data has to be seen in the context of the proprietary data that businesses themselves collect, manage, and use. The potential for open data for businesses may lie increasingly in connecting it with other sources of information and resources. Businesses can also be open data providers as well as users, and there is a growing sense that the private sector should make some of its data available in the public interest.

In France, recent legislation prepared in consultation with citizens could serve as a global model for opening up private data. The Digital Republic Act, which came into force in October 2016, has introduced the notion of "general interest" to widen the scope of private data available to everyone.[36] Although there have been no enforcements yet, this notion could help create a new paradigm for how governments see the public value of privately held data. Even if such a dramatic shift does not take place, the future value of open data will depend on public–private collaboration in the generation and sharing of data.

To fully realise the economic value of open data, we will need to overcome some of the same barriers that now inhibit the full utilisation of other kinds of data and digital technology. Countries in the Global South, for example, may lack the financial resources needed to apply and grow new business ideas for leveraging open data. Promising ideas that emerge from challenges or hackathons in these countries may not turn into viable businesses as easily as they would if they could leverage the greater investment resources in the Global North. Launching incubators or accelerators in these countries could increase the chances of business success (see box, Open data incubators and accelerators). Other strategies to support new open data companies could include establishing intermediaries that can help smaller companies leverage open data, creating technical capacity and training opportunities, and developing networks of expertise and experience.

Gender bias may also be inhibiting the development of new open data companies. Some anecdotal observations suggest that men may have greater access to the resources needed for entrepreneurial data ventures than women. Programmes, such as Mexico's Crea Communities of Social Entrepreneurs,[37] can empower and encourage women entrepreneurs and businesswomen from socially and economically marginalised areas. Other initiatives, like TechMousso[38] in the

Ivory Coast, are encouraging more women to participate in apps competitions and can help train them on different business models.

Despite the challenges that remain, open data is being applied by businesses of all kinds and has proved to be a critical resource for the private sector. The value of open data should be a key consideration as governments around the world weigh the costs and benefits of developing better open data resources. There is still a need to increase awareness of the business value of open data and provide examples and guidance on how companies can put it to use. At the same time, governments can learn new ways to improve their open data programmes from the private sector and other innovators.

Further reading

Bonina, C.M. (2013). *New business models and the value of open data: Definitions, challenges and opportunities.* NEMODE Working Papers. Guildford: NEMODE, University of Surrey. https://ofti.org/wp-content/uploads/2014/08/Bonina-Opendata-Report-FINAL.pdf

Gruen, N., Houghton, J. & Tooth, R. (2014). *Open for business: How open data can help achieve the G20 growth target.* Omidyar Network. https://www.omidyar.com/sites/default/files/file_archive/insights/ON%20Report_061114_FNL.pdf

Gurin, J. (2014). *Open data now: The secret to hot startups, smart investing, savvy marketing, and fast innovation.* New York, NY: McGraw-Hill Education.

Kaasenbrood, M., Zuiderwijk, A., Janssen, M., De Jong, M., & Bharosa, N. (2015). Exploring the factors influencing the adoption of open government data by private organisations. *International Journal of Public Administration in the Digital Age (IJPADA), 2(2),* 75–92. https://www.igi-global.com/article/exploring-the-factors-influencing-the-adoption-of-open-government-data-by-private-organisations/121537

Tinholt, D. (2013). *The open data economy: Unlocking economic value by opening government and public data.* Paris: Capgemini Consulting. https://www.capgemini.com/wp-content/uploads/2017/07/the_open_data_economy_unlocking_economic_value_by_opening_government_and_public_data.pdf

Verhulst, S. & Caplan, R. (2015). Open data: A twenty-first-century asset for small and medium-sized enterprises. *SSRN.* https://papers.ssrn.com/sol3/papers.cfm?abstract_id=3141515

About the authors

Joel Gurin is President of the non-profit Center for Open Data Enterprise (http://www.opendataenterprise.org), which works to maximise the value of open government data as a public resource for economic growth, social good, and scientific research. He is the author of *Open data now* and has held top leadership positions at the US Federal Communications Commission, Consumers Union of the US, and several non-profit organisations. Follow Joel on Twitter at https://twitter/joelgurin.

Carla Bonina is a social scientist and an expert on digital government and social innovation in Latin America. Carla provides strategic advice to governments, international organisations, and philanthropic investors, such as Avina Americas, the Organisation for Economic Co-operation and Development (OECD), the Latin American Open Data Initiative (ILDA), and the World Bank among others. She holds a PhD in Management from the London School of Economics and Political Science, and is currently a lecturer at the University of Surrey's Centre for Digital Economy (https://surreycode.org).

Stefaan Verhulst is co-founder and Chief of Research and Development at the GovLab at New York University (https://thegovlab.org) and Project Lead of the Global Open Data 500 Network. He is the co-author (with A. Young) of *Global impact of open data* (2016) and *Open data in developing countries* (2017).

How to cite this chapter

Gurin, J., Bonina, C., & Verhulst, S. (2019). Open data stakeholders: Private sector. In T. Davies, S. Walker, M. Rubinstein, & F. Perini (Eds.), *The state of open data: Histories and horizons* (pp. 418–429). Cape Town and Ottawa: African Minds and International Development Research Centre. http://stateofopendata.od4d.net

This work is licensed under a Creative Commons Attribution 4.0 International (CC BY 4.0) licence. It was carried out with the aid of a grant from the International Development Research Centre, Ottawa, Canada.

Endnotes

1. Manyika, J., Chui, M., Groves, P., Farrell, D., Van Kuiken, S., & Doshi, E.A. (2013). *Open data: Unlocking innovation and performance with liquid information*. New York, NY: McKinsey Global Institute. https://www.mckinsey.com/~/media/McKinsey/Business%20Functions/McKinsey%20Digital/Our%20Insights/Open%20data%20Unlocking%20innovation%20and%20performance%20with%20liquid%20information/MGI_Open_data_FullReport_Oct2013.ashx
2. http://www.opendata500.com/
3. http://opendataimpactmap.org/
4. http://www.opendata500.com/
5. http://opendataimpactmap.org/
6. https://exploralat.am/
7. Centre for Open Data Enterprise. (2018). *Government data for business innovation in the 21st century*. Chicago, IL: Accenture. https://www.accenture.com/t20180103T192103Z__w__/us-en/_acnmedia/Accenture/Conversion-Assets/DotCom/Documents/Global/PDF/Dualpub_26/Accenture-Open-Data-Executive-Summary.pdf

8   http://opendataimpactmap.org/
9   Berends, J., Carrara, W., & Radu, C. (2017). *Analytical report 9: The economic benefits of open data*. Luxembourg: European Data Portal. https://www.europeandataportal.eu/sites/default/files/analytical_report_n9_economic_benefits_of_open_data.pdf
10 Gurin, J. (2014). *Driving innovation with open data*. Washington, DC: US Chamber of Commerce Foundation. https://www.uschamberfoundation.org/sites/default/files/Gurin%20Article.pdf
11 https://www.zillow.com/
12 http://properati.com/
13 Verhulst, S. & Caplan R. (2015). Open data: A twenty-first-century asset for small and medium-sized enterprises. *SSRN*. https://papers.ssrn.com/sol3/papers.cfm?abstract_id=3141515
14 http://autochilango.com/
15 http://www.cityscale.com.ua/
16 https://farmerline.co/
17 http://www.spageo.co.in/
18 https://www.opendatasoft.com/
19 http://www.junar.com/
20 https://socrata.com/
21 http://codx.ca/
22 https://datapitch.eu/
23 https://web.archive.org/web/20180605052411/http://www.finodex-project.eu/
24 http://labora.io/
25 http://aseandatastartupaccelerator.com/
26 https://opendataincubator.eu/
27 http://datacollaboratives.org/
28 https://www.openbankingeurope.eu/
29 http://datacollaboratives.org/explorer
30 http://datacollaboratives.org/cases/orange-telecom-data-for-development-challenge-d4d.html
31 World Bank & Centre for Open Data Enterprise. (2015). *Open Data for Business (OD4B) Tool*. Washington, DC: World Bank. http://opendatatoolkit.worldbank.org/docs/odra/od4b_v2.8-en.pdf
32 Web Foundation. (2017). *Open Data Barometer – Global report*. 4th edition. Washington, DC: World Wide Web Foundation. https://opendatabarometer.org/doc/4thEdition/ODB-4thEdition-GlobalReport.pdf
33 Gurin, J., Rumsey, M., Ariss, A., & Garcia, K. (2017). Protecting privacy while releasing data: Strategies to maximise benefits and mitigate risks. In F. van Schalkwyk, S.G. Verhulst, G. Magalhaes, J. Pane, & J. Walker (Eds.), *The social dynamics of open data* (pp. 183–200). Cape Town: African Minds. https://zenodo.org/record/1117782#.W-mjihP7SL5
34 Berends, J., Carrara, W., & Radu, C. (2017). *Analytical report 9: The economic benefits of open data*. Luxembourg: European Data Portal. https://www.europeandataportal.eu/sites/default/files/analytical_report_n9_economic_benefits_of_open_data.pdf
35 Manyika, J., Chui, M., Groves, P., Farrell, D., Van Kuiken, S., & Doshi, E.A. (2013). *Open data: Unlocking innovation and performance with liquid information*. New York, NY: McKinsey Global Institute. https://www.mckinsey.com/~/media/McKinsey/Business%20Functions/McKinsey%20Digital/Our%20Insights/Open%20data%20Unlocking%20innovation%20and%20performance%20with%20liquid%20information/MGI_Open_data_FullReport_Oct2013.ashx
36 Republique Francais. (2016). Digital Republic Bill: Explanatory Memorandum. *République Numérique*. https://www.republique-numerique.fr/pages/digital-republic-bill-rationale
37 http://www.crea.org.mx/
38 http://techmousso.ci/

030

Researchers

François van Schalkwyk

Key points

- There has been a substantial growth in research on open data since 2007.
- Researchers cannot be described as a single, coherent open data stakeholder group. However, distinct clusters can be identified, including one cluster primarily centred around scientific institutions and another rooted in the work of the international development sector. Each cluster seeks to produce knowledge on open data but for different purposes and according to different taken-for-granted rules and procedures.
- The Open Data Research Symposium is the only regular conference for researchers focused entirely on open government data that brings researchers together from different clusters. There are a number of other conferences that include open data tracks, although these tend to have a narrower disciplinary and thematic focus. Including open data as an area of focus at these conferences has helped to stimulate research, but not necessarily a cohesive research agenda.
- Scientific articles on open government data are predominantly produced by male authors from the Global North with a trend toward co-authorship. In the development research cluster, there is greater diversity of authorship, but researchers face short and restrictive timelines for completing commissioned research.

Introduction

Over the last decade, many civil society and non-governmental organisations (NGOs) have advocated for public access to, and the use of, government data. They have drawn on arguments regarding the benefits of open data for society at large based on what intuitively seems like sound logic. Data that is open to the public increases the transparency of public institutions that routinely produce data. It can improve efficiency by interconnecting typically siloed datasets, and, because open data is free to reuse, it can resource innovation and development. In the words of Lawrence Lessig, in 2009, on the relationship between open data and greater transparency in governance, "How could anyone be against transparency? Its virtues and its utilities seem so crushingly obvious."[1]

The origins of this logic can be traced to leading governments of Western democracies in the eighties and nineties.[2] In 2007, a definitive meeting of government officials took place in Sebastopol, CA, where the logic for open data was codified into what became known as the Sebastopol Principles.[3] Subsequently, governments, donor agencies, multilaterals, and civil society have fuelled interest in, and the implementation of, open data initiatives. However, there is a problem. The logic that these open data efforts have drawn upon, while intuitively appealing, is, in most cases, premised on a hunch, and one frequently based on experience in relatively few countries and contexts. Given the scope and depth of the purported impact that open data may have on the development of society, the responsible thing to do is to seek evidence in support of claims that open data is delivering on its promise. This is a key role of research in this domain – to produce the knowledge that confirms empirically the benefits and limitations of open data. This is the role that researchers have been asked to take up over recent years.

Since 2007, researchers have responded to that demand. There has been a substantial increase in the volume of research on open data being produced. Figure 1 illustrates the increase between 2007 and 2016 in journal articles on open government data indexed in the Clarivate Web of Science.[4] While solid data is not available on the numbers of non-indexed articles and grey literature publications about open data, it can be reasonably assumed that these have also increased.

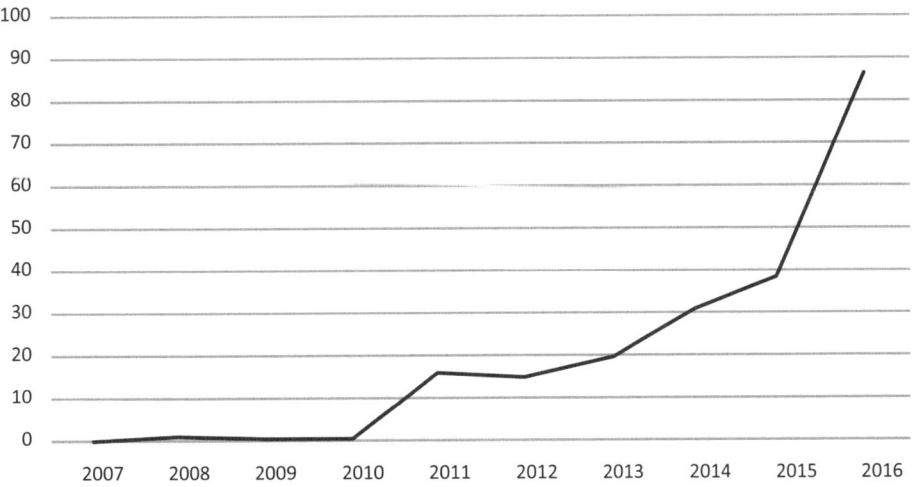

Figure 1: Number of publications on open government data indexed in the Web of Science 2007–2016 (n=216)
Source: Van Schalkwyk & Verhulst (2017).[5] See also Klein et al. (2017)[6] who find a similar publication pattern.

However, it is not possible to conclude based on this increase that questions about the impact or operation of open data have been resolved or that the most critical knowledge gaps around open data have been filled.

There may be several factors that work against the assumption that more research invariably results in more valid and reliable knowledge about open data's impacts and operations. For one, researchers do not constitute a singular or cohesive stakeholder group, and their different intents are reflected in their published articles. At best, researchers are a collective by virtue of their shared interest in the collection, synthesis, and use of evidence to advance particular objectives. While some applied researchers collect evidence to inform and shape policy or practice as their primary objective, other, more theoretical, researchers are interested primarily in the potential of evidence to confirm or advance knowledge. How evidence is collected, what counts as evidence, how evidence is scrutinised, and how it is put to use, will vary according to the objectives that bind particular communities of researchers together.

This should hardly come as a surprise. Sociologists studying organisations have argued that the behaviour of social actors (including researchers) is governed by different "institutional logics",[7] and those studying social networks call on us to acknowledge the different "programmes" that shape the actions of those who belong to particular networks.[8,9,10] However, too often the agendas behind research were left unexamined in the rush to find facts or figures to bolster the belief in open data's potential during the early phases of the open data hype cycle. This chapter puts the emphasis on the factors shaping research to redress this imbalance.

When we focus on open government data specifically (i.e. not open research data or open data created and consumed only in the private sector), then we can identify research and researchers in relation to two main global networks:

1. The science, technology, and higher education network or, in short, the "science network".

2. The transnational NGOs and social movements network or, in short, the "development network".[11]

Although individual researcher affiliations and projects may cross over between these networks, as when a researcher in academia takes on consultancy-type research that leans more toward the application of existing know-how rather than the creation of new knowledge or a researcher in a non-profit organisation produces new knowledge without any immediate apparent application. The key question to ask when assessing researchers as stakeholders in the open data world is "Which institutional or network logic are they connected to?" This chapter will argue that we should not ignore these different logics because they determine how research is conducted which, in turn, determines both the relevance and the validity of the findings behind any conclusions regarding the impacts and operations of open government data.

Furthermore, if we want to see research contributing critical knowledge that can further efforts to realise the potential of open data, and that can sensitively illuminate where that potential has been overstated, we need to pay attention to the shape of research networks and consider the diversity of viewpoints represented. Bias in research toward particular geographies, genders, organisational positions, and academic disciplines can affect the stock of knowledge that the open data field has to draw upon with significant consequences.

The sections that follow will explore questions of how current research networks around open data have been shaped and challenge the idea that researchers constitute a single stakeholder group, as well as examine what this means for the current composition of research and research impacts.

Shaping networks of research

Although research is often presented as pure inquiry directed simply at addressing some particular question, those who ultimately hold the power to shape a research field are those who provide the financial resources to conduct research and those who determine the rules and standards governing research practice. Both money and standards as influencers correspond to different types of networked power in the information age.[12] Money makes it possible to direct the focus of research and to create new spaces for research through funding particular research programmes, meetings, or events. Standards, in the form of required practices to secure publication of research, or the cultures of particular research networks and academic disciplines, establish the boundaries of particular research networks and allocate power within those networks to particular groups and institutions. In the context of open data research, these forms of power have played out differently in shaping open data research within the science network and the parallel development network.

Funders in focus

Common to both science and development research networks is the influence of economic capital. Researchers in both networks rely on financial resources for their research activities. In the case of predominantly university-based research in the science network, funding is provided by government and/or student fees but also from third-stream income in the form of financial grants from alumni, donors, and research funding agencies. Tenured and other scientists are relatively free to pursue their own research agendas, although there is increasing institutional pressure to seek third-stream income to fund research. In the case of the development network, research is most often the remit of non-profit organisations and individual consultants, relying almost exclusively on financial support from external funders. Dependency on funding from donor agencies is, therefore, more acute in the development research network, and, consequently, the type of research undertaken is more exposed to the vagaries of the strategic priorities of funders. It is also important to note that researchers dependent on funding operate in a competitive environment, and this can dampen collaboration and the development of a shared research agenda.

Looking at a sample of publications on open government data indexed in the Clarivate Web of Science (which is biased toward the science network) in 2017, Van Schalkwyk and Verhulst[13] found that the European Union (EU) was the single largest cited funder of research on open data.

Even so, EU funding only accounted for 20% of those publications that acknowledged financial support, making it clear that funding for open data research comes from a variety of sources. More ubiquitous is the finding that 64% of acknowledged funding came from national-level funding sources, reflecting perhaps a focus also on national-level studies of open data. What Van Schalkwyk and Verhulst (2017) were not able to fully address, however, is why 68% of publications in their sample did not acknowledge funding. It is known that researchers underreport when it comes to acknowledging funders, and acknowledgements, when they are provided, are not always indexed.[14] Nevertheless, the low number of research publications without funding acknowledgements could indicate that researchers in the science network are able to determine and conduct their research without external funding, and it may also reflect the relatively small size of open data research projects and the ability, at least early in the rise of interest on open data, for publication to be secured with relatively little input of resources.

It is not possible to use bibliometrics to provide a comparable analysis of publications produced by researchers in the development network because these publications are not indexed and are seldom assigned the ISBNs or DOIs needed for tracking and measurement. There is also no representative repository of publications produced by researchers in this network. However, we can look at funding of open data research across the development network using projects as a proxy in the absence of bibliometric data.

One of the first large-scale open data research projects was the Emerging Impacts of Open Data in Developing Countries (ODDC)[15] implemented by the World Wide Web Foundation as a two-phase research project from 2012 to 2015. ODDC was supported by the Open Data for Development (OD4D) programme, which is a partnership funded by Canada's International Development Research Centre (IDRC), the World Bank, the United Kingdom's (UK) Department for International Development (DFID), and Global Affairs Canada (GAC). In Latin America, the Latin American Open Data Initiative (ILDA)[16] has also received funding to conduct research on open data from OD4D and its funders plus financial support from the Avina Foundation. In addition, research in support of Africa Data Revolution Reports,[17,18] the state of open data in Eastern Europe and Central Asia,[19] as well as research on open data in the Caribbean,[20] have all also received research grants from OD4D and its funding partners. The GovLab, based at New York University but active within the development network,[21] received research project funding from the Omidyar Network for its Open Data Impact project in 2015,[22] which was extended to cover developing countries with funding from FHI 360 and the United States Agency for International Development (USAID).[23] GovLab has also received funding from the John S. and James L. Knight Foundation in support of its Open Data 500 (OD500) research project focusing on commercial reuse of open data.[24] Between 2013 and 2017, the Making All Voices Count (MAVC) project supported 61 research projects, several of which focused on open data. MAVC was funded by the Omidyar Network, the Swedish International Development Cooperation Agency, DFID, and USAID. The Global Open Data for Agriculture and Nutrition (GODAN) project,[25] while not exclusively a research project, has commissioned research on open data in agriculture. GODAN has received funding and in-kind support from various partners,[26] but funding for research activities appears to be covered primarily by its grant from DFID.

While the list of projects above is not exhaustive (given that we lack a complete database of research projects and one of grey literature publications), what emerges from the overview of open data research project funding in the development research network is the presence of a few key funders from the constellation of funders active in the broader open data space (see Chapter 25: Donors and investors). In particular, government funding through DFID, IDRC, the World Bank, and USAID, as well as private funding from the Omidyar Network, has played a significant role in directing research and in setting the open government data research agenda.

Standards, culture, and key influencers

Among open data advocates, there has often been talk of the importance of standards to make data interoperable and to tie together communities of practice around particular datasets. However, this focus, which some have termed the "magical thinking" of standards,[27] can ignore the way in which standards as fixed practices, norms, and rules also create barriers to entry and foster forms of exclusion for those who may not have the capacity to meet the standards bar that has been set. As Davies (2014) writes: "Whilst our network society can make law, markets and norms more visible and contestable, by default, code, data and standards become an embedded part of the background, rarely subjected to scrutiny, and rarely open to be shaped by those who they affect."[28] Whether for datasets or for a field of research, standards are typically set by early movers in more developed and well-resourced countries. Such standards can then set unrealistic or unfeasible expectations for later adopters. It should not be assumed that standards set for scientific research, or the datasets widely used by researchers, are apolitical as their creation and application is inevitably an expression of the will of those exercising the full extent of their influence with varying impact across different social contexts.

In the case of the science network, accepted standards and their associated practices (the derivatives of the so-called "Mertonian norms" of science)[29] include requirements to seek approval from ethics review boards, cite peers in written work, and subject written work to peer review prior to publication, all of which affects who gets to contribute to the creation and dissemination of knowledge. While, in theory, these standards are intended to be meritocratic, they may nevertheless preclude many individuals and groups from contributing to certain forms of open data research.

For example, Van Schalkwyk and Verhulst indicate that of 205 publications on open government data indexed in the Web of Science, only 0.5% of corresponding authors listed their affiliation as being an NGO, 2.0% as a private firm, and 3.0% as government.[30] In other words, over 90% of publications were authored by researchers from within the science network, suggesting that relatively little progress has been made either in bringing practitioner perspectives into academic research or in bridging between academic and development networks.

Different norms exist in the development network where rapid publication may be prioritised over peer review and there is a strong orientation toward case study research or to participatory research projects such as the Open Data Index. Values of inclusion and transparency are also often referenced by development stakeholders in their research. It is notable that the development network has had its own early movers involved in setting standards that shape the research agenda, such as technical definitions of open data (e.g. efforts by the 2007 working group on open government data,[31] the Open Knowledge Foundation,[32] and the Exploring the Emerging Impacts of ODDC project[33]), leading open data working groups and standards-setting bodies (e.g. efforts of the Open Data Working Group of the Open Government Partnership and sector-specific groups working on data standards in contracting, agriculture, etc.), and engaging in the drafting and promotion of the International Open Data Charter.[34] Instruments and assessment criteria for evaluating open data readiness, implementation, and impact have also played a significant role in shaping development network research with the World Bank's Open Data Readiness Assessment,[35] the Web Foundation's Open Data Barometer,[36] the Open Data Inventory (ODIN) from Open Data Watch,[37] and the Open Knowledge Foundation's Global Open Data Index,[38] all leading both to the secondary analysis of collected data and influencing the methodologies used by other researchers.

Although early projects emerging from the development network, such as OD4D's ODDC programme, sought to foster an interdisciplinary research agenda and contribute to academic as well as development literature, it appears to have resulted in few publications indexed in the Clarivate Web of Science. It is also worth noting that while the Web of Science does index non-English journals, they are also known to be underrepresented. The index itself, therefore, may mask and reinforce the exclusion of contributions from a segment of the research community.

[Un]welcome to science?

The Open Data Research Symposium (ODRS) is designed to be a space where researchers can share and advance knowledge exclusively on open government data. University academics, independent researchers, and researchers from NGOs are all encouraged to submit and present papers at the symposium.

For the inaugural ODRS, a policy manager from an international NGO active in the open government data space submitted a paper abstract. The abstract was reviewed and accepted for presentation as a full paper at the Symposium. After the Symposium, all authors of accepted abstracts were also invited to submit their full papers to a special journal issue on open data. Submitted papers were put through a double-blind peer review process prior to publication in the special issue. The policy manager's paper was subsequently not recommended for publication by the reviewers.

The following exchange provides a small example of a misunderstanding of the accepted norms in the science network (i.e. peer review and possible rejection) versus those of the development network (i.e. participatory and inclusive).

EDITORS: All the reviews on your paper entitled "XXX" that was submitted for consideration to the special issue on open data of the *Journal of Community Informatics* have now been received. Unfortunately, the reviewers have recommended that your paper not be accepted for publication. Once again, thank you for submitting your manuscript and for your patience as your paper went through the peer review process.

POLICY MANAGER: "What a welcoming community! Why was I invited in the first place?"

Fields and fora

We can see from the above that, in spite of some efforts, the different networks around open data research broadly operate in parallel, but still remain separate. The science network, in particular, contains a number of different disciplines which have been more or less active at different points over the last decade with the production of research on open data shaped substantially by their different research cultures.

Initial interest and research influence on open data emerged in the computer sciences, where the emphasis was on data as an object rather than on socially embedded practices. This research was largely interested in the technical aspects of open government data, focusing on methods to link open data by means of formats, languages, and standards that could result in possible efficiency gains and better data use. This research was, therefore, largely detached from the social world, seeing government data as an input but not studying the government processes that generated the data. However, as the implementation of open data initiatives matured and attention turned to the successes and failures of implementation, as well as to the terrain of policy and governance, a gradual switch toward examining social factors as determinants of success or failure emerged, bringing in a more diffuse set of researchers from backgrounds in geography, politics, economics, and business.[39] It is possible that this interest was fuelled by the concomitant interest of civil society in the social benefits of open data (e.g. countering corruption to improve service delivery). Regardless of the catalyst, social research into open data has become more established, although social research agendas are now arguably turning more to framings of data privacy,[40] data rights, data justice,[41] and social inclusion[42] as opposed to maintaining a core focus on open data.

The extent to which these new areas of enquiry are driven by an increase in media coverage, or by the shifting interests and strategies of funders, is not clear at this stage, and it remains to be seen whether this reflects a shift of interest into new fields or whether these new themes might be integrated into a coherent development network field of open data research.

Klein et al.'s analysis of where articles on open data have been published illustrates the current state of this shift. In 2017, they found that most articles had been published in the journal *Government Information Quarterly*, a journal that invites submissions from a range of both technical and social disciplines, and the distribution across the remaining journals that had either a technical or a social focus was 50/50.[43] However, by volume of publications, technical disciplines still predominate. Using the subject categorisation of published articles added by the Web of Science, rather than academic journals as a proxy for discipline, Van Schalkwyk and Verhulst found that the two most prominent subject categories in the literature published to date are both from technical disciplines: computer science (27%) and information and library science (23%).[44] Overall, Klein et al.[45] found that academic social research into open data has had a preoccupation with issues related to governance, such as transparency, participation, accountability, and collaboration, and, to a lesser extent, with the economic benefits of open government data, such as innovation and added value.

When it comes to the fora where researchers can meet, the only regular conference that focuses exclusively on open government data is the ODRS that is co-located with the International Open Data Conference with the goal of bridging academic and development research networks.[46]

Three symposia have been held to-date (Ottawa 2015, Madrid 2016, and Buenos Aires 2018). Funding for ODRS has been limited to in-kind support from the World Wide Web Foundation (ODRS 1 and 2), GovLab (ODRS 2 and 3), and the organisers of the International Open Data Conference. USAID has provided travel support for participants (ODRS 2016), and the OD4D network has also provided funding for travel grants and logistics (ODRS 2018). Although a number of other conferences related to web science and e-government have included open data tracks, these appear to have been relatively short-lived and have not led to the creation of distinct open data research sub-fields nor contributed to an overarching research agenda on open data.[47]

The state of research stakeholder networks: A snapshot

The factors outlined above, such as funding or disciplinary standards, may be difficult for individual researchers to affect. This section provides a brief snapshot of the effect of these forces shaping open data research and explores whether we are seeing an inclusive or integrated landscape of research emerge.

- Gender. Using the names of corresponding authors for articles on open government data indexed in the Clarivate Web of Science, Van Schalkwyk and Verhulst[48] found that 30% (70 out of 209) were female. An analysis of attendees at the 2016 Open Data Research Symposium found 34% of participants were female. At the 2018 Symposium, 29% of the attendees were female. These findings indicate an underrepresentation of women in open data research.[49]

- Geography. Van Schalkwyk and Verhulst indicate that 88% (189) of research publications indexed in the Clarivate Web of Science were published by authors in the Global North.[50] The trend data show that there has been an increase in the proportion of authors from the Global South, but that the gap remains wide. Zhang et al. (2017) found that most authors are from the UK and US, both in terms of theoretical and practical research on open data, while in China, for example, most researchers focus on practical research.

- Collaboration. Bibliometric analysis of research published in the science network indicates that the trend is for research publications on open data to be co-authored. Seventy-nine per cent (170) of publications were found to be authored by two or more researchers, and the average number of authors per publication was found to be 3.29.[51] Of those authors who collaborated, 33% (71) did so with colleagues in the same organisation, 23% (49) collaborated with colleagues in the same country, and 11% (23) collaborated within a region (e.g. Europe, Africa). Only 3% (7) of collaborations were between regions within the same development classification (e.g. collaboration between authors in the US and Europe), while 8% (16) of collaborations took place across development classifications (i.e. North–South collaboration).

- Impact. The impact of the new knowledge produced by open data researchers can either be measured as impact on the production of new knowledge or impact on society in terms of changes brought about that are attributable to research outputs. Neither is easy to measure, although impact on knowledge production is typically measured using citations as a proxy for impact (the greater the frequency of citation for a research publication, the greater the impact of the research in the science network). Van Schalkwyk and Verhulst (2017) have indicated a marked increase in the number of citations, which is to be expected as the number of publications on open data has increased over time, finding that, on average, each paper is cited 5.88 times.

Alternative metrics (or "altmetrics")[52] can also be used as proxy indicators for the "impact" of research among different stakeholder groups outside of the science network. The most highly cited academic open data paper according to Klein et. al.[53] was, at the time of writing, mentioned 17 times on Twitter and twice in policy documents.[54] Altmetrics for a comparable paper from the development network had 77 mentions on Twitter, two in policy documents, as well as a mention in one blogpost. In both cases, the data indicates that it can be a number of years before the publications are picked up and cited as sources.

From the data above, albeit primarily from the science network, it appears that there is a long way to go before open data research represents an inclusive stakeholder group. In particular, the lack of Global South representation and limited international collaboration are cause for concern when we consider the identified need for research to understand the role of open data in securing progress on the Sustainable Development Goals (SDGs). From altmetrics data, we also get a hint that research uptake in the wider discourse around open data is limited as well.

Reshaping research: Challenges and opportunities

Although papers and publications abound, when it comes to findings that can illustrate whether or not open data is fulfilling its promise, it is not unreasonable to ask why so little progress has been made in ten years? Why is there still so much uncertainty about the actual potential of open government data? And why has the open data research stakeholder group not managed to place research at the heart of open data discourse?

One key reason is that researchers as a stakeholder group are fragmented and uncoordinated. Those in the science network are more focused on technical aspects of open data, while those in the development network have been trying to emphasise the importance of social dynamics if open government data is to be transformative. Connections between these networks are few and far between. Entities that can function as connectors, such as GovLab at New York University, the Singapore Internet Research Centre (SiRC) at Nanyang Technological University, and the AidData lab located at the College of William & Mary, could play an increased role in this regard provided they can maintain a balanced position between both networks.

Balance is also needed in other areas. If open data research continues to be dominated by those in the Global North and does not become more collaborative (across disciplines and regions), and if it does not address the dominance of male researchers, then the knowledge produced will be of limited relevance to those regions and communities that are often touted as being the main beneficiaries of open data. This requires action from those shaping research networks and greater consideration by researchers of the collaborations they enter into and the ways in which they can contribute to a more inclusive and interdisciplinary research field.

Another key challenge to the construction of a research field, and the collation of clear findings, has been the limited duration or reduction of resources for open data research. If, as already suggested in this chapter, research in the science network is mostly undertaken without direct financial support from external funding agencies, then it is likely that, aside from the institutional pressures to "publish or perish", such research is not directly subject to external time pressures. However, the lack of external funding also suggests that independent science-led research projects are likely to be fairly small and not linked to large empirical data collection. Even EU Horizon 2020 funding, identified above as the largest single funding source for open data research, is generally split between scientific outputs and more applied research and development activities. While the duration of these projects can vary, a typical small- or medium-scale research project would generally last two to four years, and larger projects could run for three to five years.

In the development network, the time allowed to complete funded research is shorter and has been shrinking. Commissioned research by the likes of GODAN, the World Bank, and the Open Government Partnership have allocated as little as one to three months for research to be carried out. The Impact of Open Data in Developing Countries research project by GovLab was to be completed within one year. Researchers had two years to complete research for the first phase of the Emerging Impacts of Open Data in Developing Countries, but for phase three of the research project, they had just seven months. While this is not a comprehensive survey of all calls for open data research across the development network, it does indicate that the time afforded researchers to complete their research is likely to substantially constrain the kinds of studies that can be carried out and the extent to which impact studies can be conducted. Of course, not all research requires an equal amount of time. It is often possible to complete synthesis and desktop research within in shorter time frames, but empirical research requiring fieldwork and longitudinal data collection inevitably needs more time.

It may be that research in the development network has been afforded less time because of the needs and priorities of actors in that network and because the shorter time periods are suitable to the kinds of research questions being explored. If so, shorter research timelines may not be problematic, and even less so if empirical studies are completed in the science network. But there are potential risks to consider. For example, if short-term research is done without reference to relevant empirical data and is presented as definitive, or if short-term research is more concerned with "real" social issues and scientific empirical work remains abstract and esoteric, then the risk of continued reliance on weak evidence to inform our understanding of open data will become a reality. An open conversation not only about the open data research agenda, but also about the kinds of resources needed to advance that agenda, is greatly needed.

Conclusion

As this chapter has shown, the role that different research stakeholders play is being substantially shaped by funding, culture, and field building. This observation is not unique to researchers as other stakeholder groups have had their engagement with open data influenced by similar forces. Crucially, one of the reasons we still have limited evidence on the impact of open data is that impact measurement in general is notoriously difficult. There are many widely adopted social policy interventions that have a surprisingly shallow evidence base. In particular, it takes time for evidence of impact to become available, and effective measurement requires methodologies to be refined and extensive empirical data to be gathered.

However, as open data work heads firmly into its second decade, the need to provide answers to questions about its value becomes ever more critical. Short-term project-based research that values relevance and application at the expense of programmatic research that incorporates robust empirical data and theory building will ultimately result in advocacy campaigns and open data policies built on shaky foundations.

This is not to say, however, that open data research enters the next decade starting from scratch. In fact, both development and science-network researchers have completed much groundwork to date and subjected some of it to critical attention. It could be argued that open data research has created the space for new, emerging areas of enquiry, such as data justice, privacy, and rights. One the other hand, these emerging fields will need to guard against some of the challenges faced by prior open data research because they still lack the conceptual clarity needed to support open data studies. A reboot of open data research could offer the opportunity to keep and strengthen good foundations and put aside the more shaky outputs from earlier short-term projects. If the forces shaping networks of research align appropriately, it may be that open data researchers can provide the answers needed to fulfil the hopes of the Sebastopol "pioneers".

Further reading

Hossain, M.A., Dwivedi, Y.K., & Rana, N.P. (2016). State-of-the-art in open data research: Insights from existing literature and a research agenda. *Journal of Organizational Computing and Electronic Commerce, 26(1–2)*, 14–40. https://doi.org/10.1080/10919392.2015.1124007

Klein, R.H., Klein, D.C.B., & Luciano, E.M. (2017). Open government data concept over time: Approaches and dimensions. *EnANPAD 2017*, São Paulo, Brazil, 1–4 October. https://www.researchgate.net/publication/320831625_Open_Government_Data_Concept_Over_Time_Approaches_and_Dimensions_EnANPAD_2017_Open_Government_Data_Concept_Over_Time_Approaches_and_Dimensions

Van Schalkwyk, F. & Verhulst, S. (2017). The state of open data and open data research. In F. van Schalkwyk, S. Verhulst, G. Magalhaes, J. Pane, & J. Walker (Eds.), *The social dynamics of open data* (pp. 1–12). Cape Town: African Minds. https://zenodo.org/record/1117807#.XLv7v-gzZPY

Wagner, C.S. (2008). *The new invisible college: Science for development*. Washington, DC: The Brookings Institute.

Zhang, Y., Hua, W., & Yuan, S. (2017). Mapping the scientific research on open data: A bibliometric review. *Learned Publishing, 31(1)*. https://onlinelibrary.wiley.com/doi/abs/10.1002/leap.1110

About the author

François van Schalkwyk is a Research Fellow at the Centre for Research on Evaluation, Science and Technology (CREST), Stellenbosch University. His main research interests are in the areas of higher education studies, data, and scholarly communication. You can follow François at http://www.twitter.com/francois_fvs2.

How to cite this chapter

Van Schalkwyk, F. (2019). Open data stakeholders: Researchers. In T. Davies, S. Walker, M. Rubinstein, & F. Perini (Eds.), *The state of open data: Histories and horizons* (pp. 430–444). Cape Town and Ottawa: African Minds and International Development Research Centre. http://stateofopendata.od4d.net

This work is licensed under a Creative Commons Attribution 4.0 International (CC BY 4.0) licence. It was carried out with the aid of a grant from the International Development Research Centre, Ottawa, Canada.

Endnotes

1. Lessig, L. (2009). Against transparency. *The New Republic*, 9 October. https://newrepublic.com/article/70097/against-transparency
2. Gray, J. (2014). Towards a genealogy of open data. *SSRN*. https://papers.ssrn.com/abstract=2605828
3. Malamud, C. (2007). 8 principles of open government data. *Public.Resource.Org*, 7–8 December. https://public.resource.org/8_principles.html
4. https://clarivate.com/products/web-of-science/web-science-form/web-science-core-collection/
5. Van Schalkwyk, F. & Verhulst, S.G. (2017). The state of open data and open data research. *The social dynamics of open data*, 18 December. Cape Town: African Minds, p. 6. https://zenodo.org/record/1117807#.XEHZXc_7TX8
6. Klein, R.H., Klein, D.C.B., & Luciano, E.M. (2017). Open government data concept over time: Approaches and dimensions. *EnANPAD* 2017, São Paulo, Brazil, 1–4 October. https://www.researchgate.net/publication/320831625_Open_Government_Data_Concept_Over_Time_Approaches_and_Dimensions_EnANPAD_2017_Open_Government_Data_Concept_Over_Time_Approaches_and_Dimensions
7. Thornton, P.H., Lounsbury, M., & Ocasio, W. (2012). *The institutional logics perspective: A new approach to culture, structure and process*. Oxford: Oxford University Press.
8. Castells, M. (1996). *The information age: Economy, society and culture (Volume 1) – The rise of the network society*. Malden, MA: Wiley-Blackwell.
9. Castells, M. (2009). *Communication power*. Oxford: Oxford University Press.
10. Stalder, F. (2006). *Manuel Castells and the theory of the network society*. Cambridge: Polity Press.
11. Wagner, C.S. (2008). *The new invisible college: Science for development*. Washington, DC: The Brookings Institution; Castells, M. (2009). *Communication power*. Oxford: Oxford University Press.
12. Castells, M. (2009). *Communication power*. Oxford: Oxford University Press.
13. Van Schalkwyk, F. & Verhulst, S.G. (2017). The state of open data and open data research. *The social dynamics of open data*, 18 September. Cape Town: African Minds. https://zenodo.org/record/1117807#.XEHZXc_7TX8

14. Paul-Hus, A., Desrochers, N., & Costas, R. (2016). Characterization, description, and considerations for the use of funding acknowledgement data in Web of Science. *Scientometrics 108(1)*, 167–182. https://doi.org/10.1007/s11192-016-1953-y
15. https://webfoundation.org/research/exploring-the-emerging-impacts-of-open-data-in-developing-countries/
16. https://idatosabiertos.org/en/
17. https://www.od4d.net/publications/highlighting-developments-in-african-data-ecosystems-the-africa-data-revolution-report-2016.html
18. https://sdg.iisd.org/news/african-data-revolution-report-previewed-at-un-world-data-forum/
19. https://www.od4d.net/publications/open-data-in-europe-and-central-asia-final-technical-report-2016.html
20. https://www.od4d.net/publications/harnessing-open-data-to-achieve-development-results-final-technical-report-2016-latin-america-and-the-caribbean.html
21. http://thegovlab.org/
22. http://thegovlab.org/open-data-impact-studies/
23. http://odimpact.org/
24. http://www.opendata500.com/
25. http://www.godan.info/
26. http://www.godan.info/pages/resources-and-financing1
27. Van Schalkwyk, F. & Verhulst, S.G. (2017). The state of open data and open data research. *The social dynamics of open data*, 18 December. Cape Town: African Minds. https://zenodo.org/record/1117807#.XLv7v-gzZPY
28. Davies, T. (2014). Data standards and inclusion in the network society. *Open Data Impacts*, 18 October. http://www.opendataimpacts.net/2014/10/data-standards-and-inclusion-in-the-network-society/
29. Merton, R.K. (1973). The normative structure of science. In R.K. Merton (Ed.), *The sociology of science* (pp. 267–278). Chicago: Chicago University Press.
30. Van Schalkwyk, F. & Verhulst, S.G. (2017). The state of open data and open data research. *The social dynamics of open data*, 18 December. Cape Town: African Minds. https://zenodo.org/record/1117807#.XLv7v-gzZPY
31. https://public.resource.org/8_principles.html
32. https://opendefinition.org/ and https://blog.okfn.org/2013/10/03/defining-open-data/
33. https://docs.google.com/document/d/1z-T3QmmZTmWkFrKySi-x_EBDVqlt6Orr6z-C58gPGeg/edit#heading=h.6h4tjf2d83w4
34. https://opendatacharter.net/
35. http://opendatatoolkit.worldbank.org/en/odra.html
36. https://opendatabarometer.org/
37. http://odin.opendatawatch.com/
38. https://index.okfn.org/
39. Klein, R.H., Klein, D.C.B., & Luciano, E.M. (2017). Open government data concept over time: Approaches and dimensions. *EnANPAD 2017*, São Paulo, Brazil, 1–4 October. https://www.researchgate.net/publication/320831625_Open_Government_Data_Concept_Over_Time_Approaches_and_Dimensions_EnANPAD_2017_Open_Government_Data_Concept_Over_Time_Approaches_and_Dimensions
40. See, for example: Green, B., Cunningham, G., Ekblaw, A., Kominers, P., Linzer, A., & Crawford, S. (2017). *Open data privacy*. Berkman Klein Center for Internet & Society Research Publication. http://nrs.harvard.edu/urn-3:HUL.InstRepos:30340010; Gurin, J., Rumsey, M., Ariss, A., & Garcia, K. (2017). Protecting privacy while releasing data: Strategies to maximise benefits and mitigate risks. In F. van Schalkwyk, S. Verhulst, G. Magalhaes, J. Pane, & J. Walker (Eds.), *The social dynamics of open data*, (pp. 183–200). Cape Town: African Minds. http://doi.org/10.5281/zenodo.1117782

41 See, for example, Taylor, L. (2017). What is data justice? The case for connecting digital rights and freedoms globally. *Big Data & Society*, 1 November. https://doi.org/10.1177/2053951717736335; Heeks, R. & Renken, J, (2016). *Data justice for development: What would it mean?* Manchester: Global Development Institute (SEED). http://hummedia.manchester.ac.uk/institutes/gdi/publications/workingpapers/di/di_wp63.pdf; and Johnson, J. (2014). From open data to information justice. *Ethics and Information Technology*, 16(4), 263–274.

42 Bentley, C.M., Chib, A., & Poveda, S. (2018). A critical narrative approach to openness: The impact of open development on structural transformation. *Information Systems Journal*, 28 September. https://doi.org/10.1111/isj.12226; Van Schalkwyk, F. & Cañares, M. (2019). Open government data for inclusive development. In M.L. Smith & R.K. Seward (Eds.), (forthcoming), *Making open development inclusive*. Cambridge, MA: MIT Press. DOI: 10.13140/RG.2.2.29720.24325

43 Klein, R.H., Klein, D.C.B., & Luciano, E.M. (2017). Open government data concept over time: Approaches and dimensions. *EnANPAD 2017*, São Paulo, Brazil, 1–4 October. https://www.researchgate.net/publication/320831625_Open_Government_Data_Concept_Over_Time_Approaches_and_Dimensions_EnANPAD_2017_Open_Government_Data_Concept_Over_Time_Approaches_and_Dimensions

44 Van Schalkwyk, F. & Verhulst, S.G. (2017). The state of open data and open data research. *The Social Dynamics of Open Data*, 18 September. Cape Town: African Minds. https://zenodo.org/record/1117807#.XLv7v-gzZPY

45 Klein, R.H., Klein, D.C.B., & Luciano, E.M. (2017). Open government data concept over time: Approaches and dimensions. *EnANPAD 2017*, São Paulo, Brazil, 1–4 October. https://www.researchgate.net/publication/320831625_Open_Government_Data_Concept_Over_Time_Approaches_and_Dimensions_EnANPAD_2017_Open_Government_Data_Concept_Over_Time_Approaches_and_Dimensions

46 http://odresearch.org/

47 Examples include the ACM Web Science Conference (https://websci19.webscience.org/), Semantics (https://2018.semantics.cc/), European Semantic Web Conference (https://www.eswc-conferences.org/), International Conference on Theory and Practice of Electronic Governance (http://www.icegov.org), and International Conference on eDemocracy & eGovernment (https://edem-egov.org/). The IFIP WG 8.5 Electronic Government (EGOV), the IFIP WG 8.5 IFIP Electronic Participation (ePart), and the Conference for E-Democracy and Open Government Conference (CeDEM) are further examples that in 2018 merged into a single conference (http://depts.washington.edu/egcdep18/#/)

48 Van Schalkwyk, F. & Verhulst, S.G. (2017). The state of open data and open data research. *The social dynamics of open data*, 18 December. Cape Town: African Minds. https://zenodo.org/record/1117807#.XLv7v-gzZPY

49 See Chapter 20 (Gender equity) for more on the state of open data with regard to gender.

50 Van Schalkwyk, F. & Verhulst, S.G. (2017). The state of open data and open data research. *The social dynamics of open data*, 18 December. Cape Town: African Minds. https://zenodo.org/record/1117807#.XLv7v-gzZPY

51 Ibid.

52 Piwowar, H. (2013). Introduction altmetrics: What, why and where? *Bulletin of the American Society for Information Science and Technology*, 39, 8–9. https://doi.org/10.1002/bult.2013.1720390404

53 Klein, R.H., Klein, D.C.B., & Luciano, E.M. (2017). Open government data concept over time: Approaches and dimensions. *EnANPAD 2017*, São Paulo, Brazil, 1–4 October. https://www.researchgate.net/publication/320831625_Open_Government_Data_Concept_Over_Time_Approaches_and_Dimensions_EnANPAD_2017_Open_Government_Data_Concept_Over_Time_Approaches_and_Dimensions

54 Author's calculations based on Altmetric Explorer data.

Section 4: Open Data Around the World

CONTENTS

Introduction	446
Chapter 31. Eastern Europe and Central Asia	450
Chapter 32. European Union	465
Chapter 33. Latin America and the Caribbean	485
Chapter 34. Middle East and North Africa	503
Chapter 35. North America, Australia, and New Zealand	517
Chapter 36. South, East, and Southeast Asia	535
Chapter 37. Sub-Saharan Africa	549

The chapters in this section look at open data in different regions of the world.

How far have open data ideas and practices spread around the world over the last decade? And to what extent has open data developed differently across different countries and regions? The first of these questions has been addressed at some length. International indices, such as the Open Data Barometer,[1] the Open Data Index,[2] and Open Data Inventory,[3] have surveyed countries over a number of years, and the United Nations (UN) E-Government Survey has also included questions on open data.[4] Together, these studies indicate that open data has rapidly gained traction in upwards of 70% of UN Member Countries. However, translating the presence of portals and policies into reliable supplies of data on key topics and supporting a cultural change around government data have proven to be much more challenging. Addressing the second question requires a more qualitative approach, and that is the challenge taken up by the chapters in this section.

A note on regional clusters

Drawing regional boundaries for a qualitative review is fraught with difficulty. There are a myriad of possible approaches to clustering states based on geographic, economic, cultural, political, and linguistic factors, each with its advantages and disadvantages. In the end, our selection was influenced by the World Bank, the distribution of development sector funding, existing linkages between national open data communities, and the structure of the Open Data for Development (OD4D) network from which many of our authors for this section are drawn. As a result, we have used seven regional categories: Sub-Saharan Africa; South, East, and Southeast Asia; Eastern Europe and Central Asia; Latin America and the Caribbean; Middle East and North Africa; North America, Australia, and New Zealand; and the European Union. These cover the majority of countries in the world, although we note with some regret that we have not managed to capture the particular experience of all small island developing states and hope that future work can address this gap.

For each of the seven regions, the authors have also been free to identify subregional clusters of countries and explore both internal and cross-regional comparisons. This subregional approach is evident in the Latin America and Caribbean chapter and, to an extent, in work on Francophone and Anglophone activities in Sub-Saharan Africa and in distinctions drawn between the Western Balkan and Black Sea regions in Eastern Europe and Central Asia.

Different directions

In order to provide a contextualised view, the chapters in this section look specifically at regional histories of open data, and at the particular opportunities and challenges work has faced in each region. In Eastern Europe and Central Asia (Chapter 31), a narrative of open data for transparency and anti-corruption has provided a strong basis for advancement, while in the Middle East and

North Africa (Chapter 34), organisations have adopted a framing of "data driven innovation", playing down the political dimensions of open data in favour of a focus on economic development. For Sub-Saharan Africa (Chapter 37), strengthening links between open data and the Sustainable Development Goals has provided renewed impetus for open data activities Overall, the picture emerging from these chapters reveals that the peak of public excitement about open data appears to have passed across all regions, yet, instead of presaging the terminal decline of open data, these chapters suggest that regions have found different routes to sustain open data activity, creating distinct approaches that respond to local networks, political priorities, funding availability, and cultural ideas.

Crucially, in this section, the chapters offer insight into the extent to which open data has become truly global. Global not in terms of the spread of a "cookie-cutter concept" of government open data portals, but rather in terms of how and where leadership and innovation on open data may originate. Although many of the earliest identifiable activities in support of open data started in North America and Western Europe, these chapters illustrate that today, some of the most interesting ideas and activities can be found in Africa, Eastern Europe, Asia, or Latin America. These chapters also point out where innovation is likely to emerge over the next decade. For North America, Australia, and New Zealand (Chapter 35), opportunities lie in the use of open data as an enabler of cross-government collaboration and in strengthening a culture of data analytics. For Europe (Chapter 32), although evidence to date reflects that open data has had more impact on improving efficiency than social impact, the authors argue that the focus for the future must be on recapturing the social impact dimension of open data. Chapter 33 (Latin America and the Caribbean) points to the need for greater private sector engagement, and the chapters on South, East, and Southeast Asia (Chapter 36) and Sub-Saharan Africa (Chapter 37) both recognise that progress in high-income countries needs to expand to less-developed nations.

Alongside critical questions about whether open data should be seen as an unalloyed good as explored in the introduction to this volume, the emergence of different regional perspectives on the future of open data can also reinforce the sense of a growing open data identity crisis. When open data networks and movements were forming, being all things to all people may have been an effective strategy. But as the pressure grows on open data to perform, a lack of clarity about goals and values can create risks. Ultimately, readers may find that whether they see these chapters as illustrating the growth of a global open data movement or indicative of a fracturing and fragmenting open data landscape will depend upon their own views on how the future of open data should look. Views on whether the success of open data efforts depends on the alignment of political and cultural norms, or whether it simply requires the adoption of particular technical practices, will substantially determine that assessment.

Common experience

In spite of the different contours of open data activity from region to region, a number of common features nevertheless emerge. First, external funding has played a critical role in shaping the development of open data in most regions. Second, civil society plays a crucial role in supporting open data use, but successful civil society engagement only comes with approaches that are tailored to the region. Third, work on data journalism is making steady progress, although the wider journalistic and academic communities remain largely untapped as networks for data use. Fourth, data literacy building lags behind work on data supply everywhere, which currently acts as a major brake on realising broad benefits from open data.

In taking a regional perspective, it is possible to identify a number of funders who do not appear when looking at the global funding of open data work (see Chapter 25: Donors and investors). In the Western Balkans for example (Chapter 31: Eastern Europe and Central Asia), a number of funders have responded to the presence of technically savvy CSOs by adding open data components into new and existing programmes of activity. In Europe, substantial financial support through the European Union's Horizon 2020 programme has been instrumental in the creation of a private sector market around open data and in fostering cross-country collaborations, while a decline in core funding for civil society networking or open data capacity building has arguably led to a reduction in community activity and collaboration as groups compete for limited resources. The fear that funder interest will move on from open data is also a concern in a number of other chapters. In Asia, for example, the author notes that "New and innovative projects will not see the light of day without donor support" and that "pilot projects cannot be scaled without donor funding" (Chapter 36: South, East, and Southeast Asia, p. 545). Overall, there is little evidence, as of yet, that sustainable domestically funded financing models for realising the benefits of open data have been established at scale.

Although governments have a role to play in reshaping policies and data infrastructures to provide a reliable supply of open data, and the private sector may be a direct beneficiary of data provision, civil society appears throughout the following chapters as the real driver of open data activity and innovation. Yet, from region to region, the models of civil society engagement vary greatly. In the Middle East and North Africa (Chapter 34), and around the Black Sea (Chapter 31: Eastern Europe and Central Asia) it is universities that are hosting work on data use, acting as brokers between the state and citizens. In Sub-Saharan Africa and the Western Balkans, "startup" CSOs are accessing resources and developing new models of engagement based around open data, and, in Latin America, we see an interesting mix of new CSOs and established civil society groups blending a focus on open data into their existing agendas. Successful use of open data for social impact ultimately requires both technical know-how and domain expertise which takes time to establish.

When it comes to journalism, most regions have evolved a small number of journalistic organisations who have chosen to invest in building their data journalism capacity, often focusing on data visualisation as a means to communicate stories of interest. What is less clear, however, is how far journalists, as opposed to specialist data journalists, are drawing on open data sources in researching their stories. Similarly, while some academics have specialised in developing open data projects, we would expect that a much larger number would be using open data to support their research. Although universities appear as key actors in a number of chapters, the influence of open data on knowledge production across academic institutions is under-surveyed.

Different regions all started their work with open data with very different levels of technical capacity, as well as different levels of access to institutional delivery of education and training. However, across all regions, a continued lack of data literacy among both policy-makers and potential data users appears as a recurring challenge. In reflecting on the experiences of North

America, Australia, and New Zealand (Chapter 35), the authors suggest "[o]ne potentially underappreciated aspect of the open data story is that beyond the supply and demand for transparent government information, open data may be laying a broader foundation in the region for a more robust role for analytics and performance management in government, (p. 530)", pointing in particular to the way in which engagement with open data has encouraged government staff to develop their analytical skills. Given data literacy is not only key to engaging with open data debates, but is also critical for any organisations or individuals navigating an increasingly digital society, a key underappreciated argument for open data in future is that it promotes hands-on engagement with meaningful data. Instead of simply viewing a lack of data literacy as blocking progress on open data, open data initiatives themselves could play a pivotal role as tools of global data literacy building.

Shared futures

It is difficult to fully sum up ten years of open data in a single country, let alone a whole region. As such, the chapters that follow offer one set of perspectives on each region, acting as a starting point for further analysis. In the conclusion to this book, we will return to look at how the international exchange of ideas, new networks for collaboration, and the fragmentation of effort that results from a range of economic and cultural differences are likely to shape the future of global open data work.

Endnotes

1. https://opendatabarometer.org/
2. https://index.okfn.org/
3. https://odin.opendatawatch.com/
4. UNDESA. (2018). *United Nations E-Government Survey 2018: Gearing e-government to support transformation towards sustainable and resilient societies*. New York, NY: United Nations Department of Economic and Social Affairs. https://publicadministration.un.org/egovkb/Portals/egovkb/Documents/un/2018-Survey/E-Government%20Survey%202018_FINAL%20for%20web.pdf

031

Eastern Europe and Central Asia

Lejla Sadiku and Yaera Chung

Key points

- Initial enthusiasm for open data in Eastern Europe and Central Asia was rooted in the transparency and anti-corruption agenda, but, over time, there has been a shift in the narrative to focus on how open data may support efficiency gains, competitiveness, and innovation in the private sector.

- The majority of open data portals in the region are run by governments. Some governments, notably Ukraine, Georgia, and Moldova, have published vast amounts of data online.

- Notable success stories from the region include ProZorro, the open contracting data initiative created in Ukraine, and access to medicinal data initiatives in Serbia.

- The region has also seen civic technology organisations engage in substantial capacity-building efforts for data journalists, and, in Kosovo* and Georgia, networks of young women have been established, counterbalancing male domination of the civil technology sector. There are opportunities to build on these trends in future.

Note *: All references to Kosovo are in the context of United Nations (UN) Security Council Resolution 1244.

Introduction

The region of Eastern Europe and Central Asia has had a tumultuous recent history. Through the 1990s, the region underwent a transition from state-socialism with the formation of a number of breakaway republics. Countries and territories have had to develop or evolve new institutional, political, and economic systems to improve economic performance, while also confronting concerns about high levels of government corruption.[1] Today, the majority of countries and territories in the region are considered middle-income with the Western Balkans and Eastern Partnership countries and territories, in particular, receiving significant domestic and international investments over the last two decades and enjoying relatively high levels of digital government capacity.[2] However, a number of countries and territories in the region are also still being described as authoritarian states.[3] The region has long been at a global crossroads – at the intersection of diverse cultures, trade routes and relationships, political systems, and geopolitical influences.

Significant diversity in the degree of civil and political freedom, stages of development, and levels of economic transition, should partially explain the different degrees of uptake of open data across the region, and can help inform critical reflection about the different ways to secure further progress in the future. This context is also important to understanding how organisations have driven progress to date on open data, as well as the influence of transparency and economic development arguments for open data in the region. Although progress on open data to date has fallen short of realising all the social and economic potential that some had promised, a survey of the region reveals a picture of genuine innovation, increased focus, and strengthened regional networks.

This chapter will explore the various influences on open data in the region, providing a snapshot of distinctive features of open data in Eastern Europe and Central Asia to form a basis for a subsequent look at priority areas for development and growth of open data activities in future.

State of open data

Early movers: Enabling environments and evolving practice

Moldova was among the first lower-income countries to develop a government-led open data initiative, launching a programme in 2011 with backing from the World Bank.[4] The project was developed as a component of wider e-government reforms and was aligned with the European Union (EU) Digital Agenda focus on the "use of ICT as an enabler with the potential to maximise business development, communication, freedom of expression, innovation and economic growth".[5] Although civil society groups in the region were active in creating independent data portals around the start of the last decade, it was not until a number of years later that other governments caught up by launching official data portals. It appears, however, that the first-mover advantage was limited, as Ukraine, for example, only launched a national open data portal in 2015,[6] but now has arguably one of the most developed open data ecosystems and highest number of datasets online.[7] In Serbia, there has also been a significant increase in open data activities since 2017, both at the central and local level, suggesting open data adoption can take place at varied speeds.

Today, 53 open data portals that provide information in machine-readable formats have been identified in the Eastern Europe and Central Asia region, of which 18 are run by civic actors.[8] The list is by no means exhaustive and only covers supply-side initiatives, but it does provide an indication of the growth of open data in the region, as well as the approach taken by a number of governments now hosting distinct statistics, open data, and geodata portals. The volume of data on portals has also grown with Kazakhstan and Uzbekistan, for example, having created dynamic portals hosting 5 000 and 2 000 datasets, respectively, across a range of sectors. It is equally notable that a number of other countries and territories in the region are yet to substantively advance their engagement with open data. Kyrgyzstan, Tajikistan, Belarus, and Bosnia and Herzegovina all appear near the bottom of the 2017 Open Data Barometer rankings.[9] Open Data Readiness Assessments (ODRA) that took place in Kyrgyzstan[10] and Tajikistan[11] between 2014 and 2015 highlight some of the barriers that initiatives there may face, including competing political priorities and uncertainty about how changing international relationships might affect future open data policies and donor financing.

High-level political leadership on open data has been evident in a number of countries. In Ukraine, the national adoption of the International Open Data Charter (IODC) in 2016, as well as Charter adoption at the subnational level in five cities, has acted as a public demonstration of government commitment. In Serbia, Ana Brnabic, the Prime Minister, expressly came out to support the open data movement and even personally launched the open data portal for the government in 2017, drawing on narratives of both transparency and public sector efficiency,[12] In Kosovo, the IODC was endorsed through a Prime Ministerial declaration, although formal institutional structures to move open data forward are yet to follow.

Civil society has also played a pivotal role in the regional development of open data, although patterns of engagement vary between distinct clusters of activity in the Western Balkans and the Black Sea. For example, Western Balkans civil society engagement with open data benefits from stronger cross-country collaboration and more sustained activity with the Action SEE (South-east Europe) networks bringing together six regional organisations working on the intersection of transparency and technology.[13] Action SEE has attracted backing from other organisations, including the National Endowment for Democracy in the United States (US) and the United Kingdom (UK) Westminster Foundation for Democracy. One of the flagship products of Action SEE is the Openness Index, looking at over 640 institutions and providing over 25 000 indicators, including an assessment of open data publications.[14] The index, implemented with a network of country partner organisations and with financial support from the EU, is distinct from many other open data measurements in that it covers all branches of government, including the core executive, line ministries, parliament, local government, and the courts and prosecutors. Although only published once so far in 2017 (and so lacking longitudinal data to help track progress), data from the Index has been used to support country and institution-level advocacy on open data and to publish civil society-created roadmaps for action on government openness across government.[15]

Over the last decade, there have also been a number of key meeting points for civil society and for connecting civil society with other stakeholders. The POINT conference, for example, organised by Zasto Ne in Sarajevo, Bosnia and Herzegovina, is now in its seventh year and provides an annual gathering looking at the role of new technologies in political accountability.[16] As a community-driven event, it has regularly addressed issues related to open data. The Personal Democracy Forum for Central and Eastern Europe, an annual one-day event in Gdansk, Poland, which brings together civic actors in the intersection of media, technology, and civil society, is also now heading into its seventh year.[17] The Regional School for Public Administration (RESPA) has also provided a notable forum for discussions on open data.[18] Although civil society open data networks specific to the Black Sea region are less developed, Ministry of Data,[19] a regional open data challenge that brought together the regional civic tech community to stimulate the release of relevant datasets in 2016 and 2017 in the Western Balkans, also subsequently took place in the Black Sea region in 2018.

Across the whole region, the Open Data for Development (OD4D) network hub for Open Data in Eastern Europe and Central Asia (ODECA),[20] formed in 2015 and hosted by the United Nations Development Programme (UNDP) Istanbul Regional Hub, has provided convening and knowledge management support for overall efforts on open data. This has included work on liberating datasets, strengthening leadership among government actors, investing in data journalism, and creating platforms for collaboration between governments and members of the civic technology community.

Government support, civil society engagement, regional networking, and support from external funders and partners have all provided an enabling environment for open data. But has this led to substantive progress? By 2018, the majority of open data portals in this region are run by governments, and, with a few exceptions, the majority of national governments have some sort of open data activity underway. Some governments, notably Ukraine, Georgia, and Moldova, have published vast amounts of data online. Others, like Serbia, have taken a more phased approach in the development of their open data initiatives, which has included setting up horizontal structures and community development along with investments in government capacities. Twelve of the government open data portals available are focused on national statistics, which is especially important for the measurement of the Sustainable Development Goals. One of the reasons for this focus on national statistics may be the higher quality of statistical data as opposed to other data collected by governments. On non-statistics focused portals, budget data is the most commonly provided type of data, although other types of data considered relevant for anti-corruption[21] are not frequently available in open formats. The bulk of published data is that which can either be easily put into simple spreadsheets (like budget data or education statistics) or data that is already compiled for international financial institutions.[22] This suggests the focus is still on providing the easy-to-publish datasets, rather than identifying and meeting the demand for other meaningful data.

Overall, the state of open data in the region is diverse. Initial progress and investments in open data have brought quick wins, and some "low-hanging fruit" projects have taken shape. The majority of countries and territories in the region have, to some extent, created institutional infrastructures to deliver on open data, including portals, working groups, and policy commitments. However, enforcement has often been lagging. Portals are not frequently updated, and, without a consistent supply of support to open data communities, it has been challenging at times to maintain the commitment of the civic tech community to continue engaging with the topic. This, coupled with the perception that the impact of open data is lagging, especially as it pertains to social and economic development as well as business innovation, presents a growing threat to future development of general and broad-reaching open data ecosystems. It is in this light that renewed efforts to roll out open data at the city level and in particular sectors, such as procurement, are gaining momentum. However, to understand this fully, we need to go back and look at how the framing of open data has evolved in the region over the last decade.

E-government, open government, and economic agendas

At the start of the decade, civil society and donor enthusiasm around open data was primarily linked to the transparency and anti-corruption agenda. Governments, on the other hand, initially regarded open data as a component of e-government. A study by RESPA on the period from 2013 to 2015 describes how the emphasis among governments in the Western Balkans shifted from e-government to open government,[23] providing a period of tighter alignment between civil society and state agendas for open data and giving new impetus to projects involving both government and civil society. The development of a policy link between open data and open government was further reinforced through the Open Government Partnership (OGP) and is evident in the fact that the majority of OGP member countries in the region have also included open data commitments in their National Action Plans.[24] However, the link between e-government and open government has not gone away. For example, open data was promoted as a component of the Kyrgyzstan National e-Governance programme adopted in 2014,[25] and e-government programmes across a number of countries and territories have continued to be the key vehicle for advancing open data reforms.

Debates on open data have also been influenced by the EU. The path toward EU integration, or commitments to strengthening relationships with the EU among Eastern Partnership and Western Balkans subregions, has helped to frame early initiatives. This has also exposed the region to shifts in the open data discourse in Europe. Most recently, the Digital Agenda for the Western Balkans,[26] announced by the European Commission in June 2018 in partnership with Albania, Bosnia and Herzegovina, Kosovo, Montenegro, and the Republic of North Macedonia and Serbia, has been seen as a new opportunity to leverage the EU connection to promote open data in the region. However, the Digital Agenda approach arguably reflects more of a focus on the economic growth aspects of open data than on open government.

The emphasis on the economic value of open data, more prominent in recent years, is shaped by changing geopolitical influences and increasing disillusionment with transition processes, especially in terms of the economic gains delivered so far. Government discourse right across the region has begun to explore how open data and related frameworks can be used to deliver concrete results, including improved competitiveness and private sector innovation, alongside continued improvements to government efficiency. Fortunately, with the development of sector-specific open data initiatives, such as open contracting and work on open data in health providing a template, the focus on economic growth is not based on the naive assumption that the release of government datasets will lead automatically to innovation. Instead, the early outline of a more holistic approach with a focus on particular sectors and a range of models of support for entrepreneurial activity is evident. However, the extent to which work on economic growth-related uses of open data will compete with, or displace, resources and support for open data for open government is yet to be seen.

Open data in use: Focus and facilitation

Although the general mood among governments and funders may be one of uncertainty about whether open data is showing a return on investment, there are a growing number of open data use cases across the region that demonstrate both the potential and the quantifiable impact of open data. One of the most widely discussed[27,28] has been Ukraine's ProZorro platform (see box below),[29] which has made use of the Open Contracting Data Standard (OCDS)[30] and an improved e-Auction methodology[31] to create a more automated and transparent procurement system for the country, leading to claims of over USD 55 million in savings for government during the pilot phase alone.[32] Results for Development research costed the ProZorro project in 2017,[33] suggesting that, from inception in 2014 up until 2017, the work cost at least € 4.69 million with much of this accounted for by salaried labour and the substantial in-kind contribution of volunteers. This funding was split between three phases: set-up (26%), implementation (12%), and ongoing operation (62%), offering some indication of the kind of investment profile that might be needed to help scale open data use cases into operation.

ProZorro: Technology, business, and governance[34]

The ProZorro website describes the project as "a hybrid electronic open source government e-procurement system created as the result of a partnership between business, government and the civil society". Initiated in 2014 by a volunteer team, the project quickly built relationships with government and committed to an approach based on open standards, open source, and open data, such that the full data underlying any procurement can be accessed by anyone through an open application programming interface (API).

Understanding the importance of business buy-in to the project, its design supports a commercial ecosystem of intermediaries, allowing third-party electronic procurement marketplaces to provide a front-end onto the central ProZorro system. Getting this right has required substantial work on governance and the technical architecture.

Responsibility for running ProZorro was transferred to a state-owned enterprise in December 2015, although with co-founder, Transparency International Ukraine, maintaining a role through the creation of DoZorro, a procurement monitoring platform, combining business feedback with data from the ProZorro platform to provide scrutiny of procurement processes.

Much like the narrow procurement focus of ProZorro, many of the other civil society platforms working with open data in the region are sector specific, although with many acting more as demonstrators rather than as full-scale platforms. A major thematic focus of these projects remains on open and transparent public finance, perhaps reflecting transition concerns about problems in public financial management, though we are also witnessing the advent of a new generation of tools that respond more to the local issues and challenges that citizens face. One such example comes from Skopje, one of the most polluted cities in Europe, where citizens are using crowdsourced data combined with data from official sources to create visualisations and to empower citizens to make better data-driven decisions. AirCare app, which is the app to measure the air quality with non-verified hourly data from Serbia and the Republic of North Macedonia, has attracted more than 100 000 users, helping them to understand the level of toxicity in the air and providing relative information to support comparisons between days.[35] Open Data Kosovo's mapping of illegal rubbish dumps also ties in with this emerging environmental theme.[36]

Looking across the region, it does appear that the majority of uses of open data originate from within the civic sector rather than government with the caveat that when the public sector uses open data internally, it is not easy to detect. In general, civic users of open data can be divided into three main groups: (1) advocacy organisations and the media, (2) civic tech incubators, and (3) academia. For organisations in the first category, who are focused on specific social issues rather than on data, their direct use of open data remains limited without the facilitation of either civic tech organisations or external funders, including multilaterals. This appears to be as a result of both the high cost of procuring data analytics capacity and the limited existing capabilities of advocacy organisations to use data and digital tools. There are, however, some promising signs of media organisations building their data capacity with investigative platforms, such as KRIK in Serbia building data components into investigations and reporting.[37]

Over recent years, we have seen a mix of models used to bring together advocacy organisations with civic technology expertise in order to increase use of open data. The 2018 Open Data Hackathon in Serbia, supported by UNDP and the World Bank, used open data as a golden thread to link technologists and advocacy organisations to address issues from road safety to openness in procurement.[38] The hackathon model has become well established in a number of countries and territories, acting as a time-limited meeting point between different stakeholders to explore data and identify potential applications. On the other hand, existing civic tech organisations, such as Open Data Kosovo,[39] ForSet in Georgia (see box below), and SocialBoost in Ukraine,[40] have expanded their roles and responsibilities to focus on capacity building for data journalists and to build communities around open data, effectively becoming a new generation of civic tech incubators for open data ideas.

Georgia: ForSet[41]

ForSet was established in June 2017 in Tbilisi, Georgia with a mission of transforming data into narratives that resonate with the average citizen in Georgia. To date, the organisation has worked on four strands of work:

- Data storytelling[42] – developing stories based on data that can be shared using digital communication tools, working with the United Nations Population Fund, UNDP, and other external partners to use their data to build interesting narratives.

- Education – running programmes for journalists and civil society activists, researchers, government representatives, and students both from Georgia and the wider region.

- Technology development – using open source tools to parse and present data, including election data taken from scanned documents and political party budget data.

- Community building – providing outreach to municipalities to bring them into the open data movement and facilitating networking events.

Collaboration with academics has been particularly strong as a means of encouraging open data engagement and use in the Central Asia subregion. In Uzbekistan, for example, hackathons promoting the reuse of open data often involve collaboration with the universities in Tashkent. As of July 2018, a running poll on the open data portal of the Government of Uzbekistan shows that 23% of users draw on the data for the purpose of research (e.g. writing articles, degree programmes, and scientific works) as opposed to 14% who use data from the portal in order to create web applications.[43] It is notable, however, that across the open data field, very little evaluation has taken place of the impact of increased open data accessibility on academic knowledge production and the consequent benefits this may have for government and business.

Although as explored above, governments across the region have recently shifted their emphasis to look at how private sector innovation might unlock value from open data, we find relatively little evidence of active support to facilitate this. The global Open Data Impact Map, which captures cases of entrepreneurial open data reuse, is noticeably sparse in providing examples from the region,[44] although there are some promising cases emerging around particular datasets as documented for Serbia in the box below. While the scarcity of examples of private sector open data use cases may in part reflect a gap in systematic evidence gathering, it likely also reflects an underlying reality that, when the supply of relevant and reliable open data remains limited, businesses have not found it worth their while to engage with the open data agenda. When the gaps in official data sources cannot be filled by crowdsourced or self-generated datasets, private sector actors lack the incentives or cultural orientation needed for them to adopt business strategies based on open data.

Serbia: Improving access to medicines

In Serbia, the national Open Data Initiative is in its early stages, but 24 line ministries are already publishing their data in machine-readable formats. One example is the Agency for Medicines and Medical Devices.

Within two weeks of publishing their data on market-admissible medicines, a Slovenian company released an app allowing users to check the availability of a medicine or alternatives on the Serbian market. Another Serbian pharmaceutical company used the data to speed up internal processes, eliminating the need to exchange paper-based information with the agency.[45]

Investment in open data

External funding has been crucial to the development of open data in the region, where a diversity of funders offering a mix of small-scale and larger programmatic funding has appeared to be beneficial to the creation of an open data ecosystem.

In Western Balkans and Eastern Partnership countries and territories, for example, the investment in government-led open data has come hand-in-hand with investments in open data and the civic tech community, which has allowed for a smaller and more diverse subset of actors to continue working with open data in thematic areas. Civil society organisations (CSOs) in the region have been able to use both bilateral funding, including support from the UK, US, and UN organisations, alongside support from international foundations, including the National Democratic Institute, Richard Mott Foundation, and the Rockefeller Brothers Fund. Notably, most funders have a regional agenda and support projects where open data is one element of the effort rather than the primary objective of the project. In Central Asian countries, where large amounts of data have been published by governments, civil society engagement is less developed and there is a need for more investment particularly around engagement methods and the prioritisation of datasets in order to better realise the value of open data for society.

International donor investment has been a key driver in programmes that support evidence-based decision-making and focus on open data as a tool for transparency and anti-corruption. Much of this catalytic support has been provided by the World Bank and UNDP to conduct early ODRAs for open data, as well as to support data infrastructures (World Bank) in Moldova, Kosovo, and the Republic of North Macedonia. The Millennium Challenge Corporation (MCC) in Kosovo recently launched a group of funders who are supporting open data, in particular, through a "Dig Data" campaign to mine environmental data.[46] The director of MCC noted that the reason that they decided to reinvigorate the open data movement in Kosovo was that they see substantial potential, through work on open data, to raise awareness around specific issues and to support the government in designing policies that are evidence-based. In Ukraine, the Transparency and Accountability in Public Administration and Services (TAPAS) project, funded by the United States Agency for International Development (USAID) and UK Aid, has been one of the key forms of support for the open data movement in the country. TAPAS has supported a challenge series, leadership networks, and a country-level open data barometer.[47] In Serbia, the UK Good Governance Fund, the World Bank, the Swedish International Development Agency, and UNDP have joined forces on a "360 degree approach to open data", supporting the government to improve infrastructure, create co-creation spaces, and promote the reuse of data through collaborations with tech incubators, such as Startit, and the civil society sector.[48]

Other actors, such as international financial institutions, have also found routes to support sectoral open data initiatives. The European Bank for Reconstruction and Development (EBRD), for example, supports the implementation of the OCDS in the countries around the Black Sea. According to Eliza Niewiadomska, Senior Policy Officer at EBRD, the use of open data in public spending and procurement is contributing to freedom of enterprise and market access to the economy, as well as affecting the local markets. In Georgia, for example, Niewiadomska describes how better open data related to procurement can assist individuals in setting up and operating small businesses, noting that similar trends are visible in other countries like Moldova and Tunisia.[49]

> ### TAPAS Project Ukraine[50]
>
> The Transparency and Accountability in Public Administration and Services (TAPAS) project, funded for five years by the Eurasia Foundation with backing from the UK's Department for International Development and USAID, aims to support Ukrainian citizens and the Government of Ukraine in reducing or eliminating corruption in key public administration functions and services.[51] Eurasia Foundation describes how "Ukraine's Revolution of Dignity transformed the executive and legislative branches of government in 2014. Since then, the Government of Ukraine has prioritised increasing public sector transparency and accountability through eGovernance reforms, including eProcurement, Open Data, and eServices."
>
> eProcurement, Open Data, and eServices form the three components of the TAPAS programme. It seeks to support all central ministries and at least 35 municipalities with populations greater than 100 000 to publish open data regularly and to organise a series of seminars and workshops for open data managers, establishing a more reliable supply of open data and unlocking the full economic potential of open data for the country.

Looking ahead: Areas for growth

What does the future hold for open data work in Eastern Europe and Central Asia? The development and impact of open data in this region have unfolded incrementally and have been difficult to capture. According to the Open Data Barometer, while the readiness of governments in the region is high for opening data, implementation is often seen as lagging behind and evidence of impact is almost non-existent.[52] This feeds into a common feeling that the full breadth of transformative political, social, and economic results expected or anticipated at the advent of the open data movement has not materialised. However, digging deeper into the trends in the region indicates that international measurements of the impact of open data do not adequately capture the tangible examples which are, in fact, affecting people's lives on a day-to-day basis and have led to improved efficiencies in government. Given the capacity built over the last decade and the groundwork laid, there are real opportunities to move beyond the hype to embed open data approaches in public problem solving.

However, to get there, several challenges will need to be overcome, such as addressing data supply and government capacity, creating an inclusive community of data use, and improving collaboration with the private sector.

First, the production of high-quality open data remains an issue. The administrative data generated by government institutions continues, to a large extent, to be collected on a paper basis. Not only does this create inefficiencies in the system, but it also limits the potential for collaboration and complex problem-solving between different departments and the potential for engagement with businesses and civil society. With the advent of artificial intelligence, where the ability to deliver on high-tech solutions is contingent upon access to good quality data, weaknesses in data production become ever more important to address.

Second, in spite of high-level commitments to open data, the capacity of institutions to proactively publish relevant data also remains limited. While general technical capacity in the region is strong, governments are strained to supply the human and financial resources needed to capitalise on the potential of open data. The reasons for this are structural and institutional. IT departments are underpaid compared to market salaries, and making sure that data is fit to publish is not envisioned as a core task for civil servants. Additional capacities have not been put in place to support the political and open government commitments around open data. The majority of governments do not have internal protocols in place for open data, in stark contrast to the way in which other policy areas, including, for example, freedom of information legislation has been implemented. Engagement processes have also not been put in place to support two-way dialogues with communities of interest and citizens to identify the most relevant datasets and support the reuse of data. Addressing these gaps needs action by individual governments, support for governments to share best-fit practices from regional institutions, and external work to track the pace of reforms in order to support monitoring, learning, and adaptation.

Third, the open data movement in the region needs to be more inclusive. Open data activity has generally favoured issues and development activities in urban environments, while it has been less effective in enabling broad usage and engaging people. Civic tech communities have been structured around urban centres and many of the applications based on open data have been focused on governance-related issues, catering to a subset of interest groups. Furthermore, women continue to be underrepresented in the open data sector. Broad networks of young women in Kosovo and Georgia, in particular, have counterbalanced, at least partially, the male domination of technology sectors, including of civic tech, providing a model for others to follow. However, inclusion of women in the design and development of tools to address different issues is key in ensuring that gender dimensions are integrated across solutions, rather than limited to areas that are typically considered to be women's issues, such as gender-based violence and harassment.

Lastly, collaboration with, and open data use by, the private sector is still very limited. This is due primarily to three factors: insufficient government capacity to engage, limited donor strategies, and a lack of clear business models for open data engagement. Nevertheless, a study for Ukraine has quantified the economic impact of open data, directly and indirectly, at USD 700 million up to April 2018 with the potential to reach USD 1.4 billion by 2025, demonstrating the importance of improving private sector strategies.[53] The evidence base regarding interventions that can successfully engage the private sector is less developed than it should be. However, with the proliferation of use cases based on open contracting, more evidence on the related economic benefits should become available, providing potential routes to engaging more businesses with the wider open data agenda. Critical research will be needed to understand the transferability of impacts from one sector to another (e.g. from procurement to transport or medicine).

Conclusion

Open data has entered the repertoire of civil society and governments in Eastern Europe and Central Asia at an interesting point in time. Newer CSOs have embraced the strategic use of open data, responding to funders and global movements, but are also looking to link open data to pressing local issues. Governments, if not fast to adapt, have at least recognised that open data should be part of future strategies. Fully embedding the principles, values, and skills needed to make the most of open data will be the task of the next decade.

> ### Further reading
>
> Kassen, M. (2017). Open data in Kazakhstan: Incentives, implementation and challenges. *Information Technology & People, 30(2)*, 301–323. https://www.emeraldinsight.com/doi/abs/10.1108/ITP-10-2015-0243
>
> Rahmentulla, H., Tisacova, I., Jhalla, K., Custer, S., Gigler, B., & Brigham, C. (2012). *The journey of open government and open data in Moldova.* Washington, DC: Open Development Technology Alliance. https://www.researchgate.net/publication/318726993_The_Journey_of_Open_Government_Open_Data_in_Moldova?channel=doi&linkId=597a58c9a6fdcc61bb09dc64&showFulltext=true
>
> Web Foundation. (2017). *Open Data Barometer* (4th edition) – *Regional snapshot for East Europe and Central Asia.* Washington, DC: World Wide Web Foundation and Open Data in Eastern Europe and Central Asia (ODECA). https://opendatabarometer.org/4thedition/regional-snapshot/east-europe-central-asia/

About the authors

Lejla Sadiku is the Governance and Innovations Specialist at the UNDP Regional Bureau for Europe and Central Asia, where she has led work on open data, including the development of the OD4D regional hub, ODECA. You can follow Lejla at https://twitter.com/LejlaSadiku.

Yaera Chung is a consultant on Innovations for Data and Civic Engagement within the Open Government and Accountable Institutions team at the UNDP in Turkey. She has a Master's in Public Administration from Columbia University and has worked with World Vision and the World Bank.

How to cite this chapter

Sadiku, L. & Chung, Y. (2019). Open data around the world: Eastern Europe and Central Asia. In T. Davies, S. Walker, M. Rubinstein, & F. Perini (Eds.), *The state of open data: Histories and horizons* (pp. 450–464). Cape Town and Ottawa: African Minds and International Development Research Centre. http://stateofopendata.od4d.net

This work is licensed under a Creative Commons Attribution 4.0 International (CC BY 4.0) licence. It was carried out with the aid of a grant from the International Development Research Centre, Ottawa, Canada.

Endnotes

1. World Bank. (2011). *Trends in corruption and regulatory burden in Eastern Europe and Central Asia*. Washington, DC: World Bank. http://elibrary.worldbank.org/doi/book/10.1596/978-0-8213-8671-2
2. UNDESA. (2019). *United Nations e-government survey 2018: Gearing e-government to support transformation towards sustainable and resilient societies*. New York, NY: United Nations Department of Economic and Social Affairs. https://publicadministration.un.org/egovkb/Portals/egovkb/Documents/un/2018-Survey/E-Government%20Survey%202018_FINAL%20for%20web.pdf
3. Freedom House. (2019). *Freedom in the world 2017 – Populists and autocrats: The dual threat to global democracy*. Washington, DC: Freedom House. https://freedomhouse.org/sites/default/files/FH_FIW_2017_Report_Final.pdf
4. Rahmentulla, H., Tisacova, I., Jhalla, K., Custer, S., Gigler, B., & Brigham, C. (2012). *The journey of open government & open data in Moldova*. Washington, DC: Open Development Technology Alliance. https://www.researchgate.net/publication/318726993_The_Journey_of_Open_Government_Open_Data_in_Moldova
5. Ibid.
6. Anon. (2019). Ukraine's government opens over 300 datasets for citizens. *UNDP in Ukraine*, 12 November. http://www.ua.undp.org/content/ukraine/en/home/presscenter/articles/2015/11/12/ukraine-s-government-opens-over-300-datasets-for-citizens.html
7. Maddison, J. (2018). How Ukraine became an open data pioneer. *Overseas Development Institute*, 17 December. https://theodi.org/article/how-ukraine-became-an-open-data-pioneer/
8. Authors' research. Available in the online version of this chapter.
9. Web Foundation. (2017). *Open Data Barometer – Global report*. 4th edition. Washington, DC: World Wide Web Foundation. https://opendatabarometer.org/4thedition/report/
10. Zijlstra, A. (2015). *Open data readiness assessment for Kyrgyzstan*. Washington, DC: World Bank. https://www.slideshare.net/TheGreenLand/open-data-readiness-assessment-for-kyrgyzstan
11. Atoev, A. & Kosimov, R. (2015). *Open data readiness assessment Tajikistan*. Washington, DC: World Bank and Open Knowledge International. https://web.archive.org/web/20161017073358/http://ispa.tj/wp-content/uploads/2015/09/En_ODRATajikistan_20151.pdf
12. Anon. (2017). Startovao nacionalni portal otvorenih podataka: Manje korupcije i efikasnija javna uprava [The national open data portal started: Less corruption and more efficient public administration]. *Blic.Rs*, 12 October. https://www.blic.rs/biznis/startovao-nacionalni-portal-otvorenih-podataka-manje-korupcije-i-efikasnija-javna/ls0qq5t
13. https://actionsee.org/
14. https://opennessindex.actionsee.org/
15. https://opennessindex.actionsee.org/research-findings

16 https://point.zastone.ba/
17 https://pdfcee.pl/en/
18 https://www.respaweb.eu/
19 https://www.ministryofdata.info/
20 http://www.odecanet.org/
21 Garcia Aceves, R. (2018). *Open up guide: Using open data to combat corruption*. Open Data Charter. https://open-data-charter.gitbook.io/open-up-guide-using-open-data-to-combat-corruption/
22 Authors' own research. See the online version of this chapter.
23 Millard, J. & Thomasen, L. (2015). *E-government analysis: From e- to open government*. Danilovgrad, Montenegro: Regional School of Public Administration. https://www.respaweb.eu/download/doc/eGov+-+From+E-Government+to+Open+Government.pdf/d3ab1cd43fa4cd3071be9cea7e4b0cd3.pdf
24 Including Albania, Armenia, Azerbaijan, Georgia, Kyrgyzstan, Montenegro, Moldova, Serbia, the Republic of North Macedonia, and Ukraine.
25 Zijlstra, A. (2015). *Open data readiness assessment for Kyrgyzstan*. Washington, DC: World Bank. https://www.slideshare.net/TheGreenLand/open-data-readiness-assessment-for-kyrgyzstan
26 European Commission. (2018). European Commission launches digital agenda for the Western Balkans. http://europa.eu/rapid/press-release_IP-18-4242_en.htm
27 Open Contracting Partnership. (2016). Everyone sees everything. *Open Contracting Stories*, 28 November. https://medium.com/open-contracting-stories/everyone-sees-everything-fa6df0d00335
28 Manthorpe, R. (2018). From the fires of revolution, Ukraine is reinventing government. *Wired UK*, 20 August. https://www.wired.co.uk/article/ukraine-revolution-government-procurement
29 https://prozorro.gov.ua/
30 http://standard.open-contracting.org
31 Chmel, O. (2018). Prozorro e-auctions: Savings on public procurement of medicines in Ukraine. Thesis submitted for Master's in Economic Analysis, Kyiv School of Economics, Kyiv, Ukraine.
32 Bugay, Y. (2016). Ukranian Reform Success: ProZorro public procurement system is landmark victory for anti-corruption crusaders. *Business Ukraine*, 31 August. http://bunews.com.ua/politics/item/ukrainian-reform-success-prozorro-public-procurement-system-is-landmark-victory-for-anti-corruption-crusaders
33 Vissapragada, P. (2017). *Costing the ProZorro e-procurement program*. Washington, DC: Results for Development. https://www.r4d.org/wp-content/uploads/R4D_OG-ProZorro-CS_web.pdf
34 Kyiv School of Economics. (2017). Co-creation of ProZorro: An account of the process and actors. *Transparency International*, 4 April. https://www.transparency.org/whatwedo/publication/co_creation_of_prozorro_an_account_of_the_process_and_actors
35 https://getaircare.com/
36 http://www.odecanet.org/projects/od4environment/
37 KRIK. (2017). KRIK wins global data journalism award. *KRIK*, 22 June. https://www.krik.rs/en/krik-wins-global-data-journalism-award/
38 UNDP Serbia. (2018). The first Open Data Week in Serbia. United Nations Development Programme. http://www.rs.undp.org/content/serbia/en/home/presscenter/articles/2018/open-data-week-organized-for-the-first-time-in-serbia.html
39 http://opendatakosovo.org/
40 http://socialboost.com.ua/
41 https://forset.ge/
42 https://stories.forset.ge/
43 O'zbekiston Respublikasi Ochiq Ma'lumotlar Portali [Open Data Portal of the Republic of Uzbekistan]. (2018). *Data.Gov.Uz*. https://data.gov.uz/uz
44 http://opendataimpactmap.org/map.html

45 Gurin, J. (n.d.). *Open data for business tool: Enabling the private sector's use of government data for economic growth*. Washington, DC: Centre for Open Data Enterprise (CODE). http://reports.opendataenterprise.org/OD4BSummary.pdf
46 https://millenniumkosovo.org/transparent_gov/dig-data/
47 http://tapas.org.ua/en/
48 http://www.rs.undp.org/content/serbia/en/home/projects/opendata.html
49 Interview with Eliza Niewiadomska of EBRD, May 2018.
50 http://tapas.org.ua/
51 http://www.eurasia.org/Programs/ukraine_TAPAS
52 Web Foundation (2017). *Open Data Barometer* (4th edition) – *Regional snapshot for East Europe and Central Asia*. Washington, DC: World Wide Web Foundation and Open Data in Eastern Europe and Central Asia (ODECA). https://opendatabarometer.org/4thedition/regional-snapshot/east-europe-central-asia/
53 Kovalchuk, A., Khanzhyn, V., & Kudlatskiy, Y. (2018). *Economic potential of open data for Ukraine*. Kyiv: Transparency and Accountability in Public Administration and Services. https://drive.google.com/file/d/1PIg2AKrzx52b-ERjxLdQEgrV7wA7UzSk/view

032

European Union

Rufus Pollock and Danny Lämmerhirt

Key points

- European Union (EU) member countries have played a leading role in setting the open data agenda with governments pioneering open data policies, licences, and practices in Europe and globally.

- Building on existing public sector information (PSI) policies, significant work has been undertaken related to creating a "digital single market" (DSM); however, open data maturity still varies substantially among countries.

- A number of European governments and the EU have been major funders of open data initiatives, seeking to improve government practices, increase the accessibility and use of government data, and stimulate private sector engagement with open data.

- Basic open government data practices are reasonably embedded in the EU, but with other data-related policy agendas gaining attention (e.g. data protection), and volunteer advocacy in need of new energy, there are threats to the sustainability and progress of open data that will need to be addressed.

Introduction

The history of open data in the European Union (EU) began in the late 1990s and early 2000s. It was at that time that a public sector information (PSI) reuse policy space[1] established the groundwork for more public debate around open data and laid the foundations for key legislative tools in Europe, such as the PSI Directives. Debates at the time revolved around copyright, licensing, pricing, marginal cost recovery, and the political economy of information, as well as the role of citizens and private business in using government data to innovate, especially with respect to government services. Some of the questions at stake included whether government should have a monopoly on data? or should "lean government"[2] provide data to the public to stimulate economic growth? At the time, this idea of lean government overlapped with other ideas around government reform, such as "government 2.0" or "government as a platform", a term originally coined by Tim O'Reilly and later adopted by European policy-makers (still present in French open data strategies).[3]

Although the PSI Directives coexist with other open data policies developed at the national and local level, and individual countries have promoted their own open data principles framed in terms of transparency and accountability, the EU focus on creating a digital single market (DSM) cannot be ignored when seeking to understand the current state of open data in the region. The DSM strategy seeks to enhance the digital economy through cross-country data exchange, envisaging that the reuse of PSI should enable fair market competition. Debates around fair access to PSI and the role of reusable PSI for competitiveness and economic growth overlap to some extent with later open data agendas and policies; however, they also differ because PSI encompasses data and other sources of PSI, such as cultural works. For this reason, this chapter looks in depth at the role of the EU in shaping open data debates.

European countries have been the source of a number of pioneering open data initiatives from the United Kingdom's (UK) leadership on opening beneficial ownership data to the Government of France's introduction of policies directing public sector bodies to retain access to data created as a result of public–private partnerships. Key innovations, such as the CKAN data catalogue software, and organisations, such as Open Knowledge International (OKI) and the Open Data Institute (ODI), originated in Europe and have spread across the globe. However, it is also important to recognise that Europe's policy space developed in parallel with, but was influenced by, legal and policy work in the United States (US).[4] For instance, decisions in American copyright law influenced the European Database Directive, a key legal feature that influenced open licensing around the world.[5] Likewise, Gray suggests that the boom of the geospatial data community in the US supported the development of the INSPIRE Directive.[6]

This chapter will start by addressing EU regulations influencing open data before exploring the state of open data infrastructure across the continent and then looking at the ecosystem of actors who have influenced open data development both within the region and around the world.

The European Union as regulator

The Public Sector Information Directive

One key feature of the EU is the directive on the reuse of PSI, also known as the "PSI Directive". This landmark legislation paved the way for Europe's open data policies, even though its first version did not refer directly to the term open data.[7] Also noteworthy are the rules on reuse of the European Commission's own data.[8] The Commission states that "the directive on the re-use of PSI provides a common legal framework for a European market for government-held data (public sector information). It is built around two key pillars of the internal market: transparency and fair competition."[9]

First ratified in 2003, the PSI Directive established a minimum set of rules governing the reuse of PSI. This included PSI at large, covering the "material held by public sector bodies in the member states, at national, regional and local levels, such as ministries, state agencies, municipalities, as well as organisations funded for the most part by or under the control of public authorities (e.g. meteorological institutes)".[10] With recent work on revisions to the directive, some have argued that the directive should be extended further to also cover educational and research institutions.[11] EU member states implement the PSI Directive through different legal tools; some of them ratify specific legislation, others embed the directive in existing access to PSI laws, and some countries use a mix of both approaches.[12] Notably, Belgium developed individual policies for federal and regional levels, while other states issued policies only at the federal level.

Originally only a recommendation, the PSI Directive was revised in 2013 to become an obligation for member states "to make all documents re-usable unless access is restricted or excluded under national rules on access to documents".[13] This revision should harmonise rules and practices among EU member states. The PSI Directive still leaves flexibility around its implementation, allowing governments to define their own access to document regimes. It is recommended, but not required, that members determine marginal cost recovery regimes for public information, and they are encouraged to use open licences (the effect that this has on open data is discussed further below). In 2013, the directive was also expanded to cover content held by museums, libraries, and archives.

Like every EU directive, the impact of the PSI Directive is assessed at regular intervals. At the time of writing, the PSI Directive is currently undergoing a review that started in 2017. The new revised PSI Directive has not yet been agreed upon, but it is anticipated that several new aspects will be ratified, including:

- **An expansion in scope.** The new PSI Directive covers data from "public undertakings" (such as government-owned companies), legislative and judiciary government branches, and publicly funded research, although none of these data holders are explicitly obliged to proactively publish data.
- **Publication of high-value datasets** with a list of specific high-value datasets to be determined in future legal legislation, referred to as "delegated acts".
- **Limitation of protection via database rights** such that governments will no longer be able to protect data based on database rights, modifying an important aspect of EU law (see below).
- **Provisions to cover real-time access to data.**
- **Curtailing exclusive arrangements** between public and private stakeholders by mandating that governments disclose these arrangements.

However, issues persist. For example, the European Commission has debated what should count as high-value datasets, and some policy-makers considered databases, such as company registers, to be exempt.[14] There are also no public routes to provide input into the designation of high-value datasets. They are likely to be determined by expert groups only. This may raise issues regarding how "high-value" is determined and how diverging values (e.g. economic and social values) will be weighed against each other.

Some voting committees in the European Commission have also sought to change the new PSI Directive by excluding public undertakings as a source of open data, and it is questionable to what extent data from public service providers will be made open in the future. Past shifts in public ownership through public–private partnerships, public sector liberalisation, and the privatisation of key public sector activities, such as the British Royal Mail, have prevented key data from being opened up. This raises questions as to how well existing open data laws can ensure the release of key data for the public's benefit. France has addressed these issues since 2016 with its "données d'intérêt général" (data of public interest) policy,[15] which contains a clause to enable public sector bodies to demand the provision of data collected from companies that provide public services, such as waste management or transport firms. The ODI has developed a policy guideline on how procurement contracts may include open licensing provisions in order to ensure that key data continues to be available to the public, although there are no numbers on how many contracts contain such clauses.[16]

INSPIRE Directive

The introduction in 2007 of the INSPIRE Directive was another key landmark policy for EU member states. This directive sets minimum conditions for interoperable sharing of spatial data across EU member states and their geospatial communities. The INSPIRE Directive is part of a larger European Interoperability Framework and the e-Government Action Plan that contributes to the DSM.

The Directive is focused on the spatial information infrastructures of the 28 member states of the EU. To enhance interoperability, it requires member states to adopt several measures from data specifications and metadata to data sharing and monitoring requirements. The directive also covers 34 spatial data themes that are relevant for different environmental applications.[17]

The INSPIRE Directive must be fully implemented by all member states by 2021, including requirements to increase sharing services, structure and enhance data, and apply conducive licensing terms. The directive has led to the creation of the INSPIRE Geoportal,[18] a central access point for searching, viewing, and downloading spatial data.

Implementation at the member state level has been mixed. According to a recent status report, national action plans have provided momentum in member states.[19] Many states provided plans for the period 2016–2020 to tackle persistent implementation issues. According to the report, member states need to improve data sharing; strengthen national use cases of spatial data; enhance the management of spatial data, including the identification of spatial datasets; improve access to data; and align spatial data with common data models prescribed by the directive. In particular, spatial data is seen to be underused. The status report suggests that spatial data could be more strongly aligned with other e-government initiatives across Europe.

The Digital Single Market strategy

The DSM is the European Commission's strategy "to ensure access to online activities for individuals and businesses under conditions of fair competition, consumer and data protection, removing geo-blocking and copyright issues".[20] More concretely, the strategy seeks to improve access for consumers and businesses to digital goods and services across Europe, to create the right conditions for digital networks and services, and to grow the digital economy.

Adopted on 6 May 2015, the strategy includes 16 initiatives which were delivered by the Commission by January 2017. The evolution and progress of the DSM strategy can be assessed according to how these initiatives were developed. Achievements under the strategy include the ratification of the General Data Protection Regulations (GDPR). Other legislative frameworks introduced in this chapter also contribute to the DSM. For instance, the PSI Directive creates a common data space in the EU and regulates common access conditions for PSI. The copyright reform (ongoing at the time of writing) may also be a key anchor point for the DSM.

A mid-term review of the strategy in 2017 stressed that Digital Public Services were key to further advancing the strategy.[21] While the focus is on e-government and open data is not mentioned specifically, open government data programmes are likely to play an important role given their close links to other progressive ideas, such as "Government 2.0" and "government as a platform".

The role of the EU as a funder

The EU plays an important role in funding research and innovation programmes through its Horizon 2020 financial programme. The European Commission publishes the names of the projects that receive funding through the CORDIS database.[22] A query of the CORDIS database, using open data to understand the nature of EU funding of open data research under Horizon 2020, produced a result of 63 projects. Based on query results, € 223 million has been spent on the following topics and applications:

- **Mobility:** Open data protocols to be used for smart mobility.
- **Energy:** Heating and energy management with open data as one enabling component.
- **Pollution:** Publication and use of open air pollution data.
- **Agriculture:** Open data input into agricultural services.
- **Research:** Open science and citizen science, using open data as one component to exchange information across researchers (e.g. one project used open data sources to map political concerns of citizens).
- **Utilities:** Open data for water management.
- **Geo-data:** Open geospatial and earth observation data.
- **Health:** Gathering and publishing open health data and open data on clinical trials.
- **Business models:** Using open data as an enabler for business.
- **Digital humanities:** Digitising text and making it available and processable as open data.
- **Housing:** Developing an infrastructure for open and closed housing data.
- **Innovation:** Open data for public service innovation.
- **Open data:** Capacity building around open data for researchers, open data for smarter decision-making, and research on open data's contribution to the economy.

For many of these projects, only a small share of the funding focused directly on open data per se. For most projects identified, open data plays an enabling role or is a planned project outcome. This suggests, however, that a substantial number of European projects can, or might, put open data and existing open data infrastructures and frameworks to use.

Implementing PSI in national open data policies

Since 2010, open data has become a topic of national debates with member states commissioning studies and white papers, issuing decrees and executive orders, developing national open data strategies and policies, and ratifying laws to act upon new commitments to open up data. The latest report on Open Data Maturity in Europe[23] states that governments have significantly invested in developing open data policies with 27 out of 28 EU member states now having a national open data policy. Twenty of these countries have stated that their policies are more ambitious than the PSI Directive by going beyond the passive availability of data on request by proactively publishing data and making it reusable, as well as by supporting training, awareness raising, and engagement activities.[24] Motivations to develop open data policies range from enabling citizens to exert more power over the state and hold wasteful government to account to creating opportunities for small and medium-sized enterprises (SMEs), enhancing the efficiency of government, allowing for better access to government information, and making more effective use of new technologies in the public sector. This is distinct from the PSI Directive's focus on fair conditions to access PSI and the creation of an EU-internal digital market. Yet, challenges remain. The PSI Directive has to be embedded in federal and regional legislation, requiring multiple legislative documents to open up data. A particularly complex case is the UK, where, for example, the complex administrative devolution requires the development of a unique open data policy for Northern Ireland's administrative bodies and parliament.[25] Governments have started responding to this complexity by developing harmonisation agencies (e.g. Belgium's l'Agence pour la Simplification Administrative[26]), and several cities have promoted coordination with national data portals.[27]

The state of open data in the United Kingdom

The UK played a key role in promoting open data by launching the data.gov.uk portal in February 2010, listing over 42 000 datasets to date. In 2010, Conservative Party leader David Cameron made open data a part of his electoral campaign and pledged that his government would publish an "unprecedented amount of government data". As Prime Minister, he spearheaded initiatives such as the publication of the world's first open beneficial ownership register in 2016.[28]

While the UK has continuously performed well in international open data rankings, challenges still remain. Open data lost most of its momentum in late 2015 as government attention turned to the Brexit referendum and later to Brexit negotiations. Many open data advisory bodies ceased to exist or merged with others. For example, the Public Sector Transparency Board became part of the Data Steering Group in November 2015, and the Open Data User Group discontinued its activities entirely in 2015.[29] There have also been political attempts to limit the Freedom of Information Act (FOIA) based on the argument that opening up government data would be an adequate substitute.[30,31] There are still issues around publishing land ownership information across all regions, and some valuable datasets have been transferred out of government ownership avoiding publication, such as the Postal Address File that was sold off during the privatisation of the Royal Mail.[32]

Open licensing

Within existing legal and policy frameworks, most European countries publish at least some key datasets under open licences. However, Europe's open licensing landscape is fragmented, with several bespoke licences adopted by governments. Critics argue that this "licence proliferation" can increase legal uncertainty and complexity.[33] It may also cause incompatibilities with other open licences and create data use silos. The result would be an incompatible licensing system based on many individual contractual terms that may jeopardise the efforts of the European DSM strategy, prevent the free flow of public sector information, and impede the growth of data economies.

No systematic study has explored the exact extent of this problem, but there are some indications of emerging issues. The European Open Data Portal indicates that there could be up to 90 different licences currently used by national, regional, or municipal governments (although the real number may be lower when cases of the same license under different titles are taken into account). Another report commissioned by the EU suggests that small changes and variations between European bespoke open government licences can cause them to be incompatible.[34]

Database rights: A European legal phenomenon

European legislation has had significant impact on the development of open licences in Europe and worldwide. This is due to a key legislative text called the EU Database Directive.[35] It is a "database right" which protects investments made to build a database. This stands in stark contrast to the situation in regions like North America, where database records or the database structure needs to include works of creative authorship to be protected by copyright. Between 2009 and 2010, the Open Data Commons created global licences to address database rights, including the Open Database Licence 1.0 (ODbL) and Open Data Commons Attribution Licence 1.0 (ODC-BY).[36] Creative Commons updated its Creative Commons Attribution (CC-BY) and Creative Commons Attribution Share-Alike (CC-BY-SA) licences to the worldwide version 4.0 to explicitly address database rights globally.[37]

In order to govern, control, and harmonise the adoption of open licences, the EU and its member states have developed several approaches using policy, as well as governance and educational frameworks. At the EU level, the Legal Aspects of Public Sector Information (LAPSI) project, co-financed by the EU, is noteworthy, containing recommendations around the reuse of public sector data in Europe.[38] Tools such as the European Data Portal's Licensing Assistant also help governments to identify compatible licences.[39]

It should be mentioned that the PSI Directive does not require the use of standard open licences, such as Creative Commons licences, which would help further harmonise licensing regimes. National licence regimes are governed by different policy tools (laws, policies, decrees, and executive orders) and other soft policy mechanisms (see box on National governance below). However, some national governments, including Germany and Italy, have updated their bespoke licences to ensure compatibility with the Open Definition and standard open licences.

Some public sector bodies may have business models that make them opt out of using open licences. This is supported by the PSI Directive which allows public sector bodies to charge fees for data reuse at higher than marginal costs (although fees must be limited to the costs of reproduction, provision, and dissemination). Examples of datasets available for a fee include the company register in the Netherlands or land registration data in the UK. In other cases, opening up data is controversially discussed under competition law. One such example comes from Germany concerning the release of open weather data under the "Verordnung zur Festlegung der Nutzungsbestimmungen für die Bereitstellung von Geodaten des Bundes" (GeoNutzV).[40] The case suggests the potential emergence of country-specific data markets, with business associations, sometimes successfully, pushing against open data in order to maintain information oligopolies.

> ### National governance of open licences: The cases of Belgium and the United Kingdom
>
> To harmonise the open licenses used, Belgium has developed open data policies at the federal and regional levels. As part of this work, the government has appointed a committee to support agencies in making better licensing choices through a "comply-or-explain" approach. Belgian open data policies define standard open licences (CC0 and CC-BY 4.0) that are recommended for use by agencies. If an agency still wishes to use a bespoke licence, it must send a justification to the committee, which will review the justification to understand whether a bespoke licence is necessary or not.
>
> The UK has developed several mechanisms to ensure a widespread uptake of its Open Government Licence (OGL). The British government initially faced an issue with its OGL since Crown Copyright only applies to government agencies which have Crown status. This means that public sector bodies without Crown status were not able to use the OGL. Open Government Licences 2.0 and 3.0 address this issue by being applicable to rights beyond Crown Copyright. In order to help government agencies, the British government has also developed a licensing framework, providing educational and training resources for government agencies to help ensure harmonisation of licensing practices.

The unfolding impact of the General Data Protection Regulation

In May 2017, the EU ratified the GDPR.[41] This is a broad data policy spanning topics from consent and privacy by design through to an individual's rights over information about them, the lawfulness of personal data processing, and the rights and responsibilities of data controllers and data processors.

The advent of the GDPR has sparked several discussions about its potential impact on open data. The GDPR requires any processor to have a legal basis to process personal data, primarily, but not only, by gathering consent. This has prompted questions about the reusability of open data containing personal data, such as company registers or public contracting data that may include names of company directors or the disaggregated salary figures of civil servants that may be considered personal data.[42] The EU has stated that personal data, once anonymised, can be published for reuse as open data since anonymised data falls outside the scope of the GDPR.[43] Others argue, however, that, in particular, non-anonymised names in public registers are of substantial public value, including for anti-corruption purposes.

Anonymisation has proven a challenging concept for open data derived from, or relating to, personal data, particularly given it may be possible in some cases to re-identify people by linking several otherwise impersonal datasets.[44] Current open data licensing frameworks that prohibit discrimination against any particular use of data are not equipped to restrict privacy-affecting data reuse. There have also been arguments from the open research data community to suggest that the GDPR has set the standard of consent required for data processing too high and that, in the case of specific research purposes, a lower standard of consent should be set.[45]

The EU has stated that the PSI Directive is compliant with the GDPR and suggests that public sector bodies conduct a triple assessment to determine if personal data can be published. This includes determining if datasets contain personal data, identifying whether national access regimes restrict access to the PSI, and ensuring that PSI containing personal data can only be processed in compliance with data protection law. The GDPR also requires purpose limitation, which can cause problems with open licence terms. Purpose limitation means that personal data cannot be used for purposes other than the one for which the data was originally collected, whereas open licensing terms encourage any lawful use purpose. As of late 2018, these tensions remain unresolved with some institutions arguing for experimentation with different decision-making and data governance approaches.[46] We anticipate that the outcome of these debates could significantly impact the discourse as to whether privacy protection outweighs the public benefits of publishing data openly in cases where the names of natural persons are relevant for particular purposes, such as fighting corruption. This discussion will be particularly interesting with regard to high-value datasets as some datasets are argued to be high-value if they are highly disaggregated and able to link monetary transactions to individuals (e.g. spending records or beneficial ownership data).

European open data infrastructure

Beyond legal considerations, the establishment of an open, usable, and interoperable data infrastructure has been key to the development of open data in Europe. A data infrastructure includes data portals, registries, and websites, data files that meet standard formats, as well as the organisational skills and work routines that surround them.

A number of governments have linked their open data programmes to the creation of unified reference databases and registers. For example, Denmark's Danish Data Program has integrated formerly dispersed address registers, responding to the need to restructure data, as well as to share it, in order to break down departmental silos.[47] Like PSI, the concept of National Information Infrastructures pre-dates open data, but open data agendas have helped widen engagement with the task of creating such infrastructures, as well as creating space for a wider number of stakeholders to get involved.[48,49]

The most direct element of data infrastructure created by open data agendas, however, has been the data catalogue. By 2016, all EU member states had established national data catalogues, providing central access points for government data. Via web forms or application programming interfaces (APIs), government agencies can upload data to these catalogues which index their metadata, making them searchable. The European Data Portal aggregates data from many national portals to provide Europe-wide search capacity.[50]

In order to support this kind of information exchange across governments, a shared vocabulary was necessary. The DCAT Application Profile (DCAT-AP), a Resource Description Framework (RDF) vocabulary designed to facilitate interoperability between data catalogues was developed as a common metadata standard for describing public sector datasets in Europe. It is not only used by national portals, but some city ones as well. In 2017, only Denmark, Estonia, Hungary, Lithuania, Malta, and Portugal had not yet implemented a standardised approach to collect metadata from other portals in the country and only Belgium guaranteed that 100% of its data is uploaded automatically.[51]

For all the work that has taken place on data catalogues, the Open Data Barometer and Global Open Data Index both suggest that much of government data remains hard to find, is poorly indexed, or is of poor structural quality. Data may be hosted on ministerial websites, often hidden multiple clicks down and missing metadata. But metadata issues are also found on the European Data Portal (as indicated by the use of non-standard metadata for licences). Data standards are one way to address issues of data structure, representation, and interoperability; however, beyond the geographic datasets released through the INSPIRE directive, there is little evidence of the adoption of data standards for open datasets. Budget and finance datasets, for example, are notable for their different nomenclature and structure.[52] Open data and catalogue standards have made it easier to discover data across borders, but, once discovered, those datasets may lack interoperability. It is notable that while the EU has substantial programmes of work on interoperability under the European Interoperability Framework, they are not yet having a major impact on the interoperability of open datasets.

The open data ecosystem

The last two sections have outlined how open data has developed at the EU and national government level. However, the open data ecosystem in Europe includes many more actors, including an active civil society, a dynamic private sector, and an engaged research community, as well as actors working on open data at the city level. This section will take stock of recent developments in this wider ecosystem.

Cities

A large number of European cities have developed local open data initiatives, and many applications of open data have been developed at the city level. Cities and their public institutions publish a variety of data relevant for urban planning, tourism, transport, mobility, green transition, utilities, and energy management. Several trailblazers should be mentioned, including European capital cities such as Helsinki, Amsterdam, Berlin, Copenhagen, London, Paris, Stockholm, Vienna, Lisbon, Dublin, and Vilnius. Other important larger and medium-sized cities which have developed open data policies as well as portals include Barcelona, Florence, Gdansk, Ghent, and Thessaloniki.

The vision and strategies of these cities may differ, but open data policies are frequently developed as part of broader digitisation and smart city strategies. As a recent report of the European Open Data Portal notes, often these strategies are developed top-down by municipal governments.[53] Beyond merely providing open data portals, several cities have organised awareness-raising workshops, skills training, and hackathons.[54] A number of cities organise recurring events and meetups, such as Data Dive Ghent and Helsinki Loves Developers, or collaborate with local schools to include digital skills training in curricula. These events are used as opportunities to discuss the usefulness of data or to consult with citizens about their data needs. Independent civil society initiatives, such as Open Data Manchester, city-level chapters of the Code for Europe network, and chapters and affiliates of the Open Knowledge network have also played a role in organising meetups and hackathons, as well as building local networks around open data.

The European Commission plays a role in supporting the use of open data in cities. As our analysis of Horizon 2020-funded projects (see above) shows, the European Commission has given support to several city-related initiatives, including activities to improve mobility, as well as smart city initiatives like CITYKEYS and CitySDK, which have explored the possibility of creating interoperable data infrastructures at the city level. A number of European initiatives are evident in Chapter 16: Urban development.

Despite advances in European cities, there are still several open questions and challenges, not least of which concerns who gets to participate in the opportunities created by open data. The European Data Portal reports that a "lack of awareness plays a part on both the side of the data publisher and the data user, as data publishers are not always aware of the relevance and potential of Open Data, and users are not always aware of the Open Data available".[55] Although Europe ranks high in terms of education levels and technical skills, a look at open data use for citizen participation in Milton Keynes (UK) found that the majority of citizens lack key data literacies, and that building these literacies is a long-term challenge.[56] Further research is needed to more fully investigate how well current engagement, awareness raising, and capacity-building activities are designed. Beyond technical skills to use data, new literacy skills should incorporate the politics of data and the institutional embeddedness of data, foster public pathways for engaging with how open data is produced and published, and be complemented with tangential skills from the political and social sciences.[57] Crucially, future research must also ask who benefits? For example, are women engaged by hackathon approaches?; are skills training opportunities addressing the needs of marginalised communities?; or are programmes being designed to address specific problems in communities?

Enterprise and private sector

Several studies have been carried out to understand the economic benefits of open data.[58,59] These studies look into the revenue generated from open data, the types of data used by enterprise, and gains from using open data. A 2015 study by the ODI identified and analysed 270 UK-based companies using open data and reported on their annual turnover and workforce size.[60] Another Europe-wide study estimated the effects of open data on job creation, market size, cost savings, and efficiency gains, suggesting that open data will generate a total turnover of € 59.7 billion. The study noted differences in market maturity with the UK, France, Germany, and Spain currently leading.[61]

There is, however, a recognition that developing a market around open data may need some government support. From 2014 to 2017, the EU funded the Open Data Incubation Network (ODINE), supporting 57 companies in 18 countries.[62] ODINE operated as a six-month incubation programme, funding companies with up to € 100 000 and providing mentoring, business, and data training, as well as visibility at international events and introductions to investors.[63] Another initiative with co-funding from the EU was FINODEX, a virtual accelerator supporting SMEs and web entrepreneurs to develop products and services that build upon Future Internet Fiware technologies and the reuse of open data.[64] The UK-based ODI also runs its own startup incubation programme.[65] It should be noted, however, that many of the potential economic benefits of open data come not from startups but from improvements to existing business practices.

While Europe does have reasonably good private sector engagement with open data, market barriers and market competition across companies and grant-funded networks may limit the full development of open data businesses. For example, a commonly noted problem is that public procurement is not conducive to supporting lean startups that do not meet revenue requirements or other procurement rules. In addition, organisations using open data might struggle to raise capital, depending instead on grants, sponsorships, membership contributions, volunteerism, and individual resources. Future research could go deeper in investigating how government procurement patterns affect open data startups and in identifying funding needs for open data businesses, including how existing funding initiatives support social enterprise, startups, and SMEs.

Non-profits and civil society

Europe's open data ecosystem has benefited from well-developed civil society and non-profit networks working to bring together national or regional interest groups for open data. At the local and national level, groups like Open Data Manchester,[66] Open Knowledge Belgium,[67] and Open Knowledge France[68] are examples of the kind of grassroots communities that came together around open data a decade ago and have developed a range of programmes and organisational capacities to advocate for, support, and work with open data. Groups like these are brought together through networks, including the Open Knowledge network,[69] the ODI nodes,[70] and Creative Commons.[71] Other Europe-wide networks, such as Code for Europe,[72] also convene events relating to open data and connect groups across countries. In addition, policy networks, such as the European Thematic Network on the Digital Public Domain (Communia),[73] have been active on open data issues. The European Commission helps to spark cross-country collaboration by funding consortia through its Horizon 2020 programme.[74]

Interviews with members of the Open Knowledge network suggest that civil society organisations (CSOs) have often played a crucial role in establishing a culture of openness within national governments. CSOs have helped in the exchange of best practices between public bodies, business, and individuals. For example, local Creative Commons chapters helped to promote open licensing and to influence open data policies in a number of countries. Organisations like Communia continue to engage with copyright and licensing issues. Over the last ten years, several of these networks have seen a rise and fall. OKI, in particular, experienced a period of significant growth and activity between 2010 and 2014, organising a number of key regional summits and thematic working groups, but many have since become inactive. The Open Education Working Group remains as one of the active working groups in Europe (see Chapter 6: Education).

One key challenge for civil society has been accessing sustainable funding to work on open data as opposed to short-term project funding. Membership contributions and individual donations are used by some networks, such as the Swiss Open Knowledge Chapter, and individual organisations, such as Civio in Spain, to fund activities, although, in general, project grants remain the major source of funding for open data-related CSOs.

Research and development

The EU produces a substantial share of all open data-related research. According to a systematic review of open data research produced in 2016, universities like Delft University in the Netherlands, the University of the Aegean in Greece, the University of Southampton in England, or the Copenhagen Business School in Denmark, produce a large portion of all open data articles reviewed. Most studies in this review also chose activities in the EU region as their object of study.[75]

The review suggests that European research covers a fairly wide range of topics, including open data policy design in Europe, the impact of European open data policies, the use of open data for policy-making in Europe, analyses of public data infrastructures, business models for PSI reuse, or technical descriptions of European data portals and other elements of data infrastructure. Open data research has contributed theoretical, as well as empirical, case studies of European open data initiatives, drawing on several disciplines and intellectual traditions, such as information management, critical data studies, science and technology studies, new media studies, and others.[76]

Institutionally, several universities are dedicating research programmes to the study of open data, such as the University of Southampton,[77] Delft University,[78] or Ghent University.[79] Research institutions are also involved in a number of collaborations with both non-profit and private sector organisations, such as the participation of Fraunhofer Fokus[80] and University of Southampton as part of the consortium that has developed the European Data Portal.

A thriving ecosystem?

It is challenging to assess whether Europe's open data ecosystem is thriving, stalling, or receding. The history of the open data ecosystem shows volatility. A notable boom for civil society and open data communities took place between 2010 and 2013. However, since then, some communities have continued to thrive, while other national and local communities have become less active or have disappeared completely. This may not necessarily indicate a weaker ecosystem as some anecdotal evidence suggests there may have been a spillover effect of expertise transitioning from volunteer-based organisations to government and business. Along these lines, weakening civil society networks might indicate a loss of engagement with open data or a shift of the priorities of network members, but could also indicate a transition from volunteerism to professional roles with the open data community. In a similar vein, it is currently unclear to what extent different models of investment in open data, such as business incubation and hackathons, contribute to the sustainable growth of open data-related organisations.

Our conversations with the community indicate that volunteerism is a major challenge in open data and may not be a sustainable organising principle for the open data sector for much longer. There are no figures available on how much labour is provided unpaid, but interviews with several organisations suggest that continued reliance on volunteers makes it challenging for organisations to sustain themselves or to scale activities. This is especially true when volunteers rarely play a leadership role, face conflicting commitments, and have sometimes been active in their roles for more than a decade, pointing to the fact that the renewal of open data communities in Europe may be overdue.

The real measure of the effectiveness of the open data ecosystem in Europe must be its impact. While there is evidence of impact and return on investment, it is uneven across political, economic, and social domains. As the EU Open Data Maturity Report states, governments still struggle to evaluate the social impact of their open data initiatives.[81] This highlights the need for future work to improve impact measurement with a particular view to influencing strategic government investment in open data initiatives.

Conclusion

Europe played a key role in shaping the open data space a decade ago. This was demonstrated by the early adoption of rules for PSI release complementing the rise of open data, by the development of key infrastructures used for open data around the world (e.g. CKAN), by Europe's global influence on open licensing, and by the promotion of international open data principles through the G8 Open Data Charter. Significant progress has been made in the development of open data policies in almost all countries, as well as in the development of catalogues at the EU and national levels with metadata standards for the exchange of information across these catalogues.

However, the coordination of policies across different administrative levels remains a political and administrative challenge, and many jurisdictions develop their own policies with different requirements regarding access conditions, data management, licensing, and the use of data standards. The INSPIRE Directive was a key achievement for a geospatial data standard, but for other areas, such as fiscal data, harmonisation efforts are only just starting. Standard open licences are widely used, but governments continue to apply bespoke licences, possibly creating data use silos that act against the creation of a DSM. Data markets also still interpret access to data differently, and controversy persists around whether the release of some data as open will distort competition.

The data ecosystem seems to develop at different paces in some countries with France and the UK being more advanced than others. Open data networks in civil society are volatile and may thrive moving forward or they may disintegrate. Interpreting this development, or how much positive spillover is taking place as individuals move from voluntary to professional engagement with open data, requires further study. Additionally, research into the sustainability of open data enterprises needs to pay more attention to market barriers and competition among open data organisations.

A decade on, a lack of awareness and skills to use data is still seen by governments as a major impediment to impact, illustrating the need for governments to continue to invest in educational programmes and training. Finally, it remains unclear to what extent the open data ecosystem includes marginalised groups or develops solutions with and for them, and research to date indicates that the impact of open data across the region is unevenly distributed toward organisational efficiency gains and less toward social goals. This should give us pause and inspire a new set of objectives for future open data activities that place a greater focus on inclusion and social impact.

Further reading

Berends, J., Carrara, W., Engbers, W., & Vollers, H. (2017). *Re-using open data: A study on companies transforming open data into economic & societal value*. Brussels: European Data Portal. https://www.europeandataportal.eu/sites/default/files/re-using_open_data.pdf

Berends, J., Carrara, W., & Vollers, H. (2017). *Analytical report n6: Open data in cities 2*. Brussels: European Data Portal. https://www.europeandataportal.eu/sites/default/files/edp_analytical_report_n6_-_open_data_in_cities_2_-_final-clean.pdf

Cecconi, G. & Radu, C. (2018). *Open data maturity in Europe: Report 2018*. Brussels: European Union. https://www.europeandataportal.eu/sites/default/files/edp_landscaping_insight_report_n4_2018.pdf

Cetl, V., Nunes de Lima, V., Tomas, R., Lutz, M., D'Eugenio, J., Nagy, A., & Robbrecht, J. (2018). *Summary report on status of implementation of the INSPIRE Directive in EU*. Luxembourg: Publications Office of the European Union. http://doi.org/10.2760/143502

European Commission. (2014). Legal Aspects of Public Sector Information (LAPSI) thematic network outputs. https://ec.europa.eu/digital-single-market/en/news/legal-aspects-public-sector-information-lapsi-thematic-network-outputs

Hossain, M.A., Dwivedi, Y.K., & Rana, N.P. (2016). State-of-the-art in open data research: Insights from existing literature and a research agenda. *Journal of Organizational Computing and Electronic Commerce, 26(1–2)*, 14–40. https://www.tandfonline.com/doi/full/10.1080/10919392.2015.1124007

About the authors

Rufus Pollock is an entrepreneur, researcher, and technologist working to create an open information age. He is founder and President of Open Knowledge International (OKI), a leading international non-profit that empowers people and organisations with access to information and the tools and skills to make sense of it. Rufus is a recognised global expert on open data and open knowledge. He has worked with multiple governments, CSOs, the World Bank, the United Nations, and the private sector. You can follow Rufus at http://rufuspollock.com/ and learn more about OKI at https://www.okfn.org.

Danny Lämmerhirt is Research Coordinator at OKI. His work focuses on the politics of data, metrics, policy, data ethnography, organisational theory of open systems, and the data commons. Danny leads work on the Global Open Data Index and co-chairs the Open Data Charter's Measurement and Accountability Working Group. You can follow Danny at https://www.twitter.com/danlammerhirt.

How to cite this chapter

Pollock, R. & Lämmerhirt, D. (2019). Open data around the world: European Union. In T. Davies, S. Walker, M. Rubinstein, & F. Perini (Eds.), *The state of open data: Histories and horizons* (pp. 465–484). Cape Town and Ottawa: African Minds and International Development Research Centre. http://stateofopendata.od4d.net

This work is licensed under a Creative Commons Attribution 4.0 International (CC BY 4.0) licence. It was carried out with the aid of a grant from the International Development Research Centre, Ottawa, Canada.

Endnotes

1. Gray, J. (2014). Towards a genealogy of open data. *SSRN*, 15 May. https://papers.ssrn.com/abstract=2605828
2. Janssen, M. & Estevez, E. (2013). Lean government and platform-based governance – Doing more with less. *Government Information Quarterly*, 30(1): S1–S8. https://doi.org/10.1016/j.giq.2012.11.003
3. Pollock, R. (2012). Open data, technology and government 2.0 – What should we, and should we not expect. *Open Knowledge International Blog*, 13 September. https://blog.okfn.org/2012/09/13/managing-expectations-ii-open-data-technology-and-government-2-0/
4. Gray, J. (2014). Towards a genealogy of open data. *SSRN*, 15 May. https://papers.ssrn.com/abstract=2605828
5. Gupta, I. (2017). *Footprints of Feist in European database directive: A legal analysis of IP law-making in Europe*. Singapore: Springer. https://www.springer.com/gp/book/9789811039805
6. Gray, J. (2014). Towards a genealogy of open data. *SSRN*, 15 May. https://papers.ssrn.com/abstract=2605828
7. European Union. (2003). Directive 2003/98/EC of the European Parliament and of the Council of 17 November 2003 on the re-use of public sector information. *EUR-Lex*. https://eur-lex.europa.eu/legal-content/EN/ALL/?uri=celex:32003L0098
8. European Commission. (2011). 2011/833/EU: Commission Decision of 12 December 2011 on the reuse of Commission documents. *EUR Lex*. http://data.europa.eu/eli/dec/2011/833/oj/eng
9. European Commission. (2018). European legislation on the re-use of public sector information. https://ec.europa.eu/digital-single-market/en/european-legislation-reuse-public-sector-information
10. Ibid.
11. Communia. (2018). Policy paper on the review of the PSI Directive. https://www.communia-association.org/wp-content/uploads/2018/01/Communia-_-Review-of-PSI-Directive-2017-_-Policy-paper.pdf; Richter, H. (2018). Reconsidering the exemption for educational and research establishments under the directive on re-use of public sector information (2003/98/EC; 2013/37/EU) – Possible ways and legal consequences. *SSRN*, 9 March. https://papers.ssrn.com/abstract=3090337
12. European Commission. (2018). Implementation of the Public Sector Information Directive. https://ec.europa.eu/digital-single-market/en/implementation-public-sector-information-directive
13. European Union. (2013). Directive 2013/37/EU of the European Parliament and of the Council of 26 June 2013 amending Directive 2003/98/EC on the re-use of public sector information Text with EEA relevance. *EUR-Lex*. http://data.europa.eu/eli/dir/2013/37/oj/eng
14. Open State Foundation. (2018). NGOs urge European Parliament to vote for free access to company and UBO registers. *Open State*, 28 November. https://openstate.eu/en/2018/11/psidirectiverevision/
15. https://www.economie.gouv.fr/republique-numerique-ouverture-donnees-d-interet-general

16. ODI (Open Data institute). (n.d.). Guide: How to embed open data into the procurement of public services. http://training.theodi.org/Procurement/Guide/
17. https://inspire.ec.europa.eu/index.cfm/pageid/2/list/7
18. http://inspire-geoportal.ec.europa.eu/
19. Cetl, V., De Lima, V.N., Tomas, R., Lutz, M., D'Eugenio, J., Nagy, A., & Robbrecht, J. (2018). *Summary report on status of implementation of the INSPIRE Directive in EU*. Luxembourg: Publications Office of the European Union. http://doi.org/10.2760/143502
20. European Commission. (2018). Shaping the digital single market. https://ec.europa.eu/digital-single-market/en/policies/shaping-digital-single-market
21. European Commission. (2018). E-government & digital public services. https://ec.europa.eu/digital-single-market/en/policies/egovernment
22. https://cordis.europa.eu/projects/home_en.html
23. Carrara, W., Radu, C., & Vollers, H. (2017). *Open data maturity in Europe 2017: Open data for a European data economy*. Brussels: European Data Portal. https://www.europeandataportal.eu/sites/default/files/edp_landscaping_insight_report_n3_2017.pdf
24. Ibid.
25. OKI. (2017). The Global Open Data Index as a national indicator – So why do we have Northern Ireland? *Open Knowledge International Blog*, 9 May. https://blog.okfn.org/2017/05/09/the-global-open-data-index-as-a-national-indicator-so-why-do-we-have-northern-ireland/
26. http://data.gov.be/fr/conditions-dutilisation
27. Berends, J., Carrara, W., & Vollers, H. (2017). *Analytical report n6: Open data in cities 2*. Brussels: European Data Portal. https://www.europeandataportal.eu/sites/default/files/edp_analytical_report_n6_-_open_data_in_cities_2_-_final-clean.pdf
28. Companies House. (2017). Keeping your people with significant control (PSC) register. *GOV.UK*, 6 April. https://www.gov.uk/government/news/keeping-your-people-with-significant-control-psc-register
29. GOV.UK. (n.d.). Public Sector Transparency Board. https://www.gov.uk/government/groups/public-sector-transparency-board
30. Broad, E. (2015). Appeal to the FOI commission: Don't confuse open data with FOI. *Open Data Institute*, 6 August. https://oldsite.theodi.org/blog/appeal-to-the-foi-commission-dont-confuse-open-data-with-foi
31. Cabinet Office & the Rt Hon Lord Maude of Horsham. (2014). Francis Maude speech on open data and transparency. *GOV.UK*, 11 December. https://www.gov.uk/government/speeches/francis-maude-speech-on-open-data-and-transparency
32. Hope. C. (2013). Everyone's postcodes to be privatised in Royal Mail flotation, despite objections from Sir Tim Berners-Lee. *The Telegraph*, 19 April. https://www.telegraph.co.uk/news/uknews/royal-mail/9994741/Everyones-postcodes-to-be-privatised-in-Royal-Mail-flotation-despite-objections-from-Sir-Tim-Berners-Lee.html
33. Open Source Initiative. (n.d.). Report of License Proliferation Committee and draft FAQ. https://opensource.org/proliferation-report
34. Tsiavos, T. (2014). LAPSI license interoperability report. *European Commission*. https://ec,europa.eu/digital-single-market/en/news/lapsi-license-interoperability-report
35. EUR-Lex. (n.d.). Directive 96/9/EC of the European Parliament and of the Council of 11 March 1996 on the legal protection of databases. *EUR-Lex*. https://eur-lex.europa.eu/legal-content/EN/ALL/?uri=celex:31996L0009
36. See http://opendefinition.org/licenses/odc-odbl/ and http://opendefinition.org/licenses/odc-by/
37. See also https://creativecommons.org/share-your-work/licensing-considerations/version4/
38. https://ec.europa.eu/digital-single-market/en/news/legal-aspects-public-sector-information-lapsi-thematic-network-outputs
39. https://www.europeandataportal.eu/en/content/show-license

40   Venema, V. (2017). Germany weather service opens up its data. *Variable Variability* [Blog post], n.d. http://variable-variability.blogspot.com/2017/08/germany-weather-service-DWD-open-data.html

41   EUGDPR.org. (2018). The EU General Data Protection Regulation (GDPR) is the most important change in data privacy regulation in 20 years. https://eugdpr.org/

42   Hustinx, P. (2012). *Opinion of the European Data Protection Supervisor on the "Open-Data Package" of the European Commission including a proposal for a directive amending Directive 2003/98/EC on Re-Use of Public Sector Information (PSI)*. Brussels: European Data Protection Supervisor. https://edps.europa.eu/sites/edp/files/publication/12-04-18_open_data_en.pdf

43   European Data Portal. (2018). Protecting data and opening data. https://www.europeandataportal.eu/en/highlights/protecting-data-and-opening-data

44   European Data Portal. (2018). The PSI directive and GDPR. https://www.europeandataportal.eu/en/highlights/psi-directive-and-gdpr

45   Wiebe, A. & Dietrich, N. (2017). *Open data protection: Study on legal barriers to open data sharing – Data protection and PSI*. Göttingen: Universitätsverlag Göttingen. https://www.openaire.eu/legal-barriers-to-open-data-sharing

46   European Data Portal. (2018). The PSI directive and GDPR. https://www.europeandataportal.eu/en/highlights/psi-directive-and-gdpr

47   McMurren, J., Verhulst, S., & Young, A. (2016). *Denmark's open address data set*. New York, NY: GovLab and Omidyar Network. http://odimpact.org/case-denmarks-open-address-data-set.html

48   Saxby, S. (1996). The development of UK government policy towards the commercialization of official information. *International Journal of Law and Information Technology, 4(3)*, 199–233. http://doi.org/10.1093/ijlit/4.3.199

49   Saxby, S. (2011). Three years in the life of UK national information policy – The politics and process of policy development. *International Journal of Private Law, 4(1)*, 1–31. http://doi.org/10.1504/IJPL.2011.037891

50   https://www.europeandataportal.eu

51   Carrara, W., Radu, C., & Vollers, H. (2017). *Open data maturity in Europe 2017: Open data for a European data economy*. Brussels: European Data Portal. https://www.europeandataportal.eu/sites/default/files/edp_landscaping_insight_report_n3_2017.pdf

52   Lämmerhirt, D. (2016). *Making budgets attractive – Best practices from governments' financial transparency portals*. Sankt Augustin, Germany: OpenBudgets.eu. http://openbudgets.eu/assets/resources/Report-Laemmerhirt-Making-Budgets-Attractive.pdf

53   Carrara, W., Radu, C., & Vollers, H. (2017). *Open data maturity in Europe 2017: Open data for a European data economy*. Brussels: European Data Portal. https://www.europeandataportal.eu/sites/default/files/edp_landscaping_insight_report_n3_2017.pdf

54   Ibid.

55   Berends, J., Carrara, W., & Vollers, H. (2017). *Analytical report n6: Open data in cities 2*. Brussels: European Data Portal. https://www.europeandataportal.eu/sites/default/files/edp_analytical_report_n6_-_open_data_in_cities_2_-_final-clean.pdf

56   Wolff, A., Gooch, D., Cavero, J., Rashid, U., & Kortuem, G. (2019). Removing barriers for citizen participation to urban innovation. In M. de Lange & M. de Waal (Eds.), *The hackable city* (pp. 153–168). Singapore: Springer. http://link.springer.com/10.1007/978-981-13-2694-3_8

57   Beyond focusing on technical skills to enhance data literacy, we suggest that a more profound engagement with open data requires what could be called "data infrastructure literacy". This form of literacy inquires how data is being made, the institutional embeddedness and politics of data, and how data is used institutionally for a variety of purposes, including public policy. See Gray, J., Gerlitz, C., & Bounegru, L. (2018). Data infrastructure literacy. *Big Data & Society, 5(2)*. https://journals.sagepub.com/doi/10.1177/2053951718786316

58   Dekkers, M., Polman, F., te Velde, R., & De Vries, M. (2006). *MEPSIR – Measuring European Public Sector Information Resources*. Final report of study on exploitation of public sector information – Benchmarking of EU framework conditions, Part 1: Description, overview of results and conclusions. Brussels: European Commission. http://ec.europa.eu/newsroom/dae/document.cfm?doc_id=1198

59 Berends, J., Carrara, W., & Radu, C. (2017). *Analytical report n9: The economic benefits of open data*. Brussels: European Data Portal. https://www.europeandataportal.eu/sites/default/files/analytical_report_n9_economic_benefits_of_open_data.pdf
60 ODI. (2015). Open data means business: UK innovation across sectors and regions. *Open Data Institute* [Article], 31 May. https://theodi.org/article/open-data-means-business/
61 Berends, J., Carrara, W., Engbers, W., & Vollers, H. (2017). *Re-using open data: A study on companies transforming open data into economic & societal value*. Brussels: European Data Portal. https://www.europeandataportal.eu/sites/default/files/re-using_open_data.pdf
62 International Data Corporation. (2017). *Impact assessment of ODINE programme*. https://opendataincubator.eu/files/2016/01/ODINE-Final-report-by-IDC.pdf
63 https://opendataincubator.eu
64 https://cordis.europa.eu/project/rcn/191684_en.html
65 https://theodi.org/service/startups-fostering-innovation/
66 https://www.opendatamanchester.org.uk/
67 https://www.openknowledge.be/
68 https://fr.okfn.org/
69 https://okfn.org/network/
70 https://theodi.org/global-network-directory/odi-nodes/
71 https://network.creativecommons.org/chapters/
72 http://codeforeurope.net/
73 http://communia-project.eu/
74 https://ec.europa.eu/programmes/horizon2020
75 Hossain, M.A., Dwivedi, Y.K., & Rana, N.P. (2016). State-of-the-art in open data research: Insights from existing literature and a research agenda. *Journal of Organizational Computing and Electronic Commerce, 26(1–2)*, 14–40. https://doi.org/10.1080/10919392.2015.1124007
76 Ibid.
77 University of Southampton. (2015). Leading the open data revolution. https://www.ecs.soton.ac.uk/research/leading_the_open_data_revolution
78 TU Delft. (n.d.). Open data/Open government. https://www.tudelft.nl/en/tpm/research/projects/open-dataopen-government/
79 IDLab. (n.d.). Semantic knowledge generation and publication at scale. *Ghent University*. https://www.ugent.be/ea/idlab/en/research/semantic-intelligence/semantic-knowledge-generation-and-publication-at-scale.htm
80 https://www.fokus.fraunhofer.de/
81 Carrara, W., Radu, C., & Vollers, H. (2017). *Open data maturity in Europe 2017: Open data for a European data economy*. Brussels: European Data Portal. https://www.europeandataportal.eu/sites/default/files/edp_landscaping_insight_report_n3_2017.pdf

033

Latin America and the Caribbean

Silvana Fumega and Maurice McNaughton

Key points

- Shared language, regular meetings, strong civil society networks, technical capacity, and engagement from governments have all led to the growth of a distinctive Latin American open data movement with increasing focus on developing sector-specific open data initiatives.

- In the Caribbean, donor support has helped influence and resource a series of thematic initiatives on agriculture, tourism, and election monitoring with the primary actors coming from civil society and academia. However, a lack of sustained political engagement has frustrated efforts to build a wider open data movement and infrastructure.

- Comparing regional experiences is instructive, informing leaders and advocates of the challenges of working across language barriers, the different drivers for open data, and the importance of civil society in sustaining open data activity through political change.

Introduction

Latin America and the Caribbean is often considered a homogeneous region by international development agencies and multilateral organisations. In many respects, this is a misleading oversimplification and reflects an inadvertent mixing of geographical and cultural classifications. Technically speaking, Latin America refers to countries in the Americas that speak a language derived from Latin, such as French, Spanish, or Portuguese, which is not necessarily the case for the Caribbean, a region lying at the geographical axis of North and South America.

Notwithstanding decades of preferential north-bound migratory patterns, the Caribbean shares much in its cultural disposition – football (not soccer), music, and carnival – with its southern neighbours. However, with regard to open data, its intrinsic drivers, attitudes, and emergent patterns, the two regions are quite different, and the Caribbean has consistently lagged behind Latin America, which is heralded as one of the most vibrant communities in the open data field.

The divergence in the social and political legacy of the two regions, defined in part by very different colonial experiences, might provide some explanation for the differences in the way key actors in public sector administration, civil society, and the media have approached the open data agenda. This chapter aims to illuminate the trajectory and diversity of the open data agenda in these two culturally diverse regions, covering a period from 2009 until early 2018. Distilling the differences and similarities in approach will aid the principal actors in both regions to better understand causal factors and theories of change and to identify more productive synergies.

Given the distinct differences in the trajectory of open data between the two regions, the chapter is structured to address Latin America first and then the Caribbean before offering any conclusions and final remarks in terms of regional similarities and differences, as well as opportunities for greater collaboration and synergy in the future.

Latin America

The open data agenda started to gain momentum in Latin America in 2012. From that moment onward, we have seen the growing development of data portals at the national, regional, and local level (more than 200 according to the Open Data Inception project),[1] as well as promising use of open data by the private sector and civil society. Latin America has developed its own unique open data agenda with particularly strong linkages between countries and within the broader open data community.[2]

Latin American countries have shown enthusiasm in advancing their open data agenda in several ways, from events, such as AbreLatam-Condatos,[3,4] and the nine national and 24 local governments that have adopted the International Open Data Charter[5] (note that the majority of Open Data Charter adopters globally come from this region) to the development of open data policies and regulations in a large number of countries in the region. To date, seven countries in the region have consolidated open data policies (Argentina, Brazil, Uruguay, Peru, Costa Rica, Colombia, Mexico), and they have done so, in many cases, with the input of civil society experts and organisations.[6] Moreover, the Open Data Barometer (ODB) confirms the leading position that the region occupies with Mexico, Uruguay, Brazil, and Colombia all within the top 20 countries in its global ranking, while, in 2017, Argentina had the largest increase in score globally, demonstrating particularly rapid progress.[7] However, despite this advancement, there are many gaps and areas for improvement in the region.

Community

2012 was a breakthrough year for open data in Latin America. Prior to this point, there had been a number of early regional initiatives, such as Desarrollando América Latina (2011),[8] and separate open data initiatives in Montevideo (2010)[9] and Lima (2012),[10] as well as projects such as Money and Politics[11] and Bahia Blanca Public Expenditure,[12] but there was little sense of a regional open data community. Technically advanced stakeholders from the region were instead plugged into global online networks, engaging in global open data events and activities.

These global events, organised in Europe and the United States (including Open Knowledge's OKCon[13] and OKFest,[14] Sunlight Foundation's Transparency Camp,[15] and the World Bank's hosting of the International Open Data Conference (IODC)[16]) managed to gather a considerable number of activists, academics, and public officials with some representation from Latin America in the mix. Although an incipient community was brewing during these early exchanges, it became increasingly evident that there was a need to organise local and regional events where there was not only a shared interest in open data but where participants also shared a language and cultural context. Cultural context remains a key component when considering the barriers that limit collaboration on open data initiatives.

By 2012, against an international backdrop of open data networking, and drawing on the regional experience of "Desarrollando America Latina" events,[17] the local work done by policy entrepreneurs inside and outside government agencies in Montevideo and Buenos Aires,[18] and the launch of the Open Government Partnership (OGP) which held its first summit in Brasilia in 2012, a regional open data agenda was starting to develop and finding traction in government and civil society.

The first AbreLatam was organised by Data Uruguay[19] in collaboration with Ciudadano Inteligente[20] in Montevideo in 2013.[21] AbreLatam was designed with an informal and participatory approach and intended to bring together many of those who were working on open data in the region but who had not yet met or interacted. With hindsight, it is clear that AbreLatam was one of the main staging points on the journey to establish a Latin American open data community. AbreLatam was organised as an "unconference",[22] but alongside this informal and participatory meeting, another more formal event was held that brought together mainly governmental actors and representatives of intergovernmental organisations, albeit with some actors from global civil society. This was the Regional Conference on Open Data of Latin America and the Caribbean, later known as Condatos, which stemmed from a conversation among representatives from the International Development Research Centre (IDRC), the United Nations Economic Commission for Latin America and the Caribbean (ECLAC), the World Bank, and Government of Uruguay.[23]

The AbreLatam-Condatos model of twin events, each respecting the culture of their respective professional communities but providing a space for cross-over, has been a catalyst for the construction of a community with interaction and trust among all of the key actors which has arguably not been seen in other regions. Over the different editions of the conference, a range of partners have been involved, including Data Uruguay, Ciudadano Inteligente in Chile, SocialTic in Mexico, Somos Mas in Colombia, Wingu, Conocimiento Abierto y Democracia en red in Argentina, and Abriendo Datos in Costa Rica. The bonds of trust created through these events were not only between actors of the same sector but also across sectors with different groups learning to work together. Moreover, many of those actors working in the open data field, who are currently public officials, have been members of civil society organisations (CSOs) in the past and vice versa. This fluidity of roles has been a great help in maintaining momentum and ensuring the continuity of many open data policies.[24]

From 2013 onward these actors worked to create channels of communication that allowed for more ongoing interaction. At first, messaging channels created for events were routinely deactivated after the end of the event (Telegram, WhatsApp, Slack). However, after the third edition of AbreLatam in Chile in 2015, the messaging channels remained active even after the end of each event. Although informal, and without any explicit governance structure, these channels remain active through the collaboration of participating members, which, as of March 2018, exceeded 300 in number.

In spite of all the progress and the unique strength of a Latin American open data community, there are a number of areas for improvement. A session focused on a regional "collaborative agenda" held during the fifth AbreLatam-Condatos in Costa Rica identified particular challenges related to private sector inclusion and a regional strategy.[25]

In terms of inclusion, networks between civil society and government are strong, although there has, to date, been less inclusion of private sector actors from the larger corporations and from small and medium businesses.[26] Although there is a recognition that private sector companies using open data need to be included in regional discussions and activities, substantial efforts to make this happen have not yet materialised. There are several businesses working with open data and civic technology in the region, but only a small number work with civil society and governmental actors in the open data community, with firms such as Properati,[27] Junar,[28] and Dymaxion Labs[29] acting as the exception rather than the rule.

Improving regional collaboration at the project, as well as the policy level, is a topic repeatedly discussed at Latin American events. Participants have explored whether the region could develop cross-country open data initiatives that address specific topics and bring together more actors from civil society and government to carry out local projects within an overarching strategy and/ or guiding framework. Common areas of work cannot be imposed but must be developed through dialogue and agreement. At AbreLatam-Condatos in Costa Rica (2017), issues related to gender violence emerged as the potential focus for shared actions across the region in 2018. As yet, however, there are no transnational governance structures or strategies to coordinate agreed upon actions toward the creation and use of shared open datasets or data infrastructures on gender violence, and there remains significant work to be done to secure progress on commitments to thematic regional collaboration.

In addition, an observation of the actors who have been engaged in the regional open data field over the last five years points to a further area for development: regional and linguistic inclusion. At present, the Latin American open data community is largely focused on Spanish-speaking countries and actors. Although there are many successful Brazilian open data projects and actors, as Spanish is the dominant language at Latin American open data events, Portuguese-speaking actors are not as involved as they should be. A similar issue exists in the relationship between Latin American and Caribbean actors. Despite being geographically linked, there are historical, cultural, and language-related differences that currently prevent these actors from being as integrated as funders might assume based on conventional regional groupings. Language barriers also have an impact on knowledge sharing in the region. Although there is a vibrant Spanish-speaking community, comparatively little research is published in Spanish, as Latin American researchers choose to write in English to secure greater exposure for their work.

> ### Open data and startups
>
> The region has seen a number of startups emerge, exploring a range of business models. One example, Properati, was founded in 2012 as a startup focusing on online real estate operations in Argentina.[30] However, unlike the traditional business model, where real estate companies pay to place ads on a site, their business model is based on the sale of leads (interested contacts). That is, Properati charges the real estate or construction company whenever a user contacts it via the platform. To increase the chance of such leads ending in effective business relationships, Properati uses open data and provides tools that give additional information to future buyers, tenants, or investors in relation to the properties on the site.
>
> Properati has also proven to be a development ground for new open data entrepreneurs. In 2017, a couple of former Properati staff members created Dymaxion Labs in Buenos Aires.[31] Dymaxion uses satellite images and open data with the goal of extracting knowledge and providing evidence to inform public policy. Since its creation, Dymaxion Labs has developed AP Latam, a monitoring platform for informal settlements[32] with the support of Mapbox and TECHO, as well as "The Flood Monitor" used to observe and monitor the progress of floods in real time[33] and 'Detection of Changes',[34] an application used to identify possible land-use modifications.

Policy

In addition to strong civil society leadership and an emphasis in public discourse on open data projects related to accountability and public service delivery,[35] governments in Latin America have progressively developed policies and policy environments to support open data.

In 2017, the ODB revealed that most Latin American countries had either increased or maintained their scores from the past year, contrasting with declining performance in some other regions. Regional leaders, including Mexico, Uruguay, Colombia, and Brazil, saw their ODB-ranked performance increase and extended their edge over the rest of the region with Mexico and Uruguay becoming established as challengers to traditional global leaders. Yet, a number of newer players have also seen significant improvements in their policy and practice in recent years, with Argentina and Paraguay rising 14 and nine places in the ODB rankings respectively.[36]

Two exceptions to the upward trend emerged in 2017. Ecuador and Costa Rica saw dramatic declines in their ODB rankings. This can be mostly attributed to a lack of sustained political support for their initial open data commitments.[37] However, the situation in Costa Rica has started to be rectified through the process of developing and adopting an open data decree. The Organisation of American States (OAS) through its Department for Effective Public Management has deployed a participatory methodology to contribute to the development of open data policies. In partnership with OAS, the Latin American Open Data Initiative (Iniciativa Latinoamericana de Datos Abiertos – ILDA) has delivered a tailored programme of support to the Government of

Costa Rica to set up an open data policy, leading to a decree signed in May 2017.[38] This decree provides the policy leadership to support open data implementation, and ILDA was subsequently invited to design and implement a training course for 150 public officials. This online training, developed with the support of the Inter-American Development Bank (IADB), not only explains the basic concepts behind open data to officials but also helps them to realise the potential of the data in their own organisations.[39]

In the decade ahead, the regional focus will need to continue to shift from policy-making to policy execution as government officials stress the need for material and human resources and training, in addition to political support and frameworks, as the necessary elements to the successful implementation of open data commitments and policies.[40]

Data focus: Social and political development

Corruption scandals[41,42] and gender-based violence incidents[43] are high on the public agenda in Latin America. As a result, some of the main lines of work exploring the use of open data to address social, political, and economic development problems have focused on gender equity and public procurement.

Gender-based violence: The urgent need to address issues related to violence against women, and its worst expression in the form of femicides, has seen important progress in recent years via both regional and global discussions. The open data community is engaging with these issues by raising questions about the availability and use of data to track the problem, and work is being done to map gender-based violence in a number of countries,[44] as well as to develop data standards that can better join up information to support informed advocacy for policy reform.[45] This project-based work on data and tools is receiving policy support from the OGP with its launch of the Feminist Open Government initiative,[46] which provides an important opportunity to bring the data dimensions of an often sidelined issue into the spotlight.

Procurement transparency: After the launch of the OGP and the creation of the Open Contracting Data Standard, Latin America was quickly established as an early-adopter region with a number of governments seeking to open up data on government contracting, and CSOs exploring connections between procurement and other areas of transparency.[47] Projects in Mexico, Paraguay, and Colombia have demonstrated the potential of open data to address corruption and inefficiency in procurement.[48] In 2017, ILDA was selected as a regional hub to provide support to open contracting implementers within Latin America.[49]

Data use and users

The creation of public value from open data is only fully possible through data reuse. The idea that intermediaries in civil society and the private sector, educators, and public officials can work with data to secure social impacts has been key in the design of open data policies in the region and in sector-specific data-use projects looking at issues, such as cities,[50] local budgets,[51] parliaments,[52] health,[53] education,[54] and public procurement.[55]

With regard to data use, journalists have played a particularly active role acting as intermediaries. Groups, such as LNData[56] (data section for the newspaper *La Nación*), Chequeado,[57] a fact-finding organisation in Argentina, *Ojo Publico*[58] in Peru, and *La Nación* [59] in Costa Rica, are examples of journalists becoming key actors analysing data and making it accessible for a larger audience. Beyond journalism, there are numerous CSOs working with open data, as well as advancing data literacy within civil society through initiatives such as the regional adaptation of School of Data, Escuela de Datos.[60] It is also important to add that, in many cases, the data used by these organisations is not only generated by the public sector but also draws on complementary datasets created by citizens to add to and/or correct official data. One example of this can be found in the inclusion of informal settlements of the City of Buenos Aires in the official cartography that incorporates work carried out by a consortium of CSOs to map missing areas.[61]

Within the universe of non-governmental open data users, there are notable differences in terms of their perspective vis-à-vis government. Both journalists and transparency-focused organisations have adopted a "watchdog" position. By contrast, other organisations with a greater emphasis on technology rather than transparency often develop a more collaborative approach.[62] Nevertheless, data users are able to draw on a reasonable stock of accountability-related datasets. As the ODB's most recent regional report noted, "Influenced by its long held 'right to information' tradition, Latin America generally performs relatively well in opening up datasets that are key for holding governments to account. In fact, more of this type of data is available in the region than anywhere outside of Western Europe and North America."[63]

Governments have also been direct users of their own data or have established partnerships with academia or civil society to develop data-driven platforms and services, such as "To your Service"[64] or "For my Neighbourhood"[65] in Uruguay. As governments become more sophisticated in using their own data, they are also developing new services, such as the "Commercial Opportunities Map" in the City of Buenos Aires,[66] or small campaigns that make creative use of open data to raise awareness of open data policies, such as the "Popular Names in Argentina".[67] This represents a break with the idea that all governments need to do is release data and leave it to others to build something with it.

Both governments and civil society actors seeking to engage with open data in the region are reasonably well supported by funders. Organisations, such as IADB, OAS, IDRC, Omidyar Network, ECLAC, Hivos, and Avina Foundation, support open data projects in the region, and initiatives, such as Altec, allow organisations to test their ideas and to understand how to make their projects sustainable in the medium and long term. However, as welcome as external funding for open data innovation is, and in spite of some of the examples given above, direct government support for open data use remains limited.

Knowledge

As we look to the future, one of the largest challenges for open data practice in Latin America relates to the lack of systematisation when it comes to knowledge generated on open data and civic technology in the last decade. In spite of community networking, numerous investigations, and all the projects that have been developed and implemented in the region, it has been difficult to gain a clear picture of regional practice or to make sure learning is shared. ILDA has recently launched RIGA,[68] a research archive with the aim of contributing to knowledge-management efforts at the academic level, although there is still much work to do in this area. Developing a map of the open data and civic technology initiatives in the region remains important to being able to learn from existing practice and to inform future work.[69]

The Caribbean

The Caribbean could justifiably lay claim to being one of the most culturally and politically diverse regions in the world. Blessed with deep, large natural harbours and short channels to open seas, the Caribbean has had a long history of cultural and commercial "openness" situated in a geographically advantageous location astride the major East–West shipping lanes. From Cuba and the Bahamas in the north to Trinidad and Tobago and the Dutch Antilles in the south, various colonial powers from the Spanish and the British to the Dutch and the French have had their way with this archipelago of islands, leading to a multiplicity of social and cultural influences of adaptation and assimilation – European, African, Asian, and North American – leaving an eclectic legacy of influences in political, social, cultural, and administrative institutions.

Public sector organisations of the Caribbean, generally speaking, perhaps due to the perceived power of information, often consider data produced using public resources as the private property of the agency which produced it, and cultural and institutional habits often limit the active sharing and use of data and other forms of evidence for policy- and decision-making. Aside from these inherited tendencies, there are also structural/institutional barriers that arise from the limited scalability and resources of the public administrations of small island developing states (SIDS) that inhibit effective data sharing and use.

Absent the impetus of active civil society and media advocacy demanding open data, Caribbean governments have been slow to embrace the more formal open government and open data movements. As a result, the open data landscape has evolved unevenly and depended considerably on the stimulus of external funding resources and institutional actors. IDRC, the Open Data for Development (OD4D) network, the World Bank, and the United Kingdom's (UK) Department of International Development (DFID) have all been major contributors in this regard.

Nevertheless, there is an interesting and distinctive Caribbean open data narrative that spans the last ten years.

A brief history: High demand and slow supply

Very soon after the beginning of the global open data movement, IDRC convened a meeting in Kingston, Jamaica in June 2010, titled "Towards a Caribbean Open Institute: Data, Communications and Impact". The meeting brought together 40 high-level public policy specialists from across the region along with international experts, and out of the conversations that took place, emerged the Caribbean Open Institute (COI),[70] conceived as a forum and a catalyst for research, advocacy, and mobilisation of key stakeholders around a regional open data agenda.[71] This dialogue also laid the groundwork for staging the first open data hackathon in Jamaica in 2012, which experimented with the creation of the first agriculture open data portal in the Caribbean.

This fledgling event in 2012 was significant in several respects. Labelled at the time as the /*Slashroots* Open Data Conference, it was the genesis for the DevCA (Developing the Caribbean) open data conference and codesprint. With its unique multi-country model, DevCA has become the signature forum for convening open data actors, stakeholders, and experimental innovations within the region over the subsequent years. It also provided the basis for engagement and ongoing partnerships between open data actors and the Rural Agriculture Development Authority (RADA), the government agency responsible for extension services to farmers in Jamaica. This focus on agriculture has been especially significant given the enormous social and economic influence of the agriculture sector in the region.[72]

Developing the Caribbean (DevCA)

The first edition of Developing the Caribbean (DevCA) in 2012 was modelled on the Developing Latin America (Desarrollando América Latina) event as a multi-country open data conference and hackathon. DevCA has become an important pillar of regional open data advocacy, engagement, and outreach. Over the course of its multiple editions, DevCA has taken place in Jamaica, Trinidad and Tobago, Dominican Republic, Cuba, Guyana, Barbados, and St. Kitts.[73]

While many similar events have succumbed to "hackathon fatigue", DevCA continues to be relevant to the Caribbean open data discourse. Its uniquely configured conference and codesprint combination has allowed it to evolve as a significant regional innovation and engagement platform. For instance, the DevCA2016 event in the Dominican Republic focused on the country's national, provincial, and municipal election monitoring in partnership with the non-governmental organisation, "Participación Cuidadana",[74] while the event in Jamaica tackled the Zika Virus Challenge in collaboration with the Ministry of Health and their regional and international development partners, including the Pan American Health Organisation (PAHO) and Caribbean Public Health Agency (CARPHA).

Initially, the Slashroots moniker was adopted as an informal label by a community of tech enthusiasts, but it eventually morphed into the SlashRoots Foundation,[75] now one of the key civic technology actors in the region responsible for a range of regional discussions and open data projects particularly focused on agricultural development and on models for managing privacy and consent issues around open data. Another key initiative in the early phase of Caribbean open data was the *m*Fisheries project, conceptualised by the Caribbean ICT Research Programme (CIRP) based at the University of the West Indies, St. Augustine Campus, in Trinidad and Tobago.[76] The project used open data as a platform for delivering mobile-enabled services to fisher folk in Trinidad and Tobago and was an early demonstration of demand-side engagement and action research, setting a pattern that has perhaps become a defining characteristic of the COI's model.

From its early beginnings, the COI moved from a concept to a virtual coalition of a core of regional founding partners[77] and has emerged as a consistent actor in crafting the Caribbean open data narrative. In 2013, the COI became an official member of the OD4D network[78] as the regional hub for the Caribbean. Over the period 2014–2017, through the project "Harnessing Open Data to Achieve Development Results in Latin America",[79] funded by the OD4D network, the COI mobilised a portfolio of demand-side research initiatives designed to investigate, articulate, and test value impact opportunities for open data in the key sectors of agriculture,[80] tourism,[81] national statistics,[82] and marine protected areas in the Caribbean.[83] These studies have provided important insights and empirical support for the potential demand, use, and value opportunities for open data for development in the Caribbean.

Agricultural Digital Services in Jamaica

An Agriculture Digital Services pilot in 2016 explored the potential of emergent best practices in government digital services to address challenges related to data accessibility, quality, and data gaps in agriculture. This initiative employed a co-production partnership model between a government agency (RADA) and technologists (Slashroots) and demonstrated a novel approach to providing key public infrastructure and enhancing information sharing in the agriculture value chain.[84]

In parallel with these primarily demand-side research-oriented activities of the COI, the World Bank, in a funding alliance with UK's DFID, also mobilised several country-level open data initiatives in the Caribbean with the primary focus on engaging central government actors to conduct open data readiness assessment (ODRA) studies, and in some cases, to facilitate open data policy formulation and open data portal implementations. Over the period 2014–2017, this endeavour saw ODRA studies conducted in Antigua, Dominican Republic, Trinidad and Tobago, St. Lucia, Jamaica, and Haiti.[85] In some cases (e.g. Jamaica), this initiative brought a valuable supply-side orientation and attention to policy-making that complemented the work being undertaken through the COI's and OD4D's networks. More typically, however, these supply-side initiatives sparked interest for the duration of the engagement but failed to generate any sustainable momentum in national open data programmes. In a number of instances, changes in political administrations arising from national elections have considerably slowed momentum with the turnover of individual personalities and priorities.

As of early 2019 at the time of this retrospective, open data in the Caribbean is still seeking to establish a scalable and sustainable platform. There is unquestionably a solid foundation to build on, grounded in a robust demand-side community, strong levels of open data awareness, technical capacity to apply open data, and a portfolio of research and pilot initiatives that have demonstrated social and economic value opportunities for open data in the Caribbean. The region also has active representation and participation in the global open data community through the COI and regular networking opportunities through DevCA, a recognised regional platform for convening stakeholders and communities around thematic open data innovation. As the most recent ODB report for the Caribbean reflects, "There is pent up demand from businesses and entrepreneurs to take advantage of the economic opportunities offered by open data", but "[g]overnments in the region have yet to commit to developing the initiatives and policies needed to support demand-side opportunities".[86]

Unlocking potential: Future challenges

One study looking at the social and economic opportunities for open data in the Caribbean estimates a potential impact of 1–2% of GDP for key sectors, such as agriculture, tourism, and education.[87] For the majority of the countries of the Caribbean, small island developing states with limited economic resource endowments and persistent growth challenges, this represents a significant value opportunity, yet unlocking this potential requires a number of challenges to be addressed.

Political commitment

The persistent apathy of political leadership in the Caribbean toward the open data/open government agenda continues to be disappointing. Notwithstanding strong advocacy efforts on multiple fronts, most countries, especially in the Anglophone Caribbean, have realised little to modest gains in terms of focus on open data from a policy perspective. Recent changes in the political administration in countries, including Jamaica, Trinidad and Tobago, and St. Lucia, have had the effect of slowing momentum as relationships and advocacy cultivated with various government leaders have to be continually re-built. Even in cases where countries have been signatories to OGP commitments, progress on the formulation and execution of National Action Plans has been pedantic at best. The enactment and institutionalisation of national open data policies is particularly important in signalling to both public and private sector actors the extent of the commitment of the political leadership to the open data agenda, and without more action on this front, progress may remain limited.

Key actors and intermediaries

Even in cases where there is active intent, many Caribbean governments and public sector agencies typically fall short of having the internal capacity, technical expertise, and resources needed to initiate and undertake open data initiatives. In a region where SIDS struggle to cope with the lingering effects of the economic recession and fiscal policy dictates, open data must contend with a range of other socioeconomic policy demands for scarce resources and political attention. Intermediaries, with the support of multilateral funding, will continue to play a critical role as enablers of emerging open data initiatives in the Caribbean. Providing innovation fellowships, such as in the case of the Agriculture Digital Services, partnership brokering, such as in the case of Community Tourism in Jamaica, and Election Monitoring, such as in the Dominican Republic, demonstrate different models of intermediation that have catalysed valuable open data initiatives (see boxes on Agriculture Digital Services and Crowdsourced open data for community tourism).

> ### Crowdsourced open data for community tourism in Kingston
>
> In late 2015, an open geodata and Interactive Community Mapping (ICM) initiative was initiated in an inner-city community in Kingston, Jamaica, to explore how crowdsourced open data could contribute to advancing community tourism activities and provide a platform for developing new tourism products and services. The initiative brokered a partnership model with community organisations, government agencies, local businesses, and academia all involved in the creation of an open geodata ecosystem and seeking to encourage tourists to access a wider range of locally provided services outside of all-inclusive package tourism.[88]

Capacity building

The Caribbean region has been generally regarded as "data poor", not just because of limited access to high quality, locally relevant data, but also due to cultural and institutional habits and capacity limitations (both in the public and private sectors) that restrict the use of data and other forms of evidence for policy- and decision-making.[89] Building sustainable open data infrastructures and enabling the effective use of open data in the Caribbean requires actors from all sectors (public, private, media, CSOs) to invest in individual and community capacity across the whole open data value-chain. The Caribbean School of Data (CSOD),[90] hosted by the COI, is seeking to provide a comprehensive and sustainable data literacy programme that will help to develop greater awareness, attitudes, competencies, and capacity to build a stronger data culture across the Caribbean. This will be a critical and essential component of future open data initiatives. The current "Ayitic Goes Global" data literacy pilot initiative in Haiti is an important learning opportunity in this regard (see box, Ayitic Goes Global).

> ### Ayitic Goes Global – Building digital literacy
>
> Digital literacy is a critical prerequisite for sustainable digital development. "Ayitic Goes Global: Empowering Women through Digital Markets"[91] is a research initiative that seeks to increase women's access to online employment in Haiti by building digital and data capacities in the field of information technology. However, the typical assumptions about the availability of digital infrastructure and the evolution of social and cultural habits toward normative online behaviours in the digital economy are rigorously challenged in the Haiti context. This initiative has explored new pedagogical approaches for online digital education in resource-constrained environments.[92]

Regional agenda, global connections

There is growing evidence to demonstrate the potential of open data in key Caribbean sectors, such as agriculture and tourism. This creates the imperative to find strategies and business models that can scale by applying regional approaches to these common priority sectors. The implementation of shareable platforms that go beyond publishing open data and application programming interfaces (APIs) to leverage, where appropriate, international standards, such as the GODAN Agriculture Open Up Guide (see Chapter 2: Agriculture), to create strong value propositions and reduced transaction costs for data custodians and data consumers across the Caribbean will be an important enabler. To secure a stronger future for open data, Caribbean governments, together with key regional actors and stakeholders, should look to the experience of other regions and contemplate the formulation of a Caribbean Data Consensus to align efforts toward a regional data commons. A continuation of current fragmented approaches to the data for development agenda in the region will limit its effectiveness and sustainability.

Conclusion

This examination of the open data landscape in Latin America and the Caribbean demonstrates several points of convergence, as well as areas where collaboration could be fostered, including on data use, capacity building, and improving political leadership.

In the first place, both regions recognise the importance of moving from a generic approach to a sectoral focus. However, the sectors of focus vary. Where research in Latin America has unearthed significant opportunities in areas, such as health, procurement, and energy, Caribbean research has prioritised agriculture and tourism. A sectoral focus can also aid work to engage non-traditional actors and those not previously involved in the open data agenda, particularly the Latin American private sector. This may provide the opportunity to multiply the number of uses and benefits of open data that is currently available.

Second, there is still a pressing need to build the capacity of governments and society at large to engage with an open data agenda. In the case of Latin America, there is a strong organised civil society which demands, and uses, data in many of the countries. They are a powerful force in advancing the agenda, and they should continue to be part of the development of policies and other governmental activities. But making demands of government without supporting government capacity is fraught with difficulty. Training for officials and for users of data is a vital component when implementing open data policy. Public officials need to be aware of key data concepts, as well as their duties in relation to opening data. In the Caribbean, capacity-building efforts to date have focused broadly on digital competencies and data literacy through initiatives such as the Caribbean School of Data. At the political leadership level, where open data policies have not advanced at the same pace as in Latin America, there is scope for the application of initiatives to better network and support leaders, potentially drawing on the model of the OD4D-backed Open Data Leaders Network.[93] The opportunity for networking between Latin American and Caribbean leaders should also be considered. For example, the experience of building consensus to secure open data policy in Costa Rica could contribute learning to policy development processes in Caribbean countries.

Finally, while acknowledging language barriers and other socio-cultural differences, there is much value to be secured by creating stronger linkages between actors in both subregions. Despite sustained dialogue through the OD4D network, there is still a considerable gap to be bridged. Actors engaged in similar work, in spite of language barriers, should be encouraged to share their expertise and to consider joint initiatives. Events, such as AbreLatam, Condatos, DevCA, and IODC, and others, should provide the opportunities to enhance these linkages moving forward.

> **Further reading**
>
> Carranza, D. (2017). Lecciones, experiencias y aprendizajes en el ámbito de gobierno abierto: el caso de DATA Uruguay. In A. Naser, Á. Ramírez-Alujas, & D. Rosales (Eds.), *Desde el gobierno abierto al estado abierto en América Latina y el Caribe*. Santiago: United Nations Economic and Social Commission for Latin America and the Caribbean (ECLAC). https://www.un-ilibrary.org/economic-and-social-development/desde-el-gobierno-abierto-al-estado-abierto-en-america-latina-y-el-caribe_320272ce-es
>
> McNaughton, M.L., McLeod, M.T., McNaughton, M., & Walcott, J. (2016). Open data as a catalyst for problem solving: Empirical evidence from a small island developing states (SIDS) context. In *Proceedings of the Open Data Research Symposium*, 5 October 2016, Madrid, Spain. https://drive.google.com/file/d/0B4TpC6ecmrM7OEN6OVllUXh1d1U/view
>
> Naser, A., Ramírez-Alujas, Á., & D. Rosales, D. (Eds.). (2017). *Desde el gobierno abierto al estado abierto en América Latina y el Caribe*. Santiago: United Nations Economic and Social Commission for Latin America and the Caribbean (ECLAC). https://www.un-ilibrary.org/economic-and-social-development/desde-el-gobierno-abierto-al-estado-abierto-en-america-latina-y-el-caribe_320272ce-es
>
> Scrollini, F. (2017). El surgimiento de América Latina abierta: La agenda de datos abiertos en la región. In A. Naser, Á. Ramírez-Alujas, & D. Rosales (Eds.), *Desde el gobierno abierto al estado abierto en América Latina y el Caribe*. Santiago: United Nations Economic and Social Commission for Latin America and the Caribbean (ECLAC). https://www.un-ilibrary.org/economic-and-social-development/desde-el-gobierno-abierto-al-estado-abierto-en-america-latina-y-el-caribe_320272ce-es

About the authors

Silvana Fumega is Research and Policy Director of ILDA. You can follow Silvana at https://www.twitter.com/SilvanavF and learn more about ILDA at https://idatosabiertos.org/.

Maurice McNaughton is a founding member of the COI and is a Director at the Mona School of Business & Management, University of the West Indies. You can follow Maurice at https://www.twitter.com/mauriceMcn and learn more about the COI at https://caribbeanopeninstitute.org/.

How to cite this chapter

Fumega, S. & McNaughton, M. (2019). Open data around the world: Latin America and the Caribbean. In T. Davies, S. Walker, M. Rubinstein, & F. Perini (Eds.), *The state of open data: Histories and horizons* (pp. 485–502). Cape Town and Ottawa: African Minds and International Development Research Centre. http://stateofopendata.od4d.net

This work is licensed under a Creative Commons Attribution 4.0 International (CC BY 4.0) licence. It was carried out with the aid of a grant from the International Development Research Centre, Ottawa, Canada.

Endnotes

1. https://opendatainception.io/
2. Scrollini, F. & Mora, M. (2017). Precisamos políticas de datos abiertos [We need open data policies]. *ILDA*, 15 November. https://idatosabiertos.org/precisamos-politicas-de-datos-abiertos/
3. http://20187.abrelatam.org/
4. https://condatos.org/
5. https://opendatacharter.net/
6. Scrollini, F. & Mora, M. (2017). Precisamos políticas de datos abiertos [We need open data policies]. *ILDA*, 15 November. https://idatosabiertos.org/precisamos-politicas-de-datos-abiertos/.
7. Web Foundation & Iniciativa Latinoamericana por los Datos Abiertos (ILDA). (2017). *Open Data Barometer (4th edition): Latin America regional snapshot*. Washington, DC: World Wide Web Foundation. https://opendatabarometer.org/doc/4thEdition/ODB-4thEdition-RegionalReport-LATAM.pdf
8. https://web.archive.org/web/20111126233408/http://desarrollandoamerica.org/
9. Scrolini, F. (2014). *Open cities: The case of Montevideo*. Open Data Research Network. http://www.opendataresearch.org/sites/default/files/publications/Opening%20Montevideo-a%20case%20studyfinalll.pdf
10. Delfin, M. (2015). The limits of a good practice: On the need for an intercultural critique of open data and its social construction in the Global South. *2015 Open Data Research Symposium*, 27 May 2015, Ottawa, Canada. http://www.opendataresearch.org/dl/symposium2015/odrs2015-paper58.pdf
11. http://dineroypolitica.org/application/about
12. http://gastopublicobahiense.org/
13. https://blog.okfn.org/tag/okcon/
14. https://blog.okfn.org/category/events/okfest/
15. https://sunlightfoundation.com/transparency-camp/
16. https://www.opendatacon.org/
17. For more information, see https://apps.co/comunicaciones/articulos/desarrollando-america-latina-la-iniciativa-colabor/
18. Fumega, S. (2014). City of Buenos Aires Open Government Data initiative. *Opening the Cities: Open Government Data in Local Governments of Argentina, Brazil and Uruguay*. Open Data Research Network. http://www.opendataresearch.org/content/2014/663/city-buenos-aires-open-government-data-initiative.html
19. https://www.datauy.org/
20. https://ciudadaniai.org/

21. Roitberg, G. (2013). Abre Latam: Por una región de datos abiertos. *La Nacion Data* [Blog post], 26 June. http://blogs.lanacion.com.ar/data/datos-abiertos/abre-latam-por-una-region-de-datos-abiertos/
22. Bagley, R.O. (2014). How "unconferences" unleash innovative ideas. *Forbes*, 18 August. https://www.forbes.com/sites/rebeccabagley/2014/08/18/how-unconferences-unleash-innovative-ideas/#42f47b6b645b
23. Accesa. (2017). La evolución de AbreLatam: Perspectivas de sus organizadores. *Medium*, 25 August. https://medium.com/revista-sinergias/la-evoluci%C3%B3n-de-abrelatam-perspectivas-de-sus-organizadores-76c2e70607e7
24. Fumega, S. & Scrollini, F. (2017). The Latin American way. *ILDA* [News post], 12 September. https://idatosabiertos.org/en/el-camino-propio-de-america-latina/
25. Ibid.
26. Belbis, J.I. (2015). *Apertura legislativa en el Cono Sur ¿Y los datos?* Montevideo: Iniciativa Latinoamericana por los Datos Abiertos (ILDA). https://idatosabiertos.org/wp-content/uploads/2015/10/3.-Apertura-legislativa-Belbis1.pdf
27. https://www.properati.com.ar/
28. http://www.junar.com/
29. https://www.dymaxionlabs.com/
30. https://properati.com/
31. https://www.dymaxionlabs.com/
32. https://ap-latam.dymaxionlabs.com/en/
33. https://flood.dymaxionlabs.com/
34. https://cd-demo.dymaxionlabs.com/
35. Some examples are the projects funded by Altec. https://altec.lat/es/proyectos/
36. Web Foundation & Iniciativa Latinoamericana por los Datos Abiertos (ILDA). (2017.) *Open Data Barometer* (4th edition): *Latin America regional snapshot.* Washington, DC: World Wide Web Foundation. https://opendatabarometer.org/doc/4thEdition/ODB-4thEdition-RegionalReport-LATAM.pdf
37. Ibid.
38. https://web.archive.org/web/20180812235632/https://www.od4d.net/impact-series-facilitating-the-costa-rican-open-data-national-decree/
39. Scrollini, F. & Mora, M. (2017). Precisamos políticas de datos abiertos [We need open data policies]. *ILDA* [News post], 15 November. https://idatosabiertos.org/precisamos-politicas-de-datos-abiertos/
40. Fumega, S. (2018). Políticas de datos abiertos: Algunas reflexiones. *ILDA* [News post], 23 March. https://idatosabiertos.org/en/politica-de-datos-abiertos-algunas-reflexiones/
41. Anon. (2017). 5 escándalos de corrupción que ensombrecen a América Latina. *AltoNivel*, 18 May. https://www.altonivel.com.mx/empresas/5-escandalos-corrupcion-ensombrecen-a-america-latina/
42. BBC. (2018). Los presidentes y expresidentes latinoamericanos salpicados por el escándalo Odebrecht, "La mayor red de sobornos extranjeros de la historia". *BBC World*, 22 March. https://www.bbc.com/mundo/noticias-america-latina-38905411
43. See, for example, http://www.bbc.com/mundo/noticias-america-latina-37828573
44. See, for example, https://feminicidiosmx.crowdmap.com/ and https://www.zeemaps.com/view?group=1790384, http://www.ellastienennombre.org/mapa-1.html and https://cuantasmas.org/
45. Fumega, S. (2018). News of our work on data, gender and security. *ILDA* [News post], 9 February. https://idatosabiertos.org/en/algunas-novedades-de-nuestro-trabajo-sobre-datos-genero-y-seguridad/
46. Pradhan, S. (2018). The right to a glass of milk – and to live life fully. *Open Government Partnership*, 14 February. https://www.opengovpartnership.org/stories/right-glass-of-milk-and-live-life-fully
47. Florez, J., Wikrent, K., & Martín-Borregón, E. (2017). Following the money in Latin America: Reflections from Condatos. *Open Contracting Partnership* [Blog post], 15 September. https://www.open-contracting.org/2017/09/15/following-money-latin-america-reflections-condatos/
48. https://www.open-contracting.org/why-open-contracting/worldwide/

49 Deminchuck, C. (2018). Latin American Helpdesk turns one. *Open Contracting Partnership* [Blog post], 27 April. https://www.open-contracting.org/2018/04/27/latin-american-helpdesk-turns-one/

50 Bonina, C. (2015). *Co-creación, innovación y datos abiertos en ciudades de América Latina: Lecciones de Buenos Aires, Ciudad de México y Montevideo*. Montevideo: Iniciativa Latinoamericana por los Datos Abiertos (ILDA). https://idatosabiertos.org/wp-content/uploads/2015/09/1.-Cocreacion-innovacion-y-datos-abiertos-Bonina.pdf

51 Albano, C. & Craveiro, G. (2015). *Acesso a dados orçamentários (em formato aberto) na América Latina: Panorama da atuação dos intermediários nesse ecossistema*. Montevideo: Iniciativa Latinoamericana por los Datos Abiertos (ILDA). https://idatosabiertos.org/wp-content/uploads/2015/10/2.-Acceso-a-dados-orcamentarios-Albano-Craveiro.pdf

52 Belbis, J.I. (2015). *Apertura legislativa en el Cono Sur ¿Y los datos?* Montevideo: Iniciativa Latinoamericana por los Datos Abiertos (ILDA). https://idatosabiertos.org/wp-content/uploads/2015/10/3.-Apertura-legislativa-Belbis1.pdf

53 Pane, J., Ojeda, V., & Valdez, N. (2015). *Dengue open data*. Montevideo: Iniciativa Latinoamericana por los Datos Abiertos (ILDA). https://idatosabiertos.org/wp-content/uploads/2015/10/7.Dengue-Pane-Ojeda-Valdez.pdf

54 Khelladi, Y. (2015). *Datos abiertos en educación, primeros alcances y lecciones*. Montevideo: Iniciativa Latinoamericana por los Datos Abiertos (ILDA). http://riga.idatosabiertos.org//papers/datos-abiertos-en-educacion-primeros-alcances-y-lecciones.html

55 Volosin, N.A. (2015). *Datos abiertos, corrupción y compras públicas*. Montevideo: Iniciativa Latinoamericana por los Datos Abiertos (ILDA). https://idatosabiertos.org/wp-content/uploads/2015/10/5.-Corrupcion-y-compras-publicas-Volosin1.pdf

56 http://blogs.lanacion.com.ar/data/

57 http://chequeado.com/

58 https://ojo-publico.com/

59 https://www.nacion.com/data/

60 https://es.schoolofdata.org/

61 Balbi, M. (2017). "Caminos de la Villa": La plataforma argentina premiada como mejor tecnología social latinoamericana de 2017. *Infobae*, 23 December. https://www.infobae.com/tendencias/innovacion/2017/12/23/caminos-de-la-villa-la-plataforma-argentina-premiada-como-mejor-tecnologia-social-latinoamericana-de-2017/

62 Fumega, S. (2015). *Understanding two mechanisms for accessing government information and data around the world*. Open Data Research Network. https://webfoundation.org/docs/2015/08/UnderstandingTwoMechanismsforAccessingGovernmentInformationandData.pdf

63 Web Foundation & Iniciativa Latinoamericana por los Datos Abiertos (ILDA). (2017). *Open Data Barometer (4th edition): Latin America regional snapshot*. Washington, DC: World Wide Web Foundation. https://opendatabarometer.org/doc/4thEdition/ODB-4thEdition-RegionalReport-LATAM.pdf

64 http://atuservicio.uy/sobre_el_proyecto

65 http://www.municipiob.montevideo.gub.uy/comunicacion/noticias/aplicacion-por-mi-barrio

66 https://moc.buenosaires.gob.ar/

67 http://nombres.historias.datos.gob.ar/

68 http://riga.idatosabiertos.org/

69 Fumega, S., Bonina, C., & Scrollini, F. (2018). Mapeo analizará nueva era de datos abiertos y tecnología cívica en América Latina. *Blog Altec*, 2 July. https://altec.lat/mapeo-analizara-nueva-era-de-datos-abiertos-y-tecnologia-civica-en-america-latina/

70 http://caribbeanopeninstitute.org/

71 IDRC. (2010). *Towards a Caribbean Open Institute: Data, communications and impact: Summary of guidelines and recommendations*. Kingston: International Development Research Centre. http://web.idrc.ca/uploads/user-S/12826689291Towards-a-Caribbean-Open-Initiative.pdf

72 McNaughton, M. & Soutar, D. (2015). *Agricultural open data in the Caribbean: Institutional perceptions, key issues and opportunities*. CTA Working Paper. Wageningen: Technical Centre for Agricultural and Rural Cooperation ACP-EU. https://cgspace.cgiar.org/handle/10568/75489

73 SlashRoots Foundation. (2016). *DevCA 2016 Conference Report*. Kingston: SlashRoots Foundation. http://caribbeanopeninstitute.org/civicrm/file?reset=1&id=23&eid=1238

74 https://pciudadana.org/

75 https://www.slashroots.org/

76 Mallalieu, K. & McConney, P. (2015). *Caribbean Open Data Scoping Study: Fisheries and marine protected areas (MPAs)*. Kingston: Caribbean Open Institute. http://caribbeanopeninstitute.org/civicrm/file?reset=1&id=19&eid=1231

77 Mona School of Business and Management, University of the West Indies (UWI); Fundacion Taiguey; SlashRoots Foundation, Caribbean ICT Research Programme, UWI; Panos Caribbean.

78 http://od4d.net

79 https://www.idrc.ca/en/project/harnessing-open-data-achieve-development-results-latin-america-and-caribbean

80 McNaughton, M.L., McLeod, M.T., McNaughton, M., & Walcott, J. (2016). Open data as a catalyst for problem solving: Empirical evidence from a small island developing states (SIDS) context. In *Proceedings of the Open Data Research Symposium*, 5 October 2016, Madrid, Spain. https://drive.google.com/open?id=0B4TpC6ecmrM7OEN6OVlIUXh1d1U

81 McLeod, M. *Caribbean Tourism Sector Open Data Scoping Study*. Kingston: Caribbean Open Institute. http://caribbeanopeninstitute.org/civicrm/file?reset=1&id=20&eid=1232

82 Jackson, S. (2015). *Official statistics and open data: A small island developing state (SIDS) perspective*. Mona School of Business and Management & Caribbean Open Institute. http://caribbeanopeninstitute.org/civicrm/file?reset=1&id=18&eid=1230

83 Mallalieu, K. & McConney, P. (2015). *Caribbean Open Data Scoping Study: Fisheries and marine protected areas (MPAs)*. Kingston: Caribbean Open Institute. http://caribbeanopeninstitute.org/civicrm/file?reset=1&id=19&eid=1231

84 SlashRoots Foundation. (2016). *Caribbean Open Institute Agriculture Digital Services Strategic Initiative – Project report*. Kingston: Caribbean Open Institute and SlashRoots Foundation. http://caribbeanopeninstitute.org/civicrm/file?reset=1&id=26&eid=1241

85 World Bank (2017). *World Bank support for open data – 2012 – 2017*. Washington, DC: World Bank. http://hdl.handle.net/10986/28616

86 Web Foundation & Caribbean Open Institute. (2017). *Open Data Barometer* (4th edition): *The Caribbean regional report*. Washington, DC: World Wide Web Foundation. https://opendatabarometer.org/4thedition/regional-snapshot/caribbean/

87 McNaughton, M.L., McLeod, M.T., McNaughton, M., & Walcott, J. (2016). Open data as a catalyst for problem-solving: Empirical evidence from a small island developing states (SIDS) context. In *Proceedings of the Open Data Research Symposium*, 5 October 2016, Madrid, Spain. https://drive.google.com/open?id=0B4TpC6ecmrM7OEN6OVlIUXh1d1U

88 Young, A., & Verhulst, S. (2017). *Jamaica, community tourism and open data*. Brooklyn, NY: GovLab.

89 IDRC. (2010). *Towards a Caribbean Open Institute: Data, communications and impact: Summary of guidelines and recommendations*. Kingston: International Development Research Centre, pp. 5–6. http://web.idrc.ca/uploads/user-S/12826689291Towards-a-Caribbean-Open-Initiative.pdf

90 http://caribbeanopeninstitute.org/csod

91 http://ayitic.net

92 SlashRoots Foundation. (2017). *Ayitic Goes Global: Pedagogical strategy*. Kingston: SlashRoots Foundation. https://www.ayitic.net/documentos/2017/ayitic-pedagogical-strategy.pdf

93 https://theodi.org/project/open-data-leaders-network/

034

Middle East and North Africa

Nagla Rizk, Nancy Salem, and Stefanie Felsberger

Key points

- The Middle East and North Africa has seen varied progress on open data, from university-led efforts focusing on social issues to government-led open data initiatives that place an emphasis on economic development.

- The region faces the substantial challenge of data scarcity: with gaps in data collection, data publication, and a lack of continuity and updates when data is released publicly.

- Improved regional networking is needed to unite the scattered initiatives that are working directly on open data and to ensure other data-literacy and capacity-building initiatives address openness, as well as more general data skills and use.

Introduction

The Middle East and North Africa (MENA) is an expansive geographical region that extends from Morocco in the West to Iran in the East. The region is historically, economically, and socially diverse. Arabic is the most widely spoken language with several subregional dialects. As a whole, the region is resource rich, with several economies primarily based on the exportation of natural resources, oil and gas in particular. A history of colonialism and imperialism has contributed to persisting socioeconomic challenges. Large populations of young, educated citizens are common to many countries in the region, providing a key asset to increasingly digital economies.

For the past decade, MENA has been broadly associated with civil unrest. Political and social change has been unpredictable, and, in many places, tensions persist. As in much of the world, the region has also had to grapple with technological change, which has created opportunities for both governments and citizens. Data has been at the forefront of many discussions related to these issues, including the potential for open data to address socioeconomic challenges.

This chapter provides an overview of recent developments in the field of open data in the region, stressing the diversity of open data initiatives undertaken and recording the key moments over the past few years. By extending the data life cycle approach, the chapter seeks to investigate not just the spectrum of data production, access, and use, but also to consider feedback mechanisms that ensure datasets remain timely and accurate. This allows for the integration of a broader set of issues in relation to open data, particularly the ability to use data once it is open. In the MENA context, where datasets are often scarce, it is critical to address what happens when data is published to fill an identified need but is never updated or is inaccurate. The chapter will also focus on a recent surge in capacity-building initiatives and their ability to address challenges to open data in the region.

Data-driven innovation: Framing the open data debate

Regional interest in open data has often been encouraged by international engagement with a global open data community where an increasing number of governments are adopting open data commitments as a result of the expansion of international networks and programmes looking at "data for development" initiatives, as well as the influence of narratives highlighting the economic potential of data. Resulting activities have overlapped and coalesced, with no clear chronology that would confirm which of these factors is the most important in pushing forward engagement with open data in the region. However, as a result, open data initiatives in the region are often explained by these three narratives: the socioeconomic potential of data to spur innovation and entrepreneurship; the potential of data for better decision-making, efficiency, and service delivery; and data for development. In addition, many initiatives and activities have been framed within the concept of data-driven innovation (DDI).

According to an Organisation for Economic Co-operation and Development (OECD) report on Data Driven Innovation for Growth and Well-Being,[1] DDI refers to innovation, new knowledge, products, processes, and markets created based on insights gained through the analysis of large volumes of data using new data analysis technologies, such as big data analysis, machine learning, and algorithms. The concept of DDI has been adopted within many of the initiatives explored in this section, irrespective of the sector or actor from which they originate.

The focus on DDI is also partly explained by regional development priorities. MENA has a large young population. The median age in the region is 22 years, compared to a global average of 28.[2] Educational enrolment rates are generally high across the region, but youth unemployment is a concern in most countries. Internet and mobile phone usage is common among the young and educated, and an emphasis on educational and employment reform has largely focused on building digital skills. Many countries have established national digitalisation plans or strategies, looking to capitalise on skilled youth and technological innovations to address socioeconomic challenges. This focus on DDI and the potential of the MENA region's youth are accompanied by a strong emphasis on the importance of entrepreneurial activities to develop the region. MENA is witnessing a growing interest in innovation originating from university campuses, accelerators, and incubators, resulting in the creation of networks and hubs for entrepreneurship.

There are two main emerging open data trends in the region. While some countries have seen work on open data led by governments within e-government or open government initiatives, other countries have seen strong support for open data work come from universities and the private sector. While these two trends do not negate one another, very few countries have seen matched progress in both arenas.

Open and e-government: Digitalisation from the top down

Open government data is often an element of larger national digitalisation strategies. This is particularly true for countries in the Gulf Cooperation Council, which have linked the development of e-government services with open data initiatives. The United Arab Emirates (UAE), for example, has an open data portal (Bayanat.ae) that is framed in terms of their vision of promoting a digital knowledge economy.[3] Since data and data-driven decision-making are key drivers fuelling the knowledge economy, the open data movement is seen more as part of initiatives that encourage overall digital transformation strategies and projects.

Qatar's open data policy also follows the country's digitalisation initiative. As part of this policy (published in November 2014), Qatar's e-government portal, Hukoomi, makes several open datasets available.[4] Bahrain also has an open data portal, allowing users to select data by topic with an option to bulk download several datasets at once.[5] Oman's e-government service portal currently has 56 open datasets across 12 different sectors available in csv (comma-separated values) format.[6] Additionally, Oman has an Omani Open Government License with stipulations for the use of government data.[7]

Much like the region's Gulf states, Lebanon has also sought to incorporate open data into its national digital transformation strategy. In March 2018, Lebanon held a Digital Transformation Summit to highlight plans for digital government services, open data and evidence-based policies, cybersecurity, and capacity building. Their e-government portal was launched at the conference although it is still in beta phase.[8]

Other notable initiatives have stemmed from engagement with the Open Government Partnership (OGP). Three countries in the region are now members: Jordan, Morocco, and Tunisia. Since joining the OGP in 2014, Tunisia has made 20 commitments, with an additional 15 currently underway. The country's current national plan supports a range of OGP principles with initiatives falling within such thematic areas as e-government, legislation and regulation, and public service delivery. As part of these efforts, Tunisia's Ministry of Energy worked with international organisations in 2014 to implement a site for publishing hydrocarbon investment contracts along with their associated documents.[9] This followed appeals to increase transparency around projects related to the extractive industry. The data is available in machine-readable formats and is accompanied by metadata that includes country, company name, resource being extracted, signature date, and type of contract.[10]

Innovation from universities and the private sector

A focus only on public sector data and national open data initiatives can conceal critical work from universities and the private sector in the region in both using and creating relevant datasets. Although working with different datasets and areas of focus, their initiatives often still lie within a DDI framework, emphasising the potential of data-related projects to create employment through entrepreneurship.

In 2015, a research consortium led by the Access to Knowledge for Development (A2K4D) Center at the American University in Cairo, with Al-Akhawayn University in Morocco and the Center for Continuing Education at Birzeit University in Palestine, developed several pilot data and open data initiatives in the region with support from the International Development Research Centre (IDRC). Within this consortium, A2K4D in partnership with SETS North Africa used open-sourced, crowdsourced, and existing government data to capture informal transport patterns on Cairo's Ring Road (the largest freeway in Greater Cairo which connects large portions of the city's metropolitan areas) to visualise information on transport safety, accessibility, and reliability.[11] A2K4D also developed a pilot Solar Data Platform in partnership with IDRC and the German Friedrich Ebert Stiftung, providing a repository where users could openly share data on energy projects in Egypt.[12] The project places particular emphasis on the use of data to connect different business actors (distributors, installers, and suppliers) in the supply chain for solar energy projects and to create sustainable entrepreneurial networks.[13] As part of the same consortium, Birzeit University used sensors to measure air pollution in Ramallah and then trained the Ministry of Transportation on the uses of data-based technologies to monitor air quality.[14] Al-Akhawayn University also created a digital tool to crowdsource data on accident-prone highway locations.[15]

Beyond this consortium, the Open Data Impact Map, developed and managed by the Center for Open Data Enterprise in the United States (US), has documented a further seven initiatives in the region using open data.[16] The Impact Map lists two data initiatives in Lebanon: Visualising Impact from an organisation founded in Canada, with a regional office in Beirut, that combines storytelling with data visualisation[17] and the Lebanese Elections Data Analysis which monitors Lebanese elections.[18] In Egypt, Transport for Cairo (TfC), a product created in 2015 by a cross-disciplinary team of urban planners, social scientists, and computer engineers, has mapped traffic networks in Cairo using an open data methodology also employed in Kenya and London.[19] The project has sought to explore how transit mapping can contribute toward urban mobility by exploring the availability of data from private transport firms on transport affordability, safety, and environmental sustainability alongside more commonly sought transit data such as service timetables and real-time locations.[20]

Larger private sector organisations have also made efforts to release their data with varying levels of detail and openness. For example, Uber launched an open data platform called Uber Movement in 2017[21] and recently made aggregated data on its vehicle movements available for bulk download. Cairo is currently the only city in the MENA region with data available on the Uber Movement platform, but initiatives like this are set to be a valuable source of data that is not available elsewhere. The private sector may also have the capacity to be an important source of data when other parties lack the necessary resources and opportunities. A growth in private sector data provision should, however, be accompanied by a concern for user privacy and data ownership.

The growing diversity of open data and DDI initiatives reflects differing objectives and capacities to create and use open data. As discussed at greater length later in this chapter, the ability to engage meaningfully with open data can render initiatives less supply-side driven and more responsive to open data demand. It is also important to note that while acknowledging the potential of open data for new economic opportunities for small and medium enterprises, a focus on DDI does not necessarily involve advocacy for fully open data. Nevertheless, focusing on the economic potential of open data, as DDI has undoubtedly had an effect on the open data agenda in the region, and using DDI as a common starting point, can serve to spark a dialogue across stakeholders that may not initially be interested in open data.

The challenges: Data scarcity, engagement, and capacity

To further develop both DDI and parallel open data work in the MENA region, there are a number of challenges that will need to be addressed. In overcoming these challenges, there are genuine opportunities to deploy data as a tool for social and economic development.

Data scarcity

In the MENA region, data has remained scarce for varying reasons, but data collection issues are key.[22] Therefore, in discussing data scarcity, it is important to explore two main issues: data openness and the ecosystem around data collection, production, and management. Three questions are relevant: whether data is open?, whether good quality and timely data has been collected?, and whether it will continue to be collected and released? Data scarcity appears to be a common issue across the region, albeit to varying degrees and for different reasons; however, the common objective throughout the region, using data in order to support the development of the digital knowledge economy, has undoubtedly shaped decisions that affect data availability and quality.

Using Open Data Barometer data from 2015,[23] data expert Hatem Ben Yacoub estimates that only 1.48% of data in the Arab world is open. Even though the Barometer indicated that 71% of surveyed government information was available on the internet, there were technical and/or legal barriers to accessing it as machine-readable data. The Barometer data also indicated that readiness for open data development in the Arab world was lower than the global average at 32.44% and implementation rates stood at just 16%. Other measurements indicate issues not only with the quality of open data, but also with the breadth of data that is made open, although some concerns about methodology have been expressed.[24]

Initiatives like the Global Open Data Index (GODI), managed by Open Knowledge International (OKI), use crowdsourced assessments, depending on the availability of local contributors found through referrals and social media. Exploring the GODI[25] measurement of open government data in 17 countries, Riyadh Balushi and Sadeek Hasna note that a common challenge is that several governments store and publish data and records as scanned PDF documents under varying licences that affect how "open" the records can be considered.[26] Table 1 draws on the GODI and illustrates the varied progress made by countries across a range of data categories, highlighting that, in the region, there remains much room for progress on several datasets. This data was also used to prepare Figure 1.

Table 1: Open data progress in the MENA region
Source: Global Open Data Index (https://index.okfn.org/)[27]

Country	National Statistics	Legislation	Procurement tenders	Pollutant emissions	Company register	Location datasets	Water quality
Algeria	35%	35%	0%	0%	0%	0%	0%
Bahrain	80%	45%	35%	10%	45%	0%	5%
Egypt	60%	45%	0%	0%	0%	0%	0%
Iran	0%	45%	0%	0%	0%	0%	5%
Iraq	50%	45%	0%	0%	0%	0%	0%
Jordan	35%	0%	45%	0%	35%	0%	10%
Kuwait	35%	25%	45%	10%	0%	5%	0%
Lebanon	35%	45%	0%	45%	35%	0%	0%
Libya	35%	45%	0%	0%	0%	0%	0%
Morocco	35%	45%	45%	0%	15%	100%	35%
Oman	80%	75%	45%	0%	0%	0%	0%
Qatar	35%	90%	45%	35%	0%	0%	0%
Saudi Arabia	50%	45%	35%	5%	0%	0%	0%
Sudan	0%	45%	0%	0%	0%	0%	0%
Syria	0%	5%	0%	0%	20%	0%	0%
Tunisia	90%	45%	0%	5%	0%	25%	0%
United Arab Emirates	60%	35%	0%	45%	0%	0%	0%

These findings are echoed by the 2017 Open Data Inventory (ODIN), which assessed data available on National Statistical Office (NSO) websites for both coverage and openness.[28] Prepared by Open Data Watch, the inventory also offers a two-year comparison between data available from 2015 to 2017.[29] Figure 1 represents the overall ODIN score of countries in the MENA region. Findings from this assessment indicate that there is progress to be made in terms of openness, with the highest overall percentage of statistical data available as open data being 51% in the UAE. The relative openness of the region as a whole, according to ODIN, based on an accumulation of social, economic, and environmental statistics, has remained stable since the 2015 report, although Egypt's overall performance has gone up by 3 points from 2015 to 2017, while Jordan's has gone down by 1 point.

Given these findings, focus in the regional open data community has understandably been placed on releasing more open data. For the region as a whole, there is also a concern around the lack of feedback mechanisms to ensure that open data is timely and responds to the demands of users. The 2017 *Open Data Barometer, 4th Edition* found that almost all countries in MENA were regressing on open data progress made in previous years, citing, in particular, a lack of civil society engagement.[30]

Further insight into regional data scarcity is gained by looking beyond static measures of data availability to examine what happens before and after data is released. This involves placing a focus on the data life cycle, including data production, access, and use, and determining what data is produced; who has the skills, knowledge, and the financial and technological capacity to access and work with data; and how the data is used. Another important issue is the question of how long a dataset can be used before it becomes untimely or inaccurate.[31]

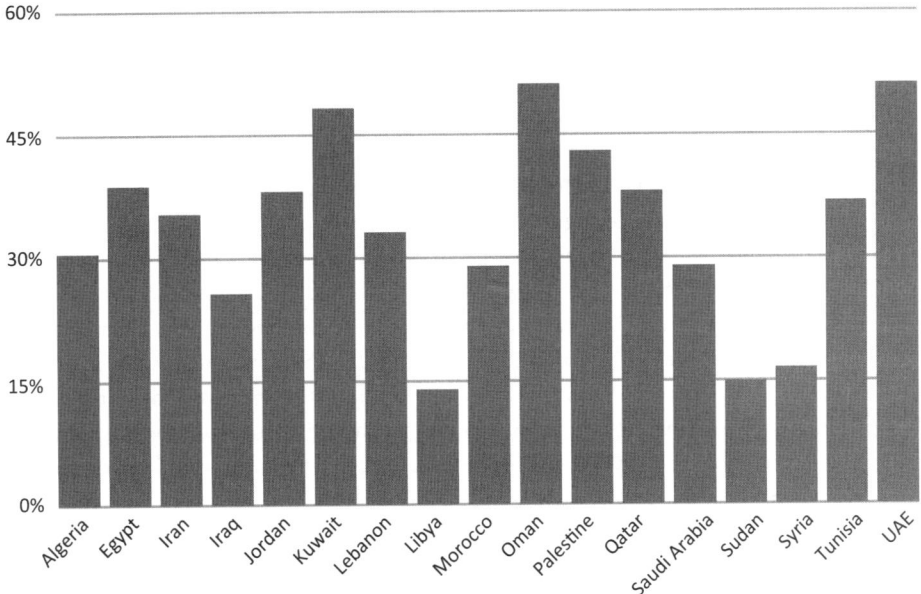

Figure 1: Open Data Inventory score of MENA countries[32]

When only limited datasets are available, they are often used far beyond their timeliness and accuracy, with the lag between data collection and use having a detrimental impact on the practical results of data analysis. What is missing in most data initiatives are feedback mechanisms about the status of datasets after their release to ascertain that they remain timely, accurate, and useful, as well as to determine whether inaccurate datasets should be updated or retracted.

Looking at current indices measuring openness, the main focus is placed on the number of priority datasets released. There is less effort, however, applied to measuring the number of datasets used by relevant stakeholders or to exploring how existing and released datasets are updated and managed. This can hide elements of scarcity in practice. When focused more on the demand-side of data, it is possible to identify gaps in how stakeholders engage in the opening up of data, the lack of feedback mechanisms supporting potential users in requesting certain datasets, or the inability to assess what data is required or requested by different stakeholders.

Data engagement and uptake has been difficult globally, and, in the early years of open data, most efforts around the world were placed on releasing data without focusing on data uptake strategies. In the case of MENA, addressing data scarcity involves encouraging new actors to take on open data initiatives, particularly in academia, which occupies a key role in the use of data for research, and advocating for more reliable, high quality, and timely data.

Engagement and uptake

Despite issues surrounding data scarcity, many local and international organisations have supported a degree of engagement with open data in the region, both through funding and development programmes. Engagement with open data, in particular as part of data-driven innovation, has been encouraged most clearly through community-building activities. Notably, this community building has looked to engage stakeholders working in the wider fields of open-source software, open knowledge, digital innovation, and development.

The role that international networks have played in setting a global agenda around open data should be highlighted. Both the Open Data Institute (ODI) and OKI have promoted open data, data use, and the issue of data standards around the world. Established network members or nodes in the region between 2013 and 2015 include the ODI in Cairo, Dubai, and Riyadh, and the OKI in Egypt and Morocco (although these appear to now be inactive and are recorded as "hibernated").[33] When active, both ODI and OKI provided a mix of open data workshops, skills training, and events that showcased the different uses of open data in contributing to innovation and development.

Code for Africa (CfA) is a continent-wide network that fosters the use of open data to solve the real-life problems of citizens. CfA places an emphasis on the importance of a thriving open data ecosystem in the region and has developed various projects to further this vision. A great example of this type of initiative is openAFRICA, the continent's largest open data repository. Although the project is focused on Sub-Saharan Africa, the network has members from Arab countries and has a hub in Morocco, Code for Morocco (CfM). Working within the mandate of CfA, CfM focuses on digital innovation and fostering data ecosystems at the local level.

A key turning point for the open data movement and community building in the region came in February 2016, when a week-long regional conference titled "Data Driven Innovation (DDI) MENA" was held in Cairo, hosted by IDRC with Cairo University, the Canadian Embassy in Cairo, United Nations Development Programme (UNDP), Information Technology Institute (ITI), and the International Labour Office (ILO).[34] Several days of events culminating in a two-day workshop at Cairo University focused on the status of DDI and digital entrepreneurship.

A central theme running through DDI Week in Cairo was the use of open data in relation to the Sustainable Development Goals (SDGs) and the potential for open data to facilitate information sharing within and between the public sector and private sector. Speakers also emphasised the potential for open data to be a critical resource for digital and social entrepreneurs. This was seen to be especially important in the MENA region which, as has been noted above, has a significant younger population with high rates of mobile phone and digital media use.

In December 2016, the first MENA node of the global OD4D network was established in the region.[35] MENAData has hosted regional events as part of its work and aims to build capacity for a locally based open data community. Through its collaboration with a number of stakeholders in the region, spanning across Algeria, Egypt, Lebanon, Morocco, Tunisia, and Palestine, the node aims to contribute to building the supply of quality open data in the region, advancing locally driven solutions, and promoting a sustainable open data ecosystem.

The 2016 DDI Week and the subsequent ongoing activities of MENAData have focused on bringing individual initiatives together into a more coordinated and cohesive network. Recognising local nuances, the establishment of mechanisms for stakeholders to share resources and best practices is important. These mechanisms may also help to address the lack of demand-side inclusion in open data if they furnish outlets that aid in the identification of gaps in current data provision. They also help to document progress on the use of data in the region. Continuation of this networking and community building remains a central priority for the region. While the past few years have looked to involve new stakeholders in open data activities, the next few should focus on consolidation, capitalisation, and investment in the networks developed to date and ongoing knowledge and capacity building.

What is evident in the most recent phase of engagement across the region is the emphasis on innovation and data for development. This focus ties in well with the development of digital transformation strategies and e-government portals built by governments as they look to capitalise on the digital economy. The DDI emphasis also links with an emphasis on data innovation in tackling growing unemployment in the region, a priority for the development agendas of many countries. In total, this has meant that some degree of stakeholder buy-in with open data has been achievable, even though it has not followed the discourse on open data for accountability that other regions have stressed. It is nonetheless clear that open data is being used for a host of activities beyond innovation, and it is premature to assess the impact that adopting the framing of DDI will have in the long term. Regardless, turning engagement into impact will also require a continued emphasis on building the capacity of users to work with data critically.

Who are the funders?

Several organisations have begun to offer support and funding to data projects in the region:

- IDRC, through the OD4D network, supports a multitude of open data activities in the region, including the Open Data for Development MENA (MENAData) node and the DDI Cairo week.

- The World Bank has provided technical assistance to governments with open data strategies and implementation, open budget data, and making the case for open data. It also offers support and grants to initiatives that use open data to address developmental challenges.

- UNICEF's Innovation Fund gives money to startups using frontier technologies, such as AI or blockchain, that have the potential to reach a very large number of children. One of their requirements is that the funded output has to be open source.[36]

- The UNDP's Innovation for Development programme has also supported the potential of big data solutions for development in the region, launching an Innovation for Development Lab in 2014.[37]

Capacity building

The sections above have identified barriers that go beyond questions of access, looking past the lifecycle of datasets to understand the impact of data in context. Ultimately, limited regional availability of data has led to the overuse of particular datasets, and widely circulated datasets are used beyond their contexts and "expiry dates". In addition, insufficient training of parties in implementing data collection processes has often meant that stakeholders do not feel included in the processes and do not trust that their privacy is being respected.[38] This suggests capacity building is not just about the development of technical data skills, but also about assisting stakeholders to adopt more critical perspectives on data. Additionally, cheaper and more accessible digital technologies have eased the collection of datasets, often creating varied representations of the same phenomenon.

Research conducted by the Centre for Continuing Education (CCE) at Birzeit University (BZU) has pointed out some critical issues with general data capacities in the region.[39] The CCE finds that wide community awareness and engagement has been limited. Specific data science courses outside of business contexts are also scarce. In an effort to combat the widening gap between data knowledge and capacity, the CCE has developed curricula and educational modules aimed at building data skills and capacities among students and professionals. Researchers at BZU have found, in particular, that there is a substantial shortage in local capacity and knowledge pertaining to the use of data with regard to decision-making and policy development.[40] Citing the lack of general awareness about the potential that data has as a key driver of economic development and service delivery, the university has developed three educational modules in Data Science.

The modules were developed with the local context in mind to provide students with both practical and theoretical tools that can be used to enhance capacity and knowledge in the region. Further to the university-level courses, BZU has also worked toward implementing a programme for school students that integrates data literacy into the existent curricula. In developing and executing educational modules, the university hopes to strengthen awareness and knowledge about the role that data plays in supporting development and advocacy in the region. By adopting an Open Educational Resource (OER) approach, teaching materials have also been made openly available through Github (Data Science Fundamentals[41] and Applied Data Science[42]) so that the modules developed can be taught at other universities in the region, including Al-Najah National University in Nablus.

In recent years, data capacity-building initiatives have also emerged in several other countries. While the focus has not always explicitly been on open data, progress toward data literacy and better awareness of the potential of data are arguably also important contributions toward the use of open data. Most activities place a focus on encouraging individuals to experiment with data and vary from short-term events to long-term initiatives that take the form of data hackathons or bootcamps. Many examples include an element of mentorship from data experts. More intensive initiatives, such as curriculum development or data labs, aim to make the use of data more common in learning. There has also been notable interest in the potential of data journalism and data visualisation in the region.[43]

One such activity was a regional hackathon led by the Arab Development Portal (ADP) in October 2017. The ADP is a knowledge depository and online database, which allows users to browse, download, and visualise data from across the Arab world.[44] Led by a number of institutional affiliates in the Arab region, the platform hosts a comprehensive database spanning 12 areas of development impacting Arab countries. It includes data gathered from the various countries' NSOs and international sources. Content on the platform is available in both Arabic and English, ensuring greater accessibility to individuals and communities in the region. The hackathon, entitled Visualize 2030, was carried out in partnership with the UNDP and centred around the UN's 17 SDGs.[45] Participants had the opportunity to attend seminars by data scientists and development practitioners in the field. In hosting this event, the ADP was able to further cultivate the open data ecosystem in the region and encourage young individuals to think critically about the potential data has for the region's inclusive growth and development.

Another initiative focused on data visualisation skills is Visualizing Impact. Under MENAData, Visualizing Impact hosted the Impact Data Lab in 2017, culminating in a four-day workshop in Amman, Jordan.[46] Dedicated to producing data visualisations for social justice in Palestine, participants received up to three months of mentorship with data experts prior to the workshop, which was held in collaboration with Columbia University Studio X Amman. While the workshop was multi-disciplinary, participants were predominantly data journalists, researchers, information designers, and web developers.

Building women's data skills in Egypt

A series of skills-building workshops were organised in 2016 and 2017 in Egypt, focusing on data visualisation skills and on building capacity for women. Two workshops were held in Cairo by Infotimes in collaboration with the Canadian Embassy in Egypt, A2K4D, and IDRC. The workshops included a Data4Women Hackathon that focused on tackling gender inequality through data visualisation. IDRC and the German Federal Enterprise for International Cooperation (GIZ) further supported data visualisation workshops in the Southern city of Aswan, in coordination with local non-profit foundation Om Habibah. These workshops focused on the economic empowerment of women.

It is clear that there is a breadth of capacity-building activity, ranging from work on basic data skills to work with a more explicit focus on economic empowerment or social justice. Data availability and engagement, as well as networking activities that can support shared learning, are the foundation for the regional advancement of open data.

Conclusion

This chapter has attempted to shed light on the current state of open data initiatives in the Middle East and North Africa, pointing to a regional diversity of open data initiatives. It has argued that predominant trends around open data can be seen as diverging efforts to respond to regional interest in open data as a resource for innovation. Open government data initiatives have now taken root in many countries, often linked to digital government reforms, while non-governmental initiatives under a narrative of "data driven innovation" have also emerged. However, issues of data scarcity and limited user feedback indicate that there is still work to be done for these divergent trends to "meet in the middle". The chapter has also identified a number of the challenges that need to be addressed around engagement, uptake, and capacity building, although a range of examples have also revealed that some progress is being made on meeting these challenges across the region. Lastly, the chapter highlighted the need to manage open data throughout its life cycle, arguing that what happens to data after it is released needs to be part of how we evaluate the success of open data in the region.

Although many examples of open data supply, engagement, and use have been explored, in the future the MENA region will require a convergence of the efforts of stakeholders and stable open data networks to ensure the sustainability of initiatives and efforts to date. Broad-based capacity building will be central to further advancing open data, specifically initiatives that aim to build the data skills of people across all sectors. It is only by ensuring a diversity of users and data from the public and private sectors that the potential of open data will be realised. Sustainability and advancement could also be strengthened by working with a wider array of donors and investors and requiring increased effort on the part of local organisations to advocate for data-driven projects.

Further reading

Alanazi, J. & Chatfield, A. (2012). Sharing government-owned data with the public: A cross-country analysis of open data practice in the Middle East. *AMCIS 2012 Proceedings*, 16. http://aisel.aisnet.org/amcis2012/proceedings/EGovernment/16

Elbadawi, I.A. (2012). The state of open government data in GCC countries. In *12th European Conference on EGovernment (ECEG 2012)*, pp. 193–200.

Web Foundation. (2017). *Open Data Barometer, 4th Edition – Regional Report for Middle East and North Africa*. Washington, DC: World Wide Web Foundation. https://opendatabarometer.org/4thedition/regional-snapshot/middle-east-north-africa/

About the authors

Nagla Rizk is Professor of Economics and Founding Director of the Access to Knowledge for Development Center (A2K4D) at the School of Business at the American University in Cairo.

Nancy Salem is a Senior Researcher at the Access to Knowledge for Development Center at the American University in Cairo.

Stefanie Felsberger is a Senior Researcher at the Access to Knowledge for Development Center at the American University in Cairo.

How to cite this chapter

Rizk, N., Salem, N., & Felsberger, S. (2019). Open data around the world: Middle East and North Africa. In T. Davies, S. Walker, M. Rubinstein, & F. Perini (Eds.), *The state of open data: Histories and horizons.* (pp. 503–516). Cape Town and Ottawa: African Minds and International Development Research Centre. http://stateofopendata.od4d.net

This work is licensed under a Creative Commons Attribution 4.0 International (CC BY 4.0) licence. It was carried out with the aid of a grant from the International Development Research Centre, Ottawa, Canada.

Endnotes

1. OECD. (2015). *Data-driven innovation: Big data for growth and well-Being.* Paris: OECD Publishing. https://dx.doi.org/10.1787/9789264229358-en
2. Youthpolicy.org. (n.d.) Middle East and North Africa: Youth facts. http://www.youthpolicy.org/mappings/regionalyouthscenes/mena/facts/
3. http://data.bayanat.ae/en_GB/dataset
4. http://portal.www.gov.qa/wps/portal/opendata
5. http://www.data.gov.bh/en/ODPolicy
6. http://www.oman.om/wps/portal/index/opendata/
7. Government of Oman. (n.d.). Open government licence – Oman. http://www.oman.om/wps/portal/index/opendata/ogl/
8. Lebanon Digital Government. (n.d.). Lebanon digital transformation. *Digital Transformation Conference 2018.* https://digitaltransformation.gov.lb/digital-conference/
9. Dreisbach, T. (2017). Information for the people: Tunisia embraces open government, 2011–2016. *Innovations for Successful Societies.* Princeton, NJ: Princeton University. https://successfulsocieties.princeton.edu/publications/information-people-tunisia-embraces-open-government
10. Heni, W. & Pedersen, A. (2016). Tunisians can now access hydrocarbon contracts in open data format. *Natural Resource Governance Institute,* 7 October. https://resourcegovernance.org/blog/tunisians-can-now-access-hydrocarbon-contracts-open-data-format
11. http://menadata.net/public/project/3
12. https://solardataegypt.info/
13. Access to Knowledge for Development Center. (n.d.). Open data in solar energy. Digitising dynamics: The solar energy sector in Egypt. *Access to Knowledge for Development* [Blog post]. http://a2k4d.tumblr.com/opendatainsolar
14. Marwan Tarazi (Director, Center for Continuing Education) in discussion with the authors.
15. Kettani, D. (2018). Enhancing road safety in the MENA region using a big data app. *Conference Proceedings: The Seventh International Conference on Advances in Computing, Electronics and Communication.* New York: SEEK Digital Library. https://www.seekdl.org/conferences/paper/details/9495.html
16. Middle East & North Africa. (n.d.). The Open Data Impact Map. http://opendataimpactmap.org/mna.html
17. https://visualizingimpact.org/
18. http://lebanonelectiondata.org/about.html
19. Transport for Cairo. (2019). Transport for Cairo: A simple map to travel through Cairo. http://transportforcairo.com/

20. Abdelaal, A., Hegazy, A., Hegazy, M., & Khalafallah, Y. (2017). *How can transport mapping contribute to achieving adequate urban mobility? The case of the Greater Cairo Region (GCR)*. Cairo: Takween Integrated Community Development and Transport for Cairo. http://transportforcairo.com/wp-content/uploads/2017/11/TfC_TICD_How-can-Transit-Mapping-Contribute-to-achieving-AUM-08-11-2017-Web-Version.compressed.pdf

21. Moon, M. (2017). Uber movement's traffic data is now available to the public. *Engadget*, 31 August. https://www.engadget.com/2017/08/31/uber-movement-traffic-data-website-launch/

22. Rizk, N., Felsberger, S., & Salem, N. (2017). Data for development in the MENA region: A narrative on paradigms, production, access and usability. Working Paper (Forthcoming). Cairo: MENA Data Platform, p. 53.

23. Web Foundation. (2015). *Open Data Barometer – Global report*. 2nd edition. Washington, DC: World Wide Web Foundation. https://opendatabarometer.org/assets/downloads/Open%20Data%20Barometer%20-%20Global%20Report%20-%202nd%20Edition%20-%20PRINT.pdf

24. Ben Yacoub, H. (2015). Why Open Knowledge's Global Open Data Index 2015 is a failure. http://www.hbyconsultancy.com/blog/why-okf-global-open-data-index-2015-is-a-failure.html

25. https://index.okfn.org/

26. Al-Balushi, R. & Hasna, S. (2016). *Open data in the Arab World: An examination of government data in the Arab world in the area of national budget, legislation, elections, and company register*. https://www.academia.edu/22800914/Report_on_Open_Data_in_the_Arab_World

27. The table was created by A2K4D using the Global Open Data Index.

28. Open Data Watch. (2017). *Open Data Inventory 2017 annual report: A progress report on open data*. Washington, DC: Open Data Watch. http://odin.opendatawatch.com/Downloads/otherFiles/ODIN-2017-Annual-Report.pdf

29. Open Data Inventory. (2019). Open Data Inventory 2018/2019. http://odin.opendatawatch.com/

30. Web Foundation. (2017.) *Open Data Barometer – Regional report for Middle East and North Africa*. 4th edition. Washington, DC: World Wide Web Foundation. https://opendatabarometer.org/4thedition/regional-snapshot/middle-east-north-africa/

31. Rizk, N., Felsberger, S., & Salem, N. (2017). Data for development in the MENA region: A narrative on paradigms, production, access and usability. Working Paper (Forthcoming). Cairo: MENA Data Platform, pp. 63–64.

32. The chart was created by A2K4D using the data from Table 1.

33. https://okfn.org/network/

34. http://www.eg.undp.org/content/egypt/en/home/presscenter/events/2016/february/big-data.html

35. http://od4d.net/about/

36. https://www.unicef.org/innovation/

37. http://www.eg.undp.org/content/egypt/en/home/ourwork/development-impact/overview.html

38. Rizk, N., Felsberger, S., & Salem, N. (2017). Data for development in the MENA region: A narrative on paradigms, production, access and usability. Working Paper (Forthcoming). Cairo: MENA Data Platform, pp. 53–55.

39. Birzeit University. (2019). Research and projects. https://www.birzeit.edu/en/research

40. Khooli, Abed A. (2016). *Curricula development and capacity building component: Background research*. Working Paper (Forthcoming). Birzeit, Palestine: Birzeit University.

41. Abdel-Razzak. (2017). Data science fundamentals. *GitHub* repository. https://github.com/Abdel-Razzak/DSF

42. Khooli, Abed. A. (2017). Applied data science (ADS 2). *Github* repository. https://github.com/abedkhooli/ds2

43. See https://infotimes.org/ and http://www.arabdevelopmentportal.com/viz2030

44. Arab Development Portal. (2019). About us. http://arabdevelopmentportal.com/node/6142

45. Arab Development Portal. (2017). Beirut hackathon – Visualize 2030: The first SDGs data dive camp in the Arab region. https://tinyurl.com/y7ww7vll

46. Impact Data Lab. (2019). Visualizing Palestine. https://visualizingpalestine.org/impact

035

North America, Australia, and New Zealand

David Eaves, Ben McGuire, and Audrey Carson

Key points

- The shuttering in 2017 of open.whitehouse.gov illustrates the risks that face open data movements in Australia, Canada, New Zealand, and the United States (US) as high-level leadership on open data and access to certain datasets are vulnerable to changes of administration. However, open data practice at local levels has proven reasonably resilient so far.

- The last decade of open data work has encouraged governments to perceive their data as an asset that needs to be managed and to improve internal capacity on data use and analytics. In particular, open data has played an important role supporting cross-agency collaboration.

- Direct citizen demand for data from national open data portals remains low and highly concentrated. This can leave initiatives struggling to define success when they operate on the simple logic that open data will boost citizen engagement.

- More work is needed to both define what success looks like for open data initiatives and to monitor progress toward it with the right kinds of tools.

Introduction

One of the Trump administration's early decisions after taking office in 2017 was to shutter open.whitehouse.gov, a portal set up by the Obama administration to house public information on visitor logs, financial disclosure reports, and other personnel data. The White House Communications Director at the time, Michael Dubke, suggested that the move was in response to "the grave national security risks and privacy concerns of the hundreds of thousands of visitors annually".[1] To open data advocates, the disappearance of this data was an early sign that "American leadership on open government will not come from this Presidency".[2]

And while the closure of open.whitehouse.gov could serve as a reminder of how fragile gains in open government can be, the reality is that federal rules and legislation, like the DATA Act, continue to build and preserve open data sources across government, and the administration has publicly committed to improving the way it uses and supplies data to the nation.[3] The events of last two years also suggest that, even without executive leadership, officials at the state and municipal level have generally been able to continue to develop open data activities within their own areas of work. The past decade has been an extremely exciting time for open government and transparency in the United States (US), Canada, Australia, and New Zealand. Across these nations, there are powerful stories about open data initiatives that demonstrate a greater government commitment to, and the potential benefits of, making information more transparent.

But despite the robustness of open data initiatives during the transition to new governments with different political stripes across North America, Australia, and New Zealand, the news is not all positive. Participation remains extremely unequal across national and subnational jurisdictions. While the number of datasets on federal open data portals initially proliferated as agencies scrambled to comply with national standards, the usability and relevance of this data is often still in question. Early success stories related to geospatial data, metropolitan transportation, and legislation-tracking applications have not translated to success across all geographies or sectors. Instead, pockets of urban innovation continue to dominate the demand for, and supply of, open data, while the participation of local governments remains vulnerable to political crosswinds.

Even with these gaps and challenges in mind, the public servants, open data advocates, and private sector partners surveyed for this chapter continue to find reasons to be cautiously optimistic about the present and future of open data. While the use of open data by the general public lags behind the most optimistic predictions, usage by government staff and intergovernmental cooperation is increasingly becoming a driver of open data's value. Whereas early efforts focused on the volume of open data produced as a measure of success, governments are now becoming more sensitive to tracking usage and demand, and taking a more user-centred approach to future reforms.

Also worth noting is that the incorporation of open data as an expected practice at all levels of government has helped to build the capacity for proactive data management and analytics. Indeed, it could be argued that the open data movement's biggest accomplishment may not be the raft of new applications created by third parties, but rather the fact that it has prompted governments to perceive their data as an asset that needs to be well managed to be effectively leveraged. Jurisdictions that adopt open data aggressively tend to also manage and use data more effectively, understanding its implications on issues such as privacy, as well as how it can be used to improve operations. Open data adoption may have given some governments a jumpstart on digitising and modernising their governance.

This chapter lays out trends in open data across the region over the last decade, focusing closely on signals of progress, persistent gaps, and the potential long-term analytics value of open data investments. While powerful and positive anecdotes reflect the strength and creativity of the open data movement, due to challenges in defining shared goals, maintaining sustained investment, and matching the supply of datasets to citizen demands, stagnation and drift might better characterise the current general state of open data in this region.

Signs of progress

In 2013, the Government of Canada officially re-launched its open data portal, and, in the US, President Barack Obama signed an executive order making open and machine-readable the new default for government information. These landmark federal actions came just five years after the City of Washington in the District of Columbia launched its open data portal (2007), leading to an explosion of open data portals that included fast followers like Vancouver (2009), San Francisco (2009), New Zealand (2009), New York City (2012), and Chicago (2012), among others.[4] In the years since these first major open data breakthroughs on the North American national stage, public servants, citizen hackers, and software companies have all played a role in driving spotty but real progress in the world of open data.

To fully assess the recent progress of the open data movement across North America, Australia, and New Zealand, interviews were conducted with open data leaders across the public and private sectors. Among the participants were a state Chief Data Officer from the US, an Australian provincial Information Commissioner, government practitioners at the federal and local levels tasked with implementing open data directives and scaling open data portals, and the directors of well-known civil society organisations and academic research groups specialising in open data.

Taken in aggregate, their accounts reveal a qualified optimism about the present status and future trajectory of the open data movement. While most believe that progress has been harder and slower to come by than expected, nearly all were also able to point to major milestones that have been reached, as well as other compelling instances of progress. They universally agreed that the adoption of open data standards has gradually broadened, and that open data programmes are beginning to yield positive public benefits from greater government transparency to improved bureaucratic efficiency. Due to the efforts and investments of these open data advocates, as well as other committed individuals and organisations, it is evident that slow but steady steps have been taken to increase the ubiquity and usefulness of open data in a number of jurisdictions in these regions.

Open data leaders emphasise different goals when describing what drives the open data movement, whether it be ensuring government accountability, spurring private sector innovation, or improving bureaucratic decision-making by breaking down barriers to the access and reuse of public information. It is heartening to see that in specific instances, open data programmes have made headway against all of these goals. Highlighted below are a few anecdotal examples of the positive impacts that policies and products, fueled by open data, have had within different sectors or open data communities:

Transportation – Some of the most visible applications to date have been in the field of transportation. In New Zealand, ANZ Bank has taken advantage of open data on the traffic flow of trucks and heavy vehicles in order to forecast GDP, which is published monthly under the "Truckometer" name.[5] Another example of open data at work in the realm of transportation comes from the Australian province of New South Wales, where developers have pulled data from the province's open data portal on the location of petrol stations and station-specific petrol pricing to provide consumers with a transparent look at where they can be cost effective when filling up their tank.⁶ In fact, practitioners have indicated that this application has helped prevent petrol price gouging across the province and encouraged more consistent pricing across stations, producing a net benefit for consumers. The increase in accessible data has drawn new actors into the space, such as Google with Google Maps, as well as new companies, like Remix, which provides an advanced planning tool that transit agencies can use to test transit variables and schedule complex transit services.⁷

Health – The US State of Connecticut is at the forefront of utilising publicly accessible data to monitor threats to public health and make data-driven adjustments to policy and programmes to better serve the needs of its residents. In particular, the state has used open data as a tool to help fight the opioid epidemic that has seized the US in recent years. Using data about the location of pharmacies that prescribe opioids, dispense Naloxone (a medication used to reverse an opioid overdose), and provide prescription drug drop boxes, as well as opioid overdoses and related deaths, the state has been able to trace the movement of the opioid epidemic from one neighbourhood to the next. These findings, in turn, have been used to prioritise treatment for opioid addiction over treatment for other conditions at treatment centres in certain heavily affected neighbourhoods and to more effectively stock pharmacies located in the epicentre of the epidemic with Naloxone in order to avoid life-threatening drug shortages.⁸ Some US municipalities have also been able to utilise a similar cross-departmental approach to solve less severe, yet still entrenched, public health problems, such as the disproportionately high (and expensive) utilisation rates of emergency services by a relatively small portion of the population. The town of Cary, North Carolina has attempted to solve this problem by aggregating data across agencies from health, law enforcement, and other social services to identify root causes and provide better preventative, non-emergency care to these high-need individuals, thereby reducing the overall cost of the health system. Indeed, by investing a relatively small sum (around USD 200 000) to publish this data and conduct the relevant analyses, Cary was able to make adjustments that local practitioners estimate now saves the city more than USD 8 million annually in health costs.

Environment – The boreal forest is central to Canada's natural environment, history, and culture, but it is also an important economic resource that is regularly harvested, contributing significantly to the country's overall GDP. The 2010 Canadian Boreal Forest Agreement was a landmark conservation initiative that brought together industry, environmental groups, and government to broker a consensus on forest management techniques in the region. Central to the agreement was an accord to prohibit logging in certain vulnerable forest areas and adopt data-driven sustainable harvesting practices across the region.⁹ In return for these protections, Canadian environmental groups committed to no longer boycott forestry goods produced by the participating lumber companies, which increased the value of their stock by stabilising consumer demand. Much of the data on forest health used throughout the negotiations was open data provided by Environment Canada, such as woodland caribou range data. By serving as a single source of truth throughout the negotiations, Environment Canada provided a common foundation for both sides when debating the best way to integrate economic and environmental values. Without this open data, it is likely that the accuracy and sophistication of the debate would not have been possible and that an agreement would not have been reached. In this case, open data was a foundational ingredient for two competing interest groups to engage in productive, evidenced-based policy-making.

Law enforcement – Across these nations, the utilisation of open data by police departments stands out as a particularly high-potential and effective application of open data for public benefit. In the US, the Police Data Initiative, which started in the White House of President Barack Obama, but continues under the stewardship of the Police Foundation, provides a consolidated and interactive listing of open and soon-to-be-opened datasets identified by more than 130 local law enforcement agencies as important to their communities.[10] In this context, open data is used to encourage joint problem-solving, innovation, enhanced understanding, and accountability between communities and the law enforcement agencies that serve them. Most recently, the organisation has called on local agencies to publish data about hate crimes and has received a promising response from heartland American cities in Nebraska, Oklahoma, and Indiana. Other local police departments, such as the Toronto Police Service, have launched their own open data sites to share data directly with the public.[11] The adoption of a publish-by-default approach, as is the case with New Zealand's police agencies,[12] is a truly important development in the evolution of the open data movement, representing an impressive maturation in the way local agencies engage with open data. Notably, regular publication of New Zealand Police's crime statistics has led to detailed investigative journalism in both print and online media.

Elections and government accountability – Election data has proven to be one of the most popular types of data published on open data platforms. For example, Elections BC, a non-partisan office of the British Columbia legislature that is responsible for conducting all public elections in the province now releases all of its election results as open data.[13] Small municipalities, like the Township of Langley, Canada, have also found that election-related data is among the most heavily accessed data via their open data portals. Independent initiatives, like OpenSecrets.org produced by the Center for Responsive Politics, have also meaningfully expanded citizens' access to in-demand campaign data. For other open data applications, the aim is not so much to document the outcomes of elections as it is to empower citizens to hold government accountable at the ballot box. Some civic hackers in New York City, for example, have used public utility data revealing insufficient heating in the city's public housing projects to advocate for new leadership at the local and state level, ensuring proper funding of the New York City Housing Authority.[14] Other open data applications in the US, like GovTrack[15] and Councilmatic,[16] have helped to increase civic engagement by making it easier for citizens to stay up-to-date on their elected representatives' voting history, as well as pending legislation and special events.

While the developments detailed above from across this region are diverse, taken together, they speak to a number of common trends underlying the state of today's open data movement. First, increased collaboration on open data across government units, such as when a public health department shares anonymised data with a police department when both are tasked with treating the same problem, has allowed for unprecedented analytics and insights into the complex causes of various public policy outcomes. Second, publishing more and better data has enabled the development of applications that have netted measurable benefits for citizens and residents. Citizens and activists who have the ability to easily access vast quantities of government data are empowered to more accurately assess and act on information in both their private and public lives.

Above and beyond these trends, however, two developments stand out that seem likely to bend the arc of the open data movement by accelerating its adoption and impact: the move toward internal usage and the move toward quality over quantity.

Internal usage

Among the first wave of state and local open data portals, the primary objective was to publish anything at all, regardless of whether it would actually be accessed or not. In this environment, releasing data was driven by a need to comply with the requirements of overarching data directives, not by the specific uses and desires of downloaders. Over time, however, government departments and agencies tasked with publishing open government data began to refine their criteria for success, adopting goals related to the external usage of data by citizens. In this second wave, success was more often assessed via key performance indicators that measured the number of datasets downloaded. With limited means to assess how data made available was being used, government entities focused on sheer citizen demand for open data to justify their programme costs. Underlying this operating model was a primary objective to make government data available outside of government for use by citizens.

In recent years, however, there has been a shift within the departments and agencies that publish open data. This shift has been driven by a need to rationalise the costs of maintaining an open data programme and to convince internal stakeholders and bureaucrats of the practical value that open data programmes can provide for the day-to-day delivery of government. Today, open data portals are increasingly designed to maximise the usage, sharing, and analysis of open government data by government employees themselves, with the end goal of supporting evidence-based policy-making and improved performance management.

Under this new operating model, the value of the open data programmes as a whole can be measured partially by the incidence of government employees actually utilising the data to make data-informed decisions, both when developing policies and when adjusting existing policies to reduce costs and improve outcomes. While a mandate to "defend the spend" may not sound as lofty as proclamations to advance open data as a transparency tool, the shift toward internal usage is a truly positive development. Justifying the value of open data portals internally helps to secure their long-term sustainability, ensuring that both government employees and the public are empowered to extract meaningful value from open data in the years ahead.

Quality over quantity

The open data practitioners interviewed for this chapter frequently cited a struggle between the desire to publish a large quantity of data and the desire to publish high-quality data. In the early years of the open data movement, efforts to rapidly scale up open data programmes, either in response to real user demand or in order to match or exceed benchmarks for success, had the unintentional effect at times of encouraging the publishing of non-standard or non-machine-readable data. While the quantity of datasets published on open data portals increased rapidly during this time, actual utilisation of this data often stagnated, hobbled by the data's overall low quality and usability.

Today, governments like Canada's lead the pack in a larger effort to shift the emphasis from sheer quantity of data to the quality, consistency, discoverability, and coherence of data. To this end, governments have begun publishing data inventories and indexes to assist with data discovery, organising datasets to allow more coherent analysis, and developing additional user tools, such as data maps and visualisations, to help laypersons better understand the data hosted on their platforms.

Canada's Information Management and Open Government team has even gone so far as to suspend the practice of including the number of datasets available in reports on the health of the country's open data programme because this metric has little bearing on the platform's utilisation and overall success. Indeed, in recent years, the number of datasets available on Canada's open data portal has dropped from around 300 000 at its peak to approximately 80 000 today. This decline is a testament to the government's commitment to painstakingly auditing the datasets on the platform and replacing non-contextual, non-machine-readable data with more consolidated, accurate, and digestible data resources that will actually be used.

Emerging challenges

Alongside the trends above that demonstrate a maturing of the open data agenda across North America, Australia, and New Zealand, initiatives are also facing a number of challenges.

Slowing or stagnating data publication

Despite the many signs of progress and anecdotal success identified in the preceding section, a dominant narrative on open data at the end of its first decade is one of stalled progress, in which both advocates and practitioners are forced to reassess early expectations in light of unexpected technical, political, and cultural limitations. Early ambitions for rapid adoption fuelled by innovative open data applications in venues like New York City subways or gas stations in New South Wales have given way to a recognition that further gains will not come simply by increasing the supply of data or enacting legislation. Despite optimism about the future of open data, one practitioner in the US related a common thesis that "open data has become a bit stagnant here as we continue to focus on broader adoption and more open data instead of on what data may be the most valuable in a national context".[17] Rather than increasing transparency and the uses of open data year over year, these countries are still struggling to maintain and drive further adoption and compliance.

One insight into this trend can be found by looking at comparative international data from the Open Data Barometer.[18] Examining the results of country-level surveys,[19] it is possible to explore how 16 data categories are rated on a scale from 1 to 100 based on standardised factors, such as openness, including open licensing, machine readability, cost, and timely updating. Since 2013, several of the data categories have obtained consistent high ratings (e.g. mapping, trade, elections), while others rise (e.g. company) or fall (e.g. spending) due to issues related to outdated or inconsistent published data. These variations aside, the overall picture is one of relative stability (see Figure 1).

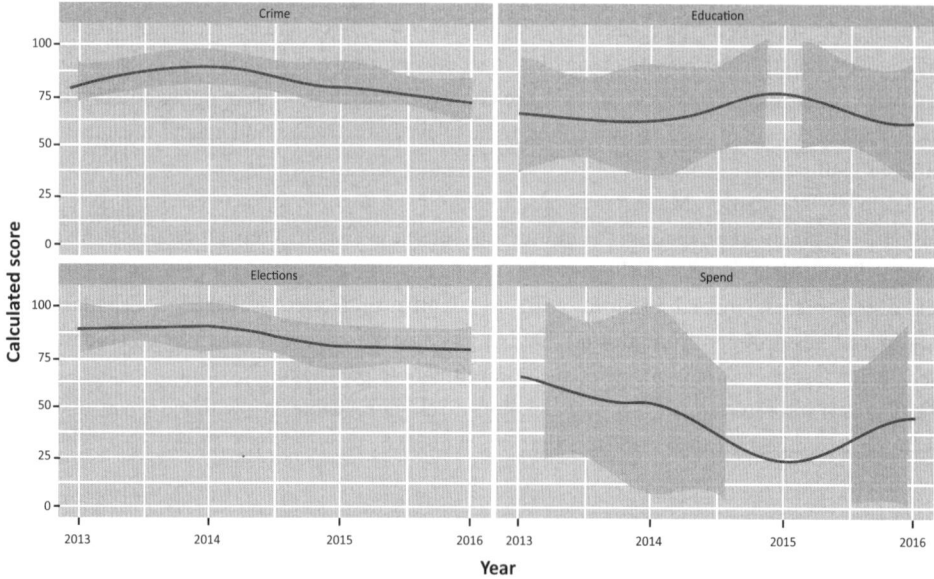

Figure 1: Average regional sector openness scores (2013–2016)
Source: Open Data Barometer 2017, consolidated data: https://opendatabarometer.org/4thedition/data/

Stagnation does not only plague the general state of data openness and access. A closer look at national open data portals in North America, Australia, and New Zealand indicates that a slowdown has also occurred in terms of the data being uploaded to flagship sites. While advocates rightly celebrate the increasing participation of various agencies within governments in the release of open data, the broader story is one of early adopters and laggards. By and large, the picture today is very much the same as it was five years ago.

In the US, the national open data portal Data.gov collects hundreds of thousands of datasets into a single, searchable database. With over 365 000 total datasets uploaded to date, the federal government has been by far the greatest contributor to the Data.gov repository, accounting for 85% of the total datasets. State governments account for only 5% of the total. Within organisations, the distribution of datasets uploaded by individual offices can be extreme. On the low end, 50% of all offices have uploaded five datasets or fewer. At the high end, three federal agencies (Commerce, Interior, NASA) account for over 60% of all datasets on Data.gov.

The temporal pattern of uploads to Data.gov over the last decade also tells a story of inconsistency and occasional spikes of activity linked perhaps to major policy announcements, which are followed by limited ongoing participation. While the metadata on site uploads over time is not available for all countries within the group discussed here, practitioners interviewed for this chapter suggest that a similar pattern of stagnation in agency participation on open data portals is a significant problem within and across their home countries.

It is not clear, however, whether this represents the demise of open data initiatives or simply the demise of the open data portal as the organising device within such initiatives. As agencies shift to focus on data for targeted groups of users and to internalise open data practices, they may be making more use of their own websites to distribute datasets, providing specialist data platforms instead of using national portals. For example, in New Zealand, geospatial data is provided through the LINZ Data Service,[20] which users may first discover via the national data portal (data.govt.nz), but once found, it becomes the more direct destination for geospatial data.

It is clear that national open data initiatives in the region have, in general, been experiencing a sense of disillusionment that characterises many new technologies that move beyond the peak of a hype cycle, a challenge that other nations across the world may soon have to grapple with. According to the open data advocates interviewed for this chapter, this slowdown in high-level participation is rooted in four distinct challenges:

- The struggle to agree on definitions for goals and success.
- Uneven adoption within and across government at all levels.
- A reliance on champions who do not maintain their roles over the long term.
- A focus on performance metrics related to supply rather than demand and use.

How these challenges are addressed will shape the development of open data in the next decade.

The struggle to define success

The public presentation of open data and the stated aims of public programmes frequently trumpet transparency and the potential for civic engagement. However, many actors also believe that the potential economic benefits from sharing data as a "natural resource" will increase the efficiency of government services or facilitate new opportunities for economic growth, essentially meaning that open data programmes would pay for themselves. The potential tension between the "good government" and "economic benefit" perspectives can sometimes lead to confusion when trying to prioritise which datasets to share and, in the medium term, can make it difficult to agree on how to define programme success.

In the early stages of the open data movement, the US and Canada stressed transparency and civic engagement as the primary motivations for making information more available. At the opening of Data.gov, the Sunlight Foundation's Executive Director referred to the launch as "a dramatic breakthrough in the role of government".[21] In New Zealand, government's framing of its open data initiative was broader, linking open data with open government agendas, but also maintaining a degree of distinction between the two. Regardless, many arguments for open data focused on its broad potential as a resource for change without setting out explicit measurable policy goals. This constructive ambiguity in defining the goal of open data initiatives and the subsequent way in which different groups have engaged with open data, has, over time, made the identification of success or failure a significant challenge.

According to practitioners interviewed for this chapter, many early adopters primarily understood open data as a "transparency tool" that would provide citizens with "more access to the inner workings of government" while driving new "civic participation and accountability in the public sector".[22] Early experimental and creative apps that took advantage of new datasets promised an explosion of citizen data use, but in the decade that has followed, such a transformation has yet to materialise. Instead, as government budgets have held steady or shrunk, there has been increasing pressure to defend open data as an investment and to define a return value. Even ardent advocates admit that transparency is "hard to quantify, to implement, and defend from a budget perspective".[23]

As US and Canadian narratives shifted away from transparency justifications and moved toward discussions of open data as an asset and a tool for making government more efficient, practitioners tried to drive value by uploading lots of data in the hope that beneficial uses would organically emerge. As one practitioner described this period, "We put up what we thought people wanted to see."[24] For advocates and practitioners, the shift to prioritising economic value raised the immediate expectation of revenue or savings from open data, but these also were not necessarily forthcoming or easily quantified in the short term. Ultimately, it is difficult to "make the change and articulate the overall benefit in the long run of early government investments, which will reap tax revenues or efficiencies from uncertain new ventures".[25]

One dangerous consequence of this lack of agreement over goals has been a reversion to competition and comparison to other governments, rather than increasing the focus on measuring the value of local investments by the good they do for consumers and citizens. Programmes like the Open Cities Index[26] or the Open Data Barometer[27] were never intended to be the final definition of success, yet some municipal open data practitioners are forced to define their success via these tools even when they "don't really understand the criteria used to judge",[28] because they impress elected officials.

Uneven adoption within and across governments

While inter-agency and inter-governmental collaborations are exciting developments in some areas as noted earlier in this chapter, a sizable challenge to broader engagement with open data and sustained citizen involvement is the difficulty that many governments still have working together. This problem is particularly acute at the subnational level (state and provincial), where there may not be clear consumer demand for data due to a lack of public awareness or lack of demonstrated use cases. In contrast, for large cities, the density of the population and volume of data produced, especially for services like transportation, has allowed for sustained buy-in, but, beyond questions related to scale and opportunity, there remain significant data quality, governance, and definition challenges, which inhibit progress.

Many practitioners interviewed for this chapter suggested that the open data movement has struggled because there has not been enough attention paid to interjurisdictional collaboration and data standardisation. As a result, open data plans at the national level tend to dominate the agenda, while the coordination between levels of government, which practitioners believe could produce the greatest value, is often forgotten. This challenge manifests not only at the federal level between different agencies, but is also a significant problem where regional and municipal governments have begun to set up open data federations. While these cooperative groups represent one of the largest current opportunities in the open data movement, they face huge hurdles in coordinating datasets across levels of government and with private sector partners. One of the complex barriers to cooperation is data ownership, particularly when private data is involved, or when both public and private sector organisations are involved in the same project. However, where cross-sector data co-operatives are able to form, such as the Sault Ste. Marie Consortium in Ontario, Canada, which has 22 organisational members of different sizes,[29] they are able to leverage skills from across the partnership to share skills and generate analysis based on shared data.

At the state and local level, practitioners report that a simple shortage of skills prevents them from reaching the sort of scale and value realisation that is frequently identified in large cities. One practitioner related a common lament that there is still a "long way to go with smaller local governments, because they don't have the political support or capacity to move on their own".[30] A huge part of the challenge in this area is simply based on volume and demand. There are few organisations or individuals seeking public data from states and small cities relative to very large metropolitan areas because the minimal volume of data produced there does not produce as many obvious opportunities. Until these regions can cooperate more effectively or find ways to drive increased demand, it is likely that subnational open data movements will continue to struggle outside of the largest cities.

Reliance on local champions to build and sustain initiatives

The ultimate goal of open data advocates and practitioners is that data will become "open by default"; however, no governments have reached this goal as a steady state, and many still closely guard access to most of their datasets. In some cases, this may be because "authoritative publishers, particularly in government, are paralysed by a fear of publishing poor quality or incorrect data"[31] for fear of damaging any existence of trust with constituents. Consequently, practitioners admit that, in many cases, "open data programmes need to have very strong-willed champions or demonstrated return, or else they'll wither off".[32] When political turnover or other factors result in the removal of these key personalities, open data programmes can falter or even disappear.

Virtually all of the practitioners and advocates interviewed for this chapter suggested that open data movements in the context of their own experiences could not have succeeded without a handful of strong local champions. However, few could articulate an effective way to hand off the administration and maintenance of programmes to the next generation of potential leaders, and many admitted that open data remains very susceptible to budget cuts that result from political turnover. The challenge is distinct within and across the countries discussed in this chapter. In New Zealand, for example, public service chief executives are appointed on five-year contracts independent of political change, unlike their counterparts elsewhere in this group of nations. Personality-driven projects can result in open data initiatives that are siloed in one part of an organisation, and, if open data is seen as an IT project rather than a strategic asset for example, long-term sustainability is a challenge.

Citizen demand for data remains limited and highly concentrated

The most consistent gap cited by those interviewed for this chapter related to the measurement of outcomes and, in particular, how to best track the relationship between open data producers and potential users. In the earliest years of the open data movement, the release of large amounts of open data represented a kind of progress, but practitioners now suggest that creating more datasets "doesn't allow value to be realised" because producers have largely "failed to create an authentic feedback loop between users of data"[33] and government.

One way to explore this problem is by looking at usage metrics from national open data portals to see not only how the demand for data has changed over time, but also what total demand looks like relative to a nation's population and how concentrated demand is for specific datasets. When per capita uptake is low, this could suggest that open data in general has not been adopted by the public for mainstream use. When use is highly concentrated among a handful of consumers, this could suggest that rather than serving a diverse set of interests, open data tools are essentially catering to a specific power user base.

In the US in 2016, there were about .009 recorded views of datasets on data.gov per resident with internet access. In Australia, the equivalent figure for 2017 was .14, and in Canada, it was .04 (New Zealand does not make the metadata required to calculate this ratio available). This data suggests that larger countries may suffer when judged by the volume of completed downloads (and perhaps also hints that the size of an open data community is not directly proportional to nation size); however, it could also suggest that approaches to advertising open data portals to the public have had different levels of success within different countries.

We can also use portal metrics to explore trends in the uptake of open data. A first glance at monthly visits to Data.gov suggests a noisy but discernible upward trend in site visits (see Figure 2 below).

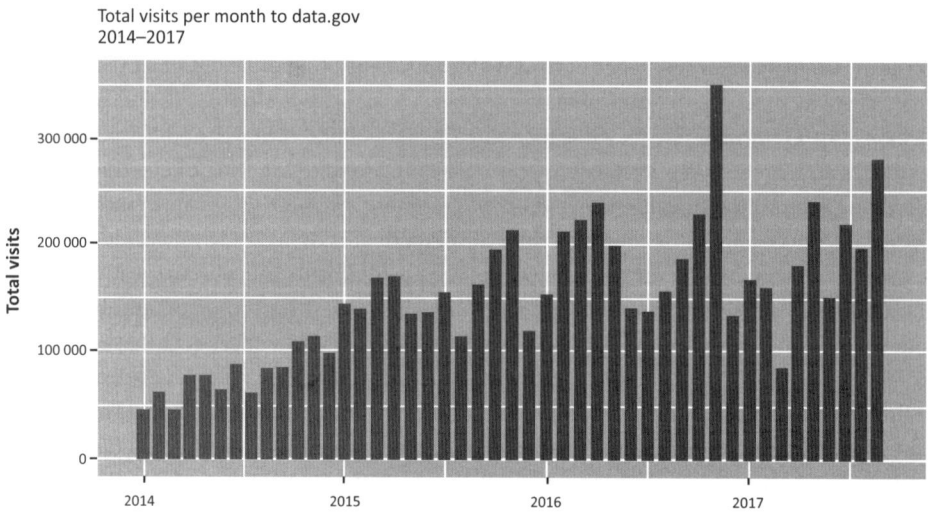

Figure 2:   Monthly visits to data.gov (2014–2017)

A closer look at the monthly visits indicates that there is significant variation within and across years, but that most datasets remain consistently below 2 500 monthly views. In fact, most agencies have had an effectively static rate of page views since 2014. Instead of showing a general upward trend, the data suggests that overall increased traffic stems from a few outlier datasets that have received much higher traffic. Notably, the ten largest agencies by dataset count (about 4% of agencies releasing data) account for 75% of total downloadable files and 40% of total views.

In Australia, a similar upward trend emerges over time (see Figure 3), providing an encouraging sign that more citizens are taking advantage of the portal. However, as with the US data, examining publisher popularity on data.gov.au shows that visits are dominated by a small handful of agencies. Datasets published by the Department of Human Services alone account for 47% of all visits to the site since 2013, and the ten most popular publishers account for 84% of total visits. By far, the most popular resources on data.gov.au are a small sample of location search resources, with the locations of Medicare offices accounting for 27% of total historical visits and the Location of Centrelink Offices accounting for another 14%. Essentially, two out of 70 000 datasets account for 41% of all visits. The distribution of downloads rather than visits is slightly less skewed toward the most popular resources, with the ten most popular datasets accounting for about 54% of visits, but only 21% of downloads.

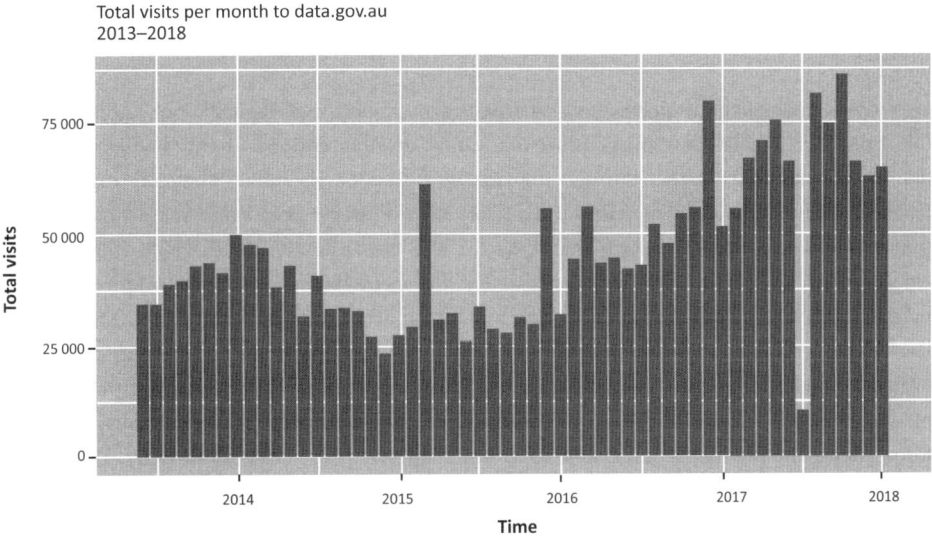

Figure 3:   Visits to data.gov.au

Other countries in this group do not provide this kind of data, but additional analysis and anecdotal evidence suggests that demand is similarly highly concentrated on a small percentage of available data, indicating that much of the information that has been made public does not serve any specific consumer need. Should administrators interpret the gap between what users are accessing and the vast resources available as a problem that needs to be solved? Some practitioners suggest that this skewed distribution was an inevitable result of experimentation and reflects the fact that many users are simply not aware of what is available. Others argue that there are legitimate "difficulties in identifying who currently uses open data, who might use it if certain changes were made, and how all users think about the reliability and usefulness of government datasets relative to other tools".[34] Even the best anecdotes about users and their open data success stories rarely translate to strategies for how to promote the use of other data. Establishing lines of communication with users that can reveal their preferences can be difficult and time-consuming when both data and user needs change over time.

Hidden benefits: Analytics and performance management

One potentially underappreciated aspect of the open data story is that beyond the supply and demand for transparent government information, open data may be laying a broader foundation in the region for more robust analytics and performance management in government.

Generating and making sense of open data forces staff to develop skills to manage, analyse, visualise, and interpret complex datasets. Furthermore, investments in open data elevate data managers and analysts into strategic discussions and help enable nominally operational teams to take on strategic roles. Open datasets have formed the foundation of some of the most promising public sector innovations in predictive analytics,[35] and, in many cases, large cities in the region that are leaders in data-driven governance have built up their expertise based upon earlier work with open data.[36]

From a management perspective, increasing organisational capacity for discussing and interpreting data helps develop a culture that can be more intentional about establishing shared definitions, defining success through metrics, and creating incentives that rely on common datasets. None of this obviates the critical role of progressive and aggressive leadership, but practitioners argue that "making public sector agencies actually use the data internally for evidence-based policy-making in order to defend the spend has caught on like wildfire".[37] Within private sector partners that work with government agencies, such as Socrata[38] and ESRI,[39] there has been a sizable shift from simply managing open data platforms to building capacity to visualise and manage real-time government performance data. Whether or not performance management will take hold across countries and levels of government, there is a growing demand for products and platforms that enable data-driven governance.

Many pundits have opined that data is the new oil.[40] The value and strategic importance of data in modern government suggests a critical role for the open data movement. In many ways, making government information more transparent and available transcends arguments about the right success markers, the roles of champions, adoption rates, or attentiveness to user demand. Truly opening up public data holds the promise of creating a more level playing field, ensuring that early movers and big players do not dominate the use of public data sources. As government becomes a more sophisticated and smarter user of data in establishing and pursuing its goals, open data may well form the bridge that connects data-informed policy objectives to citizen engagement.

Conclusion

This chapter opened with the shuttering of open.whitehouse.gov, signalling both the political risks that face the open data movement in Australia, Canada, New Zealand, and the US and just how robust and dedicated the open data community has become in these countries. The stories of progress and the remaining gaps to be addressed are not intended to represent all that has happened in open data in recent years, but rather a summary of the most important trends that practitioners and advocates have identified as having an impact on their work.

Based on the challenges identified and best practices that have emerged, policy-makers should focus on three distinct areas of reform. First, foster more standards around the collection and publishing of open data, particularly at the local level. Second, push government staff and departments to share and make use of each other's data, in particular, by investing in tools that enable them to share and a culture that encourages public servants to leverage each other's data when drafting policy and improving operations. Third, publish open data in response to demand and work to identify the kinds of public problems for which the use of open data can help create innovative solutions.

The stories of progress identified here demonstrate that the hard-fought victories to increase the availability of open data have created real value for the governments, citizens, and businesses of North America, Australia, and New Zealand. On the other hand, the persistent challenges facing the advance of open data in these countries should also serve as a warning. For open data to move beyond early successes and quick wins, governments must address the uneven demand for open data, better identify the users and use cases of open data, and push for long-term local adoption. The state of open data in these nations is currently neither a crisis nor a celebration, but these steps will be critical to ensuring that open data becomes a truly integral, sustainable, and effective pillar of 21st century governance.

Further reading

Civic Analytics Network. (2017). An open letter to the open data community. *Data-Smart City Solutions*, 3 March. https://datasmart.ash.harvard.edu/news/article/an-open-letter-to-the-open-data-community-988

Manyika, J., Chui, M., Groves, P., Farrell, D., Van Kuiken, S., & Almasi Doshi, E. (2013). Open data: Unlocking innovation and performance with liquid information. *McKinsey Digital*. https://www.mckinsey.com/business-functions/digital-mckinsey/our-insights/open-data-unlocking-innovation-and-performance-with-liquid-information

Tauberer, J. (2014). *Open government data: The book* (2nd edition). https://opengovdata.io/

About the authors

David Eaves is a public policy entrepreneur and expert in information technology and government. He has worked closely with municipal and federal leaders in Canada and the United States on the intersection of technology, open data, and governance. He is currently the Faculty Director of digital HKS at the Harvard Kennedy School of Government. You can follow David at http://www.twitter.com/daeaves and learn more about his work at https://eaves.ca.

Ben McGuire is a public policy master's candidate at the Harvard Kennedy School. He previously worked in strategy research in the education sector, as well as in organising and data analytics in American political campaigns. You can follow Ben at http://www.twitter.com/bean_mcguire.

Audrey Carson has contributed to technology and public policy research at the Harvard Kennedy School, the Berkman-Klein Center at Harvard Law School, and the MIT Media Lab. She currently works as a strategic communications consultant advising companies and organisations on external communications, corporate positioning, and public affairs.

How to cite this chapter

Eaves, D., McGuire, B., & Carson, A. (2019). Open data around the world: North America, Australia, and New Zealand. In T. Davies, S. Walker, M. Rubinstein, & F. Perini (Eds.), *The state of open data: Histories and horizons*. (pp. 517–534). Cape Town and Ottawa: African Minds and International Development Research Centre.
http://stateofopendata.od4d.net

This work is licensed under a Creative Commons Attribution 4.0 International (CC BY 4.0) licence. It was carried out with the aid of a grant from the International Development Research Centre, Ottawa, Canada.

Key informant interviews

In the process of researching this chapter, interviews were conducted with the following key informants:

Diego Cuesy, Former Open City Coordinator at Laboratorio para la Ciudad in Mexico City; Jay Daley, Managing Director of techobscura Ltd and former CEO of the .NZ registry; Valentina Delgado, Open Data Strategy Consultant at Laboratorio para la Ciudad in Mexico City; Jason M. Hare, Open Data Principal at Jason M. Hare Associates; Alannah Hilt, Business Lead, Open Government Portal, Treasury Board of Canada Secretariat; Tyler Kleykamp, Chief Data Officer for the State of Connecticut, United States; Scott McQuarrie, Geomatics Coordinator for the Township of Langley, Canada; David Moore, Executive Director of the Participatory Politics Foundation and Co-founder of Sludge; Andrew Nicklin, Director of Data Practices at the Center for Government Excellence at Johns Hopkins University; Denice Ross, Phaze Zero Project at New America; Gabe Sawhney, Executive Director of Code for Canada; Paul Stone, Open Government Data Programme Leader for the Secretariat for Open Government Data and Information Programme, New Zealand; David Wasylciw, Founder of OpenNWT.

Endnotes

1. Miller, Z.J. (2017). The White House will keep its visitor logs secret. *Time*, 14 April. http://time.com/4740499/white-house-visitor-logs-public-record-trump/
2. Tarantola, A. (2017). Trump administration is killing its open data portal. *Engadget*, 14 April. https://www.engadget.com/2017/04/14/trump-admin-killing-open-data-portal/
3. President's Management Council and Executive Office of the President. (2018). *President's management agenda*. https://www.whitehouse.gov/wp-content/uploads/2018/03/Presidents-Management-Agenda.pdf
4. Knell, N., Pittman, E., Towns, S., & Mulholland, J. (2014). Open data policies in state and local government. *GovTech*, 17 March. http://www.govtech.com/data/Are-Governments-Committed-to-Open-Data-Interactive-Map.html
5. https://www.anz.co.nz/about-us/economic-markets-research/truckometer/
6. Byrne, D.P., Nah, J.S., & Xue, P. (2018). Australia has the world's best petrol price data: FuelWatch and FuelCheck. *Australian Economic Review*, *51(4)*, 564–577. https://doi.org/10.1111/1467-8462.12302
7. https://www.remix.com/
8. https://www.tylertech.com/resources/blog-articles/connecticut-data-sparks-winning-app-for-opioid-crisis
9. Riddell, D.J. (2014). From the ground up: The story of the Canadian boreal forest agreement. https://www.researchgate.net/publication/303328044_From_the_Ground_Up_The_Story_of_the_Canadian_Boreal_Forest_Agreement
10. https://www.policedatainitiative.org/
11. http://data.torontopolice.on.ca /
12. http://www.policedata.nz/
13. https://elections.bc.ca/resources/voting-results/provincial-by-elections-results/
14. https://www.digital.nyc/startups/heat-seek-nyc
15. https://www.govtrack.us/
16. http://www.councilmatic.org/
17. Key informant interview.
18. Web Foundation. (2017). *Open Data Barometer – Global report*. 4th edition. Washington, DC: World Wide Web Foundation. https://opendatabarometer.org/4thedition/report/
19. https://opendatabarometer.org/4thedition/methodology/
20. https://www.linz.govt.nz/data/linz-data-service
21. Madrigal, A. (2009). Data.Gov launches to mixed reviews. *Wired*, 21 May. https://www.wired.com/2009/05/datagov-launches-to-mixed-reviews/
22. Key informant interview.
23. Key informant interview.
24. Key informant interview.
25. Key informant interview.
26. https://publicsectordigest.com/open-cities-index-results-2017
27. https://opendatabarometer.org/
28. Key informant interview.
29. https://communitydata.ca/SaultSteMarieConsortium
30. Key informant interview.
31. Key informant interview.
32. Key informant interview.
33. Key informant interview.

34 Key informant interview.
35 Goldsmith, S. (2015). Chicago's data-powered recipe for food safety. *Data-Smart City Solutions*, 21 May. https://datasmart.ash.harvard.edu/news/article/chicagos-data-powered-recipe-for-food-safety-688
36 Howard, A. (2012). Predictive data analytics is saving lives and taxpayer dollars in New York City. *O'Reilly Media*, 26 June. https://www.oreilly.com/ideas/predictive-data-analytics-big-data-nyc
37 Key informant interview.
38 https://socrata.com/
39 https://www.esri.com/en-us/about/about-esri/overview
40 Anon. (2017). The world's most valuable resource is no longer oil, but data. *The Economist*, 6 May. https://www.economist.com/leaders/2017/05/06/the-worlds-most-valuable-resource-is-no-longer-oil-but-data

South, East, and Southeast Asia

Michael Canares

Key points

- From 2012 to 2014, several open data initiatives emerged in Asia, but they were often little more than "data dumping" and plagued by data quality problems. More recently, substantial progress has been made with improvements to the quality and coordination of initiatives.

- Civil society organisations are active in creating and curating access to data in order to support development planning and, in some cases, political advocacy and scrutiny of governments, although there are concerns around their sustainability.

- Open data use is increasing but is largely concentrated in higher-income countries. Supply-side initiatives are primarily at the national level and still need to permeate to the local level.

- The ODAsia 2020 vision calls for national governments to show stronger leadership and commitment to open data, improve collaboration on open data initiatives, and increase citizen capacity to use and benefit from open data.

Introduction

Asia[1] is the world's most populous region, accounting for at least 40% of the global population and home to two of the world's largest countries in terms of land size. Diversity characterises the region in terms of political, economic, and social characteristics. It is home to both mature and fledgling democracies. It hosts some of the world's fastest, as well as the slowest, growing economies, resulting in a high level of inequality within countries, meaning a high degree of affluence for some and chronic destitution for others. Asian countries have varied origins, cultures, and colonial histories, painting a complex tapestry of religion, beliefs, and practices that underlie the regional identity.

The significance of the region on the global stage cannot be discounted. Emerging economies, such as China and India, are the source of a large proportion of the services and products distributed globally. Advanced economies, like Japan, have also been consistently large providers of development aid. Importantly, the volatile geo-political condition within the region has been a cause of concern for decades, including the perceived threat to global security caused by North Korea's missile programme.

The record of countries in the region in terms of transparency and accountability is poor. In the latest Corruption Perceptions Index[2] released by Transparency International, more than half of Asia's countries scored below 50, with at least a quarter of those countries considered to have issues with systemic corruption. Nevertheless, there have been significant attempts by several countries to install transparency measures and to make commitments toward greater openness. Indonesia and the Philippines, for example, are founding members of the Open Government Partnership (OGP). Five more of the region's countries have since joined the OGP and are preparing or implementing national action plans to foster greater transparency, accountability, and citizen participation within their jurisdictions. At least a dozen Asian countries have Right To Information (RTI) laws that legislate citizens' fundamental access to government information.

In the 4th edition of the *Open Data Barometer*,[3] the region performs comparatively better when compared to Africa and Latin America as it includes early adopters such as South Korea. Among lower-middle-income countries in the Global South, the Philippines leads the rankings in terms of open data implementation and impact. In a recent survey conducted by OpenDataSoft,[4] at least 23 countries in the region have web-based portals that publish open data on a regular basis.

But how do we describe the overall state of open data in the region? This chapter will attempt to describe the state of open data in Asia by discussing emerging trends that have characterised the journey of national governments in advancing open data initiatives.

Emerging trends

When the International Development Research Centre of Canada (IDRC), working with the World Wide Web Foundation, issued a call for proposals for a global research project "Emerging Impacts of Open Data in Developing Countries"[5] in 2012, there were very few open data initiatives in the region. Indonesia and the Philippines were at the preliminary stages of their open data initiatives, launching open data portals in 2013 and 2014 respectively, and there were hardly any visible user groups identified, although there was some publishing of government data online, albeit in closed formats.

As a matter of fact, research on the state of open data in the region between 2012 and 2014 concluded that open data was still in its infancy[6,7] and country initiatives were plagued by data quality[8,9] problems that had led to more data dumping than use.[10,11] But since then, significant improvements have been observed, along with attendant challenges.

Data availability is improving but limited

The *Open Data Barometer*[12] indicates that progress has been made in terms of data disclosure as governments in the region, both at the national and subnational levels, have initiated open data platforms as a means of data disclosure. To date, over 200 portals have been launched by different levels of government[13] to disclose various datasets on a range of government activities from budgeting and spending to water quality and land use, among many others. The *Barometer* also illustrates, however, that many of the key datasets required for holding governments accountable are not generally available in Asia. This includes data on land ownership, public contracting, company ownership, and elections. Japan, for example, is the only Asian country that the Barometer reports has disclosed spending data.

In the region, it must be noted that providing access to key datasets is not a task that is only taken seriously by governments. In Cambodia, as an example, a group of civil society organisations worked together to launch an online platform that publishes key datasets that are necessary not only for development planning, but also for research and advocacy.[14] In Malaysia, the Sinar Project has worked with researchers and activists to assemble data to visualise the intersection of public and private interests in national politics.[15] The same is true in India, where a civil society organisation collects and shares data on the quality of electricity supply.

> ### CSO publishes power quality data[16]
>
> Across the developing world, roughly 1.2 billion people do not have access to electricity. Of this number, at least 30% live in India. In addition, at least 247 million people in India experience irregular access to electricity with many receiving only four hours of service a day.
>
> In 2007, the Prayas Energy Group, an Indian non-governmental organisation, launched the Electricity Supply Monitoring Initiative (ESMI) to collect real-time power quality information by installing Electricity Supply Monitors (ESMs) in various locations in the city of Pune, India. The data generated by the ESMs has been made available for free at a website set up by Prayas and it is presented in three different forms:
>
> 1. Minute-by-minute voltage information of all monitored areas.
> 2. Reports that analyse voltage data for each location.
> 3. General analysis of the aggregated data that considers the voltage situation at the regional as well as the national level.
>
> The availability of data is argued to have improved power quality, increased consumer satisfaction, and enabled evidence-based advocacy in the power sector.

Interestingly, many governments in the region have embraced the notion of open data within wider narratives on the pursuit of "smartness". The Government of India, for example, has announced the development of 100 smart cities across the country, although this ambitious plan only draws upon a narrow notion of openness. Very often, cities are selectively opening up datasets to spur innovation and economic growth with less attention given to datasets that can aid transparency or government accountability.

Data use is increasing – but concentrated in high-income countries

The Open Data Impact Map[17] reports that many organisations in East Asia and the Pacific region, most of which are in the private sector, are using open data in a variety of economic sectors. However, these organisations are largely concentrated in higher income countries (see the box on South Korea). The same is true in South Asia, especially India, where IT, health, and geospatial companies are using open data; however, widespread use of open data, especially by non-state actors outside the private sector, is limited. While there are a few stellar examples of open data use in some countries (e.g. Kawal Pemilu[18] for election monitoring in Indonesia in 2014, Sakay.ph[19] for commuting in the Philippines, and gov.tw on budget monitoring in Taiwan), these are exceptions rather than the rule. This is largely because capacity issues are still prevalent for users[20] along with the persisting problems associated with the digital divide.[21]

Nevertheless, it is important to point out that data quality (i.e. timeliness, completeness, comparability, comprehensiveness, relevance) is a key factor in eliciting use. This is fundamental to users being able to use data, find relevance in engaging continuously with it, and develop products based on it. Unfortunately, except for advanced economies in the region, data quality is a systemic problem in most countries (e.g. the Open Data Readiness Assessment completed for Malaysia recommended that the country specifically work on improving data quality).[22] This is one of the reasons often given by government agencies for their reluctance to release datasets and often the main reason used to actively deny user requests for data publication. In Indonesia, the government is in the process of issuing a One Data Policy, putting a focus specifically on data quality and management systems in recognition of the inferior quality of many data assets.

South Korea: Generating economic value from open data[23]

Because of the high volume of datasets made publicly available in South Korea and a robust enabling environment that encourages the use of public data for innovative products and services, several private companies have benefited significantly. One of these companies in South Korea is AD Ventures, developers of "MediLatte", which was launched publicly in 2012. This application provides customised hospital information services to South Koreans. AD Ventures made use of hospital information provided by the National Health Insurance Service and those of local governments to provide users with information on hospitals, their location, services, number of doctors, times of operations, peak hours, and service reviews to enable them to select which health service provider to use and for what purpose. For hospitals, the app added value by reducing marketing costs and ensuring better health service delivery through customer feedback.

As of 2015, MediLatte had earned USD 1 million in revenue and another USD 1 million in capital investments. The app has been used by 600 000 users and received 30 000 daily visits.

Nevertheless, governments should not use data quality as a main reason for foregoing data disclosure. As a matter of fact, research conducted by the Open Data Institute (ODI)[24] has shown that opening up data sets has a consequent effect on improving data quality which then benefits the government's ongoing use. Other examples from the Open Data Lab in Jakarta[25] have also shown that publishing datasets will reveal inconsistencies in the data, alerting government agencies to institute improvements in their data collection and aggregation processes.

New civil society actors and networks are emerging

In the last three years, we have seen a growing number of actors in the open data space in most countries in the region. Figure 1 below shows a preliminary inventory of stakeholders that have been active in the open data space. Though the figure is not exhaustive, it illustrates how widespread the open data movement is across the region with different actors working in-country on different issues and concerns related to transparency and accountability, public service delivery, and innovation in a range of thematic sectors, such as education, health, environment, transport, and economic development. As a result, new cross-regional partnerships have emerged, including the Sinar Project in Malaysia working with Phandeeyar in Myanmar to develop an app for monitoring legislative activities.[26]

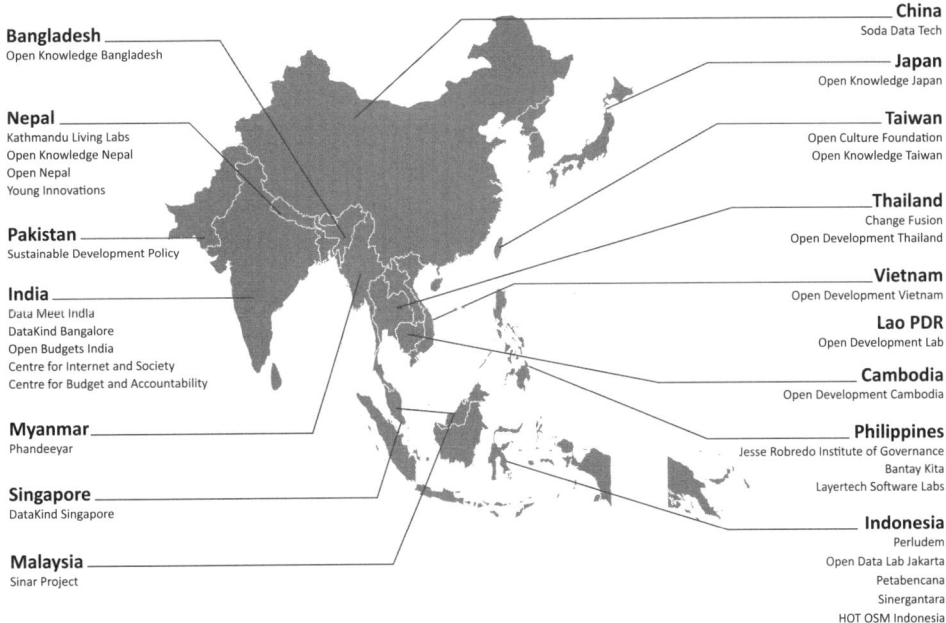

Figure 1: Civil society organisations working on open data
Source: Author

Ongoing cross-country networks have also emerged, some formal, others informal. For example, Open Development Mekong is a network of countries publishing open data in countries within the Mekong region, while Asia Open Data Partnership is a network of organisations in different countries working on open data particularly in the private sector that has held annual conferences of its partners in the last three years. Informal networks also exist, such as the group of stakeholders who gathered in 2014 to define the Open Data Agenda for Asia to 2020. Within countries, there is also the increasing emergence of open data networks. For example, Open Nepal, initially established in 2013, is a growing community of practice in Kathmandu that meets regularly to share open data experiences and plan collective action on an open data agenda. Informal networks based on social media platforms are also growing, including Indonesia's open data WhatsApp group which now has 144 open data advocates and the Philippine's open data Facebook group which has more than 8 900 followers.

Yet for the most part, these networks remain disconnected from each other, and there is no one single network of open data actors in the region as yet with the individual networks mentioned above frequently operating mostly in silos. Major obstacles to collaboration in the region are the lack of a common language across countries, differences in political and economic trajectories, and the lack of opportunities to work together and coordinate.

CSO-led initiatives are increasing in number, but lack sustainability

The emergence of new actors and partnerships has increased the number of open data initiatives in the region. In several countries, different organisations, including those mentioned above, have developed and led several open data projects in many sectors, such as health, education, natural resource governance, and public administration. However, many of these interventions are donor-funded, creating issues around the sustainability for these projects and raising questions about their ability to scale in order to achieve wider and more pervasive results.

The rush by donors toward achieving measurable impacts has also significantly constrained the ability of organisations to obtain funding beyond the pilot stage. In several cases, pilots remain pilots only because of a lack of donor support beyond initial implementation. While private companies using data can attract private investment even during the startup phase, this is hardly the case for non-profits whose aim is to improve transparency and accountability in governments, improve public service delivery, or promote economic inclusion of the disadvantaged. These are big challenges and complex problems that initial pilots will not be able to solve outright, much less achieve lasting impact over the short-term timelines often demanded by funders.

In the last two years, organisations like Code for Nepal, the Sinar Project, and the Open Data Lab Jakarta, among others, have faced funding constraints and been unable to continue pilot projects beyond the pilot period, losing precious human capital in the process as staff move on to more stable employment. This also restricts the ability of these actors to explore new avenues of open data work, such as those related to gender, public service delivery, youth and children, and inclusive development.

Open data outcomes exist, but solid evidence of impact is elusive

Open data initiatives have started to show significant outcomes in a few countries, but with fewer "quantifiable" concrete impacts as yet. Funders are hungry for stories of impact, but the *Open Data Barometer* (3rd edition) reports that while "there is an increasing evidence that open data is improving government efficiency", open data has not yet "translated into concrete improvements in the lives of ordinary people, especially the traditionally marginalised groups".[27] Although there is evidence that points to achievements at the outcome level (e.g. changes in practices and behaviour), it is still difficult to identify improvements in the lives of people that can be directly attributed to open data. Nevertheless, there are specific instances when open data has been cited as lifesaving (see the box on Nepal). While quantifying the specific impact of open data is not possible, such cases do highlight that having clearly defined problems to be addressed by open data is critical to gathering evidence that can ultimately determine its ability to make a difference.

Nepal: Using open data for post-disaster relief operations[28]

Natural disasters occur frequently in Asia, and in most cases, aid delivery to the most affected areas is hampered by logistical problems and a lack of data. After two devastating earthquakes occurred in Nepal in 2015, the government, aid organisations, and other early responders faced significant problems in identifying and prioritising needs related to support and assistance. Several open data activists in the country used open data to identify areas affected, prioritise needs, target relief efforts, and ensure timely aid delivery. This work resulted in post-quake maps that were used by responders to locate Nepalis needing urgent assistance, facilitate timely response, and ensure accountability in aid delivery. At the same time, initiatives allowed opportunities for affected citizens to share feedback with the government (e.g. Kathmandu Living Lab's Quake Map, Young Innovation's Earthquake Response Transparency Portal, and Code for Nepal's Rahat Payo (did you get relief) initiative).

While it is difficult to ascertain how many lives were saved, anecdotal evidence suggests that open data initiatives enabled the mapping of 80% of quake-affected areas. This information was used by responders to ensure that aid delivery reached affected communities.

Open data actors need to find ways to navigate political environments

For several countries in the region, open data initiatives have thrived due to a strong enabling environment. This includes the presence of a legal framework that strengthens citizens' rights to information and data, the political commitment of country leaders to promote openness, a thriving civil society, and a free press. But recent political events have risked the sustainability of open data initiatives undertaken by governments because of fledgling or fluctuating political commitments and increasingly constricted civic space even in leading countries.

Indonesia and the Philippines were two of the pioneering countries behind the founding of the OGP, but, more recently, concerns have been raised with regard to the shrinking of civic space in these countries (see the box on the Philippines). This is also true in Myanmar, where even freedom of speech is curtailed and speaking against the policies of the ruling government is a criminal offense.[29] In China, "shortfalls in civic and political rights arrest the benefits of open data at an early stage".[30] Attacks on basic democratic freedoms in several countries in the region have prompted the Association of Southeast Asian Nations (ASEAN) and European Union (EU) parliamentarians to issue calls to respect human rights and the rule of law in the region.[31] In Cambodia, for example, the national government has issued laws to restrict the freedom of expression and coordinated attacks against media,[32] while in Vietnam, the government has used legislative processes to potentially control dissenting voices by requiring tech companies to store locally important data and take down offensive content at the request of government.[33]

Philippines: Open data initiatives and changes in the political environment

The Open Data Barometer identified the Philippines as the most improved country in their 2016 report, but the assessment only covered the period up to June 2016 as the country was still transitioning to a new political leadership. With the new administration of President Rodrigo Duterte, open data has taken a back seat. Following the election, the government's open data portal was inactive for two months to allow for redesign, but when it was launched again, historical information previously available could no longer be found, including procurement data. The focus was also shifted to the reactive disclosure of information as the president issued an executive order on the right to information that covered only the executive branch of government.

Several reports have confirmed that civil society and freedom of speech have also been assailed and dissenting voices targeted for repression. One senator who has been vocal against the president's war on drugs is currently serving jail term, and the Chief Justice of the Supreme Court was recently removed from office for political reasons. News outfit Rappler, which is perceived to be critical of the president, has also had its licences revoked, and human rights groups have been accused of being used by drug syndicates to undermine the government's efforts against drug trafficking.

However, civil society organisations have found creative ways to implement open data initiatives and use the right to information as a substitute platform. It is still to be seen whether these initiatives can withstand all the current challenges brought about by the changing political climate.

Open data activists in the region are finding alternative means to engage in open data work, including working with other information providers to piece together accountability stories as with the Sinar Project in Malaysia,[34] using legal channels to resist state-sponsored attacks against journalists as with the media company Rappler in the Philippines,[35] or engaging directly with government agencies who are willing to open up data sets to innovators who can use data to create innovative products as in Shanghai, China.[36] While far from desirable, it is likely that open data actors in the region will have to continue to adapt to changes in the political environment with significant creativity over the coming years.

National initiatives still need to permeate to the local level

In most cases, open data initiatives are orchestrated at the national level except in China, where regional governments have steamed ahead of national commitment to publish open datasets.[37] Unlike other countries, such as the United States and Canada, countries in Asia demonstrate relatively few examples of open data initiatives that have originated at the state or local level of government. For example, only four of 29 states and seven union territories in India have an official open data portal. Similarly, the Bangladesh Open Data Strategy,[38] approved in 2016, focused only on the release and publication of data at the national level.

This noted, there are some examples where countries have had more success establishing subnational initiatives. In the case of Indonesia in particular, more and more local governments outside the capital city of Jakarta have been successful not only in publishing data sets, but also in eliciting public use of that data (see the box on Indonesia).

> ### Indonesia: Encouraging open data at the subnational level
>
> Indonesia is one of the few countries in the region that has successfully encouraged the publication and use of open data at the subnational level. While the capital city of Jakarta is one of the forerunners in the region in terms of data publication and the use of data to solve specific problems associated with traffic (e.g. Waze), flooding (e.g. Petabencana), and public service delivery (e.g. Qlue), more and more subnational governments are joining the journey toward greater openness in the country.
>
> The city of Banda Aceh has shown how proactive data disclosure can support better education planning and contribute to better economic opportunities for local producers. In the regency of Bojonegoro, citizen input was included in the budgeting process, and the resulting budget data has been disclosed publicly so that citizens can communicate their level of satisfaction with how their articulated priorities were handled by the government. In the city of Yogyakarta, a local civil society organisation has worked with the local government to make budget data widely available to the public to promote more discussions on gender-related budgeting and spending.
>
> Contributing to this spread of open data initiatives are the government's efforts to promote open governance. In 2016, Indonesia was the only government in the region to include subnational targets in its National Action Plan for the Open Government Partnership, and government efforts in this area are complemented by local actors who have matched the government's publication of key datasets with their own efforts to encourage data use.

Conclusions and looking ahead

Back in 2015, a group of actors from countries in the region gathered together in Jakarta, Indonesia, to define what they would like to see in the open data movement by 2020.[39] The group identified three key desired outcomes that are listed and illustrated in the figure below:

1. Governments show strong leadership and commitment to open data at both national and subnational levels.
2. Stakeholders and sector actors collaborate on open data initiatives.
3. Citizens have the capacity to use and benefit from open data.

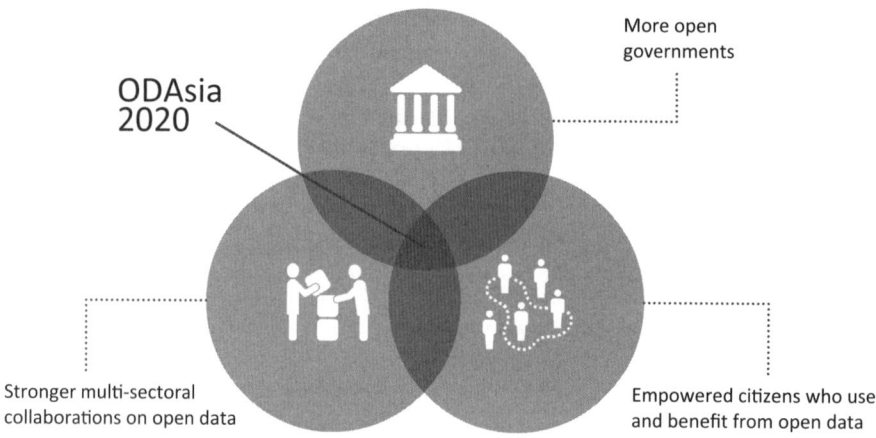

Figure 2: Desired outcomes of the open data movement
Source: Web Foundation. (2015). *Open data agenda-setting for Asia 2015*. Jakarta: World Wide Web Foundation, p. 8. http://labs.webfoundation.org/wp-content/uploads/2015/04/ODAsia2015_WorkshopReport.pdf

The trajectory of the region has included significant strides toward these three outcomes, not only in terms of governments providing users with access to key datasets, but also by encouraging data use to achieve social, economic, and political impact. At the same time, new actors have emerged who have made use of publicly available data to solve specific problems, improving public service delivery, strengthening government bureaucracy and accountability, and catalysing economic growth. Reviewing what has been achieved to date and comparing the current state of open data to when the open data movement was at its infancy stage at the start of this decade, significant milestones have been achieved to lay the foundation for more openness, better transparency, and strengthened accountability through open data.

Notwithstanding these achievements, several challenges remain across the region. Data availability is far from optimal, especially for some critical accountability datasets. For most countries, data quality remains an issue, necessitating the reform of data management systems, and unstable political climates pose threats to the open data movement and the success of open data initiatives. Finally, several open data initiatives face sustainability issues, owing largely to decreasing sources of funding for open data initiatives on the ground. There are several core areas of activity to be pursued to strengthen open data activities in the region:

1. Open data activists need to advocate for countries in the region to open more quality datasets. Toward this end, international indices, such as the Open Data Barometer and the Global Open Data Index, are useful levers to help lobby for reforms with government officials. Many countries, including South Korea, Taiwan, and Malaysia, have used these indices as the basis for structuring their data disclosure practices. Advocacy is also needed to push for new legal frameworks to enable data disclosure, and, in particular, to secure right to information laws, as well as national open data policies. For OGP member countries, advocates should work to secure commitments to more data openness are included in the National Action Plans.

2. Strengthen coordination among open data stakeholders for knowledge sharing, collective action, and scaling impact. There are already existing networks within and among countries in the region. This momentum can be continued by creating a common platform where networks and organisations can share resources, lessons learned, good practices, and skills to foster greater collaboration. Consolidating currently available networks needs to be considered to improve coordination and the efficient use of resources, as well as strengthen collective impact.

3. Project implementers, researchers, and academics need to improve documentation and research on the impacts/outcomes achieved by using open data. While there have been a few research programmes documenting what has been achieved by open data initiatives, there are many stories of change that have not been adequately documented and made widely available. Universities and research institutes in the region should document these practices, looking not only at successes but also failures, so that lessons from implementation can be shared and used to influence the design and implementation of future open data initiatives.

4. Donors need to continue funding new open data initiatives to help scale existing successful activities. Currently, open data initiatives, particularly those that are intended to strengthen transparency and accountability in governments and improve service delivery, need donor funding until such time that appropriate business models are identified for their sustainability. New and innovative projects will not see the light of day without donor support and pilot projects cannot be scaled without donor funding through their initial phases.

5. National governments should promote open data activities at the subnational or local levels. Ensuring that subnational governments are participating in open data initiatives is critical because open data is often argued to have more tangible impact at the local level.[40] Public data often includes granular information capable of addressing the kinds of problems that citizens face day-to-day, and it can be used to generate customised solutions that have tangible impact.

Sustainable impact resulting from open data activities in Asia is not as yet guaranteed, but with the right research, action, and investment in the five core areas discussed, the movement has every chance of expanding and maturing in the years ahead.

Further reading

Canares, M. & Shekhar, S. (2016). Open data and subnational governments: Lessons from developing countries. *The Journal of Community Informatics, 12(2).* http://ci-journal.org/index.php/ciej/article/view/1260

Davies, T. (2014). *Open data in developing countries: Emerging insights from phase 1.* Washington, DC: World Wide Web Foundation. http://webfoundation.org/docs/2017/09/Phase-1-Synthesis-Full-Report.pdf

Lu, F. (2016). *Private and open data in Asia: A regional guide.* Sebastopol, CA: O'Reilly Media.

Stagars, M. (2016). *Open data in Southeast Asia: Towards economic prosperity, government transparency, and citizen participation in the ASEAN.* Singapore: Palgrave Macmillan.

Verhulst, S. & Young, A. (2017). *Open data in developing economies: Towards building an evidence base on what works and how.* Cape Town: African Minds. http://www.africanminds.co.za/wp-content/uploads/2017/10/AM-OD-in-Developing-Economies-COMPLETE-R-WEB-10Nov2017.pdf

Web Foundation. (2017). *Open Data Barometer 4th Edition: East Asia and the Pacific regional snapshot.* Washington, DC: World Wide Web Foundation. https://opendatabarometer.org/4thedition/regional-snapshot/east-asia-pacific/

About the author

Michael Canares is the Senior Research Manager for Digital Citizenship at the World Wide Web Foundation. He has more than ten years of research and development work experience in Southeast Asia and has led research at the Foundation's Open Data Lab in Jakarta.

How to cite this chapter

Canares, M. (2019). Open data around the world: South, East, and Southeast Asia. In T. Davies, S. Walker, M. Rubinstein, & F. Perini (Eds.), *The state of open data: Histories and horizons* (pp. 535–548). Cape Town and Ottawa: African Minds and International Development Research Centre. http://stateofopendata.od4d.net

This work is licensed under a Creative Commons Attribution 4.0 International (CC BY 4.0) licence. It was carried out with the aid of a grant from the International Development Research Centre, Ottawa, Canada.

Endnotes

1. Asia, in this paper, refers to the countries that the World Bank classified as East Asia and the Pacific and South Asia. For purposes of this paper, the Pacific Islands are explicitly excluded.
2. Transparency International. (2018). Corruption Perceptions Index 2017. http://www.transparency.org/cpi2017
3. Web Foundation. (2017). *Open Data Barometer – Global report*. 4th edition. Washington, DC: World Wide Web Foundation. https://opendatabarometer.org/4thedition/report/
4. https://www.opendatasoft.com/a-comprehensive-list-of-all-open-data-portals-around-the-world/
5. http://www.opendataresearch.org/emergingimpacts
6. Ritter, W. (2014). *Open data in Asia. An overview of open data policies and practices in 13 countries*. Hong Kong: Knowledge Dialogues. https://knowledgedialogues.files.wordpress.com/2014/07/open-data-asia-09-2014.pdf
7. Srivastava, N., Aggarwal, V., Soni, A., Bhattacharjya, S., Nayak, P., Meenawat, H., & Gopalakrishnan, T. (2014). *Open government data for regulation of energy resources in India*. New Delhi: The Energy and Resources Institute (TERI). http://www.opendataresearch.org/sites/default/files/publications/Full%20-%20TERI%20OGD%20and%20energy%20resources%20July%202014-print.pdf
8. Shekhar, S. & Padmanabhan, V. (2014). *The quality of civic data in India and the implications on the push for open data*. Ottawa: Open Data for Development (OD4D). https://idl-bnc-idrc.dspacedirect.org/bitstream/handle/10625/55352/IDL-55352.pdf
9. Ona, S.E., Hecita, I.J., & Ulit, E.D. (2014). *Exploring the role and opportunities for open government data and new technologies in MHCC and MSME: The case of the Philippines*. Manila: De La Salle University. http://www.opendataresearch.org/sites/default/files/publications/Open%20Data%20Opportunities%20in%20Maternal%20Health%20and%20Child%20Care%20and%20MSMEs-print.pdf
10. Canares, M. (2014). Opening the local: Full disclosure policy and its impact on local governments in the Philippines. ICEGOV'14. In *Proceedings of the 8th International Conference on Theory and Practice of Electronic Governance, Guimaraes, Portugal, 27–30 October 2014* (89–98). https://dl.acm.org/citation.cfm?id=2691214
11. Chattapadhyay, S. (2014). *Opening government data through mediation: Exploring the roles, practices and strategies of data intermediary organisations in India*. http://www.opendataresearch.org/sites/default/files/publications/sumandro_oddc_project_report_0.pdf
12. Web Foundation. (2017). *Open Data Barometer 4th edition: East Asia and the Pacific regional snapshot*. Washington, DC: World Wide Web Foundation. https://opendatabarometer.org/4thedition/regional-snapshot/east-asia-pacific/
13. https://www.opendatasoft.com/a-comprehensive-list-of-all-open-data-portals-around-the-world/
14. Canares, M., Young, A., & Verhulst, S. (2017). Open Development Cambodia: Opening information on development efforts. Brooklyn, NY: GovLab. http://odimpact.org/case-open-development-cambodia.html
15. Canares, M., Yusof, K., & Meng, S. (2017). *Collaborating for open data: Building a database on politically exposed persons in Malaysia: A case study*. Washington, DC: World Wide Web Foundation. http://webfoundation.org/docs/2017/08/RP-Collaboration-For-Open-Data-082017.pdf
16. Canares, M., Dinesh, A., Young, A., & Verhulst, S. (2017). India's ESMI: Civil society complementing government data in an open manner. Brooklyn, NY: GovLab. http://odimpact.org/case-indias-esmi.html
17. See http://opendataimpactmap.org/eap.html
18. http://www.kawalpemilu.org/#0
19. https://sakay.ph/
20. Canares, M. & Shekhar, S. (2016). Open data and subnational governments: Lessons from developing countries. *The Journal of Community Informatics, 12(2)*. http://ci-journal.org/index.php/ciej/article/view/1260

21 Stagars, M. (2016). *Open data in Southeast Asia: Towards economic prosperity, government transparency, and citizen participation in the ASEAN*. Singapore: Palgrave Macmillan.

22 Zijlstra, A.A., Vaira, C.L., & Boothe, R. (2017). *Open data readiness assessment: Malaysia*. Malaysia Development Experience Series. Washington, DC: World Bank Group. http://documents.worldbank.org/curated/en/529011495523087262/Open-data-readiness-assessment-Malaysia

23 Jung, K. & Park, H.W. (2015). Open Data 500 Korea goes live. *GovLab* [Blog post], 29 November. http://thegovlab.org/open-data-500-korea-goes-live/

24 ODI. (2018). *Using open data to deliver public services*. London: Open Data Institute. https://theodi.org/wp-content/uploads/2018/03/Using-open-data-to-deliver-public-services.pdf

25 Canares M. & Pawelke, A. (2015). *Open data and fiscal transparency: How can we unlock the benefits? – Learnings from pilot projects in Indonesia and the Philippines*. Jakarta: Open Data Lab. http://labs.webfoundation.org/wp-content/uploads/2015/09/OD4T-Lessons-Learned-EN-Screen.pdf?pdf=LLP-OD4T-EN

26 http://openhluttaw.info/

27 Web Foundation. (2016). *Open Data Barometer 3rd edition. Regional report: East Asia and the Pacific*. Washington, DC: World Wide Web Foundation. https://opendatabarometer.org/doc/3rdEdition/ODB-3rdEdition-EastAsiaPacificReport.pdf

28 McMurren, J., Bista, S., Young, A., & Verhulst, S. (2017). *Nepal earthquake recovery: Open data to improve disaster relief*. Brooklyn, NY: GovLab. http://odimpact.org/case-nepal-earthquake-recovery.html

29 McPherson, P. & Diamond, C.W. (2017). Free speech curtailed in Aung San Suu Kyi's Myanmar as prosecutions soar. *The Guardian*, 9 January. https://www.theguardian.com/world/2017/jan/09/free-speech-curtailed-aung-san-suu-kyis-myanmar-prosecutions-soar

30 Stagars, M. (2016). *Open data in Southeast Asia: Towards economic prosperity, government transparency, and citizen participation in the ASEAN*. Singapore: Palgrave Macmillan.

31 Human Rights Online Philippines. (2017). ASEAN and EU parliamentarians decry shrinking civic space; unite with CSOs in defending human rights and rule of law. *Human Rights Online Philippines* [Press release], 12 November. https://hronlineph.com/2017/11/12/press-release-asean-and-eu-parliamentarians-decry-shrinking-civic-space-unite-with-csos-in-defending-human-rights-and-rule-of-law/

32 Smith, R. (2019). Cambodia daily closure a major blow for freedom of information and expression in the country. *The Conversation*, 5 September. http://theconversation.com/cambodia-daily-closure-a-major-blow-for-freedom-of-information-and-expression-in-the-country-83472

33 Nguyen, M. (2018). Vietnam lawmakers approve cyber law clamping down on tech firms, dissent. *Reuters*, 12 June. https://www.reuters.com/article/us-vietnam-socialmedia-idUSKBN1J80AE

34 https://sinarproject.org/en/projects/popit-api-database

35 Regencia, T. (2018). Government targets Rappler, website critical of Duterte. *Al Jazeera*, 16 January. https://www.aljazeera.com/news/2018/01/philippine-government-seeks-close-rappler-website-180115084959311.html

36 http://sodachallenges.com/en

37 Zheng, L. & Gao, F. (2016). Assessment on China's open government data platforms: Framework, status and problems. In *Proceedings of the 17th International Digital Government Research Conference on Digital Government Research (dg.o '16)* (pp. 408–414). https://dl.acm.org/citation.cfm?id=2912160.2912213

38 Government of Bangladesh. (2016). *Open government data strategy*. Dhaka: Statistics and Informatics Division, Ministry of Planning. https://sid.portal.gov.bd/sites/default/files/files/sid.portal.gov.bd/notices/e1531b3c_460d_49a6_82bf_36b9b61b8b1d/Open%20Government%20Data(OGD)%20Strategy%202016.pdf

39 Web Foundation. (2015). *Open data agenda-setting for Asia 2015*. Jakarta: World Wide Web Foundation. http://labs.webfoundation.org/wp-content/uploads/2015/04/ODAsia2015_WorkshopReport.pdf

40 Canares, M. & Shekhar, S. (2016). Open data and subnational governments: Lessons from developing countries. *The Journal of Community Informatics, 12(2)*. http://ci-journal.org/index.php/ciej/article/view/1260

037

Sub-Saharan Africa

Leonida Mutuku and Teg-wende Idriss (Tinto)

Key points

- The open data movement in Sub-Saharan Africa has evolved substantially over the last seven years, but is still far from mature. However, there are promising examples of civil society intermediaries using data to support citizen engagement with government.

- Although the main source of data is often official statistics, open government data initiatives are rarely hosted by National Statistics Offices (NSOs), but instead by technology and communications ministries or ministries of finance. Private sector engagement is very low compared to other global regions.

- Open data is seen as a secondary priority, separate from other development agendas, such as physical infrastructure, agriculture, education, water, and health. There remains a perception that open data is an external priority that is owned by funders, rather than adopted and valued to serve domestic agendas.

- Strict definitions of open data can act as a barrier to data production. There are opportunities for data to be made more accessible and to be used to address social or government needs, even if not fully open.

Introduction

A story is often told of a group of open data civil society advocates in Uganda who requested that the government make budget information available as open data. The government official who responded could not understand why they were making this request in the first place. "But the data is already open!" was the response before he went on to point out to them that if they looked at various newspapers, they would see that the government regularly published summaries of approved budgets. This anecdote points out the importance of considering nuance and context when one reviews the successes and failures of African open data initiatives.

The norm for policy-making on the continent is for it to be based more on perceptions and personal experience, without the necessary data analysis that would help to paint a more accurate picture of any given issue or situation. Additionally, the open data movement in Africa has emerged against a backdrop of state-driven cultures within which it is considered sufficient to have public institutions alone responsible for control and monitoring of executive functions.

Historically, in many African states, data access was governed by the infamous "Secrets Acts", a remnant from the colonial era (for British colonies in particular) when most government information was considered pertinent to national security and not for public disclosure. However, mounting pressure from donor institutions and a well-informed and digitally connected citizenry have provided the necessary incentives to kick start the open data movement. This has led to improved governance practices, including constitutional provisions for citizen participation (directly or indirectly via civil society organisations (CSOs)) and the establishment of national consultation frameworks for government planning related to resource allocation, as well as the monitoring of policy implementation by public institutions. The effectiveness of these mechanisms, nevertheless, is dependent on an informed citizenry; therefore, the right to access information, and by extension, open data, is a critical tenet for democratic states that value citizen involvement in the governance process.

Since Morocco launched the first open data initiative in Africa in 2011, open data movements on the continent have remained vibrant, with several countries and institutions rolling out new initiatives each year. More than 20 countries, regional organisations, and international groups have launched open data initiatives specific to Africa. However, this chapter will also address how many initiatives have struggled to find solid ground or have been deemed unsustainable by failing to show evidence of value and impact to the citizenry, the ultimate beneficiary of open government initiatives.

The progression and regression of different open data initiatives in Africa over the past few years has been attributed to several factors. For open data initiatives to thrive on the continent, they require "proper infrastructures, a high technology literacy rate, adapted national policies and strategies, national leadership, local intermediaries, local competencies and plenty enthusiasm among public institutions, civil societies, ICT companies, non-governmental organisations (NGOs) and academics".[1] This chapter will focus on an analysis of open data ecosystems on the continent with a focus on Sub-Saharan Africa, providing a view of the state of open data in both Anglophone and Francophone countries. It will seek to describe the African open data landscape by unpacking the catalysts for the progress made to date and explore why some gaps persist in many existing open data initiatives across the continent.

The African open data ecosystem

The initial premise for launching open data initiatives was to advance democracy and drive economic growth in African countries. These outcomes were expected to result from increased transparency, accountability, data reuse, and technology innovation, so accordingly, when we examine the African open data ecosystem, many different stakeholders have emerged, each potentially driven by different motivations.

Government institutions

Within the open data ecosystem, government institutions have primarily been designated as open data producers, hosting national data portals and developing the frameworks required to govern the release of open data. However, in the Sub-Saharan African context, there is rarely any general consensus on which government institution is designated to host the national open data portal. While the majority of the data released is based on official statistics, National Statistics Offices (NSOs) are not necessarily the custodians of open data initiatives. There are notable situations where government open data initiatives are hosted by specific ministries, such as the ICT/Communications Ministry in the case of Ghana and Kenya or the Ministry of Finance in the case of Tanzania.

More recently, local governments have also become involved in the open data ecosystem, setting up their own portals, often complementary to their national counterparts. Local initiatives provide more granular and thematic data specific to the locality (e.g. City of Cape Town open data initiative in South Africa and the Edo State initiative in Nigeria). Similarly, multilateral organisations, such as the UN Economic Commission for Africa (UNECA),[2] have initiated open data initiatives that provide comparable data at a regional level on a range of topics, including population, health, national accounts, and other development indicators.

Development partners

The history of open data in Sub-Saharan Africa, and more generally, in developing countries, cannot be told without featuring the prominent role played by development partners. For instance, the World Bank is credited with being the critical catalyst for the emergence of an open data ecosystem on the continent, providing both financial and technical support to at least ten open data initiatives. This involvement has often integrated high-level dialogue with governments and the completion of Open Data Readiness Assessments[3] in countries such as Rwanda, Mauritania, and Ethiopia, providing them with an understanding of their baseline positions in terms of the availability of data that can be reflected in planned open data initiatives.[4] In several cases, such as in Kenya, Tanzania, and Ghana, this support has resulted in the development of customised roadmaps and funding to implement open data initiatives.

In addition to providing external support to national initiatives, development partners have been credited as being producers and aggregators of open data. As an example, the Africa Information Highway,[5] an umbrella open data platform, was launched by the African Development Bank in 2013 with the aim of solving the difficulty in accessing data on key socioeconomic indicators for African countries. It allows each African country to have its own open data portal hosted on the platform, and the national data is mainly provided by each country's NSO, donors, and other international institutions.

Other key development partners that have been critical to the growing African open data movement include the United States Agency for International Development (USAID), the Department for International Development in the UK (DFID), and the International Development Research Centre (IDRC). All of these organisations have open access policies that require that data from supported projects be made available in open formats, although with some exceptions. IDRC, together with the World Bank, DFID, and the Government of Canada, has also funded and supported knowledge generation and the development of thriving open data ecosystems in Africa through the Open Data for Development Partnership (OD4D). USAID has similarly actively supported capacity building for stakeholders in the open data ecosystem by providing grants for influential open data initiatives such as the Data Collaboratives for Local Impact programme.[6]

Civil society organisations

NGOs have been instrumental to the growth of African open data ecosystems. These organisations mainly support the implementation of open data initiatives and build capacity for the use of open data to increase access to information in support of advocacy and service delivery.

Some notable institutions actively promoting the development of the open data ecosystem in Africa include Open Knowledge International, the Open Data Institute (ODI), and the World Wide Web Foundation. These organisations have rolled out several initiatives with grassroots communities, providing thought leadership and creating knowledge resources and capacity building for open data government champions[7] and civil society, as well as supporting annual Open Data Day activities.[8] Other institutions, such as the International Budget Partnership, Extractive Industries Transparency Initiative (EITI), and Development Initiatives, have also been champions for thematic open data access and use with regard to budgets, the extractives industry, and poverty, respectively.

CSOs have also been instrumental in the growing demand for open data to support technological innovation. In particular, open data is increasingly used to develop effective civic technologies, especially those that enhance citizen–government engagement. Initiatives, such as Code*for*Africa,[9] have developed citizen-focused applications utilising open data, while others, such as the Africa Open Data Collaboratives,[10] have supported the convening of civic hackers, data journalists, and other open data stakeholders at regular conferences, such as the Africa Open Data Conference, as well as online events.

Private sector and academia

The private sector and academia have not been particularly active in the African open data ecosystem to date, with their participation traditionally limited to internal data production and the use of data for research and business purposes. However, more recently, as the private sector and academia look to contribute to the sustainable development agenda, there are emerging examples of the role that they can play as partners in growing the open data ecosystem. For instance, IBM and Ericsson have been involved in Smart Cities initiatives,[11] in partnership with government and development partners. The Smart Cities blueprint for Africa recognises the role open data will play in building efficient technology-driven cities via the management of city infrastructure, flows, and services.[12]

Academic institutions are also embracing open data policies in governing the dissemination of their research outputs, recognising the major impact that open access to the related data can have on development and other research. Electronic Information for Libraries (EIFL) is working in partnership with a consortium of library partners toward the creation of open access repositories for academic research, which include data developed within research institutions.[13] Academia is also contributing to the open data ecosystem through the completion of research on open data itself, such as the work undertaken by the University of Cape Town.[14]

To illustrate the potential interaction of African open data stakeholders, an initial model for the Kenya Open Data ecosystem (see Figure 1) was conceptualised by Rahemtulla et al. for the World Bank in 2012, describing the emerging and fluid relationships between civil society as drivers of demand for open data, development partners as supporting partners, and government officials serving as champions and agents of change.[15]

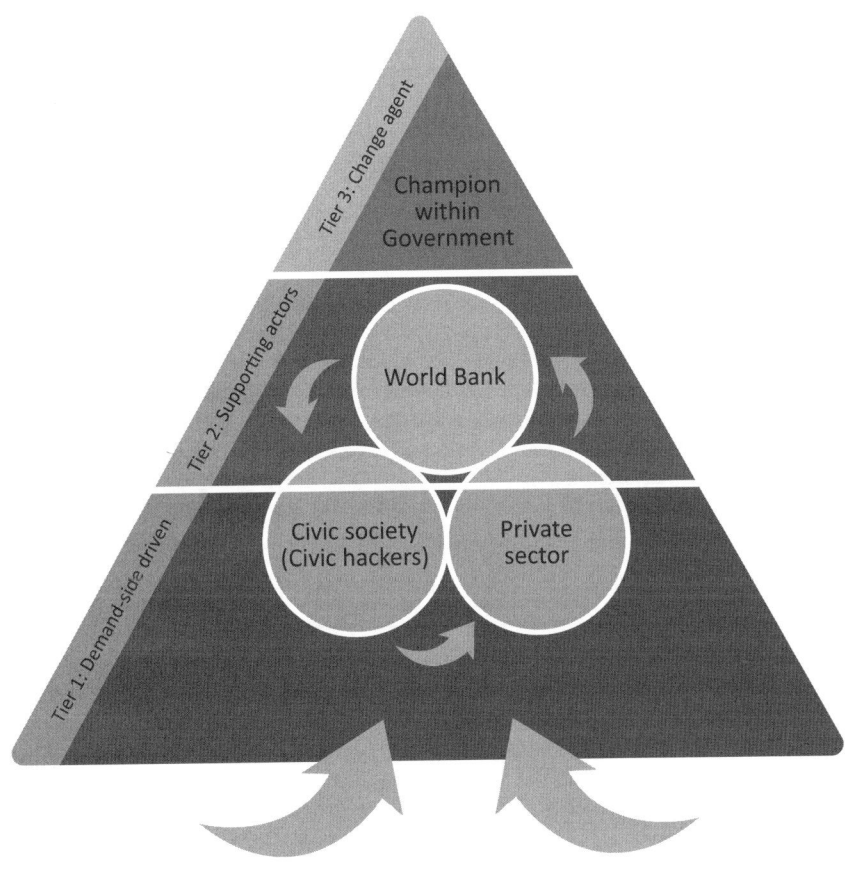

Figure 1:   Kenya open data ecosystem as envisioned by Rahemtulla et al. (2012)

This "government/civil society/development agency" model can easily be extrapolated to many African country contexts. While relationships and the influence of open data stakeholders may vary in extent within the context of each country, they ultimately fulfil more or less the same role, although this model has started to become outdated as African open data ecosystems have evolved to include more actors with broader and multi-level interactions. For example, citizens have begun to feature more prominently in the open data ecosystem: first, as the ultimate beneficiaries of the value created by open data and, second, as the producers of alternative open data via crowdsourcing activities.

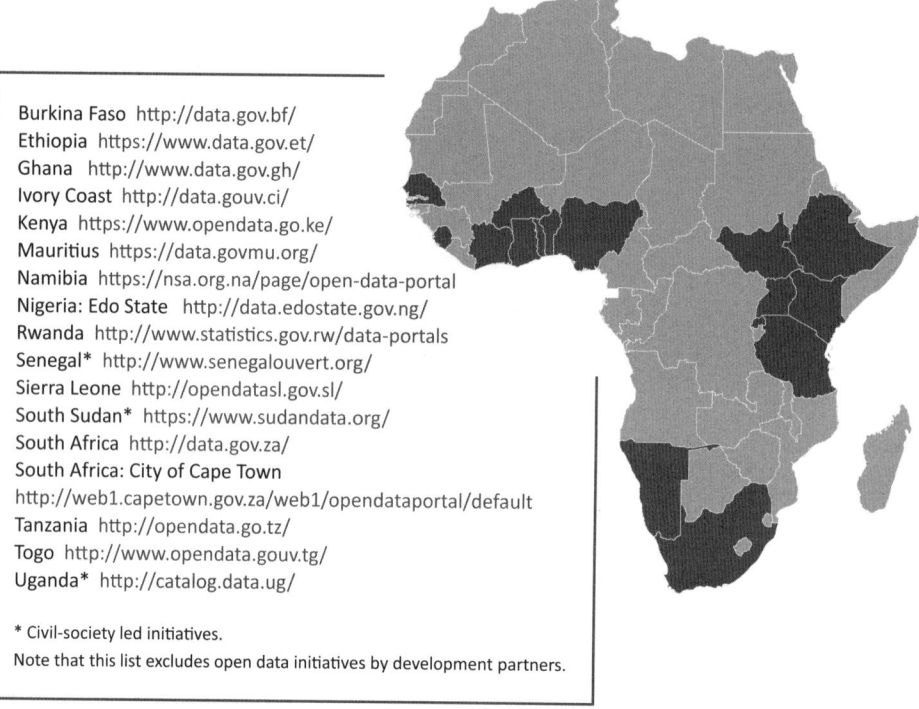

Figure 2: Countries in Sub-Saharan Africa with local open data initiatives
Source: Authors

Production and access to open data

Production of open data

During the past seven years of the global wave of open government activities, more than 15 Sub-Saharan African countries have launched open data initiatives (see Figure 2). Countries in the region with national open data portals can be classified into two categories: those with an official government-led open data initiative or open data portal, and those whose main open data initiatives are civil society driven. Initial efforts to build open data ecosystems began with English-speaking countries launching portals and initiatives beginning in 2011, followed by countries from Francophone Sub-Saharan Africa who started their initiatives in 2012.

Most African open data portals make data available in machine-readable formats;[16] however, very few datasets can be categorised as truly open (based on principles provided by the Open Data Charter).[17] A review of these open data portals via global measurement tools, such as Open Data Watch,[18] the Open Data Index,[19] and the Open Data Barometer,[20] reveals that the most common datasets available cover demographics, education, healthcare, agriculture, budgets, economic data, procurement, oil/energy, and water. Of these datasets, it seems that census and budget data are the most commonly available on most portals, most likely because of the historical need for these datasets for planning purposes and resource allocation. While the majority of open data is created from government statistics, in some instances, development partners, CSOs, and research organisations have also made available the open data from projects that they have supported.

Production of open data has not been without its challenges, with several African countries struggling to produce and provide high quality and accessible open data. Data from the last three years of the Open Data Barometer shows a decline in readiness and implementation of open data across most of the Sub-Saharan African countries that were studied.[21] This implies a consequent decline in the quality and quantity of updated open data available for public access even though the demand for data in new categories is increasing.

The Open Data Barometer further indicates that only two out of 375 datasets in the Africa regional analysis met the full definition criteria for open data.[22] This is first and foremost attributed to the fundamental issue of data licensing. Despite the availability of data via open data portals, many datasets are subject to copyright and disclaimers are provided that restrict the reuse of the data.[23] In other instances, data is available in the form of scanned documents or as printed booklets, rendering its reuse very difficult without an additional process of manual or technology-enabled extraction of the data, which, in most cases, is an expensive exercise. For example, detailed data on government expenditures in Kenya is available from the controller as scanned documents, but only compiled reports are available online.[24]

In addition, for some published open datasets, it is difficult to establish provenance as not all datasets are published with proper metadata, and it is not uncommon to find variations of the same datasets on different government sites. Some ministries and other public institutions are known to publish data on their own websites, but not via portals, making open data discovery and availability quite fragmented and difficult to trace.

Open data initiatives in Sub-Saharan Africa have been criticised for not generating high value datasets in open formats and more disaggregated data in thematic areas, such as healthcare, agriculture, and education. Most datasets on official government open data portals are rarely updated. Additionally, despite the fact that a few cities have launched open data initiatives, granular/localised datasets are still not widely available. It seems that institutions working on the supply side of data are still not collecting granular data, nor are they sufficiently supported to collect this data at the grassroots level. Yet these datasets are critical if development is to be localised.

Access to open data

Open data is produced and made available for access on digital platforms, but an essential requirement to access and use of open data is digital literacy. On a continent where more than 50% of the population is still without access to digital tools and mobile phones,[25] the lack of connectivity and technology is a barrier to the proliferation of open data initiatives, especially at the grassroots level. While the continent has leapfrogged the curve of technology uptake through the widespread adoption of mobile technology, crucial infrastructure elements, such as mobile internet, are still beyond the reach of many, with the penetration at just 38% in 2017.

Even with connectivity, open data is, in practice, only useful to those who are data literate and able to synthesise it into actionable insights. There is still poor use of open data by both government officials and CSOs due to limited data literacy. The literacy gap is large, especially for those CSOs that operate at the grassroots level, where they are expected to play a critical intermediation role between the citizen and public institutions.[26] Similarly, government officials are often unable themselves to leverage open data to support policy-making.

Language barriers also exist, further distancing potential access and the use of open data locally. For instance, open data literature is frequently in English only, which is a limiting factor that can exclude people who could benefit from open data if guidance was also available in local languages.

Key role for intermediaries in open data use

Although direct access to open data can be challenging, citizens still have the right to access the necessary information to make decisions and engage with their public institutions on policy-making. This necessitates some form of intermediation. Open data intermediaries play a critical advocacy role, as well as offering tools and access to information for potential users at the community level. In particular, traditional institutions, such as media outlets and religious institutions, have played an important role in relaying government information to grassroots communities in Sub-Saharan Africa.[27]

To combat the barriers to access related to limited data literacy and technological capacity, intermediaries have taken up the role of distilling open data and creating products and information packages in formats that can be accessed offline.[28] Common tools used by intermediaries include citizen town halls and visual presentations that allow information synthesised from open data to be shared with citizens. For instance, the Open Institute in Kenya has worked with community members from Lanet, Nakuru County to collect local household data, which they then visualised in dashboards in order to share findings with community leaders.[29]

CSOs, technologists, and data journalists have emerged as central open data "intermediaries". Civic hackers and technologists have also created a variety of applications that are based on open data synthesised with other information to make data more readily available to citizens. For example, BudgIT[30] in Nigeria and PesaCheck[31] in East Africa are promoting participatory governance on budget issues, enabled by synthesised open data that they are disseminating to local communities.

Similarly, there has been demonstrated growth in data journalism efforts on the continent. In 2016, the African Network of Centers for Investigative Reporting demonstrated the role of open data in investigative journalism by publishing articles on illicit financial flows mined from the leaked Panama Papers.[32] The Sudan Evidence Base Programme has also promoted data journalism as it encourages journalists and civil society members to use a storytelling approach to monitor development, government policies, and the use of government resources.

Legal, economic, and political frameworks for open data

More than half of the countries in Sub-Saharan Africa have either a constitutional mandate or right to information legislation in place, granting citizens the right to access information held by the state or public institutions.[33] Additionally, the advent of the Open Government Partnership (OGP) and the implementation of the African Peer Review Mechanism by African Union member states have been monumental in advancing the creation of government open data initiatives.

The OGP, through their support for the development of National Action Plans, has advocated for member states to commit to open data initiatives. These OGP commitments have been the channel through which countries, such as Côte d'Ivoire, have launched their open data initiative. Sierra Leone, South Africa, Ghana, Tanzania, and Kenya also have commitments related to open data as part of their OGP National Action Plans.[34]

However, neither a Right to Information Law nor an OGP commitment necessarily translate to the existence of a thriving open government data initiative. In fact, it has been noted that several of these laws are insufficient or have significant weaknesses. These include restrictions within the laws on what information can be released, vague provisions that allow for withholding of information as deemed necessary, and difficult procedures for requesting information held by the state.[35] It has also been observed that much of the existing legislation related to open data is not backed up by any government policies or regulations that ensure the enforcement of these laws.

The impact of laws that are poorly implemented is visible in that some of the pioneering open data initiatives, such as the stalled Nigeria and Ivorian open data initiatives, were unsustainable as they were unable to transcend changes of government. Open data in African countries mainly thrives due to strong political will from open data champions within government; however, if this political will is not institutionalised, governments that must transition to new administrations are at significant risk that limited interest from the subsequent governments will undermine any pre-existing open data initiatives. Similarly, some open data initiatives are not funded sustainably and are threatened once funding from development partners ends if there is no custodial ownership from host government institutions.

Some institutions, including NSOs, face legal restrictions even where there is willingness to open up data for the general public to access. NSOs are also, in some cases, mandated to sell data in the form of publications to generate revenue in order to fund their complex work collecting and structuring national datasets. As a result, some data is available, neither openly nor for free, but solely in printed compendiums that have to be purchased.

Within data lies power, and those who hold data hold the power. Government officials, therefore, without the guidance of regulations and policies to publish open data are likely to be reluctant to publish this information, claiming that once open, data is subject to misinterpretation, challenge, or contradiction if citizens are free to manipulate government data without restrictions. The Statistical Act of Tanzania, published in 2015, restricts unauthorised communication and the dissemination of data that has not been sanctioned by the National Bureau of Statistics.[36] In this way, the law is running counter to the government's commitments to open data.

Given that many African governments are still not culturally open by nature, several have found difficulty to establish sustainable policies. There is a need for a "blueprint" for open data policies that can account for the many different contexts for African governments. However, successes do exist, such as Kenya's public participation frameworks that have been put in place to ensure citizen input on legislation, budgets, and resource allocation.[37] These frameworks are promoting active and meaningful participation in governance processes by prescribing the publication of relevant data and information in advance of barazas (town hall meetings), and could still be inspiration for development of local open data policies.

The African Data Consensus developed at the High Level Conference on Data Revolution held in Addis Ababa in 2015 attempted to provide principles that African governments could fall back on as they establish data initiatives. The document included specific references to ensuring government data is licensed as open by default, the use of technology, and the production of disaggregated data;[38] however, this document was never formally adopted, and open data advocates must rely on collaborative efforts within the open data ecosystem to domesticate the principles presented in the consensus.

Open data in the context of African development

Evidence of the use of open data in policy-making has been observed in several contexts; however, the most impactful outcomes from uses documented to date are in the area of governance and technology innovation. The drivers of these initiatives are mainly non-governmental actors: non-profits and civic technology innovators.[39] These stakeholders are the demand drivers and early adopters of open data in the African ecosystem, yet the private sector is conspicuously missing, unlike on other continents, where open data is also used directly to create innovation in business as well as for business research.

Throughout the continent, technology innovators and CSOs are employing open data in their projects. Examples of the impact of open data are found in several sectors. For instance, in Ghana, Where My Money Dey? is a volunteer built project that aims at improving public accountability of allocated funds in Ghana,[40] and Farmerline aims to impact the agriculture sector by offering an SMS-based service that provides small-scale farmers with up-to-date agricultural data.[41] In 2014, during the serious Ebola outbreak in West Africa, a number of data-driven initiatives were established to improve the quality of information available to the humanitarians working to address the crisis, including work by the National Ebola Response Centre, United Nations Humanitarian Data Exchange, and the Ebola GeoNode.[42]

Despite these exciting outputs resulting from open data use, such initiatives do not publish the extent of their impact (i.e. how many citizens or policy-makers have been affected by these initiatives). Therefore, their impact is not seen as widespread especially within government. In fact, according to the Open Data Barometer, the continent scores poorly on impact,[43] which is calculated as a composite of political, social, and economic impact. The first major limitation to wider impact of open data initiatives is the limited funding available to open data projects. In African countries, priority is given to investments in physical infrastructure, agriculture, education, water, health, and sanitation. Open data is seen as a separate project from these priority development agendas. Even after starting an open data initiative, governments will often prefer to direct follow-up investment toward development projects that are more visible to the electorate, rather than to data-related innovation.

As a result, open data projects are often funded by external donors and development partners, and they exist within a limited time period. Accordingly, it is inevitable that there is a potential disconnect between the objectives of those funding open data initiatives and those of the implementing governments and institutions. For instance, although the initial argument for open data initiatives was to promote good governance practices, such as transparency and accountability, it is challenging to find support for this narrative without giving consideration to the current institutional contexts and other political motivations. Therefore, open data initiatives are perceived as not grounded in reality and development priorities for host countries, but rather aligned with external priorities set by funding partners.

As discussed previously, the demand for open data has mostly stemmed from technology innovators, international organisations, and CSOs. Their efforts in some ways have been siloed, alienating public institutions and resulting in little to no ownership or commitment by government institutions, either as suppliers or advocates. Once again, without this institutional ownership, open data initiatives remain low on the priority scale and consequently receive little to no resources once donor funding runs out. Initiatives become dormant or regress in open data readiness as a result.

A second limitation to the developmental impact of open data initiatives in Sub-Saharan Africa is related to technical capacity at the government level. There is inadequate evidence of the use of open data to actually enhance government efficiency even though this has been identified as one of the key benefits touted by the open data movement. There are varying levels of data literacy both within policy-making and implementing institutions, presenting a challenge to actually using open data to drive development processes and produce high economic value. Collaborative initiatives such as OD4D, the Open Data Leaders Network, and similar fellowships for government officials are working to address this issue.

Additionally, there have been concerns that important data communities are currently not engaged in ongoing open data initiatives in the region, whose strengths could be leveraged to bridge gaps in development activities. Data communities are defined as "a group of people who share social, economic, political and/or professional interests in data across the entire data value chain – production, analysis, management, dissemination, use, and storage".[44] For instance, the statistics community plays a pivotal role in harnessing the data revolution to achieve Sustainable Development Goals (SDGs). However, over the past seven years, empirical research has noted that this particular data community has more recently been side-lined, with more importance being attached now to technology entrepreneurship and innovation communities. Nevertheless, NSOs will be very important to promote standards adoption for open data and ensure high levels of data quality, as explored in more depth in Chapter 13: National statistics.

Other important data communities that are not a mainstay within the region's open data ecosystems include agriculture associations, health professionals, and education experts, as well as gender experts, all of whom are not active at this time in helping to contribute toward achieving national development goals. We argue that it is necessary to mainstream open data further into these and other thematic communities to build capacity to use open data within these settings.

Partnerships for open data

As we have seen previously, different stakeholders in the open data ecosystem bring different skills to the table; however, there is limited collaboration documented between the different users of open data, particularly between government and civil society actors, despite their mutual interest in using open data being for policy-making, governance, and economic development.

Currently, efforts in this space are highly fragmented, and these siloed efforts result in repetitive initiatives, each with limited impact which could have been expanded with opportunities for peer-learning or a greater legacy footprint if they had a broader resource base. This leads to a chicken-and-egg situation where impact is necessary to compel additional resourcing for open data initiatives, but, at the same time, resources are required to implement these initiatives in the first place to fully realise the impacts.

This calls for the establishment of beneficial partnerships as advocated for by SDG 17 (Strengthen the means of implementation and revitalise the global partnership for sustainable development) and the African Data Consensus. The Communauté d'Afrique francophone des Données Ouvertes (CAFDO) and the Africa Open Data Networks (AODN) are two communities on the continent established to promote open data use to achieve Africa's development goals. They have been established as nodes of the OD4D initiative and are convening open data stakeholders across the data value chain, working to drive supply and demand for open data in the context of development and to mobilising the requisite resources and human capacity toward this goal. Through these kinds of collaborative efforts, the open data community can pool resources and strengthen its capacity to tackle the continent's most pressing needs.

Outlook for open data in Sub-Saharan Africa

While the open data movement on the African continent has definitely evolved over the past seven years, it is still far from mature. The number of open data portals and initiatives implemented is impressive; however, several of these are neither sustainable nor have they shown evidence of mass impact. Access to, and the use of, open data is still skewed to benefit a select few as the digital divide prevents widespread open data access. Regardless, the capacity of those with access to use open data, particularly those from grassroots communities, is questionable. Those with access are curtailed in their role as conduits to communicate the needs of every citizen and compel action by government institutions in delivering required services. Any capacity building activities should be geared to enable institutions with access to open data to become better intermediaries in order to expand access more widely.

Weak institutions and weaker legal infrastructures are limiting the extent to which open data can impact developmental outcomes. Despite the existence of political will and laws that preserve the citizen's right to access information in most countries, it is vital to establish strong leadership to promote the production of open data that meets quality standards to provide maximum benefit to those who access and use it. To realise impact from such use, it is necessary to strengthen the capacity of open data stakeholders to create solutions to real problems based on the data. Therefore, the next step for the growth of the African open data movement involves ramping up advocacy efforts that can identify and support champions of open data within government institutions. To further strengthen these champions, there is also a need to promote the establishment of more sustainable open data initiatives by providing these initiatives with the support of appropriate policies and local resourcing modelled to the nuances of Sub-Saharan Africa's data ecosystem that will institutionalise open data within governments.

There is also an opportunity to resource open data initiatives via public–private partnerships to overcome existing funding gaps. Additionally, getting private sector actors more actively involved in open data initiatives can complement government open data with the non-competitive data that they may be holding. Combined with this is a need to systematically document outputs from active open data initiatives and their impacts on society, which could amplify these impacts through further research and other knowledge sharing platforms. Establishment of open data networks, such as CAFDO and AODN, are examples of efforts in this area that will go a long way in boosting open data initiatives and supporting stakeholders across the ecosystem. To realise the full potential of open data in Africa, these networks will have to galvanise the different data communities operating in Africa to work with governments at all levels to accelerate the supply, demand, and use of open data.

Further reading

Ochieng, C. (2016). *The Africa data revolution report 2016*. Addis Ababa: ECA Printing and Publishing Unit. http://www.africa.undp.org/content/rba/en/home/library/reports/the_africa_data_revolution_report_2016.html

Rahemtulla, H., Kaplan, J., Gigler, B.-S., Cluster, S., Kiess, J., & Brigham, C. (2012). *Open Data Kenya: Case study of the underlying drivers, principal objectives and evolution of one of the first open data initiatives in Africa*. Washington, DC: Open Development Technology Alliance. https://www.scribd.com/document/75642393/Open-Data-Kenya-Long-Version

Web Foundation. (2017). *Open Data Barometer regional snapshots – Sub-Saharan Africa*. Washington, DC: World Wide Web Foundation. https://opendatabarometer.org/4thedition/regional-snapshot/sub-saharan-africa/

About the authors

Leonida Mutuku is the founder of Intelipro, an African company that builds analytics platforms for financial institutions and retail organisations. Leo is also the project lead at Africa Open Data Network (AODN), a community of Africans and friends of Africa, who believe in the continent's development agenda and how open data can help make it a reality. You can follow Leo at https://www.twitter.com/c_leo_patra and learn more about AODN at https://www.africaopendatanetwork.org.

Teg-wende Idriss (Tinto) is an open data advocate with more than six years' experience, both in government as a technical lead and with a CSO as a founder and project lead. Tinto is currently the coordinator of the Francophone Africa open data community (CAFDO) that is a regional hub for OD4D. You can follow Tinto at http://www.twitter.com/titinto_ and learn more about CAFDO at https://www.cafdo.africa.

How to cite this chapter

Mutuku, L. & Tinto, T.I. (2019). Open data around the world: Sub-Saharan Africa. In T. Davies, S. Walker, M. Rubinstein, & F. Perini (Eds.), *The state of open data: Histories and horizons.* (pp. 549–564). Cape Town and Ottawa: African Minds and International Development Research Centre. http://stateofopendata.od4d.net

This work is licensed under a Creative Commons Attribution 4.0 International (CC BY 4.0) licence. It was carried out with the aid of a grant from the International Development Research Centre, Ottawa, Canada.

Endnotes

1. Alais, O. (2016). The status of open data initiatives in West Africa. *ICTworks*, 29 June. https://www.ictworks.org/the-status-of-open-data-initiatives-in-west-africa/
2. https://www.uneca.org/pages/eca-databank
3. World Bank. (2015). *Readiness assessment tool*. Washington, DC: World Bank. http://opendatatoolkit.worldbank.org/en/odra.html
4. World Bank Group. (2017). *World Bank support for open data – 2012–2017*. Washington, DC: World Bank. http://hdl.handle.net/10986/28616
5. https://www.afdb.org/en/knowledge/statistics/africa-information-highway-aih/
6. https://www.mcc.gov/initiatives/initiative/mcc-pepfar-partnership
7. See, for example, https://theodi.org/project/african-open-data-leaders-network/
8. http://opendataday.org/
9. https://codeforafrica.org/
10. https://www.meetup.com/AODC17/
11. https://smartafrica.org/membership-and-sponsors/private-sector/
12. Smart Africa, Republic of Rwanda. (2017). *Smart sustainable cities: A blueprint for Africa*. Kigali: Smart Africa, Republic of Rwanda. https://smartafrica.org/IMG/pdf/smart_africa_sustainable-cities_a_blueprint_for_africa.pdf.pdf
13. Electronic Information for Libraries. (n.d.). Open access in Kenya, Tanzania and Uganda. http://www.eifl.net/eifl-in-action/open-access-kenya-tanzania-and-uganda

14 https://www.datafirst.uct.ac.za/dataportal/index.php/catalog/central/about
15 Rahemtulla, H., Kaplan, J., Gigler, B.-S., Cluster, S., Kiess, J., & Brigham, C. (2012). *Open Data Kenya: Case study of the underlying drivers, principal objectives and evolution of one of the first open data initiatives in Africa*. Washington, DC: Open Development Technology Alliance. https://www.scribd.com/document/75642393/Open-Data-Kenya-Long-Version
16 Bello, O., Akinwande, V., Jolayemi, O., & Ibrahim, A. (2016). Open data portals in Africa: An analysis of open government data initiatives. *African Journal of Library, Archives & Information Science, 26(2)*, 97–106. https://www.researchgate.net/profile/Olayiwola_Bello/publication/312057417_Open_Data_Portals_in_Africa_An_Analysis_ofOpen_Government_Data_Initiatives/links/586d634608ae6eb871bced07.pdf
17 Open Data Charter. (2015). International Open Data Charter. https://opendatacharter.net/principles/
18 https://opendatawatch.com/
19 https://index.okfn.org/
20 https://opendatabarometer.org/
21 Web Foundation. (2017). *Open Data Barometer – Global report*. 4th edition. Washington, DC: World Wide Web Foundation. https://opendatabarometer.org/4thedition/report/
22 Web Foundation. (2017). *Open Data Barometer regional snapshots – Sub-Saharan Africa*. Washington, DC: World Wide Web Foundation. https://opendatabarometer.org/4thedition/regional-snapshot/sub-saharan-africa/
23 Lämmerhirt, D., Montiel, O., & Rubinstein, M. (2017). *The state of open government data in 2017*. Cambridge: Open Knowledge International. https://blog.okfn.org/files/2017/06/FinalreportTheStateofOpenGovernmentDatain2017.pdf
24 https://cob.go.ke/publications/
25 GSMA Intelligence. (2018). *The mobile economy: Sub-Saharan Africa 2018*. London: GSMA Intelligence. https://www.gsmaintelligence.com/research/?file=809c442550e5487f3b1d025fdc70e23b&download
26 Davies, T., Perini, F., & Alonso, J.M. (2013). *Researching the emerging impacts of open data – ODDC conceptual framework*. Working Paper. Washington, DC: World Wide Web Foundation. http://www.opendataresearch.org/sites/default/files/posts/Researching%20the%20emerging%20impacts%20of%20open%20data.pdf
27 Chiliswa, Z. (2014). *Open government data for effective public participation: Findings of a case study research investigating Kenya's Open Data Initiative in urban slums and rural settlements*. Nairobi: Jesuit Hakimani Centre. http://www.opendataresearch.org/sites/default/files/publications/JHC%20Publication%20April%202014%20-%20ODDC%20research.pdf
28 Davies, T., Perini, F., & Alonso, J.M. (2013). *Researching the emerging impacts of open data – ODDC conceptual framework*. Working Paper. Washington, DC: World Wide Web Foundation. http://www.opendataresearch.org/sites/default/files/posts/Researching%20the%20emerging%20impacts%20of%20open%20data.pdf
29 Open Institute. (2016). Developing the right tools for citizen participation. https://openinstitute.com/developing-the-right-tools-for-citizen-participation/
30 http://yourbudgit.com/
31 https://pesacheck.org/
32 Sharife, K. & Van Schalkwyk, F. (2016). *The Panama Papers and investigative journalism in Africa: Lessons learned from and about the data*. Washington, DC: World Wide Web Foundation. http://webfoundation.org/docs/2016/12/WF-LL-Panama-Papers-in-Africa-Update.pdf
33 Freedom Info. (2017). Alphabetical and chronological lists of countries with FOI regimes. http://www.freedominfo.org/2017/09/chronological-and-alphabetical-lists-of-countries-with-foi-regimes/
34 Based on http://www.opengovpartnership.org/explorer/all-data.html
35 http://www.rti-rating.org/country-data/
36 Twaweza. (2015). Rapid analysis and key questions on Tanzania's Statistics Act. https://www.twaweza.org/go/stats-act-analysis

37 Ministry of Devolution and Planning & Council of Governors. (2016). *County public participation guidelines.* Nairobi: Republic of Kenya. http://devolutionasals.go.ke/wp-content/uploads/2018/03/County-Public-Participation_Final-1216-2.pdf

38 UNECA. (2015). *Africa data consensus.* Addis Ababa: United Nations Economic Commission for Africa. https://www.uneca.org/sites/default/files/PageAttachments/final_adc_-_english.pdf

39 See the Open Data Impact Map for Africa at http://opendataimpactmap.org/afr.html

40 http://wmmd.codeforafrica.org/

41 http://farmerline.co/

42 OSM. (2018). 2014 West Africa Ebola response. *OpenStreetMap Wiki.* https://wiki.openstreetmap.org/wiki/2014_West_Africa_Ebola_Response

43 Web Foundation. (2017). *Open Data Barometer – Global report.* 4th edition. Washington, DC: World Wide Web Foundation. https://opendatabarometer.org/4thedition/report/

44 Ochieng, C. (2016). *The Africa data revolution report 2016.* Addis Ababa: ECA Printing and Publishing Unit. http://www.africa.undp.org/content/rba/en/home/library/reports/the_africa_data_revolution_report_2016.html

Conclusion and recommendations

The State of Open Data project set out to explore how effective open data has been in addressing challenges related to social and economic development and to democratisation around the world. In this concluding chapter, we contemplate the impact that open data has had in addressing these challenges, reflect on the current strengths and weaknesses of the open data movement, and set out a series of recommendations with the goal of strengthening the future contribution of open data to sustainable and democratic development.

Meeting the challenges

Our look at the history and horizons for open data across sixteen sectors, seven regions, and the work of seven different stakeholder groups provides numerous examples of open data deployed as a tool for change. Open data has become a key element of the policy toolbox and proven its value in fields as diverse as agriculture, anti-corruption, and environmental research. A proliferation of pilots and prototypes have turned into ongoing projects and initiatives, working to establish new data infrastructures for corporate governance, transparent public procurement, or monitoring progress toward the Sustainable Development Goals (SDGs). In a number of cases, these initiatives can point to solid results, such as supporting environmental research, increasing access to healthcare, and enabling improved humanitarian coordination.

Yet, those seeking a quantitative measurement of effectiveness may still not be satisfied. To a substantial degree, this can be attributed to a lack of research that goes beyond ad hoc case studies. Few, if any, of the open data interventions described in this book have been subject to rigorous independent and longitudinal impact evaluation, although, increasingly, decision-makers seek this kind of robust evidence. Although it might be argued that it is still too early to talk in depth about measuring impact, the current evidence gaps, when set against early claims of large economic or social impact to be secured from open data, have undoubtedly fuelled perceptions that open data has not lived up to the hype.

We are more optimistic. Recognising Amara's adage that "[w]e tend to overestimate the effect of a technology in the short run and underestimate the effect in the long run",[1] we see evidence that many open data communities have been putting solid foundations in place for future impact, and are, in many cases, quietly creating substantive change with relatively meagre resources. In a number of instances, practitioners have made rapid progress in addressing the data components of a problem space but have been much slower at converting insights gathered from the use of data into policy and operational decision-making. For example, back in 2012, open data on doctors' prescribing behaviour enabled new analysis which identified the potential savings to the United Kingdom's health service from the better use of generic drugs, but it has taken another six years to develop the tools, processes, and communication approaches needed to present this information to decision-makers for action. We should keep in mind the complex contextual elements of effective open data interventions[2,3] and the time needed to secure alignment of all factors toward desired outcomes when seeking to track the extent to which open data projects are achieving impact.

The increasingly sectoral focus of open data work also provides an opportunity to strengthen collaboration between open data generalists and domain specialists. There are few contemporary social, economic, or democratic challenges where the solutions will not have at least some data component. Although it may initially appear easier to forgo openness and use data to address problems inside of organisational silos, evidence from across this collection suggests that the additional effort required to incorporate effective open data approaches can create a wide range of opportunities for innovation, collaboration, and value added. The question now for the broad open data movement is how to scale up and sustain the stakeholder engagement, infrastructure building, governance processes, capacity development, and cross-community networking that appear central to successful long-term open data initiatives, while not losing sight of the value of simply making data available and progressively enhancing its usability and usefulness over time.

Analysis and recommendations

The different lenses used across this book (sectors and communities, cross-cutting issues, stakeholders, and regions) provide a range of vantage points from which to assess the state of open data. They reveal sectors and communities at different stages of development: some sectors embedding open data ideas, others with a solid but marginal open data community, and still others where open data ideas are yet to move to the fore. They outline how each stakeholder group has a unique contribution to make, and they reveal some of the tensions that may characterise work in the coming years, such as between governments focused on institutionalising reforms, looking to prioritise engagement with larger established civil society actors just at the time when civil society is being encouraged to create space for smaller and more agile actors to engage with open data. The chapters reviewing cross-cutting issues reveal how open data movements have, over the last five years, engaged more and more with critical questions of data literacy, privacy, and gender equity, while, at the same time, revealing unresolved questions of how open data initiatives should respond to calls for Indigenous data sovereignty. Finally, regional chapters show how the state of open data varies between and within regions, leaving us with a number of different narratives at play within the broad global open data movement and different cultural and linguistic communities placing emphasis on different aspects of open data.

So where does the broad open data movement go from here? For all the differences across regions, stakeholders, and sectors, we believe there is a strong case for continued development of distinct work on open data as a key input into discussions of the future of data in our societies. We suggest a number of key areas for action relevant at this particular inflection point in the development of open data ideas and practice. The 12 recommendations below, three for each of the audiences identified in the introduction, are not exhaustive and are offered in addition to those put forward in particular chapters. Our hope is that they provide useful guidance in both strengthening existing work and identifying new avenues forward to secure the role of open data as a tool to meet sustainable development challenges.

Practitioners: Think politically and increase inclusion

Power is a recurring theme throughout the chapters in this book. Data is seen as a source of power, and advocacy for open data as a strategy to redistribute that power. There is clear evidence of this working in practice, whether enabling new market entrants to challenge established businesses providing geospatial data or supporting researchers to independently model extractives deals and reveal how countries could be securing higher revenues from their natural resources. However, there has also been growing recognition that, in conditions of unequal access to the skills and resources to work with data, or with wider existing patterns of exclusion and disadvantage, opening up data may not always lead to desirable outcomes. Indigenous scholars in particular have outlined how the models through which open data is put into practice often ignore important considerations about community rights to privacy and the control of data, failing to take into account the systematic biases built into existing government datasets.

It is evident from the work on corporate ownership and beneficial ownership disclosure that in some sectors, the open data community is at the heart of working out how to strike the balance between privacy and publicity, as well as between ad hoc data publication and the creation of high-quality datasets. This work is inherently political. While open data work has, for a long time, been able to maintain a broad-based appeal to actors across government, civil society, and the private sector, future projects will involve negotiations over the shape of data infrastructure that may make keeping everyone on board in a broad coalition much more challenging. We believe that unpacking the particular governance challenges in individual sectors, the specific interests and agendas of different stakeholders, and the range of dynamics in different regions, is essential for open data actors to be able to think more politically in the future. Future work must recognise that, while some aspects of open data practice can be positioned as a general public good, other aspects will entail maintaining and communicating a clear position on the kind of development to be pursued in order to build support.

The politics of data is particularly evident in debates around urban governance and "smart cities". Within the urban macrocosm, choices are playing out with regard to who will build, own, and operate data infrastructures, and how open they will be. As Landry explores in Chapter 16: Urban development, while open data is likely to play some part in the future urban landscape, there are other competing technological visions, focusing on centralised big data systems, corporate-owned sensor networks, and algorithmic decision-making. In general, open data discourse still reflects its origin in opposition to government data hoarding, yet the new landscape of data collection and use in 2019 calls for a re-articulation in opposition to emerging models of data power in our societies. In summary, practitioners need to:

- **Engage with the politics of data.** Thinking politically involves considering the agency and agendas of those who create and use data and exploring the opportunities and constraints that affect their actions. It involves addressing collective action problems and building coalitions, recognising that there may be different ideologies and interests at play and particular data-use projects may not please all stakeholders all of the time. Acting politically may, at times, involve the need to look beyond the technical quick-wins to the real change needed in the longer term and also require a greater diversity of people and organisations to solve a given problem.[4]

Understanding history and context is essential to support a more political approach, and this calls for deeper collaboration between open data practitioners and long-established civil society organisations.

- **Prioritise inclusion and equity.** Data is a team sport.[5] If work on open data is going to help deliver on the SDGs, it is important to build diverse and inclusive teams. This may not always be a comfortable or easy process as it may involve questioning assumptions or creating new shared organisational cultures. Brandusescu and Nwakanma, in Chapter 20: Gender equity, explore how both equity and inclusion involve questioning whose reality is represented within available datasets and who undertakes the labour or directs how data is used. Ultimately, every practitioner is potentially capable of sharing or distributing the power of data and data analysis in some way by taking action to support inclusion.

- **Provide renewed leadership for openness.** Communities and movements benefit from engaged leadership on all open data initiatives from local open data projects to global sectoral collaborations. When, as Howard and Constantaras (Chapter 27: Journalists and the media) describe, democratic governance and openness are under threat on a number of fronts, the open data movement needs renewed leadership that can bring together technical and political agendas and ensure that the many individual open data projects working to address particular sustainable development challenges add up to more than the sum of their parts. The horizon for open data needs to represent more than just a narrow technical strategy. To avoid losing its transformative potential, the multipoint open data movement of the future requires diverse leadership that, rather than being distracted by the latest technology, revisits and reinforces the core values that underlie work on open knowledge and open data.

Policy-makers: Pick a problem to solve

Eaves, McGuire, and Carson, in Chapter 35: North America, Australia, and New Zealand, argue that open data has been central to the development of wider governmental discourse around data and analytics over the last decade. Although many policy-makers are now looking at a much wider spectrum of closed, shared, and open data, it is not unreasonable to suggest that without the last ten years of open data, policy and public discourse would be far less equipped to respond to the rise of algorithmic governance, AI, and concerns about invasion of privacy through the use of large private datasets. In taking government data outside of its own "black box" and giving both government officials and citizens greater awareness of what data can do, open data initiatives have helped many people to hone their technical intuition in important ways.

However, as we look to the decade ahead, emphasis is shifting from "open by default" to "publish with a purpose" and to the strategic use of open data. Policy-makers are starting to understand that their role is not just to release data, but also to play an active role in governing data infrastructure and use, making sure, as Ubaldi describes in Chapter 26: Governments, that distinct streams of work on regulation, technology, engagement, and value-creation are aligned under a common vision and strategy. There is a risk, however, that further institutionalisation of open data policy will lead to some of the generative space around open data being closed down, re-creating government as gatekeeper, rather than as platform provider and engaged collaborator. Publishing with a purpose should be introduced alongside, rather than instead of, the default of "raw data now" which can be improved over time (at least for non-privacy impacting datasets). This requires policy-makers to adopt parallel tracks of activity that:

- **Embed open data approaches in problem solving.** Any time an organisation is commissioning a new data system, reviewing the data it collects, or seeking to carry out data analysis, it should be able to consider: (a) the existing data it may be able to access from others; (b) whether the data to be collected and shared could be provided openly and meet common standards; and (c) the outside actors who might be engaged as partners in working with that data. This may involve taking open data ideas further out into sectoral communities in the attempt to integrate open data into domain-specific expertise.

  In short, open data should no longer be the sole responsibility of specific data or technology teams, instead it needs to be considered a methodological element across different policy domains and initiatives. This should come with the recognition that, while effective open data approaches do require a level of technical skill, they also involve complementary work on strategy, governance, collaboration, and public communication, and frequently need vision and leadership that can bring together different stakeholders.

- **Maintain space for innovation and civic engagement.** Many of the successful applications of open data explored in this volume, from transit apps to budget data websites and air quality monitoring platforms, were not conceived of as part of top-down policy initiatives. Instead, they emerged when interested parties identified a need and were able to discover open data that could help address it.

  It remains central to the value proposition of open government data that the proactive publication of "open by default" data can enable outside parties in civil society, the private sector, and other government agencies, to find value in datasets in ways not foreseen or realised by the original data owner or steward. As data availability, quality, and more widespread data literacy develop, it will also be important to revisit and renew engagement models, such as hackathons, open data day events, and networking activities, to increase their inclusivity, while embedding the idea that open data is not only a tool for government-led problem solving, but can also create new civic spaces that can be used to connect different stakeholders and communities.

- **Explore openness as a golden thread across data policy.** Open data is sometimes seen as competing with, or in opposition to, other important data agendas around privacy, machine learning, and data analytics. Yet each of these other areas of data policy can be approached with a focus on openness. For example, much open data and privacy activism has shared roots in a common concern about who has access to the power that data creates, and the open data field has already developed tools to strike a balance between open, shared, and closed data. Beyond this, open data may be a tool to bring greater transparency to questions of how data is being governed and who has access to certain sensitive datasets. In AI policy, governments have widely recognised the role of open data as a source for innovation, and there is space to further explore the role of open data in supporting the independent audit of algorithmic outcomes.

Ultimately, although some groundwork has been laid, the narratives that treat open data as a strategic tool for problem solving and that link open data with other areas of data policy remain underdeveloped. Policy-makers have a key role to play in promoting the integration of open data into other areas of work, while not losing sight of the simple idea that the data governments collect should, whenever possible, be shared as a resource for all citizens.

Researchers: Rebooting the research agenda

The global spread of open data has been tracked by studies such as the Open Data Barometer (ODB) and Open Data Index; however, both the ODB and this collection are highly reliant on case studies of open data use in order to generate an understanding of impact. This can lead to a degree of bias in the evidence base, capturing more about case study research that has been funded, rather than producing a representative picture of impact on the ground. Although substantial work has taken place on input variables affecting open data projects (described as enabling conditions and disabling factors in Verhulst and Young's useful periodic table/logic framework),[6] much less has been written about the range of impacts that open data has beyond those captured in a supply-demand-use framework or about the comparative benefits of adopting open data problem-solving strategies. Smith and Reilly (2013) describe openness as "a complex process, not a state",[7] and the chapters in this volume illustrate that the complex processes that lead to data use also enable and support new relationships, collaborations, and strategies for sustainable development. These must be better captured in future research.

We also note that research on open data faces particular methodological challenges. Because open data is by definition available for anyone to reuse without permission, gaining an accurate sampling of all those affected by data release can be extremely challenging. Our hunch, albeit a hard one to confirm based on current research, is that the impact of open data has been substantially underestimated in case studies, since many beneficiaries of open data will simply be unaware that the information they have used for research, advocacy, or decision-making is only accessible as a result of open data policies. Current case studies generally only capture projects that are conceived of as open data projects in the first place, when project architects have opted to frame their work within open data narratives, rather than identified as work undertaken to address social, environmental, and political challenges and that has benefitted, knowingly or otherwise, from open data interventions. We also note that, just as Van Schalkwyk describes research (see Chapter 30: Researchers) as an output that may be discovered and able to influence policy many years after it was first published, open data that, at first, may appear to have limited value, may end up having a much longer and more useful life.

As a result, we see the opportunity to reboot the current research agenda around open data, such that researchers:

- **Document the history of open data initiatives**. Moving forward more strategically will benefit from a greater understanding of the past, particularly at the end of the first decade of open data. Studies of open data initiatives in their historical, cultural, and political contexts, that provide accessible documentation of the journey to date, can be instrumental to support reflection and learning and to enable new actors to become informed, involved, and empowered participants in the future of the open data movement.

- **Compare open and non-open models.** In light of the broader data agenda that has developed over the last decade, instead of asking "What was the impact of open data?", research should place more of a focus on "How do open data strategies compare to shared data or closed data approaches in addressing sustainable development challenges?" Methodologies should consider the potential added costs or added value of open data approaches in order to support better resource allocation decisions.

- **Improve quantitative evidence through natural experiments**. For example, when historical data is also made available as part of open contracting interventions, it provides an opportunity for a natural experiment, comparing procurement outcomes before and after data was openly available. Although the robust quantification of outcomes from a particular open data intervention does not provide generalisable evidence of open data impacts, it is essential for testing the null hypothesis and establishing a level of confidence in open data theories of change.

Rebooting the research agenda also needs specific action to address the current disconnects within the research community that Van Schalkwyk diagnoses (see Chapter 30: Researchers) in order to build better interdisciplinary and cross-continental research collaborations. We note that the resources for much of this work may not, however, come in the form of open data funding per se, but instead from support for thematic and sectoral research agendas, where work to understand the role of data could and should pay particular attention to the openness of the data or the potential for open data to directly support project goals.

Funders: Mainstreaming, movement building, and data literacy

Funders have a pivotal role to play in shaping the next decade of a global open data movement. Bringing together different stakeholders around common data challenges and building data infrastructures to support the public good will not happen at scale without continued support from donors and investors. However, it is clear that open data has passed its peak on the hype cycle and that funders whose support was based on open data as an emerging technology are rapidly shifting their focus to other areas, such as AI. Although, in some areas, open data work has garnered support from a range of funding sources, including sector-specific funders or programmes, in other areas, open data work is more vulnerable to a complete loss of funding based on a dependency on just one or two open data-focused funding schemes. There is already evidence to suggest that, if not well managed, competition for funding between open data organisations will drive further fragmentation and undermine more collaborative ways of working. There is a delicate balance to be struck between the need to support sector-specific funding programmes to identify how open data can help to deliver their project goals and the ongoing need to ensure that the core of the open data movement does not become hollowed out, undermining the essential need for continued knowledge sharing, innovation, and the development of open data techniques, ideas, and approaches.

While many funders have, in recent years, explored a shift from focusing on open data supply to looking at open data use, many chapters in this volume also call for an increased and broader focus on data literacy. Data literacy is not just about open data, but open data can be an invaluable asset for inclusive and empowering data literacy-building programmes. We suggest that an underinvestment in data literacy building has been a major factor in limiting both the quality of data supply and the uptake and use of open data over the last ten years, and that investment in intermediaries, while valuable, does not obviate the need to see the majority of organisations and individuals engaged in social change and development work having direct access to much higher levels of data literacy.

In short, across the community of funders involved in work on open data, there is a clear need for funders to:

- **Continue to invest in a core open data movement and in shared open data infrastructures.** The open data movement has yet to develop the kinds of professional associations or institutional structures that offer the potential for self-sustaining knowledge management, networking, and professional development. Even where sustainability mechanisms do emerge, developing and maintaining the inclusivity of the global open data community will require resources, as will public-good open data infrastructures that may not ever be self-funding. While funding may increasingly fall under wider "data rights" or "digital economy" headings, or be drawn from sectoral funding programmes, without enhanced donor coordination around open data initiatives and programmes, the full return on investments from the last decade may not be realised.

- **Integrate open data approaches within sectoral funding programmes.** The idea of "mainstreaming" in international development funding has a mixed history. However, funding teams who have worked on directly resourcing open data work over the last decade will in the future have a larger role helping other thematic funding teams to identify the open data elements in their work. This does not mean trying to force open data into all projects, but instead should involve identifying where a project is already adopting a data-driven approach and exploring the extent to which an open data approach could enhance this. Much as governance or gender advisors have helped development-related donor programmes explore new dimensions of their work, data and open data specialists could have a major role to play in supporting funders in the coming decade.

- **Focus funding on (open) data literacy.** Securing the benefits of open data, and mitigating risks associated with the abuse of data by powerful actors, requires much more widespread data literacy. Models for capacity building exist, but few have been tested at scale. Funders should set an ambitious vision for increased data literacy, both as a focus in its own right and as an element of other sustainable development projects.

  Fundamentally, open data literacy is not just about technical skills. It involves a critical awareness of the right to know, the power of data, and how data can be explored and questioned. As Montes and Slater state in Chapter 19: Data literacy, the "focus should be placed on the value of openness in fighting inequality, versus focusing solely on the value of data analysis".

While presented as recommendations for funders, implicit in the points above is a call for practitioners to also give long-term consideration to ways to self-fund networking and knowledge sharing, and to explore opportunities for open data approaches to be used within sector-specific projects, as well as to give more space to data literacy building in programme design.

Looking over the horizon

The history of open data over the last decade has seen open data become a well-established tool within the global policy toolbox with a wide community of supporters across many sectors. There are few development problems today that do not have a data dimension and, thus, will not have an open data dimension in the future. The risk that funders, policy-makers, and practitioners who were among the first to engage with open data as the "bright new thing" will shift their attention to emerging technologies in the next decade is real. But there is a strong foundation now in place for open data advocates to argue that open data must also continue to share the spotlight – as a complementary and, at times, corrective element of emerging public, private, and civil society data initiatives.

It could be argued that our conclusions and recommendations reflect the kind of "dogged optimism" that Wilson finds characteristic of civil society's engagement with open data, always calling for a "fresh push in a long struggle that is just on the precipice of success" (Chapter 24: Civil society, p. 361). Yet, this optimism is rooted in the evidence found across this collection that, over the last ten years, open data policy and practices have matured significantly. While shared learning and proven best practices from the past decade are not evenly distributed, they still offer the basis for a strategic way forward and substantial progress in the years ahead. The short essays in this volume are packed with examples, organisations, and innovative ideas that illustrate open data in practice, indicate the distance travelled, and highlight critical questions for the future. It is our hope that they inform and inspire new investment, research, and collaboration that will widen the effective use of open data.

As we look to the horizon, we cannot easily predict what the open data landscape will look like a decade from now. However, if there is a doubling-down on data literacy, an ongoing commitment to community and capacity building, and a deeper recognition of the politics and power dynamics around data, as well as of the vital strategic role of openness in protecting society from the darker side of data, then there is good reason to expect more opportunities to realise open data benefits for all.

Endnotes

1. Ratcliffe, S. (Ed.). (2016). Roy Amara 1925–2007, American futurologist. In *Oxford Essential Quotations*. 4th edition. Oxford: Oxford University Press.

2. Davies, T. & Perini, F. (2016). Researching the emerging impacts of open data: Revisiting the ODDC conceptual framework. *The Journal of Community Informatics*, *12(2)*. http://www.ci-journal.net/index.php/ciej/article/view/1281

3. Verhulst, S.G. & Young, A. (Eds.). (2017). Introduction. In *Open data in developing economies: Toward building an evidence base on what works and how* (pp. 1–3). Cape Town: African Minds. http://www.africanminds.co.za/dd-product/open-data-in-developing-economies-toward-building-an-evidence-base-on-what-works-and-how/

4. Leftwich, A. (2011). Thinking and working politically: What does it mean, why is it important and how do you do it? In *Politics, leadership and coalitions in development: Policy implications of the DLP Research Evidence, Research and Policy Workshop* (pp. 3–11). Frankfurt: Development Leadership Programme. https://gsdrc.org/document-library/thinking-and-working-politically-what-does-it-mean-why-is-it-important-and-how-do-you-do-it/

5. Slater, D. (2017). Data is a team sport: Enabling learning. *School of Data*, 6 June. https://schoolofdata.org/2017/06/06/data-is-a-team-sport-episode-1/

6. Verhulst, S.G. & Young, A. (Eds.) (2017). Introduction. In *Open data in developing economies: Toward building an evidence base on what works and how* (pp. 1–3). Cape Town: African Minds. http://www.africanminds.co.za/dd-product/open-data-in-developing-economies-toward-building-an-evidence-base-on-what-works-and-how/

7. Smith, M.L. & Reilly, K.M.A. (Eds.). (2013). Introduction. In *Open development: Networked innovations in international development* (pp. 1–13). Cambridge, MA and Ottawa: MIT Press and International Development Research Centre. https://www.idrc.ca/en/book/open-development-networked-innovations-international-development